Pinstripe Empire

Baseball's Best: The Hall of Fame Gallery (with Burt Goldblatt)
Thurman Munson: An Autobiography (with Thurman Munson)
Batting Secrets of the Major Leaguers
Tom Seaver's All-Time Baseball Greats (with Tom Seaver)
Hardball: The Education of a Baseball Commissioner
(with Bowie Kuhn)
The First Book of Baseball
Yesterday's Heroes
My Nine Innings (with Lee MacPhail)
Joe DiMaggio
Working the Plate (with Eric Gregg)
Yogi Berra
Great Moments in Baseball (with Tom Seaver)
When You're from Brooklyn, Everything Else Is Tokyo (with Larry King)
Slide, Kelly, Slide
Baseball: 100 Classic Moments in the History of the Game
(with Joseph Wallace and Neil Hamilton)
Now Pitching for the Yankees
Munson: The Life and Death of a Yankee Captain
162–0: The Greatest Wins in Yankee History

PINSTRIPE EMPIRE

*The New York Yankees from
Before the Babe to
After the Boss*

MARTY APPEL

BLOOMSBURY

New York · Berlin · London · Sydney

Published by Bloomsbury USA, New York

All papers used by Bloomsbury USA are natural, recyclable products made from wood
grown in well-managed forests. The manufacturing processes conform to the environ-
mental regulations of the country of origin.

LIBRARY OF CONGRESS CATALOGING-IN-PUBLICATION DATA

Appel, Martin.
Pinstripe empire : the New York Yankees from before the Babe to after
the Boss / Marty Appel.—1st U.S. ed.
p.   cm.
ISBN 978-1-60819-492-6 (hardcover : alk. paper)
1. New York Yankees (Baseball team)—History.   I. Title.
GV875.N4A664 2012
796.357'64097471—dc23
2011039006

First U.S. Edition 2012

1 3 5 7 9 10 8 6 4 2

Typeset by Westchester Book Group
Printed in the U.S.A. by Quad/Graphics, Fairfield, Pennsylvania

To those who ignited my love of baseball: Bob Fishel with his Yankee yearbooks, Mel Allen with his broadcasts, Sy Berger with his Topps baseball cards, Willard Mullin with his World-Telegram & Sun *cartoons, Dick Young with his columns, Frank Graham's* Lou Gehrig: A Quiet Hero, *the* Daily News *Sunday magazine,* The Little Red Book of Baseball, *Ethan Allen's All-Star Baseball, Sharpie the Gillette parrot and World Series theme music,* Pride of the Yankees *with Gary Cooper, the Turkin-Thompson* Official Encyclopedia of Baseball, *the Chip Hilton baseball novels by Clair Bee, Manny's Baseball Land, "Baseball and Ballantine," the Hall of Fame, the* Dell Baseball Annual, *Ed Fitzgerald's* Sport *magazines with Ozzie Sweet's photography,* Who's Who in Baseball, *the* Sporting News, Baseball Digest, *Tom Meany's* The Magnificent Yankees, *John Rosenberg's* The Story of Baseball, *Harry Simeone's "It's a Beautiful Day for a Ballgame," Mickey Mantle, Bobby Richardson, and the New York City Police Athletic League for my early "career" in Maspeth, Queens.*

Contents

Foreword by Yogi Berra   ix

Preface by Bernie Williams   xi

Special Introduction by Frank Graham Jr:
Growing Up Yankee   xiii

Author's Introduction and
Acknowledgments   xv

Chapter One   I

Chapter Two   15

Chapter Three   30

Chapter Four   40

Chapter Five   63

Chapter Six   78

Chapter Seven   94

Chapter Eight   108

Chapter Nine   118

Chapter Ten   133

Chapter Eleven   140

Chapter Twelve   151

Chapter Thirteen   158

Chapter Fourteen   172

Chapter Fifteen   187

Chapter Sixteen   200

Chapter Seventeen   216

Chapter Eighteen   226

Chapter Nineteen   236

Chapter Twenty   255

Chapter Twenty-One   267

Chapter Twenty-Two	274
Chapter Twenty-Three	286
Chapter Twenty-Four	301
Chapter Twenty-Five	317
Chapter Twenty-Six	330
Chapter Twenty-Seven	347
Chapter Twenty-Eight	358
Chapter Twenty-Nine	373
Chapter Thirty	384
Chapter Thirty-One	397
Chapter Thirty-Two	411
Chapter Thirty-Three	425
Chapter Thirty-Four	439
Chapter Thirty-Five	452
Chapter Thirty-Six	462
Chapter Thirty-Seven	473
Chapter Thirty-Eight	482
Chapter Thirty-Nine	492
Chapter Forty	503
Chapter Forty-One	512
Chapter Forty-Two	523
Chapter Forty-Three	532
Chapter Forty-Four	543
Chapter Forty-Five	552
Chapter Forty-Six	558
Chapter Forty-Seven	568
Appendix: Yankees Year-by-Year Results	575
Bibliography	583
Index	599

Foreword by Yogi Berra

Sometimes people ask me what it was like to play with Babe Ruth—I have no idea. I met him once, even got my picture taken with him when I was a rookie in 1947, before he died. Shaking hands with him was like touching history.

I learned once you're a Yankee, you're always in touch with that history. You sense it all around you, the pinstripes, the stadium, the tradition. On all the teams I played on, with DiMag, Whitey, Mickey, all of us felt responsible to our team. Being a Yankee meant something and still does.

To this day I owe an awful lot to Bill Dickey, who made me into the catcher I became. Bill came up in 1928, and then came out of retirement to learn me all his experience, as I used to say. Bill was a great man and a coach on many of our championship teams. Being around him and some of the guys on the legendary '27 team at our Old-Timers' Days was special. We'd lend them our gloves or shoes for the game, it was like a big family reunion.

What I like most about the Yankees is that connection, like we're all related. I'm proud a guy like Posada came along to continue our connection at catcher—Dickey, me, Ellie Howard, Munson. Not many teams have that kind of tradition. I'm glad Jorgie appreciated the connection, he got it.

Even nowadays, at spring training or in the new stadium, the current guys like seeing the old guys like me. They know they're part of a big family. Guys like Jeter, Posada, and Rivera know it best. We have fun together every time I see them.

I'm not one to dwell in the past; I follow today's team as close as anyone. But I always get a kick out of Old-Timers' Day because it's great to see everyone again. When I was a young player, we had newspapermen like John Drebinger and Frank Graham traveling with us—they also covered the Lou Gehrig teams. We heard a lot of great stories from those guys.

Talking baseball is what I still love. I was with the Mets when Marty joined the Yankees, but we caught up when I was hired as a coach in '76—he was the PR guy. Boy, he knew his stuff. I would call him to talk about the latest gossip. He knew how to separate the truth from the rumors. That's a good thing to know if you're writing the history of the team.

I've written introductions to many books, but this will probably be the last. This book is the last word on the Yankees. It's a great history and I've been lucky to witness a lot of it. Some of it pretty close up.

Preface by Bernie Williams

I was sitting by my locker before the first game of the '99 ALCS against Boston. It was my habit to be quiet before big games, sort of get into my game frame of mind. Yogi Berra was there to throw out the first pitch, and he thought I looked nervous.

"What's wrong?" he asked.

"Nothing," I said. "Just a big series. It'll be a tough one."

"Don't worry about it," he replied. "These guys have been trying to beat us for eighty years."

He was right. He always was.

That was Yogi, a man of great baseball wisdom, who always made you feel terrific in his presence. And what he was saying was "We've got your back," speaking for ninety-seven seasons of Yankee baseball and all the great players who had come before. No one carried Yankee history more than he did.

For me, there were other important personal links to the past. I once had a three-minute conversation with Joe DiMaggio, who always intimidated me a little, and he said, "Great job—keep up the good work." It meant so much. And Mickey Mantle signed a ball for me on Old-Timers' Day and said, "I've heard a lot about you, keep working hard." Those were just passing moments to them—but so meaningful to me, as a young player trying to find my place.

I grew up in Puerto Rico rooting for Puerto Rican players more than any one team. I was ten when I watched the Yanks' Ed Figueroa become the first Puerto Rican to win 20 games. What a big moment that was for us. And I came of age as a fan in 1977 and 1978 when the Yankees were on top. I found myself drawn to them. I ate Reggie bars. I watched Bucky Dent in the Macy's Thanksgiving Parade and thought that was very cool.

When I first got to the Yankees in 1991, the team was down, but the organization was first-class, even in the minors. It was my first brush with feeling like a rock star. The facilities, the travel, the things that were required of us—no beards, dress right, wear a tie—it all made us stand out against other organizations.

I was part of the generation of homegrown players who began to make their marks with the Yankees, a shift in the mentality of the way the team was built. Hensley Meulens, Kevin Maas, Oscar Azocar, Pat Kelly, Andy Stankiewicz, Jim Leyritz: They came just ahead of me, with Jete, Mo, Andy, and Jorge on the way. It was a transitional time and I was just proud to put on the Yankee uniform. We may have been down, but we had a following wherever we went. Good days were coming; you could feel it.

Yankee Stadium was magical. Maybe it was just my overwhelming excitement, but while the area around it seemed gray and gloomy, you'd walk into the ballpark and even the sky seemed bluer. It was like I had changed to new glasses. I walked out to the monuments, to the retired numbers, and took it all in. I was going to learn who all these old players were.

You learn about Yankee history because it's all around you. I first wondered why the team would spend so much time marketing the past when you had this emerging team coming along. But I came to realize it's what connected generations of fans and how important that shared experience was. The PR department would get us to record trivia questions for the scoreboard, or we'd watch the historic moments on the board during the game, taking it all in. (You think we don't watch?)

That I could be with the Yankees during a championship era in their great history means the world to me. I'm proud to have been a player for this very special franchise, and proud to be part of the telling of its story.

Special Introduction by Frank Graham Jr.: Growing Up Yankee

I was born predisposed to become a Yankee fan, as other tots are born into their religion. My father was a sportswriter for the old *New York Sun*, covering first the Giants and later the Yankees. I spent my earliest years in a Brooklyn apartment, hearing not great symphonies or birdsong but illustrious names from the sports world. The most prominent was that of a person I understood to be called Bay Bruth.

In 1933 my father took the whole family to St. Petersburg, Florida, where the team had its spring training camp. I saw the great players close up. One day my father and I joined the players on a ferry shuttling them across Tampa Bay for an exhibition game. Tony Lazzeri, Earle Combs, Lefty Gomez, and others who had been simply names to me until then patted this eight-year-old on the head. As we waited on a dock for the return ferry, I wandered over to where the Babe and Lou Gehrig had dropped a fishing line into the water. I stood close to them as they pulled up a blowfish and shared their wonder as the little creature, hitting the air, swelled like a toy balloon.

For the next decade I exulted or grieved with the Yankees' fortunes, following their results faithfully in the newspapers. Better still, I read the daily column in the *Sun* bylined "by Frank Graham," which often recounted the conversations in the clubhouse and dugout my father had overheard and transcribed with such skill. I tagged along with him sometimes to Yankee Stadium, where the two of us always visited manager Joe McCarthy in his office before the game, and later I would sit in the dugout beside some of my heroes. I posed for a picture with Gehrig, wearing the great man's cap. Lazzeri offered me a batboy's uniform so I could go to the outfield and shag flies during batting practice. But I stubbornly declined his offer, envisioning myself skulled by a high fly ball and carted, ignominiously, off the field.

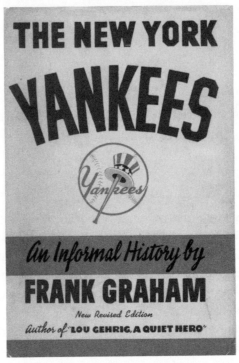

The 1943 Frank Graham history.

That era ended with the onset of World War II. In 1943 my father published the first full-fledged history of the Yankees. I had already gone off to war, serving far from home. But the day my copy of his book arrived at mail call and I began to read about the exploits of those fabulous players from the very beginning—the disasters and triumphs of this greatest of baseball franchises, all set down in print by my old man—I was the proudest apprentice seaman in the United States Navy.

I believe my father would be pleased that Marty Appel has used his original history as his own base for continuing this unique saga well into the twenty-first century. The story is still in good hands, written once again by a man who knows much of what he describes from his own deep personal experience.

Author's Introduction and Acknowledgments

In the 1940s and 1950s, Putnam published a series of sixteen team histories, of which *The New York Yankees* by Frank Graham was the first and most successful. It was published in 1943 and updated in 1958 after fourteen printings. Graham, who worked at the time for the *New York Journal-American*, "knew people who knew people" who went back to the origin of the team in 1903. When he used "Griff" for Clark Griffith, you knew he wasn't just making up a nickname.

Graham would not be surprised to learn that the Yankees have maintained their winning ways, but he would be surprised by the internationalism of the "brand" and the enormity of the business. And, yes, by the salaries.

I think he'd also be surprised that in all these years, the Yankee story has yet to be retold in a traditional narrative. It is our hope that this book fills that void.

The best advice I received early in this project came from my friend Darrell Berger, a Detroit Tigers fan who said, "Remember, a down time for the Yankees was a pretty good time for fans of other teams." That kept my focus on the assignment—to try and tell a story anyone can relate to, not just for the Bronx faithful.

I was privileged to work for the team, and later to produce its telecasts over a span of some twenty-five years, and I was smart enough to appreciate being surrounded by observers who went back to the 1920s. I listened. And I'd like to salute the authors, beat writers, broadcasters, and columnists who chronicled the team over the years and left a trail of information to be combed over by people like me for just such a project. They did their profession proud.

I also had an all-star team gracious enough to read some of this material and lend their thoughts, and I especially wish to cite Doug Lyons, Paul

Doherty, Tony Morante, Rick Cerrone, Jordan Sprechman, Tom Villante, Bob Heinisch, and Bill Madden for their time and counsel.

Others who were gracious enough to help with this project include Maury Allen, Dom Amore, Norm Appel, Peter Bavasi, Mary Bellew, Kathy Bennett, Howard Berk, Yogi Berra, Peter Bjarkman, Arline Blake, Ron Blomberg, Jim Bouton, Ralph Branca, Bruce Brodie, Bill Burgess, Neill Cameron, Bill Chuck, Jerry Cifarelli, Joe Cohen, Dan Cunningham, Pearl Davis, Lou D'Ermilio, Steve Donahue, Frank Fleizach, Whitey Ford, Sean Forman, Steve Fortunato, Bill Francis, Bruce Froemming, Joe Garagiola, Joe Garagiola Jr., Peter Garver, Pat Gillick, Frank Graham Jr., Joe Grant, Ross Greenburg, Bill Guilfoile, Bob Gutkowski, Michael Hagen, Jane Hamilton, Fran Healy, Henry Hecht, Roland Hemond, Dr. Stuart Hershon, Brad Horn, Arlene Howard, Jeff Idelson, Stan Isaacs, Steve Jacobson, Bill Jenkinson, Mark Katz, Lana Kaufman, Pat Kelly, Jason Latimer, Jane Leavy, Mark Letendre, Dan Levitt, Lon Lewis, Terry Lefton, Phil Linz, Lee Lowenfish, Sparky Lyle, Jeffrey Lyons, Nathan Maciborski, Lee MacPhail, Rich Marazzi, Michael Margolis, Tim Mead, Ernestine Miller, Gary Mitchum, Toni Mollett, Gene Monahan, Leigh Montville, Mickey Morabito, Tomas Morales, Craig Muder, Ken Munoz, Kay Murcer, Ian O'Connor, Juliet Papa, Tony Pasqua, Phil Pepe, Fritz Peterson, Dr. Joseph Plantania, Tim Reid, Bobby Richardson, Kurt Rim, Ray Robinson, Mark Roth, K. Jacob Ruppert, Frank Russo, Richard Sandomir, Al Santasierre III, Harvey Schiller, Jerry Schmetterer, Ron Selter, Jay Schwall, Bill Shannon, Danny Sheridan, Tom Shieber, Al Silverman, David Smith, Tal Smith, Jeff Spaulding, Mark Stang, Steve Steinberg, Brent Stevens, Tom Stevens, Sheldon Stone, Bert Sugar, Randall Swearingen, David Szen, Bob Thompson, John Thorn, Dan Topping Jr., Kimberly Topping, Juan Vene, Mike Wach, Larry Wahl, Suzyn Waldman, Willie Weinbaum, Irv Welzer, Bill White, Roy White, Tim Wiles, Bernie Williams, Ralph Wimbish Jr., Bob Wolff, Jason Zillo, and Andrew Zimbalist. Special thanks for extended interviews to Randy Levine, Lonn Trost, Brian Cashman, and Gene Michael.

At Bloomsbury, I would like to thank George Gibson, Ben Adams, Mike O'Connor, Will Georgantas, Nate Knaebel, Michelle Blankenship, and Patti Ratchford; my agent, Robert Wilson, and Team Appel—Brian, Deb, and especially Lourdes, who accepted the hours on the computer and the stacks of reference material cluttering our home.

Thanks too to John Rogers and Will Means at Rogers Photo Archives in North Little Rock, Arkansas, for their newspaper, *Sporting News*, and *Sport* magazine photo files, and to Phil Castinetti of Sportsworld for providing scorecards back to the days of Hilltop Park. Art depicting Yankee Stadium, 1923, was researched and produced by David Kramer, Matt O'Connor, J. E. Fullerton, Michael Hagan, Scott Weber, Michael Rudolf, Dennis Concepcion, and Chris Campbell.

Chapter One

P HIL SCHENCK WALKED GINGERLY across the soupy ground that would
soon become Manhattan's newest baseball diamond. As the newly
appointed head groundskeeper of what would be, after all, a major
league facility, he had to be intimidated by what lay ahead. Opening day
was April 30.

This new franchise had only been approved on March 12, 1903, and a
playing field was a hurried afterthought. So difficult had been the struggle
to get an American League team stationed in New York that the playing
field, with so much barren space available in New York, seemed somehow
less important.

Unless you were Phil Schenck.

"There is not a level spot on the whole property," reported the *Sporting
News* in its March 21, 1903, edition. "From Broadway, looking west, the
ground starts in a low swamp filled with water, and runs up into a ridge of
rocks . . . The rocks will be blasted out and the swamp filled in."

Joe Vila, thirty-six, approached Schenck and sympathized with his
plight. The *New York Sun* sportswriter had played a significant role in
bringing this franchise to reality. Now he wanted to see how "his" field was
taking shape.

It wasn't very impressive. It would be a haul for fans to get to this field,
and they would expect something worthy of the journey, worthy of a paid
admission. The new team had to give them a product that felt big-time. And
the clock was ticking.

Vila was born in Boston and had spent two years at Harvard before quitting to become a brakeman and baggage handler on the B&O Railroad. He joined the *New York Morning Journal* in 1889, and moved to the *New York Herald* a year later. He had been with the *Sun* since '93.

As a Harvard man he was well aware that in July, ground would be broken for a grand concrete structure in Allston, Massachusetts. It would be home to the Crimson football team, an edifice worthy of being called a stadium. The idea of building a "stadium" for a baseball team was just silly. The small wooden structures cropping up around the country were not up to the name. Hell, they were burning down with regularity and befit the smaller position baseball held in the American consciousness. College football was the big sport of the land, and Harvard Stadium, the first to be called a stadium in the U.S., deserved it. When it opened in the fall, it would seat more than fifty thousand.

Still, Vila's enthusiasm was genuine. It was exciting to have played such a prominent role in the birth of a franchise, and he could honestly say he did.

In 1892, he was in New Orleans for the John L. Sullivan–Jim Corbett heavyweight championship fight. It was a most important sporting event, the first staged under the Marquis of Queensbury rules, with both fighters wearing gloves and a sense of civility in the brutal sport. It was the fight that made boxing "acceptable."

The nation's newspapers sent reporters to cover the event. There Vila met a stocky, cigar-smoking reporter from the *Cincinnati Commercial-Gazette*, one Byron Bancroft Johnson. The two formed a friendship.

While Vila continued to work as a New York journalist, Johnson, better known as Ban, harbored other ideas. As baseball grew in popularity, he saw an opportunity to develop a second major league that competed with the existing National League, putting franchises in the major cities of the day and winning over enough fanatics ("fans") to make money for the owners. For the most part, Johnson would hand-pick the owners and put his own stamp on his league.

Just a year after the Corbett-Sullivan fight, Johnson was elected president of the Western League, placed there by John T. Brush, the owner of the Cincinnati Reds, and by Charles Comiskey, the manager of the team. He would lead that minor league for six years, giving up his conflicting role as sports editor of the paper after the first one.

With his wide girth, Johnson looked every bit the picture of prosperity as the nineteenth century drew to a close. The U.S. presidents of the era—McKinley, Cleveland, Roosevelt, and Taft—all looked well nourished and prosperous. It was a look that represented success and confidence, recaptured years later by George M. Steinbrenner III, who would not have been Steinbrenner in Woodrow Wilson's frail frame.

Disgusted by the National League's inability to curtail drinking and gambling in the ballparks, by the blatant abuse of umpires by rowdy fans, and by the ballparks themselves offering environments unfriendly to women and children, Johnson saw the opportunity for a more civil league with a friendlier ballpark atmosphere, and enough star players for a second major league.

By 1899, his Class A Western League included Buffalo, Columbus, Detroit, Indianapolis, Kansas City, Milwaukee, Minneapolis, and St. Paul.

In 1900 he renamed it the American League, replacing Columbus and St. Paul with Chicago and Cleveland. It was still a minor league but Johnson had the full intent on converting it to a major league by raiding National League players for 1901.

Showing no fear of Johnson's ambition, the twenty-five-year-old National League decided to establish a salary cap at this time. The league's wage ceiling was $2,400 (around $60,000 in 2011 dollars), small even by 1901 standards.

This was the opening Johnson needed. He declared his league to be major and induced players like Cy Young, Nap Lajoie, and Clark Griffith to jump leagues for higher pay. Baltimore and Washington replaced Buffalo and Indianapolis. Connie Mack came in to manage Philadelphia; John McGraw Baltimore.

The league was an immediate hit. In 1901, the American League drew a reported 1,683,584 fans without even having teams in New York or Brooklyn. The National League, with New York and Brooklyn, drew a reported 1,920,031. It was a remarkable success story.

Then as now, New York was the biggest city in the country. More than 3.4 million people resided there, 1.8 million of them in Manhattan. Philadelphia, with almost 1.3 million in the 1900 census, was the second-biggest city. New York was a glaring absence if the American League was to be big-time.

The history of New York and baseball had been charmed. The "New York Game" was the dominant amateur game as rules began to take form in the mid-eighteenth century. Firemen from Manhattan would sail across the Hudson and play at Elysian Field in Hoboken, New Jersey, likely the true birthplace of the game. The ninety-foot distance between the bases, about as perfect a concept as mankind has ever produced, was established in New York. The game's first superstar was Jim Creighton of the Excelsior team of Brooklyn. Candy Cummings, also an Excelsior, is generally credited with discovering the curveball—a tactic that relied on the seams on the baseball, making one wonder whether the game's creators stumbled onto it by accident or had planned it all along. The first great chronicler of the game, the inventor of the box score, was Henry Chadwick, a New Yorker.

The National Association, both amateur and pro, started in 1857 and featured teams largely based in Brooklyn. (Brooklyn was incorporated into New York City in 1898.) The National League was formed in 1876, and the New York Giants joined in 1883. The American Association, born in 1882, featured the Metropolitans.

But of course one didn't need rules to pick up a wooden stick and hit a round object, as many children did in the streets of New York, inventing their own versions as fit the terrain. New York was in love with base ball. (It was two words back then.)

In his American League, the problem franchise for Johnson proved to be Baltimore. It was not a city he truly wanted, with its population of only half a million. In its favor was its rich tradition: The Baltimore Orioles had been a great championship name while playing in the National League and included John McGraw, Wilbert Robinson, Willie Keeler, Joe Kelley, Hughie Jennings, and Kid Gleason. Johnson managed to bring Robinson back into the fold for his American League entry in 1901 and tapped McGraw as manager.

But McGraw's legendary temper and antics, popular with the rowdy fans of the day, translated poorly into what Johnson sought to accomplish with his more genteel game. His scrapes with umpires and incitement of the fans played poorly with the American League's aspirations.

Frequently Johnson had to suspend McGraw for inciting riots against the umpires. On June 28 he again went into a crazed argument, and was again suspended, this time indefinitely.

Incensed, McGraw asked for his release. "Johnson's down on Baltimore and would like to see it off the map," he said. "I am sick and tired of the whole business, and I don't care if I never play in the American League again."

He was playing both ends. He had been negotiating with the New York Giants to manage their team, and in a sense arranging for his own departure. But Johnson was glad to see McGraw get his release and depart for New York. "Let the National League have this maniac," he must have thought. "It better makes my point."

"Johnson's ultimate ambition was to get a club in New York," wrote McGraw in his memoirs. "If he succeeded, this meant, of course, that Baltimore again would be dropped and someone would be left holding the bag. Baltimore was the weakest team in attendance. If it failed to hold its own, that would be a good excuse to the public for dropping it."

The McGraw action set in motion a series of events essentially rendering the Orioles impotent. Six more players were released, among them Roger Bresnahan, Joe McGinnity, Kelley, and Robinson, and a majority of stock in the team was transferred to Andrew Freedman, owner of the Giants. Freedman now had a piece of the American League.

Decimated, the Orioles were restocked with players essentially given away by the other teams in order to play out the schedule. Not surprisingly, they limped to a last-place finish and were done.

Rather than rebuild in Baltimore, Johnson set about putting a team in New York. He would have eight months to get a franchise established, stock it with players, find owners,* locate grounds for a ballpark, hire a manager, and start selling tickets.

In 1902, Johnson's league drew more than two million fans, almost four hundred thousand more than the National League, even without New York. He was ready for a fight.

After the 1902 season, Freedman sold his Giants to the Reds' owner, John Brush, who in turn unloaded his Cincinnati stock. But Freedman, with his strong political connections, would remain a nuisance to Johnson as a member of the Giants' board of directors.

The sale came about despite the efforts of another suitor for the Giants, a young Manhattan congressman named Jacob Ruppert Jr. He would be heard from again.

With just days left in the 1902 season, James C. Kennedy, a sports promoter, of "whom no better man could be found to manage successfully a rival baseball club in this city," emerged as a man to possibly head a new team.

"I am not at liberty to say where they will locate," said Kennedy. "For the present, let me tell you that we have options of three sites, one of which is admirably situated, and when its location is made known will cause no little surprise. New York is not a sentimental city, it is a business center, and its people will demand the best article and support those who give it."

---

* Among the candidates was Hall of Fame owner and innovator Barney Dreyfuss, who owned the Pittsburgh franchise. It was said, "He is too good a sportsman. His place is with the American League. He has given every indication that he is sick of the National League, its schemes, and his associates." But Dreyfuss stayed in Pittsburgh.

Kennedy had been working hard, traveling to Chicago to meet with Ban Johnson, beginning to make plans to run the new team should it become a reality.

"Kennedy's name should be a sufficient guarantee to the baseball public that the American League means business," said someone with knowledge of the American League's thinking.

Jimmy Kennedy, thirty-five, was considered by most to be the new team's logical owner. He was a boxing promoter at the Seaside Athletic Club in Coney Island and ran the very popular Six-Day Bicycle Races at Madison Square Garden in partnership with Patrick Powers.

Kennedy was all set to take command of the team, and his name began appearing more and more in the newspapers as the logical choice. Yet he seemed wedded to playing home games on Manhattan Field, presenting it as if it were already a fait accompli.

Manhattan Field had actually been a major league facility in 1889–90; the Giants played there prior to moving into the newly constructed (and adjacent) Polo Grounds. But despite Kennedy's plans, Manhattan Field had been leased to the National League as parking and the American League was unlikely to secure it. Furthermore, although it was now unused land, the free vantage points overlooking it hardly made it a worthy site for paid admissions. There wasn't enough time—or money—to build a grand structure to block the views.

Kennedy left by steamship for Europe at the end of October, noting, "I have not seen Ban Johnson this week, but that fact of my going away on a business trip does not mean that I have abandoned the idea of managing the new club. Matters are at a standstill regarding that venture, and nothing can be done for a few weeks toward a definite settlement as to its management. I will be back again within four weeks, and when I return, things may have shaped themselves so that they can be given publicity."

Yet Kennedy's opportunity to own the team was gone in a week. (And, as fate would have it, Kennedy was found dead in a subway car in lower Manhattan in April 1904.)

While he was abroad, Ban Johnson was spotted looking at other sites. South Field, on 116th and Broadway, was land owned by Columbia University. But Columbia would lose its tax break if admission was charged on its property. No good. One Hundred Twenty-sixth Street and First Avenue would require a road closing. No good. One Hundred Forty-fifth Street at the Harlem River merited a look. It was just two blocks from the elevated rail. But, no good. At 142nd Street and Lenox Avenue was the Curtis estate; the wealthy August Belmont Jr. (who would build Belmont racetrack in 1905) was willing to buy the property and an adjacent piece of property owned by the Rapid Transit Company and lease it to the American League. But Andrew Freedman, serving as a director of the Rapid Transit Company, refused to lease the strip of land, causing Belmont to step aside.

The American League had a ten-year option on land on Berkeley Oval, in the Morris Heights section of the Bronx (the site of all the city's top track meets), and there was talk of Ambrose Park in south Brooklyn. Both Kennedy and Johnson found them too far removed, and the search continued.

Johnson, meanwhile, focused on lining up players. Johnson later wrote that

Jack O'Connor, catcher for Barney Dreyfuss' Pittsburgh team, had been on friendly terms with us for some time and had kept us posted on the desires of the players to switch to our league.

When we decided to . . . form the New York club, I wired O'Connor that we were prepared to raid the Pittsburgh team, and for him to make arrangements to let me know how the land lay. I was going to Atlantic City with Charley Somers [owner of the Cleveland team and a major benefactor of the American League] and . . . the train took us through Pittsburgh.

In the train station O'Connor found us and as he passed us he spoke out of the corner of his mouth, pretending not to see us.

"They are wise to us," he said. "Get in a cab at once and go to the Lincoln Hotel."

My telegram [to O'Connor] had gone astray. It had fallen into the hands of the Pittsburgh club officials or an operator had tipped off Dreyfuss that the American League was prepared to strike.

We met O'Connor at the Lincoln Hotel and he urged us to take immediate action if we wanted to sign any of the Pittsburgh players. The Pittsburgh club, forewarned by the telegram, was trying to forestall our raid, he informed us, by getting the signatures of the players on iron-clad contracts. [O'Connor would be suspended by Pittsburgh.]

We realized that it was the time to act and before the next day dawned we had scoured Pittsburgh for the stars we wanted and had signed . . . [Wid] Conroy, [Jack] Chesbro, [Jesse] Tannehill, [Lefty] Davis and several other players, seven or eight in all.

> I postponed my trip to Atlantic City and decided to go to Cleveland. There still remained the task of giving the players [who had] signed their advance money to bind the contracts and not wanting to let the enemy know that I was in Pittsburgh. I took elaborate steps to get out of town without anyone seeing me. I left the hotel by the freight elevator and went to the train by a circuitous path. I climbed aboard the train and was congratulating myself on having outwitted the opposition when out there behind the corner of the coach I saw Harry Pulliam [secretary] of the National League. I certainly had gone to a lot of trouble to run right into the eyes of the enemy.

Johnson evaded Pulliam and pulled off his caper. In December, Pulliam was elected National League president. At their league meeting, the National League owners adopted a committee "for the purpose of conferring with representatives of the American League . . . to ascertain upon what basis [peace] can be accomplished."

The resolution was in sight. The National League wanted no part of a bidding war.

Johnson was staying at the Criterion Hotel in Longacre Square (soon to be renamed Times Square) for his own league meeting on December 11 when he saw the three-man committee from the National League approaching him.

"I knew in an instant the purpose of their visit . . . They informed me they composed a committee of the old league to wait on me and see if peace terms could be arranged. We've always advocated peace," he told reporters.

> Now that the other side is willing to meet us I feel confident that we can come to an amicable arrangement whereby clashing of playing dates can be prevented . . . We have careful preparations to place an American League club on Manhattan Island, and we would have announced our plans and the location of our playing grounds ere this were it deemed advisable by our legal representatives.
>
> We will hold the American League annual meeting here within two weeks, and then everything will be ready for the widest publicity. New York's baseball enthusiasts can rest assured that we will do our utmost to give them first-class baseball and as the American League has fulfilled all that it promised so far, there is

no good reason why we cannot continue to do so. We are fully prepared to go our way, whether it be peaceful or warlike, but we are now, as always, anxious for peace on any fair business basis.

These salvos eventually led to a January 19 agreement in Cincinnati. Terms included acceptance of a team in New York and the AL's agreement not to place one in Pittsburgh or Baltimore. There was also a matter of settling contract claims with those who had jumped prior to 1902, and those after.

Two teams opposed the agreement, the Giants being one of them. But John Brush, seeing its passage a certainty, gave in to make acceptance unanimous.

Now came the work of finding owners, a manager, more players for the team, and a place for them to play—with the season only three months away.

GAMBLING IN NEW YORK was illegal at the turn of the century but still operated fairly openly, thanks in part to cushy relationships between gambling hall owners and the city's politicians. Many of these gambling dens were tucked into the area along Broadway from Battery Park to the streets of the mid-Twenties.

There, card games like faro were played and betting on sports was enjoyed, especially horse racing, where results were sent by telegraph from tracks around the country.

Big Tim Sullivan, a big shot in the New York Democratic political machine known as Tammany Hall, had managed to get as far as the U.S. Congress and was considered the man to know if you wanted to make sure your business wasn't shut down. Nobody missed his annual public pig roasts. Little Tom Foley was another politico to know. They could open doors.

This brings us to Frank Farrell, "the Pool Room King," thirty-seven years old, one of the more prominent owners of gambling houses in New York, and a good friend of Sullivan's. He had grown up on the Lower East Side of the city with Al Smith, the future governor and presidential candidate. Farrell owned racehorses, including the champion Roseben. The biggest of his slews of gambling houses, a veritable palace on Thirty-third Street with steel doors and connecting passageways, had been raided by district attorney William Travers Jerome. Apparently, someone had forgotten to make a payoff.

No problem. Farrell knew Big Bill Devery, thirty-eight, who in one breath would be called the greatest police chief New York ever had and in another the most corrupt. The two were not mutually exclusive.

Farrell was sued in March of 1903 to recover losses sustained at one Commercial Clerks Club, a gambling den that he was said to own. Although newspapers the year before announced FARRELL'S NEW GAMBLING PALACE [OPENS] AT 33 WEST 33RD, Farrell denied ever having been in a pool hall, let alone owning one. He'd never seen a roulette wheel and couldn't recall ever having placed a bet even though he owned racehorses. He was acquitted.

Just a few days after the January 19 meeting in Cincinnati, Joe Vila had a conversation with his old pal Ban Johnson.

"You've got your franchise, Ban, do you have an owner? Is the league going to own it?"

Vila was asking not as a reporter but as a broker.

"I'd like to introduce you to Frank Farrell. He's a sportsman. Owns some saloons and gambling halls. Owns the famous racehorse Roseben, in fact. He's got money."

Actually, Farrell owned as many as 250 "pool halls" at which all sorts of commerce took place. If it hugged the line between legal and illegal, you could probably find it at a Farrell establishment. You could go in, do some opium, win at roulette, spend your winnings on a prostitute, and arrange for a backroom abortion all at once. Or so it was said.

Johnson was, nevertheless, curious to meet Farrell. Vila arranged a meeting.

At the meeting, Farrell presented Johnson with a certified check for $25,000 and said, "Take that as a guarantee of good faith, Mr. Johnson. If you don't put this ball club across, keep it."

"That's a pretty big forfeit, Mr. Farrell," Johnson replied.

At which point Vila said, "He bets that much on a race, Ban!"

Farrell told Johnson that he would bring in Big Bill Devery as a partner. He had it all figured out: While he could afford to buy the team on his own, Devery would bring in the political muscle he needed to overcome the Giants' behind-the-scenes opposition.

Johnson had a problem. The point of his league, apart from being a profitable business, was to do away with the unseemly behavior of fans of the National League.

And now he was talking to a guy who owned gambling houses and might bet $25,000 on a race.

Farrell appreciated the hesitation when Johnson expressed the lofty goals of the league.

"Tell you what, Mr. Johnson," said Farrell, who had another solution at the ready. "We'll find a team president and he'll be the one the public comes to know."

Farrell and Devery would own the team, and a mild-mannered coal-mining executive named Joseph W. Gordon would be installed as president.

Apart from the coal-mining résumé, a term in the New York State Assembly (1888) and a year as New York's superintendent of buildings (1901), Gordon had a baseball background. He had been president of the New York Metropolitans of the American Association and was a part of the New York Giants management team. He had been a young pitcher at PS 49, playing games in Central Park. He had some blueblood credentials, too: a member of rowing clubs and the New York Athletic Club. He lived in a nice apartment on West Eightieth Street, was tall, gray-haired, and distinguished looking, and met with Johnson's approval.

At the "press conference" to announce the team, Gordon was front and center; Farrell and Devery weren't even present. All of Johnson's dealings with the team, after these initial meetings, would be with Gordon. Gordon remained on the scene for three years, and then Farrell became the face of the team as the new president.

Devery had little to do with the running of the team, but his celebrity far exceeded Farrell's and he could occasionally be called upon for a ceremonial first pitch.

"I BOUGHT THE baseball team as a hobby," Devery told people, "and I never had any intention of making any money from it."

He didn't need to, having earned considerable wealth from artful graft during his career with the New York Police Department. In retirement, on an estate in Far Rockaway, Queens, when his wealth was said to grow with healthy real estate investments, he would proudly show off a collection of thirty-six scrapbooks featuring cartoonists and editorialists having at him. He was known far beyond New York's borders, and for a time was as recognizable as the various mayors he served. In 1902, the *World* reported that this civil servant was worth $750,000.

For the New York newspapers—the *Times*, the *Herald*, the *Sun*, the *Evening Telegram*, the *Tribune*, the *Press*, the *World*, the *Globe*, the *Journal*, the *American & Journal*, the *Morning Telegraph*, the *Mail and Express*, and the *American*—he was a reporter's dream.

He'd been born near Third Avenue and East Twenty-eighth Street in 1857 and joined the police department in 1876. He advanced to sergeant in 1882 and captain in 1891, and soon made friends with a powerful political boss, Richard Croker. Croker began to oversee Devery's rise in the department. It was while he was captain of the West Thirteenth Street police station that he first met Farrell, who had one of his saloons at Thirteenth and Sixth. Devery made sure that the establishment ran smoothly, so long as tribute was properly rendered.

While captain in 1894, Big Bill was arrested for bribery and extortion, fired, and then reinstated when the conviction was overturned a year later. A month later, he was made deputy chief of police. In 1896, the Board of Police, headed by Theodore Roosevelt, filed a complaint against him that should have led to his removal, but he fought it off with a legal maneuver, claiming the board was not bipartisan as required. In 1898, while Roosevelt was running for governor, he became chief of police.

Mayor Robert Van Wyck was under pressure to remove Devery from office in 1901, but Croker arranged for Van Wyck to make him deputy police commissioner.

His greatest strength seemed to be in managing the corruption that had invaded the police department, and then as deputy commissioner, serving as judge at the trials of his cops. "His wonderfully shrewd judgment of police human nature; his accurate knowledge of all the small tricks of the lazy or dishonest patrolman and his frankness in revealing his familiarity with them at trials was at once the joy and the astonishment of the city," wrote John M. Sullivan in 1904.

Lincoln Steffens, a leading journalist and editor of his day and one of the city's most famous muckrakers, loved to write about Devery. "As a character, as a work of art, he was a masterpiece," he wrote. "I think we never printed a paragraph against this crook that did not betray our involuntary liking for his honesty, courage and character."

Perhaps Devery's finest hour was in carefully organizing a parade to honor Admiral George Dewey, the hero of the Battle of Manila Bay during the Spanish-American War. The parade, up Broadway on September 30, 1899, would become the model for the ticker-tape parades that became such a part of New York—and that would later be held many times for championship Yankee teams starting in 1977. (There was one on October 29, 1999, with no one noting the connection to Devery, who had devised the route a century before.)

In 1902, Farrell and Devery purchased Empire City Race Track in Westchester (today Yonkers Raceway), Farrell having purportedly retired from the pool-hall business after the '01 elections. The same year, Devery quit the police force, his "reputation" secure. The new mayor, Seth Low, who had been president of Columbia University, wanted no part of Devery or his Tammany Hall political connections. Just a few months later, Devery, feeling betrayed by Croker, declared his candidacy to lead the Ninth Assembly District of New York while presiding over his "interests" from a saloon called the Pump on Eighth Avenue and Twenty-eighth Street. Once its darling, he was now taking on Tammany Hall.

Devery won the election, but when the Tammany leaders refused to recognize him, he organized a new party, the Independent Peoples Party, and ran for mayor in 1903 following his first season in baseball. He lost badly, despite offering free beer at his rallies.

Given the reputations of Farrell and Devery, a strong commissioner would no doubt have turned them away. But now they were poised to buy into the American League.

The purchase price for the franchise was $18,000 (about $440,000 in 2011 dollars). It remains a question of historical debate whether this was for the ownership of the Baltimore franchise that was to be moved to New York, or whether it was for a brand-new franchise with no Baltimore roots. In either case, it would be replacing the Orioles in the American League.

Devery's name wasn't even listed as a stockholder, although he had clearly put a lot of money into the cost of the team and the ballpark site. "Me a backer?" he had said. "I only wished I did own some stock in a baseball club. I'm a poor man and don't own stock in anything. Besides, how could I pitch a ball with this stomach?"

If it was a franchise shift, it included new owners (as with the St. Louis Browns' move to Baltimore in 1954), almost entirely new players (unlike the Montreal Expos' move to Washington in 2005), and a new spring training site (the Orioles had been in French Lick, Indiana, in 1902; the New Yorkers went to Atlanta in 1903). Though many historians feel the Yankees and Orioles were the same franchise, greats like McGraw, Robinson, Bresnahan, and McGinnity are never listed as Yankee Hall of Famers. There seems little to really connect the two teams other than one replacing the other. The first baseball encyclopedia, published in 1922, makes no connection. The Yankees themselves begin their record keeping with the 1903 season.

On March 14, just six weeks from opening day, the Greater New York Baseball Association was incorporated. The directors were John R. Bushong, Samuel C. Worthen, Jerome H. Buck, Bernard T. Lynch, and Henry T. Randall, names that were seldom heard from again in the operation of the team. A happy group of new "team officials" including Ban Johnson hired wagons to deliver them uptown to survey their soggy new site on that very day.

What would one day be a billion-dollar franchise had been born.

Chapter Two

WITH OWNERSHIP SECURED AND a team president in place, Ban Johnson then took personal charge of hiring a well-credentialed manager to run the team. That was thirty-three-year-old Clark Griffith.

Johnson had committed to taking a personal interest in this franchise. Farrell and Devery were neophytes, and Gordon had been out of it since his American Association days.

Among the things that Griffith brought to the table was a dislike of Mc-Graw, which Johnson found appealing. Griffith's distaste had much to do with on-field incidents, but the chance to compete against him in New York was a strong incentive for Griff to listen to Johnson's offer.

Griffith, known to baseball people as the Old Fox, owned the Washington Senators from 1919 to 1955 but was still a young fox when he was approached by Johnson.

Born in Clear Creek, Missouri, in 1869, he was raised in a log cabin by a single mother, his father having been killed in a hunting accident when Clark was two. The family had moved west by covered wagon, making this a genuine pioneer tale.

He had been a professional baseball player since he was eighteen, and became a pitcher of note with Cap Anson's Chicago Colts beginning in 1893. Although only five foot six and 156 pounds, he was a 20-game winner six times, owing largely to a variety of pitches that involved legal foreign substances. He jumped to the Chicago Americans in 1901 and won 20 again, serving as both player and manager and winning the first AL pennant.

Well respected in the game and thought of as one of the bigger stars raided from the National League, Griff had the credentials to be a high-profile leader of the fledgling New York team and still provide a contribution on the field.

Next came the ballpark. Freedman and Brush had outmaneuvered Johnson on several possible locations but had pretty much ignored areas north of the Polo Grounds, an option they thought doomed to failure.

Even as late as March 3, with players beginning to gather for spring training, no site had been announced, although Johnson had promised April 22 as a home opener. Not until March 10 was the area in Washington Heights finally announced, and someone calculated that fifteen sites had been considered in all. "Someone has guessed [the site]," said the *Evening Telegram*, "because every vacant lot has been seized upon by somebody as the available place." In making the announcement at the Fifth Avenue Hotel in Manhattan, Johnson said, "If the plan to secure this site had fallen through, we would have leased the Astor estate property at 161st Street and Jerome Avenue."

He was describing the land that two decades later would become the site of Yankee Stadium.

Griffith met his men at Union Station in Washington on the seventeenth, and they headed to Atlanta together. On March 25, the day of their first workout at Piedmont Park in Atlanta, blasting began to eliminate the rocks of what would be known as Hilltop Park. The excavation, estimated at $200,000, was far more expensive than the cost of constructing the park. Spring training moved ahead with no sign of what the home ballpark would ultimately look like. They would find out on opening day.

The area north of the Polo Grounds was not quite wilderness in 1903, but it was far enough north, and seemingly so unusable, as not to be considered prime real estate or a threat to Giants ticket sales.

A subway was being planned, and the 157th Street station of the Interborough Rapid Transit Company, by the Polo Grounds, would be opening in the fall of 1904. (It is today the 1 line.) The stop at 168th Street, where the Americans would play, would not open until March of 1906. So the new team would spend three seasons way uptown, counting on people either taking surface transportation like trolley cars, available at 125th Street (horse-drawn buses were being phased out and replaced by double-decker, electric-engine models), or trying out one of those new motorcars seen on occasion up and down Broadway. The streetcar lines that traversed Broadway would run special cars on game days, and the Third Avenue and Sixth Avenue lines would also take fans to within walking distance of the park. By opening day, most people had decided to use the streetcars and walk two blocks.

The ten-minute walk from the Polo Grounds stop, beginning in '05, was no big deal really, particularly in the company of fellow fans who shared the fun of the new underground experience. So high was the hilltop and so submerged was the subway that the 168th Street station, then as now, required an elevator from platform to street; there were no stairs. Even when the line was built, some fans chose to walk to 157th Street to avoid the slow and crowded elevators to the subway platform.

Broadway was on the eastern side of the hilltop property; Fort Washington Avenue was on the west, with West 168th Street at the north and West 165th Street at the south. St. Nicholas Avenue, another main street, converged with Broadway at 168th. You could look over the third-base line and over the top of the Deaf and Dumb Institute on Fort Washington Avenue and see the Palisades on the New Jersey side of the Hudson. It was a beautiful, pastoral view, an absolutely wonderful backdrop, unexpected in site selection, that would turn an afternoon at a ballgame into a true escape from the daily rigors of city life. "It is useful rather than ornamental," wrote *Sporting Life*, "and the view is a visual treat." Games were always over before the beautiful Palisades sunset, but the whole experience nevertheless contributed to what was being recognized as our "national pastime."

The entrance would be on Broadway, about ninety feet south of the end of the right-field foul line, where large painted letters said N.Y. above the team's office windows and AMERICAN LEAGUE. below, above three turnstiles, a period following "League." From there fans would walk along a passageway behind the seats, as far as the left-field bleachers, passing fifty-two private boxes. There was a little room left on the 165th Street side for a modest parking lot to accommodate carriages and, in just a few years, more motorcars. The words AMERICAN LEAGUE PARK. appeared again in six-foot letters on the wooden walls on either side of the entrance.

The land itself was leased to the baseball team for ten years by the New York Institute for the Blind, which was also known as the Blind Asylum. Public School 169 rested across Broadway at 168th and was a quite visible landmark beyond right-center field. A series of three five-story apartment buildings, still standing, loomed over dead center field on 168th.

The neighborhood was called Washington Heights, with the Hudson River just two blocks west. The George Washington Bridge would be constructed ten blocks north in about twenty-five years. Alex Rodriguez would be born in this neighborhood in 1975, when it was becoming largely populated by Dominican immigrants. In 1903, it was made up largely of Irish immigrants.

TODAY WE THINK the field was commonly called Hilltop Park, and the team commonly called the Highlanders. But in the first decade, while actually in use, the park was better known as the American League Grounds, sometimes just as "up on the hilltop" or "up the rockpile." Sometimes newspapers called it "the American Park."

The team was also better known as the New York Americans or the Greater New Yorks. On opening day, the *Telegram* called them the Deveryites. Sam Crane in the *Evening Journal* was determined that they be the Invaders. In those days, team nicknames were far less formal. It was, for example, more common to say the Bostons or the Boston Americans than to call them the Red Sox or the Pilgrims.

There was a well-known British military regiment called Gordon's Highlanders, and some fans thought team president Joe Gordon had suggested it as the team's nickname. "Hilltoppers" was also used on occasion, and as early as April 7, 1904, the *Evening Journal* used YANKEES BEAT BOSTON in a headline. ("Highlanders" didn't even appear in the *New York Times* until March 1906.) "Yankees" spoke to patriotism, certainly of northern patriotism (post–Civil War) going back to the Yankee Doodle days of the American Revolution, and baseball executives loved to consider the sport a uniquely American one. This was a particularly nationalistic time in the country's history, with victory in the Spanish-American War having come in 1898.

Writing for *Baseball* magazine in 1922, Fred Lieb reported,

> [Highlanders] was awkward to put in newspaper headlines. Finally the sporting editor at one of the New York evening papers exclaimed "The hell with this Highlanders; I am going to call this team 'the Yanks,' that will fit into heads better."
>
> Sam Crane, who wrote baseball on the same sheet, began speaking of the team as the Yankees and Yanks. When other sporting editors saw how much easier "Yanks" fit into top lines of a head, they too [decided against] Highlanders, a name which never was popular with the fans.

Mark Roth of the *Globe* was an early proponent of "Yankees," while Jim Price used it in the *Press*.

An irony to all of this is that if the major league baseball cities had been outside of America's Northeast at the start of the century, and if the team had ever envisioned selling its brand nationally, "Yankees" might have been rejected. Less than forty years removed from the Civil War, with Confederate veterans still in abundance, feelings still ran strong in the South against the term. It might have been considered insensitive.

The year 1903 was itself remarkable in America, with eighty-eight automobile manufacturers opening their doors, including Ford and Buick. Among companies founded that year were Harley-Davidson, Kraft Foods, Steuben Glass, Sanka coffee, and Lionel Trains. On April 22, a magnificent new building opened on Broad and Wall streets to house the New York Stock Exchange. People were running to movie houses to see a twelve-minute silent film called *The Great Train Robbery*. In December, the Wright Brothers made their first successful flight at Kitty Hawk.

Among the people born in 1903 were Bing Crosby, Bob Hope, Benjamin Spock, Walter O'Malley, and two who would have strong connections to the Yankees: a future restaurateur named Toots Shor, and a baby named Henry Louis Gehrig, born June 19 at 1994 Second Avenue near 103rd Street, about equidistant from Hilltop Park and the future Yankee Stadium.

FORMER POLICE COMMISSIONER Thomas F. McAvoy headed the construction of the American League grounds, a rush project that needed extensive dynamite work to clear five thousand cubic yards of rock from where the grandstand would sit, the filling in of a swamp that ran near the Broadway side of the park, the uprooting of trees, and the leveling, as best as possible, of the playing surface. The total area of the grounds was 9.6 acres. McAvoy was awarded contracts for both the excavation work and the construction work. Conveniently, he was the Tammany Hall leader of the Washington Heights district.

Much of the construction force was made up of some five hundred Polish, Italian, and Irish laborers, paid $1.50 a day, who were not otherwise part of the twelve-thousand-strong team digging up the subway tunnel. They would work night and day, in rain and chilly weather, with the home opener now moved to April 30.

Farrell and Devery spent $200,000 to level the site and $75,000 in construction costs for what would be a park with a capacity of sixteen thousand, largest in the league. (The league may have assumed some of the cost.) It was the last "five-figure" ballpark built for a major league baseball team. The two-story clubhouse wouldn't be ready by opening day, so the players would change in their hotel, two blocks east on Amsterdam Avenue, and would walk to the field amidst admiring crowds. Not only was the grandstand not going to be finished by opening day, there would be no roof over it; only the support posts to eventually support a roof. Plans for a second deck never did materialize, as attendance didn't seem to warrant it.

Additionally, Farrell set up an office in the new Flatiron Building at Twenty-third and Broadway, where Ban Johnson also would maintain an office (and where, coincidentally, the publisher of this book would be housed more than a century later). He later moved the team office to the Reed and Barton Building at 320 Fifth Avenue.

The park was made almost entirely of yellow pine and spruce wood, which remarkably never burned. Most wooden ballparks eventually met this fate: Parks in Philly, Boston, Baltimore, and Chicago all burned in one season in 1894. The first row was sixteen inches higher than the playing field, the twentieth and last row thirty-four feet above field level. Six aisles in the grandstand separated the sections and provided access to the field. After games, fans could exit through these aisles and across the field, a practice the Yankees maintained until 1966 wherever they called home.

When the clubhouse was ready, Gordon hired a young man to manage it named Fred Logan, twenty-three, who had been working for the Giants since he was ten but now switched over. He would remain with the Yankees until his death in 1947, the last original team employee.

Another part of the original cast was Harry Mosley Stevens, who had been selling scorecards and snacks at Giants games and now added the Hilltop to his growing concession business. Considered by some to have introduced hot dogs to ballparks, Harry M. Stevens Inc. would be the concessionaire for the Yankees on into the early sixties, with the team continuing to assign the rights until 2008, when it formed a partnership with the Dallas Cowboys football team to operate its own concessions.

Stevens produced the official scorecard for the team (five cents), calling the team the American League Base Ball Club and its field American League Park. There was no reference to Highlanders or Hilltop. The twelve-page program, with rosters and room to score in the centerfold, included advertising for such products as Philip Morris cigarettes, Dewar's scotch, Coca-Cola, Horton's ice cream cones, automobile oils and greases from Atlas, Pommery champagne, and Henry Rahe's Café just opposite the 168th Street subway station, where you could order Jac. Ruppert's Extra Pale, Knickerbocker, and Ruppiner.

There was also an ad that said, "Any baseball player who will hit the 'Bull' Durham cut-out sign on the field with a fairly batted ball during a regular scheduled league game will receive $50.00 in cash."

On the front of the scorecard was a notice from the telephone company stating that "Public Telephone Booths on Grand Stand, rear aisle, northerly end. Patrons expecting inward calls should leave their seat number with the operator."

While the Giants used Pinkerton agents to police the Polo Grounds during games, the Highlanders, with Devery's connections, chose to use retired policemen.

Joseph Gavin was hired as team secretary, charged with making travel arrangements, paying the players, counting the gate, keeping the books, and answering the occasional question from the press. His duties would be assumed a year later by Abe Nahon, Farrell's right-hand man throughout his gambling-hall days and a man Farrell trusted with the team's checkbook and to make immediate business decisions. Nahon, a Columbia Law School graduate known as "On the Level Abe" by racetrack acquaintances, was officially the team's secretary-treasurer.

Team finances were not complicated. Income came from ticket sales and concessions. Expenses were salaries, travel, and rent, plus assorted clubhouse purchases including a large iron safe made by Mosler, which would house the players' personal "valuables" during the games—their wallets, jewelry, and keys. Once you opened the master door to the safe, which was about four feet high, you would find twenty-four small drawers, each stenciled with a player's name: Chesbro, Keeler, and so on. The safe, bearing the original names, would ultimately be the last vestige of the Highlander years, kept at Yankee Stadium before disappearing during renovations in 1973.

By then I was working for the Yankees and knew the importance of the safe. It had been moved to the Polo Grounds when the team relocated there, then hauled to Yankee Stadium in 1923. And there it rested, first in the original clubhouse and then in the "new" clubhouse built in 1946. I spoke to Pete Sheehy about it. Pete was the clubhouse man, an employee since '27; Logan's assistant and then successor.

"Pete, they will be tearing down this place in two weeks. Do you think we should get this moved out early to protect it?" I asked.

I think he nodded. He was a man of few words.

Sadly, the safe never made it to Shea Stadium, where the rest of the team's belongings were being stored during the construction.

The worst part of the new ballpark was surely the mess in right field. Try though he might, poor Phil Schenck could do nothing about this less-than-big-league condition. Willie Keeler, it was reported, "had to stand on a wooden platform placed over the impromptu ravine."

Schenck was unable to get sod over the muck that was right field, and so after a good rain there was a big mud puddle, and it was anything but level. The only good news for Schenck was that the first homestand lasted just six games, and by the time the team got back from its road trip, green paint had been applied to the grandstand, a roof was added, and, remarkably, right field was level and sodded.

Left field was 365 feet and right field began as 385, but was reduced to 290 for the balance of the first season before being restored to 385 (1904–06) and then 365 (1907–12). Right-center field was the deepest part of the field at 424, with center field at 420. The fence in left was eight feet high, then twelve feet in center and right. A modest scoreboard in left field stretched for some twenty-five feet near the foul pole, providing a line score along with the scores of other American League games, while an adjacent board labeled "National League" kept a line score of the Giants game. In 1907 the Bull Durham tobacco sign was placed in center (later shifted to right). The sign was not unique to New York but was part of the origin for the term "bullpen," where relief pitchers could warm up.

Of course, the dimensions were fairly meaningless in the deadball era. Few home runs ever cleared the fences. Hitters of the time adjusted to placing the ball between fielders as best they could. Although a muscular male athlete might be expected to try and hit the ball as hard as possible, the futility of having it caught on the fly made the practicality of good placement the secret to success.

Hilltop Park would in fact be a haven for inside-the-park home runs and a nightmare for over-the-fence ones. In its first eight seasons, before center field was shortened, only 23 balls cleared the fences on the fly (15 of them in 1903 when the right field fence was 290), while 175 inside-the-parkers were achieved. According to research reported in *Ballparks of the Deadball Era* by Ronald Selter, 61 percent of home runs in the American League were inside-the-parkers between 1904 and 1910, but 95 percent of home runs hit at the Hilltop failed to clear a fence.

The first two over-the-fence homers at Hilltop were hit by Buck Freeman of Boston on the same day, June 1, 1903. Ernie Courtney hit the first for New York in the ninth inning of the same game. Of the 23 over-the-fencers, just 12 were hit by Highlander players in those eight seasons—five of them by pitchers (Jack Chesbro two, Griffith, Harry Howell, and Jack Powell one each), with the others by Herm McFarland (four, all in 1903), Jimmy Williams, and John Ganzel. Between 1904 and 1910, there were only eight over-the-fence homers at Hilltop Park.

APART FROM GRIFFITH, the most prominent new member of the team was Wee Willie Keeler, who had batted an amazing .371 during twelve National League seasons. This included a .424 year for Brooklyn six years earlier, with 239 hits, 199 of them singles, and a forty-four-game hitting streak. His move to New York was engineered by Johnson, who "found him an easy man to deal with."

Of course he was easy. Keeler was given a $10,000 contract, making him the highest-paid player in the game.

A native of Brooklyn, a student at PS 26, and then a lifelong bachelor who lived with his father at 376 Pulaski Street, Keeler's lifetime Highlander average, .294, would fall far short of what he had accomplished earlier on. He would choke up on his twenty-nine-ounce bat and smack the ball pretty much wherever he wanted it to land. He was also known to have some sort of no-strikeout streak covering perhaps 700 at-bats during the 1890s, although the actual mark is not researchable.

"As I recall it," said Keeler, "I started my record the tag end of the season of 1895, went through the entire season of 1896 without whiffing, and played a number of games in the spring of 1897 before I was retired over the strikeout route."

At five foot four, and 140 pounds, Keeler contributed one of the best-known expressions to the game's legend. Asked his batting secret, he told Abe Yager of the *Brooklyn Eagle*, "Keep your eye clear and hit 'em where they ain't."

"He was a nice little guy, very friendly, always laughing and kidding," recalled Sam Crawford to Lawrence Ritter in *The Glory of Their Times*.

Until Lou Gehrig came along, Keeler was certainly the best native New York player in major league history.

Of course, Keeler probably didn't expect to be starting the season negotiating mud puddles and standing on planks of wood. In fact, on the very first play of the very first game, Keeler was almost lost to the team attempting to make a play in right with sordid consequences.

Stocking the rest of the roster also involved Johnson's fine hand, with Griffith getting more involved as the days passed. The Pittsburgh connection provided the Americans with a terrific spitball pitcher in Chesbro, who had led the National League with a 28–6 record in 1902, a quality starter in Jesse Tannehill, who had been 20–6 as Chesbro's teammate, the infielder Wid Conroy, plus the go-between catcher, seventeen-year veteran Jack O'Connor, and outfielder Lefty Davis. The Pittsburgh players, apart from Griffith, were the first Yankees in terms of date of agreeing, and with Pittsburgh having won the National League's 1902 pennant, these were huge defections.

Griffith may have agreed to play for New York as early as August 1902, even without the club secured, and had been talking up the new team to possible defectors all along. It was said he was even responsible for a delay in Christy Mathewson finally re-signing with the Giants.

Five players who finished 1902 with the Orioles found themselves on the '03 Highlanders: right-handed pitcher Harry Howell, second baseman Jimmy Williams, pitcher Snake Wiltse, and outfielder Herm McFarland. Third baseman Ernie Courtney played just one game for the '02 Orioles.

Longtime star Boston shortstop Herman Long, thirty-seven, joined the team as its senior citizen, along with Dave Fultz, from Brown University, who came over from the Athletics after leading the league in runs scored in '02.

Others who rounded out the roster were Doc Adkins, a pitcher, John Ganzel, a first baseman recovering from smallpox, Monte Beville, a rookie catcher, and pitchers Barney Wolfe and John Deering. (On June 10, New York would send Long and Courtney to Detroit for Kid Elberfeld—the franchise's first trade.)

Cameo appearances during the first season would be made by Pat McCauley, Jack Zalusky, Paddy Greene, Tim Jordan, Fred Holmes, Ambrose Puttmann, Elmer Bliss, and Eddie Quick: a total of twenty-eight different players who could claim to be original Yankees.

Mike Martin was hired as the team's trainer, and over the next few years, the team would add a trio of scouts: Toronto-born Arthur Irwin (who would also emerge as a sort of general manager), Eugene McCann, and Duke Farrell, a former Boston catcher.

Irwin, a former infielder and manager of the 1896 Giants, was the best-known of the three, a veteran of the game who saw himself as a "baseball anarchist" because of his opposition to a World Series, which he felt made the regular season and the pennants less important, hurting fourteen of the sixteen teams.

Williams, a St. Louis native, had a great rookie season for Pittsburgh in 1899, compiling hitting streaks of twenty-seven and twenty-six games and finishing fifth in the National League with a .355 average. (The twenty-seven-game hitting streak is still a Pirates club record, better than Honus Wagner, Paul Waner, or Roberto Clemente.) In 1901 he jumped to Baltimore and moved to second base, with McGraw playing third. He led the American League with 21 triples in '02. He would live until 1965, making him the longest-living principal member of the original team.

Chesbro (name actually pronounced "Cheez-bro") came from North Adams, Massachusetts. Although we tend to look with scorn at his unsanitary spitball today (the pitch was declared illegal in 1920), it was a legal pitch in his day, and he was a leading practitioner. He would be the team's number-one starter and would teach the spitball to Howell, who achieved greater success than he ever had before.

Chesbro's Pittsburgh pitching partner, Tannehill, did not find the success in New York that Chesbro did. He had been released by Pittsburgh, rather than allowed to jump, because owner Barney Dreyfuss felt he was a ringleader of talks with Ban Johnson. But he hated Hilltop Park. "The grounds are on a high bluff overlooking the river and the cold wind blows over the diamond morning, noon, and night," he said. "A man would have to have a cast iron arm to pitch winning ball under these circumstances."

William "Wid" Conroy, twenty-six, from Camden, New Jersey, played for Connie Mack at Milwaukee in 1900. In 1902, he actually jumped from the American League to the National, joining Pittsburgh and taking over at shortstop from Wagner, who moved to the outfield. He jumped to New York in '03 and moved from short to third when the team acquired Elberfeld.

Fultz wasn't a jumper: His contract had been purchased by New York in March of '03. He would later go on to earn a law degree and become president of a players' union formed in 1912. His brief New York career ended in 1905 when his jaw was broken in a collision with Elberfeld.

"Popup John" Ganzel, who came from Kalamazoo, Michigan (later famous as Derek Jeter's hometown), hit the first home run in Yankee history on May 11, 1903, in the team's seventeenth game. He was one of four brothers who played pro ball, and his older brother Charlie preceded him into the majors. The Ganzel family was known as the "first family of Michigan baseball." On May 5, 1903, Ganzel, playing first base at Hilltop Park, caught a liner, stepped on the base, and threw to Long at shortstop. The team had a triple play before it had a home run.

McFarland, just five foot six, played five seasons in the majors, and his only year in New York would be his last. He'd batted .322 for Baltimore the year before, but it turned out to be a season well above his skills. He had played for Griffith in Chicago in 1901–02, and in spring training of '02 suffered a scare on a ten-minute run in Excelsior Springs, Missouri. Running over a train trestle high above ground, he, Griff, and two others heard a train coming and had to grab onto a railroad tie and dangle over the river, clinging for dear life.

Herman Long's defection to New York after thirteen years in Boston was a tough blow for National League fans. Four times he had batted .300 for the Beaneaters, and with Fred Tenney, Jimmy Collins, and Bobby Lowe had been part of what was called the Big Four. But his stay in New York lasted only two months.

"Ladies and gentlemen," as a PA announcer might say today, "these are your 1903 New York Americans!"

The team opened its season in Washington on Wednesday, April 22, with a lineup of Davis in left, Keeler in right, Fultz in center, Williams at second, Ganzel at first, Conroy at third, Long at short, O'Connor catching, and Chesbro pitching.

Getting uniforms made quickly was a challenge, but it was accomplished thanks to the experience of the A.G. Spalding company, provider of team uniforms. Griffith himself had a hand in designing the look, a look that some considered gaudy and inappropriate for a stately New York franchise.

The players wore navy-blue wool jerseys and knickers with four buttons down the front to midchest. On each side was a white letter: N on the right, Y on the left. They wore white belts and gray wool socks. The caps were also dark blue with white stripes emanating from the top center, and no lettering.

Over time, the Highlanders hitters came to use the N.Y. letters to signal baserunners whether they would be swinging on the next pitch—touching the Y for "yes" if swinging, or touching the N for "no" if not—as they plotted hit-and-run plays.

The New Yorkers lost their opener 3–1 to Washington pitcher Al Orth, with Williams driving in Keeler for their only run, in the first inning. The game took an hour and forty-five minutes and was played before 11,950 witnesses to history, a sellout. Farrell sat with Ban Johnson.

The next day, they beat Washington 7–2 for their first victory, with Howell getting the win.

AFTER FINISHING THEIR first road trip at 3–4 on April 29, the team took the train from Philadelphia to New York for the big home debut the next day.

Would the Americans be a hit with the public? Would fans find their way to Washington Heights?

An overflow crowd of 16,243 passed through the revolving turnstiles of Hilltop Park, with each fan receiving a small American flag to wave. (The team's first "promo day"!) "Street fakirs, selling everything from a fake score card . . . vied with each other as to who had the most vigorous and resounding lung power," wrote Sam Crane in the *Telegram*. The crowd was almost totally adult males, most in coats, ties, and hats, a style that would be the norm at New York baseball games for decades to come. Many watched for free from perches across the street on Broadway known as "Rubberneck Flats." While not a record-breaking crowd, (18,675 had seen a Philadelphia-Chicago game the summer before, in which Rube Waddell beat Clark Griffith 2–1), it was certainly enough to bring satisfaction to Johnson, Farrell, Devery, and Gordon. Clearly, fans wanted to see American League baseball, were curious about the new team, and had no trouble finding their way uptown. This was going to work!

The players from both Washington and New York exited their new, unfinished clubhouses beyond right-center field and lined up at 3:00 P.M., set to parade toward the infield, each also holding a small American flag. Ropes were drawn across the back part of the outfield, with any ball hit in there counting as a double. The box-seat crowd paid a dollar each to sit on movable folding chairs; eight thousand others filled in the grandstand benches at fifty cents each. Smaller bleachers, along the outfield, held an additional twenty-five hundred at twenty-five cents each. All the seating was placed over concrete foundations.

The opening lineup at the American League Grounds was the same as the road opener, except Courtney was at short instead of Long. Washington's star was Big Ed Delahanty, who would die in a mysterious fall off the team train crossing near Niagara Falls two months later.

For a home uniform, the Highlanders reversed things. A white wool uniform went with blue socks, a blue belt, and a blue collar. Again there were buttons halfway down the chest, with a blue N on the right and a blue Y on the left. The cap was white with a blue visor and blue stripes originating from the top center. Although the weather was perfect for late April, the Highlanders wore maroon coats over their uniforms for the parade across the outfield at the start of the game.

The gates opened at 1:00 for the 3:30 game, with live music provided by the 69th Regiment Band under the direction of Bandmaster Bayne, who led the crowd in singing "The Washington Post March," "*Columbia* the Gem of the Ocean" (the most popular patriotic tune of the time), "Yankee Doodle," and "The Star-Spangled Banner." The crowd stood, cheered, and waved their flags. (Farrell wanted game times at 4:00 to accommodate the Wall Street workers; 3:30 was a compromise to the deadline needs of newspapers.)

(In an oversight, rainchecks were not part of the ticket, and one day early in the season, the consequence of that was felt when fans at the hilltop were invited back—on their honor—after a game was called. Needless to say, thousands more showed up when word of free baseball spread, breaking down a fence and overrunning the field.)

Joe Gordon was the prominent New York club official involved in the ceremonies. Farrell and Devery were present but did not take part.

While the facility was reported as being only "half-complete," the *New York Times* reported that "the diamond has been sodded and rolled until it looks as level as a newly covered billiard table, but the outfield is in a rough and rugged condition." The *Evening Journal* used NEW PARK A MARVEL as a subhead.

"There is a good deal of filling in to be done in right field and ground rules will be arranged in regard to the value of hits made in that direction," reported the *Times*.

> Only six games have been scheduled for this and the following playing days, and then the teams will go over the circuit. It is hoped that by the time the players return from the Western trip everything, to the merest detail, will be completed and that the new club and its team will have a successful season in every respect.
>
> While the big gathering was not overdemonstrative, the absence of fault finding was in itself an assurance to the management that the patrons fully appreciated the difficulties which beset

the new club, and due credit was given to the almost herculean efforts of the officials who had accomplished so much in such a brief time.

The sod had not yet turned fully green in the outfield, but the infield was beautiful. Phil Schenck was lauded for his efforts.

The hastily assembled park had the biggest seating capacity in the league and remained the biggest until Sportsman's Park in St. Louis expanded to 17,000 in 1906. Boston's Huntington Avenue Grounds rose from 9,000 to 12,500 in the decade; Chicago's South Side Park seated 14,000; Cleveland's League Park held 11,200; Detroit's Bennett Park went from 8,500 to 10,500; Philadelphia's Columbia Park went from 10,000 to 13,600; and Washington's two American League parks held steady at 7,000. The Polo Grounds, just down Broadway, also had a seating capacity of 16,000 for its Giants.

As FOR THE first home game, Ban Johnson threw out the ceremonial first pitch to the umpire Tom Connolly, and the band struck up "The Star-Spangled Banner" just as Washington's first batter was stepping in to hit. Then it was a 6–2 New York victory, played in ninety minutes. The Highlanders scored single runs in the first and second innings and added two in the fifth and two in the seventh. Keeler, who walked, was the first baserunner. Fultz had the team's first home-field hit and scored its first run. Ganzel had the first RBI (not really a statistic that was yet maintained). The biggest cheers were reserved for Keeler. Chesbro went the distance for the seven-hit victory, holding Delahanty 0 for 5 as New York looked just like what Ban Johnson wanted them to be: world beaters. Everyone went home happy. American League baseball had officially landed on Manhattan Island.

Chapter Three

TO THE DISAPPOINTMENT OF Ban Johnson, the Americans weren't more than ordinary in 1903. Griffith tried many lineups and relied heavily on Chesbro and Tannehill, but each step forward seemed followed by a step back. He himself got in trouble early, arguing too vehemently with umpire Tom Connolly in just the team's fourteenth game and finding himself suspended by Johnson for ten days. Keeler took charge.

Ballpark improvements continued, but fans weren't flocking to the Hilltop, as word spread that it was "unfinished" and "hard to reach." The opening-day glitter quickly wore off.

As for the play on the field, some questioned Griffith's leadership. The sage eighty-year-old baseball historian Henry Chadwick wrote, "The failure to secure services of a team manager of [Ned] Hanlon-like experience and ability was at the root of their failings." (Hanlon was the highly regarded Brooklyn manager.)

Chadwick's dismissal of Griffith's work could not be taken lightly. No figure in baseball was as respected as the aging Chadwick, despite his being "just" a journalist. "Father" Chadwick was the man whose writings in the annual *Baseball Guide* and in an assortment of newspapers was always taken seriously. He is today the only journalist in the Baseball Hall of Fame.

With Chadwick as the leader and Joe Vila as an early catalyst in the formation of the Yankees, the relationship between the team and the press was established early. From the humble beginnings to the entry of radio, then television, and then the Internet, it has been a marriage of necessity, with the requisite highs and lows of any marriage. Newspapers knew that coverage of the team would attract more circulation, thus enabling them to sell advertising at a higher rate. Teams knew that the coverage was free promotion for their product, and that they were in a much better position than other forms of entertainment such as Broadway or the cinema, where the show would get a review and then be forced to rely on paid advertising. Baseball, however, received daily free coverage, with each story helping to sell the product by reinforcing its importance and making the players celebrities.

Over the decades, there would be times when the team hated its coverage, and there would be times when the newspapers would want to ignore the team. But in the end they needed each other. It was just good business.

And so the teams regularly paid for the journalists to travel with them, covering most of their expenses. Not until the late fifties did the growing Long Island newspaper *Newsday*, under sports editor Jack Mann and reporter Stan Isaacs, decide that the free perks could be seen as compromising its role and tell the Yankees it would assume all the costs on its own. Other papers followed, with the *New York Times* forbidding its writers to serve as official scorers or to vote for awards or the Hall of Fame, let alone accept travel or Christmas gifts from the teams.

The '03 Highlanders were 17–23 after a win on June 9 when Ban Johnson helped to implement the first trade in franchise history. New York sent Courtney and Long to Detroit for Norm "the Tabasco Kid" Elberfeld.

Kid Elberfeld, twenty-eight, the youngest of ten surviving children born to German immigrant parents in Pomeroy, Ohio, was a light-hitting shortstop of whom much was expected on defense.

Tabasco sauce, made from spicy tabasco peppers, had been on American tables since 1868, and it provided a fitting nickname for this pepperpot of a figure, a five-foot-seven, 158-pounder who could spice things up.

He was an immediate favorite with fans of the era who liked their athletes rowdy. He was the anti-Keeler, the bad boy that young fans were not supposed to emulate (which of course they did). At the same time, he would be high maintenance for the team and the league: He was known to pick fights, go after opponents with baseball bats, stomp on umpires' toes, curse loudly, deliberately get hit with pitches and then charge the mound, earn suspension after suspension, and suffer through periods of indifference or questionable injuries.

While he was not what Johnson felt was an American League player, Johnson knew the Kid would spark fan interest, and indeed Elberfeld was much influenced by McGraw himself, for whom he hoped to play in 1903.

However, letting him go from Detroit to the Giants would have been seen as upending the peace agreement between the leagues, so he was forced to remain with Detroit until an intraleague trade beckoned. There he played for manager Ed Barrow, the Yankees' future general manager. Barrow had just suspended the Kid a week before the trade for "loaferish conduct." Rejuvenated by the move to New York, Elberfeld gave the team a quick lift and they won five of their first six games with him. In early July they won seven straight, went over .500, and began to play decent baseball, even while failing to move up in the standings.

But the lineup would ultimately fail as often as not. Getting "Chicagoed" (shut out) ten times, they never really contended. The best they could say was that as a new team, finishing in the first division (fourth place, out of eight teams, ten games over .500) was an accomplishment. One newspaper reporter suggested that the failures of the season might be owed to the "unfit physical condition of some players."

Keeler's .313 led the team but was well below his National League performances, while Chesbro (21–15), Tannehill (15–15), and Griffith (14–11) were too often just ordinary. Tannehill would be dispatched to Boston after the season and would win 43 games over the next two seasons there.

In the end, Elberfeld was a bright spot, hitting .287, exceeding expectations at the plate.

The Highlanders drew 211,808, seventh among the eight teams in the league, a disappointment after the big opening day. It meant they averaged just about 3,400 per game. (They played nine doubleheaders.) The euphoria of opening day faded.

The Giants, meanwhile, with 61 victories from Christy Mathewson and Joe McGinnity combined, led all of baseball with 579,530, and one could say successfully headed off the American League's threat to their territory.

The Highlanders were just not a very exciting ballclub. And with only one exception, almost all of their next seventeen seasons would feel like 1903— some better than others, some disasters, but just not very exciting. Certainly it would be the case throughout the Farrell-Devery years, and of course through the years at Hilltop Park.

The one exception was 1904.

IN 1904, THE Highlanders made their home caps all white and put horizontal stripes on their socks. Like their annual spring training sites that were ever shifting (Atlanta in 1903–04, Montgomery in '05, Birmingham in '06, Atlanta in 1907–08, Macon in '09, Athens in 1910–11, Atlanta in '12, Bermuda in '13, Houston in '14, Savannah in '15, Macon in 1916–18, Jacksonville in 1919–20, Shreveport in '21, New Orleans in 1922–24), so too were tweaks to the uniform an annual event.

In 1905 they had an awkward interlocking "NY" on both home whites and road grays. In '06 they were back to their original look. In '07, gray replaced navy as the road color. In '08, a navy cap appeared for the first time. In '09, the now familiar interlocking NY debuted on the sleeve. In 1910, the NY appeared for the first time on caps—red on navy at home, blue on gray for the road. In 1911 the words "New York" first appeared on road jerseys. In 1912, a pinstriped home uniform looking much like today's debuted, accompanied by a pinstriped cap with a blue brim. But the pinstripes were replaced in 1913–14 by a solid white with the interlocking NY over the heart, and for the first time, the "New York" road grays were worn all season. In 1915, the pinstripes returned for good, but by 1917 the NY on the chest had vanished, not to reappear until 1936. (Babe Ruth never wore it.) The navy caps with the NY were used for a time only on the road, and full-time starting in 1922.

The interlocking NY was designed by Tiffany and Company for the New York Police Department in 1877: It was used in a medal for a fallen police officer, John McDowell. Police symbolism was appropriate to Bill Devery's legacy. There was a long-standing admiration between the New York police and fire departments and the Yankees, no better demonstrated than when George Steinbrenner created the Silver Shield charity to look after the families of fallen police and firemen.

1904, THE FIRST year of a 154-game schedule, would produce the franchise's first pennant race and the first great New York–Boston rivalry. Had New York won the pennant in '04, it would have been an enormous triumph for Johnson and by extension Griffith, accomplishing so much so quickly.

But they didn't win, so it didn't become a year of great Yankee history, distantly connected to all the other championship teams. But it was the best of all the pre–Babe Ruth teams.

Rumors that Griffith might be replaced by the Cubs' Frank Selee were put to rest when Selee signed a new contract with Chicago in July. With that tension removed, New York and Boston battled back and forth, New York never going ahead by more than two games or falling behind by more than a game and a half.

Al Orth, thirty-one years old and the man who beat New York in their first-ever game, came over from Washington to pretty much replace Griffith as a starting pitcher, going 11–6 while Griffith limited himself to just 16 starts. The spitball was Orth's signature pitch, and some credited him with being one of its originators. He certainly helped to popularize it, along with Chesbro.

An interesting pickup that season was forty-year-old Deacon McGuire, purchased from Detroit. He was the oldest player in the league, having debuted in 1884. The onetime Brooklyn star caught 97 games for New York, with Red Kleinow handling 62, including most of the final month.

On June 17, Boston traded popular outfielder Patsy Dougherty to New York to play left field. The trade raised eyebrows: New York had surrendered only a utility infielder named Bob Unglaub. Was this the hand of Ban Johnson working to strengthen New York again? Dougherty, who had been feuding with Boston management, was the league's leading run scorer, a statistic rated only below batting average by fans and players. Unglaub played only nine games for Boston. (He would briefly manage the club in 1907 and then was replaced by Deacon McGuire, whom by then New York had released.)

Also new to the team in 1904 was an outfielder named John Anderson, who accidentally gave his name to baseball slang when he tried to steal second base with the bases loaded. On into the 1930s, such a boneheaded play would be called a John Anderson. Mercifully for his family, the expression eventually faded from use.

The roster also included a couple of fresh-faced pitchers of diverse backgrounds. The team signed one of the nation's most heralded amateur prospects, Harvard's Walter Clarkson, brother of the great nineteenth-century star John Clarkson. He was immediately banned from Harvard's team after signing, so he went right to the major leagues, debuting on July 2 with a 3–2 loss. He won only one game that year, and only 18 in five big-league seasons.

Then there was Ned Garvin.

Garvin joined the team from Brooklyn with a month left in the season and was an undistinguished 0–1 in two games. But Garvin had an amazing history of barroom brawls, some involving gunplay, while on more sober days he wrote poetry. Known as "the Navasota Tarantula" (he came from Navasota, Texas), he made Elberfeld seem like a choirboy.

Ten days after the 1904 season ended, Garvin was involved in another assault, this time beating up an insurance salesman who wouldn't engage him in conversation. So seventy-five years—almost to the day—before Billy Martin fought a marshmallow salesman and got fired as Yankee manager, this marked the end of Garvin's major league career. He died less than four years later at age thirty-four, a victim of consumption.

The season also saw the first appearance on the field of photographer Charles Conlon, who would become a fixture at New York baseball games on into the 1940s, shooting posed photos and occasional action pictures onto glass negatives and providing the earliest looks at American League Park and its players that we know.

KEELER AND CHESBRO, of whom so much was hoped for in 1903, delivered in '04. Keeler played as he had in his National League days, batting .343, while Happy Jack had the winningest twentieth-century season of any man who stepped onto the mound, recording 41 victories in 51 starts, tossing 48 complete games and 455 innings—including 44 consecutive shutout innings—and posting a 1.82 ERA (although that statistic was not officially recorded until 1912). His 239 strikeouts would be a team record for 74 years until Ron Guidry broke it in 1978. His 14 straight victories was a team record until Roger Clemens won 16 straight 97 years later. While pitch counts were certainly not kept, one can assume he threw about 150 pitches a game, often with only a day or two off. Most of his pitches were spitballs, which were no less taxing on the arm than fastballs or curveballs were.

What a finish the 1904 season provided! A "death struggle," said Irving Sanborn of the *Chicago Tribune*. For excitement, rivalry, star power, competitiveness, and the total engagement of fans of the two cities, one could truly place the final contests with all the great Yankees–Red Sox games that would follow over the next century. Not only were the rivals geographically close, but their cities were hotbeds of the game's very origins and their fans among the most rabid and knowledgeable. Boston, managed by Jimmy Collins, was the defending World Series champion; New York, the team built to contend for this honor in a hurry.

"There may be closer races . . . in future years," wrote Sanborn, "but there can be no pennant battle which will have more to enthuse over and less to regret than did the American League's of 1904."

This had everything that Ban Johnson could have dreamed up, except that Brush and McGraw of the Giants, who had clinched the National

League championship weeks before, were not about to do what Barney Dreyfuss had done in 1903—play a World Series. Pittsburgh had lost to Boston in '03, an embarrassment to the National League, and they would have no more of it. The Giants' excuse was that their opponents would be cheated out of playing against champions should they lose a World Series, as Pittsburgh had the year before, devaluing their appeal. A number of angry Giants players, looking to bag the extra money a Series would bring, spoke out against McGraw's position and offered to play all the games at Hilltop Park. A petition signed by ten thousand New Yorkers demanding a series was presented to the Giants, but there would be no postseason as long as McGraw had his way.

AFTER THE GAMES of Wednesday, October 5, Boston led New York by half a game. Five games against each other remained on the schedule, three in New York and two in Boston. It was, essentially, a best-of-five playoff series for the American League pennant.

For the game on Friday, October 7, New York arrived home from St. Louis just after noon for the 3:30 game. It had been nearly a twenty-eight-hour trip. New York wore its road dark blues, and Boston, arriving from Chicago, wore their road grays. Boston sent Norwood Gibson (17–13) against Chesbro (40–10).

Over nine thousand fans turned out as New York won its fifth straight to move into first place with a 91–56 record to Boston's 92–58. The score was 3–2 with Chesbro winning for the 41st time; the fans, totally caught up in the thrill of the race, carried Happy Jack on their shoulders to the outfield clubhouse after the final out. Patsy Dougherty, recovering from malaria, scored twice and drove in what proved to be the winning run in the seventh.

The next morning, the teams boarded New York Central trains for the five-and-a-half-hour trip to Boston and a doubleheader at Huntington Avenue Grounds. (Farrell had rented out Hilltop Park to Columbia University for a football game.) Even though Griffith had told Chesbro he wasn't needed and should stay home, Jack showed up at Grand Central. He pitched the next game.

Enough tickets were sold in advance that temporary seating had been created to handle the overflow crowd of more than twenty-eight thousand, while thousands more stood downtown in front of newspaper offices, following the game on outdoor scoreboards.

Alas, Chesbro, on no days rest, couldn't get past the fourth inning, and his reliever, Clarkson, was also ineffective, as Bill Dinneen won, 13–2, to put Boston back in first.

In the third game, thirty-seven-year-old Cy Young, who in May had pitched a perfect game against Philadelphia on these very grounds, stopped New York 1–0, the winning run scoring in the fifth in a game called after seven innings due to darkness.

Now New York would have to win both of the remaining games—a doubleheader on Monday back at Hilltop—to win the pennant.

So this was it, the final day of the regular season, Boston and New York, two must-win games, and the most important ones yet played by the Highlanders. Some two hundred Royal Rooters wearing WORLD CHAMPIONS badges came down from Boston, although if any wore HIGHLANDERS SUCK T-shirts under their suits and ties, it went unrecorded. They were seated together on the left-field side while the rest of the standing-room-only crowd of 28,584 cheered for their New Yorkers.

Someone found a ladder and a lot of fans scrambled up to the grandstand roof only to be shooed back down. Ropes were placed in the outfield to pack extra fans there. One can only imagine the pregame revelry as so many thousands headed up Broadway via buses and on foot for this great final showdown. Streetcar was still the way to go: The 145th Street subway station, the northernmost stop of the IRT, about a mile short of the ballpark, would not open for three more weeks.

The Royal Rooters had adopted a Broadway theme song, "Tessie," which they delighted in singing but which was quickly taken up in a mocking way by the New York fanatics with rolled-up megaphones whenever their team staged a rally. Dueling "Tessies."

Boston also brought along a mascot, an "aged Negro" who danced atop their dugout to "Dixie" and "Old Black Joe."

It would be Chesbro, of course, well rested now with a full day off, taking on Dinneen. So enchanted were the fans with Chesbro's season that the game would be halted as he came to bat in the third inning, when fans from his hometown of North Adams presented him with a fur-lined overcoat.

New York scored two in the fifth for the delirious faithful, but Boston tied it in the seventh. They went to the ninth tied 2–2.

In an inning for the ages, Boston's Lou Criger beat out an infield single and was sacrificed to second by Dinneen. On a grounder to Elberfeld at short, Criger somehow sneaked past the ball and got to third. And so with two out and Criger dancing off third, Freddie Parent at bat, and the count 2 and 2, Chesbro took the sign from his catcher, Red Kleinow, and delivered. The ball sailed over Kleinow's head and went all the way to the backstop, ninety-one feet behind him. Criger scored standing up and the crowd groaned, then fell silent. Forty-one victories in a season, but a horrific wild pitch in the final inning on the final day had given Boston a 3–2 lead.

In the last of the ninth, Dougherty struck out with runners on first and second and the game was over, making the second game, a 1–0 New York win, meaningless.

Sportswriter Mark Roth later told people he saw Chesbro "crying like a baby" on the Highlanders bench after the inning ended, while the Bostons danced in front of their dugout.

"How did I make the wild pitch?" Chesbro told the *Boston Post* in January. "How does any pitcher make one? I used a spitball, but the spitball had nothing to do with it. I simply put too much force into the throw. Dinneen had been using the spitball and had made the ball rather slippery. I am not blaming Dinneen, however. I put too much force into the ball and that's all. It hit the grand stand and it's a long story of what happened. We lost the pennant."

Boston won it by eight percentage points. Had New York won both of those final games, they would have won by six percentage points. There were no plans to replay New York's four tie games. (It did complicate the understanding of the standings for fans of both teams, who argued all week over what was needed to win.)

Chesbro's wild pitch was played over and over in people's minds and discussed for years. Could Kleinow have caught it? Was their some superhuman effort that could have kept the ball from sailing out of range? As years passed, some indeed felt it might even have been a passed ball.

Almost forty years later, writer Fred Lieb ran into Kid Elberfeld and asked what he thought. He'd been at shortstop.

Said the Tabasco Kid, "That ball rode so far over Kleinow's head that he couldn't have caught it standing on a stepladder."

"They said it was a wild pitch, and I'll let it go at that," said Chesbro years later. "But I think the ball might have been caught."

In 1938, Griffith, attending the Winter Meetings in New Orleans, told the press that he always thought it was a passed ball. "Kleinow . . . was the man who blew the championship," he said. "[He] had been out celebrating the night before. His vision was none too keen and he missed the pitch that would have given New York its first American League pennant."

Like Babe Ruth's "called-shot home run" in the 1932 World Series, it would be seen differently by every eyewitness and be one of the most debated moments in Yankee history, so long as people who lived through it remained.

It was certainly the most exciting moment of the Yankees' first seventeen seasons, even if it didn't work out for them. Boston had maintained bragging rights and would again fly the pennant. But the beginning of a great rivalry was born.

The final attendance for New York was reported as 438,919, fourth in the league, and more than double the 1903 total. The Giants led all of baseball with 609,826, an increase of thirty thousand from the previous year.

Chapter Four

DURING THE YANKEES' FIRST TWO decades, one issue above all stood out in public debate.

Sunday baseball.

All of professional baseball had been dealing with the matter long before the American League came along, so it certainly didn't catch Farrell and Devery by surprise. But they joined in efforts to reverse the ban on playing games on Sunday, one deeply set in America's traditional ties to the church. A politician was more likely to win votes with the support of clergymen than with their opposition.

At the start of the twentieth century, Chicago, St. Louis, and Cincinnati were the only major league towns that allowed Sunday baseball. It was not until the 1910s that Detroit, Cleveland, and Washington joined them, recognizing how wartime workers needed a day at the ballpark to unwind.

But New York, Boston, Philadelphia, and Pittsburgh remained holdouts. Bills were periodically introduced in the state legislatures, but they made little progress.

Today, Sundays are the the most lucrative attendance day of the week. It's the reason that baseball leagues never have an odd number of teams: If they did, someone would be idle on Sunday.

The main argument against Sunday baseball had always been that it distracted people from church attendance. While charging admission was the most severe flaunting of the law, even amateur teams could find themselves under arrest, depending on the passion the local police held for enforcement. It was supposed to be a day of rest. For organized groups like the

Anti-Saloon League and the Sabbatarians, the passion of this fight was equal to today's polarization over abortion. It would occupy the battlefield of public opinion for decades. The ban lasted in Boston until 1932 and in Philadelphia and Pittsburgh until 1934. Few fans today even know that it was once such a great issue.

Proponents argued that baseball had grown into a wonderful leisure activity, a national pastime that embodied wholesome qualities. Wealthier people were going off to play golf or ride horses on Sunday, but the working class—people who commonly worked six days a week—were being deprived.

It was pointed out that teens could sneak into saloons on Sunday but didn't have a baseball game as an option. There were cases of arrests and fines for those even caught playing the game recreationally.

Of course, Frank Farrell owned so many saloons, he tended to be quiet on the matter. He was going to be fine either way.

New York's teams sought ways around the ban. A ten-thousand-seat field in Ridgewood, Queens, called Wallace's Ridgewood Grounds was a place to play on Sunday, even if the games were billed as exhibitions. It was located at the crosshairs of Wyckoff and Irving avenues and Weirfield and Covert streets. Teams would get around the no-admission rule by allowing everyone in for free but requiring that they purchase a scorecard for the equivalent of a ticket. Ordinarily a scorecard was five cents. At Ridgewood, it could be as much as seventy-five cents. And there you might see the Highlanders take on a team like the Brooklyn Field Club, or whatever team was available to face Keeler and Chesbro and the rest. The players would share in the proceeds of the Sunday games. On occasion the local gentry protested, sometimes even getting Griffith himself arrested.

In 1909, the Highlanders played a Sunday exhibition in Jersey City, and the club owners handed out notices to fans not to cheer, so as not to arouse suspicion among the local police. The game was played in silence.

The Brooklyn Superbas (forerunners of the Dodgers), claiming they had territorial control over Ridgewood, tried to stop the Highlanders from playing there, forcing them to appear only when Brooklyn was out of town. Ultimately, the Highlanders ceded the territory to the Superbas and found other places to play. But for New Yorkers, Ridgewood Field was ground zero for the Sunday baseball feud, largely because Queens judges had a more enlightened interpretation of the Sunday laws. (Brooklyn twice played regular-season Sunday games there: The first, in 1904 against Boston, produced no arrests, but the second, against Philadelphia, featured several arrests of players, ending the "experiment.")

A Sunday exception was granted for a benefit exhibition game in April of 1906, played at Hilltop Park before fifteen thousand fans and raising $5,600 for San Francisco earthquake relief. The game was played between New York and the Philadelphia Athletics—two American League opponents— and many in the stands were not sure whether it was an exhibition or a league game. It was an exhibition, and it was pitched by Louis LeRoy, New York's first Native American Player.

In 1908, Father Thomas McLoughlin of New Rochelle reported on a meeting he had with President Theodore Roosevelt, claiming that the president "fully approved" of Sunday baseball.

"I told the president that I did not see how there could be any harm in persons playing baseball or attending the National game on Sunday, after their religious duties had been discharged," he said. "The president replied, 'That is the kind of talk I like to hear from a clergyman.'"

The Giants also played the Yankees in a Sunday exhibition game at the Polo Grounds in 1912, a benefit for survivors of the *Titanic*, which raised nearly $10,000 in program sales without charging admission. Farrell jumped on the PR benefits of the endeavor, hoping to win favor with politicians. "I am pleased to say that the men who devote their time and talents to the national game are always ready to give freely of both time and talents . . . in the case of a national disaster."

In 1915, state assemblyman Martin McCue told his colleagues, "I live up to my religion as well as any practical man can, and there is nothing in my religion that says I can't go to a baseball game Sunday afternoon if I go to church in the morning. I think if I watch the Giants perform on a bright Sunday afternoon I am keeping the day holy as the Master intended it should be kept holy."

But shortly after his speech, a bill to allow Sunday baseball was defeated.

"I shall try again!" he said. "It's sunshine, outdoors and peanuts against dives, gambling and vice!"

In April of 1919—after the war had relaxed some of the more rigid standards in society—the New York State Senate and Assembly finally passed a Sunday baseball (and movies) bill, stating that no game could begin before 2:00 P.M. The bill was led by state senator Jimmy Walker, the future mayor of New York. Governor Al Smith, a devout Catholic, signed the bill, which allowed for a local opt-out. It was done.

On May 4, 1919, both the Giants and the Dodgers played Sunday home games against National League opponents. The Yankees followed a week later, Sunday, May 11.

And the earth didn't tremble.

THE 1905 HIGHLANDER season, a sixth-place finish, saw the debut of first baseman Hal Chase, who was drafted from the Pacific Coast League. His comings and goings from California "outlaw" leagues to the American League would, over the years, test the patience of the major leagues and their willingness to put up with players spending the off-season in makeshift West Coast leagues.

It was just one of a number of issues that made Hal a controversial figure.

Chase, handsome and tall at six feet and 175 pounds, batting right but throwing left, almost immediately became the team's most popular player. Although he batted just .249 in his rookie season, he would hit .323—third in the league—the following year. *Sporting Life* magazine called him "perhaps the biggest drawing card in baseball."

He was often seen in the company of Broadway showgirls. He lived for a time in the same apartment building as John McGraw, and then in Suffern, New York, with his fiancée, Nellie Heffernan. He drank, he played poker, and while he loved New York, he would always hold out the possibility of retiring to California for outlaw league baseball as leverage in his contract negotiations.

Chase quickly became known as the best fielding first baseman the game had yet produced. Even by midcentury he was still included in the debate of who was the best first baseman ever.

His dazzling plays seemed to make up for a large number of errors, but it was all part of what made him exciting. He was also an adept base stealer, and his 248 steals while with New York was a team record that stood until Rickey Henderson passed him in 1988.

"His first base wizardry is beyond dispute, but Hal committed an amazing number of errors for one possessing his skill," wrote Fred Lieb.

But a shadow came to follow Chase's career: accusations that gambling may have caused him to deliberately throw games, perhaps accounting for the high error totals. This would take on increasing significance in later years.

He readily admitted to betting on games, but always denied that he bet for or against his own team. "My limit was $100 per game and I never bet against my own team," he said. "That was easy money."

His future teammate, shortstop Roger Peckinpaugh, recalled "a few times I threw a ball over to first base, and it went by him to the stands and a couple of runs scored. It really surprised me. I'd stand there looking, sighting the flight of the ball in my mind, and I'd think, 'Geez, that throw wasn't that bad.' Then I'd tell myself that he was the greatest there was, so maybe the throw was bad. Then later on when he got the smelly reputation, it came back to me and I said, 'oh-oh.' What he was doing, you see, was tangling up his feet and then making a fancy dive after the ball, making it look like it was a wild throw."

(With runarounds like Elberfeld and Chase playing key roles on the team, it is worth noting that on August 4, 1905, the Yankees started a battery of Jim "Doc" Newton on the mound and Mike "Doc" Powers catching. Both men were physicians.)

Near the end of the 1905 season, a collision between Dave Fultz and Elberfeld at the Hilltop silenced the crowd of twenty thousand as three doctors (including Newton) ran onto the field. The two men lay motionless for ten minutes. Elberfeld suffered bad cuts over his right eye, chin, nose, and cheek, while Fultz went into shock and was taken to a hospital, unconscious. He had broken both his jaw and his nose, and his baseball career ended.

IN 1906, GRIFFITH's men were once again contenders. Maybe it was the long-awaited opening of the subway station at Hilltop Park, which helped attendance jump from 309,100 to 434,700, providing a more encouraging audience.

A crowd of fifteen thousand turned out on opening day to visit the new subway station and see Chesbro outduel Cy Young 2–1 in 12 innings with Chase driving in the winning run. Old-time star John Montgomery Ward, now a forty-six-year-old lawyer in New York, threw out the first pitch, the band played "Yankee Doodle," and the fans began inventing songs for the different players. It was a great day at the ballpark, and the two legendary pitchers shook hands after the game, admiring each other's performance.

Griffith, having pretty much wound down his playing career, coached at third and turned over the starting rotation to Chesbro (23–17), Orth (27–17), Bill Hogg (14–13), Clarkson (9–4), and Newton (7–5).

Hogg, who hurled a one-hitter against Boston on May 1, was in the starting rotation for New York from 1905 to 1908, but then died at twenty-nine of kidney disease after pitching for Louisville in 1909.

The Highlanders were in first place as late as September 24. They had been boosted by a fifteen-game winning streak surrounding Labor Day. But hurt by a suspension of Elberfeld, the team would win only five of its remaining thirteen games and finished second, three and a half behind Chicago. Elberfeld's suspension followed what the *Times* called a "disgraceful attack" on umpire Silk O'Loughlin.

No one knew, of course, that this would be the team's last serious pennant race under the ownership of Devery and Farrell. What would follow would be a string of mediocre to bad seasons and not a very good attraction for baseball-crazed New York fans.

1907 WAS A big step backward. In fact, the Yankees were the only American League team sharing a city with the National League who failed to outdraw its rival. Attendance fell to 350,020 while the Giants' reached 538,350. (Brooklyn drew 312,300.)

"If it gets any smaller, they'll have to put fractions on the turnstiles," wrote Mark Roth in the *Globe*.

Griffith was starting to feel the pressure of not producing a winner. The team started strong, with a deliberate worker named Slow Joe Doyle hurling shutouts in his first two outings, but then found themselves essentially out of the running by mid-June.

(Doyle won only 22 games in his career, but a variation of his T-206 tobacco trading card—the set containing the famous Honus Wagner card—sold for $329,000 in a 2009 auction simply because it erroneously identified him as being with the New York Nat'ls, not Americans.)

On June 12, with his players starting to openly complain about his managing, Griffith exited Hilltop Park through the right-field exit and encountered a fan complimenting Ty Cobb on a game well played. Griffith struck the fan in the jaw, and the victim threatened to seek a warrant for Griff's arrest.

On June 28, a rookie catcher named Branch Rickey, the man who would one day bring Jackie Robinson into the major leagues, was given a start despite a sore arm. Rickey that day set a record which still stands, allowing 13 stolen bases.

"My arm was numb and I was helpless to do anything," he explained.

Keeler, sidelined by injury, was replaced in right field by Rickey on July 6. During the game, Rickey nearly broke his arm sliding into third and was essentially done as a ballplayer. He said good-bye to Griffith in mid-September.

CHASE, MEANWHILE, WAS enjoying a twenty-seven-game hitting streak. Yet he was often high drama.

He was living with his fiancée, Nellie. On July 26, the day he hit in his twenty-seventh straight, Nellie and her friend Ethel Martin (who was newly married to the team's trainer, Mike) were arrested in Suffern, charged with the unlawful disposal of a dead infant. Ethel had delivered the baby seven days before, apparently stillborn. Ethel and Nellie went to gruesome means to destroy the baby (think fire and stray dogs), and a tip to the police led to their arrest.

It could have been Devery's connections with the area police that brought the case to a quiet close, but clearly Chase had a knack for meeting "interesting" women, and Mike Martin was not much better.

JOE GORDON, WHO had taken long summer vacations in '06 and '07 and who had been "demoted" to vice president, was ousted by Farrell before the 1908 season began.

Gordon did not go quietly. He sued Farrell, claiming he was due to receive half ownership of the team, something he believed was understood when the parties first came together. Farrell countered that he was only due the dividends on $10,000 worth of stock. Both sides admitted that establishing Gordon as team president in 1903 was a "front" to present a more reputable owner to the public. Farrell further claimed that he kept Gordon on the team's stationery only to help Gordon's coal business.

Documents introduced at trial allow a look into the finances of the club, which showed a nice profit: receipts being about $240,000 for a season, operating costs about $80,000. Not until January 1912 did the court dismiss Gordon's complaint, with Judge Bischoff stating he found no evidence that any contract of partnership existed.

THE HIGHLANDERS OPENED the 1908 season well and were in first place as late as June 1. Griffith took his team to the White House during a series in

Washington, and the players got to meet Teddy Roosevelt. It would be the team's first White House visit, but Teddy's son Quentin was not at home and was described as "inconsolable" at missing a chance to meet his heroes. The *Times* reported that Quentin "worshipped" the players in both leagues and knew all of their records.

But six weeks later, with the Highlanders going through a 3–27–1 stretch, the time had come to bring down the curtain on the Clark Griffith era. It would be the first firing of a manager in team history.

On June 24, Griff issued a statement: "In justice to Mr. Farrell and myself, I think a change in management will give better results. Whenever the team had a chance to win the pennant luck broke against us . . . I want it distinctly understood that Mr. Farrell and myself are good friends. He always treated me fine and spared no expense to get a winner."

Griffith was probably fired and paid for the rest of the season, and the breaking point was likely a difference over the value of Elberfeld to the team. The Tabasco Kid was forever getting into ugly umpire feuds, getting suspended at critical times, and not really providing enough value to balance those misdeeds. Griffith was fed up with him, but Farrell seemed to like the rogue. He said he wouldn't sell him for $50,000. So he did the logical thing: He fired Griffith and replaced him with Elberfeld.

It was believed that Farrell's first choice was actually Keeler, now thirty-six and slowing down. That season he played only 91 games and hit just .263. He wasn't the player he'd been, blaming the slowdown in his game on "one of the most trying [sun fields] in the country." But he was still enormously popular with the fans. The question for Farrell was, could a man barely five foot four lead a baseball team?

Maybe even Keeler thought he could not. And so it came to be believed that as Farrell sought him out to take over the team, he in fact fled from the hotel in Philadelphia where the Yankees were staying, determined not to be found. Farrell understood and turned to the thirty-three-year-old Elberfeld instead. All five foot seven of him.

Chase, who was mild-mannered and not a big fan of Elberfeld's style of play, was reportedly upset that he had been passed over. In September he left the team and headed back west, joining Stockton in the outlaw California State League. He hit .383 in 21 games for Stockton and was banned from the major leagues by the governing National Commission. It could have been the end of Hal Chase.

Griffith would emerge as the manager of Cincinnati in 1909, the start of a three-year stint. He took the Highlanders trainer Mike Martin with him (and presumably his impetuous wife, Ethel), and then in 1912 took him to Washington when he became manager of the Senators. Martin remained in Griffith's employ until he died in an auto accident in 1952, one of the last ties to the Highlanders still in the game. (Harry Lee succeeded Martin in New York.)

By 1920 Griffith took off the uniform for the last time, acquired majority interest in the team, and devoted the rest of his life to running the Senators. He became friends with U.S. presidents, an elder statesman of baseball, and gave his name to the Senators' ballpark. He seldom reached back and hired anyone from his New York days. In fact, when he arrived and took over the Senators in 1912, he released the team's third baseman: a fellow named Elberfeld who had gone there in 1910.

Griffith would never really be "family" to the Yankees, but at the 1952 Yankees Old-Timers' Day, marking the franchise's fiftieth season, they saluted the Old Fox, with Tannehill, Conroy, Ganzel, and Fultz, 1903 Highlanders all, among the guests that day to honor him. He would live until 1955, his last great act being the signing of Harmon Killebrew.

ELBERFELD WAS GREETED by a floral horseshoe and seven thousand happy customers in his first game as manager at Hilltop, a crowd that included Griffith, who stayed to wish him well before departing for his Montana ranch. All the players pledged support. Everyone said nice things about one another, and the press hailed Griff as courteous, fair, and luckless.

As for the Tabasco Kid, it went as some had feared. He wasn't long into the job when he had a terrible argument with umpire Silk O'Loughlin again and found himself suspended indefinitely. Defiantly, he managed the team's first game during a July 4 doubleheader in Washington, sitting in a box next to the Yankee dugout. The umpire that day, Rip Egan, chose to allow this behavior despite great protests from the Washington manager, Joe Cantillon. But Elberfeld was sent to the clubhouse for the second game and watched from the porch.

Suffering from an injury, Elberfeld turned over much of the shortstop play to Neal Ball, while he coached at first. (Ball earned fame with Cleveland the following year, pulling off the first unassisted triple play in history.) By July 8, the Yanks already seemed doomed to finish last, then endured a twelve-game losing streak later in the month.

The horrible season would include the embarrassment of being no-hit by Cy Young, the oldest pitcher in the game at forty-one. It was an 8–0 gem at the Hilltop on June 30 in front of just fifteen hundred people, most of whom were cheering for Young from the sixth inning on. It was nearly a perfect game—New York's leadoff man in the first walked and was thrown out stealing. Young also had three hits, drove in four runs, and made a sensational catch on a bunt attempt by Neal Ball. It was the first no-hitter against the Yankees.

Then twenty-year-old Walter Johnson, seeking to establish himself in his first full season, shut out New York three times in four days (with no game on Sunday, of course), September 4, 5, and 7, pitching 27 innings, allowing no runs, 12 hits, and one walk. With these games, he served notice that he would be a formidable foe for years to come. He did, in fact, defeat the Yankees 60 times in 101 decisions during his career, far and away the most wins against the franchise. (Lefty Grove and Ed Cicotte had 35 each, tied for second place.)

Elberfeld would be 27–71 as a manager that year, an awful .276 percentage. With 103 losses, this would be the first of only three teams in club history to finish last.

And so Farrell was prepared to admit a mistake and make a change, and the Kid would return to play shortstop in '09 under a new manager, without complaint.

THE NEWS THAT George Stallings would be the new manager was made official just weeks after the 1908 season ended. It competed for attention with news that Willie Keeler was retiring to take care of his growing real estate interests in Brooklyn. Then, as Stallings was being named, Keeler said he would return after all, but would be hopeful of moving out of the "sun field"—right field in Hilltop Park.

Keeler would in fact play one last season for New York, playing 95 games in right field and batting .264.

The 1909 season was also the farewell for Jack Chesbro, who was 128–93 in his seven years with the club. Chesbro attempted a comeback with New York in 1912, failed to make the team, and then retired for good to his home in Conway, Massachusetts, where he lived until his death in 1931.

At the end of the '09 season, Kid Elberfeld was sold to Washington. Thus 1909 marked the farewells of Elberfeld, Keeler, and Chesbro, the last of the 1903 Highlanders.

Stallings, forty-one and a personal friend of Frank Farrell's, had managed the Philadelphia Phillies in 1897–98 (where Elberfeld had been a rookie), the Detroit Tigers in 1901, and most recently the Newark team in the Eastern League, finishing third. Among his players was a .196-hitting catcher named Paul Kritchell, who would one day figure prominently as a Yankee scout.

Jimmy Austin, a second-year infielder on the team, told Larry Ritter in *The Glory of Their Times* that "Stallings was a fine manager. One of the best . . . [but] talk about cussing! Golly, he had 'em all beat. He cussed something awful. Once, in a game, he gave me a real going over. Later that night he called me in and said, 'Jim, I'm sorry about this afternoon. Don't pay any attention to me when I say those things. Just forget it. It's only because I get so excited and want to win so bad.'"

Stallings, the son of a Confederate general, was a VMI grad and a friend to Cobb and Wagner, who visited him often on his five-thousand-acre cotton plantation in Haddock, Georgia, called the Meadows. There he employed "600 negroes" and, according to *Sporting Life*, "considers them all 'his children' and looked after the welfare of the happy-go-lucky darkies as if they were not paid employees." It could not have been easy for him to call this team the Yankees; "Highlanders" worked a lot better for him. He was handsome, wealthy, a "man's man," and a popular figure among the baseball crowd. And, yes, he liked to drink.

Farrell helped out Stallings by bringing Hal Chase back from the outlaw California State League. Farrell had been quite angry at Chase, but Stallings, with irony awaiting him, persuaded him to reach out and re-sign him.

Chase, unfortunately, contracted smallpox during spring training in Macon, Georgia. It was originally diagnosed as malaria, but despite the frightening scourge of the disease and its large toll on human life, he recovered and rejoined the team on May 3.

Farrell also let Stallings bring along his own trainer for the team, James Burke. In February, the much-respected Abe Nahon resigned as team secretary, replaced by Farrell's brother-in-law, Tom Davis.

Also new to the club in '09 were pitchers Jack Warhop and Jack Quinn, as well as the speedy outfielder Birdie Cree. Warhop and Cree debuted the same week in September 1908 and became the senior players on the team by 1915.

The well-cultured Cree would hit .348 in 1911, the highest average in the team's first seventeen seasons. He came out of Penn State, where, despite being only five foot six, he had a football scholarship. His Yankee career was almost derailed when Walter Johnson hit him in the head with a pitch in the sixth game of the 1910 season, but he returned to the lineup the next day.

Spitballer Quinn, a right-hander born Joannes Pajkos in Austria-Hungary, was signed by Arthur Irwin after going 14–0 in the minors in 1908. He would have a twenty-three-season pitching career in the major leagues, with two tours of duty on the Yankees. He spent his first four seasons in New York, posting an 18–12 record in 1910, and then returned for three more years, beginning in 1919. He was with the Yankees in 1920 when the spitball was banned, but it was still permitted for those whose career was defined by it. When he appeared in the 1921 World Series at age thirty-seven, he was the only Highlander to have finally made it into the Fall Classic as a Yankee.

Warhop, a five-foot-eight submariner, was considered a steady yet un-lucky right-hander on the team, with a dismal 69–92 career record but a 3.12 earned run average. While he was 23 games under .500 in his Yankee career, the Yankees were shut out when he pitched on twenty-one occasions.

It was said that a dozen teams sought to sign him after he was 29–7 for Williamsport in the Tri-State League in 1908, but it was Stallings who got him for New York. With a better lineup behind him, he would certainly have had more to show for his eight seasons.

The '09 Highlanders didn't play very well, but they did arouse contro-versy when the Detroit trainer, Harry Tuthill, discovered that an open or closed O on an outfield sign was tipping off New York hitters whether a fastball or a breaking ball was coming. Some had wondered why the team hit so much better at home, and this may have been the answer. New York had been caught cheating.

The board of directors of the American League would ultimately exon-erate the Highlanders, but said anyone found guilty of this in the future would be "barred from baseball for all time." For Stallings, who had come to town as a distinguished gentleman of the game, it was an embarrass-ment.

The team finished fifth, three games under .500.

STALLINGS RETURNED IN 1910, with the Yankees now training at his behest in Athens, Georgia, having abandoned Macon after the smallpox episode of

1909. There were four new hurlers on the staff, Ray Caldwell, Ray Fisher, Russ Ford, and Jim "Hippo" Vaughn. The foursome would have to adjust to a redesigned baseball, with a cork center having replaced solid rubber. The *Reach Guide* called it "the greatest improvement made in the most important part of the game, the baseball [itself]."

The change was deemed necessary to beef up the hitting. The American League had just two .300 hitters in 1905, Keeler being one of them. The champion White Sox of 1906 hit .230 as a team and were called the Hitless Wonders. The league hit .239 in 1908 and .244 in 1909.

Ray "Slim" Caldwell put in nine years with the Yankees, and it was always thought that he should have done better than his 96–99 mark, with 37 of the wins coming in 1914–15. But he was forever a discipline problem, both to the team (hard drinking and disappearances) and to police authorities (problems with women and at least four marriages). He learned the spitball late in his career and managed to pitch until 1933, the last eleven years all in the minor leagues.

Ray Fisher, educated at Middlebury College, was, with Quinn and Caldwell, one of the spitball pitchers allowed to continue throwing the pitch after the 1920 ban. Fisher hurled for the Yankees from 1910 to 1917, was in the army in 1918, and then went to the Cincinnati Reds in 1919–20, pitching in the notorious rigged 1919 World Series. He wound up being banned from the game by Commissioner Kennesaw Mountain Landis—not for any betting activity surrounding that series but for leaving the Reds on seven days' notice to coach at the University of Michigan, instead of providing the required ten days' notice.

Ray coached Michigan baseball for thirty-eight years; the ballpark there was eventually named Ray Fisher Stadium. He coached future Mets owner Fred Wilpon in baseball and Gerald Ford in football. In 1980, Commissioner Bowie Kuhn reversed Landis's ban and called him a "retired player in good standing." Ray lived to be ninety-five and attended Yankee Old-Timers' Days as the oldest living Yankee player as late as 1982.

Russell Ford, master of the illegal "emery ball" (scuffing the ball with an emery board but claiming it was a spitball), was born in western Canada and raised in Minneapolis. He broke in with eight shutouts and a 26–6 rookie season in 1910—still, after more than a century, the American League rookie record for wins.

Ford picked up his famous emery ball pitching for Atlanta in the Southern Association, when a wild pitch hit a cement upright and came back to him nicely scuffed. His catcher was Ed Sweeney, who would be his Yankee batterymate. After watching the pitch break, he concluded that while he couldn't hide concrete in his glove, a little emery would do. "The Boy Wonder" or "Matty of the Yankees" would pitch only four full seasons before jumping to the Federal League in 1914 and then dropping into the minors. The secret of his pitch got around the league after his second year, and he ultimately lost his effectiveness.

Hippo Vaughn, 13–11 for the 1910 Yankees with a 1.83 ERA, went on to win 20 or more games five times for the Chicago Cubs from 1913 to 1921. At six foot four and 215 pounds, the big left-hander from Texas was said to have the best physique in the game and stood out among players of his day for sheer size. His mound presence was not unlike that of CC Sabathia's a century later. But only his rookie year was distinguished for New York, and he was waived to Washington in 1912 before finding success in the National League.

Right-hander Tom Hughes, an otherwise middling player on the team, pitched the first no-hitter in Yankee history that year. A later revision of baseball rules invalidated it from being so listed, as he allowed two hits in the tenth and five more in the eleventh innings in losing the game. But through nine, only an error marred what could have been a perfect game.

It would be a season of improved play under Stallings: The team finished second, although it was never in the race after July 4. Most of the drama for the season came in the final two weeks and involved the manager and his star first baseman.

Stallings openly claimed that Chase, by now team captain, was "laying down" on plays. It would not be the first time that such charges were leveled at Hal, but the whispers usually involved gambling. When you made as many great plays as Chase did, the ordinary ones that got past him were sure to arouse suspicion. His teammates were suspicious. Some felt he was a master at arriving at the base just a moment too late to nail a runner. In this case, some felt he was undermining Stallings in an effort to get him fired and succeed him.

By mid-July Stallings was increasingly upset by Chase's play. After two questionable games against the St. Louis Browns, he was replaced in the lineup by John Knight. In the next two series came more Chase errors, and soon Knight was being written into the lineup each day. Starting August 9,

Chase went missing for ten days. He claimed to be suffering from dizzy spells. In fact he'd been visiting with Frank Farrell, imploring him to make a managerial change.

Most of the players, seeing Chase's work at first, tended to side with Stallings.

Stallings gave Chase a tongue-lashing but put him back in the lineup. On September 18 at St. Louis, New York lost to the last-place Browns; Chase was hitless and let a throw from Fisher get past him. That was all Stallings needed to see. He directly confronted Chase and accused him of "lying down." Players had to pull the two apart to keep them from fighting.

The next day in Chicago, Chase missed a hit-and-run sign while trailing 1–0 in a game they would lose 3–0. An impatient Farrell asked Stallings to take the Twentieth Century Limited back to New York to see him. Stallings turned the team over to the team secretary, Tom Davis, and departed. Davis asked Chase to be the temporary manager.

Farrell and Stallings met at the Flatiron Building, and Stallings unloaded on Chase. Then Farrell headed to Cleveland to meet with the players and get their feedback. Ban Johnson was there too. The plot thickened.

Johnson, still closely involved with the fates and fortunes of his New York franchise, didn't like Stallings much, especially after the sign-stealing scandal from the year before. Stallings had few allies, and Johnson demanded his resignation.

"Stallings has utterly failed in his accusations against Chase," said Farrell of his onetime close friend. "He tried to besmirch the character of a sterling player. Anybody who knows Hal Chase knows that he is not guilty of the accusations against him."

No owner of gambling halls could have stated it better. Stallings was gone; Chase, just twenty-seven, was to be the fourth manager in team history. He got a two-year contract.

On September 26, Chase officially took over with fourteen games left in the season. In his first game, he was presented with floral tributes and the players on both teams stopped to salute him. He was obviously a popular choice: Stallings's strategy of discrediting him had failed.

Chase won ten of his games, including the last five in a row. He was now well positioned to guide the team for 1911 and, he hoped, for many years after. Left unspoken was the fact that Chase was being watched at every turn; it was now suspected that he might "lie down" from time to time.

But first came one last and very important assignment for 1910. John

McGraw and John Brush had at last agreed to a Giants-Yankees series: the championship of Manhattan! It would be a best-of-seven series, played alternately at the Polo Grounds and the Hilltop, and it would prove to be so interesting to fans that many newspapers felt it exceeded the World Series— Cubs vs. Athletics—for national interest.

The games began on October 13, five days after the regular season ended, with the teams well rested. The World Series didn't begin until the seventeenth, so attention turned to New York.

The *Times* forecast, "New Yorkers will watch with interest the battles between the Cubs and the Athletics for the highest honors in baseball, but they care less for this fight than they do for the battles which will decide the baseball supremacy of Greater New York."

The Giants won the series, four games to two with one tie. The great Christy Mathewson won three of the games and saved the fourth (although it was not a stat at the time) but never managed to pitch at Hilltop Park. A crowd of 27,766 attended game three at the Polo Grounds, larger than any at the 1910 World Series. Warhop and Quinn had the Yankees' two victories, and the top crowd at Hilltop Park was 13,059. Each Highlander got a $706 bonus check and each Giant got $1,111. Chase's bold managerial move was having his pitchers hit eighth and infielder Jimmy Austin ninth.

Wrote John B. Foster, "The games . . . were the most successful in the history of organized baseball."

The fans loved the event, but when the Giants won pennants from 1911 to 1913, the series was suspended so they could play in the World Series. The New York series was played one last time in 1914, with another Giants win before much smaller crowds.

HAL CHASE'S MANAGERIAL run with the Yankees lasted just one full season, 1911. He brought the team home a disappointing sixth with a .500 record, twenty-five and a half games out of first.* They lost their last five games to kill a first-division finish. Chase was soft on discipline, including his own, and just didn't set a good example. Plus, he made 36 errors at first base.

Still, the fans delighted in having Prince Hal as manager. Generally acknowledged as the most loyal of all fans was Edward Everett Bell, a safe

---

* Oddly, it was the only .500 season in the team's history.

manufacturer, who always closed his office and headed for the Hilltop when the Yankees were at home. He always sat in the same grandstand seat and truly believed he brought the team luck.

Bell was the best-known of a group of die-hards who attended games over the years. There would be Bill "Pee Wee" Scheidt, the savant Bill "the Baker" Stimers, Chris Karelekas (with his YES WE CAN banners in the seventies), "Freddie Sez" Schuman (with his spoon and frying pan), Ali Rameriz, the founder of the Bleacher Creatures, and "Bald Vinny" Milano, who would chant the names of each player (except pitcher and catcher) until they acknowledged him—this "roll call" can be heard in the first innings of Yankee games today.

For many fans who devoted decades of their lives to box scores and baseball cards and stats and autographs, or to following the team by Western Union updates outside newspaper offices, then later by radio, television, and streaming video, their investment in the team was in many ways mightier than that of any player, executive, or even owner who passed through.

The Yankees—and baseball—saw people through illness and through war, provided happy and sad moments, marked births (with baby-size Yankee caps in photos) and weddings, and came to define a person's very existence to friends and family. When a generation gap might curtail conversation within families, there would still be baseball to share.

The game lent order to the lives of its fans from the beginning of spring training to the final day of the season, and then all over again the next year.

There was a fan named George Raft. Later nationally known as a tough-guy movie star (with a propensity for off-screen association with gangsters), Raft and his pal Charlie Schrimpf were Hilltop Park regulars, sweeping up the bleachers in exchange for game tickets and delivering the dirty uniforms to Charlie's mom after the games. Raft, about eleven at the time, was a mascot and a batboy and would cart the bats to the dugout in a wheelbarrow. He had a reputation for being the brightest kid in the neighborhood when it came to memorizing baseball statistics.

Raft remained a fan, played baseball and boxed, but drifted off to the stage and then to Hollywood. Ironically, his adult friendship with Leo Durocher (a onetime Yankee player but by then the Brooklyn manager) got Durocher in trouble—some of Raft's associates were gamblers—and he was ordered to break off the association.

Charlie Schrimpf remained a lifelong fan.

"I worked for Fred Logan in 1912 until they hired a regular bat boy, a guy named Hunchy, to replace me," he wrote to announcers Phil Rizzuto and Jerry Coleman in 1969.

> He got a uniform and all. My brother Bob was assistant ground keeper to Mr. Phil Schenck. George Raft and I had to go over early in the morning, get a broom and sweep up under the bleachers. Then we would secure a slip of paper to get into the game.
>
> After school [PS 169, across the street from Hilltop Park], all the kids would stand on the Ft. Washington Avenue side of the park and wait for a ball to be knocked over—then you took the ball to the man at the little door and he would let you into the game.
>
> My mother did the laundry for the team. She never wanted to see Hal Chase's uniform because the left leg was so dirty, and let us not forget these all had to done with the washing board. There were no dryers or washing machines in those days, just the old coal stove. George Raft and I had to bring the uniforms to the clubhouse before going to school and collect 35 cents.
>
> When we got a broken bat that was like a gift. We would get a two cent roll of tape and a few nails and we were set. And a baseball, when the stitches were broke, we would tape it up and played just fine.
>
> In my time I saw the best—Walter Johnson, Ty Cobb, [Bert] Daniels,* Chesbro—last but not the least, Hal Chase, the greatest first baseman of them all in baseball.

In the early 1970s, Charlie's younger brother Frank was still a ticket taker outside gate 4 of Yankee Stadium, the employee with the longest family ties to the franchise.

THIRD BASEMAN ROY HARTZELL, twenty-nine, from Golden, Colorado, was the key new addition to the team in 1911, and he hit .296 and drove in 91 runs (including eight in one inning)—the most by a Yankee third baseman

---

* Daniels, an outfielder, skilled base stealer, and hit-by-pitch specialist, played for the Yanks from 1910 to 1913.

until Graig Nettles had 93 in 1976. This was Cree's .348 season, fifth high-est in the league, and Chase hit .315 (and starred in a silent movie, *Hal Chase's Home Run*).

Throughout the season—a sixth-place finish—Farrell pondered that his lease would be running out in another year, and a decision had to be made on where to play his home games. He settled on property known as Kings-bridge Grounds, at 221st Street and Broadway in the Bronx, just north of Manhattan, a plot of land that would require excavation similar to what greeted him in Washington Heights in '03. (The 225th Street subway sta-tion had opened in 1907.) This time, with more time to plan, he had a nice design, featuring an enhanced clubhouse with "shower baths, a plunge and lockers," as well as club offices. He was anxious to get away from the slow elevator problems at the 165th Street station. The park would be double-decked and hold twenty-two thousand. Work on filling in a creek that ran through the grounds began cautiously in the spring of 1911, and it was hoped the park might be ready in midseason of 1912, with Farrell prepared to jump out of his lease a few months early if he could. But so far it was a lot of talk and no real construction.

The big news of the 1911 season was a terrible fire at the Polo Grounds that forced the Giants to share Hilltop Park with the Yankees.

The fire broke out around 12:40 A.M. on April 14 and began with an ex-plosion. Fred Lieb, in his first season covering the Yankees, wrote that the fire was "one of New York's biggest and most spectacular . . . Almost totally out of control, it lit up the night sky in upper Manhattan, the Bronx, and western Queens."

The flames were nearly one hundred feet high and were brought under control around 2:00 in the morning, when all but the left-field bleachers and the clubhouses had finished burning. The field was not harmed; pitcher Bugs Raymond actually stood at the mound watching the grandstand and dugouts burn.

The fire spread and destroyed thirty elevated subway cars. John McGraw abandoned his late-night billiards game and rushed to the scene. The chal-lenge was just too great for the FDNY, who sped there in their horse-drawn fire trucks. The real cause was never found: Some thought it could be traced to the concession storage areas maintained by Harry M. Stevens, and some thought it was nothing more than smoldering peanut shells from that afternoon's game, perhaps set off by a cigar ash. Stevens had just stocked a season's worth of inventory in his storerooms.

At first McGraw thought games could still be played and temporary chairs set up, but that proved impractical and unsafe. So where could they play? It couldn't be in Brooklyn, because the two teams were often home at the same time. But by design, the Yankees and Giants were never home at the same time, so Hilltop was the logical choice. And it wouldn't be much of an inconvenience to ask Polo Grounds fans to go the extra ten blocks north.

Farrell and team secretary Tom Davis were in Philadelphia for games with the Athletics. Davis went back to New York the very next morning to offer the Giants use of his field. It was a fine gesture, and of course good news for Phil Schenck and his ground crew, who would now have additional paydays with the field in constant use. John Brush showed the proper amount of appreciation for the offer and accepted at once. It would be the first shared ballpark in major league history.

The Giants played twenty-eight games at Hilltop while the Polo Grounds was repaired, morphing into the fourth version of the field, the one that would last on into 1963—where Bobby Thomson would homer, Willie Mays would debut, and the New York Mets would play.

The first Giants games at Hilltop were against the Brooklyn Superbas, marking the first and only time that Brooklyn would play there. The Giants, with all new bats, drew over fifteen thousand for their first game at Hilltop and won 6–3.

The new Polo Grounds was ready on June 28. Brush called it Brush Stadium, the first use of *stadium* for a baseball park, and that is what it said on the Yankees scorecards during the first seven years they would play there. The Giants thanked their hosts and returned home to win a pennant and host a World Series. But an important step had been taken; a warm gesture from the Yankees had eased the competitive thaw that still hung in the air, even after the 1910 postseason series. Loyal Giants fans curtailed their Highlander hatred. The Hilltop scoreboard, which now showed out-of-town scores, would evoke cheers from Yankee fans when the Giants were shown to take a lead. On Memorial Day in 1912, the Giants lent the Polo Grounds to the Yankees to help them achieve maximum attendance for a doubleheader, since they had been hurt at home by numerous rainouts all season. When the Giants won the 1912 pennant, the Yankees stayed in town one day extra to work out with them at the Polo Grounds as a World Series tune-up. Farrell had played this well with Brush. "Mr. Farrell's generosity," wrote the *Times*, "will be remembered as the brightest spot in local baseball competition."

About six weeks after the 1911 season ended, Chase visited Farrell during a break in the Joe Gordon trial, and the two agreed to end his managerial reign. Whether he resigned or was fired was uncertain; the public announcement was that he had resigned and would remain with the team as its first baseman, receiving the same salary he had made as player-manager.

The managing job was then offered to Harry Wolverton, who, like Casey Stengel thirty-seven years later, was managing Oakland of the Pacific Coast League. *Baseball* magazine called him a "forceful character," a good credential to succeed Chase. A former major league infielder (he had been captain of the Phillies), he was still a full-time player for Oakland. The thirty-eight-year-old Wolverton would still play a little third base and serve as a pinch hitter for the Yankees, hitting .300 in 50 at-bats.

"I can assure all . . . that Chase and I agree perfectly and will get along together admirably," he said. "I consider him the greatest first baseman the game has ever known. He doesn't want my job, and I couldn't fill his, so we are both satisfied. I have the friendliest of feelings for him and I know that he has for me. I am sure he will be a great source of strength to the club."

Wolverton preferred calling his team the Highlanders rather than the Yankees. This would be the final season of the ten-year lease at Hilltop Park, and if it was to be the end, they would go out as Highlanders, at least as far as Harry was concerned. The season gave birth to the Yankee pinstripe look, and they became the first American League team so adorned; Chicago, Boston, and the 1911 Giants had worn it in the National League.

The Highlanders lost the first five games of the regular season and then headed to Boston, where they would serve as visitors for the opening of Fenway Park on April 20, 1912, a 7–6 Boston win. (The *Titanic*, carrying many New Yorkers, had sunk on April 15.)

On May 12, Ty Cobb delivered a shocking burst of his legendary temper at Hilltop Park. This time, he couldn't control himself while being heckled over his ancestry by a fan named Claude Lueker, a pressman at a New York newspaper. Cobb looked for Farrell to have the fan removed and couldn't find him. Teammate Sam Crawford goaded Cobb, saying, "You going to take that?" In the middle of the game, Cobb ran into the stands to beat up the man. It turned out Lueker had lost one hand and two fingers on his other hand and was defenseless. Heckling, as ugly as it might be, had to be ignored by players.

When Lueker's handicap was reported, Cobb said, "I don't care if he got no feet . . . When a spectator calls me a 'half-nigger' I think it is about time to fight." Cobb was suspended by Ban Johnson, who happened to be at the game. Three days later, his teammates refused to take the field against Philadelphia in support of what they thought was justified action. The result was Detroit fielding a team of amateurs recruited from local sandlots who would lose to the Athletics 24–2. (They all got their names into the *Baseball Encyclopedia*.) It became an important piece of Cobb's life story and also led to the establishment of the Base Ball Players' Fraternity, a labor union headed by the ex-Highlander Dave Fultz. Highlander catcher Ed Sweeney was elected a vice president, along with Mathewson and Cobb.

Wracked by injuries to many of their regulars, devoid of a top scout—Arthur Irwin was now a stay-at-home business manager—and distracted by Hal Chase's ugly divorce (he'd shed Nellie, found a new girlfriend, and missed three weeks with a nervous breakdown), the team was going nowhere fast. Farrell was concentrating on his new ballpark in the Bronx, and the Wolverton experiment was failing. The team finished in last place, 50–102, fifty-five games out of first and with the lowest percentage—.329—in team history. They drew only 242,294, about a third of what the Giants drew.

The final game at Hilltop Park was played on October 5, the same day the Giants played the Superbas in the final game at Washington Park, prior to the opening of Ebbets Field. This would be the last Highlander game: The team would officially become the Yankees in 1913.

The opponents were the Washington Senators, now managed by one Clark Griffith. Remembering all the pomp and pageantry of the 1903 opener could only have been painful to people who had hoped for so much more from this franchise. And this final game was one of baseball's sad stories.

Barely five thousand fans turned out to see the 8–6 New York victory. After hearing other scores that rendered this game meaningless in the standings, Griffith sent Nick Altrock and Germany Schaefer into the game, two "coaches" who were really clowns, generally assigned to entertain the fans with zaniness in pregame warm-ups.

Altrock made his only appearance of the season that day, first announcing himself as "batting for Ty Cobb," then pitching a loony inning in which he was charged with the loss. He was relieved by old man Griffith, forty-two, who pitched in his first game in three years and allowed a home run to Chase, the only batter he faced. It was the last one hit at the Hilltop. At that point, Altrock took out Griffith (his manager) and called on Schaefer, an infielder, who took the mound for two thirds of an inning, his first pitching appearance in fifteen years as a big leaguer.

It might have passed for an exhibition game, but it was an official league game made farcical by Griffith's actions—and perhaps a bit of payback for perceived slights in New York four years before. After his firing, Griffith surely noticed that his successors—Elberfeld, Stallings, Chase, and Wolverton—had not distinguished themselves.

And that was the end of Hilltop Park and the Highlanders. Ten seasons, best remembered for a wild pitch by Chesbro that ruined their only shot at a pennant. Their best player may have been throwing games, their chief scout was a bigamist, the owners skirted the law, and maybe the best thing you could say about the ballpark was that it never burned down.

No band played "Auld Lang Syne" as the fans exited one last time. In 1914 the park would be torn down, and in 1928 replaced by a magnificent hospital complex, Columbia Presbyterian. One can still see the hospital today, up on the hilltop, across the Harlem River from Yankee Stadium. It is two miles and a century away.

In 1993, the Yankees placed a bronze plaque, shaped like home plate, in the spot where home plate would have been in 1903, commemorating the original ballpark. In a ceremony attended by Highlander pitcher Red Hoff, the last surviving Hilltop Park player (1911–13), the plaque was placed in the courtyard garden just outside the Presbyterian Building of the medical complex, where the Yankees of the twenty-first century send their injured players. The garden includes the area where right field—still level—had been.

Chapter Five

FOUR QUESTIONS FACED THE YANKEES as 1913 dawned: who would manage them, what they would be called, where they would play, and, above all, how they would improve.

On November 6, Farrell fired Wolverton from his only major league managing job. He returned to the PCL the following year, and when his managing career ended, he settled in Oakland and sold automobiles until his death in 1937. Farrell, meanwhile, set about looking for someone new.

As for a nickname, that was the easy part. "Yankees" was now in common use, and the team no longer played in New York's highlands.

But where *would* they play? While Farrell had big plans for his park on Broadway in the Bronx, it was a long way from being a reality, and there was already some community opposition to the work ahead, especially filling in the creek. Washington Park in Brooklyn was now available, but that was too far from the team's fan base. It would be like starting over. The Polo Grounds it would be.

Giants owner John Brush, long in failing health and wheelchair ridden, attended the 1912 World Series, appearing even more feeble following a September auto accident. After the Series, he went west by train for recovery in better weather, but died en route. He was succeeded as club president by his son-in-law Harry Hempstead, who would become the Yankees' landlord at, ahem, Brush Stadium.

So they would haul their clubhouse safe and equipment and move down to Coogan's Bluff. (James Coogan owned the land.) Short-term, maybe a year. The detente between the Yankees and the Giants, brokered over the

1911 fire, easily allowed this accommodation. And for the Yankees it meant express trains from Wall Street delivering fans to a park with a greater capacity, with perhaps more celebrities attending their games (though the Giants attracted most of the bigger fish). And of course playing in a newly reconstructed, state-of-the-art facility gave them a more "big-league" home.

The Polo Grounds wound up being the Yankees' home for ten years, as long as Hilltop Park was. It was never easy being guests in someone else's home for so long. The Giants enjoyed the rent, which ranged from $50,000 to $100,000 as the years passed, but the field took a beating. By September of each year, there wasn't much grass left in the diamond. There were few off days to tend to it.

The Polo Grounds was horseshoe shaped: Center field was 460 feet from home, and the foul lines were just 277 to left and 258 to right, making for a very odd configuration. *Baseball* magazine called it "the greatest ballpark in the world," "beyond imagination of the baseball enthusiast of the past. It is built entirely of steel, marble and reinforced concrete, and it is fireproof." (Elevated outfield clubhouses, along with a second-deck outfield grandstand, were added in 1923.)

Part of the rebuild, as a gift to the city by the Giants, was an eighty-step concrete stairway from the high reaches of Coogan's Bluff to the low ground where the park sat. In 2010, the Yankees and San Francisco Giants both contributed to the restoration of this staircase, which is all that remains there now.

When Farrell heard that "the Peerless Leader," Frank Chance, was in a salary dispute with Chicago Cubs management, he found his manager. Chance, the man who had won four pennants with the Cubs, was coming to the Yankees.

Johnny Evers, Chance's second baseman (they were two thirds of the poetically celebrated Tinker-to-Evers-to-Chance infield), said, "A man who can get together a team that has won 530 games in five years and lost but 235 is, in my opinion, the peer of all leaders."

Wrote *Sporting Life*, "If you had informed anybody five years ago that in 1913 Chance would be managing the cellar team of the American League you would have been hauled to the batty bungalow. There several doctors armed with all sorts of torture prongs would have picked out your brains and dried them before a gas heater."

Make no mistake about it, this was big. This was the kick that this valuable franchise in the biggest city in America needed.

ITS MASTER STROKE . . . LANDING CHANCE IS AMERICANS BIGGEST TRIUMPH . . . PEERLESS LEADER TO DIVIDE WITH JOHN MCGRAW WORSHIP OF FANDOM IN NEW YORK CITY, headlined the *Sporting News*.

Added *Baseball* magazine in a headline to an eleven-page story on the move from the Cubs: A RED LETTER DAY IN THE TRIUMPHANT CAREER OF THE AMERICAN LEAGUE! They called it "the greatest deal in baseball history."

Chance issued a statement for the press:

> The contract existing between Mr. Farrell and myself is for three years. The terms of this contract have been widely discussed, and I may say they were entirely satisfactory to us both. I can give little information as to the make-up of my team until I have had an opportunity to try out the material at hand.
>
> We shall train this season in Bermuda. I believe it will offer an almost ideal climate. As for my connection with a new organization, I can say that I always wanted to work for the American League, and have long considered New York the best town to work in. I shall give my players a fair and equal opportunity and the good people of New York may count to the full upon my giving them the best I have in me.

Chance wanted the team named simply "New York," and to display it on their home uniforms just that way. But "Yankees" won the day. The fifteen-year veteran had been an elite player, but he was really done a year earlier following a beaning that caused him great headaches. He played just a dozen games for the Yanks. He'd been a player-manager since he was twenty-eight, a total of eight seasons. In his first full season in charge, the Cubs had won 116 games, producing the highest winning percentage in baseball history. And he was a symbol of success, residing in the off-season at his "Cub Ranch" in Glendora, California.

Sportswriter Joe Vila would again play an intermediary role in securing Chance, first reporting it as a rumor in late December of 1912. Farrell gave Chance a three-year deal at an almost unimaginably high $25,000 a year. (It may have been less, and enhanced with attendance incentives.)

That left just one big question: how to improve on the 1912 disaster. The team didn't make any great additions that year. A twenty-two-year-old shortstop named Roger Peckinpaugh came over from Cleveland on May 25, and on August 20 they outbid a couple of other teams and paid $12,000 for a hot Baltimore third baseman named Fritz Maisel. Ed Sweeney, the team's regular catcher since '08, was really the only regular to last through the season without turning over his position. Forty-four different players wore the uniform that year. The team had a new trainer in Charlie Barrett, succeeding Harry Lee.

The biggest addition may have been the subtraction of Hal Chase. Almost at once, Chance and Chase clashed. Chase took to making fun of Chance's mannerisms, including his being deaf in one ear. Chance began to scrutinize Chase's play in minute detail, suspecting that the rumors around him were true. He came to believe that the man was throwing games.

"I want to tell you fellows what's going on," Chance told a couple of sportswriters, including Fred Lieb. "Did you notice some of the balls that got away from Chase today? They weren't wild throws; they were only made to look that way. He's been doing that right along. He's throwing games on me!"

Hal Chase's days as a Yankee were done. He was batting in the low .200s. A few times, although he threw left-handed, he even played second base, with Chance playing first. On July 1, Chase was traded to the White Sox for Babe Borton and Rollie Zeider. Borton, in the lingo of the day, was an "onion," an insignificant player. Zeider suffered from bunions on his feet. It was too much to resist. Mark Roth, writing in the *Globe*, said the Yankees had "traded Chase to Chicago for a bunion and an onion." Everyone loved that line.

Chase, the former manager, the most popular player in the team's history, had put in nine years for the Yankees, batted .284, and stole 248 bases—and maybe a few victories—along the way. His hitting improved in the National League: He won a batting title with the Reds in 1916, but in 1918 the Reds charged him with throwing games, and he went before the National League president for a hearing. He played one more year, 1919, and then he was done. He wasn't banned from the game with the Black Sox (all of whom played in 1920), but his reputation was such that it was time to go, and everyone knew why.

Chase never really denied his gambling habits, and after his playing days often spoke of them with regret. Still, he was a baseball outcast. He returned to California, worked menial jobs, and died penniless and repentant in 1947 at the age of sixty-four, hopeful of clearing his name but realizing that it wasn't likely to happen.

Despite all these changes, the 1913 Yankees moved up only to seventh place, losing 94 games. They lost their first seventeen games at the Polo Grounds and didn't have a home victory until June 7. They were in last place all summer. They hit only eight home runs. Farrell was grinding his teeth. A $25,000 manager, and now this.

The Yanks drew 357,551, while the Giants won another pennant and led the majors in attendance with 630,000. It was also clear to Farrell that his great new ballpark was not going to be ready for 1914, and so he needed another season of shared quarters. The Giants were fine with it. The rent checks were clearing.

1914 AGAIN FAILED to provide any new star-quality players while the Federal League began its first of two seasons, with a team in Brooklyn, the Tip-Tops, playing at Washington Park. Said Jimmy Gilmore, the president of the Feds, "New York is the largest city in the country and a great baseball city, but we are aware of the conditions. The New York Americans have never succeeded in getting more than a foothold in New York, as New Yorkers can see nothing but their Giants. We would not place a team in Manhattan and know enough about baseball to know that we cannot get New York fans to go to the suburbs while the Giants and New Yorks are playing in the Polo Grounds."

Fritz Maisel, perhaps the most heralded player on the team, stole 74 bases in 1914, still the most ever for a third baseman. It would be the single-season Yankee record for seventy-one years, until Rickey Henderson swiped 80 in 1985. The Yankees, of course, became known for power hitting and never really sought base stealers.

Chance took to relying on his many superstitions, like rubbing a rabbit's foot on his players' bats. It usually failed to work. The Peerless Leader had peers after all.

Infielder Angel Aragon, from Havana, Cuba, came up on August 20 and got into six games. He would be the first Latin American player in the franchise's history. (A more substantial contributor would be Cuban outfielder Armando Marsans, who played for the Yankees in 1917 and 1918 at the end of an eight-season career, appearing in 62 games.) Aragon and Marsans were, of course, light-skinned Cubans; no dark-complexioned players would enter the major leagues until 1947 or join the Yankees until 1955.

Then there was catcher Pius "Pi" Schwert, a Wharton School product who got into a dozen games over two years. Schwert wasn't much of a base-ball player, but in 1938 he would be elected to his first of two terms in the U.S. Congress, representing the Buffalo area. He remains the only Yankee player ever elected to Congress.

Yet none of this did much for the hapless '14 team. Farrell and Devery were not making much money with baseball or any other business. Atten-dance was lower than the peak years at Hilltop. They were said to be "less chummy" then they had been; some said they weren't even speaking. They were losing even more with the ill-fated Kingsbridge ballpark project, or with some scheme for a ballpark on a "floating island" off Manhattan.

After a late-season game, the two of them walked into the clubhouse and overheard Chance complaining about them. A losing manager complain-ing about owners not getting him better players is as old as baseball itself, but this time it became confrontational, and the players had to pull Chance and Devery apart.

It could not have helped matters that at this time, over in the National League, none other than George Stallings was leading his Boston Braves to a "miracle" pennant, coming from last to first in the second half of the season.

Another issue had been Farrell forgiving Ray Caldwell's various fines for bad behavior, an undermining of Chance's authority. Farrell had feared that Caldwell would jump to the Federal League if he didn't get his money refunded, and he gave in. Chance was furious. Plus, Chance con-cluded that Arthur Irwin was just a lousy scout who hadn't helped the team at all.

With the team in seventh place, Chance and Farrell worked out a parting of the ways. Chance wanted to be paid in full for his third year. Farrell re-sponded with a diplomatic letter saying no:

> Dear Frank: I received your letter yesterday but it was too late to send an answer to Washington. Of course you know it was your own propo-sition to give up the management of this club on Sept. 15 which I ac-cept much against my wishes. Your request for full salary I cannot see my way clear to grant you, as I know you do not want to take money you do not earn. I will see you after the game.
>
> Very truly yours, Frank J. Farrell.

This great figure of the game, who had won four pennants with the Cubs, could do nothing with this sorry team. It was an embarrassment all around after all the excitement following his hiring.

The remaining twenty games of the season would find the youngest player on the roster, twenty-three-year-old shortstop Roger Peckinpaugh, taking over as manager, winning half his games and moving the team up to a sixth-place finish with 70 wins. (The Yankees also lost their postseason exhibition series to the Giants.) The Wooster, Ohio, native remains the youngest man to ever manage a major league team. It was a curious pick, but clearly leadership was seen in this lantern-jawed youngster, who worked up the nerve to ask Farrell for an extra $500 and got it.

I met Peckinpaugh in the early seventies when he was living near the Yankees' spring training site in Fort Lauderdale. I had invited him to a spring training game, and although he declined, he did invite me to his home one evening.

It had been almost seventy years since he had been a Yankee manager, and he'd gone on to enjoy a nice seventeen-year big-league playing career followed by service with Cleveland as both manager and general manager, taking him up through 1946. He was a proud man, and in making small talk, I tossed out a compliment, saying, "You sure oughta be in the Hall of Fame, Mr. Peckinpaugh!"

That was his opening. "Whaddya mean, oughta be!" he said. And with that he shuffled into his bedroom, rummaged through his sock drawer, and came out with a folded and yellowed newspaper clipping from the twenties, long before the Hall of Fame had been established.

OUR MAN PECK: A HALL OF FAMER FOR SURE, said the headline.

I apologized at once for thinking that somehow he wasn't in! This was all the proof he needed: Never mind what the Cooperstown folks thought. And we had a great evening together. He told me it was Chance who suggested he ask Farrell for the $500.

He had come to the Yankees in a trade from Cleveland in May 1913 and wound up putting in nine years at short for New York, becoming the team captain in '14 and the only player from the 1915 club—taken on by new ownership—to make it to a Yankee World Series (1921). While only a .257 hitter in his nine seasons with the Yanks, he did enjoy a .305 season in 1919, which included a twenty-nine-game hitting streak.

With Chance gone, it was again time to take stock. Twelve seasons into their history and the Yankees were no closer to contending than they had been at their birth. It was easy to conclude that this franchise was still one big flop.

"How much longer shall the American League allow a glaring business blunder to exist?" wondered a writer in *Baseball* magazine.

NOT LONG AFTER the 1914 World Series, Ban Johnson and his top aide James Price began to orchestrate the departure of Farrell and Devery and set up the sale of the team. Devery seemed to want out first; the pair had lost about half a million dollars on the franchise. A final issue between them involved Farrell's securing a $50,000 loan from the league without informing Big Bill.

After twelve seasons, Johnson's hope for a big-time attraction in New York had been a failure. It was time to start over. He needed new owners, men of means, men who would be taken more seriously than the gambler and the crooked cop. The game had matured, and the quality of ownership needed to reflect that.

Johnson was not only going to find new owners: He was going to provide the Yankees with a new manager, a new business manager, some new players, and plans for a new ballpark. It was to be one grand statement. Of course, at the same time it was going to be 1903 all over again.

Farrell, preparing to exit baseball (there was scant mention of Devery), said, "Certainly I am sorry to retire from the game which I love. But I feel that I have been repaid for all the efforts and disappointments. I confess that my luck as a promoter was not such as I had hoped. For the new owners, I have the warmest friendship."

JACOB RUPPERT JR. was spending the fall and early winter of 1914 at the resort hotel in French Lick, Indiana where the wealthy would regularly converge to experience "the cure"—a vacation built around the miracle healing powers of the local mineral waters. It was the sort of thing that rich people did, and Jacob Ruppert qualified.

Born in New York City in 1867, Ruppert was the son of Anna and Jacob Ruppert, who had developed a great $30 million brewery on Third Avenue between Ninetieth and Ninety-second streets in the German-speaking Yorkville section of Manhattan. His grandfather Franz, a Bavarian, had brought his brewing skills to New York in 1851 and established the foundation of the family business, a modest beer garden and brewery at First and Forty-fifth.

Junior worked menial jobs and learned the business inside and out until he was made general manager in 1890. He was well prepared to one day succeed his father, but first came the distraction of politics. At twenty-two, he joined the staff of New York governor David Hill, where he took on the honorary title of colonel of the New York National Guard. He kept the position when Governor Roswell Flower assumed office in 1891, and was the principal speaker a year later when the great monument honoring the four hundredth anniversary of Christopher Columbus's discovery of the new world was erected at what became Columbus Circle. He was all of twenty-five.

With Tammany Hall backing, Ruppert was elected to Congress in 1898 out of New York's Fifteenth Congressional District (later the district of Adam Clayton Powell and Charles Rangel), which to that point had normally voted Republican.

While in Congress, he served on the Committee on Immigration and Naturalization and the Militia Committee. His first bill was intended to provide tariff relief to Puerto Rico, a newly annexed territory, which brought forth all sorts of questions about the extent of its relationship with the U.S. In a compromise, Ruppert's bill passed, ultimately leading to no tariffs, a measure in place to this day. In his role on immigration and naturalization, he brought forth a petition to amend immigration procedures at the Port of New York on behalf of immigrant Jews.

He was reelected three times, serving eight years, before he declined to run in 1907. He thus retired undefeated and returned to help run the brewery, the principal product being Ruppert beer.

The brewery of George Ehret was the biggest in New York (Ruppert later bought it), with the Ruppert Brewery second, which probably made both of them among the top five breweries in the nation—sharing honors at various times with Schlitz, Seipp, Engel, Philip Best (later Pabst), and Ballantine. There were no "national" brands as we know them today. In 1917, Ruppert Brewery surpassed one million barrels annually and later peaked at one and a half million.

Jacob Sr. owned trotting horses, but the Colonel preferred thoroughbreds. He also bred champion Saint Bernards, owned yachts, had massive collections of rare first-edition books, jade, and porcelain, and lived in a fabulous fifteen-room mansion at 1120 Fifth Avenue. His twenty-five-room country estate in Garrison, New York, was also the home to a large collection of monkeys. He had butlers and servants, maids and chauffeurs, the finest silver serving pieces, and a magnificently tailored collection of three-piece suits. He was the very definition of the well-bred fellow who joined all the right clubs and knew all the right people. In 1933, he helped to finance the exploration of Antarctica by Rear Admiral Richard Byrd, whose fleet of cargo vessels included the *Jacob Ruppert*.

A lifelong bachelor, he frequently escorted Helen "Winnie" Weyant to social events; she was often at his side at his Fifth Avenue or Garrison homes. When he died, the *Times* obituary, perhaps mindful of rumors that accompanied lifelong bachelors, made a point of saying, "He was distinctly of the masculine type, and this was reflected in his business office, which was paneled in dark wood. There were no curtains. The only ornaments were two bronzes of American Indians, a bronze of an American eagle and a gold-fish aquarium. They all stood on marble pedestals."

Ruppert eventually sold off his rare book collection, some buildings, and his racing and breeding interests, in part out of recognition that Prohibition would cut back on his brewery profits. He laid off very few employees and produced a legal "near beer" during its time. He sold his near beer at Yankee Stadium, and the brewery continued to other syrups, soda-bottling services, and a sweetener called Maltone. The closing of half the city's breweries meant greater market share for Ruppert.

In 1915, Jacob Sr. died and the Colonel took over the family business, expanding it to 1.25 million annual barrels of Knickerbocker, Ruppert's Extra Pale, and Ruppiner beer by 1917. Jacob Jr.'s younger brother George became vice president.

Sizing up the Colonel in a 1915 interview in *Baseball* magazine, their reporter said, "Col. Ruppert is in every sense a man of big business, quick of speech, decisive in his statements, yet courteous and discriminating in his treatment of the men who approach him in a continual stream on a thousand varied errands."

Ruppert's new business partner was Tillinghast L'Hommedieu Huston, two years younger than Ruppert and a man clearly in need of a nickname. He would answer to Til and would sometimes be called Cap (his rank in the Spanish-American War while serving in Cuba) and later Colonel (his rank while serving in France during the Great War). When people wanted to refer to him and Ruppert together, it was the Colonels. If referring to one and not the other, it was the Colonel and the Captain.

While Ruppert looked like the sort of fellow who expected to be handed a towel each time he washed his hands, Huston looked more like a fellow who would give a quick glance toward the sink and decide he could skip it.

Both were season-ticket holders at the Polo Grounds but did not know each other. And so as Christmas 1914 approached, Huston set off for French Lick to meet his potential partner in this baseball investment. The meeting was arranged by John McGraw, who was a member of the Havana Club with Huston and the Lambs Club with Ruppert.

Huston, stout and outspoken, dowdier than the elegant Ruppert, was a civil engineer and, in his earlier years, a railroad developer in his father's employ. He had made his fortune in Cuban land development after the Spanish-American War. He remained in Cuba for nearly a decade, developing harbor fronts and learning his way around the political minefields of the country.

McGraw mentioned him to Ruppert as a man who might make a good baseball owner (both would have preferred the Giants). They split the $460,000 sale price of the Yankees and pledged to go out and purchase better players, with Johnson lobbying the seven opposing teams to make some good ones available.

Johnson also believed that the Yankees would have a home of their own, ready to go, sometime during the 1916 season. It wasn't going to be the property in Kingsbridge, however: That plan was now dead.

"Many said that we were buying a 'pig in a poke,'" said Ruppert, "and that it was unwise to make such an investment with the Great War bearing down upon our country. At that time, they were certainly a poor team, but we believed that by acquiring a smart manager and good ball players, we could make the New York Yankees into a top-notch baseball club. We knew that it would be difficult, if not impossible to draw the fans away from the Giants, but we hoped that we could offer New York an answer to the otherwise unanswerable Giants."

Ruppert spoke with a German accent that would become more pronounced as his voice rose. Some thought that surely he had been born in Germany, not realizing that he was a second-generation, American-born industrialist. In manner and bearing he looked the part of a man of prosperity and was every bit the sportsman, philanthropist, and patron of the arts—one of those arts being baseball.

"There was anti-German sentiment in America at that time," notes K. Jacob Ruppert, great-grandson of Jacob Sr. "I'm sure he suffered considerably, notwithstanding his strong political ties with Tammany Hall and Washington from his congressional days. The family has said that during this time he 'dropped' his German accent. He never really had one, but did speak German fluently. He just used the accent when it was favorable to do so."

"He insisted that everything he possessed in the entire world be clean and well groomed," recalled his later pitching ace Waite Hoyt. "He was the first owner to buy four sets of home uniforms and four sets of road uniforms and insisted that they be dry-cleaned every day so his team would look like champions."

IN THE LATE afternoon of December 31, 1914, the sale was closed. Ruppert paid his half with a certified check, Huston in thousand-dollar bills. Huston said he would not return to Havana and would stay in New York to attend to the team. A celebratory dinner was offered for the new owners at the New York Athletic Club, with Farrell in attendance.

Ruppert became the team's president and Huston the secretary-treasurer. Around that same time, on November 25, another key piece of the Yankee future arrived. Giuseppe Paolo DiMaggio was born in Martinez, California. People would come to call him Joe.

Farrell and Devery faded into the sunset, no longer on speaking terms. Farrell had at least legitimized his reputation: He was no longer just the Poolroom King of New York. Devery, however, remained identified with his shady police tenure, and his obituaries barely made note of his baseball connection.

Devery died at his home in Far Rockaway, Queens, in 1919, forty-two months after selling his interest in the team. He never lived to see his old team win a pennant, nor did he reconcile with Farrell. He had just returned from a business trip to Washington when he was stricken, the cause of death listed as apoplexy—a stroke. He was sixty-five, and his wife and four grandchildren were at home with him when he collapsed. "No more spectacular policeman than Big Bill Devery ever wore a uniform of the New York Department," said the reigning police commissioner, Richard Enright.

Neither Farrell nor anyone from baseball attended Devery's huge funeral, but then again, neither did Mrs. Devery, who was reportedly home and "prostrated by grief."

Farrell died at sixty of a heart attack on vacation at the Ritz Carlton in Atlantic City in 1926. The press reported that he was a millionaire at the time of his death. Governor Al Smith called him a "close personal and family friend for more than 25 years," and he attended the funeral in Manhattan, where Farrell lived on West End Avenue. Farrell lived long enough to see world championships, Yankee Stadium, and Babe Ruth in pinstripes, just not on his watch. Among those at his funeral were Charles Stoneham, who now owned the Giants; Tim Mara, who owned the fledgling football Giants of the new NFL; and Joe Vila. No one associated with the Yankees, present or past, attended.

While neither man made much money with the team, the sale to Ruppert and Huston presented them with plenty to divide. Despite reports that Devery was worth over $1 million, both he and Farrell were pretty much broke when they died. Devery left $1,023 and Farrell $1,072. As both men liked to wager, Farrell might claim to have won by forty-nine dollars.

THE NEW YEAR'S EVE announcement would have been plenty big with just the sale of the club, but with it went rumors of the new manager to be. And that would be Wild Bill Donovan, who was in the small group rumored to have been considered (a group that included Hughie Jennings, Miller Huggins, Joe Kelley, Wilbert Robinson, and even Connie Mack). Johnson backed Donovan. Kelley, a future Hall of Famer who had been managing in Toronto, would become a Yankee scout and spring training coach for several years.

Donovan agreed to terms on January 2. Peckinpaugh would return to his role as team captain.

Like Buck Showalter many decades later, Donovan, thirty-eight, would be the manager just as the team was on the brink of success. Donovan would precede Miller Huggins; Showalter, Joe Torre.

(Donovan was not related to another "Wild Bill Donovan," a contemporary who had starred in football at Columbia and went on to a distinguished military and intelligence career.)

Wild Bill's initial impact in New York came while pitching for Brooklyn, where he won 25 games in 1901 to lead the National League. After winning 17 in 1902, he jumped to the American League, joining Detroit, for whom he'd win 139 games over the next nine seasons, including a 25–4 record in 1907 and pennants in 1907, 1908, and 1909. In 1913–14 he was the manager and part-time pitcher for the Providence Grays of the American Association, where he managed a twenty-year-old first baseman named Wally

Pipp, a twenty-two-year-old pitcher named Carl Mays, and a nineteen-year-old pitcher named Babe Ruth.

Donovan's hiring was well received, and he said, "I shall treat my players with every courtesy and friendship for I feel that I will always be one of the boys. I shall try to encourage every man of the squad and give all a square deal. I have not the least apprehension that any player will try to take advantage of me."

Donovan brought back coach Charlie "Duke" Farrell, another Brooklyn alum who had been an early mentor and who had coached for the Yankees in 1909 and 1911, and trainer Jimmy Duggan, who had been with him in Detroit and Providence. Ruppert and Huston named Harry Sparrow as business manager. Sparrow was a popular New York sports figure who had capably served as business manager for the world tour undertaken by the White Sox and Giants after the 1914 season. With Arthur Irwin off to manage Lewiston in the Northeast League, Sparrow was given broad powers and often acted as general manager as we know the job today. Ruppert and Huston came to trust him with their checkbook and with his judgments.

Also brought aboard were Mark Roth and Charlie McManus, the dual traveling secretaries who would come to be known as Nip 'n' Tuck. Roth, who was also the de facto publicity director (and hence my "great-grandfather" in that position), had covered the team for the *Globe* since they had played their first game, lived until 1944, and would be the longest-standing insider witness to the team's history from its inception. (Fred Lieb, the journalist who lived until 1980, did not cover the team until 1911.) Since hotels would often mix up Roth and Ruth when assigning rooms, Mark would sometimes get the luxurious suites saved for Babe; it was said that this led to the practice of traveling secretaries getting suites on a regular basis.

McManus would eventually become an assistant business manager and then the stadium manager when Yankee Stadium opened.

Irwin, it turned out, was a scandal waiting to happen. On July 15, 1921, while managing Hartford, he climbed aboard a steamship headed for Boston. When he went missing on the ship, authorities found the stool from his stateroom on deck and concluded that he had probably committed suicide and jumped overboard. His body was never found.

In sorting out his affairs, it turned out that he had a wife and two daughters in Boston and another wife and son in New York. Managing Hartford must have seemed like the perfect job for him. It was, apparently, all too much.

The new hirings—Sparrow, Roth, and McManus—were an important step in the maturity of the team as a business operation. Offices at 30 East Forty-second Street (telephone Murray Hill 3146) were inherited from Farrell and maintained until 1920 when they moved to the Cohan and Harris Theater Building at 226 West Forty-second Street (Bryant 2300). In 1928 they went to 55 West Forty-second (Pennsylvania 6-9300).

THE REMAINING PIECE of business for Ruppert and Huston was a ballpark of their own. Attention now returned to Manhattan Field, adjacent to the Polo Grounds, also owned by James J. Coogan and also leased by the Giants, who used it as a parking lot. It was still not a great choice because the free view from the top of the hill—Coogan's Bluff—was a hard thing to accept.

Ban Johnson liked the idea of a ballpark in Long Island City, just across the East River in Queens. The Dodgers waived territorial rights and accepted it. Subways ran there. Yet Johnson was outvoted. Ruppert and Huston felt the Queens site was too removed from the fan base. In July, Houston wrote to Johnson about a site in Forty-second Street, but acknowledged that it would be costly. They made a quick deal with Harry Hempstead to keep the Yanks in the Polo Grounds through 1916 if necessary, and it appeared it surely was. They would keep searching.

Chapter Six

THE 1915 TEAM TOOK ITS PINSTRIPES down to Savannah, Georgia, for training camp, and Donovan, going through a messy divorce, was glad to focus his attention on baseball.

As for the five new players he had been promised, Wally Pipp, whom he had managed at Providence, was a nice waiver-price pickup. Pipp had played a dozen games for Detroit in 1913 and then batted .314 at Rochester in 1914 before the Yankees purchased him. At six foot one and 180 pounds, the Chicago native was a big man for his time, and at twenty-two, offered hope for a good long stay at the position.

The others—Bunny High from the Tigers, Walter Rehg from the Red Sox, Elmer Miller from the Cards, and Joe Berger from the White Sox, were onions. Getting five players sounded better than it really was. Nobody was giving away good talent.

The pitching staff would get 73 starts out of its three Rays—Keating, Fisher, and Caldwell. Caldwell, coming off 18 wins in 1914, would win 19 in 1915 and would even deliver consecutive pinch-hit homers. Fisher would go 18–11 with a 2.11 ERA in his sixth Yankee season.

Bob Shawkey, who would go on to become the leading winner (168) in Yankee history by the time he departed, was purchased from the Philadelphia Athletics on June 28. Just twenty-four, he was the kind of prospect the Yankees had been hoping to find for years. The right-hander from Slippery Rock University, usually distinguished by the red sweatshirt he wore under his uniform jersey, had been a 15-game winner for Connie Mack, who occasionally liked to sell off his players for cash. The Yankees paid $3,500 for Shawkey.

Sometimes, of course, good signings would get away. Take Dazzy Vance. The Yankees bought Vance from Pittsburgh in April, and he was 0–3. They farmed him out for a couple of years, and he returned in 1918 to hurl just two innings. Back to the minors he went, with Brooklyn finally purchasing him as the 1922 season beckoned. He was thirty-one and had yet to win a single game in the major leagues.

Daz would go on to win seven consecutive strikeout titles for Brooklyn and make it all the way to Cooperstown. Nobody on the Yankees saw that one coming.

SADLY, 1915 WAS another well-intentioned season that went nowhere. New ownership, new manager, new players, new hopes—same old results.

The team finished fifth, with one fewer win than the year before. Even worse, despite all the enthusiasm and publicity that went with the changes, the team drew just 256,035—less than four thousand a game. In the remodeled Polo Grounds, capacity thirty-four thousand, one can only imagine what Ruppert and Huston must have been thinking. *"What have we purchased?"* It was said they lost $30,000 in that first year.

There wasn't a .300 hitter to be found. Only the Giants finishing last (with the same 69 victories as the Yankees) deflected attention away from the lack of progress. It was just a bad year for Manhattan baseball.

As 1916 approached, an important development was taking place in Boston, where star center fielder Tris Speaker was holding out and experiencing a very bad relationship with Red Sox owner Joe Lannin. With no Federal League to use as leverage, Speaker was in no position to bargain, and Lannin was prepared to move him. He was a lifetime .337 hitter for Boston, one of the true talents in the game. For many years, historians would put him in an "all-time outfield" with Ruth and Cobb. His defense was as heralded as his hitting.

Lannin spoke to Huston and Ruppert about him at the American League meetings in February. Rumors made their way to the newspapers. TRIS SPEAKER TO YANKEES IF MAGNATES AGREE TO TERMS, headlined the *Washington Post*.

This was the time for Ban Johnson to step in and help make this happen.

After all, he had pledged to the Colonels that he would get them some good players. Here was his moment. This could drive the Yankees to a pennant at last.

Two days before opening day, Speaker wound up traded to Cleveland for Sam Jones, Fred Thomas, and $55,000, the most money ever included in a player deal. The Yankees had been talking about Fritz Maisel and cash, but could certainly have added more. Where was Johnson?

It was complicated. Just a few weeks before, he had helped to find a buyer for the Indians, bailing out his friend Charlie Somers, who had helped bankroll the American League at its start. In finding a buyer—James Dunn—Johnson had apparently made a similar pledge as he had made the year before to Ruppert and Huston: "I'll get you some players." Now he used his influence to move Speaker to the Indians, where he continued onward with his Hall of Fame career. Maisel went to center for the Yankees. Unfortunately, the speedy Maisel's promising career never played out. He broke his collarbone on May 15, and by 1918 he was done.

And Jake Ruppert would remember that Johnson hadn't come through.

THE YANKS WENT north with Frank "Home Run" Baker, who was no Speaker but still one of the great stars of the American League. Baker, a third baseman with a .321 career average, was celebrated as part of Connie Mack's "$100,000 infield," winners of pennants in 1910, 1911, 1913, and 1914, three of them world championships. Baker hit only 93 career home runs, but he's the only player so nicknamed in baseball history, partly because of his sense of good timing. He led the league in home runs four times during those years (a high of 12 in 1913), and he hit two big ones in the 1911 World Series against the Giants, one off Christy Mathewson and one off Rube Marquard. He got Marquard again in the first game of the 1913 World Series at the Polo Grounds.

So renowned did those games make him that soon afterward, his monstrous fifty-two-ounce bat was auctioned off for $250 and won by Broadway producer-composer George M. Cohan, a big baseball fan.

After the Athletics lost the 1914 World Series to the Braves, Mack began to sell off his star players. Baker chose to retire, sitting out the 1915 season, playing just Saturday and holiday games with a local team near his Trappe, Maryland, farm.

But in 1916 he decided to return, and working with an agent, a lawyer named Vernon Bradley, he was sold to New York for $37,500 and signed a three-year, $36,000 deal with the Yankees. The deal was hammered out in Ruppert's brewery office with Baker, Ruppert, and Mack all present.

Baker, like Keeler a decade before him, was not the player he had been, but his presence indicated that the team could pay top dollar for top-tier players.

But so often, things just didn't play out right for the Yankees. They signed a catcher named Al "Roxy" Walters from San Francisco, and *Baseball* magazine did a three-page story on "the Yankees' Great Young Backstop, Who Looks Like the Niftiest Catcher on the Circuit." "Al should become the Yankees' first-string backstop next year," they reported, "and . . . will be recognized as one of the greatest maskmen in either league . . . And oh, how that boy could hit!"

Walters spent three seasons with the Yanks but never did become a regular. After hitting .266 and .263, he hit .199 in his last year, and then went to Boston where he hit .193, .198, .201, and .194. He never hit a home run. Just surviving in the majors with that performance was an accomplishment. No star, he.

Then there was Lee Magee. The former Cardinals outfielder had batted .323 in the Federal League in 1915, third in the league, and was considered a hot pickup for the Yankees. He was the first player to return to "organized baseball" from the Feds, and the Yanks paid $25,000 for him. But he hit a disappointing .257 and was gone the following year, and then, along with Hal Chase, was kicked out of baseball for gambling after the 1919 season. (Also kicked out—after 1920—was the Browns' Joe Gedeon, a second baseman who played for the Yanks in 1916–17 and whose name was linked to meetings with the gamblers who attempted to fix the '19 Series.)

Gentlemanly Bob Shawkey, on the other hand, burst through with a 24-victory season, tops in his career. He started 27 games, relieved in 26, and was credited with eight saves as we know them today, as Donovan tested a new concept of using pitchers in dual roles.

Ray "Slim" Caldwell's battles with alcohol continued. This was one of the saddest stories in early Yankee history. His name is barely remembered today, yet he might have been one of the all-time great Yankee hurlers— maybe even a Hall of Famer. "He has one of the best curves in the business, and his fastball is a peach," said an unidentified star pitcher to *Baseball* magazine in 1918. "He might be the best all-round pitcher in the American

League." When he died in 1967, he was still ranked seventh all-time among Yankee right-handers with 96 victories. At six foot two and 190, he was a top-tier star on the sports stage of New York.

He was a good hitter too: .248 lifetime.

But alcohol was his ruin. Like many of his contemporaries, he thought imbibing to excess was a sign of "manliness." Athletes often took measure of each other by whether they could hold their liquor. It was an ongoing problem for baseball from its earliest days. Some handled it better than others. Caldwell did not handle it well at all.

He really tested the patience of the easygoing, player-friendly Donovan. But in midseason of 1916 Donovan suspended him for two weeks, and when the suspension ended, Caldwell didn't materialize; the suspension was extended until the end of the season. Although the *Sporting News* reported that he was in a St. Louis hospital for alcohol "treatment," no one could find him during the entire off-season. His wife had to sue him for divorce, charging desertion. When he emerged from wherever he had been, it was due to an arrest for the theft of a ring.

Caldwell reported late to spring training in 1917, and although he'd contribute 13 victories that year, he was again suspended for excessive drinking. He was killing off his own career by the day.

He'd play one more season for New York, 1918, going 9–8 before being traded to Boston, released on August 4, and then signed by Cleveland two weeks later. In his first start for the Indians, he had a lead with two outs in the ninth when he was struck by lightning on the pitcher's mound. For a time he was unconscious, the hometown fans sitting silently in fear.

"My first thought was that I was through for all time," he recounted, "living as well as pitching. But when I looked up and saw I was still in the diamond and that fans were in the stands, just as they were before I was hit I just had to laugh with joy. I never was so glad to be living in all my life, and wouldn't it have been tough luck for me to be stricken just as I had won my first game for a club that was willing to give me a chance when other clubs thought me through. I tingled all over and just naturally sank to the ground. I guess it was almost a minute before I saw Spoke Speaker and the others running toward me and realized the trumpets were not sounding for me yet."

When he regained consciousness, he insisted on finishing, and he recorded the final out for the victory. What a debut!

Seventeen days later, he made his first start in the Polo Grounds against his old teammates, the Yankees. It was enough to attract a big crowd for a

Wednesday doubleheader. Caldwell pitched the opener and proceeded to toss the only no-hitter in the American League that season, a 3–0 victory in which he faced only twenty-nine batters.

"A large and noisy gathering of 25,000 folks saw Caldwell pitch the no-hit game with their own eyes," wrote the *Times*. "If they hadn't been there in person, many of them would never have believed it . . . A lot of the electricity is still lurking in Caldwell's system . . . At times Slim's voltage was higher than others."

Seemingly rejuvenated, the spitballer won 20 for the first time in 1920, helping the Indians to their first world championship and pitching in his first World Series.

And then it all came crashing down on poor Slim Caldwell again. He made only 12 starts in 1921, and manager Speaker had to suspend him yet again. His final big-league appearance was against the Yankees, and he took the loss in a 21–7 drubbing with the teams tied for first late in the season.

And that was it.

He spent most of the rest of that decade pitching in the minors, never to return to the big stage. He was again a 20-game winner at age forty-two with Birmingham. He threw his last game in 1933 at age forty-five. The man could pitch. After his career, he owned a bar, tended at others, and returned to his original profession as a telegrapher. Briefly he was a greeter at the Golden Nugget in the early days of Las Vegas hotels. But mostly he lived quietly with a third wife about sixty miles south of Buffalo. He died in 1967 at the age of seventy-nine.

By many measures, 1916 was a year of improvement. The Yanks were in first place as late as July 30, when a nine-game losing streak ended the temporary trip into rare air. The streak including losing a six-game series to the Browns in St. Louis, in which they scored only four runs in consecutive doubleheaders. With a payroll of $125,000, the Yanks finished fourth, their first first-division finish since 1910. (World Series money didn't extend to first-division finishers until 1918.) Attendance kicked up to 469,211, although the Giants did 551,000 for *their* fourth-place finish.

At the end of the season, the Yankees happily re-signed Donovan and announced that they had plans for a fifty-thousand-seat, double-decked ballpark in place for 1919. In the meantime, it would be back to the Polo Grounds, writing out rent checks to the Giants.

War was looming as the 1917 season unfolded, and in fact had been looming since the *Lusitania* was sunk in May of 1915. But the U.S. did not officially enter the war until April 6, 1917, when President Wilson declared war on Germany. The next day Cap Huston, nearly fifty, reenlisted, offering his engineering skills and effectively ending his day-to-day involvement with the Yankees as he headed off for France. He was the first member of the "baseball family" to enter the war effort; Braves catcher Hank Gowdy enlisted on June 1, making him the first player.

Although ballplayers were not exempt from the military draft, the Yankees lost none of theirs to war service in 1917. But the team did its patriotic part by performing marching drills, bats on shoulders as though rifles, in pregame exercises, a practice designed by Huston. On June 17 they played the Browns in the first-ever Sunday game played at the Polo Grounds—so permitted because the game raised $10,000 for the First Reserve Engineers Regiment of New York, which was soon to deploy. In pregame ceremonies before almost twenty-five thousand, in addition to "The Star Spangled Banner," singer Harry Ellis sang a new George M. Cohan song called "Over There."

"Spread the word, spread the word, over there . . . that the Yanks are coming, the Yanks are coming, the drums drum drumming over there!"

The fans sang along lustily once they learned the refrain, loving the use of the word "Yanks" in the song. Since the Civil War, the word had stood for the north. Now Cohan made it a word of national pride. And the Yankees were proud to seize its patriotic symbolism.

In 1917 the Yanks dropped back to sixth place and attendance fell to 330,294. No pitcher won more than 13, and Maisel hit just .198. Baker hit .282 with just six homers and found himself suspended by Donovan toward the end of the season when he refused to play in a Sunday exhibition game. The headstrong Baker decided to retire, and not until Ruppert intervened did he return. It was a blow to Donovan's authority.

A rare high point was the first no-hitter ever thrown by a Yankee left-hander. On April 24 at Fenway Park, George Mogridge squeaked out a 2–1 win after a ninth-inning rally and an error. Mogridge, twenty-eight years old and just 9–11 that year, was a journeyman from Rochester whom the Yanks had purchased in August of 1915. Through 2011, Mogridge is the only visiting left-hander to pitch a no-hitter in Fenway Park—and in fact one of only four visiting pitchers to throw a no-hitter there at all. The others, all right-handers, are all Hall of Famers: Walter Johnson, Ted Lyons, and Jim Bunning.

So Donovan had three seasons to impress his bosses, and he didn't. He needed to improve on his fourth-place finish in 1916, and he failed. Like the others before him, he was shown the door, and the search for the next great hope would begin.

Donovan was a very likeable figure in the game, and had he found a way to stick around a little longer, he could have been the beneficiary of the greatness to come.

He went back to the Tigers to coach in 1918, managed Jersey City in 1920, the Phillies (with outfielder Casey Stengel) for part of 1921, and New Haven in the Eastern League in 1922 and 1923. On December 9, 1923, he and his boss, New Haven president George Weiss, were passengers in a New York Central Twentieth Century Limited train carrying a number of baseball officials from Grand Central Terminal to league meetings in Chicago.

"We had a compartment and Bill was a cigar smoker," recalled Weiss to sportswriter Harold Rosenthal years later.

> I was one of the few people who didn't smoke in those days. While he was filling up the compartment with tobacco smoke I figured I'd go out into the club car and have a drink. Prohibition? I forgot how, but we managed in those days. I guess I had two or three because by the time I got back Bill had gone to bed. He had taken the lower berth even though it figured to be mine because I was the boss. Since he was asleep I didn't bother to awaken him. Instead I undressed and hopped up into the upper. In those days it was no problem.
>
> There was this horrible crash that awakened me and when I looked around I realized I wasn't in any train but lying there on the tracks. I had nothing on except the neck-ring from my pajama top. There were dead and dying people all around me. I learned later Donovan was among them.

At 1:30 in the morning, the train had crashed into a standing train at a crossing in Forsyth, New York (along Lake Erie, south of Buffalo). Blame was put on the engineer. The actor Douglas Fairbanks Jr. was among the survivors. Weiss, miraculously, survived with just cuts and bruises. Years later, of course, he would become the Yankees general manager.

"The news hits me very hard," said Colonel Ruppert, who was leaving on another train for Chicago.

I can't express my sorrow at hearing of Bill's untimely end. He was still in his prime and one of the greatest managers in baseball. I say this because I know. When he was with the Yankees Donovan had more hard luck than I have ever seen on a ball field. One player after another was injured, but still Donovan kept plugging ahead, and he never forgot how to smile.

He was a wonderful fellow and a great leader. He was our first manager in New York after Colonel Huston and I bought the club and I still think that barring injuries and hard luck Bill Donovan would have brought the Yankees their first pennant. The hardest thing I ever had to do was to release him. Well, Bill died with his boots on. When he died he was on his way to a baseball meeting on business for his club. I think that is the way he would have liked to go.

FINDING A MANAGER for 1918 was complicated by Huston being away in France. He had a first choice and he felt strongly about it: Brooklyn's Wilbert Robinson. But he wasn't there to fight for him.

Ruppert's candidate was Miller Huggins. He gave Robinson a quick interview at the brewery and wasn't impressed. He thought Robbie, at fifty, was too old. So many managers of that era were playing managers, a move that saved a salary, or at least a full one.

His meeting with Huggins went better, although Hug almost didn't take him up on the invitation. It took Taylor Spink's encouragement to get him to take the meeting—Spink was publisher of the *Sporting News*, which was based in St. Louis, and knew Hug well.

"Uncle Robbie" was a lovable character and a respected baseball man, linked in history to John McGraw, with whom he had played and for whom he had coached. When he moved over to manage Brooklyn, the team became known as the Robins (and for years afterward, the derivative the Flock) and he won the 1916 pennant. He hadn't done as well in 1917 and Huston thought he could sign him. The two were hunting buddies, brought together through Huston's friendship with McGraw.

Ban Johnson was encouraging Ruppert to sign Huggins, thirty-nine, who had been manager of the Cardinals. The owner of the Cardinals, Helene Britton, a widow who'd inherited the team from her husband, was looking to sell.

She summoned Hug to her home and told him he could get a group together and buy it.

Hug, a Cincinnati native, partnered with yeast magnates Julius and Max Fleischmann, former limited partners in the Reds. But before he could present the proposal, Britton sold the team to a local group and left him in the lurch. He was angry and ready to move on.

On October 26, 1917, Ruppert signed him to a two-year deal. It was the beginning of a frost between Huston and Ruppert that never really melted. Huston was furious, even suggesting that Ruppert had taken advantage of a solider in uniform. Had Huston not been off in France, he might have been better able to argue the issue, and history might have turned in favor of Robbie. Robinson continued to manage the Robins until 1931 and wound up in the Hall of Fame, although the rest of his managerial career was mostly second-division stuff, save for another pennant in 1920.

Huggins was little. There was no getting away from it. Sports people liked their men big; the *Reach Guide* called Hug "a man of high mentality but of physical inferiority." For most of his playing career, he was the smallest player in the game, a second baseman who stood about five foot five and weighed, by his own account, 120. But to make it to the majors at that size—and to even hit .304 one year—he proved his worth. He played thirteen seasons for the Reds and the Cards, led the league in walks four times, and had been managing the Cardinals since 1913, overseeing the emergence of Rogers Hornsby. In fact, he would bring with him to the Yankees the scout who found Hornsby, Bob Connery, along with Paddy O'Connor to coach.

Despite Hug's diminutive size, he could hold his own. A thoughtful pipe smoker not given to smiling very much, nowhere near as talkative as Donovan, he went about his job in a businesslike fashion, took the game very seriously, and used his law degree from the University of Cincinnati to argue his points. He was never one of the boys. He had no hobbies, no family, and no business interests. He was all baseball. Grantland Rice thought he was somewhat of a lonely figure, tagging behind his players at train stations rather than leading them. But Huggins commanded respect. Of course, his greatest challenges would lie ahead when a certain incorrigible player named Ruth would come to the Yankees. But for 1918, he seemed like a sound choice.

There wasn't much new to the team for 1918, although they did wear red-white-and-blue armbands on their left sleeves in a show of patriotism. Del Pratt was a good addition, coming from the Browns with the great pitcher Eddie Plank on January 22 for five players, including Maisel, who was pretty much done. Pratt would hold out until mid-March in a contract dispute before coming aboard to play second base. (Plank, the game's oldest player at forty-two, retired after the 1917 season, but it did not cause the trade to be restructured.)

Pratt had spent six seasons with the Browns and was considered the best second baseman in the league except for Eddie Collins. Now thirty, he had tied for the RBI lead in 1916, rare for a second sacker. His .275 in 1918 was the best by a Yankee second baseman since 1909.

"For several years, I had my eye on Pratt," said Ruppert. "How did I get him? I paid fifteen thousand dollars in cash and gave away a number of good players for him. But what can you do? I needed this player, everyone knew I needed him. One thing was certain; I couldn't come back empty handed. I had to do something to build up the club after the loss of several valuable men to Army service. And I got what I went after, though I had to pay out of all reason for him."

The other pickup of note was outfielder Ping Bodie, real name Francesco Pezzolo, of San Francisco, who came from the Athletics in a three-way trade involving Detroit. A colorful player who like Baker swung a fifty-two-ounce bat, the thirty-year-old Bodie was popular with New York's Italian community, popular with kids because of his nickname and his roly-poly appearance, and would be a Yankee regular in the outfield for three years before going back to the Pacific Coast League. He was considered influential in starting the stream of great Italian Yankees who came from the Bay Area (Tony Lazzeri, Frankie Crosetti, and Joe DiMaggio), and is famous for denying that he was Babe Ruth's first Yankee roommate, claiming, "I only room with his suitcase."

(In spring training of 1919, Huston, back from the war, arranged for a spaghetti-eating contest between Ping and an ostrich named Percy. It was staged in a boxing ring, and Bodie emerged the winner with the eleventh serving, Percy staggering away from his plate after ten rounds.)

The 1918 season was scheduled to slim down to 140 games, but the war forced a Labor Day cutoff (except for the World Series) and essentially a 125-game season.

On May 23, a "Work or Fight" order was issued by U.S. Provost-Marshall Enoch Crowder, requiring men twenty-one to thirty to either report for duty or take a military-related "essential job." While those in show business were excluded, War Secretary Newton Baker ruled on July 20 that baseball was not considered essential, and its players not exempt. And so by August, players began deserting their rosters, taking war-related jobs or enlisting. Rosters could be filled with those outside of the twenty-one-to-thirty age group or otherwise exempt.

Fourteen Yankee players went into the service, including Fisher, Pipp, Shawkey, Ward, Sammy Vick, Muddy Ruel, Walter Bernhardt, Neal Brady, Alex Ferguson, Frank Kane, Bill Lamar, Ed Monroe, Bob McGraw, and Walt Smallwood. From other rosters, enlistees included future Yankees Herb Pennock, Carl Mays, Ernie Shore, Mike McNally, Urban Shocker, and Casey Stengel, plus former Yankees Les Nunamaker and Fritz Maisel.

Home Run Baker, because he was thirty-two, was the best player they were able to retain.

The team did its part by turning over 10 percent of profits from games during the July 4 week to the Red Cross, and by contributing $13,000 to the Reserve Engineer Regiment and the benefit of their dependents.

A CURIOUS CASE developed involving the old Highlander pitcher Jack Quinn. Quinn had last been a Yankee in 1912, but he proved resilient in the minors and found himself pitching for Vernon, California, in the Pacific Coast League in 1918. White Sox owner Charles Comiskey got permission from the National Commission chairman Garry Herrmann to make a deal directly with Quinn if he wished, and to pay Vernon the draft price if he was retained after play resumed in 1919. Comiskey followed the instructions.

The Yankees wanted Quinn too, and decided to acquire his rights directly from the Vernon club. Quinn reported to the White Sox and went 5–1 down the stretch for them before the National Commission ruled, on August 24, that the Yankees were entitled to him. The season was pretty much over by then, but since both teams were in the American League, Ban Johnson stepped in and ruled that the Yankees had the clearer title to Quinn for 1919 and should prevail.

This caused a permanent rift between Comiskey and Johnson, but it kept Quinn off the 1919 Black Sox and returned the ancient spitballer to the Yanks for three more seasons, including a pennant-winning one.

IT IS HARD to pass judgment on any team's 1918 performance, but the Yanks did return to the first division, finishing fourth despite a 60–63 record. They were tied for first place going into July 4, but were badly outplayed in the second half. Baker hit .306 and Pipp .304 before he departed, and Mogridge led the team with 16 wins.

In December of 1918, the Yankees made their first trade with Harry Frazee, who had purchased the Red Sox twenty-five months earlier. They dealt Caldwell and three lesser names, along with a reported $15,000, for pitchers Ernie Shore and Dutch Leonard and the popular outfielder Duffy Lewis, who had been part of the great Harry Hooper–Speaker–Lewis outfield in Boston for six years. (Leonard refused to report and instead went to Detroit.) This did not turn out to be a blockbuster deal in any sense, but the relationship between Frazee and Ruppert was soon to take on monumental importance.

Huston returned from his war duty right after New Year's and met Huggins for the first time at the club's office on Forty-second Street. It wasn't warm or cordial. He seemed determined not to like Huggins.

"I wouldn't go through again, for all the money in the world, the years from 1919 to 1923," Huggins would later say, talking about the time Huston remained on the scene.

THE YANKS WRAPPED up spring training of 1919 by playing thirteen games with Brooklyn en route north, winning ten of them.

While most fans remember 1919 for the Black Sox and the damage the fixed World Series did to the game, most of the final months of the regular season were dominated by news of the Yankees' purchase of pitcher Carl Mays from Boston.

Not only did this continue a process of obtaining big stars from the Red Sox, but it also launched the era when the Yankees' ability to outspend others would be realized, when the power of the Yankees seemed to surpass the power of the league president, and when the still pennantless Yankees began to see good times on the horizon.

Mays, twenty-seven, was a submarine pitcher who threw with great speed and liked to pitch high and tight. He may not have been a very popular player, but he was a good one. He'd joined the Red Sox in 1915 and had helped them to two pennants, winning two games in the 1918 World Series. He had 61 regular season victories from 1916 to 1918 and had led the league with eight shutouts in '18 despite the abbreviated season.

While the scouting report on Mays was "surly and ill-tempered," his teammates thought of him as more of a loner. He once explained that his teammates were better educated than he was, and he was more comfortable retreating from them than engaging them in conversation. He was, by most accounts, a clean-living, highly competitive guy who was frustrated by pitching problems in 1919. Working on a 5–10 record when he took the mound on July 12 in Chicago, he left in the second inning, trailing 5–0, four of the runs unearned.

He lost his temper when manager Ed Barrow came to take him out. Startled fans saw him throw the ball against the backstop and storm into the clubhouse. Was he angry at his teammates who had made errors behind him? Whatever it was, it was a final straw. He swore to never pitch for the Red Sox again.

Barrow suspended Mays once he learned that he had headed back to Boston, cleaned out his Commonwealth Avenue apartment, and drove to his in-laws' home in Pennsylvania with his wife, Freddie. The Boston newspapers were ravaging him, and it helped not at all that Mays was of German descent and anti-German sentiments were still strong in the country.

Barrow decided to get rid of Mays. He viewed it as an opportunity to clear himself of a problematic player and to exert his authority for future benefit. Either Barrow or Frazee called the Yankees to see if they had interest in him.

They sure did. They were in a pennant race, and this would be a player from the defending champions. According to Mays, he got a long-distance call on July 29 that went like this: "Carl, this is Cap Huston of the Yankees. I called to find out if you would be interested in pitching for the Yankees. If you are, there's a good chance of my swinging a deal for you tonight, but I didn't want to get all tangled up in negotiations if you wouldn't pitch for us."

"Well, how about the money?" Carl said he asked.

"We'll have no problems there. Just pack your bag, and by the time you get here we'll be ready to talk contract."

And so that very day, the Yankees traded pitchers Allen Russell and Bob McGraw to Boston, added $40,000, and had themselves one of the best pitchers in the game. This was a big day in Yankee history: a statement from Ruppert that they were ready to do what it took to build a winner.

But wait a minute.

Ban Johnson didn't like this one bit. First, the Red Sox had sold a player who was under suspension and who, it could be argued, initiated his own trade with his actions. And he had come out better off for it! Johnson nullified the deal. He wanted the money returned and Mays to return to the Red Sox. This was his league, he founded it, he was president, and he decided whether this trade should go through.

Ruppert and Huston were now feeling pretty powerful themselves. And nobody pushed the Colonels around.

They weren't returning Mays. They ordered him to remain with the Yankees, and they said, "If necessary, we will go to the courts!"

No one in baseball ever liked going to the courts. It was an industry that policed itself. There might be an occasional court proceeding from outside—like the Federal League—but most matters were settled before the National Commission or the league offices. This was defiance!

On August 6, Justice Robert F. Wagner of the New York State Supreme Court, a future U.S. senator and the father of future New York City mayor Robert F. Wagner Jr., granted a temporary injunction, seeking additional briefs. The Colonels provided them and ordered Huggins to pitch Mays.

Detroit's Frank Navin, siding with Johnson, intimated that the Tigers might not take the field against the Yankees if Mays was on their club. Chicago's Charles Comiskey opposed Johnson, something that might have been unthinkable years earlier. The injunction held. Mays took his regular turn with the Yankees as Johnson stewed. He won his debut on August 8 at the Polo Grounds and went on from there with great success. He made 13 starts, 12 of them complete games, and went 9–3 with a 1.65 ERA. Johnson's power had been struck down. Ruppert and Huston had prevailed.

In one last attempt at relevance, the National Commission, of which Johnson was a member, decided to withhold the Yankees' third-place money from the World Series because they had used an "illegal player." The Colonels paid the players out of their own funds while the players, led by Shawkey, Peckinpaugh, and Pratt, argued over how to divide the money and whether to include trainer Al "Doc" Woods and Phil Schenck. But ultimately the commission backed down. It was the end of Johnson's power, a recognition that the Colonels had emerged as more powerful than he was. And they had made it clear that they were prepared to open their checkbooks for available stars.

This was a monumental case. The 1920 *Reach Official American League Guide* presented a synopsis of the case, covering seventeen pages. The editors sided with Johnson.

The Yanks were 29–18 after obtaining Mays, and although they fell short of their first pennant, they wound up third, thirty-two games over

.500 and just seven and a half games out of first. They drew 619,164, the most they had ever attracted and just twenty-five thousand shy of leading the league for the first time. (The Giants led the majors with 708,857.) Peckinpaugh hit .305, Baker hit .293 with 10 homers, Pratt hit .292, and Bob the Gob Shawkey was again a 20-game winner.

A couple of interesting 1919 call-ups were outfielder George Halas, who would go on to own and coach the Chicago Bears the following year (he played a dozen games and had two singles), and pitcher Lefty O'Doul, who was both an outfielder and a pitcher and who would play briefly for three seasons before finding his real niche in the National League, where he batted .353 over seven seasons (1928–34).

It was also the year that Sunday baseball became legal in New York. Fred Lieb observed:

> Sunday baseball in this state and town have been vindicated . . .
> Before the war there were gloomy forebodings that Sunday ball
> would lead to disturbances, organized roughhouse, and what not.
>
> Yesterday I watched 45,000 fans file out after the game. It was
> a refreshing sight.
>
> Leisurely, good-natured, without unnecessary pushing or shov-
> ing, the big throng dispersed. It was entirely different from the rush-
> hour jam in the subway, when it is a case of every man for himself.
>
> The lady fans grow more numerous with each passing year.
> Never is this more noticeable than in the Sunday crowds. At least a
> quarter of that crowd yesterday were women.

Indeed, the Polo Grounds was becoming more female-friendly.

An oddity worth noting was the fastest game ever played by the team, when the Yanks beat the Athletics 6–1 on September 28 in just fifty-one minutes.

For Huggins, despite the tension with Huston, it was a solid season, a year that had people taking New York seriously in the first postwar test of whether the Yankees were indeed on the move.

Now what could the Colonels have in mind to make the team even better in 1920?

Chapter Seven

THE COLONELS DISPATCHED HUGGINS to Los Angeles to catch up with the vacationing Babe Ruth and deliver news of his new team in person.

It did not go well.

Babe had never been impressed by short men in leadership positions. It was the beginning of a tough relationship for both of them, a constant test of Huggins's ability to lead, a constant test of Ruth's ability to follow.

But let there be no mistake: This was the biggest deal in baseball history. It changed the fortunes of two high-profile franchises for decades.

Babe Ruth would take baseball soaring into a new era as the number-one game in the Golden Age of Sports. It is always difficult to say any athlete is bigger than the game. But Babe Ruth may have qualified.

He certainly became an overnight celebrity when he came to New York, and may have been the best-known American after the president throughout the remainder of his career. Many European immigrants first became aware of baseball by his presence—his easy to remember name, his easily identified look, his love of celebrity. If they could talk about Babe Ruth and smile when his name was mentioned, they were on the road to assimilation.

He looked different. His moon face with the boyish grin, atop a barrel chest and skinny legs, made him easy to pick out in any group photo. He wasn't fat but was rather top-heavy, and not until late in his career did he occasionally let himself get out of shape. He could run the bases well and cover a lot of ground in the outfield: Otherwise, Barrow might have converted him into a first baseman.

And he was lovable. Even when he'd get himself into a tight spot, he'd win over the fans with a humble apology, like a child scolded and sent to his room. He had a gift for saying the right things in interviews and being the all-American boy for kids even if he really wasn't. Today's players know how to answer media questions because they grew up watching the process on TV. In Ruth's day, he was inventing it as he went along, and he usually got it right.

He visited hospitals and inspired sick children. He signed more base-balls than anyone in the game. A joke long after his playing days was that there is nothing as rare as a ball not signed by Babe Ruth. A Sinclair Oil ad on the back of the 1937 Yankee scorecard promised five hundred Ruth-signed baseballs as contest prizes.

By June of his first season in New York, the *Times* reported that he was so popular, "girls in the field boxes bring their cameras and take snapshots of him as he walks to the plate."

He also broke new ground in having a personal trainer during off-seasons (Artie McGovern's gymnasium on Madison Avenue) and in having an agent (Christy Walsh) to ghostwrite stories for him and find him promotional deals—and to some extent to manage his image, although he never moder-ated his behavior.

Of this there can be no doubt: He became the face of the Yankees as they emerged as the best-known team in sports. All discussions of Yankee great-ness, dynasties, and success begin with the Babe. Obtaining him proved to be the greatest transaction a team ever pulled off, and keeping his name and image front and center proved to have enduring qualities for the franchise. With baseball hurting from the notorious Black Sox scandal of 1919, after which eight Chicago White Sox received lifetime suspensions for taking money to lose the World Series, Ruth was a welcome sight.

FOR ALL OF his immaturity and humble education, he was aware of his worth. In 1920, Ruth was locked in the beginnings of a contentious dispute with Red Sox owner Harry Frazee, seeking $20,000. He felt he'd signed a bad deal in 1918: three years at $10,000 a year.

After signing that deal, he was converted to a full-time outfielder by Sox manager Ed Barrow for 1919, and responded by hitting a record 29 home runs, driving in a league-leading 114, and batting .322. He also pitched 15 games and compiled a 9–5 record, making him 89–46 lifetime for Boston (17–5 against the Yankees). He knew his worth.

The 29 homers had broken the mark set in the nineteenth century. It was truly amazing in the deadball era; Ruth himself had led the league the previous year with just 11. No one is exactly certain when the Spalding Company put more juice into the baseballs (the conversion to cork centers didn't do it), but it wasn't in 1919 and it probably wasn't in 1920 either. Yet Ruth was hitting the ball a ton. The 29 home runs were almost triple what the runners-up hit—10 each for Home Run Baker, George Sisler, and Tillie Walker.

Frazee, though, was starting to think that life after Babe might not be so bad. He thought Babe was as much a disruption to discipline as he was a good player. He had survived the sale of Speaker; he could survive this.

He'd also become an ally to Ruppert and Huston in opposing Ban Johnson over his sale of Carl Mays. So the parties were good pals now and able to talk freely about doing business together, as though off on their own crusades.

By mid-December of 1919, they were heavily engaged in talks. Frazee was a New Yorker, and this was holiday party season. His office was on West Forty-eighth Street, about six blocks from the Yankee offices. Ruppert and Frazee would meet as snow fell over New York, a spirit of good fellowship between them, a shared sense of having put one past Johnson in the Mays deal.

At one point the Colonels sent Huggins to see Frazee, and it was he who returned with the news that the Babe could be had for $100,000. Interest on the payment schedule made the price $125,000.

The formal papers were signed the day after Christmas. The Yanks' longtime attorney Byron Clark prepared the documents. Included was a reported loan of $350,000, without which Frazee might have defaulted on his mortgage payments. In effect, the Colonels would be the mortgage holders on Fenway. The loan is what put the deal over the top.

The Yankees would also take out an insurance policy on Ruth for $150,000.

"I'm not surprised," said Ruth of the sale. "When I made my demand on the Red Sox for $20,000 a year, I had an idea they would choose to sell me . . . and I knew the Yankees were the most probable purchasers in that event."

Babe also tried to get $15,000 of the sale price from Frazee, to no avail.

Over the years, as the effects of the trade became apparent through Yankee successes and Red Sox failures, Frazee would be vilified in Boston history as simply the "man who sold Babe Ruth." His manager, Ed Barrow, told him, "You're making a mistake, Harry. You know that, don't you?"

It was said Frazee was using the money to finance his play in development, *No, No, Nannette*, which wouldn't open for five more years. That, argues Red Sox historian Glenn Stout, is unlikely, although it became accepted wisdom. Leigh Montville, in *The Big Bam*, his biography of Ruth, cites a drama produced by Frazee called *My Lady Friend* that opened in December 1919 as the beneficiary on the Ruth money. The Red Sox, who'd won the league's last legitimate World Series, wouldn't win another until 2004—by which time the Yankees had won twenty-six.

George Vecsey of the *New York Times* first referred to a "Babe Ruth curse" during the 1986 World Series (Bill Buckner vs. Mets), and in 1990 Dan Shaughnessy wrote a book called *The Curse of the Bambino*, which made the term part of the culture. There was no curse discussed before then, but baseball fans knew how the fortunes had reversed after the sale.

The immediate reaction in January 1920 (the sale was announced in newspapers on the sixth, ten days before Prohibition took effect) was mixed. To be a baseball "purist" in 1920 was to respect the deadball way of playing the game, the Cobb-Wagner way of moving runners along with well-placed hits. With Ruth socking home runs, all strategy was changing, and the purists didn't like it.

In the *Reach Official Guide*, the sale was reported with this lack of enthusiasm:

> We question the judgment of the New York Club in buying another player who has no respect for his obligations, who is not a team player in any sense of the word, and who is a constant trouble-maker, according to Mr. Frazee's confession; and that too, at a price which is out of all reason. However, leaving the price out of consideration, where will the New York Club come out artistically? With Mays' assistance the New York Club could finish no better than a scant third, while Boston, with Ruth was lucky to finish fifth. By adding Ruth to its team, the New York simply gains another undesirable and uncontrollable player, adds enormously to its expense account and its salary roll, and gains absolutely nothing except the probability of boosting Ruth's home-run record, which never did and never will win any pennants. This was proven by Boston's experience last year, despite Ruth's home-run record.

Of course, this was not an opinion shared by all. A headline in the *Sporting News* of January 15 said, BOSTON FANS UP IN ARMS AND THREATEN DIRE VENGEANCE ON HARRY FRAZEE.

The life story of Ruth quickly became required knowledge for any American schoolboy who fancied baseball. He was born in Baltimore on February 6, 1895, and when his parents found him too difficult to raise, he was sent to St. Mary's Industrial School for Boys in 1902, where he discovered baseball and learned both the game and a manner of discipline from Brother Matthias Boutlier, a six-foot-six Canadian who managed to control young George Herman Ruth.

That baseball could "save" this waif was the part of the life story that publishers loved. But as Montville writes in his biography, "How bad could he have been" to be sent off at age seven as "incorrigible"?

St. Mary's remained his legal guardian when at nineteen he found his calling and joined the Baltimore Orioles, the local International League team, to begin his professional career. The team owner was Jack Dunn, and soon after he was referred to as "one of Dunnie's babes." This grew into Babe Ruth. His teammates would call him Jidge, a remake of George. He would, of course, also become the Sultan of Swat, the Bambino, and an assortment of off-color racial "jokes" that players used to taunt him over his heritage.

He was never good with names, and even longtime teammates were forever "kid" to him. Once he visited a hospital with teammate Red Ruffing, couldn't remember his name, and just called him Meathead in introducing him around. How hard could it have been to remember "Red" for a red-haired teammate?

On July 14, having been sold to Boston after just a few months in the minors, Babe made his pitching debut for the Red Sox and discovered the fast life of the major leagues and his ability to succeed and enjoy it there. It all agreed with him.

The Red Sox won pennants in 1916 and 1918, and Babe was 3–0 in the World Series with a record 29⅔ consecutive scoreless innings pitched, a record that would later be broken by two Yankees—first by Whitey Ford and later by Mariano Rivera.

With the move to the outfield by Barrow in 1919 and his astounding 29 home runs, he was already a gate attraction and a celebrity. But so much more of that was still to come in the spotlight of New York.

I was fortunate to begin my career with the Yankees in 1968, and thus got to know a number of people who had been close to Babe Ruth during his Yankee days. *New York Times* sportswriter John Drebinger, a member of our PR department when I arrived, was a hard-living fellow himself and used to enjoy telling stories of how Babe would pay everyone to keep a speakeasy open past closing time.

Jackie Farrell was a Jersey guy who was a *Daily News* sportswriter and editor and was smaller than even Huggins. He had a misstep in the forties when he passed up a chance to become Frank Sinatra's manager, but smartened up when he left the *News* to join the Yankees and became a lifelong friend of the Babe's. Jackie, with whom I would share an office for four years, never missed a chance to talk about what a terrific friend the Babe was. One of his assignments would be to accompany him on his personal appearances around town. Babe even called him Jackie, not "kid," perhaps the ultimate honor.

I knew Claire Ruth, Babe's second wife. I knew his daughters Julia Ruth Stevens and Dorothy Ruth Pirrone, and I knew his teammates Hoyt, Dugan, Shawkey, Ruffing, Earle Combs, and Lefty Gomez. And of course clubhouse man Pete Sheehy.

But the best of all was Little Ray Kelly. Little Ray, who insisted on that nickname even as a fully grown accountant for Mobil Oil, was the Babe's mascot.

Little Ray was only three when Babe spotted him having a catch with his dad on the park across from Riverside Drive, where they both lived. The cute three-year-old with good throwing and catching skills simply caught the Babe's eye. Although he hadn't even started kindergarten yet, Ray could read and knew baseball statistics. Babe asked Ray's father to bring him to the Polo Grounds the next day. They sat in the dugout, and afterward, Ruth said, "I'd like to make Little Ray my personal mascot. "

And so, for the next eleven years, there was Little Ray, sitting next to Babe in the dugout, bringing him good luck, and bringing him in-game hot dogs from the clubhouse. Sometimes Babe even took him on road trips, a scary proposition for the child, as Babe simply roomed him with the adult, alcoholic batboy, the hunchbacked Eddie Bennett.

"I was scared to death rooming with him," said Little Ray. "I guess the Babe's judgment wasn't the best on that. But he might have thought Eddie was also a kid. He didn't pay close attention to everything."

"How did the other players feel about Babe having his own mascot in the dugout?" I asked him.

"Are you kidding? He was Babe Ruth! He could do anything he wanted. He put a lot of money into his teammates' pockets with all those World Series!"

"How about just the way guys talk in the dugout, Little Ray. Did they have to watch their language in front of you?"

"Hell, no," he said. "How do you think I learned to talk like this?"

Yes, to a point, Babe could pretty much write his own rules. For instance, the team's trainer kept an ice bucket in the dugout. In it would be placed a head of cabbage. That was for the Babe only. Every inning on a hot day, he would peel off a cabbage leaf and put it in his cap. Nobody else had access to that air-conditioned cabbage head.

THE IMPACT OF Ruth on attendance was immediate, and in preparation, ticket prices at the Polo Grounds (for both teams) were raised to $2.20 and $1.65 for box seats, $1.10 for grandstand (from 85 cents), 55 cents for the distant center-field bleachers, and 75 cents for left- and right-field bleachers. While some fans grumbled that "the game has just become a business now," it really didn't matter. The Babe's Hall of Fame plaque would one day say GREATEST DRAWING CARD IN THE HISTORY OF BASEBALL, and in his first year with the Yankees, 1,289,422 paid to see him in the Polo Grounds, an American League record and the first time a team passed a million. It would be the Yanks' largest season attendance until after World War II, more than even the new Yankee Stadium would draw in any of its first twenty-four seasons. (The Cubs exceeded 1.4 million in 1929 and 1930.) The Giants, long the dominant team in town, drew 929,609 and clearly felt threatened by their tenants.

In early May, Charles Stoneham (who had bought the Giants in 1919) and John McGraw announced that this would be the Yankees' last year as tenants. A week later, they reversed course and said they would consider a new lease. Ruppert and Huston, of course, now had grand designs of their own and were looking around for architects and properties, an attractive one being available at the Hebrew Orphan Asylum at 135th and Amsterdam Avenue. But by the Winter Meetings of 1920, a new two-year lease was signed to remain at the Polo Grounds, slowing the urgency of the process.

The Colonels meanwhile engaged Osborn Engineering of Cleveland to draw up plans for a new ballpark, choosing to take this step before identifying the land on which it might sit. Osborn had designed the new Polo Grounds, as well as Fenway Park, Griffith Field in Washington, League Park in Cleveland, and Navin Field in Detroit.

HOME RUN BAKER thought of retiring in 1920, his three-year contract having run out, but he decided to come back for another year. "I feel I owe the game of baseball a great deal," he said. "It is because of my sense of duty and devotion to the game that I feel it almost obligatory to return."

But those plans ended on February 17, when his wife, Ottilie, died from scarlet fever at thirty-one. Baker was left with two young daughters, and everyone understood his need to retire. His place in the lineup would be taken by Bob Meusel, twenty-three, a Pacific Coast League star who would join the Yankees the same year as Ruth. He had been recommended to the Yanks by PCL manager Bill Essick, who would go on to become a top Yankee scout.

Meusel split the season between third base and the outfield, where he had a rifle arm, eventually settling into the Yankee outfield as his brother Emil "Irish" Meusel had done for the Giants. Bob would hit an impressive .328 that year, setting eleven Yankee rookie records, most of which would last until Joe DiMaggio came along.

Bob was well liked by his teammates, but like many players before and after, had a less satisfying relationship with the press. He was said to have two personalities and could turn them off and on at will when a newspaperman approached.

"Bob Meusel is of a different type," wrote *Baseball* magazine. "For one thing he has a rather unemotional face, and praise or criticism doesn't affect him the same way as it does Ruth. He looks on apparently with languid indifference."

"Meusel was very quiet . . . drank a lot," said Mark Koenig in a 1979 interview. In an era when so many players were heavy drinkers, to be called out like that by Koenig he must have made quite an impression.

Later, with his career winding down, he arrived in spring training and seemed to have a big smile and a hardy handshake for all the newspapermen he had shunned for so long. It was Frank Graham who said, "Bob Meusel learned to say hello, just when it was time to say goodbye."

Aaron Ward became the team's regular at third in 1920. A native of Booneville, Arkansas, Ward graduated from Ouachita College with the intent of going to law school but couldn't resist baseball. As a part-time job, he once read bills before the Arkansas State Senate.

Ward was a durable performer who played 567 consecutive games from 1920 to 1924 and held down third base through the 1925 season.

THE YANKEES' GOOD-NATURED business manager Harry Sparrow died on May 7, leaving a gaping hole in the front office. Flags at the Polo Grounds were lowered to half staff for a man who loved nothing more than sunshine on the morning of a game. Sparrow was only forty-five and had been in declining health, losing thirty pounds, since a case of food poisoning in spring training in 1917. His death was a tough one for the team in an important season. Charlie McManus became the acting business manager.

After an exciting spring training in Jacksonville, Ruth hit his first home run as a Yankee in the team's twelfth game, off Herb Pennock of Boston. It was a "sockdolager," according to the *Times*, launched high over the right-field grandstand and into Manhattan Field, where only Joe Jackson had previously hit a ball. Babe swung a forty-two-ounce bat, occasionally more, and was the only player in the game who wound the handle of his bat with tape for a better grip, a style later copied by many.

ON THE MORNING of Monday, August 16, Carl Mays awoke at his apartment in the Roger Morris Hotel on Edgecombe Avenue, atop Coogan's Bluff. The Yanks had lost in Washington on Sunday to fall to third place, a half game behind Chicago and Cleveland, who were tied for first. They had then taken a train back to New York. That afternoon, Mays (18–8) would face Cleveland's Stan Coveleski (18–9) in a game that could put them in first.

Mays had not raised his popularity in his first full season in New York, but with so much attention on Ruth, he, like his teammates, proceeded somewhat unnoticed. About twenty-one thousand were on hand for the big game. Neither the Yankees nor the Indians had ever won a pennant; the White Sox were defending champions, but there was still much talk about their shady performance in the 1919 Series defeat to Cincinnati. They were not the popular favorites.

Mays drove his car from his garage, down the bluff, and parked behind the Polo Grounds so he could arrive near the outfield clubhouse entrance.

Mays was the only submarine pitcher in the game, and was known to throw hard and inside. He'd hit five batters that season, and there was nothing extraordinary about that.

The Indians' popular shortstop, Ray Chapman, liked to crowd the plate. And so he did when he came to bat in the fifth inning, with the Indians leading 3–0.

With the count 1 and 1, "my arm reached the farthest point of my back-swing [and] I saw Ray shift his back foot into the position he took for a running bunt, a push bunt," said Mays to author Bob McGarigle in the 1972 book *Baseball's Great Tragedy*.

> So at the last split second before hurling the ball, I changed to a high and tight strike pitch. Usually a batter would fall away from such a pitch. But Chapman didn't, there was a sharp crack, and the ball bounded like a bunt between myself and the third-base line. I ran over, fielded the ball and winged it over to Wally Pipp at first base.
>
> Then I watched as Wally prepared to start the ball around the infield. But he never did. Just as he was about to throw to Peckin-paugh he stopped with the ball up around his ear and looked in toward home plate.
>
> It was only then that I realized Chapman had not run to first. I turned toward home plate and saw Ray on the ground. [Catcher Muddy] Ruel was trying to help him, as were several of the Cleve-land players who had come off the bench, and Tris Speaker, who had been in the on-deck circle. Home-plate umpire Tom Connolly sought to summon a physician from the stands.
>
> After a few moments that seemed like an hour Ray got to his feet with the help of his teammates and walked to the bench. A substitute was put in for him as a runner and the game continued just like any other in which a player had been struck by a pitched ball.

The fans in the ballpark did not realize that Chappie's skull was frac-tured. He was taken to St. Lawrence Hospital on West 163rd Street. A deci-sion to operate was made by Speaker, the Indians' secretary Walter McNichols, and McManus, the Yankees' acting business manager. The morning papers had him in "grave condition" following a three-hour midnight operation to make an incision at the base of the skull. Small pieces of skull were re-moved. Bones had lacerated his brain.

He died shortly before 5:00 A.M.

The American League considered a cash donation to Chapman's widow, but settled on a letter of sympathy.

It would be more than thirty-five years until players were required to wear helmets. (In 1999, Yankee coach Don Zimmer was "beaned" in the dugout by a batted ball, and the next day, as he jokingly wore an army helmet with a Yankee logo, wire fencing was added across the top of the dugout steps to prevent a repeat.) Getting beaned was considered the risk of being a player. Almost all experienced it.

There had been two known minor league deaths from beanings—one in 1906 in the New England League and one in 1916 in the Southern League. Mike "Doc" Powers, the 1905 Highlander who had formed half of a doctor-doctor battery, died of peritonitis in 1909, two weeks after running into a wall while playing for the Athletics. Chapman's death, however, is generally cited as the only on-field death in major league history.

The Yankees' Russ Ford had hit Chicago's Roy Corhan in 1911, leaving him unconscious for three days and forcing Ford to take a two-week leave of absence. Kindly Walter Johnson, the hardest thrower in the game, beaned the Yankees' Jack Martin in 1912 and was so distraught that he suffered more than Martin did. (Martin not only survived but was the oldest living Yankee when he died in 1980 at ninety-three.)

The Yankees had witnessed something like this for one of their own during spring training of 1920, an event that still haunted the team. Yankee outfielder Chick Fewster had been beaned on the left temple by Jeff Pfeffer of the Dodgers. He lay unconscious for ten minutes before Doc Woods could bring him around. Hospitalized and without the power of speech, he lay, barely alive, for three days with a fractured skull. He was moved from Florida to his hometown Johns Hopkins Hospital in Baltimore, where a piece of his skull was removed and a silver plate placed inside. It was assumed he would never play again.

But on July 5, Fewster returned to action. The Yankees had a batting helmet designed for him, but he didn't wear it. He played in just 21 games that year and was on the bench when Chapman went down. The Yankee players surely had him in mind as they watched Chapman walk off the field. Chick survived—surely Chappie would too.

But he didn't, and oh, what a loss it was. Chapman was an enormously well-liked player, a total contrast to Mays. How odd that all of this would happen in 1920, the very year in which the spitball was banned, safety being one of the reasons.

Reaction, predictably, was very anti-Mays.

Mark Roth, the Yankees' traveling secretary, went to Mays's apartment early on Tuesday morning.

"Carl, I've got some bad news for you," he said. "Ray Chapman died at five o'clock this morning."

A police car arrived soon after and Mays, met at the precinct house by a Yankee lawyer, spoke to an assistant district attorney from the homicide division.

"It was," he told them, "the most regrettable incident of my career, and I would give anything if I could undo what has happened."

The assistant DA was satisfied that it was just a horrible accident in the normal course of a baseball game, and no charges were filed. No other witnesses were called. Mays was sent home, where his wife informed him of two telephone death threats that had already been received.

Cap Huston met with Speaker on Tuesday to express his condolences on behalf of the Yankees. It was a tense meeting. Mays did not go to the funeral home on Amsterdam Avenue—"I couldn't bring myself to look at his lifeless body," he said—but he did meet with reporters at his apartment on Tuesday afternoon.

"Many players get hurt in baseball," said Ruppert, "and I don't see how they can hold Mays responsible for yesterday's unfortunate accident. There is no ground for any belief that Mays hit Chapman intentionally. There is not the slightest ground in my estimation for any such action as is reported as being planned by the Boston and Detroit players."

Mays's lack of popularity did not help his situation. Four teams, the Red Sox, Tigers, Browns, and Senators, spoke out for going on strike in any game pitched by Mays if he wasn't thrown out of baseball. Cobb was the leader of the Tigers in this movement.

No one struck, but some reasonable voices thought he might just take the rest of the season off to deal with the emotional incident. Mays wasn't having any of that. He did agree, though, when Cap Huston asked him not to travel to Cleveland.

The Indians mourned their fallen shortstop and went out and won the pennant "for Chappie." Umpires began supplying clean baseballs for pitchers from that point on, thinking scuffed balls more easily went out of control and were harder to see. Mays went on to lead the Yankees with 26 victories. But his reputation was made. He would forever be known as the man who killed a batter with a pitch during a game. He would be booed wherever he appeared on the road. He put up borderline Hall of Fame numbers but never got serious consideration.

"My attitude toward the future is very simple," he said in a story written for *Baseball* magazine. "I have played baseball for all there was in it. I have tried to make myself a successful pitcher and within reasonable limits have succeeded. Even my enemies will admit that. Unfortunately for me, I have never seemed to make friends easily and many people with whom I come in contact have developed a dislike for me . . . I have been told that I lack tact, which is probably true . . . If you wish to believe that a man is a premeditated murderer there is nothing to prevent it. I cannot prevent it, however much I may regret it, if people entertain any such idea of me."

THE 1920 YANKEES won a team-record 95 games, but although favored to win the pennant, finished third, three games out of first. No one was critical; the pennant winners, Cleveland, had become the sentimental favorites after Chapman's death.

And the Ruth "experiment"? What a success that was! Besides smashing attendance records and stirring excitement (even making a silent movie called *Headin' Home*), the Babe delivered 54 home runs, including some of the longest ever seen, breaking his own mark of 29 while batting .376, a team record. Throughout his career, whether in spring training, barnstorming, in the regular season, or in the World Series, people were always talking about "the longest ball ever hit in this ballpark" and the thrill of "going to the game and seeing the Babe smash one." At the Polo Grounds they had to paint white lines on the face of the upper deck to help umpires determine fair or foul.

His slugging percentage was an unimaginable .847, still a major league record, and his on-base percentage equally unimaginable at .532. His OPS—on-base plus slugging—was 1.3791, which stood for eighty-two years as the highest ever until broken by Barry Bonds in what was assumed to be a steroid-aided season. (His 1.1636 career mark remains supreme, even if players of his era were unaware of the stat.) While his strikeouts were legendary and almost as dramatic as his long hits, by today's standards they were small. He never struck out 100 times in a season—his high was 93—but he did walk over 100 times in twelve different years. Unsophisticated fans, not alerted to watching the fielders, would think every pop-up, every fly ball was going out, and if he'd hit the ball into the air, the reaction from the stands was a spine-tingling "*Ohhhhhh! Ahhhhhh!*"

And all this was taking place without anyone really believing that the ball had been juiced up. After all, no one else's output was dramatically increasing. His 54 homers were more than the total of any *team* in the majors except for the Phillies, managed by Gavvy Cravath, who had 64. Cravath, the career home run leader at the time, hit his 119th and final home run that year, making him an easy target for Ruth in '21.

After the season, Harry Sparrow's front-office role was filled by none other than Barrow, Ruth's Boston manager, the man who had moved him to the outfield. Barrow would join the Yankees as business manager, and it was on to glory and the Hall of Fame from there.

As for Huggins and Huston, well, Cap Huston had become a fan. Not so much of Hug's, but of Yankee baseball and Babe Ruth. He pretty much kept out of the business side now and just sat back and enjoyed his investment.

Chapter Eight

THE YANKEES AGAIN LOST THE pennant in 1920. Huston was certain that his choice, Wilbert Robinson, was a better manager than Huggins. But he'd lost that battle and was publicly quiet on the subject, knowing that Hug was coming back.

Shortly after the Brooklyn Robins won the 1920 World Series, with most of the year spent in chatter about whether the 1919 one had been cooked, baseball took the bold step of retiring the National Commission and seeking a commissioner with broad oversight—a single figure not tied to any ballclub, with total authority to do what was necessary to restore the game's integrity.

The movement had its roots with the Carl Mays case, when the autonomous authority of Ban Johnson was first compromised. The trio of defectors from the AL—the Yankees, Red Sox, and White Sox—remained opposed to "BanJo" and were prepared to undermine him as the decision on a commissioner approached. They joined the eight National League owners in supporting the so-called Lasker Plan to overhaul the game's hierarchy.

Albert D. Lasker, a Chicago lawyer, had a vision of a new three-man panel, one mightier than the other two, all of them "civilians" with no conflicts of interest. There was even talk of the three AL opponents of Johnson moving into a twelve-team National League, the closest the Yankees would ever come to changing leagues.

On November 12, the owners instead chose federal judge Kenesaw Mountain Landis as the game's first commissioner. The battle lost, the Johnson loyalists fell in line behind the new authority. Ruppert was the most prominent figure in the group photo hovering over Landis as he signed his contract.

His first act was to ban for life the eight Black Sox players who, although acquitted in court of charges to fix the Series, were now untouchables in baseball.

The White Sox wouldn't win another pennant for forty years.

EDWARD GRANT BARROW's arrival at the Yankees' Forty-second Street office in the fall of 1920 marked the beginning of an association that would ultimately take him to the Hall of Fame as one of the most significant executives in baseball history.

Variously known as "Simon Legree" and "Cousin Egbert" during his long career, Barrow's name could evoke fear in the hearts of the innocent ballplayer. "His eyebrows—you never saw anything like them," Phil Rizzuto said to me. "If you had to go see him, you'd tremble at those ferocious eyebrows."

Barrow, son of a Civil War veteran, had as full a career as one could imagine even before he resigned as Boston manager and was named the Yankees' business manager at the age of fifty-two.

He'd really done it all: journalist, bare-knuckle boxer, catering partner with Harry M. Stevens, salesman, hotelier, amateur ballplayer, coach, minor league manager, minor league president, major league manager. He even had a hand in the discovery of Honus Wagner.

In 1898 he bought Arthur Irwin's shares and became manager and part owner of the Toronto franchise in the Eastern League. He sold his stock and became the manager of Detroit in 1903. After resigning in 1905 over disagreements with Tigers owner Frank Navin, he returned to the minors, managed at Toronto and Montreal, became president of the Eastern League (and renamed it the International League, as we know it today), and finally returned to the majors in 1918 as Red Sox manager, winning the world championship and then converting Ruth from pitcher to outfield.

Now he would run the Yankees.

The Colonels, in rare agreement, entrusted him with running both the business and baseball sides of the team. And Barrow was prepared to support Huggins.

"You're the manager," he said to Hug, "and you're going to get no interference or second-guessing from me. Your job is to win, and part of my job is to see that you have the players to win with. You tell me what you need, and I'll make the deals—and I'll take full responsibility for every deal I make."

The makings of a beautiful working relationship were in place. With him from Boston came a coach, Paul Krichell, who would become the best-known scout in baseball and who would, within a year, observe a game between Columbia and Rutgers and sign the Columbia first baseman, Lou Gehrig, to a Yankee contract.

Krichell would build a two-man scouting staff to twenty and go on to sign Rizzuto, Red Rolfe, Vic Raschi, Whitey Ford, and others. It was not the least of Barrow's contributions to the coming fortunes of the franchise.

Barrow had no misgivings about ongoing trades with the Red Sox, and Frazee continued as a happy trading partner. On December 15, just weeks after Barrow had settled into his new office, he obtained Waite Hoyt, Wally Schang, Harry Harper, and Mike McNally for Muddy Ruel, Hank Thormahlen, Del Pratt, and Sammy Vick.

It was hard to part with Ruel, who was occasionally thought of as the best catcher in the league, but Schang turned out to be a fine replacement and was, in fact, first thought to be the key player in the deal.

But it would prove to be Hoyt, a right-hander, who would emerge as the star of the litter.

"Wake up, wake up," shouted Hoyt's father as he slept in the family's Brooklyn home. "Your Christmas present is here! You've been traded to the Yankees!" Without any pennants to show for their history, this cry of elation wasn't expressed very often, but by 1921 it was beginning to be heard.

The Brooklyn-born Hoyt, a product of Erasmus Hall High School, was signed to a New York Giants contract at fifteen. His father was a fellow member of the Lambs Club with McGraw. But instead of being a local phenom who made good, he shuffled around from minor league town to minor league town, pitching just one game for the Giants in three seasons of generally unimpressive performances.

But Schoolboy Hoyt was nothing if not cocky and self-confident, and after 1918 he quit. He pitched for an independent team, went to officer's candidate school, and then in 1919 had his contract purchased from New Orleans by the Red Sox, where he would join Ruth, Sam Jones, and Herb Pennock in the Boston rotation. Then came the trade.

The big right-hander would find his game under Huggins, put in ten seasons with the Yankees, and make the Hall of Fame largely on his Yankee accomplishments. This included a dazzling 1.64 World Series ERA in 11 appearances.

Casual on the mound, his work seemed almost effortless. "Always a smooth worker," wrote Tom Meany, "he didn't have a great variety of stuff, but from the way he flourished in tight, low-score games and the manner in which he could finish a nine-inning chore in less than two hours, it seemed that he must have had every sort of [trick pitch]."

New York was his town. He became a vaudeville star in the off-season, using his accomplished singing voice. He would also run a funeral business in Larchmont and became known as "the Merry Mortician." Cincinnati fans would later know him as a beloved broadcaster of Reds games, famous for filling rain delays with Babe Ruth tales.

THE YANKS WERE now the biggest draw in baseball, and it was embarrassing to Stoneham, who wanted them gone. That was fine with Ruppert; he'd been thinking like that since the day he bought the team. On Saturday, February 5, 1921, drawings of their new stadium were unveiled (triple-decked all around), with excavation to begin within a few weeks on ten acres between 157th and 161st streets in the Bronx, bounded by Doughty and River avenues, property acquired from the estate of William Waldorf Astor. (Doughty Avenue would later become Ruppert Place.) This would be Yankee Stadium. The cost of the land was a reported $675,000. Currently in use as a lumberyard, it was across the Harlem River from the Polo Grounds, which was clearly in view. The IRT elevated subway (today the number 4) ran to the park; the IND (today the B and the D) would be built underground ten years later.

It was, it seemed, a last-minute decision. As early as January, the Colonels were said to favor land between 136th and 138th streets in Manhattan just off Broadway, where the Hebrew Orphan Asylum sat.

As for the site in the Bronx, the *New York Times* reported, "An effort will be made by the owners of the team to induce the New York Central Railroad authorities to agree to put in a station near the grounds, which are quite near to the tracks of that line."

Just eighty-eight years later, the station, now run by Metro North Railroad, opened.

The '21 Yanks featured the return of Home Run Baker, who made arrangements for his daughters to live with him and a housekeeper in New York. He was up there in years now—thirty-five—but his bat was welcomed back.

It was also the year that Eddie Bennett, an orphan of seventeen, joined the team as a mascot, batboy, and road roommate of Little Ray. Bennett, who barely weighed one hundred pounds, had been a part-time batboy for the notorious Black Sox in 1919 and had moved to his hometown Brooklyn Dodgers in 1920, another pennant winner. That was all that was needed for players to think he was good luck. Waite Hoyt knew him because they'd both gone to Erasmus Hall. Bennett had a hunchback, and players of that era felt it was good luck to rub his back.

Thirty-seven-year-old Jack Quinn remained in the starting rotation. He was one of seventeen pitchers permitted to continue throwing the spitball after it was ruled illegal in 1920. Mays, Hoyt, Shawkey, and Rip Collins rounded out the rotation, with Mays's 27–9 season tops on the staff.

The infield featured Pipp, Ward, Peckinpaugh, and Baker, and the outfield had Meusel, Ruth, and an assortment of center fielders including the recovered Chick Fewster. Schang was the regular catcher, catching 134 games and hitting .316.

On June 10, 1921, Ruth hit the 120th homer of his career, a 420-foot liner into the right-field upper deck at the Polo Grounds off Cleveland's Jim Bagby Sr. It put him one past Gavvy Cravath as the all-time home run champion, a position he would hold until Hank Aaron homered off Al Downing in Atlanta on April 8, 1974, a total of 53 years—19,252 days as the game's home run king. (Coincidentally, it was Jim Bagby Jr., also of Cleveland, who would be one of two pitchers to stop Joe DiMaggio's fifty-six-game hitting streak in 1941.)

On September 15, facing Bill Bayne in St. Louis, Babe hit his 55th home run of the season to set a new single-season mark, breaking his 54 of the previous year. And on October 2, off Curt Fullerton in Fenway Park, he hit his 59th and final home run of the season, which would set the new standard for the record books—at least for the next six years.

For the season, which may have been his best, he had an .846 slugging percentage, a .378 average, and 129 extra base hits. His slugging percentage was 240 points better than that of the runner-up, Harry Heilmann. He scored 177 times (45 more than the runner-up) and knocked in 171 runs (32 more than the runner-up). In park after park he hit the longest home run ever seen, 16 of them over 450 feet and nine of them over 500 feet, according to research by Bill Jenkinson, a scholar of Ruth's homers. He hit one about 575 feet to center field in Detroit on July 17 off a Bert Cole fastball, a 1-and-1 pitch, which may have been the longest home run in all of baseball history. No one measured it, but Jenkinson concludes, "There are no other home runs in Major League history that have been confirmed to have flown so far."

His on-base percentage of .512 was 60 points higher than runner-up Ty Cobb. He walked 145 times (42 more than the runner-up). His 59 home runs were 35 better than runners-up Bob Meusel and Ken Williams. He even missed the triples title by just two, belting 16, and he was second in doubles to Speaker with 44. Only seven players stole more bases than his 17.

And no one can be certain that this was yet a lively ball, although it was, of course, thought to be. "The manufacturers [Spalding and Reach] have consistently denied that the ball is any different from what it used to be, except that they admit that the quality of yarn used in winding it may be somewhat better than it was during the war," reported the *Reach Official Guide*.

A decade later, the *Spalding Guide* looked back at the power revolution and noted, "Beginning in 1921, the managers of major league clubs began to allow more latitude to their batters than they had in the past. They took off some of the shackles of forearm and place-hitting and permitted the batters to take a toehold and a free swing. The result was an immediate increase in the number of home runs and an alarming decrease in the number of sacrifice hits."

All of this, it should be mentioned, came in a season in which Ruth was involved in a bad auto wreck. Players were allowed to skip the team train and drive on their own to eastern cities. Babe, accompanied by his first wife, Helen, with teammate Fred Hofmann and coach Charlie O'Leary in the backseat, crashed, the car rolling over twice. O'Leary was tossed from it, and Babe thought he was dead. Miraculously, though, there were no injuries, just another day in the life of Ruth. They resumed their trip to Philadelphia by taxi and saw the headline in the morning paper: BABE RUTH KILLED IN AUTO ACCIDENT.

The '21 Yanks won 98 games, a club record to that point, but didn't coast to the pennant. On the morning of Sunday, September 25, they were tied for first with the defending champion Indians, with Mays facing their old teammate Ray Caldwell and first place on the line. This was arguably the biggest game the Yankees had played since Chesbro's famous wild-pitch game of 1904, and an overflow crowd of forty thousand packed the Polo

Grounds despite periodic afternoon rain, equaling the record crowd to see a Yankee–Red Sox doubleheader fourteen days before, at which a reported sixty thousand were turned away.

The team played without Home Run Baker, whose mother had died. Mike McNally, one of the players who came in the Hoyt-Schang trade, played third, and would continue to do so on into postseason games, with Baker's star clearly in decline.

The game was a 21–7 Yankee romp, with the Yanks on top 15–4 after four innings and the outcome clear. Mays went the distance for his 26th win, while Caldwell failed to get out of the second inning. Meusel and Fewster homered, Chick hitting his first of the season as he took over for Ruth in left in midgame, allowing Babe to coach third, something Ruth often had fun doing when he wasn't due to bat.

The Yanks led by one game.

On Monday afternoon, the Yanks won again, this time 8–7, with Ruth hitting his 57th homer and Hoyt, in relief of Quinn, beating Coveleski. (It being after September 15, the unofficial end of straw-hat season, the crowd could no longer throw their hats into the air after a Ruth homer.) Mays, with no rest, pitched the last 1⅓ innings for his seventh save of the season. Jake Ruppert couldn't bear to watch the last batter; he went to the bullpen and let Hofmann update him.

Mays struck him out. The Yanks led by two.

On Tuesday, Urban Shocker of the Browns shut them out 2–0, and with the Indians idle, the lead was back to one and a half games with four games left in the season. Hearts were racing; could a pennant be at hand? At last?

The Yanks won every one of the four remaining games, and the pennant clincher came in the first game of a doubleheader on Saturday, October 1, with Mays winning his 27th, tying Shocker for the league lead and topping the Athletics 5–3 before twenty-six thousand delirious patrons at the Polo Grounds, on hand to witness history. Thousands more stood before scoreboards outside newspaper offices in Manhattan, where Western Union reports kept them informed pitch by pitch. The Yanks broke a 3–3 tie in the seventh, with McNally scoring from first on a hit-and-run single by Schang.

Elmer Miller caught Chick Galloway's fly ball for the final out, and the Yankees, now in their nineteenth season, became the sixth of the eight American League teams to win a pennant: Only Washington and St. Louis remained winless. Yes, the Yankees had won the pennant!

Wrote Damon Runyon: "Miller Huggins, the little manager of the New York club, tamped across the yard in the wake of his men, his head bowed in a characteristic attitude. In happiness or sorrow, Huggins is ever something of a picture of dejection. The crowd cheered him as his familiar Charley [sic] Chaplain feet lugged his small body along, and Huggins had to keep doffing his cap."

What a moment for Ruppert and Huston in their seventh year as owners. And for Barrow, in his first year as business manager! What a moment for the fans who had been there since '03, or for Phil Schenck the groundskeeper (who now shared Polo Grounds duties with the Giants' Henry Fabian), and Pop Logan in the clubhouse, the senior employees, or portly Jack Lenz, the PA announcer with his large megaphone, or Quinn, the only Highlander now on the field. For Ban Johnson, at long last. For Harry M. Stevens, who had been there as concessionaire from the start. The old guys—Farrell, Chesbro, Griffith, Chase—scattered like the wind, what must they have been thinking? And poor Willie Keeler in Brooklyn, suffering from a heart condition, in need of medicine and other necessities of life—so much so that a bunch of Brooklyn baseball guys headed by Charles Ebbets began a fund to raise money to help him.

And of course the Bambino, who pitched in relief in the second game that day and won it. The big lug had been under the pressure of living up to expectations since the day he arrived, and seemed not to have felt any pressure at all. He hit number 59 the next day in the meaningless season finale for his latest new standard. What were Red Sox fans, the Royal Rooters, thinking of all of this!

The first is always special, but with so many pennants to follow, 1921 sometimes gets lost in the shuffle. It shouldn't. It was a great pennant race in the season that followed the Ray Chapman death and the banishment of the Black Sox players.

FOR THE BEST-OF-NINE World Series, with all games to be played in the Polo Grounds, gambling resumed as though nothing had happened in 1919 and ticket scalpers were out in force, getting what they could for $6.60 box seats. This would be the first World Series ever broadcast, with Tommy Cowan in a studio at WJZ in Newark, getting reports by phone and delivering a play-by-play for the few listeners who had wireless sets. Most fans who couldn't get to the games would again pack the streets outside newspaper offices to follow along on Play-O-Graphs, pitch-by-pitch scoreboards that kept fans posted of the game's progress, including men on base.

This was the taciturn Huggins against the outspoken McGraw, the Giants returning for their sixth World Series and first in four years. The legendary McGraw had so far won only one World Series.

"The Star Spangled Banner" was played before the game, and the crowd included Irving Berlin and George M. Cohan. Frank Farrell was in attendance, as was Arnold Rothstein, who despite his dirty hands in the Black Sox scandal was unpunished and even engaging in business with Stoneham.

The Yankees won the first two games, getting steals of home (McNally and Meusel) in each one. The Giants took the third, and then Carl Mays had an eighth-inning meltdown in game four, blowing a 1–0 lead, and the Yanks lost 4–2, missing a chance to go up 3–1 in the Series.

Mays then became the victim of a whispered assault on his performance, which had included five no-hit innings and a two-hitter through seven. Fred Lieb, perhaps influenced by asides from Huggins (who cared not a bit for Mays), began to tell people that Mays's wife, Majorie, may have received a bribe at the start of the eighth, then waved a handkerchief to signal to her husband that the money had been received. Mays then gave up a leadoff triple, a single, fell down fielding a bunt for a single, and then after a sacrifice came a double, wiping out the lead. The story first appeared in print in a 1947 biography of Commissioner Landis, and then in Lieb's 1977 memoir. Lieb said the game kept Mays out of the Hall of Fame (he was a voting member).

True? Impossible to say. If a fix was in, why wait for the eighth inning? After the Black Sox, everyone was suspicious of everyone.

Another controversy emerged in the game. Ruth showed up with an abscess near his left elbow, and whether he could play was in question. He did play—in fact he hit a home run. The abscess was drained for game five, but he was playing in an obviously weakened state. Joe Vila accused him of being overly dramatic, while others rushed to his defense. In the top of the fourth, after taking mighty practice swings in the on-deck circle, the Babe dropped a bunt down the third-base line and legged it out to first. It was a shocking sight. Meusel then doubled and Babe made it all the way home: He "staggered into the dugout, collapsed, and passed out." The team doctor, Dr. George Stewart, revived him with ammonia. The press box (behind home plate) was informed that Babe had fainted.

Wrote Sid Mercer, "Surely no greater exhibition of gameness has ever been featured in baseball."

One can only imagine the cheers of the crowd when the Yankees took the field and, after a delay with no one in left, Babe emerged and ran out to his position.

Game five would be the Babe's last hurrah in the Series. The abscess remained an issue; it kept him out of games six and seven (lost by Mays 2–1) and limited him to one pinch-hit appearance in the decisive game eight, a ninth-inning, leadoff groundout.

(Keeler attended the sixth game, rooting for his pal McGraw but reminding others, "Don't forget, I'm a charter member of the Yankees." It was the last game he would ever see.)

Without Ruth, these weren't the pennant-winning Yankees. The Giants won all three of those Ruth-less games and the world championship. The Series ended abruptly after Ruth's groundout. Ward walked, then Baker hit a shot to Johnny Rawlings at second, who made a terrific play, nailing Baker at first. But Ward decided to make a dash for third and was nailed on a tag play, George Kelly to Frankie Frisch. The Yanks lost 1–0.

The best player in the Series was Waite Hoyt, who won two, lost one, and pitched 27 innings without allowing an earned run, striking out 18.

A full share for each losing player was a record $3,510, thanks to having all the games played in the biggest ballpark in the country.

And so the Yankees lost their first World Series, but the fans could talk about what "could have been" if not for the Babe's abscess.

Chapter Nine

IMMEDIATELY AFTER THE '21 World Series, the fully recovered Babe jumped on a train and headed to Buffalo to begin a series of exhibition games. His compensation for touring with the Babe Ruth All-Stars would be $30,000, well above his full season's salary. He gathered up teammates Schang, Mays, Meusel, Bill Piercy, and Tom Sheehan to play with him, and off they went.

Ruth was told that this violated a major league rule prohibiting postseason exhibitions by World Series players. The rule was sound: It was intended to prevent the watering down of the Series by having players stage rematches around the country. Of course, this could hardly be considered a rematch since no Giants went, and only four of the Babe Ruth All-Stars were star players.

Still, Judge Landis was insistent that these games not take place. Fearing retribution, Mays and Schang dropped out. But Babe kept playing, giving fans well beyond major league territory a chance to see the biggest big leaguer of them all in person.

Ruppert and Huston feared they would all be suspended for the entire 1922 season. They were actually relieved when Landis delivered just a six-week suspension to Ruth, Meusel, and Piercy. Seemingly unconcerned, Babe then signed a three-year, $52,000-a-year contract to take him through 1924. But the season would begin without him.

Some felt the punishment would hurt the Yankee team more than Babe himself, and in that sense saw it as unfair.

ON FEBRUARY 14, a few weeks before spring training began, Ruth took the subway to the future stadium site, removed his winter topcoat, stood at "home plate" with a bat, and took some pitches from a reporter. He didn't reach the imaginary seats, but he did "christen" the stadium that day by hitting a few into the snow-covered outfield.

Ruth and Meusel were permitted to train with the team, and Landis even showed up to take in an exhibition game and to buy a signed Ruth ball ($250) for a Salvation Army benefit.

Three former Red Sox players had joined the team. The Yanks preyed on Frazee again in picking up Everett Scott, Joe Bush, and Sam Jones, all twenty-nine, for Peckinpaugh, Quinn, Rip Collins, and Piercy, and they added Whitey Witt from the Athletics to play center.

Sad Sam Jones, a six-foot righty from Woodsfield, Ohio, had gone to Boston in the Tris Speaker trade of 1915 and would eventually pitch for six of the eight American League teams. He was coming off a 23-victory season when the Red Sox shipped him off to New York. He'd pitch until he was forty-three and would win 229 games in the big leagues.

Bullet Joe Bush was a five-foot-nine right-hander from Minnesota, and like Jones was in the 1918 Red Sox pitching rotation with Ruth. He was coming off a 16-victory season in 1921 and his specialty pitch was the forkball.

Shortstop Everett "the Deacon" Scott came to the Yanks with an 832-consecutive-game playing streak, which he would extend to a record 1,307 over the next four seasons. He was just five foot eight and 148 pounds, and he had played for all three Boston pennant winners in the teens, being the last player to go from the 1915 champions.

Witt, just five foot seven, was a product of Goddard Seminary in Vermont and had gone right to the Athletics with no minor league seasoning, putting in five years under Connie Mack before moving to New York.

The Yankees opened their season on April 12 in Washington, with President Harding on hand to throw out the first pitch and Ruth seated in the stands with Huston and Ban Johnson. Harding kept a full box score and stayed until the end.

Fred Lieb wrote, "How many readers have seen the picture of Ruth taken while seated in a box at the opening game of the American League in Washington . . . Ruth's face . . . tells the story of his entire suspension. It is the face of a well-dressed kid, with a nice bow tie and clean collar, watching several of his intimate acquaintances on hands and knees shooting marbles. All the longing to be with them is expressed there, but an irate Mamma has told him he must stay dressed up, sit on his own stool and not play with those little ragamuffins."

The home opener, on April 20, also against Washington, marked the first time the Yankees would raise a championship pennant as part of the festivities. Huggins, along with rival manager Clyde Milan, did the honors; the Colonels accompanied the players (including Peckinpaugh, now with Washington, and Ruth and Meusel, in civilian clothes) to the flagpole. "The Star Spangled Banner" was played and the red-white-and-blue flag reading CHAMPIONS AMERICAN LEAGUE 1921 was hoisted. Unfortunately, as Mayor John Hyland prepared to throw out the first ball, the wind caught the huge pennant, took it from its mooring, and it floated down over the bleachers. A glitch in the program; laughter for the fans.

Ruth and Meusel returned on May 20 in front of a sellout crowd at the Polo Grounds to find the Yanks in first place without them. Ruth was even made team captain, but just six days later lost the position as part of disciplinary action by Ban Johnson after he went into the stands to confront a heckler. Scott, a Yankee for just one month, succeeded him.

A KEY PICKUP for the team came on July 23 when Barrow announced another Boston deal, this time getting third baseman Joe Dugan and outfielder Elmer Smith for Fewster, Elmer Miller, Lefty O'Doul (named later), and a rookie shortstop, plus $50,000.

The trade was so one-sided that the moans could be heard around the country. Former Boston mayor John Fitzgerald, grandfather of future president Kennedy, said Harry Frazee "is willing to smash the club and get his money in trades rather than at the turnstiles." Speaker, managing Cleveland, said, "It's a crime! The Yanks got all the best of it, as usual."

The slick-fielding Dugan, a Holy Cross product from the coal-mining region of Pennsylvania, was hitting .287 and would immediately take over at third from McNally. At twenty-five, he was in his sixth big-league season, having broken in with the Athletics in 1917 before moving on to Boston in January. He was known as Jumping Joe, not for his footwork but for jumping the Athletics and going home when the Philly fans were booing him. The *Reach Guide* said, "He was temperamental . . . and when things did not go to his liking, he would desert the team." Owner Connie Mack always took him back.

After his departure, though, the Philadelphia fans never let up on him. "I wanna go home," they'd taunt him through the rest of his career.

Dugan, who lived until 1982, became a great drinking buddy of Ruth's and was still able to hike his pant legs and delicately hop over the baseline when introduced at Old-Timers' Days on into the 1970s, accepting his nickname for its alternative meaning.

In 1922, the St. Louis Browns gave the Yanks a good run at the pennant as they sought to do what the Yanks had done the year before—win for the first time. But on September 8, Mays beat Walter Johnson 8–1 while the Brownies lost 8–3 to Detroit, putting New York on top.

Their final regular-season home games in the Polo Grounds were a Sunday doubleheader victory over Philadelphia on September 10 before forty thousand fans. Dugan was the last Yankee to homer in the Polo Grounds in a regular-season game.

On September 16–18, the Yankees took two of three from the Browns at Sportsman's Park with Shawkey winning his game 2–1 and Bush winning his 3–2, despite George Sisler running his hitting streak to forty.

In the September 16 game, near tragedy unfolded when Witt, in center, was struck between the eyes by a glass bottle thrown from the bleachers. It knocked him unconscious, and he was carried off with a concussion and a deep cut. Ban Johnson offered a $1,000 reward if the person who threw the bottle could be found.

"I never saw the bottle before it struck me," said Witt. "I was running toward the crowd from which the bottle was thrown when it struck me square in the forehead. It literally knocked me off my feet."

The shocking incident in the normally great baseball town of St. Louis took the enthusiasm out of the series. Some wanted the game called and awarded to the Yankees. When Witt played in the second game, his head bandaged, he received a great cheer from the crowd. The Browns' spirits seemed to be broken.

In the end no one was arrested, and, unbelievably, the official finding was that Witt had stepped on a bottle already on the field and had hit himself with it.

Witt delivered an emotional two-run single off Urban Shocker in the ninth inning two days later, where a victory would have left the Browns just a half game behind. Witt's single was probably the most important hit of the year, starting a string of six straight wins for New York. It was also Shocker's seventh loss of the season to New York; the Browns were only 8–14 against the Yanks.

Still, the Brownies fought on, Ken Williams socking a league-leading 39 homers to steal the title from Ruth (who hit 35 despite his six-week suspension) and Sisler hitting .420 to capture a rare batting title away from Cobb. The Yankees, who played their final eighteen games on the road, didn't clinch until Saturday, September 30, the next-to-last day of the season, when Hoyt beat Boston 3–1 at Fenway. The final margin of victory was just one game.

The Yanks drew 1,026,134 in their final year in the Polo Grounds, while the pennant-winning Giants led the National League with 945,809.

The '22 Series, again, all in the Polo Grounds, would be the first broadcast live on radio, with Grantland Rice and William McGeehan announcing. This time the format was best of seven, as it has since remained, and this time the Giants were dominant, the Yanks managing only a tie in the five games played. (The tie, called with about fifty minutes of sunlight remaining, left fans howling, and the commissioner donated the receipts to charity.) The Yankee bats were dead: only 11 runs in the five games, with Ruth managing just a double and a single in 17 at-bats and the team hitting just .203.

Joe Vila, no fan of the modern game, wrote of Ruth, "The exploded phenomenon didn't surprise the smart fans who long ago realized he couldn't hit brainy pitching. Ruth, therefore, is no longer a wonder. The baseball public is on to his real worth as a batsman, and in the future, let us hope he will attract just ordinary attention."

Bush, the team's 26-game winner, lost both of his starts and had a 4.80 ERA.* Huggins, sensitive still to the lasting effects of the 1919 scandal, believed Vila's claims that Bush may have bet on his games. He put him in a category with Mays and later told Fred Lieb that he'd help any of his old players who were in a jam—except for Mays and Bush. "If they were in the gutter I'd kick them," he said.

This was a rough one for the Colonels. They felt so puffed up by their apparent supremacy over the Giants—outdrawing them, owning the Babe, being the talk of baseball. But yet when all was said and done, they'd manage to lose two World Series to their rivals, leaving the Giants with bragging rights and the Yanks without a world championship after twenty seasons of play.

Limited to just one at-bat and replaced by Dugan, Home Run Baker

---

* Bush set the record that year for most wins in a season without a shutout.

called it a career. Huggins wanted him back for the new stadium—he was sent a contract—but he had remarried, was going to have a new baby, and felt the time had come.

A week after the Series, Ruppert re-signed Huggins to a contract for 1923, putting down talk that he would be replaced or would voluntarily retire.

IN MID-DECEMBER, RUPPERT gathered the press at the team's Forty-second Street office to announce that he was to purchase Huston's half of the team and become sole owner. The reported price was $1.25 million (about $15.9 million in today's dollars). "We have had no serious trouble in our seven years together," said Ruppert. "He simply wants to retire and enjoy himself, believing that he has reached the point where such an action would be most profitable."

The formality of the sale wouldn't take effect for some weeks; Huston continued to assist with advice on construction and would be very much a presence for opening day of Yankee Stadium.

Joe Vila tried to read between the lines. "There is no doubt Colonel Ruppert had grown weary of financing the Yankees' sensational deals for star players and the building of the magnificent stadium . . . without receiving due credit in the metropolitan newspapers. Colonel Huston manipulates the publicity. He was quoted at length whenever the occasion required. He was pictured as the chief rooter for the Yankees . . . But all the time Colonel Ruppert handled his check book . . . and prevented the railroading of Miller Huggins . . . I understand that Colonel Ruppert always has regretted the row over Carl Mays and the personal attacks made on President Johnson in connection with that affair."

Years later, Dan Daniel reported that Ruppert had actually given thought to selling out around 1922—before Yankee Stadium opened—receiving an offer from E. F. Simms of Simms Petroleum of Texas. "But the transaction fell apart," wrote Daniel.

THE BUYOUT DIDN'T happen until the spring. The deal fell apart not over money, but over a clause restricting Huston from buying into another team. On opening day of the new stadium, Huston was still half owner and very much part of the festivities.

The buyout became final on May 24. The new officers would be Ruppert as president, his younger brother George as vice president, Barrow as secretary, and a Ruppert relative, John Gillig, as treasurer. The board of directors would include the Ruppert brothers, Barrow, Ruppert's lawyer Ed Grant, and, to some surprise, Huston, who was left with this nugget.

Cap Huston lived another fifteen years. He wanted to buy the Dodgers, but Charlie Ebbets wasn't selling, and so Huston remained a gentleman farmer on his plantation in Brunswick, Georgia. He was seventy-one when he died.

WEE WILLIE KEELER died of heart failure in Brooklyn on New Year's Day, 1923. He was only fifty. His real estate business had fallen on hard times, and so had he. Wid Conroy, his Highlander roommate, was the most prominent Yankee figure present as Keeler was laid to rest in Calvary Cemetery in Brooklyn. Mark Roth was there from the Yankees' front office; McGraw, his old Orioles buddy, was there to see him off as well. The departures of Huston and Baker, and to a lesser extent the passing of Keeler, felt like a changing of the guard; the 1923 Yankees were already a far cry from their hapless beginnings on the Hilltop, but that year was to be the beginning of something more.

ALL THROUGH THE 1922 season, eyes were on the construction of the new ballpark across the Macombs Dam Bridge in the Bronx.

While Osborn Engineering designed the new stadium, the White Construction Company, headed by James Escher, received the contract for the labor, and ground was broken on May 5, 1922—almost a year later than hoped. (Ruppert and Huston had wanted the 1922 World Series played there if the Yanks got in.) Construction began on May 10. On peak days, some five hundred men worked on the project. Two million pounds of structural steel, a thousand tons of reinforcing rods, and more than forty-five thousand barrels of cement were employed. There were ninety-three subcontractors, including Allied Window and House Cleaning, which stayed on for nearly eighty years, contracted by the Yankees to provide the ground crew and maintenance workers. (They ultimately became Ogden Allied.)

The park would be ready in 284 working days, a remarkable accomplishment after a late start, particularly with delays awaiting street closings, strikes, and late changes slowing the process considerably. Closing Cromwell Avenue and 158th Street took a full year for approval.

Not only was the timeline rough, but heavy rains prevented the timely curing of the concrete, a railroad strike slowed shipments of materials, and there were political difficulties in condemning roads at the site. The Yankees were also slow to pay, according to the Escher family.

The triple-decked ballpark would be the first in the country, although the architects insisted that it was double-decked, plus a nineteen-row mezzanine. "A triple-decker would have required a much greater height, which would have been prohibitory," they declared. It was also a defense against the city's refusal to approve a triple-decked stadium.

It was not the top deck that was the wonder, but the ability to tuck in a mezzanine. And for years, fans accepted "obstructed views" as a necessary evil, for it was unimaginable that the stands could hold up without them.

The *Times* explained, "The mezzanine deck is made possible by carrying it out only to the front columns and not so far as the upper grandstand and by tilting the supporting mezzanine trusses. This has been done to gain headway over the lower grandstand without increasing the height at this point. It is believed that the seats in the mezzanine will find great favor with the fans, as most of those who have inspected the grandstand consider that the seats there are the best in the entire stadium. On the mezzanine deck are 19 rows of seats accommodating approximately 10,000 persons."

No one paid attention to this architectural talk. Not then, and not in the future. It was, to all eyes, a triple-decker. Ramps, not stairways, led people from one level to the next, offering teasing glimpses of the expanse of green grass that was soon to be before them.

The seats were painted a grass green. The first four rows of seats on all three levels were not bolted in but would be movable, wooden Windsor chairs with five bevels supporting the high backs. A box for four could accommodate a guest from a neighboring box, who could bring his chair with him. The architectural drawings called those rows "box chairs."

It would be called the Yankee Stadium, with the first word staying in general use on into the late 1950s. People would say "I'm going to the Yankee Stadium" more often than "Yankee Stadium." Of course, Ruppert could have put his own name on it and let it serve as an advertisement for his brewery, too, but he didn't. (Ruppert Stadium in Newark would house his powerful minor league team later on.)

It was not the first use of "stadium," although it was perhaps the first arena worthy of the word. Beginning with Harvard Stadium, college football fields had begun using the name in 1903. But they were all single-deckers. Wembley Stadium, then called Empire Stadium, the best-known soccer field in England, would open on April 28, 1923, just days after Yankee Stadium.

John Brush had tried to rename the Polo Grounds as Brush Stadium, and in Washington, Clark Griffith renamed National Park as Griffith Stadium in 1920 after assuming ownership of the team. But it was hardly fit for such a grand name; a two-deck structure that held thirty-two thousand.

Lost to history is the name of the person at Osborn who designed the copper frieze that would gracefully hang from the roof of Yankee Stadium, giving it a majesty unlike any other. But it could have been the chief architect, Bernard Green.

The *American Architect* magazine called the frieze "rather idiotic," but conceded that it provided for a "festive air."

Thomas Edison's concrete company was hired to construct the shell of the stadium and the platforms onto which seats would be installed. There were red shutters at the window openings, and dual, circular patriotic symbols looking vaguely like the presidential seal over the main entry gate. The outer concrete would be painted light brown. The twenty-four-foot-wide cinder track around the field was intended to be used for track events, perhaps one day even for an Olympics. A football gridiron could fit and would accommodate major college games, an eventual fixture there. The park was made ready for boxing with the installation of electronics in a fifteen-foot-deep vault below second base to allow easy placement of a ring. A fight was already scheduled for July of 1923, with Benny Leonard defending his lightweight championship.

The structure was 108 feet high, supported by 118 columns. The frieze hung sixteen feet down, and in the eyes of Sandy Koufax, pitching there decades later, "It made you feel as though you were playing in the Grand Canyon."

Baseball magazine said, "It looms up like the great Pyramid of Cheops from the sands of Egypt."

The original Osborn plans called for the park to be triple-decked on all of its sides, although it would come in stages. For the opening of 1923, the decks would end at the foul poles, and the long wooden planks of bleacher benches would extend pole to pole with almost unknown capacity as people shoved in. It was assumed that some eighty thousand could fill the place if put to the test, even without extra decks over the bleachers, as first planned.

(The Yankees liked to fill the twenty-one thousand or so bleacher seats end to end rather than erect a black screen in the "batter's eye." Today, as a matter of safety, it would be against the rules to have the hitters looking into white shirts in the bleachers.)

IT WAS DURING the winter of 1927–28 that the second and third decks were added in left-center field; the right-field portion was completed in 1937. Ruth, therefore, would never be hitting fair balls into the upper decks of right field. He only belted them into the bleachers, a section known as Ruth-ville. (McGraw derisively called the site of the stadium Goatville.)

So imposing were the dimensions that not even Ruth ever managed to hit a fair ball out of the park and onto River Avenue, or onto the elevated train tracks of the IRT Lexington Avenue line. (If the doors opened at just the right moment, the home run could have gone all the way to New Lots Avenue in Brooklyn.) According to Bill Jenkinson's log, Ruth reached the last row of the bleachers on at least three occasions.

The original dimensions—257 down both lines and nearly five hundred to dead center—lasted only a year. In 1924, home plate would be moved up ten feet and the field tilted a bit more toward right, making it "harder to bounce home runs into the grand stand seats" and creating more foul terri-tory for infielders to catch pop flies, according to the *Times*. The rules of the day allowed for "bounced home runs," but none of those were hit by Ruth. These became ground-rule doubles in 1931.

Beginning in 1924 it was 281 down left, 294 down right, but the walls quickly spread until dead center field was 490 feet away, making it just fine to place a flagpole in fair territory without worrying about it interfering with play. Left-center field, which would come to be known as Death Valley to right-handed hitters, was 402, and then 457 in center.

Yankee Stadium would define the Yankees. Visiting players would say, "Now I feel like I'm in the major leagues!" when they first played there. National League players might take the subway there early in the day just to take a look at it. Yankee players, already cocky after winning two pennants, could add the pride of playing in this fabulous home park to their self-image. It became a tourist attraction for New York and gave the Bronx an anchor just off the Grand Concourse, a street billed as New York's answer to the Champs-Elysées.

The Concourse Plaza hotel would open on the Grand Concourse and 161st Street in October 1923, and with its efficiencies and apartments, it would serve as "home" to generations of Yankee players up until Horace Clarke checked out in 1973. (By then, sadly, it had fallen into disrepair and was largely housing welfare citizens, but Clarke loved the convenience.) The hotel, considered the gateway to the Concourse, was a presence in photos and camera shots over left field of the stadium for the next eighty-six years of the ballpark's life.

The Bronx County Court House, which became a landmark structure over the right-field vantage, was built in 1933.

The neighborhood was home to tens of thousands of largely European immigrants or their offspring, all of whom seemed to embrace baseball and talk endlessly of growing up "in the shadows of Yankee Stadium." Becoming a baseball fan was a way for immigrants—and especially their children—to assimilate into the U.S., and the blocks surrounding Yankee Stadium were a microcosm of Europeans becoming Americans through baseball. They all shared the Yankees.

Some apartments along River Avenue offered free views over the bleacher walls. Free glances were there for the taking from the elevated train platform. The stadium was truly part of the neighborhood, yet those entering and traversing its ramps en route to a seat would marvel at the 3.5 acres of manicured grass and brown dirt. The entire footprint was 11.6 acres. There were thirty-six ticket booths and forty turnstiles. The total cost was $2.5 million.

When I first went to work there and had the ability to wander onto the field itself, I was somewhat surprised to discover that the outfield was not perfectly level, as it appeared on television, but rather given to waves of small gullies, just inches in variation, but certainly not as flat as I had thought.

The Yankees occupied the third-base dugout and their clubhouse was on street level—that is, two flights up from the field. This was a late change to the original design, which had it on the first-base side. Upon arrival, players could enter from street level on the third-base side, but they went to the field and returned to the clubhouse by climbing two flights of steps on the opposite side of the entry door.

Phil Schenck finished placing the last of 136,000 square feet of sod on the field on November 27, before snow fell. It gave the field plenty of time to "take." He supervised installation of a drainage system and sifted every piece of topsoil through a sieve, removing, as best as humanly possible, all pebbles.

Schenck couldn't have been happier. It had been twenty years since he laid out the field at Hilltop Park. During the Polo Grounds years, he'd essentially been "off duty," as the Giants' ground crew handled the field. The Yankees had kept him on the payroll assisting the clubhouse men with baggage and equipment. ("His occupation long was a jest," wrote Fred Lieb.) Now older, more roly-poly than before, but still a man who loved to work the soil, he was back in his game. And a hard game it could be, especially with power-driven lawn mowers a decade away and a vast stadium outfield to care for.

THE VALUABLES SAFE, still stenciled with the names of Griffith and Chesbro and Keeler and their teammates, was carted from the Polo Grounds across the Macombs Dam Bridge, along with PA announcer Jack Lenz's megaphone; Pop Logan's trunks of uniforms, bats, balls, resin bags, and spittoons; Doc Woods's training equipment, rubbing liniment, bandages, and scale; Dr. Stewart's medical supplies; Mark Roth's notebook with travel plans for the new season and his blank cards to fill in daily attendance data; Huggins's desk and blank lineup cards; and anything else that didn't belong to the Giants.

Charlie McManus, who would serve as the stadium superintendent from 1924 until his death in 1953, took charge of the logistics of the move. If you were a ticket seller, an usher, a carpenter, a plumber, or a groundskeeper, you reported to Charlie. Pop Logan or Michael "Pete" Sheehy, who was hired as a seventeen-year-old assistant to Logan in 1927, might hire you as a batboy, but you did your paperwork at McManus's office to get on the payroll.

The new manually operated scoreboard above the bleachers, at sixty by thirty feet the biggest in baseball, had a clock at the top center, the four American League games on the left—showing inning-by-inning scores and runs-hits-errors summaries—and the National League on the right side, covering their four games of the day. Below would be the familiar balls, strikes, and outs, and one line at the bottom to indicate the next game. It even provided a little rain and sun protection underneath for lucky bleacher patrons. It required up to three operators, depending on how many other games were in progress (usually seven), to keep it timely.

Lineups would be superfluous until uniform numbers were adopted in the seventh year of the ballpark.

As was the case with all ballparks of the time, a path ran between the catcher and the pitcher, largely to avoid the grass being worn down anyway during trips to the mound. The path remained until 1949.

The bullpens were just inside the center-field fence between the bleachers and the left-field end of the grandstand. Under the lower deck were the umpires' locker room, the visiting locker room, and storage space for Harry M. Stevens.

OPENING DAY, APRIL 18, 1923, drew 74,200 announced fans (though Barrow told friends it was more like sixty thousand), the previous major league record having been 42,620 for a game in the 1916 World Series in Boston. Many thousands more were said to be turned away. Some made it to the Bronx by automobile, and many experimented with their first trip to the Bronx via subway. (It was a subway, despite the station being elevated; the train emerged from underground only a few hundred feet from the platform on northbound trains.)

The Yankees felt a little shortchanged by the location of the station, out by the left-field bleachers. People departing the trains would thus encounter the cheapest seats, among them $1.10 for the grandstand. Like all ballparks, the stadium had to be laid out so that the sun didn't set in the batter's eye and so that the pitcher's left arm (his "southpaw") faced south. Moving the subway exits would have been good business but an impossible feat.

At one point during a private VIP reception before the first game, Huston asked for a moment's silence and saluted the team's late business manager. "Harry Sparrow should have lived to have seen this day," he said. "Then he could have died happy."

Babe Ruth was the center of attention and posed for many photos with his mascot, Little Ray. Tom Connolly, who had umpired the first Hilltop Park game in 1903, was the home-plate umpire for this one as well. The players, in their long gray button-down sweaters with the interlocking NY on the heart, marched to the flagpole for the raising of the American flag and the 1922 American League pennant, with Huggins, in his long-sleeved jersey, and the new Red Sox manager, none other than Frank Chance, doing the honors with Commissioner Landis, who had come uptown by subway. Ban Johnson, who had dreamed of this day for years, was said to have the flu, and

Mayor Hyland was under the weather as well. The great John Philip Sousa guest-conducted the Seventh Regiment Band (Ruppert's unit) and played the requisite patriotic songs of the time, many by Sousa himself. Red-white-and-blue bunting was displayed over the railings along field level, a practice that would remain in style for future opening days and World Series games.

John Drebinger, who in his younger days had crossed the country in a covered wagon, would be there taking it in, just a few weeks before officially joining the *New York Times*. John lived until October of 1979 and for a time, after his *Times* retirement in 1964, was part of our public-relations department. He didn't have many duties, but one was keeping an immaculate box score on Old-Timers' Day, which the New York papers would run. He wore a hearing aid and would conveniently turn it off if he wasn't interested in the surrounding conversation. And, oh, he loved baseball and loved to regale people with stories of his unbroken string of covering every World Series game from 1929 to 1963. Always in his storytelling was the magnificence of that opening day in 1923, when baseball seemed to jump from a game to a business. "Imagine, seventy-four thousand people coming to see one event," he'd say to me. "A lot of American cities aren't that big!"

Harry M. Stevens produced a commemorative opening-day scorecard, triple the normal price at fifteen cents, which included the message, "The temporary subway station at 161st St and River Ave will be replaced by an appropriate permanent station during this year. All the streets around the Stadium will be paved with asphalt early this season. The very few touches needed to complete the Stadium will be added at once."

Back by home plate, Huggins received a floral lucky horseshoe, the custom of the day, and Ruppert plucked a rose and put it in his lapel. Governor Al Smith threw out the first ball to Wally Schang.

"I'd give a year of my life to hit the first home run here," Ruth said.

The gates opened at noon. The game began at 3:30. Bob Shawkey, in his red flannel sweatshirt—and who with Pipp was the senior member of the team—delivered the first pitch to old teammate Chick Fewster of Boston, who grounded to Everett Scott at short. Whitey Witt would be the first Yankee hitter, with Howard Ehmke on the mound for the Red Sox.

The game was scoreless going to the bottom of the third, when Ruth cracked a three-run homer—a line drive twenty rows up in the right-field bleachers, a distance of about four hundred feet—driving in Witt and Joe Dugan ahead of him. The ovation was deafening. It was exactly what the crowd wanted to see.

The Yankees won 4–1 in just over two hours. Their lineup included Pipp at first, Ward at second, Scott at short, Dugan at third, Schang catching, and Meusel, Witt, and Ruth left to right in the outfield. It was a day for firsts, and a day when baseball moved into its next era of what would be "big-time base-ball."

Fred Lieb is believed to have christened the new stadium the House That Ruth Built, although the men in the two rows forming the mezzanine press box behind home plate could all have been verbalizing similar thoughts. Lieb called it a "moment of inspiration." The fact was, it may have been true financially—Ruth's presence making such a park possible—but if he'd really built it, it might have looked a bit different. The attractive distance down the right-field foul line notwithstanding, the fences seemed to sprint away from home plate, and the placement of very short foul poles may have cost Babe a lot of homers simply due to poor umpire calls over the years. Given Ruth's propensity for home runs, on this matter the architects just didn't get it right.

In early 1927, Ruth told Frank Graham, "All the parks are good [to hit in] except the Stadium. There is no background there at all. But the best of them all is the Polo Grounds. Boy, how I used to sock 'em in there. I cried when they took me out of the Polo Grounds!"

Ruth scholar Bill Jenkinson believes there were many Ruth shots down the foul line that entered the bleachers fair but landed in foul territory, and without the aid of a high foul pole were often mistaken by the umpires. At least at the Polo Grounds, the tops of the foul poles were "extended" by having a rope drawn from them to the second deck. Jenkinson thinks as many as 80 would have met this fate; obviously some were indeed foul, but clearly a great many were lost to this oddity. Nevertheless Ruth loved the Yankees, and the Yankees loved Ruth.

Yankee Stadium was open for business.

Chapter Ten

THE '23 YANKEES ADDED YET ANOTHER top Boston pitcher before the season began, obtaining Herb Pennock for three bench players. It was another steal, and it gave the Yanks' starting rotation a left-hander to augment the right-handed diet of Shawkey (16–11) Hoyt (17–9), Bush (19–15), and Jones (21–8). Mays's star was fading, as he won just five games in his final season with the team. Of these six pitchers, all but Shawkey had come to New York from Boston.

Pennock was twenty-nine and yet was a ten-year veteran, having come up as an eighteen-year-old without any minor league experience when he joined the Athletics in 1912. He came from Kennett Square, Pennsylvania, close enough to be a "hometown" player for the Athletics. Claimed on waivers by Boston in 1915, he was 62–59 with the Red Sox and had gone 10–17 in 1922. No one thought of him as an elite pitcher.

But in his first year with the Yankees, he led the American League in winning percentage with a 19–6 mark.

The gentlemanly Pennock was a perceptive and devoted student of the game, even serving as an unofficial hitting coach for the Yankees. He regularly invited players to accompany him and his treasured hounds in hunting silver foxes on his estate, a very upscale pastime for a ballplayer. His nickname was "the Squire of Kennett Square."

Baseball people loved Pennock, who later had a five-year career as general manager of the Phillies at the time Jackie Robinson broke in. There, his reputation was somewhat sullied as he allegedly told Branch Rickey that his Phillies would not take the field if Robinson was playing. Jackie played;

the Phillies took the field; the crisis passed. At his passing less than a year later, it was his Yankee years that were remembered, and with great fondness. His Robinson misstep would attain greater notoriety some years later when historians looked back on the burdens of Jackie's entrance into the major leagues.

AFTER THE DRAMA and excitement of opening day, the second game of the season more or less set the tone for the year: a Yankee win before a reported ten thousand fans. "Looking at the crowd and then at the wide expanse of vacant seats, you might have guessed that 3,000 or 4,000 were there," reported the *Times*.

"All the clamor and color of opening day were only memories . . . the umpires had to throw out the first ball themselves. The American flag was pulled up by as humble a personage as the groundkeeper and there was no band to play the national anthem while the flag was going up. The only parade was the one that the Yanks staged around the bases in the sixth."

Indeed, for the balance of the season, the team averaged less than thirteen thousand per date (including two September doubleheaders that drew an estimated 110,000) and barely topped a million for the year—1,026,134. And while they were the only team in baseball to draw a million, it was a drop of some two hundred thousand from the last year in the Polo Grounds. They wouldn't get back to their peak Polo Grounds attendance until 1946. Perhaps that extra five minutes on the subway into the Bronx was more daunting than imagined. But Ruppert expressed no disappointment, at least not publicly.

For those who wondered why the president of the United States hadn't chosen to attend opening day: Not to worry, Warren Harding attended a week later, Tuesday, April 24, and had a special box designed for him with presidential bunting draped over the front. He saw Sam Jones beat Washington 4–0. And that may have been why he didn't attend opening day—he was waiting for the Senators to play.

ALTHOUGH HUSTON-RUPPERT DISAGREEMENTS were minor, Ruppert was too gentlemanly to ever let them detract from the team or become overtly obstructive. Still, with Huston departing the scene on May 24, a sort of peace was felt in the organization. It was an era of good feeling. It was an era of relief for Miller Huggins.

(Dan Daniel later reported that Ruppert, in the interest of peace, was finally prepared to give in to Huston's desire for Wilbert Robinson. But Robinson had no desire to step into that situation and instead used the offer to get a new five-year deal to manage Brooklyn.)

The team was good and they knew it. And as the *Reach Guide* reported, "The team changed completely from a tempestuous go-as-you-please mob of stars to a harmonious and well disciplined team which played the game with excellent system and was entirely amenable to discipline. One of the big factors in the complete reversal of Yankees team form was Babe Ruth who amply made good on his promises of reform . . . [after his] inadequate [1922] World Series showing."

The Yankees took over first place on May 5 and led the rest of the way. They finished sixteen games ahead of the Tigers and won fifty-two of their seventy-six road games.

At Yankee Stadium on June 15, the Yanks beat the Browns 10–0, and in the ninth inning, Huggins sent a rookie in to play first base for Pipp. Thus Lou Gehrig, four days shy of his twentieth birthday, made his major league debut, recording a putout but not going to bat. Three days later, he pinch-hit for Ward in the ninth, and, after hitting a hard foul down the first-base line, struck out. No one could realize the significance of his arrival. The first signing of note by scout Paul Krichell, he would just play a bit in '23: 13 games, 26 at-bats, a homer, and nine RBI.

The Paris-born Krichell, forty, who had caught two seasons for the Browns, had watched Gehrig play for Columbia in a game at Rutgers. According to Gehrig biographer Frank Graham, he told Ed Barrow, "I saw another Ruth today."

Krichell followed Gehrig to a game against Penn on the Columbia campus. There, "Lou hit a ball out of South Field with such force that it cleared 116th Street, the northern boundary of the field, and struck on the steps of the library across the street.

" 'I was right,' [Krichell] yelled exultantly over the telephone to Barrow after the game. 'He's another Ruth!!' "

He was Ruth without drama, Ruth without nightlife, Ruth without scandal. He lived with his parents. He said things like "swell" and "gosh." He had muscles to spare when players did no weight training and tended to be lean and lithe. He could read and write in German. Lou Gehrig would become the idol of every boy who loved baseball for his quiet presence, clean standards, and heroic deeds. He was polite and humble. He would park his car three blocks from Yankee Stadium to avoid notice. Graham would eventually write *Lou Gehrig: A Quiet Hero,* and if you were a boy growing up and loving baseball in the forties or fifties, you read it. Many people became Yankee fans because of what Lou Gehrig meant to the Yankees.

Wrote Paul Gallico, "There is no greater inspiration to any American boy than Lou Gehrig. For if this awkward, inept, and downright clumsy player that I knew in the beginning could through sheer drive and determination turn himself into the finest first-base-covering machine in all baseball, then nothing is impossible to any man or boy in the country."

He did, of course, play in the shadow of the Babe, but it wasn't as though he competed for attention. The less he had the happier he was. Ruth and Gehrig could never be close friends—they had little in common. But together they were the greatest one-two punch a baseball lineup would ever see.

ON SEPTEMBER 4 in Philadelphia, Sam Jones hurled the third no-hitter in Yankee history, beating the A's 2–0 in eighty-three minutes and allowing just a first-inning walk.

Jones then pitched the pennant clincher on September 15, beating Chicago 10–4. There was still more in the tank, though; on September 28, the Yanks recorded a team record 30 hits in beating Boston 24–4, scoring 11 runs in the sixth inning.

RUTH HIT A club record .393 for the season, with his home run output at 41. Another four hits would have put him at .400. The reduced number of home runs had a certain appeal to the old-time purists, who saw him as a more complete player. He was unanimously elected winner of the League Award, which predated the baseball writers' Most Valuable Player Award that began in 1931. It was the only MVP award he ever won, since the rules were that a player couldn't win it twice. It was chosen by a vote of the Trophy Committee, a single writer in each American League city, eight in all.

There was to be a $100,000 monument erected in East Potomac Park in Washington on which the winning player—only for the American League— would have his name inscribed each year. The player himself would receive a replica trophy and a medal. But by 1924 the plan was scrapped; it required congressional approval and spending, and never found enough votes to pass.

FOR THE THIRD year in a row, the Yankees and the Giants would meet in the World Series, this time in their own respective ballparks across the Harlem River. Game one, the first World Series game in Yankee Stadium, drew 55,307 fans—the biggest crowd since opening day. American flags flew proudly, draping the three decks. (In later years, the championship pennants would be hung over the frieze at the annual Old-Timers' Day.) Sadly, the infield grass was a dried-out yellow, having been destroyed by a rodeo that had played there in August.

Would Ruth hit the first World Series home run in Yankee Stadium? No, that honor, with great irony, would fall to the aging reserve outfielder Casey Stengel, a McGraw favorite. Stengel, thirty-three, was in his twelfth year and had played just 75 games in the regular season. But McGraw had him batting sixth and playing center field, and with the score 4–4 in the ninth, Casey lined a changeup from Joe Bush deep to left center. As Witt and Meusel chased it down, ol' Casey put it into high gear and headed around the bases. As he rounded second, his shoe seemed to fly off his foot. Now running with a hobble to slow him down even more, he rounded third and headed for home as Meusel's throw came in. "You could hear him yelling, 'Go Casey, go, go go, Casey, go," said third baseman Joe Dugan. "It was the damnedest thing."

He eluded Schang's tag and scored. The first World Series home run in Yankee Stadium was an inside-the-park job, and it was hit by perhaps the slowest man on the field that day, the man who would one day manage the Yankees in ten World Series. The Giants won, 5–4, on a play that was the stuff of legend.

"The warped old legs, twisted and bent by many a year of baseball campaigns, just barely held out under Casey Stengel until he reached the plate, running his home run home," wrote Damon Runyon in the *New York American*. "Then they collapsed."

The "lost shoe" home run became part of Casey folklore. Actually, when his teammates helped him up after his ferocious slide, they asked him why he was hobbling so as he ran. "I lost a shoe at second base," he said.

"Lost a shoe?" said Hank Gowdy. "How many were you wearing?"

It turned out it wasn't exactly a shoe he lost, but a sponge inside the shoe to protect a blister.

Game two shifted to the Polo Grounds, itself nicely upgraded by Stoneham. Here at his favorite park, it was Ruth's turn to shine. He became the third player in history to belt two home runs in a World Series game, lifting Pennock and the Yanks to a 4–2 win, evening the Series and ending a streak of eight straight Giant World Series wins (plus a tie).

In the third game, back at Yankee Stadium, it was Stengel again, this time hitting a home run into the right-field bleachers that would be all the Giants needed in a 1–0 win over Jones. Responding to catcalls from the Yankee fans, Casey thumbed his nose at them as he rounded the bases. To the Yankee players, he blew a kiss. Ruppert thought he should be fined or suspended for such behavior. Landis said, "A fellow who wins two games with home runs may feel a little playful, especially if he's a Stengel."

Shawkey, who vexingly liked to count to one hundred before each pitch, won game four with relief from Pennock. Bush, his forkball dancing, won game five with a three-hitter; game six, at the Polo Grounds on October 15, would be the possible clincher as Pennock faced Art Nehf. The Giants led 4–1 after seven. But in the eighth the Yanks loaded the bases with the top of the order coming up. Here Huggins sent Bush to hit for Witt, and he drew a walk to make it 4–2. Rosy Ryan relieved Nehf and walked Dugan to make it 4–3 as Ruth came to bat. The crowd was all standing, but Ryan reached back and struck out the Bambino—probably the biggest moment of his career.

Unfortunately for Rosy, Meusel then delivered a two-run single, with a third run scoring on a Giants error. Five runs were in, and the Yankees led 6–4. For one moment, Ryan was on top of the world. Then he handed the Yanks the lead. That's baseball.

The last six outs would be the responsibility of Jones. He stopped the Giants in the eighth, and in the ninth, with 34,172 holding their breath on each pitch, he retired George Kelly on a pop-up and Frank Snyder on a comebacker. Jack Bentley, an extraordinarily good-hitting pitcher, was all that stood between the Yankees and their first world championship. He would pinch-hit for Ryan.

Bentley hit a grounder to second. Ward, who batted .417 in the Series, fielded it and threw to Pipp for the final out. Pipp jumped in the air. In their twenty-first season, the Yankees were the world champions at last.

The Yankees ran, jumped, and skipped across the outfield to their newly built locker room, up the stairs in deep center field. Ruth was the first to start hugging Meusel, pulling him, tugging at him, shouting in his ear.

Attention shifted to Huggins. Everyone was pumping his hand, congratulating him over and over again. "This is the day, boys, this is the day!" Hug shouted.

Ruth and Bush jumped on the trainer's table and asked the players to gather around. Ruth spoke. "Boys, we've won the world championship and we owe a lot of the accomplishment to the guiding hand of Mr. Huggins. He has done a great job this year in managing the team, and we want to present you with this ring in token of the esteem in which we hold you."

Yes, somehow the Babe had arranged for a diamond ring to be "on hand" in case of victory. Huggins was lifted on the shoulders of his players, and the Yanks shouted, "Speech! Speech!"

"Fellows," Huggins said, "it is a fine thing to win the American League pennant; it is still finer to go out and win the world's championship, but this ring which you have given me has brought me more real happiness than any of the victories we have won on the diamond. It is the association with such players as you, players who go on fighting in the face of odds and never give up, that brings the most happiness.

"We have had our little arguments during the season, but they were not real hard feelings; they only appeared so at the time. Underneath it all and when it is all over there can't help but be a great friendship between all of us who have fought the greatest battle of all and come out on top. This token of your friendship is one that I shall always treasure and I want to thank you all for the loyal spirit in which it is given."

"Three cheers for Huggins!" shouted the players. "Hip-hip hooray!"

"It's the happiest day of my life," said Ruppert to Commissioner Landis, informing him that there would be another celebration that very evening at the Hotel Commodore.

The joy of victory would be increased a day later when the winner's share was announced: $6,143 per man. For many it was almost a season's salary. In addition, each player received a gold watch.

The world champion New York Yankees. It would be spoken many times over the course of history, but this day, October 15, 1923, was the first.

Chapter Eleven

THE 1924 ROSTER WAS ESSENTIALLY unchanged, although Mays was presumed finished. He was sold to Cincinnati and he went out and won 20 games for the Reds, and then 19 two seasons later. He would forever be an enigma.

The new center fielder was supposed to be Earle Combs, who didn't have a great throwing arm but had batted .380 at Louisville the year before and looked ready to replace an aging Witt in the outfield. But Combs, hitting .412, broke his leg sliding home on June 15, the kind of injury from which some players never fully recover. Witt went back to center.

A six-foot product of Kentucky, Combs would resume play a year later and do just fine. After being discovered in an industrial league, he had played two minor league seasons for manager Joe McCarthy in Louisville. Sold to the Yankees, he became the first in a long line of great Yankee center fielders, a stretch of baseball history that would make center field of Yankee Stadium the most hallowed ground in all of baseball. The bleacher fans came to love him; in 1928, they contributed their pennies, nickels, and dimes to purchase an engraved watch for him, which he treasured his whole life.

He also hit leadoff, a strategic breakthrough by Huggins, since the lead-off man was typically under five foot ten and strictly a singles hitter.

Two days before Combs went down, the Yanks got into a massive brawl in Detroit when the Tigers' Bert Cole threw at Ruth's head, and then hit Meusel in the ribs. Meusel went after player-manager Cobb with his bat as thousands of fans stormed the field, resulting in a forfeit victory for the

Yanks. It was thought to be a rallying moment and they were tied for first after a win at Chicago on September 15, but ultimately they couldn't catch up to Washington, who won their first pennant by two games. On that team was Goose Goslin, whose lifetime 32 homers at Yankee Stadium were the most ever by an opposing player. For owner Clark Griffith, it was a long-awaited triumph, and for the "Boy Manager" Bucky Harris, twenty-seven, a terrific accomplishment. Fans across the country were thrilled that the great Walter Johnson would at last get to a World Series.

Pennock, 21–9, was the Yanks' leading pitcher, while Ruth hit .378 for his only batting championship, adding 46 homers and 142 RBI. The Yankees had managed a strong season; it was just the Senators' turn.

THE YANKEES MOVED their spring training site to St. Petersburg, Florida, in 1925, in what would become a thirty-six-year stay there, with just a few interruptions. Al Lang, president of the Florida State League, was the former mayor of St. Pete, and he persuaded Colonel Ruppert to try spring training in his city. St. Petersburg would benefit greatly over the years from the presence of the Yankees, hosting the team through the Huggins, McCarthy, and Stengel eras. For the newspapermen and front-office staff who followed the team south each spring, it became a second home.

The team played at Waterfront Park, which was renamed Al Lang Field in 1947. The field would be used continuously until 2008 when the Tampa Bay Rays moved their training site. The Mets trained there from 1962 to 1987, maintaining the New York presence for fans and writers. The field was easy to spot in photos: A wire backstop protected the entire grandstand, not just the area behind home plate, because St. Petersburg was largely populated by senior citizens whose reaction time to foul balls was slow.

Ruth was said to have hit some legendary homers at this field, as he did most everywhere he played. The one most talked about was a batting-practice homer around 1930 that may have hit the West Coast Inn across First Street, which would have made it about 624 feet, a seemingly impossible distance. Logic suggests that it probably bounced on the way to the inn. But late in his life, visiting St. Petersburg one last time, Ruth was asked about his longest home run there, and without hesitation he said, "The one off the [expletive] hotel." So it was a moment engraved in his memory too, whether real or imagined.

The Yanks would also use Crescent Lake Field, a practice field on Fifth

Street North, lined beyond the outfield fence by Australian palm trees. It would be renamed Miller Huggins Field in 1931 and Huggins-Stengel Field in 1962. Phil Schenck came down from New York to personally supervise the field's construction in '25.

Crescent Lake itself was 530 feet from home plate, down the right-field line, and on March 6, 1928, Ruth was reported to have hit six batting-practice home runs into the body of water to the amazement of onlookers. He was the only person ever to reach the lake.

The Boston Braves and later the St. Louis Cardinals would share Waterfront Park with the Yanks. The Browns had been the first to train there, going back to 1914, but the arrival of the celebrity-filled Yanks helped put St. Petersburg on the map. From 1920 to 1930, the city's population tripled.

The Yankees by now were playing exhibition games with the Dodgers while en route north each season, and in Asheville, North Carolina, Ruth collapsed at the railroad station. Several newspapermen abandoned the team and went on a different train to New York with the stricken Ruth, reporting on his condition at each stop. There were rumors of a social disease, as well as rumors that he had died (again!). He was rushed to St. Vincent's Hospital in New York.

The incident became "the bellyache heard round the world," a phrase typed by W. O. McGeehan of the *Tribune*. Babe's wife, Helen, from whom he was estranged, was admitted to St. Vincent's too—she had suffered a nervous collapse. And Claire Hodgson, the future Mrs. Ruth and his current mistress, only complicated visiting hours.

He stayed in the hospital into May, not meeting reporters until May 2 when they visited his hospital room. He wasn't released until the twenty-fourth and didn't play in a game until June 1. He had lost weight and the team had fallen onto tough times without him. This was going to be just a horrible year in Yankee history, a year when their big stars got old all at once.

Combs took over center and Pee Wee Wanninger replaced Scott at shortstop, with rookie Mark Koenig waiting in the wings. The unhappy Scott's playing streak came to a close at 1,307 consecutive games when he was benched by Huggins on May 7. It was written that the record would likely never be broken.

Twenty-five days later, June 1, Lou Gehrig batted for Wanninger, and the next day ran his playing streak to two when Pipp, who had been beaned in batting practice, went to Huggins complaining of a headache and was given the day off. Gehrig started at first. He started the next day, too, and the next and the next, and for fourteen years his name was in the lineup every day. The Pipp headache would become a symbol: Stay fit or lose your job. Long after players had any idea who Wally Pipp was, the idea of a regular missing a game and his replacement having a big day came to be considered a potential "Wally Pipp" moment.

If Pipp had any chance of reclaiming his job, it skittered away a few weeks later when he was again hit in the head in BP, resulting in a two-week hospital stay. First base was all Lou's. Pipp would finish the season with the Yankees, but then, like Mays, would be sold to Cincinnati. In his eleven years with the Yankees, he had twice led the league in homers, been the regular first baseman on three pennant winners, enjoyed three .300 seasons, and hit 121 triples, first all-time on the Yankees when he left and still fourth behind only Gehrig, Combs, and DiMaggio. Still, he is best remembered today as the man whose headache opened his job up to Gehrig.

And there were some who were still around when I began working there who would laugh and say, "Headache? He wanted a day off to go to the racetrack."

Wanninger wasn't going to be a long-term shortstop, so the season also introduced Mark Koenig to fans. Koenig was a late-season addition, obtained in a rare trade with the minor league St. Paul Saints, for whom he had batted .308. The Saints were owned by the old Yankee scout Bob Connery.

Major league teams didn't often engage in trades with the minors, but the Yanks, acting on Krichell's advice, sent three players to St. Paul for Koenig, and he played pretty much every day for the rest of September, getting prepared by Huggins to take over the position in '26.

Koenig, who was a baby during the 1906 San Francisco earthquake, was just an ordinary player—but fortunate to be with a team destined for greatness. "I was ordinary, a small cog in a big machine," he told the *Sporting News* in 1980. He would be the last survivor of these great Yankee teams of the twenties, living until 1993.

A returning face in 1925 was Urban Shocker, who had been traded to St. Louis after the 1917 season following two years with the Yankees. Shocker, now thirty-four, had matured into a quality right-hander with the Browns, winning 20 four times. He was one of the seventeen legally permitted to continue throwing a spitball. Generally considered one of the smartest pitchers in the game, Shocker had not been getting along well with his Browns manager, George Sisler, and word was he was available. The Yanks sent three players to St. Louis, including Joe Bush, to get him.

Huggins always liked Shocker and made him the team's opening-day pitcher.

Combs, recovered from his broken leg, enjoyed a delayed rookie season by hitting .342 with 203 hits, while Gehrig, in his first full season, hit .295 with 20 homers. Ben Paschal, a rookie outfielder from Alabama, hit .360 in 275 at-bats, which stands as a rookie record for the Yanks. But there wouldn't be many other bright spots, and fans and reporters began to criticize the team. Babe Ruth was not used to being questioned, and Huggins was not prepared to be second-guessed by his unmanageable right fielder. One could almost feel something big was going to happen. On August 29, it did.

With Ruth hitting .266 and the Yankees in seventh place, the team lost a 1–0 game at St. Louis. After the game, Ruth stayed out all night, enjoying the pleasures St. Louis offered, spending some of his $52,000 salary.

When he arrived late the next day, Huggins told him not to bother getting into uniform.

"What are you talking about?" said the Babe.

"I'll tell you, Babe, I've talked it over, and I've come to the decision you're fined $5,000 for missing curfew last night and being late today. You're fined and suspended. The suspension runs the rest of the season."

Furious, Ruth bolted from the clubhouse and took the next train back to New York to see Ruppert. The Colonel supported his manager. Huggins prevailed on all counts, his authority intact. He did relent and let Babe back on the team after nine days, and Ruth hit .345 with 10 homers in his final 29 games to salvage something of the season. He'd been taught a lesson. For now.

The Yankees finished 69–85, in seventh place. The fans knew a lousy product when they saw one; only 697,267 went to the Bronx that year, a drop of three hundred thousand. It was their only second-division finish between 1918 and 1964. Without that, they would have had forty-six consecutive years in the first division.

RUPPERT WAS CONCERNED over the 1925 finish but had confidence that Barrow could remold the team. Barrow in turn had great confidence in his four-man scouting department—Krichell, Joe Kelly, Ed Holly, and Bob

Gilks—and in his manager. Knowing he needed to remake an aging ball-club, Huggins rolled the dice in 1926, playing rookies Tony Lazzeri, twenty-two, at second, and Mark Koenig, twenty-one, at short. To take such a chance in the middle of the infield was extreme. Wanninger was traded to St. Paul for catcher Pat Collins, twenty-nine, who would become the regular catcher in '26. Schang's time had passed: He was shipped off to the Browns. At this point in Yankee history, Schang was the best catcher the team had ever had, although Huggins would ponder it and sometimes say he quit too soon on Muddy Ruel.

Dugan, twenty-nine, would be the senior member of the infield, holding down third, while Gehrig, just twenty-three, was at first. Combs, twenty-seven, was in center, with the old men Meusel (twenty-nine) in left and Ruth (thirty-one) in right. And so the team that would become the legendary 1927 Yankees was fully assembled in '26 and ready to return to contention.

The kids in the infield were doing the job. On one day's coverage, the *Times* reported that Koenig "ran over near second and excavated the grounder at top speed, but if you think that was handsome, examine what Signor Lazzeri did in the second. Tony dashed almost behind second base, stopped Luke Sewell's hopper with his bare hand, took a header and leaped up in time to nail his man at first."

The next day: "Dugan is also no wooden Indian around third. He ran over to his left, and broke down [Bucky] Harris's hot grounder, then whizzed a throw to Gehrig that nailed the Senator as he slid madly into the bag."

Tony Lazzeri was the first great Yankee of Italian heritage. He was a physically tough kid with little schooling, often getting into scrapes, and considered a boxing career. He was quiet but comfortable needling Ruth, to his teammates' delight. He had forearms that revealed his work as a union-member boilermaker. He was, almost overnight, the second-most popular player on the team, and wherever the Yankees traveled, Italian-American clubs would hold banquets in the rookie's honor. In an age before political correctness, he was called Poosh 'em Up, owing something to fans encouraging long drives to clear the fences.

He'd been a much-heralded rookie, having blasted 60 home runs the year before for Salt Lake City, where he played shortstop in 197 games on the endless Pacific Coast League schedule, scoring 201 runs and driving in 222.

There was one problem: Lazzeri suffered from epilepsy. Other teams passed on him. "Without that disease," wrote Barrow, "I doubt that he ever would have come to the Yankee Stadium." The Yankees got glowing reports from their scout Ed Holly. To confirm, Barrow asked Bob Connery to leave St. Paul and check him out in Salt Lake. Again the reports were glowing. "I don't care what he's got," said Connery. "Buy him. He's the greatest thing I've ever seen." The Yankees paid $50,000 for him, along with future players. As for the epilepsy, according to Koenig, "it was never a problem when he was on the field."

Koenig was rooming with Lazzeri one day when "he was in the bathroom, naked, combing his hair. The comb went whipping out of his hand and he went down and started having convulsions. I was stripped naked and I ran out into the hallway looking for Hoyt. He was an undertaker in the off-season. Hoyt took care of him."

Barrow said he had one seizure on a train coming north from spring training in '26, and another one in the clubhouse before a game in St. Louis. "I heard of a couple of others, secondhand," he added. The Yanks were able to get a good-sized insurance policy on him; the trainer, Doc Woods, learned how to deal with an attack; and the fans by and large never knew of the affliction. Writers never mentioned it in their Yankee coverage.

SHOCKER WAS 19–11 for the '26 Yanks, while Pennock, with 23, was the biggest winner. This club would not only bounce back in the standings but would bring fans back to the Bronx. To assemble a roster so formidable this quickly was a tribute to Barrow's work as business manager and to Huggins for bringing along young players in a hurry.

The Yankees won the 1926 pennant by three games over Cleveland, rebounding with a 91–63 record. They didn't clinch until the final weekend, but a sixteen-game winning streak in May, the longest in the league in thirteen years, pretty much silenced all who doubted that the team could return to former heights.

Ruth hit 47 homers and batted .372, and despite his bad publicity of '25 was again cheered by fans in all ballparks. Gehrig hit .313 with 16 homers, but it was Lazzeri who really dazzled, as the rookie came through with 18 homers (third in the league) and 114 RBI (second in the league) at a position from which such offense was not expected.

Having won their fourth pennant, the Yankees were poised to meet the Cardinals, who'd just won their first. This would be a World Series with more than its share of memorable moments.

The days of crowding City Hall Park and other haunts to watch the pitch-by-pitch outside newspaper offices were pretty much over. Now fans were buying radio sets like mad along Radio Row—Greenwich, Fulton, Liberty, and Nassau streets. (The stores would make way for the World Trade Center forty years later.) The way to follow the World Series action now was by listening to the radio, available coast-to-coast, with play-by-play delivered by Graham McNamee. Game one was said to have had fifteen million listeners, and when a Yankee got a hit, you could hear shouts of joy from open windows all around town.

The Series opened at Yankee Stadium, its seats freshly repainted grass green after just four years. Phil Schenck led Commissioner Landis on a tour before game one. More than sixty-one thousand turned out to see Pennock hurl a three-hitter and win 2–1. In game two, old Grover Cleveland (Pete) Alexander turned the tables, stopping the Yanks on four hits and winning 6–2. The scene shifted to Sportsman's Park in St. Louis.

Game three was a Cardinal win and game four was epic, as Babe Ruth slammed three home runs, scored four times, and led the Yanks to a 10–5 win. Two of Ruth's homers were said to travel 515 and 530 feet, respectively, the second of them breaking a window in a Chevrolet dealership across Grand Avenue. Babe was the first player to ever hit three in a Series game.

One of the radio listeners was Johnny Sylvester, eleven, hospitalized with osteomyelitis in Essex Falls, New Jersey. During game two, Johnny's father, a vice president of National City Bank, contacted both teams to request autographed baseballs for his son. Both teams sent team-signed balls and on the Yankee one, Babe wrote, "I'll knock a homer for you in Wednesday's game." The balls were air-mailed to Johnny at the hospital. Miraculously, he returned to health while listening to the Babe's big game on a radio. Alerted to the story, the press covered it widely, and it became part of Babe's biography forever after in books and film. Babe went to visit Johnny in his hospital room right after the Series ended, where he was "at a loss for words."

Sylvester not only recovered but went on to graduate from Princeton, serve in World War II, and work for a machinery company. In 1947 he visited a dying Ruth in Babe's Riverside Drive apartment to wish *him* well. He brought the signed ball from 1926 with him. Johnny Sylvester lived until 1994, when he died at age seventy-eight, forever part of Yankee lore.

The fifth game was a ten-inning thriller with both Pennock and Bill Sherdel pitching the distance. In the top of the tenth, Koenig singled and Ruth walked. Huggins then had his cleanup hitter, Meusel, sacrifice them into scoring position. Lazzeri hit a sacrifice fly and the Yanks led 2–1. Pennock set the Cards down in order in the last of the tenth, and the Yankees took a 3–2 lead in the Series, heading home.

The Cardinals won game six in a blowout, 10–2, with Pete Alexander going the distance for another big win at age thirty-nine. Like Lazzeri, Alexander suffered from epilepsy, but his more immediate problem was the pleasure of good whiskey. And after such a big win in the World Series, he felt entitled to celebrate on Broadway long into the night and then sleep it off in the bullpen the next day.

On October 10, Hoyt took the mound against Jesse Haines for game seven. Heading into the last of the seventh, the Cards were leading 3–2, with Ruth having hit his record fourth Series homer in the third inning.

The Cardinal runs were unearned. With one out in the fourth, Koenig couldn't handle a grounder, and his fourth error of the Series put a man on first. Two batters later, Meusel messed up an easy fly ball, scoring one and loading the bases. Then Tommy Thevenow singled to right, scoring two. Despite the two errors, Hoyt had otherwise been brilliant.

Combs led off the seventh with a single and Koenig sacrificed him to second. Ruth was intentionally walked. Meusel forced him at second, with Combs, the tying run, going to third. Gehrig walked, and the bases were loaded for Lazzeri.

At this point Rogers Hornsby, the player-manager, came in from second base and decided to relieve Haines with Alexander. (Adding to the drama, Hornsby's mother had died on the eve of the Series, but he chose to play on.) Pete had to be briefed on the situation as he arrived on the mound, as the game couldn't be seen from the bullpen. Reports said he staggered in. He was not expected to be called on, but Hornsby went with his hunch against the Yankee rookie.

Ruth would later say, "Just to see Ol' Pete out there on the mound, with that cocky little undersize cap pulled down over one ear, chewing away at his tobacco and pitching baseballs as easy as pitching hay is enough to take the heart out of a fellow."

With 327 career victories, Alexander took his warm-ups and got ready to pitch. On a 1-and-2 offering, Lazzeri swung and missed for strike three. Ol' Pete had fanned Tony and held on to the 3–2 lead.

The moment did not end the game; there were six more outs to go. In the last of the eighth, Alexander got Dugan, Collins, and Pennock, who had entered in the seventh.

The Cards failed to score in the ninth, Alexander taking his turn at bat, and then in the last of the ninth, the Series on the line, down by a run, Combs and Koenig both grounded to third. And up came the Babe, who drew his 11th walk of the Series.

Now the potential winning run was up in Meusel. On the first pitch—a swing and a miss—the best baseball player in the land made an unthinkable play. Babe Ruth tried to steal second! Bob O'Farrell, the catcher, threw to Hornsby, who tagged Big Bam out, and the Cardinals had won themselves a world championship.

Said Hornsby, "He didn't say a word. He didn't even look around or up at me. He just picked himself up and walked away."

O'Farrell said that the next time he ran into Ruth, he said, "Why the hell did you try to steal second base?" And that Ruth said to him, "I thought Alex was sleeping out there and I thought I could get a good jump on him."

It was baffling.

For all the plays in the Series, Alexander striking out Lazzeri was the most remembered. In his later years, in failing health, trying to scrape out a living, you could pay a dime and enter a Times Square sideshow and hear Ol' Pete tell the story in his own words. As for Lazzeri, this was a moment at the end of his great rookie season that he'd always be forced to talk about as well. And the two men, epileptics both, were forever bonded by this game for the ages.

In September 1926, fifteen-year-old Michael Sheehy was lurking outside Yankee Stadium waiting for the bleacher gates to open. Fred Logan, "Pop" to the players, asked him if he could help load some equipment into the clubhouse in exchange for a free ticket. He did, and Logan asked him on several other occasions and then made him his full-time clubhouse assistant. 1927 would be his first full season. Logan handled both Yankee Stadium and the Polo Grounds home clubhouses; Sheehy would just be at Yankee Stadium.

He came to be called Silent Pete because he never spilled clubhouse gossip. Eventually the name Pete replaced Michael, and he became Big Pete when he hired "Little Pete" Previte to assist him after he was made clubhouse chief following the death of Logan in 1945.

Sheehy was beloved by players for his loyalty to them and for the efficiency with which he ran the clubhouse. He would be in charge of doling out numbers for the new players, ordering equipment, getting team base-balls signed (he could forge some of the big names himself, before auto-graphs took on a cash value), and mostly keeping confidences. Gehrig was his favorite player.

Although he was already legendary by the time I arrived in 1968, I am proud of putting him in team photos and suggesting that the home club-house be named for him, which came to pass in the remodeled 1976 stadium.

Chapter Twelve

THE 1927 NEW YORK YANKEES.

Even today, the words inspire awe. There may be contenders for the title of "greatest team ever," and certainly the Yankees' own squads of 1939, 1961, and 1998 qualify for the discussion, but all baseball success is measured against the '27 team.

In fact, as early as July that year, sportswriters were already speculating on whether this was the greatest team in baseball history. When they beat the Senators 21–1 on July 4, Washington's Joe Judge said, "Those fellows not only beat you but they tear your heart out. I wish the season was over."

They played the whole season with just twenty-five men. Not a single roster change.

So the bench players, who barely seemed needed, should take a bow in the same way that the chorus line goes first after the final curtain at a show. Ladies and gentlemen, a hand for Ray Morehart, Mike Gazella, Cedric Durst, Ben Paschal, Julie Wera, Myles Thomas, Joe Giard, and Walter Beall for being part of the team. And one for a fellow named Don Miller, the greatest gate crasher of all time, who got into the team photo in uniform without ever being part of the team. (He pitched in two exhibition games.) And for the coaches, Art Fletcher and Charley O'Leary, with the presence of Fletcher now freeing Huggins from third-base coaching duties.

There were three catchers: Pat Collins, Johnny Grabowski, and Benny Bengough. Bengough was probably the best of the three, but a sore arm kept him on the bench most of the season as Collins and Grabowski alternated. So one might argue that this great team did lack an all-star-type catcher.

But no matter. They went 110–44, tops in team history. They clinched by Labor Day and finished nineteen games ahead.

Gehrig, Lazzeri, Koenig, Dugan, Meusel, Combs, and Ruth were the rest of the lineup, day after day. And the pitchers—Hoyt, Pennock, Shocker, and Shawkey—were joined by Dutch Ruether, Wilcy Moore, and George Pipgras to round out the roster.

They started the season 6–0 and were in first place wire to wire. They were 57–19 at Yankee Stadium, 53–25 on the road. They won 20 or more games in June, July, and September, 19 in May. They were shut out only one time, by Lefty Grove. They beat the Browns 21 times in 22 games, losing only the final game they played. They were 18–4 against Boston. The team batting average was .307. They led the league in home runs, runs scored (131 more than the runner-up), triples, walks, and slugging percentage. Their pitchers led in ERA, shutouts, fewest hits, and fewest runs.

Ruth led the league in home runs, runs scored, on-base percentage, slugging percentage, and walks. Also in salary, signing a three-year, $210,000 contract as spring training beckoned, after first insisting on $100,000 for the year. The grand signing event took place at the Ruppert Brewery offices and orbited Ruth's income past that of Cobb, Speaker, and even Commissioner Landis.

Gehrig, in his breakout year, led in games played, total bases, extra-base hits, doubles, and RBI. He would win the league's MVP Award. Combs led in singles, plate appearances, and hits, his 231 a Yankee record that stood for fifty-nine years.

Hoyt tied for wins and led in won-lost percentage; Moore led in ERA and saves.

"You never knew when that batting order was going to push the handle down," wrote Paul Gallico. "But when it went down, you could hear the explosion all the way to South Albany, and when the smoke cleared away, the poor old opposing pitcher wouldn't be there anymore. And Yankees would be legging it over the plate with runs, sometimes in single file but more often in bunches or twos and threes as home runs cleared the bases."

"Just putting on a Yankee uniform gave me a little confidence," said Koenig. "That club could carry you. You were better than you actually were."

"The '27 Yankees were an exceptional team because they met every demand," said Hoyt. "There wasn't any requirement that was necessary at any particular moment that they weren't up to."

"We never even worried five or six runs behind," said Ruth. "Ruth-Gehrig-Lazzeri-Combs . . . wham, wham, and wham!—no matter who was pitching."

Wrote Richards Vidmar of the *Times*, back in 1927, "As for the Babe and the Buster, they cheer each other's success as enthusiastically as they enjoy their own. When the Babe hits one for a non-stop flight around the bases, he always finds the Buster waiting with a merry quip and a welcoming hand at the plate. When the Buster hits one with the Babe on base they meet at the last stop and chat gaily as they walk to the dugout arm in arm. It's the greatest act in baseball."

OPENING DAY WAS the first regular-season Yankee game ever heard on radio, as Graham McNamee did the game over WEAF and WJZ—the only broadcast until the World Series. Broadcasting opening day would remain a tradition for eleven years.* Mark Roth helped set up a broadcast location within the press area behind home plate—the "press coop," it was sometimes called, being behind the wire backstop.

Some seventy-two thousand showed up on opening day, buying up Harry Stevens's specialties that included ginger ale, sarsaparilla, "charged" mineral water, hot dogs, peanuts, and Cracker Jack. The menu did not include popcorn or, of course, beer.

The Yanks were good and they knew it. After another win, they'd walk down the tunnel toward their clubhouse singing, "Roll out the barrel, we'll have a barrel of fun." "The Beer Barrel Polka" was a theme song for them, a song of delight and merriment usually led by Fletcher.

The Yankees of that era came to be known as Murderer's Row. Not surprisingly, the term had its roots in the Tombs, New York's notorious prison from the mid-nineteenth century, where those charged with murder were placed all in a row on the second floor.

Ironically, the first use of the term in baseball came in 1918 and was applied to the Yankees in Huggins's first year as manager. A newspaper article said, "New York fans have come to know a section of the Yankees' batting

---

* Until 1939, when the radio ban was lifted, evening re-creations were common with Jack Ingersall, the best-known of the announcers.

order as 'murderers' row.' It is composed of the first six players in the batting order—[Frank] Gilhooley, Peckinpaugh, Baker, Pratt, Pipp, and Bodie. This sextet has been hammering the offerings of all comers."

Working from that, the cartoonist Robert Ripley (of *Ripley's Believe It or Not*), portrayed Pratt, Pipp, Bodie, Baker, and Peckinpaugh all in single jail cells, side by side. So the use of the term in the late twenties was actually a revival. And the things that it led to! "Break up the Yankees" was first uttered by sportswriters and fans. "Five o'clock lightning" came to symbolize Yankee victories late in the afternoon. It quickly became the most awe-inspiring team yet assembled.

Charles Lindbergh came to Yankee Stadium on June 17, three days after his ticker-tape parade on Broadway to salute his Atlantic flight to Paris. Five hundred policemen led him to his seat—*five hundred*—where he was greeted by Colonel Ruppert as the fans yelled, "Lindy! Lindy! Lindy!"

Oh, was Yankee Stadium the place to be on a holiday weekend. On July 5, 71,641 packed the place, all there for a doubleheader sweep of the Senators. On another patriotic occasion, the Yankees traveled to West Point to play Army, something they went on to do twenty-one times between 1927 and 1976 (winning them all).

It was almost a miracle that the Yankees added Wilcy Moore to their roster in '27. What an unlikely hero he was.

A tobacco-chewing dirt farmer from Hollis, Oklahoma, he'd been pitching in the minors for six years. He was twenty-eight, or maybe thirty; no one seemed to know for sure. Even after going 30–4 for Greenville of the Sally League in 1926, he didn't expect to go to the majors. He was pretty much resigned to throwing his sinker at some other distant locale in '27.

But Barrow read about his season in the *Sporting News* and then bought a mail-order subscription to the Greenville newspaper to follow him more closely. He bought him for $3,500. If you go 30–4, he figured, you must have something. Who ever heard of a record like that?

Moore did not disappoint. He appeared in 50 games—12 starts, 38 in relief, of which he finished 30. He was 19–7 with a league-leading 2.28 ERA and an additional win in the World Series. And he had 13 saves by today's measurement. The term was indeed used by John Kieran in the *Times*, who wrote, "He has saved more games than half the pitchers in the league will win this year." Who was this mystery man who pitched 213 innings?

He never had a year like it again. He pitched only six seasons, including 1931–32 for the Red Sox before returning to New York. He never showed the brilliance of that rookie season. "Brilliance" was an understatement—he was probably the best pitcher on the 1927 Yankees. This was a time long before relief pitchers were ever thought of as stars. Rarely did they come into a game—starters were expected to stare down the final out no matter how many pitches had been thrown. There was little appreciation of the job that evolved to be a glamorous "closer" position.

Yet people spoke of Moore that year almost with the reverance reserved for Mariano Rivera eighty years later.

And so Moore, at least for that one year, would become the first in a long line of great Yankee relief pitchers, long before teams even thought like that.

The Yankees also gave 26 starts to left-hander Dutch Ruether (13–6) and 21 to rookie George Pipgras (10–3). Ruether, thirty-three, had been around since 1917, and the Yankees were his fifth team. He'd been a star for the 1919 world champion Reds and he'd won 21 for Brooklyn in '22. He'd won 18 for the '25 Senators, and had come to the Yanks in the midseason of '26, starting one of the World Series games against St. Louis.

Pipgras, who was right-handed, had briefly pitched for the Yanks in '23 and '24, then went back to the minors and won 22 for Connery's St. Paul Saints in '26. Now he was back with the Yankees, on the big stage in a very big year. (After his career, he became an American League umpire.)

With not much of a pennant race to focus on in September, the nation's attention turned to Babe Ruth's pursuit of his own home run record of 59. It hadn't been talked about all summer because he entered September still 17 shy, and no one had ever hit that many in a month. But what a month he had, enjoying, perhaps, his new gift from Ruppert—his own suite on road trips. His roommate days were over. Ruppert thought a suite might keep him in the hotel.

The Yankee team was on its way to 158 homers—more than one a game— a new record. Lou Gehrig came into his own by slugging 47 and driving in 175 runs, and Lazzeri hit 18, third best in the league (including three in one game, the first Yankee to do so in the regular season).

Ruth was sitting on 59 on the next-to-last day of the season, September 30. He came up in the eighth inning to face Washington's Tom Zachary and hit a liner into the right-field bleachers, about halfway up and close to the foul pole. Most of Ruth's homers were high arcs, but this one was a solid line drive, estimated at 435 feet.

"The demonstration which followed was the greatest seen in New York in years," wrote Fred Lieb. "Everyone was on his feet, cheering and yelling . . .

When Ruth went out to his position in the 8th, it started all over again. This time the rightfield bleacherites welcomed their own and started a new demonstration."

"Sixty!" Ruth said in the clubhouse. "Let's see some son of a bitch try to top that one!" He had hit 59, and may have thought he'd hit 61 one day, but there was something nice and round about the number 60, and maybe he knew that was the limit.

The nation, awed by his prowess, felt much the same way. Imagine! Sixty in one season! Few could have imagined that it would be baseball's magical number for the next thirty-four seasons. Twice players got to 58—Jimmie Foxx and Hank Greenberg—but nobody made it to 60, and certainly not in Ruth's lifetime.

Zachary, meanwhile, would come to the Yankees in '28, win a World Series game, and then go 12–0 for them in '29, the best-ever perfect record in baseball history.

Even at this stage, deep into Ruth's career, with everyone focusing on the long ball, there were enough champions of "old school" baseball to cast disdain on playing the game "that way." The publication *Who's Who in Baseball*, issued by *Baseball* magazine, waited until 1939 before listing home runs among a player's stats. And that wasn't the burden of redoing the format; they added other columns along the way, just not home runs.

THE WORLD SERIES was anticlimactic, of course. The opponent was the Pittsburgh Pirates in what would be their last Series appearance until 1960. Legend has it that they were so intimidated watching the Yankees take batting practice in Forbes Field before game one that they mentally lost any hope of winning.

The outcome fit well with the tale. The Yankees took the Series in four straight, with Hoyt and Pipgras winning the first two (Shocker, ill, was unable to do more than pitch batting practice), and then Pennock hurling 7⅓ perfect innings before yielding a single to Pie Traynor in the eighth, but winning game three 8–1 on a three-hitter. Then Hug handed the ball to Wilcy Moore for the clincher, which he delivered with a 4–3 victory in Yankee Stadium.

The Yanks were not without their defensive gems, a part of their game seldom talked about. In the seventh inning of the third game, Dugan at third made as dazzling a play as most could remember seeing. Wrote Ed

Pollock in the *Philadelphia Bulletin*, "As [Hal Rhyne] choked up on the bat, Dugan leaped into action. It was a perfect bunt. The ball rolled close to the foul line and obviously it would remain in fair territory. At a full gallop, Dugan stopped and snatched the ball. At this point he was flying through the air, horizontally. Without looking and with the continuation of the same motion used in picking up the ball, he fired under his body and then sprawled in the dirt base path. The runner was out by a clear margin."

The Yanks hit only two homers in the Series, both by Ruth, including a two-run blast in the fifth inning of the finale. For all the power of the Yanks, they actually won the final game in the last of the ninth on a wild pitch by Johnny Miljus, scoring Combs with the winning run while Lazzeri was at bat.

Koenig hit .500 for the Series, avenging his four errors from the year before when he'd been one of the Yankee goats.

So the Yankees won on a wild pitch. And in North Adams, Massachusetts, Jack Chesbro must have smiled. It had been twenty-three years since his notorious wild pitch cost the Highlanders a pennant.

THE WINNING SHARE was $5,592. For Ruth, with his $70,000 salary, it was a nice bonus. Huggins made $37,500. Pennock made $17,500. Shocker got $13,500. Meusel, Dugan, Hoyt, Combs, and Shawkey were all between $10,500 and $13,000. Ruether made $11,000 and was released. Gehrig's salary in 1927 was still just $8,000, the same as Lazzeri's. (He would eventually peak at $39,000.) Koenig made $7,000. Moore made just $3,000. For the first time, a Yankee team was awarded World Series rings, designed by Dieges & Clust. The '23 champs had received pocket watches.

Roll out the barrel!

Chapter Thirteen

URBAN SHOCKER'S ILLNESS, WHICH kept him out of the '27 World Series, lingered into the 1928 season and created drama all its own. The Yankees didn't know what was going on; he was a quiet man who shared little of himself with teammates. He liked to read the morning newspapers by himself while others were enjoying the camaraderie of the breakfast table. A lot of players would run up to a place called the Blossom Heath Inn in Larchmont to watch Benny Bengough sit in with the big bands on his sax. Not Shocker. He was never one for socializing with his teammates.

But he had a heart disease which may have gone back as far as three years. He just didn't talk about it with anyone. Still, there were signs.

Some had heard that he had to sleep standing up. This may have been exaggerated, but he was spotted on sleeper cars fast asleep sitting upright. To lay prone would cause undue stress on his heart. Or so the rumors had it.

Despite his 19–11 record in 1926 and his 18–6 record in 1927, he was done. But he didn't level with the team. He was, in fact, angry with the Yankees over not receiving moving expenses when he'd been traded. Huggins at one point offered to pay him out of his own pocket, but Shocker refused. He wanted a Yankee check for $1,500.

"Shocker is a stubborn chap," wrote John Kieran of the *Times*. "Urban took offense at a [Browns] rule which provided that the wives were not allowed to travel with the team. He walked off the mound over it, and appealed . . . from the league President to Commissioner Landis and he was preparing a brief to submit to the League of Nations . . . when he was traded to New York."

His illness continued at his St. Louis home during the off-season. His weight reportedly slipped to 115 pounds. But he didn't tell the Yankees. He told them he was going to retire, take up aviation, and open a radio store.

When he failed to report for spring training, and having not signed the new contract Barrow sent him, the Yankees suspended him.

On March 8, Huggins said, "I'm not going to waste any more time or telegraph tolls on Shocker. He says he has quit and so I'll take him at his word. He's on our voluntarily retired list.

"Naturally I could have used a pitcher like Shocker this year, what's the sense of denying that obvious fact? But he is not indispensable, and his place on the roster will be taken by one of my young pitchers who otherwise would have been farmed out. Or maybe I'll make Wilcy Moore a starting pitcher."

Shocker's spot went to Hank Johnson (14–9), with some starts going to thirty-eight-year-old Stan Coveleski, a 210-game winner and future Hall of Famer who had recorded five 20-win seasons in his illustrious career.

Shocker, meanwhile, perhaps feeling better, notified the commissioner in April that he wished to come off the voluntary retirement list. He began to work himself back into playing condition.

But while pitching batting practice at Comiskey Park in May, he collapsed. It went unreported.

He would pitch in only one game in New York, a two-inning relief effort in a Memorial Day game before seventy thousand fans. It would be his final major league appearance.

During the July 4 weekend, he did an interview with Bill Corum in the *Journal-American* and opened up a bit.

"I've had a bum heart for some time. You've seen me sitting up late at night in my Pullman berth. I couldn't lie down. Choked when I did."

Corum asked if Huggins knew of his bad heart.

"Oh sure," he said.

Speaking of his long-simmering demand for the $1,500 from the club, he told Corum, "It took me nearly four years, but I got it. My July 1 check squares the promise."

Then, tapping his heart, he said, "I'm going to Denver to fight this thing."

The Yankees released him on July 6.

On September 9, he died of complications from pneumonia at the age of thirty-eight. The Yankees were to be in St. Louis on September 15, and the funeral was delayed until the entire Yankee team, along with many Browns, could attend. Hoyt, Gehrig, and Combs were among the pallbearers.

"Without seeing the reports, it sounds like dilated cardiomyopathy," said cardiologist Dr. Joe Plantania, who treated Joe Torre. "We sometimes call these one-pillow, two-pillow, three-pillow, or four-pillow cases, depending on how many the patient has to sleep on to breathe properly. Shocker sounds like a four-pillow case."

An autopsy showed that indeed his heart was greatly enlarged. He had been mysterious and courageous all at once, and the first of a number of 1927 Yankees to die young.

DURING THE WINTER of 1927–28, the Yankees extended the grandstand in left field past the foul poles and on into the bleacher area, the first major renovation of the ballpark. The contractor was L.M. Neckermann and Son, who would also handle a 1937 expansion of the left-field grandstand. Included was ornate latticework that "finished" the edges of the structure, a design element that was removed in 1962 for reasons unclear. The park was also the setting for the filming of a silent Buster Keaton film, *The Cameraman*, in which Keaton's character lugs his movie camera and tripod around town, including a stop in Yankee Stadium, where he pretends to hit an inside-the-park homer before the empty seats while the camera records it all. It provided a magnificent view of the five-year-old park, including the elevated train going past the bleachers.

The 1928 season also saw the arrival of two other figures who would one day be Hall of Famers, one as a Yankee and the other for accomplishments elsewhere: Bill Dickey and Leo Durocher.

Durocher would one day go to the Baseball Hall of Fame on the merits of his managerial career. He was one of baseball's best-known celebrities during those years, Leo the Lip or Lippy, known even to non–baseball fans. He was a stylish sort, known for his well-tailored suits, four wives, show-business friends, and a propensity to get himself in trouble.

The fact that his career began in 1925 as a shortstop for Hartford and ran through 1973 as manager of Houston made for an amazing journey. He got to St. Paul in 1927, which had become a bit of a Yankee feeder club, and was sold to the Yanks. His main benefactor was Huggins, who liked his aggressive style a lot. None of the players seemed to, especially when he was accused of stealing a watch belonging to Ruth and Gehrig's 1927 World Series ring. It was thought that Ruth nicknamed him "the All-American Out."

But he got into 102 games as a twenty-two-year-old rookie in '28, trying to unseat Koenig, and batted a credible .270. He'd play over 100 games the following year as well, but once Huggins was gone he had no allies left, and off he went. He was well suited to the Cardinals' Gashouse Gang assemblage in the thirties, before he began his long managing career at Brooklyn.

William Malcolm Dickey would make his Yankee debut on August 15, 1928. "We have bought a young man who is destined to be one of the greatest catchers in the game," said Huggins.

Born in Louisiana but raised in Little Rock, Arkansas, he would become the team's regular catcher in 1929 after Grabowski broke a finger and would catch more than 100 games for thirteen years in a row, a record. The Yankees bought him from Jackson, Mississippi (where he was on option from Little Rock), for $12,500. What an investment that was. Durable, classy, a leader on the field, a brilliant catcher, and an outstanding hitter, he would not only be a key figure on eight championship teams but would in many ways set the standard of professionalism that would come to symbolize the Yankee organization. A lifetime .313 hitter over seventeen seasons, all with the Yankees, he would be in the debate with Mickey Cochrane and Gabby Hartnett over who was the greatest catcher of his time. Others would enter the debate later on, but in his day, Yankee fans knew they were watching an all-time great.

IT COULDN'T HAVE been easy to be the '28 Yankees, coming off a season already considered legendary.

The Yanks won 101 games but didn't clinch the pennant until the final weekend of the season, finishing two and a half games ahead of the Athletics. The key showdown for the season came in a standing-room-only doubleheader against the A's at Yankee Stadium on September 9, with the Yanks just a half game ahead going in. They won the doubleheader behind a shutout from Pipgras in the opener; a grand slam by Meusel decided the nightcap. (In '28 Meusel hit for the cycle for the third time in his career; he is still the only American Leaguer to achieve the feat three times.)

The team's sixth pennant under Huggins set the stage for a World Series rematch against the Cardinals, their 1926 opponents.

The Yanks were hurting in the Series: Pennock was sidelined with a tired arm and Combs had a broken finger, leaving Cedric Durst and Ben Paschal to play center; Lazzeri was nursing a bad arm, allowing Durocher to play the final innings at second; Ruth had a bad ankle. The team used only three pitchers, all hurling complete games—Hoyt, Pipgras, and Zachary, with Hoyt winning twice.

These were still the Murderer's Row Yankees, and they had no trouble knocking off the Cards in four straight. As if saving up for a grand finale, the fourth and final game featured Gehrig's fourth homer of the Series (he had nine RBI) and three homers by the hobbled Ruth, giving Babe and Lou seven homers and 13 RBI in the four games. Ruth's average was .625, Gehrig's .545. It was as though a tornado had passed through St. Louis.

The final blow came in the seventh inning of the last game. After Ruth and Gehrig had homered back-to-back, Meusel singled. Cards manager Bill McKechnie brought in forty-one-year-old Pete Alexander to once again face Lazzeri, restaging the big matchup of 1926.

Lazzeri got his revenge with a double to left center in what would wind up being a four-run inning to set up the championship celebration. The Yankees had now won eight straight World Series games.

On the victory train ride home, Huggins, who seldom overdid the alcohol (this was, after all, the Prohibition era), managed to overindulge just enough to lose his false teeth somewhere on the train. For what would be his last World Series, it was a small price to pay.

The players voted $4,800 of their World Series money to Urban Shocker's widow in St. Louis. All the players received wristwatches, since most had rings from '27. Joe Dugan's watch was also a parting gift; he was sold to the Braves on Christmas Eve after an injury-riddled season.

IN THE WEEKS leading up to the 1929 season, Colonel Ruppert created a stir by announcing that the Yankees would wear "football-style" numbers on the backs of their jerseys for the season. Because Yankee Stadium was so large, distant fans could not always tell who was who. The numbers would help, and perhaps boost scorecard sales.

"Colonel Ruppert's innovation will be watched with interest and may some day be universally adopted if it is a help to the man who makes the game possible, the turnstile spinner," noted the *Reach Guide* for 1929.

And so the first assignment of numbers reflected their normal starting lineup: 1—Combs, 2—Koenig, 3—Ruth, 4—Gehrig, 5—Meusel, 6—Lazzeri, 7—Durocher, 8—Grabowski, 9—Bengough, 10—Dickey, 11—Pennock, 12—Hoyt, 14—Pipgras, and on through the coaches, 33—O'Leary, and 34—Fletcher. Huggins didn't wear one. Nobody got unlucky 13 until Spud Chandler in 1937.

The Indians and the Cardinals had experimented with numbers on their sleeves in years past, without it catching on. This new idea certainly took hold. By 1931 the rest of the league had all followed up, and the National League fell in line a year later.

On a technicality, the Indians actually wore numbers first. The Yankees' opener was rained out, and the Indians, who donned them on home uniforms only, played that day and got to claim the "first," even if they had jumped in after the Yankees' announcement. The idea belonged to the Colonel.

On Sunday, May 19, about fifty thousand people braved a bad forecast to see the Yanks take on Boston at the stadium. After just fifty minutes, with the Yanks leading 3–0 on homers by Ruth and Gehrig, a ferocious thunderstorm struck. There was no time for fans to duck out of the impending rain, and instead a stampede took hold, with fans in the right-field bleacher section clawing over each other to flee. Across the river at the Polo Grounds, the Giants had introduced the majors' first public-address system on July 5. It could have been something that helped with crowd control on this day, but the Yankees didn't have one until the 1936 World Series.

At the gate leading to River Avenue, under the elevated train, the terrible tragedy unfolded. Two fans were killed and seventeen hospitalized. The dead were Eleanor Price, a seventeen-year-old student at Hunter College, and Joseph Carter, a sixty-year-old truck driver.

According to the *Herald-Tribune*, Ruth, playing right, went into the stands and was found sitting on the ground, holding Ms. Price.

An eyewitness said the gate was closed and guards refused to open it. Ruppert refuted that, and the district attorney, John McGeehan, agreed, calling it a "wild rush of people down a narrow chute." "It is one of those unfortunate things that cannot be helped," said Ruppert. "Sudden thunder showers have sent crowds rushing from the bleachers many times before. This time, the shower was unusually sudden, but even then, there would have been no casualties if persons in the crowd had not fallen down."

Ruth visited the injured at Lincoln Hospital and gave them signed baseballs.

The death of Mr. Carter fit the general demographic of ballpark attendees at the time. Ms. Price's death was notable in that seventeen-year-old coeds were not commonly seen at baseball games.

ON SEPTEMBER 15, Waite Hoyt was knocked out early while pitching against Cleveland. Art Fletcher had to remove him from the game because Huggins was in the clubhouse, nursing an infected and painful carbuncle on his cheek.

Hug was sitting next to Doc Woods's training table with a heat lamp pointed at him.

"What happened to you?" he asked Hoyt.

"Oh, Joe Hauser hit one in the seats with a couple on, so here I am," he said.

Huggins asked Hoyt how old he was. Hoyt said he'd just turned thirty.

"Tomorrow, go down and get your paycheck. You're through for the season. You just weren't in shape. Get in good shape this winter, come down next spring and have the year I know you can have."

The next day, Huggins was taken to St. Vincent's Hospital. He had erysipelas, a bacterial skin infection, often fatal.

On Wednesday the twenty-fifth, with just six games left in the season, the Yankees were in Fenway Park. They were alerted that back in New York, the end might be near for their manager. Visitors at St. Vincent's included Ruppert, Barrow, and their old scout and St. Paul owner Bob Connery. The three left for lunch and left behind Hug's brother and sister-in-law, his sister Myrtle (with whom he lived), the wife of Babe Ruth's agent, Christy Walsh, a minister, and a surgeon. Hug dropped into a coma and passed away at 3:16 P.M.

Back at Fenway, the Red Sox alerted a groundskeeper to lower the flag to half staff as soon as a call came with the news. The flag was lowered in the third inning, but the game continued and no decision was made on informing the players or the fans. Some players figured it out.

In the fifth, the Yankee players assembled in the dugout and were told the news. There was silence, and then Combs broke down and began to cry.

Someone came into the dugout and approached Ruth for a comment but he was waved off.

Before the sixth inning, the players of both teams were summoned to home plate, where they gathered with the umpires and removed their caps. The Red Sox public-address announcer lifted his megaphone and asked "for a minute of silent prayer in memory of Miller Huggins, manager of the Yankees, who has just died."

Not everyone could hear the announcement, and the news had to be spread back through the crowd. Finally, there was silence.

They finished the game.

The funeral was held on Friday the twenty-seventh at the Church of the Transfiguration, also known as the Little Church Around the Corner, on East Twenty-ninth Street. The team came up from Washington, where they had played on Thursday, and then returned after the funeral to play Saturday. All Friday games in the majors were canceled.

"I'll guess I'll miss him more than anyone," speculated Gehrig. "Next to my father and mother he was the best friend a boy could have. He told me I was the rawest, most awkward rookie that ever came into baseball. He taught me everything I know.

"He gave me my job. He advised me on salary. He taught me how to invest my money and because of him I have everything anybody could ask for in a material way. There never was a more patient or more pleasant man to work for. You can't realize that he won't join us again."

Ruth, who made Hug's life miserable but who shared in his triumphs, said, "You know how I feel about it. He was my friend. He was a great guy and I got a kick out of doing things that would help him. I am sorry he couldn't win the last pennant he tried for. We all will miss him more every day."

Huggins was just fifty-one. His body was taken to Cincinnati for another service and for burial. In 1932, with his sister doing the unveiling, a monument was dedicated to Hug in center field by the flagpole, as Ruppert and Mayor Jimmy Walker looked on. It was modeled, to a fashion, after a monument at the Polo Grounds erected in 1921 for Eddie Grant, a Giants player who had been killed in the Great War. It would be the first plaque or monument for a Yankee, the start of a special part of Yankee culture.

ART FLETCHER MANAGED THE Yanks for the remaining games of the lost season (the Yanks finished eighteen games out), and then the search was on for the new manager. One who wanted strong consideration was Ruth. Player-managers were common, and he wanted in. He was thirty-four, a sixteen-year veteran, and thought he'd earned the chance. He'd hit his 500th home run on August 11; it was time to think of his future. But Barrow and Ruppert wouldn't give it a thought. "He can't even manage himself" hovered in their conversations. Ruth was not happy.

Barrow's first choice was Donie Bush, who had managed the Pirates to their 1927 pennant. But Bush was already committed to managing the White Sox.

Next it was Eddie Collins, but he chose to coach for Connie Mack and turned it down.

Next it was Fletcher, who had once managed the Phillies. It hadn't been a good experience and he said he'd never manage again. Fletch would continue to coach for New York until 1946.

So the fourth choice was the winner, and it was Bob Shawkey, the mild-mannered Yankee veteran who had retired after the '27 season but came back in '29 to coach the pitchers.

It was announced on the very same day that Bob Meusel had been sold to Cincinnati, ending his ten-year run in the Yankee outfield.

The Shawkey announcement was a well-received choice, but some felt he was too easygoing to handle the job.

It was a transitional year, to be sure. The stock market crashed on October 29, 1929, and though the Ruppert family, fortunately, was not invested in the market, the economics of both the nation and of ticket-buying customers would be severely tested.

Harry Frazee had died in '29, but perhaps in his memory, on May 6 the Yanks robbed the Red Sox one more time, trading outfielder Cedric Durst for Red Ruffing. Ruffing, only 39–96 lifetime, a man who had lost 47 games in 1928–29, would go on to be a stalwart for fifteen years. Lefty Gomez also made the club as a twenty-one-year-old left-hander and would team with Ruffing for thirteen seasons and 408 victories between them.

Ruth, pouting but still producing, went out and hit three homers in Philadelphia on May 21, the only time he ever hit three in a regular-season game as a Yankee.

On June 2, before playing an exhibition game in Cincinnati against Meusel, Durocher, and the Reds, the Yankees visited Spring Grove Cemetery and placed wreaths at Miller Huggins's grave.

On July 4, the Yankees dropped a doubleheader in Washington. Fans were starting to realize this season might not be working out. One who actually cried that day was a little baby born in Rocky River, Ohio, named George Michael Steinbrenner III. The future impatient owner was born in the midst of a seven-game losing streak.

Three weeks after the Ruffing deal, they sent Hoyt and Koenig to Detroit and installed Lyn Lary at short. Ben Chapman replaced Dugan at third.

Jimmie Reese, born James Herman ("Hymie") Soloman, also saw time in the outfield. He would much later in life become a beloved coach with the Angels, and another who loved talking about rooming with Babe Ruth's suitcase. His signing, and his being Jewish, were hardly noted. (The first Jewish Yankee was a 1905 pitcher named Phil Cooney, born Cohen.)

Much more attention was paid to Detroit's signing of the Bronx's Hank Greenberg, who would become the greatest Jewish hitter in history. A first baseman, he saw his path blocked by Lou Gehrig and turned down a Yankee offer for a faster path to the majors.

Couple the player moves with the first year of the Great Depression and the nervousness and uncertainty hovering over the business of baseball, and it was not an easy time for Shawkey to take over.

Still, in a year that the major league batting average was .296, the Yanks batted .309. Ruth, now earning his peak of $80,000 a year, also took the mound for the last game of the season and beat Boston 9–3, pitching a complete game. Ruppert, addressing Babe's salary, said, "This is financial madness. There is no $80,000 player even with the Babe in the field. There never again will be an $80,000 player."

The Yanks finished a noncontending third, and Shawkey was out after just one season.

I knew Shawkey late in his life, and I could see why people liked him so much. He was a gentleman. One day I asked him about his brief stint as manager.

"I got screwed," he said. "They gave Huggins four years before he won his first pennant. They gave McCarthy two. Me, I had one year and they fired me. I would have won in '31. I would have won all those pennants McCarthy won, and I'd still be going . . . I might have won all those pennants Stengel won too."

He meant it. He felt genuinely wronged. It was sad to see the old fellow's hurt feelings come pouring out as they did that day.

Shawkey would manage Jersey City in '31, Scranton in '32 and '33, and would return to the Yankees organization in 1934 as manager of their top farm team, Newark.

JOE MCCARTHY WAS no fourth choice to succeed Shawkey. He was a highly regarded, pennant-winning manager with the Cubs, and before that with Louisville, where he'd managed Combs.

Warren Brown, the Chicago sports columnist, bumped into Barrow at a prizefight in New York in September of 1930. He shared with Barrow his unpublished knowledge that McCarthy was looking to move on. McCarthy felt that Cubs owner Bill Wrigley wanted to install Rogers Hornsby in the job, and McCarthy wanted to walk before he was fired.

"You'll never get anyone better than McCarthy," said Brown to Barrow. Prophetic words.

McCarthy resigned on September 25, just before the season ended. At the World Series, Barrow sent Krichell to talk to Joe; a meeting was arranged at Ruppert's Fifth Avenue apartment. There, a five-year, $30,000-per-year contract was agreed upon.

Again Babe was passed over without much consideration. Ruth and McCarthy would never have a close relationship. But then again, neither did Ruth and Huggins. And for that matter, neither did Ruth and Gehrig, over some slight involving their wives that occurred after Lou married in 1933. And Mrs. Ruth didn't speak to Mrs. McCarthy.

McCarthy, forty-four, was a minor league infielder for fifteen years, never once playing in a major league contest. He'd managed for ten years in the minors (including seven at Louisville) before being hired by the Cubs in 1926. He won the National League pennant with them in 1929 and finished second in 1930. Some felt Shawkey deserved another year, but few questioned the selection of McCarthy.

Joe made his home in Tonawanda, outside Buffalo, New York. He had his prejudices, including one against southern players, whom he considered hot-tempered and defiant. "They're all moonshiners back there," he told Barrow. "And they're just naturally against the law. They resent any kind of rules or discipline."

McCarthy brought a work ethic to the Yankees that had not previously been attempted. The ballpark, he felt, was a place of business. Players were not to arrive unshaven or in sloppy dress. They were provided with three uniforms so that one would always be dry-cleaned and immaculate. (In keeping with tradition, the players had to pay for their uniforms, approximately $30 a set, which was refunded at the end of the season when they turned them in.)

Furthermore, with Ruppert's blessing, the team traveled in style. Where most teams used a single Pullman car, with the regulars sleeping on the lowers and the reserves on the uppers, the Yankees reserved two cars, always in the rear so as to be undisturbed, and everyone had a lower berth. The manager, his coaches, and trainer had full compartments. The players appreciated the privacy; in an era before air-conditioning, they would enjoy playing bridge in their underwear as the train journeyed to its next destination.

McCarthy himself would wear a long-sleeved jersey, a style that continued among Yankee managers through Stengel's early years. The team would wear jackets to the hotel dining halls, even for breakfast, and be seated by 8:30. McCarthy eventually banned card playing. He didn't want the players thinking about card games or the losses they were suffering when their focus needed to be on the game of the day.

With Gehrig now a mature veteran and Dickey a natural leader and wise beyond his years, the personality of the team began to shift to a more corporate style, rather than the good-time days of the Ruth era. That era wasn't done by any means—Babe and "Marse Joe" would be together for four seasons. But this was now McCarthy's team, and his ways were not Ruth's ways.

CHARLEY "RED" RUFFING and Vernon "Lefty" Gomez were a fine inheritance from Shawkey.

Gomez was more of a craftsman on the mound; Ruffing more of a workhorse.

Lefty, born in Rodeo, California, was purchased from San Francisco in 1929 and assigned to St. Paul in '30 under Bob Connery's watch. Just twenty-one, he was very thin, maybe 160 pounds on his six-foot-one frame, but he threw hard. His father was born in Spain and his mother in Ireland, so while not Latin American, he could be called the first Hispanic star of the Yankees. A writer once erroneously reported that he was Mexican, which tended to get picked up many times over the years in biographical sketches of him.

Gomez's teammates loved him. He had a marvelous, self-deprecating sense of humor and could get away with teasing even the biggest stars on the team. He always credited his outfielders for running down his mistakes, his relief pitchers for saving his wins, and his hitting for being "unappreciated." He was a terrible hitter, but an example of his humor came when Carl Hubbell struck out Ruth, Gehrig, Foxx, Al Simmons, and Joe Cronin in order in an All-Star game—then allowed a single to Dickey before fanning Gomez.

"That Dickey," he'd say. "If he'd only struck out too, my name would have been included among all the great hitters he struck out in a row."

Then there was the time Gomez threw a double-play grounder to Lazzeri, standing some twenty feet from second base, instead of shortstop Frank Crosetti, who was on the base. "Why me?" asked Lazzeri in a quick mound conference.

"Tony, all I have read in the papers lately is about how smart you are. I just wanted to see what you'd do with the ball when you didn't expect it."

I once had to bring a 1932 team photo into the clubhouse to get Pete Sheehy to identify all the players for me. "That would be the year that Gomez and Ruth showed up late for the picture," he recalled. "No telling where those two were." He was right. Babe and Lefty, in the middle of row two, obviously just threw their jerseys over their street clothes and ran out for the photo. Their jerseys clearly hang out over their pants, no visible belts. It appears that the Babe may have taken Lefty under his wing for a late night.

Ruffing, from Granville, Illinois, lost four toes on his left foot in a mining accident when he was fifteen. Had it been his right foot, he almost certainly could never have competed in major league baseball. One might never have guessed he'd become the winningest right-hander in team history (only southpaw Whitey Ford, in 1965, would surpass him) and the winningest World Series pitcher, with seven victories, until that too was broken by Ford.

Ruffing, best known to fans as Red but to insiders as Charley, would later reveal that he pitched most of his career with a sore shoulder. "It hurt so much I'd keep going to doctors. But I wouldn't tell the ballclub. They'd have traded my tail out of there. So I had to spend my own money. I'd pull into a town, pull down the telephone book and look under chiropractors for a likely looking name."

Unlike Gomez, he was also a terrific hitter, often called upon by McCarthy to pinch-hit. A converted outfielder, he was a .269 lifetime hitter with

36 home runs, and he batted as high as .364, in 1930, his first year with the club.

When I would be responsible for Old-Timers' Day, Gomez was always a delight, and he would bring along his wife, Broadway actress June O'Dea. Sometimes known as El Goofy, Gomez remained on the baseball scene in his later years, working for Rawlings sporting goods. Ruffing, on the other hand, would grumpily refuse to come because the invitation did not include travel expenses for wives. This was consistent with his annual salary disputes with the Yankees, including one in 1937 in which he wanted to be paid an extra $1,000 for his good hitting. He wound up sitting home until May.

His last baseball job was as pitching coach for the woeful 1962 Mets under Casey Stengel.

Chapter Fourteen

McCarthy headed for St. Petersburg for his first Yankee training camp, accompanied by a new trainer, Earle "Doc" Painter, and a new coach, Jimmy Burke, to replace Charlie O'Leary. Joe would initially coach third himself. Burke had been McCarthy's minor league manager at Indianapolis when McCarthy was a struggling infielder back in 1911. Joe had four pitching mounds added to the training site so relief pitchers wouldn't throw off game-like "mounds." He eliminated lunch from training; only two meals a day.

The Yanks' new practice field was now known as Miller Huggins Memorial Field.

On the way north to open the season, the Yankees stopped in Chattanooga for an exhibition game with the Lookouts, a Southern Association team, where a local seventeen-year-old girl named Jackie Mitchell struck out Ruth and Gehrig on six pitches in the first inning to earn a place in baseball lore.

McCarthy also had a new infielder, Joe Sewell, the onetime replacement for Ray Chapman in Cleveland and now, moving to third, a fine number-two hitter who hardly ever struck out. Sewell, a University of Alabama product, had been released by the Indians and signed with New York as a free agent. Now thirty-two, he would give the Yanks three seasons at third, make 1,753 plate appearances, and would strike out only 15 times. His ability to put bat on ball was uncanny. In the last nine seasons of his career, he never reached double figures in strikeouts; in '32, he would strike out only three times in 576 appearances. There has never been a contact hitter quite like Joe Sewell.

McCarthy coaxed 94 wins out of his '31 Yanks, but it was still not good enough to unseat the Athletics, and they settled for second place. He got 37 wins from Gomez and Ruffing, with Lefty winning 21 at the age of twenty-two.

Outfielder Ben Chapman stole 61 bases, the first of three years in a row he would lead the league. This was the highest total in the league since 1920, and the most on the Yankees since 1914. Chapman "did more to revive the art of base running than any other individual player in ten years," noted the *Spalding Guide.*

Gehrig finally tied Ruth for the homer championship with 46 (aided by a six-game homer streak in late August), but lost a homer in April when baserunner "Broadway" Lyn Lary (whose 107 RBI, in 1931 remains a Yankee shortstop record) ran to the dugout instead of heading home. Gehrig, circling the bases, was ruled out for passing him. Still, he hit .341 and drove in 184 runs, an American League RBI record. Along the way, Ruth belted his 600th homer.

Ruppert was pleased. McCarthy let it be known that to him, second place wasn't good enough.

Attendance was off about a quarter million, reflecting an adjustment to the Great Depression that the whole baseball industry would feel throughout the thirties, as the game did its best to provide affordable entertainment and present an attractive product to cash-strapped fans. The effects were surely felt. National unemployment would reach nearly 25 percent. There were about five thousand apple sellers working New York City streets. In '33 Yankee attendance would fall under 750,000, and in '35 under 660,000, an average of just 10,436 per date. (They played fourteen home doubleheaders that year.)

On September 24, the Giants, Yankees, and Dodgers played a doubleheader at the Polo Grounds to aid the city's unemployed. More than forty-four thousand turned out to see Brooklyn beat the Giants in the first game, a series of relay races, throwing and running and fungo-hitting contests between games (the latter won by Ruth), and then it was Brooklyn vs. the Yankees in the second game, with the Yankees declared the champions and $48,135 raised for the charity.

On October 20, in the northeast corner of dust bowl–ridden Oklahoma, a baby boy was born. His dad, a big fan of the Athletics' catcher Mickey Cochrane, decided to name his son Mickey Mantle.

BRANCH RICKEY BEGAN the farm system for major league teams to develop prospects more cost-effectively, with the parent team's oversight. It was seen by Rickey as better than purchasing players from independent minor league operators. St. Paul had been an accommodating partner for the Yanks in securing players, thanks to their relationship with Connery, but by 1932 Barrow was seeing the merits of Rickey's innovation. Although not as strong a proponent of the system as Rickey (he loved tryout camps run by Krichell), he saw the game trending that way and went with it.

Ruppert was all for the new system. "We paid $103,000 for Lyn Lary and Jimmie Reese and that deal has taught me a lesson," he said.

To implement the system, Barrow hired George Weiss, who, while operating New Haven, had survived the train wreck that took Bill Donovan's life. Weiss had proven himself a tough operator and had even battled Barrow over an exhibition game at his park, for which Babe Ruth failed to show up. It was the only traveling exhibition game Ruth ever missed, and it embarrassed Weiss in front of his customers. He let Barrow know it and withheld the Yankees' money.

By the 1931 Winter Meetings, Weiss was general manager of the International League's Baltimore Orioles. Barrow was sitting with Ruppert in the hotel lobby when he spotted Weiss, nudged Ruppert on the shoulder, and said, "That's our guy."

Weiss, thirty-seven, born in New Haven and a graduate of Yale, was all business and hardworking. He would spend twenty-eight years with the Yankees, eventually succeeding Barrow as general manager. A tough negotiator, he was no favorite of the players. But he was a tireless employee who hired good scouts and pushed the right buttons.

The Yankees purchased the Newark Bears franchise in 1932 and renamed their ballpark Ruppert Stadium. They added the Pacific Coast League's Oakland Oaks in 1935 for three years, and the Kansas City Blues of the American Association in 1937, also calling their park Ruppert Stadium.

That original Yankee farm team in Newark featured George Selkirk, Red Rolfe, and Johnny Murphy. Shawkey managed them in 1934, and before the thirties concluded, Tommy Henrich, Charlie Keller, and Babe Dahlgren were also maturing there. The Oakland team produced Spud Chandler, Ernie Bonham, and Joe Gordon. Kansas City would deliver Phil Rizzuto, Johnny Lindell, and Johnny Sturm. It was an affirmation of a good farm system taking hold.

By 1932, the Yankees' farm system also included teams in Springfield, Massachusetts; Binghamton, New York; Cumberland, Maryland; and Erie, Pennsylvania. The system would grow to as large as twenty-four teams after World War II before settling into a more manageable seven or eight clubs.

The Bears, wearing hand-me-down pinstriped uniforms and playing just a short train ride from Manhattan's Penn Station, were almost joined at the hip to the parent club. It was easy for Weiss and Barrow to watch players there anytime they felt like it. From 1932 to 1942, the Bears won the International League pennant seven times and are still considered one of the great minor league franchises in history.

"When I lived in Newark," recalls Yankee fan Irv Welzer, "we would get seven games at Ruppert Stadium for a nickel, all the tickets printed on perforated paper, torn off one at a time. Now that was a *terrific* bargain!"

THE 1932 YANKEES won 107 games and their seventh American League pennant. Only eight players remained from their '28 World Series team; the rest of the roster was newly crafted by McCarthy and included a shortstop from the San Francisco Seals, Frank Crosetti, twenty-one. He'd been playing there since he was sixteen.

McCarthy knew it was a tall assignment to put a 135-pounder like Cro into a pennant-contending lineup. Just meeting Babe Ruth was a dream come true for him. And when Ruth said to him, "Remember, when you hear me boom 'my ball!'—get out of the road!" Crosetti answered, "Yes sir, Mr. Babe."

Crosetti became a master of the "hidden ball trick," picking runners off second when they thought the pitcher had the ball, something you'd expect to see on a sandlot. Later on, Crosetti passed on the skill to Gene Michael. Crosetti put in a remarkable thirty-seven years with the Yankees, first as a regular, then as Rizzuto's mentor and backup, and then as the team's third-base coach. He picked up twenty-three World Series checks, seventeen of them winning shares, for about $143,000 in total earnings. With those checks, he became the symbol of the value of being in the organization and being a good company man.

I knew Crosetti late in his coaching career, and I knew him to be a play-by-the-rules guy. When batting practice began, prior to the gates opening, only the early-arriving concession people would be in the stands. Crosetti was in charge of the ball bag—the supply of BP baseballs. If a ball went into the stands and a concessionaire pocketed it, Cro would jump the fence and run the guy down to get the three-dollar baseball back. No foul balls were lost before the gates opened. That was the rule. It said a lot about him. He could follow McCarthy's rules, play his game as best as he could, and yes, he could be the team's regular shortstop at twenty-one. It would work.

The '32 Yanks won by thirteen games and were never shut out all season. Ruth, at thirty-seven, showed little sign of slowing down—his 41 home runs may have been off his peak years, but he batted .341 and drove in 137. His weight, 225, was down nineteen pounds from 1928, twenty-six from '27, and thirty-one from 1925, mostly due to Artie McGovern's tough three-times-a-week winter workouts. He gave up in-season golf. Gehrig hit .349/34/151 and became the first twentieth-century player—and the only Yankee in history—to hit four home runs in a game. Making the day even more remarkable was that on his final at-bat of the afternoon, Lou hit his longest shot, 450 feet to dead center, but the ball was caught by Al Simmons a few steps from the wall. (Later that year, Gehrig posed with sixty-eight-year-old Bobby Lowe, who first accomplished the feat in 1894.)

Gehrig, so often overshadowed by Ruth, even had this big game overshadowed—by the announcement at the Polo Grounds that John McGraw was retiring as Giants manager.

It was a big year for Gomez, who started 13–1 and finished 24–7. Rookie right-hander Johnny Allen went 17–4, including a ten-game winning streak, to lead the league in winning percentage.

The product of an orphanage, Allen had a terrible, almost frightening temper that McCarthy couldn't stand, and he was shipped out after just four years. But he was 50–19 as a Yankee, a .725 percentage. Later, when he pitched for Cleveland, his manager Lou Boudreau would say, "He was just plain mean . . . You never wanted to go near him anytime anything went wrong."

At home, the Yankees were a remarkable 62–15. This would prove to be a pattern during the McCarthy years. For his run as Yankee manager, he was 704–365 at home, a .659 winning percentage. Between 1936 and 1943, he would be .707. And those were the post–Babe Ruth years.

IN THE NATION's capital on July 4, the Senators' Carl Reynolds slid hard into Dickey at home plate. It was bad timing on Reynolds's part—Dickey had been knocked unconscious on a similar play just the day before in Boston. Dickey, infuriated, flattened Reynolds with a sock to the jaw, breaking it in two places. It was a shocking incident, all the more so because Dickey, while a strong presence on the field whenever he was out there, was not known to be hot-tempered or excessively emotional. He wound up with a thirty-day suspension and a huge $1,000 fine.

It did give his understudy, Norwegian-born Arndt Jorgens, a rare chance to play. Because of Dickey's durability, Jorgens was seldom used. In eleven years as a Yankee, he got into just 307 games. He was on five world championship teams without ever appearing in a World Series game, Dickey catching every inning.

THE 1932 WORLD Series, which would turn out to be Babe Ruth's last, was sweet revenge for McCarthy, who would have been fired by Cubs owner William Wrigley had he not resigned at the end of the 1930 season. It was the only pennant the Yankees won between 1929 and 1935, and almost certainly it kept McCarthy from being fired.

At shortstop for the Cubs was none other than Mark Koenig. After his time with the Tigers, Koenig had gone back to the minor leagues before being purchased by Chicago in late August, in time to play 33 games and to hit .353 in helping the Cubs secure the pennant.

A half share of World Series money, as voted by his teammates, was usually fine for that amount of service time, but the Yankees thought the Cubs had been cheapskates toward their old pal and were really letting them have it. (The Yanks generously rewarded their batboy Eddie Bennett, who had been in a bad auto accident early in the season.) The dialogue often turned bitter. The Cubs' players were riding Ruth about being "Grandpa," also suggesting he had negro blood, a familiar refrain in those days.

Ruffing and Gomez won the first two contests with complete-game efforts, and the action shifted to Wrigley Field, where attendance reached nearly fifty thousand thanks to temporary bleachers erected over Waveland and Sheffield avenues to expand bleacher capacity.

In the third game, with Pipgras opposing Charlie Root, Ruth came up in the fifth inning with one out, none on, and the score tied 4–4. Babe had homered in the first inning, and New York governor Franklin Roosevelt was among the fans who sat in the windy chill enjoying the action.

But the taunting continued. As Ruth strolled to bat, a lemon rolled his way, a symbol of derision. Lemons were the weapon of the day; he'd been seeing them all afternoon.

Root's first pitch was a called strike, and the Babe held up a finger, saying something like "It only takes one to hit it," though only catcher Gabby Hart-nett and umpire Roy Van Graflan could hear. After two balls, the next pitch was another called strike, and Ruth raised two fingers and pointed at either Root, the bleachers, or nothing in particular. Babe also pointed his bat to-ward the Cubs dugout. He apparently shouted something at Root. The crowd was booing.

The next pitch turned into baseball history and folklore. With a mighty swing, out it soared. The ball traveled a reported 490 feet, the third longest in World Series history to that point.

It was history because it was Babe's 15th World Series homer, a record that would stand for thirty-two years.

It was folklore because it came to be known as the Called Shot, the time Babe pointed to the bleachers and homered. Gehrig followed with a homer (he had hit one in Wrigley years earlier playing in a high school tourna-ment), and the Yanks went on to win the game 7–5, with Pennock saving it in the ninth to put the Yanks up three games to none.

Most journalists reported that Babe pointed to the bleachers and then homered. Players had mixed feelings. Sewell said he was pointing to the Cubs' bench. Chapman said he was pointing at Root. Ruffing said he had no doubt he was pointing to center field. Crosetti thought Ruth's finger "just happened to be pointing to center, when he indicated he had one strike left." Gomez was sure he called the shot but remembered him pointing his bat. Trainer Doc Painter remembered Pennock saying, "Suppose you had missed, you would have looked like an awful bum," when Ruth got to the bench, and Ruth laughing and saying, "I never thought of that!"

Charlie Grimm, the Cubs' manager, said he was pointing at Root. Hart-nett, awfully close to the scene, denied he'd pointed to the bleachers. Koe-nig said he pointed, but "You know darn well a guy with two strikes isn't going to say he's going to hit a home run on the next pitch."

"I give him the benefit of the doubt but I don't think he actually pointed to center field. I think he was acknowledging that he had two strikes," Koe-nig added.

As for Charlie Root, he told people that if Ruth had done that, the next pitch would have gone straight into his ribcage. "I guess I should have wasted the next pitch, and I thought Ruth figured I would too," he said. "I decided to try to cross him and came in with it. The ball was gone as soon as Ruth swung. It never occurred to me then that the people in the stands would think he had been pointing to the bleachers. But that's the way it was."

Little Ray Kelly, no longer Babe's mascot but still a pal, flew to Chicago with his dad as guests of the Babe. They had choice box seats. "Damned right he pointed and hit it out," maintained Little Ray. "I'll swear it to the day I die."

The *Reach Guide* reported that "Ruth hit a ball over the centerfield fence—a tremendous drive—after indicating by pantomime to his hostile admirers what he purposed to do—and did!"

Matt Kandle was an amateur photographer at the game that day, shooting home movies. They quietly remained in the family until his great-grandson Kirk released still photos, and then the actual film, in 1982.

This was seismic news, a Zapruder film for baseball. But although the film contained absolute proof of Babe pointing, it didn't end the debate. Even viewing the film makes it impossible to know for certain where he was pointing or what the gesture meant.

Ruth was publicity-skilled enough to maintain that it surely did happen. "The good Lord was with me that day," he told newsreel photographers. And so the Called Shot took its place among the greatest of all baseball stories.

My father was born in Brooklyn but wasn't much of a baseball fan and didn't attend a game until he took me to Ebbets Field in 1955. It was the first game for both of us. Once, when we were discussing Hank Aaron breaking Ruth's home run record, he said to me, "Oh, but Ruth used to call his home runs." So for the average American, the story made it into popular culture; the translation wasn't always perfect, but no one can really be sure what happened that afternoon.

The fourth game saw the Cubs score four in the first inning and knock Johnny Allen out of the box, but Moore and Pennock allowed just two runs the rest of the way while the Yanks scored 13, with Lazzeri homering twice. The Yankees won 13–6 for their fourth world championship, running their World Series win streak to twelve games.

If they had named World Series MVPs back then, it would have been Gehrig, whose superlative play was again upstaged by Ruth's theatrics. Gehrig hit .529 with three homers, nine runs scored, and eight RBI in the four games.

THERE WAS A remarkable similarity to the 1933, 1934, and 1935 seasons, each finding the Yankees finishing second, seven games out of first in '33 and '34, three games out in '35, averaging 91 wins a year.

They ran their streak of games without being shut out to 308—almost two full years—before Lefty Grove stopped them on August 3, 1933.

A year after the Dickey-Reynolds fight of '32, the Yanks and Senators squared off again in April. This time it was Chapman sliding hard into the Senators' second baseman Buddy Myer that got things going. With Vice President John Nance Garner looking on, Myer responded to the slide with a kick to the thigh. Chapman got off a series of punches as both benches emptied. There were suggestions that Chapman unloaded some anti-Semitic remarks at Myer, who was Jewish.

Myer and Chapman were both ejected but had to exit together through the Washington dugout. Not surprisingly, things were said to Chapman as he walked down the dugout steps, and in a flash he was exchanging punches with Washington's Earl Whitehill, knocking him out. With this, Senators fans battled their way onto the field, grabbing bats from the dugout in the process. The Yanks' Dixie Walker (later a star with the Dodgers) went into the stands after taunting fans, who pinned him down; Dickey, Lazzeri, and Gomez went to rescue him. It all felt like something that belonged in nineteenth-century baseball. There has never been as big a brawl involving the Yankees as this one, with fans storming the field.

The Jewish community was troubled by the incident. People seemed to know that Chapman had no love for Jews. The players knew it too. Birdie Tebbetts, the longtime catcher and manager who finished up his career as a Yankee scout, wrote of another play in his autobiography a few years later,

> He [Chapman] had the same kind of reputation as Ty Cobb, and I know because I'd heard it myself that he was one of the most brutal Jew-baiting tormentors of Hank Greenberg. So about the middle of the ballgame, on a close play at the plate, when Chapman roared in from third and slammed into me, spikes high, I just blew my stack. I threw off my mask and started throwing punches . . . Both of us were tossed out of the game, fined and suspended.
>
> After that episode, the next stop . . . was Yankee Stadium. There was a place under the stands near the Yankee dugout where players could gather and grab a smoke before going out on the field, and as we were standing there, a bunch of Yankees wandered by. One of them was Lou Gehrig [who had recently broken Everett Scott's consecutive-game streak]. He stopped, looked us over, and said, "Which one of you is Tebbetts?"

I said, "I am."

He looked at me and said, "Did you land a good punch?"

"Yes, sir."

"Would you fight him again?"

"Yes, sir."

"Well, if you ever do and you land two good punches, I'll buy you the best suit you will ever own."

And with that, Lou Gehrig turned and climbed the staircase, grabbed a bat and stepped into the batting cage.

The Yankees won the Myer-Chapman game 16–0. That was more like 1930s Yankee baseball.

Chapman, Myer, and Whitehall were all suspended for five days. Five fans were arrested. The era of both teams leaving through the same dugout was drawing to a close. Three years later, Chapman was traded to Washington, of all teams, in exchange for Jake Powell, who would bring his own problems to New York. Chapman and Myer were now teammates.

Babe Ruth continued to be exasperated watching a manager who had never played a major league game running the show. In Ruth's time, so many of his contemporary stars had had their shot at being player-managers: Cobb, Speaker, Walter Johnson, Joe Tinker, Chance, Bill Terry, Hornsby—the list went on, and Ruth fumed. He had "saved" baseball, they said. He had been the greatest drawing card in history. He thought he deserved his shot. Ruppert offered him the managing job at Newark for 1934; he turned it down. "To ask me . . . to manage a club in the minors," he said, "would be the same . . . as to ask Colonel Ruppert . . . to run a soda fountain."

On July 6, 1933, Babe hit the first home run in All-Star Game history. Always one to rise to the occasion, he blasted one out in Comiskey Park after sportswriter Arch Ward's idea for an All-Star Game became reality. But '33 would be his last .300 season, and his 34 homers were his fewest as a Yankee except for the bellyache season of '25.

There was a sense that 1934 would be his swan song. He hit his 700th home run on July 13, but only 11 after that. (Gehrig, suffering from lumbago, almost saw his playing streak end that very day, leaving in the second inning, but he was able to return the next day.) And when Ruth went 0-for-3 with a walk in the final game of the year, a 5–3 loss at Washington, many sensed that it was over for the Babe at age thirty-nine. Before the game, the band from his old school, St. Mary's in Baltimore, performed, while a scroll signed by President Roosevelt and many others was presented. He had batted just .288/22/84.

After the season he went to Japan, China, and the Philippines with a touring All-Star team that also included Gehrig and Gomez. He hit .408 with 13 homers in the 22 games, but his game in Manila on December 10 was to be his last representing the Yankees (although he wore a special uniform, not a Yankee one).

Before embarking, he told sportswriter Joe Williams that he wouldn't be back with the Yankees in 1935 "unless I'm manager. Don't you think I'm entitled to the chance?"

According to Barrow, the story caught him by surprise. McCarthy, according to Barrow, offered to resign. The Yankees wouldn't hear of it.

"Surprising as it was, it was also a great relief," he wrote. "The Babe had made things easier for the Colonel and myself." Ruppert, in conversation with Boston Braves owner Emil Fuchs, agreed to allow Babe to sign with the Braves. Ruth, Ruppert, Fuchs, and Barrow gathered at the brewery office on February 26, 1935, to announce Ruth's release and his return to Boston, this time with the Braves.

And so it ended. He would be going to St. Petersburg to train with Boston, awkwardly sharing facilities with the Yankees, and then he would play just 28 games and hit his final three home runs (all in one game), rounding it out at 714.

Ruth held thirty-four major league or American League records and twenty-six World Series records. Over fifteen Yankee seasons, he'd hit .349 with 659 homers. Gehrig, the 1934 homer champ with 49, was next on the all-time AL list with 348 to Ruth's 708 (including his Red Sox clouts). As a Yankee, Ruth led the league in homers ten times, in slugging percentage eleven times, in on-base percentage eleven times, and in walks eleven times. He played for seven pennant winners and four world championship teams. He'd made a lot of money for himself and for his teammates, and he achieved fame far beyond the baseball field. He had his times of high drama, but what he did for baseball, and for the Yankees, was unquestioned.

How big was this release? By most measurements, everyone could see that Babe Ruth's career was winding down. His age, his stats, and his expanding waistline all screamed out with the reality. But when it finally happened, it just had an empty feel to it.

Babe's name would be part of any experience at Yankee Stadium. You couldn't watch a game without thinking of him. When he made occasional visits to the ballpark, he always seemed to call attention to himself by dressing in light-colored clothing while everyone else was in dark attire. He would always stand out.

Some forty years later, when I was in the front office, the effect was still lingering. I'd make a mistake, perhaps an incorrect stat in the press notes, or someone else would make one, and we'd try to assess the damage. "How serious might this be?"

"Hey, they released Babe Ruth!" would be the response.

New York would remain Babe Ruth's home for the remaining thirteen years of his life. After marrying Claire in 1929, they had lived at 345 West Eighty-eighth Street, in an eleven-room apartment on the seventh floor, down the hall from Claire's mother. In 1942 they moved to 110 Riverside Drive, at Eighty-third Street, where Claire lived until her death in 1976.

Babe was the best goodwill ambassador the game could ever have, but he kept his Yankee Stadium appearances sparse, not wishing to overstay his welcome. "The only times [Ruth and Ruppert] ever met after the Babe left the Yankees," wrote Richards Vidmer in the *Tribune*, "was at such affairs as the World Series, the opening game of the season, or at a dinner of celebration. And at those times they merely clasped hands and smiled for the benefit of the photographers."

Many would feel that not making Ruth manager was wrong, and that Ruppert owed him the opportunity. In talking to Dan Daniel for an autobiography project that was never completed, Ruppert later offered this view:

> Ruth could have remained with the Yankees forever. Even if I had had any idea of letting him go, I could not have fought public opinion so strongly.
>
> When Miller Huggins died in 1929, I did not make Ruth the manager because I felt that as soon as he got the reins he would look for an easy seat on the bench and retire as a player. I know that when you make a great player a manager he gets lazy. You lose the great player and get an indifferent leader.
>
> Later on I asked Ruth to go to Newark and work into the trick of running a ballclub. But he unwisely refused, and then asked me to release him to the Boston club of the National League. That was the biggest mistake of Ruth's life. It was not my fault.

Attendance fell from 854,682 in 1934 to 657,508 in '35, a 23 percent drop.

THE '34 YANKEES won 94 games and introduced their trio of players from Newark: Red Rolfe, Johnny Murphy, and George Selkirk. They also signed the forty-year-old spitball pitcher Burleigh Grimes. They released Pennock and made Sewell a coach.

Grimes was not a success with the Yankees—he was signed on May 28 and released on July 31—but it is worth noting that on July 17, he faced eight batters in one inning, and in that inning delivered the last legal spitball in Yankee history. Grandfathered in 1920 as one of those permitted to continue throwing the pitch, he would be the last to retire of those seventeen pitchers, although he went on to pitch in eight more games for Pittsburgh after his Yankee effort.

Rolfe, twenty-five, was a product of Dartmouth and later its baseball coach. He would succeed Harvard's Charlie Devens on the roster, who with Columbia's Gehrig was keeping the Ivy League represented. (Yale's Johnny Broaca was also on the team.) Rolfe hit .287 as a rookie, .300 as a sophomore, and then .319 in his third year. He quickly made a claim to being the best Yankee third baseman to date, and one of the smartest. Red would keep a ledger of every at-bat in his career, who the pitcher was, what pitches he saw, and what he did with them. It was very advanced record keeping for the time. He later managed the Tigers.

Murphy, a local boy who went to Fordham, would evolve into a relief pitcher at a time when such an assignment was seen as second-class. He made it anything but, becoming a key member of the coming championship seasons, frequently lauded by the team's starting hurlers and happily enjoying the nickname "Fireman Johnny." Later, as a player rep, he was instrumental in the institution of baseball's first pension plan in 1947. Murphy would become the general manager of the 1969 world champion Mets.

George "Twinkletoes" Selkirk, called up on August 12, was the man the Yankees had in mind to succeed Ruth in '35, which he did. He even got Babe's uniform number 3 a year later. The Ontario native hit .313 in his 46-game debut in 1934, a prelude to a .312 showing in the full season of '35. Selkirk would later manage Mickey Mantle in the minors and became the general manager of the Washington Senators in 1962.

Finding Selkirk in '34 helped cover for the loss of Combs, who on July 24 crashed into a concrete wall in St. Louis, broke his left shoulder, fractured his skull, and drifted in and out of consciousness. So frightening was his condition that players from both teams rushed to his aid, and he was hospitalized in critical condition. He was done for the year and finished as a regular. He'd play 89 games in '35 and call it a career.

1934 would also see the passing of a number of people important in early Yankee history. Among them were:

- John McGraw, a worthy adversary who influenced many of the team's early decisions. Barrow led the Yankee contingent to St. Patrick's Cathedral.
- Harry M. Stevens, their concessionaire since their first season.
- Wilbert Robinson, Huston's coveted choice for manager over Huggins.
- Joe Vila, who had chronicled the team's growth for more than thirty years, at times influencing their decisions. He was recalled as the man who introduced Farrell and Devery to Ban Johnson. Vila's funeral was attended by the owners of the Yankees, Dodgers, and Giants, as well as by George M. Cohan, Clark Griffith, Connie Mack, Casey Stengel, Bill Terry, Emil Fuchs, Joe McCarthy, and Ed Barrow.

In January 1935, batboy-mascot Eddie Bennett, thirty-one, was found dead in his rented room at West Eighty-fourth Street by his landlady. He'd spent fourteen years with the team. The autopsy cited alcoholism. After reading the account of his sad demise, Ruppert had the Yankees pay for his funeral and burial, and the office staff attended.

LOU GEHRIG WAS named captain by McCarthy in 1935 after winning the Triple Crown in 1934—.363/49/165. It was the only season in which he didn't share the spotlight with Ruth or Joe DiMaggio. He was the first captain of the Yankees since Everett Scott, but it was an "off-year" for Larrupin' Lou, who hit .329/30/119.

The 1935 season also saw the breakthrough of radio broadcasting, not just re-creations, in a number of cities. The '35 Cubs were the first to broadcast all of their games to fans. By 1936, all teams except the three New York clubs were doing radio. Ruppert was outspoken in opposing broadcasts. Since 1932, all three New York teams were living up to a five-year prohibition of any radio broadcasts coming out of their ballparks, even by the visiting team.

"The idea of spending money to provide a healthful form of outdoor recreation and then let everybody in free, of course, is ridiculous," said Ruppert.

> Radio broadcasting comes under that head. Giving out details of games over the air to thousands of fans who otherwise would pay admission to the Stadium is a menace to the National Game.
>
> All of the clubs in both leagues have invested heavily in real estate and in construction of modern ball parks. They are, like myself, battling with the times. Some of them must economize, which means reductions in salaries and other overhead expenses. Now, can you understand why club owners who want to save money are willing to let broadcasters give away their business for nothing? As far as I am concerned, you can say that there will be no broadcasting at the Stadium next year or at any other time. I simply take this stand for the protection of my investments and I think all of the other club owners should view the situation in the same light.

Similarly, and in conjunction with all the other American League teams, Ruppert voted against installing lights and playing night games. On May 24, the Reds hosted the first night game in major league history. The Yankees were more than a decade away.

IN DECEMBER OF 1935, the first election for the new Baseball Hall of Fame in Cooperstown was held, and Ruth, along with Cobb, Mathewson, Walter Johnson, and Wagner, were the first five electees. Although Cobb and Wagner both recorded more votes than Ruth, the Babe had been retired for only seven months, and few questioned his standing in the election.* It was not seen as a referendum on "greatest player ever."

---

* The five-year waiting period for the Hall of Fame was not enacted until 1954, but waived for DiMaggio because of his strong support immediately after his retirement.

Chapter Fifteen

THE EARLY DAYS OF THE YANKEES' player-development operation included the hiring of two scouts to supervise West Coast operations: Joe Devine and Bill Essick.

Devine was the first to witness a teenage prodigy from San Francisco named Joe DiMaggio. Born in Oakland in 1895, Devine served as a scout for the Pirates (signing the Waner brothers, Joe Cronin, and Arky Vaughn), and most recently managed Mission in the Pacific Coast League (1931–32), after which he became a Yankee scout. He knew all the good players in the Bay Area, and he certainly knew about the DiMaggio brothers: older brother Vince, who struck out a lot, middle brother Joe, who seemed to do everything right, and little brother Dominic, who wore glasses, was the runt of the litter, but who could also play the game.

It was still an age when hot prospects could be secretly scouted without everyone knowing about them, but not so in the hotbed of the PCL, a nearly major league–caliber outfit until the majors expanded westward in the sixties. In today's game, the top 750 baseball players are in the majors. But when there were only sixteen teams and four hundred players, then the next best 350 would be found in the Negro and triple-A leagues.

All teams knew about DiMaggio, who had quit Galileo High School in tenth grade, determined to be a ballplayer and not a fisherman like his immigrant father. In 1932, at eighteen, he signed with Charley Graham's San Francisco Seals, and after just a brief debut batted .340 in 1933 and compiled a sixty-one-game hitting streak, still a professional baseball record. It made him the talk of the nation. Everybody wanted Joe.

There was talk that Graham could sell him for $100,000—amazing in the throes of the Depression. But the deal suffered a setback in May '34 when Joe stepped awkwardly from a taxi and tore cartilage in his knee. Suddenly all the scouts went away. The perfect specimen of an athlete was no longer perfect.

Devine, however, paid twenty-five dollars for an orthopedist to examine him, who determined he could recover. This is where Bill Essick took over.

Essick, the fellow who had recommended Bob Meusel to the Yankees, was now a scout in their employ. A graduate of Knox College in Galesburg, Illinois, he was known as "Vinegar Bill" because in German, *essig* was vinegar. Essick had a brief pitching career with Cincinnati but achieved greater success as a manager, winning three straight pennants for Vernon of the PCL. He became a Yankee scout in 1926.

Essick called George Weiss and said, "Don't give up on DiMaggio. Everyone out here thinks I'm crazy but I think he's all right. Let me watch him a couple of weeks more."

"If it had been anyone else but Essick," said Weiss, "I would have called him off. But I had complete faith in Bill."

In November 1934, Colonel Ruppert authorized sending five minor leaguers and $25,000 to Graham for DiMaggio's contract. Joe would play the 1935 season at San Francisco—and bat .398. The kid was going to be fine, and at a bargain price to boot.

DiMaggio was a tribute to good scouting, faith in the scouts, and a commitment to keep signing the best players. Essick and Devine were forever associated with DiMaggio. Devine would later sign Bobby Brown, Jerry Coleman, and Gil McDougald. Essick was involved in the signings of Lazzeri, Crosetti, Gomez, Joe Gordon, and Johnny Lindell.

BY THE TIME DiMaggio got into Lazzeri's car with Crosetti to drive from San Francisco to St. Petersburg, the whole baseball world knew of him. The game may never have had as heralded a rookie. Radio and newsreels were now making the game more "national" than ever, and smart fans, even those who weren't reading the *Sporting News*, were becoming aware of players all over the country.

And New York, in the heyday of its daily papers, couldn't wait. Ten daily papers were filled with biographical sketches, cartoons, and progress reports on Joe, especially after he signed in '35. Young writers like Tom Meany, Dan

Daniel, Max Kase, Ken Smith, Jimmy Powers, and Louis Effrat were wait-ing for "their guy," much in the same way Lieb and Rice and Frick had "owned" the Babe.

DiMaggio had been "schooled" and sophisticated by Lefty O'Doul, the San Francisco native and onetime Yankee who was an enormously influen-tial baseball figure in that part of the country. While Joe had not finished high school and had never been to New York, he would very quickly go from being Joe Di-*madge*-e-o to being Joe Di-*mahj*-e-o, a more polished prod-uct than his upbringing would suggest. He had a proud sense of his own value—his holdouts became legendary—and a powerful presence. Lefty Go-mez could needle him, but most of his teammates kept a modest distance from him. He would make his own friends on the road. His outfield part-ner Tommy Henrich would tell people he was never invited to dine with Joe, not once. Phil Rizzuto would talk of the awe in which he was held. "I used to like to just watch him shave," said Rizzuto.

Whereas Mickey Mantle would suffer for years with media and fan com-parisons to DiMaggio, Joe never bore that scrutiny with comparison to Ruth or Gehrig. He was his own man.

Joe would wear the finest clothing. He would marry a movie actress not once, but twice, the second being Marilyn Monroe, the greatest movie star of her day (although the partnership would last only nine months).

He never had to open his wallet. People jumped through hoops to cater to his needs. And while he could feel a slight even when no one else noticed and could hold a grudge for years, the Yankees meant everything to him. By the late sixties, when I was beginning my front-office career, I met many fans who'd lost interest after DiMaggio. He was an era-defining player.

Those close to him could find him prickly, distant, and perhaps a little full of himself. But that didn't matter to his fans. He was loved and ad-mired, and people could hardly remember him ever making a mistake on the field. He could do it all with style and grace. A poll in 1969, the centen-nial of professional baseball, named him the greatest living retired player. (Ruth was named the greatest of all.) That sounded just fine to Joe, who requested that it be his introduction whenever an introduction was neces-sary. Arrogant? To some. But on the other hand, it was probably true. He was awfully close to perfect. He was, in many ways, the most admired player ever, a hero to the whole generation of fans who came of age in the thirties and forties, a man of dignity and class, one of the greatest Italian-American heroes in the nation's history, and a player who gave it his all every day because, in his own words, "There may be somebody in the stands who is seeing me for the first time."

Some thought Joe wouldn't dive or make an attempt to catch a ball that might make him look bad. But Yogi Berra claimed otherwise: "You never saw him dive 'cause he was always in the right position. In those days, you played each team twenty-two times. You knew where to play. And Joe knew better than most of us."

His baserunning was seldom marred by bad judgment, and he attained great acceleration with a very long stride. It was not a base-stealing era, but he was fast.

As he arrived two years after Ruth's last Yankee season, he joined a club led by Gehrig and Dickey, but in fact it was his from the start. He had that sort of commanding presence. Gehrig, for all his greatness, never sought that spotlight. Joe basked in it. And so under McCarthy's guidance, the Yankees took on a businesslike persona as never before. The team dressed right, arrived on time, played the game right, looked sharp on the trains and in the dining halls, and went about their business as though writing a textbook on how to be a Yankee. It made Ruppert proud, to be sure. It was just the way he had always wanted the team to appear. Ruth had held that back.

Combs, badly injured in '35, was done. He'd become a coach, joining Fletcher and Johnny Schulte. After starting out in right, Joe would take over center field, and it would remain his until he was ready to turn it over to Mantle.

He had a late start: A burn from a diathermy machine treating a spring training ankle injury delayed his debut until May 3. On July 29 in Detroit, he was involved in a full-speed collision with the center fielder, Myril Hoag, that was nearly fatal. Two days later, Hoag was found unconscious in his hotel room and rushed to the hospital with a brain clot. He could have died, but he survived the primitive brain surgery of the day, missed the rest of the season, then went on with his career.

In only 138 games, Joe rang up 206 hits and batted .323/29/125. He scored 132 runs. He struck out only 39 times in 668 plate appearances, and in fact would fan only 369 times in his career while hitting 361 home runs, an astonishing statistic. Those 39 strikeouts must have been due to his rookie adjustments—he never had that many again. There was no Rookie of the Year Award before 1947, but Joe's 1936 season set a standard few rookies could ever dream of.

Joe was the first rookie to play in the All-Star Game, and from 1936 to 1942 he played in every inning of every one.

It was in 1936 that Hyman Rotkin opened the Jerome Cafeteria on River Avenue, where fans could dine off a tray before or after games. The cafeteria was almost as much an institution as DiMaggio until it closed in 1976.

In addition to DiMaggio, the Yanks would also welcome Jake Powell from Washington (the Chapman trade, in mid-June) and Monte Pearson from Cleveland, obtained in a trade for Johnny Allen. Pearson for Allen was the trade of two temperamental yet talented players, and Allen was far from done—he would go 20–10 in 1936, 15–1 in 1937 (losing on the last day), and 14–8 in 1938. Pearson, a six-foot right-hander from the University of California, had broken in with the Indians in '33 with a 2.33 ERA but had fallen to 8–13 by '35. Considered both temperamental and a bit of a hypochrondriac, he was made trade bait by the Indians, who were set to give Bob Feller his place in the rotation in '36. Monte would give the Yankees five seasons and compile a 63–27 record, a .700 percentage.

The Yanks also added a workhorse, Irving "Bump" Hadley, a big right-hander, in another trade with Washington. Hadley was thirty-one when he joined the Yankees and had posted nine seasons of double-digit wins to that point.

With DiMaggio exciting the baseball world, the Yankees went about their business to reclaim their position atop the standings after a three-year absence. The 1936 team won 102 games to finish first by nineteen and a half, pretty much wrapping it up in early August. Attendance jumped by 220,000, and Gehrig, not undone by all the DiMaggio attention, had a .354/49/152 season, his high-water mark in home runs. He scored 167 runs and won his second MVP Award. Dickey hit .362, a record for catchers that stood until it was equaled by Mike Piazza in 1997 and broken by Joe Mauer in 2009.

Lazzeri, batting eighth, participated in a 25–2 win at Shibe Park on May 24, a Yankee record for runs in a game. Tony hit three homers that day, two of them grand slams, had 15 total bases, and drove in 11 runs in the rout. Crosetti belted two that day and DiMaggio one. The car poolers from San Francisco could barely have anticipated anything quite like this just twelve weeks earlier as they climbed into Tony's Ford for the cross-country journey to Florida.

THE FIRST SUBWAY SERIES in thirteen years found the Yankees and the Giants facing off, as they had in 1921–23. This would be their first Series without Babe Ruth. President Roosevelt, running for reelection, attended game two at the Polo Grounds, departing in the seventh inning with his party of forty-eight as automobiles drove across the field to the center-field exit.

The turning point for the 1936 World Series was game four at Yankee Stadium, with Pearson, 19–7 in the regular season, beating Carl Hubbell 5–2. It broke a seventeen-game winning streak for King Carl, including his win in the opening game of the Series, and it gave the Yanks a 3 to 1 lead in front of 66,669, a Series record attendance. After losing game five, the Yankees wrapped it up at the Polo Grounds the next day with a 13–5 win as Gomez won it with 2⅔ innings of relief work by Murphy. Jake Powell scored eight runs and hit .455 for the Series, making the new guy very much welcome, while Lazzeri added a grand slam and drove in seven, capping his last big season with the Yankees.

Dickey hit only .120 in the Series, but it was later discovered that he had played with two broken bones in his left wrist after being hit by a pitch late in the season. He asked Doc Painter to keep his secret, and he didn't miss an inning.

As was the custom at the Polo Grounds, where the clubhouses were in the outfield, the fans exited with the players across the field, celebrating with the Yankees and consoling the Giants until the players climbed their staircases to continue on their own. It was a practice unimaginable today. Even in Yankee Stadium, fans would exit across the field toward the exits under the bleachers, although there, the players escaped to their respective dugouts.

(The practice of letting the fans onto Yankee Stadium's field after the games ended in 1966, when some aggressive fans headed straight for Mickey Mantle, determined to reach him. From that day forward, the Yankees assigned a special "Mantle detail" of ushers to form a flying wedge around him as he trotted off the field.)

IN 1937 YANKEE STADIUM redefined the bleachers, moving them in toward the flagpole and the Huggins monument from 490 feet to a less preposterous 461. Again engaging Osborn Engineering, they originally planned to double-deck the bleachers and enlarge the ballpark's capacity to eighty-four thousand, but that plan never played out.

In '37 the Yankees again won 102 games and their ninth pennant—tying the Athletics for the most in the American League—and their sixth world championship, the most of any franchise. It is a distinction they've maintained ever since.

Gomez and Ruffing were both 20-game winners. Gehrig hit .351 and ran his consecutive-game streak to 1,965. After the season, he went off to Hollywood to make *Rawhide* after shooting the opening scene at Grand Central Terminal.

DiMaggio, in his second season, led the league with 46 homers and 151 runs scored while batting .346. The 46 homers by a right-handed hitter stood as a club record until Alex Rodriguez hit 48 in 2005 (and then 54 in 2007).

The team drew just under a million in the year that finally saw the right-field grandstand extended into fair territory, creating a right-field bullpen to separate it from the bleachers. The upper deck that was never there for Babe Ruth was at last in place.

The season also saw the arrival of young Tommy Henrich. Henrich, from the sandlots of Massillon, Ohio, signed with the Indians in 1934 but found himself going nowhere fast in the Cleveland organization. By the end of 1936, there was confusion over which team was actually controlling him—the Indians, their New Orleans farm team, or the independently owned Milwaukee Brewers, to whom New Orleans claimed to have sold him. Henrich and his dad decided to write to Commissioner Landis about his situation. He met with Landis personally, bringing no legal representation with him. The teams sent their most eloquent officials. Landis sided with Henrich and declared him a free agent, stating Henrich "has been 'covered up' for the benefit of the Cleveland club and that his transfer by New Orleans to Milwaukee was directed by the Cleveland club and prevented his advancement."

"The judge could have let it go," said Henrich, "but because he didn't like [Cleveland] scout Cy Slapnicka, and because I think he got a kick out of me writing to him and standing up for my rights, he declared me a free agent."

He signed with the Yankees in April of '37 for a $25,000 bonus, rejecting eight other offers, and was farmed out to Newark.

In early May, after losing two in a row at Detroit, McCarthy overheard his outfielder Roy Johnson saying, "What's the guy expect to do, win every day?"

Johnson, a thirty-four-year-old veteran, should have known better. As soon as McCarthy returned to the team hotel, he phoned Barrow. "Get rid of Johnson," he said. "I don't want him with us anymore. Get rid of him right away."

"Why the big rush?" asked Barrow.

"I won't play him again," McCarthy said adamantly. "Send me the kid who's at Newark." And that was how Henrich got to the major leagues.

McCarthy could be like that. All business. Some years later, his backup catcher, Buddy Rosar, wanted to leave the team to go to Buffalo where his wife was having a baby. McCarthy said no, and Rosar went AWOL. End of Buddy Rosar.

Henrich didn't let this opportunity get away. The man who would come to be known as Old Reliable hit .320 in 67 games for the Yankees that year as he began an eleven-season run (interrupted by war for three years) that would get him to nine World Series.

1937 also marked the strange demise of Johnny Broaca.* He'd pitched for ex–Red Sox star Joe Wood at Yale, and although a bad arm forced him from the team, he did graduate from the prestigious school and entered pro baseball. He joined the Yankees in 1934 and in his third start pitched a one-hitter against St. Louis, striking out 10.

The native of Lawrence, Massachusetts, would go 12–9 in that rookie season, then 15–7 in 1935. He was 12–7 in the world championship year of '36, and then got married after the season. But on July 16, 1937, with his wife eight months pregnant, he abruptly left the team, leaving no trace of his whereabouts, not even to his wife. He disappeared. No player had ever jumped the team since Ruppert owned it.

When a reporter asked McCarthy if it might cost him his World Series share, McCarthy snapped, "Might? He's lost that already!"

By September his wife had filed for divorce, and the proceeding, on Cape Cod, was the stuff of tabloid journalism. She accused him of beating her, chasing her out of the house in her underwear, threatening to cut her throat or shoot her in the head before giving her any money.

When, late in '38, the Yankees made an overture to bring him back, he insisted on being reimbursed for medical expenses. "Forget it," he was told. He had tried his hand at pro boxing but hadn't won a fight. The Yankees sent him off to Cleveland, where he pitched in relief in 1939. He went to the Giants in 1940 but never got into a game. They released him, and he was done.

---

* Broaca is believed to have been the first Yankee to wear glasses.

After domestic duty during World War II, he returned to Lawrence and earned a living as a laborer. The Yale grad and owner of a World Series ring—teammate of Ruth, Gehrig, and DiMaggio—was now digging ditches. He had no contact with his son. He lived in a small apartment. His fellow workers knew to never ask him about baseball. And he died in 1985, his son never having a clue about what went wrong.

ON MAY 25, the baseball world was shocked by what looked like a repeat of the horrific Mays-Chapman moment of seventeen years earlier.

The Yanks were hosting the Tigers, whose player-manager, Mickey Cochrane, was in the lineup facing Bump Hadley. In the third inning, Cochrane tied the game 1–1 with a home run. He came to bat again in the fifth with a man on. The count was 3 and 1 when Hadley threw a fastball that struck Mickey in the head. He threw up his right arm to protect himself, but it was too late. Dickey watched him fall to the ground, screaming, "God almighty!"

Cochrane was carried on a stretcher to a waiting ambulance and on to St. Elizabeth's Hospital. Some players cried; others prayed. Cochrane was one of the most well-liked players in baseball. He hovered between life and death for forty-eight hours. A leading brain specialist attended to him, along with Dr. Robert Emmett Walsh, the Yankees' team doctor. Hadley went to the hospital, but didn't get to Mickey's bedside. Bump said, "I don't know why the ball sailed; it just did."

Cochrane suffered a triple skull fracture. Ten days went by before he was placed on a special railroad car to Detroit. Fortunately for Hadley, he did not have Mays's reputation as a headhunter, and given the circumstances—a 3-and-1 count, a runner on—no one thought this was intentional. To his great relief, Detroit fans cheered Hadley when he pitched there on June 5. Cochrane recovered, but never played another game. That was how his Hall of Fame career ended.

The Yanks won the '37 World Series over the Giants in five games, as Lazzeri batted .400 to lead all hitters in his farewell to the Yanks. He would be released later in October, the Yankees having his replacement, Joe Gordon, ready to move up from Newark.

(On August 6, 1946, Tony Lazzeri died at forty-two. He suffered a fall down the stairs at his Millbrae, California, home and was discovered about thirty-six hours later by his wife, who had been returning from vacation.

Whether brought on by a heart attack or an epileptic fit, it was an unexpected loss for his friends in the Yankee organization.)

Gomez won the first and last games with complete-game gems, with Ruffing and Pearson winning the other two. Only Carl Hubbell could stop the Yanks, winning game four 7–3 over Hadley. The clincher was again at the Polo Grounds, and again the Giants had to sit in their silent clubhouse and listen to "The Beer Barrel Polka" being belted out next door by the jubilant Yankees.

IN 1938 IT was Gordon at second, already being called the best second baseman in the league. Nicknamed "Flash" after the comic book character, he became the first second baseman to top 20 homers, and his 25 was a rookie record for second basemen until Dan Uggla of Florida broke it in 2006. Gordon was born in Los Angeles but raised in Arizona and Portland, Oregon. He played halfback for the University of Oregon and was signed by Essick after his sophomore year.

As his daughter lovingly explained at her late father's induction to the Hall of Fame in 2009, Joe was also a classical violinist, a cowboy, and a ventriloquist.

This time the Yanks won 99 and finished nine and a half games on top in winning their tenth pennant. So deep was the Yankee organization by this time that the 1938 "Little World Series" for the minor league championship pitted Newark against Kansas City—both Yankee farm clubs.

Gehrig's streak passed 2,000 and went to 2,122, although his hitting fell off and he batted under .300 for the first time: .295 with 29 homers. There was no evidence of an illness or an injury, and some spoke of the natural progression of age. But if he was in the early stages of his illness, then it was a remarkable year, playing every game and belting his record 23rd career grand slam.

Henrich took over in right while Selkirk shifted to left. DiMaggio held out almost all of spring training, looking for $40,000, accepting $25,000—and when he signed, he had to miss two weeks of the season to get in shape. The Yanks were 6–6 without him, and when he returned, he collided on a short fly ball with Gordon, knocking out both players. He heard boos when he returned to Yankee Stadium for the first time, but they didn't last long.

On Memorial Day, May 30, a crowd of 81,841 crammed into the stadium for the biggest crowd in club history. Fire-safety laws were loosely enforced at the time, and so long as people were lined up for tickets, they were ushered in.

The Yankees held their first Ladies' Day on April 30, 1938, allowing 4,903 women in for free. (The announced Saturday crowd was sixteen thousand.) Ladies' Day would continue until 1972, when a few men brought suit against the team, claiming the free admission discriminated against them. They won, and that was the end of Ladies' Day for everybody.

ON AUGUST 27, Monte Pearson, working on two days' rest, hurled the first ever no-hitter at Yankee Stadium, with Gordon and Henrich each homering twice in a 13–0 pounding of his old team, the Indians. Pearson, who won his tenth straight and went to 13–5, walked two in the third no-hitter in team history. The thirties was such a hitter's era that there were only eight pitched in the majors for the entire decade.

Thirty-year-old Spud Chandler was 14–5 in his first full year with the team. A product of Georgia, Chandler had started his minor league career at twenty-four. He was unspectacular in the minors, and his 14–13 record at Newark in '36 hardly foretold big-league stardom, but the six-foot righthander was a battler. He had graduated from the University of Georgia and played halfback for the Bulldogs. He lived in Royston, Ty Cobb's hometown. Chandler had fought his way up the ladder to reach the majors, and by the time he was done, he had the highest winning percentage of any pitcher with 100 victories (he was 109-43, .717), and he would be the only Yankee pitcher to capture an MVP Award, winning in 1943.

If the season had a low moment, it was provided by Jake Powell. With radio still fairly new, Powell agreed to do a pregame interview on Chicago's WGN with White Sox announcer Bob Elson prior to the July 29 game. Elson asked, "What do you do in the off-season to keep in shape?" Powell, who had barnstormed against Negro League teams in the off-season, responded, "I'm a policeman in Dayton, Ohio, and I keep in shape by cracking niggers off the head with my nightstick."

Certainly in the all-white clubhouses of 1938, a line like this would have gotten its share of laughter and would have been forgotten. One might even have suspected that a player could get away with such a statement to a broader audience. There was little thought to racial sensitivities. Judge Landis had always maintained that there was no color line in baseball. "If a

Negro player was ever to show the kind of talents necessary to play in the Major Leagues, there is no rule to stop it," Landis said, in various ways, over the years. But if not under pressure, Landis would probably have ignored Powell's ill-chosen words. After all, they weren't recorded, were heard only once, and outright denial or saying it was "out of context" seemed available choices.

But the words were overheard in Chicago, word spread, and outrage grew. A group of negro leaders went to Landis (who was headquartered in Chicago) demanding that Powell be banned for life.

This demand actually gave Landis wiggle room. He could reject the demand and still punish Powell, winning on all scores. That he did punish Powell was seen by some as no less than startling, giving his previous lack of any sensitivity on matters of race.

He suspended Powell for ten games, the first time that a major league player had ever been suspended for a racist remark. Furthermore, Barrow and Ruppert, after hearing talk of a possible negro boycott of Ruppert's beer, ordered that Powell make an "apology tour" of black newspapers and black-owned bars in Harlem. As outrageous as Powell's remarks were, it was equally surprising that Landis and the Yankees then did what was viewed as the "right thing." It would still be eight years before the Dodgers would sign Jackie Robinson, but the Powell affair was a stepping stone, a moment when the white press had no choice but to visit bigotry in the game.

After the 1940 season, the Yankees sent Jake Powell to the minors, although he would later return to play during the war with the Senators and Phillies.

In November of 1948, he and his girlfriend were brought in for questioning over a bounced check at a Washington hotel. He asked if he could speak to his girlfriend alone, at which point he apologized for the bad check and asked her to marry him. She told him no, admonished him for getting into the mess, and went home. He gave her taxi money and shouted at her, "To hell with it. I'm going to end it all."

And he did. He took out a handgun and shot himself in the right temple. He was forty.

THE '38 WORLD SERIES was again against the Cubs (marking Powell's return to Chicago), and this time the Yanks gave them a 4–0 pasting in rapid style, with Ruffing, Gomez, and Pearson winning the first three and Ruffing winning the finale at Yankee Stadium. Frankie Crosetti became a hero in game two when he took Dizzy Dean deep in the eighth inning at Wrigley Field to give the Yanks the lead, although DiMaggio added a two-run homer in the ninth for dessert.

The Yankees, in winning their seventh world championship, became the first team to win three in a row, and "Break up the Yankees!" was a cry gaining more momentum. They were just too good.

Playing in his final World Series, Lou Gehrig played errorless ball at first but managed only four singles with no RBI.

Chapter Sixteen

THE YEAR 1938 HADN'T BEEN A healthy one for Colonel Ruppert. He wasn't in the clubhouse to celebrate the World Series victory; he listened at home over the radio. His old partner, Tillinghast L'Hommedieu Huston, died on his plantation on Butler Island near Brunswick, Georgia, on March 28. The Colonel issued a statement remembering the man with whom he'd entered baseball, but he couldn't attend the funeral.

In April he had some setbacks, notably phlebitis, that began to confine him to his 1120 Fifth Avenue apartment. He went to opening day, but only one other game all season. In November he had to skip his usual winter trip to French Lick, Indiana, and was treated at Lenox Hill Hospital. He got through Christmas and New Year's, but then deteriorated rapidly. News stories alerted people that his final days might be near. He was seventy-one, and had owned the Yankees for twenty-four seasons.

Babe Ruth, keeping posted via the newspapers, was just leaving the hospital himself after some heart tests.

On Thursday, January 12, 1939, Ruth phoned Al Brennan, the Yankees' treasurer and the Colonel's secretary of twenty-seven years.

"I want to see the Colonel," he said.

"Come right up," said Brennan. It was around 7:00 P.M., and Ruppert had been in an oxygen tent since 4:30. It was removed for the Ruth visit.

He managed to tell his nurse, "I want to see the Babe." But Ruth was already in the room. He held and patted Ruppert's hand.

"Colonel," he said, "you're going to snap out of this and you and I are going to the opening game of the season."

That got a faint smile out of the old brewmaster, and as Ruth prepared to leave, the Colonel was heard to say, "Babe . . ." and nothing more.

Ruth left in tears. It was the only time the Colonel had called him that. Ruppert called everyone by his last name, and in his German accent, Babe had always been "Root." That evening, Ruppert was given Last Rites of the Catholic Church.

On Friday the thirteenth, Ruppert awoke, drank some orange juice, and fell into unconsciousness. At his bedside were Brennan, his brother George, his sister and her son, and his late sister's daughter. He died at 10:28 A.M.

Barrow took Brennan's call at the Yankees' Forty-second Street office and began alerting the world. Within minutes, messages of condolence were being read on the radio. Ruppert had been so many things—a baseball man, brewer, patron of the arts, real estate investor, and more.

The *Times* reported that he was one of the richest men in the world, despite going through Prohibition and then the Great Depression. They estimated an estate at up to $100 million, where it had been $60 million before the crash. They attributed this good fortune to his real estate investments, said to be worth $30 million. These included the thirty-six story Ruppert Building at Fifth and Forty-fourth St., a thirty-five-story building at Third and Forty-fourth, and a twenty-three-story building at Madison and Fortieth. In 1915, when Ruppert had inherited his estate from his father, it was valued at just under $6.5 million.

Ruppert's place among the wealthiest Americans was a tribute to fortitude. He had survived anti-German feelings in the throes of World War I. He had survived Prohibition and laid off few workers by making near beer (sold at the stadium), producing syrups and sweeteners, and bottling soda. He had survived the Great Depression by quietly selling off his rare book collection, many of his racehorses, and the Hudson River Stock Farm/Driving Park (where Poughkeepsie Speedway now sits).

Funeral services were first scheduled for Monday at St. Ignatius Loyola on Eighty-fourth and Park, but it was clear they had to be moved to St. Patrick's Cathedral, which held so many more. The police estimated that some fifteen thousand lined the streets along Fifth Avenue and across the street into Rockefeller Center to watch the spectacle of this famous man on his final journey.

From baseball, Ruth represented former players and Gehrig the current team. Honus Wagner was there, as was Clark Griffith, Barrow, Weiss, McCarthy, tap dancer Bill "Bojangles" Robinson (who used to dance atop the dugout to entertain the fans), Mayor Fiorello LaGuardia, Al Smith, Senator

Robert Wagner, former mayor John Fitzgerald of Boston, Horace Stoneham of the Giants, Marie Mulvey of the Dodgers, as well as the owners of Schaefer and Rheingold breweries and William Burckhardt, a forty-nine-year employee of Ruppert Brewery.

A fifty-car motorcade departed St. Patrick's for Kensico Cemetery in Valhalla, New York, about a forty minute drive into Westchester County. There he was interred in the family mausoleum along with his parents.

He was laid to rest as defending world champion. He would have liked that. He was a man who liked winning a World Series in four straight, never mind the extra revenue the additional games might bring.

Barrow said he had no knowledge of what Ruppert's wishes were for the team, "but I know that whatever they are, he wanted the Yankees to go on, and that we will do."

On opening day of the 1940 season, a plaque honoring Jacob Ruppert was hung on the center-field wall behind the Huggins monument, saying GENTLEMAN-AMERICAN-SPORTSMAN, and of course the Seventh Regiment Band played Ruppert's favorite, "Just a Song at Twilight."

BARROW WAS RELIEVED to see how careful Ruppert was with the Yankees. He appeared to have taken better care of them in his will than any of his other holdings. He instructed his estate to pay all inheritance taxes on the Yankees and to furnish the necessary funds to continue to run the team at existing levels. Of all his holdings, only the Yankees were left "intact and inviolate."

However, it took almost six years to settle the estate, and it wasn't anywhere near as good as expected.

He did a most unusual thing with the ownership and management of the team. He left the club to three women in his life—his nieces, Helen Ruppert Silleck-Holleran and Ruth Rita Silleck-McGuire (the married daughters of his sister Amanda Ruppert Silleck Jr.), and a "friend," Helen Winthorpe Weyant.

The nieces lived in Greenwich, Connecticut, and had shown little interest in baseball, occasionally attending an opening day or a World Series game and asking little about the club.

"Winnie" Weyant, on the other hand, was a constant companion to the Colonel. Journalist Dan Daniel visited Ruppert at his estate in upstate Garrison and found Miss Weyant very much engaged in the team's operation, very much a student of baseball.

"She wasn't sure about Gordon succeeding Lazzeri," recalled Daniel. "When I told her Gordon would jump right in and make good, she laughed, and doubted it," he wrote.

"So many people are worried about Tony," Ruppert chuckled.

Weyant, thirty-seven, was a former actress who had last acted off-Broadway in 1929. She never attended a game with Ruppert but was seen with him at social events, notably at the announcement that the Colonel was to help fund Admiral Richard Byrd's second Antarctic expedition in 1934. She was clearly the woman of the house at the four-hundred-acre estate in Garrison, walking the Saint Bernards and guiding Daniel around.

Informed by reporters at her West Forty-fifth Street apartment of her inheritance, she was described by the *Times* as having spent a "semi-hysterical day." She said she had "no idea why so much money had been left to her."

"I feel very honored by it all," she said. "I'm surprised and frightened." When asked when she had first met the Colonel, she said "he had been a friend of the family for a number of years." Asked what her father did for a living, she replied, "He was a businessman, let it go at that."

Now she owned a third of the New York Yankees.

Her brother Rex, in fact, had been assistant traveling secretary to Mark Roth for the previous three years. (A footnote: Weyant succeeded Roth and had no assistant. Neither did any of his successors. But the popular 1990s TV show *Seinfeld*, which regularly lampooned George Steinbrenner, had the character of George Costanza serve in just that position during two seasons of the show's run.)

The three women owned the team in equal parts. However, it was a four-person group of trustees who would actually run the team. They included Amanda's husband, Henry Garrison Silleck Jr.; Jacob's brother George; Byron Clark, Ruppert's personal attorney; and Barrow. When George Ruppert stepped aside, he made Barrow president of the team, claiming he was entitled because of his years of service, his stature in the game, and his knowledge of the business. George, although nearly seventy himself, ran the brewery.

George Weiss was promoted to secretary (and heir apparent) to Barrow.

Any decision to sell the team could be made only by unanimous consent of the four trustees, with no involvement by the three owners, although they could request the trustees to vote on it. The club could be sold only as a whole, not in pieces.

———

DESPITE THE EARLY predictions of an estate worth up to $100 million, by 1945 it was finally resolved that the gross value was just $9.5 million, and the net $4.7 million. Ruppert owed Barrow half a million dollars. According to family historian K. Jacob Ruppert, the unveiling of the final numbers was a shock to many, owing largely to late tax filings, properties mortgaged to the hilt, and not enough cash on hand to meet the deadlines for the estate taxes. It was a far more complicated organization of the estate than was first believed.

Ruppert's Yankee stock was actually held by the Jacob Ruppert Holding Corporation, which oversaw his real estate, and Manufacturer's Trust had a lien on the company. Had they chosen to do so, the bank could have become the owners of the Yankees.

Despite the woeful financial setback, the Yankees would continue to be the model for sports operation in America. Barrow, Weiss, and McCarthy enjoyed a wonderful relationship in which no man stepped on the other's toes. Separating the owners from the management team proved very effective. George Steinbrenner liked to say that "buying the Yankees was like buying the *Mona Lisa*," which meant Ruppert was Da Vinci.

Ruth Rita Silleck-McGuire died in 1962, and Helen Ruppert Silleck-Holleran died in 1978.

Winnie Weyant never married, lived in Westchester County, and died there in the 1980s. She left her money to various Catholic charities.

SINCE RUPPERT HAD enjoyed the World Series on the radio, the coming at last of broadcasting to Yankee fans in 1939 should not have been a surprise. The three New York teams had resisted this move for a long while. If it was his last "blessing" for Yankee fans, it was a meaningful one.

One could almost hear the dialogue in the Forty-second Street offices: "Radio? Give away the product for free? No one will ever pay to come to a game!"

The forward thinkers who understood marketing could see that properly done, broadcasting could be used to make the in-park experience something to be coveted, to produce "I wish we were there!" moments—and then there was the announcer telling you when the next game was, and how you could get tickets!

With the five-year agreement to black out radio in New York having expired, it was Larry MacPhail of the Dodgers who took the lead, hiring Red

Barber from Cincinnati and broadcasting all 154 regular-season games. It was a masterstroke; Red, despite his unfamiliar southern accent, was a big hit. And there was something "exotic" about listening live to out-of-town games.

The Yankees and the Giants would play it safer. They would do only home games (which seemed like a backward philosophy if they were worried about cutting into attendance). Since they were never home at the same time, the same station—WABC—and the same announcers, Arch McDonald and his young assistant Melvin Allen Israel, could do both teams.

McDonald, the more senior broadcaster, moved to Washington the following year and became a fixture there. As for Melvin Allen Israel, he was Mel Allen on the air, and he would become the Voice of the Yankees.

Just twenty-six when he sat in Yankee Stadium on opening day of 1939, he delivered the game as Barber had—with a smooth southern accent, only not as pronounced. Few New Yorkers could have told you that he was from Alabama.

After studying at the University of Alabama, Mel worked his way to New York for a job with CBS before winning an audition to do the joint Giant/Yankee assignment. After McDonald left, he did Yankee games with screen actor Jay C. Flippen and Giants games with Joe Bolton, who would later be "Officer" Joe Bolton on WPIX children's programming.

Mel went into the army in 1941 and returned in 1946, when the two teams separated their broadcasting (the Yanks on WINS) and Mel worked with Russ Hodges for three years. There were few Yankee games broadcast during the war, so Red Barber and the Dodgers owned the New York airwaves. But from 1946 until he departed after 1964, Mel Allen was as big a star as any of the players he reported on. He got almost as much fan mail—and responded to all of it. So big did he become in broadcasting circles that it would be unthinkable to have anyone else known as the Voice of the Yankees, even a half century following his initial departure from the booth. (He would later come back to do cable broadcasts from 1978 to 86.)

And "man, oh, man," could he sell that Ballantine beer and those Yankee home games. Giant fans and Dodger fans couldn't stand to hear his voice. They were convinced that Mel was a Yankee fan through and through, and all of his broadcasts showed that prejudice. But he never said "we" or "us" about the team; he delivered it very straight compared to his contemporaries elsewhere. It was just that his voice so often translated into a Yankee victory, and the ones who rooted against the Yanks couldn't stand the sound of it.

As important as radio and then television advertising would be to baseball, it is worth noting that stadium billboard advertising in its time, appearing in newsreels and newspapers, was the major place for advertisers
to put their money before broadcasting truly caught on. No billboard advertiser was more prominent in Yankee Stadium than Gem razor blades, which
dominated the outfield billboard signage, and before that, the fronting of
the left-field bleachers right at field level, going back to opening day of Yankee Stadium in 1923 and on through 1957.

LOU GEHRIG WAS clearly slipping in 1938, but that was considered the normal aging in the life of any athlete. No one realized he was playing with a
serious illness.

But in spring training in '39, he played like someone who would be cut
in the first round of roster trims, if he hadn't been Lou Gehrig. He was
unsteady. Doc Painter saw him fall down when he couldn't lift his leg high
enough to slip it into his trousers. No one moved to help him; "He was lying there like a helpless puppy," said Painter. "We dared not help him up.
He finally crawled to his feet . . . There was a tear in his eye."

He made errors on simple plays. He had no oomph in his bat. Teammates
were patting him on the back if he hit a routine fly ball. His great muscula-
ture was clearly diminished.

The press wasn't being discreet. Everyone was writing about his awful
spring and signs that he might be done.

The Iron Horse just wasn't cutting it. Babe Dahlgren, who was going to
play some third base and spell Rolfe, was quietly taking ground balls at
first—just in case.

Gehrig took some days off during spring training but hadn't improved
by opening day. Still, he was out there: He was the team's captain, and he
hadn't missed a game since 1925. If he was going to come out of the lineup,
it would be his call, not McCarthy's. He deserved that.

On April 30 in New York, he played in his 2,130th consecutive game. He
went 0-for-4. The team then boarded a train for Detroit. Lou knew what had
to be done.

In the lobby of the Book-Cadillac Hotel in Detroit, sitting next to sportswriter Charley Segar, Gehrig spotted McCarthy and asked if he could talk
to him in his room. The two men went upstairs.

There, Gehrig told him that he was taking himself out of the lineup "for

Brooklyn native Wee Willie Keeler, the highest-paid player in the new American League at $10,000, could "hit 'em where they ain't" and could keep his mitt in his back pocket too. Well, they all could. (Rogers Photo Archives)

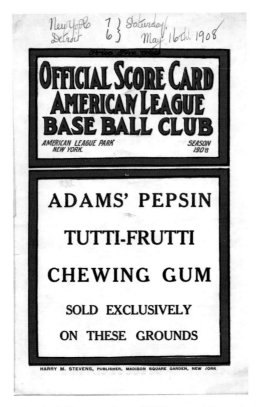

Even by 1908, neither "Highlanders" nor "Hilltop Park" was included on score-cards, despite belief today that they were commonly used names.

Hal Chase was a great fielding first baseman, except for the times when he was thought to be a little slow covering the base (in games on which he might have also bet). He also managed the team in 1910–11. (Rogers Photo Archives)

Clark Griffith, the team's first manager, and still an active pitcher at the time, shown here in Hilltop Park. New York batters would brush the N on their jersey for "no" and the Y for "yes" in hit-and-run situations. (Rogers Photo Archives)

Artist William Feldman painted this view of Hilltop Park during a game between the Highlanders (white uniforms) and the Chicago White Sox. The apartment complex towering over right center field still stands on West 168th Street. The billboard for Bull Durham tobacco contributed to the use of the term "bullpen." (Bill Goff/GoodSportsArt)

Ray "Slim" Caldwell had 96 wins for the Yankees starting in 1910, then went to Cleveland, where he no-hit his old teammates two weeks after being struck by lightning and knocked unconscious while on the mound. (Rogers Photo Archives)

Considered "the most corrupt police chief in New York history," Big Bill Devery was the man who laid out the route for ticker tape parades on lower Broadway, and was co-owner of the Highlanders with Frank Farrell. He lost a bid for mayor of New York in 1903, but a few buttons survive. His obituary made little mention of his ownership of the team.

Frank Farrell, New York's Pool Room King (seated with his elbow out), in the owner's box in the Polo Grounds, to which the Yankees moved in 1913. He first set up the team's offices in the new Flatiron Building on Twenty-third and Broadway. (Bain News Service)

Artist Bill Purdom captures Babe Ruth taking a mighty swing in the Polo Grounds in 1922, the Yankees' final season there, and a championship year for both tenants, the Yanks and Giants. Although the new Yankee Stadium would be called "the House That Ruth Built," Babe confessed to actually finding the Polo Grounds more to his liking. (Bill Goff/GoodSportsArt)

Joe McCarthy Day in 1951 brought six Yankee managers together: (l to r) Bucky Harris (1947–48), Bob Shawkey (1930), Clark Griffith (1903–08), McCarthy (1931–46), Casey Stengel (1949–60), and Roger Peckinpaugh (1914). The team's sleeve patch honored the golden anniversary of the American League. From 1936 to 1943, McCarthy had a .707 home winning percentage. (Rogers Photo Archives)

Frank "Home Run" Baker led the AL in homers four times while with the Athletics, then joined the Yankees in 1916, employing an agent to negotiate a three-year contract. He was part of their first two pennant winners, in 1921 and 1922. (Rogers Photo Archives)

Carl Mays's purchase by the Yankees, while under suspension by Boston, was a highly charged issue for baseball and helped establish Yankee power even over league president Ban Johnson. Then in 1920, Mays's high inside submarine pitch fatally struck the Indians' Ray Chapman. Mays was taken to the local police station but not charged with any crime. (Rogers Photo Archives)

After Lou Gehrig became the first twentieth-century player to hit four home runs in a game (1932), he had a "photo op" with the only nineteenth-century player to do it—sixty-seven-year-old Bobby Lowe, who did it in 1894. (Rogers Photo Archives)

In 2011, a team of graphic artists and researchers created the first full-color look at Yankee Stadium as it appeared in its opening season in 1923. In the exterior drawing, the entrance to the Yankee clubhouse is to the left of the lead parked vehicle, with the windows running along the third-base line and offering the players a street view. Of note in the interior drawing is the wide running track, intended for track meets, the loose chairs occupying the first few rows of box seats, the elevated subway line running beyond the outfield, and the distant Concourse Plaza Hotel, which opened in October of that year. The Gem razor blade advertising was a fixture until 1957. (David Kramer, Matt O'Connor, J. E. Fullerton, Michael Hagan, Scott Weber, Michael Rudolf, Dennis Concepcion, and Chris Campbell)

Urban Shocker returned to the Yankees from the St. Louis Browns in 1925, and, in the championship seasons of 1926–27, won 37 games. But an enlarged heart, which forced him to sleep in a near sitting-up position, claimed him in 1928 at the age of thirty-seven. The family waited until the Yankees arrived in St. Louis to play the Browns so that the team could attend his funeral. (Rogers Photo Archives)

Lefty Gomez (l) and Red Ruffing (r) won 420 between them for New York. Ruffing, who came to the Yanks after a 39–96 record at Boston, would be the winningest right-hander in club history for many years to come, with 231. Gomez, known for his easy personality, rarely smiled for photographers, but was always quick with a joke. (Rogers Photo Archives)

Babe Ruth loved the spotlight and—with Charles Lindbergh, Charlie Chaplin, and whoever was president—was the biggest celebrity in the land. Ruth never wore the interlocking "NY" logo on his jersey as a player, as it wasn't reinstituted until two years after he left the Yankees. (Rogers Photo Archives)

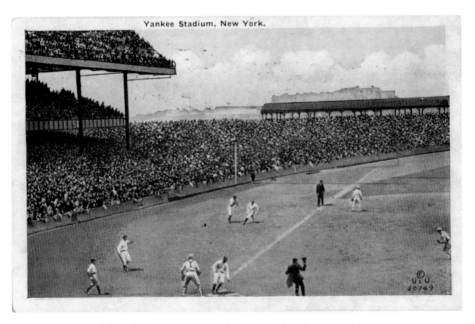

An early postcard from Yankee Stadium shows a packed house watching Ruth (presumably) heading for home with a throw on the way. The left-field grandstand did not extend to the foul line until 1928. The right-field grandstand was extended in 1937, and thus, Babe never hit one into the upper deck in right, which was all bleachers while he played.

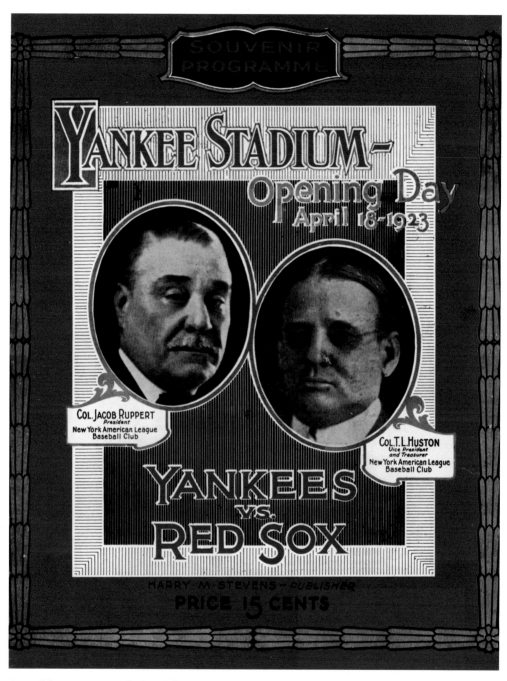

A special program was designed for opening day of Yankee Stadium in 1923, featuring the team's co-owners, Col. Jacob Ruppert and the soon-to-depart Col. Tillinghast L. Huston. A reprint of the full twenty-page program was given to all fans at the old park's final weekend in 1973.

The "Murderer's Row" Yankees of the late 1920s featured an infield of (l to r) Lou Gehrig at first, Tony Lazzeri at second, Mark Koenig at short, and Joe Dugan at third. The 1927 Yankees used just twenty-five players without a roster change all season. (Baseball Hall of Fame)

Manager Miller Huggins (l) with his ace right-hander Waite Hoyt, from Erasmus Hall High School. Hoyt regaled Cincinnati radio audiences with his Ruth stories during a long broadcast career with the Reds. (The Yankees switched to their now-familiar navy-blue caps in 1922 after winning their first pennant.) (Rogers Photo Archives)

The Yankees outfield of (l to r) Tommy Henrich, Joe DiMaggio, and Charlie Keller after winning the 1941 World Series at Ebbets Field. Henrich, who hit the first "walk-off" home run in World Series history in 1949, was sixth on the team's all-time home run list when he retired, just one behind Keller. DiMaggio played in every inning of every All-Star Game from his rookie season of 1936 through 1942. (Rogers Photo Archives)

The first Yankee locker room—used from 1923 until a new one opened in 1946 on the first-base side, where open stalls replaced metal lockers. The Gehrig and Ruth lockers were given to the Hall of Fame. Pop Logan and Pete Sheehy ran Yankee clubhouses from 1903 to 1985. (Rogers Photo Archives)

Lou Gehrig Appreciation Day, July 4, 1939, when Lou delivered his unscripted remarks in what came to be considered "Baseball's Gettysburg Address." His 1939 teammates, his 1927 teammates, the Washington Senators opponents, and the ground crew (in neckties, at rear) all stood by, with many fans hearing Lou's strong New York accent for the first time. This was the first year Yankee games were broadcast on radio. (Rogers Photo Archives)

In September 1938, *Life* magazine sent artist Howard Brodie on assignment to capture "life on the road" with the team. With the pennant nearly clinched, Brodie saw a relaxed team at work, and a two-page spread in the October 3 issue of the popular magazine featured twelve of his sketches, six of which are reproduced here. Brodie died in 2010 at the age of ninety-four. (Brodie Family)

Pitcher Bump Hadley uses a slingshot and rolled-up tinfoil to target (l to r) Bill Dickey, Jake Powell, and Joe DiMaggio.

Bill Dickey checks himself out in the mirror. Brodie reported that he did it five times in a half-hour.

Yankee trainer Doc Painter rubs down an unidentified player on the training table. The man seated at the left, fighting a bad cold with hot towels, is reporter Rud Rennie of the *Herald-Tribune*.

Lou Gehrig and Joe DiMaggio listen to manager Joe McCarthy talking about cures for sore arms.

Lou Gehrig, wearing an old-fashioned long nightgown, heads off to bed at the team hotel. This would be Lou's last month as a productive ballplayer. By the spring of 1939, ALS had robbed his body of its strength. In all likelihood, he was already carrying the disease at this time.

Breakfast in bed for DiMaggio (in just his third year) as he begins his day in red silk pajamas, with swing music on the radio and a cigarette in his mouth.

In 1941, Joe DiMaggio tied the major league hitting-streak record of 44 games and went on to reach 56, a record many feel will stand forever. After his failed attempt at 57, he hit safely in 17 more, for 73 out of 74. (Rogers Photo Archives)

the good of the team." In his mind, he thought maybe he'd take two days off, maybe play after the Detroit series.

There were probably tears in the room. Gehrig was a sensitive man, and both he and McCarthy had been in baseball a long time. They knew the significance of what was happening, and they probably understood that there was more to this story. How could this great man have deteriorated so quickly?

McCarthy returned to the lobby, gathered the New York writers around him, and informed them that Lou would not be playing that afternoon.

"What Lou had thought was lumbago last year when he suffered pains in the back that more than once forced his early withdrawal from games was diagnosed later as a gall bladder condition for which Gehrig underwent treatment all last winter," wrote James Dawson in the *Times*. "There had been signs for the past two years that Gehrig was slowing up. Even when a sick man, however, he gamely stuck to his chores . . . out of a driving desire to help the Yankees, always his first consideration."

At the ballpark, Lou dressed. Yankee uniforms that season had a sleeve patch for the 1939 World's Fair in Queens. Photographers gathered around him, taking dramatic shots of his peering onto the field from the dugout. The Tigers would play in this field for another sixty years. It would always be hard to look at the small visitors' dugout without recalling those photos.

Dahlgren and Gehrig met privately before the game, and Dahlgren reportedly tried to talk Lou out of his decision. But Lou slapped him on the back and said, "Go on, get out there and knock in some runs." Dahlgren hit a homer.

Gehrig, as he often did as captain, took the lineup to the plate at the start of the game. There were 11,379 fans on hand as Detroit broadcaster Ty Tyson took the public-address microphone and said, "How about a hand for Lou Gehrig, who played 2,130 games in a row before he benched himself today!"

The fans cheered as Lou walked to the dugout. He tipped his cap in appreciation, took a drink from the water fountain, and welled up in tears. Remarkably, one of the fans in the stands that day was Wally Pipp, who lived in Grand Rapids and had come to see his old team play.

Lou continued to travel with the team, and even went with them for a June 12 exhibition game with the Yanks' Kansas City farm team. Phil Rizzuto was the Blues' shortstop. Lou decided to play. Maybe something magical would happen.

He grounded out meekly to second base in the second inning. He made two errors at first base. A line drive "knocked him down and he fell on his back," wrote Kansas City catcher Clyde McCullough in 1982. At the end of the inning he left the game, and at the end of the day, he left the team and flew to the Mayo Clinic in Rochester, Minnesota, for a thorough analysis of his condition.

He spent a full week at the clinic. If amyotrophic lateral sclerosis was suspected, no one discussed it—yet—with Gehrig. ALS had been first diagnosed in 1874, but was so rare that only deeply schooled physicians would have even pondered it. It was likely that by the time he left Rochester, he had some awareness of the possibility that he had the disease, and what it meant.

In 2010, a report emerged that certain brain traumas could result in symptoms that mimic ALS. A review of his career indicated a few times when he received head trauma—a pitch that resulted in a concussion in a 1934 exhibition game in Norfolk, Virginia, being especially noteworthy. Today it would be unthinkable to come back and play the next day, but that's what Gehrig did, calling it just a bump on the head. Was it possible that the disease, which came to be called Lou Gehrig's disease, was not the cause of his decline? A medical mystery was raised.

Lou returned to his apartment at 10 Chatsworth Avenue in Larchmont, about a half mile from Barrow's home on Howard Street. There he composed letters to his doctors, asking key questions, trying to get a better read on his fate and on possible treatment. His wife, Eleanor, became a wonderful life partner through this strange journey. Lou's parents, in nearby Mount Vernon, were part of "Team Gehrig," with him at every turn.

A doctor at the Mayo Clinic prepared a letter for Lou to share with the Yankees, which was released to the media. The term *amyotrophic lateral sclerosis* was used, and it said, "In lay terms . . . a form of infantile paralysis." Said Barrow to the press, "We have bad news. Gehrig has infantile paralysis . . . The report recommends that Lou abandon any hope of continuing as an active player."

Polio was a disease the public was familiar with, and that was what was generally used to describe his condition. Nowhere was "fatal" uttered. Lou himself didn't know, at least then, whether it was curable.

But with his career over, the Yankees made plans for a July 4 Lou Gehrig Appreciation Day. He had batted .340 with 493 home runs. He had the love and admiration of the nation. He was a shining star to every parent who wanted his child to have a hero. In a way, Lou Gehrig Appreciation Day had been every day for baseball fans. Now one would take its place in the pantheon of historic Yankee moments.

July 4, a warm summer day in New York, saw more than sixty thousand pack Yankee Stadium for a tribute to Lou and a doubleheader with the Senators. This wasn't called Old-Timers' Day, but it would come to be considered the first held by the Yanks. All of Lou's living teammates from the 1927 team were invited back, lining home plate to the mound, facing current players—two of the greatest teams in baseball history.

From the '27 team: Combs (a Yankee coach) and Bengough (a Washington coach); Pipgras (umpiring that day); and in street clothes, Lazzeri, Pennock, Koenig, Dugan, Hoyt, Shawkey, Meusel, plus Schang, Pipp, and Scott from earlier teams. And there was Babe Ruth, looking robust in a white suit. Ruth and Gehrig hadn't spoken in years. Their relationship had ended on a tense note due to some slight involving their wives. It was a shame. Although so different in temperament, they had at first been wonderful pals.

The stadium ground crew, headed by Walter Owens, lined up respectfully behind the mound.

Held over forty minutes between games, the event included gifts for Lou and remarks by emcee/sportswriter Sid Mercer, Mayor LaGuardia, and others. Ed Barrow, in his first appearance ever on the field at the stadium, announced that Gehrig's number 4 would be retired, the first time such an honor had ever been bestowed on a player. Lou's best gift was a trophy from his Yankee teammates with an emotional inscription written by John Kieran of the *New York Times*:

> *We've been to the wars together,*
> *We took our foes as they came;*
> *And always you were the leader,*
> *And ever you played the game.*
> *Idol of cheering millions;*
> *Records are yours by sheaves;*
> *Iron of frame they hailed you,*
> *Decked you with laurel leaves.*
> *But higher than that we hold you,*
> *We who have known you best;*
> *Knowing the way you came through*
> *Every human test.*
> *Let this be a silent token*

Of lasting friendship's gleam
And all that we've left unspoken

      —Your pals on the Yankee team.

Finally, at McCarthy's encouragement and with fans cheering "We want Lou!" Gehrig himself stepped up to the microphone.

The PA system's echo came to be imitated as though part of Lou's remarks, but the crowd was silent and attentive. No one at the time knew his illness was to be fatal, but everyone knew it was serious, and everyone could see the baggy uniform barely hanging onto his weakening body.

Ray Robinson, later a Gehrig biographer, was a kid in the bleachers that day. He had once sought to interview Gehrig for his school newspaper (it didn't work out), but had been given free tickets to a game by his hero. Now he was just a face in the crowd, taking it all in.

"Lou had done some radio interviews over the years," said Robinson, "and he had done that *Rawhide* movie, but by and large, no one really knew what his voice sounded like until that day. I think many were surprised by the pronounced New York accent."

An exact transcript of Lou's speech, which was delivered without notes, does not exist. For a fiftieth-anniversary segment on WPIX, director John Moore and I (as producer) visited the archives of Fox Movietone News and found more footage than we previously knew to exist. We pieced together (with other sources) the following:

> Fans, for the past two weeks you have been reading about a bad break I got. Yet today I consider myself the luckiest man on the face of the earth. I have been in ballparks for seventeen years and I have never received anything but kindness and encouragement from you fans. Look at these grand men. Which of you wouldn't consider it the highlight of his career just to associate with them for even one day? Sure I'm lucky. Who wouldn't consider it an honor to have known Jacob Ruppert? Also, the builder of base-ball's greatest empire, Ed Barrow? To have spent six years with that wonderful little fellow, Miller Huggins? Then to have spent the next nine years with the outstanding leader, that smart student of psychology, the best manager in baseball today, Joe Mc-Carthy? Sure, I'm lucky. When the New York Giants, a team you

would give your right arm to beat, and vice versa, sends you a gift, that's something. When everybody down to the groundskeepers and those boys in white coats remember you with trophies, that's something. When you have a wonderful mother-in-law who takes sides with you in squabbles with her own daughter, that's something. When you have a father and mother who work all their lives so that you can have an education and build your body, it's a blessing. When you have a wife who has been a tower of strength and shown more courage than you dreamed existed, that's the finest I know. So I close in saying that I might have had a bad break, but I have an awful lot to live for. Thank you.

At that point, Ruth's sense of the dramatic took hold. He walked to Gehrig and embraced him, holding the pose for the still photographers and newsreel men.

Irv Welzer, later a Tony-winning Broadway producer but then just another twelve-year-old kid in the bleachers, recalled,

> I lived two subway stops up from the Stadium. I always tried to make doubleheaders because seeing two games for 55 cents was a good bargain.
>
> So I would have gone anyway, but since it was Lou Gehrig Appreciation Day, well, that was a bonus. And really, we knew it was the end of his career, but we didn't really understand the seriousness of his illness or thought for a moment he might be dying. We just wanted to pay tribute to our guy, a hero to us all.
>
> So I squeezed into the bleachers with all these guys, maybe 100 across, seven hours in the hot sun—all men, mostly white, all smoking. Mostly cigarettes, but a lot of cigars, and the fog of smoke over us was a constant. I always came home feeling ill.
>
> When Lou began to speak, the Stadium fell into a silence that I'd never heard before at a ballgame. People today remember the line, "luckiest man on the face of the earth," but the line that really got people reaching for their handkerchiefs—was when Lou said, "I might have been given a bad break . . ." At that moment, the seriousness seemed to hit all of us. Until then, we thought it was some illness that we couldn't pronounce, but we never thought of the enormity of this until that moment.

Gehrig stayed with the team for much of the remainder of the '39 season, even going on the road with them, but he was just a cheerleader now, watching one of the great teams in history put up a sensational record without him. He was in the 1939 team photo, but wearing only his jersey over his street clothes. In December, in a special election, Lou would be voted into the Hall of Fame. The Yankees offered him no job after '39, but La-Guardia put him on the New York City Parole Board, and he moved from Larchmont to Riverdale in the Bronx to meet residency requirements.

Gehrig's streak of 2,130 consecutive games was long considered the one record—perhaps with Joe DiMaggio's fifty-six-game hitting streak—that would stand forever. Even in the late eighties, it could be found on such a list. It was a shock to many when Cal Ripken Jr. broke it in 1995. DiMaggio, representing his teammate Gehrig, was there that night in Baltimore when the record fell.

THE '39 YANKEES, with a hefty payroll of $300,000, would win 106 games and capture their fourth straight pennant by seventeen games. DiMaggio batted .381, a mark higher than Gehrig ever achieved, as he won the batting championship and MVP Award. His 126 RBI was second to Boston rookie Ted Williams. In August, eight days apart, he homered 450 feet into the left-field bleachers, then ran down a Hank Greenberg drive to center, about 455 feet from home, catching it with his back to home plate, past the Huggins monument and flagpole. For years, people would call this the greatest catch ever at Yankee Stadium. As for his .381, an eye infection in September likely cost him a legitimate run at .400. For a long time, it looked as if he might achieve it.

Ruffing had his fourth straight 20-win season. Atley Donald, a twenty-eight-year-old rookie right-hander from Mississippi known for his nervous tics, started the year 12–0 and finished 13–3. (It wasn't his final contribution to the team: As a scout thirty-two years later, he would sign Ron Guidry.) Another rookie, Marius Russo, from Richmond Hill High School in Queens and Brooklyn College, won the pennant clincher on September 16. Yet another rookie, muscular Charlie Keller, a farmboy from Middletown, Maryland, and the University of Maryland, came up to play 111 games in the outfield and bat .334. Johnny Murphy recorded 19 saves.

Keller's signing was a good example of the abilities of Yankee scouts to get their man. Barrow, hearing that other teams were interested in him, called Krichell and told him to drop everything and rush to a semipro game in Kinston, North Carolina, where Keller was playing. He was met there by fellow Yankee scout Gene McCann. The two men took Keller for a walk at six in the morning and told him they would meet his best offer from any other team. They signed him while the other scouts slept.

The Yanks were a combined 55–11 against Chicago, St. Louis, and Philadelphia.

On May 27–28, Selkirk hit four consecutive home runs—against the same pitcher! Poor rookie Bob Joyce started on the twenty-seventh and relieved on the twenty-eighth and had the infamous honor of giving up the blasts.

On Monday, June 26, the Yankees played the first night game in their history, losing 3–2 at Philadelphia in front of thirty-three thousand. It would be seven years before they played one at home.

Two days later, they hit 13 home runs in a doubleheader against the Athletics.

ON JUNE 12, baseball's attention turned to Cooperstown for the formal opening of the Hall of Fame and the induction of the first four classes of electees. It was the one hundredth anniversary of the "birth of baseball," although the story of Abner Doubleday and baseball's invention was by then known to be a myth.

Fifteen thousand people packed the small village for the ceremonies, and Babe Ruth was the principal attraction, stopping at a drugstore to refill his cigar supply and signing autographs while saying, "I didn't know there were so many people who didn't have my autograph!"

The fact that these would ultimately sell for small fortunes at auction defied the laws of supply and demand.

Each team sent two players to represent them at the ceremonies and to play an exhibition game—two players removed from their roster for the day, as regular-season games continued to take place. The Yanks sent Selkirk and Jorgens. McCarthy and Barrow accompanied them on the trip.

Ruth, inducted that day alongside the late Willie Keeler, browsed through the museum and spotted Huggins's uniform, saying, "Gee, he was a tough little guy, and the only one who knew how to handle me."

Babe was the last to take the microphone that day. "They started something here, and the kids are keeping the ball rolling. I hope some of you kids will be in the Hall of Fame. I'm very glad that in my day I was able to

earn my place. And I hope the youngsters of today have the same opportunity to experience such a feeling."

In the "celebrity game," Babe popped out to the catcher (Jorgens) as a
pinch hitter. But everybody cheered.

Cooperstown would remain a joyous place to visit as the years rolled on,
and with more Yankee players inducted than any other team—and New York
the closest major league city—there would always be a strong Yankee connection to the Hall.

MAJOR LEAGUE BASEBALL's All-Star Game was played at Yankee Stadium
for the first time on July 11, 1939, with Gehrig in uniform as the American
League's honorary captain. Manager McCarthy had six Yanks in the starting
lineup, and the American League won 3–1 in front of 62,892 as DiMaggio
homered in the fifth inning to give the hometown fans a treat.

The '39 World Series gave the Yankees four straight world championships,
along with their record eighth overall. This time the Yankees faced the Cincinnati Reds, whose traveling secretary was Gabe Paul, many years later to
be the Yankees' team president. The Reds also featured Willard Hershberger
as a backup catcher. Hershberger had come up through the Yankee system
and had played for their great Newark teams. He'd been traded to the Reds
in December of '37.

Ten months after the Series, in the midst of the '40 season, it was Gabe
Paul who was summoned back to the Reds' hotel in Boston, where he found
Hershberger had taken his own life. While best remembered as a Cincinnati
Red, he had been a minor league teammate of more than a dozen Yankees,
and the Yanks as a team took the news hard as well.

As for the '39 Series, Ruffing, Pearson, Hadley, and Murphy (in relief of
Oral Hildebrand, who thought the Yankees were prejudiced against Protes-
tants) were the four winners as the Yankees swept again, winning the clincher
7–4 at Crosley Field as Reds fans sat quietly watching the inevitable unfold.
Pearson's win was a gem, a no-hitter for seven and a third innings, just five
outs from history. Reds catcher Ernie Lombardi broke it up with a single to
center.

The most memorable play of the Series came in the tenth inning of that
final game, when DiMaggio singled, scoring Crosetti to give the Yanks a
5–4 lead. But when Ival Goodman bobbled the ball in right, Keller (who hit
.438 with three homers in the Series) also scored, crashing into Lombardi

as the ball arrived. His slide stunned Lombardi. He dropped the throw and seemed to lie unconscious. That let DiMag score, too, in what came to be known as Lombardi's Snooze.

"I'll give you the true story on that one," teammate Johnny Vander Meer told author Bill Gilbert years later. "The throw from the outfield came in a short hop and hit Lom in the cup. You just don't get up too quick. Somebody put out the word that Lombardi went to sleep, took a snooze. But he was paralyzed! He couldn't move. With anybody but Lombardi, they'd have to carry him off the field."

Coach Art Fletcher, who received his eleventh World Series check, led the singing of "The Beer Barrel Polka" and "Sidewalks of New York" as the team, including Gehrig, celebrated its triumph.

The Yanks had begun the season with a trip to Arlington National Cemetery to visit the grave of General Abner Doubleday. They ended the year on a "snooze" from Lombardi. In between, it was perhaps the most news-filled season they ever experienced.

AT THE LEAGUE meetings after the season, a piece of legislation was introduced by Washington owner Clark Griffith, the Yanks' original manager, designed to do something—anything—to halt the Yankees' success. Griffith proposed that no rival American League team be permitted to trade or sell anyone to the defending championship club. Only a waiver purchase would be permitted. This was the first attempt to stop the Yankees by edict, and the measure passed. It would be a short-lived and weak effort to break up the Yankees.

Chapter Seventeen

TALK OF SELLING THE YANKEES began early in 1940 and waxed and waned over the next five years. The name most associated with the purchase was former postmaster general James Farley, a one time amateur first baseman from Haverstraw, New York, who went on to become the chairman of the Democratic Party and a close associate of Franklin Roosevelt. And so when Farley spoke of his interest, it was news.

Farley had been a season-ticket holder beginning in 1923 and remained so until his death in 1976, a few weeks after he was honored at opening-day ceremonies for the remodeled Yankee Stadium. (I escorted him onto the field.) He could be counted on to wear a proper straw boater in season, and was especially admired by Phil Rizzuto, who saw greatness in the man.

"He would have been a wonderful owner," Rizzuto told me on many occasions. "He loved baseball, loved the Yankees, and certainly knew how to use his political clout!"

Usually his interest—in the neighborhood of $6 million—was met with denials, but as early as the summer of '40 there was confirmation from H. Garrison Silleck Jr., one of the executors of the Ruppert estate.

Different Farley partners emerged every few months, including the owner of Phillips Petroleum and Governor James Cox of Ohio, who had run for president against Harding in 1920. Another was Basil O'Connor, who had been FDR's law partner and a creator of the March of Dimes. He was a powerful money-raiser and could have assembled a consortium for Farley to head.

The sale did not happen, but it remained part of the rumor mill.

AFTER FOUR CAKEWALK seasons, the Yankees found themselves in a terrific pennant race throughout 1940. If you lived and breathed Yankees, 1940 was enough to cause anxiety attacks. In fact, in a doubleheader loss to the Tigers at the stadium on a hot July Sunday before 68,590, the fans did lose it. On a questionable umpiring call by Joe Rue on a fair-foul dispute with Henrich, fans began pelting the poor umpire with bottles, half-eaten food, and rolled newspapers and scorecards, an uprising "the like of which has never before been seen either at Yankee Stadium or the Polo Grounds," said the *Times*. Police finally led Rue off the field for his own protection.

Around this time, with the Yankees slumping, *Daily News* columnist Jimmy Powers chose to write, "Couldn't the polio germ be the cause?" The statement infuriated Gehrig, who instituted a lawsuit against Powers, the *News*, and its parent, Tribune Company. It was a scurrilous thing to write, and Gehrig settled the case for $17,500.

To McCarthy, criticized by some as a "push-button manager" blessed with so much talent, it very much came down to a single play in a doubleheader in Cleveland on September 11. The consequences of what happened that day can only be fully appreciated in what would unfold in the coming years, not just days.

The doubleheader was played at vast Municipal Stadium, a park that could hold more than eighty thousand and that would one day be called the Mistake by the Lake. In the forties, it was used mostly on weekends and holidays by the Indians, who played the rest of their games at smaller League Park.

Cleveland fans were pelting the Yankees this day, especially the vulnerable coaches Art Fletcher and Earle Combs, with an assortment of tomatoes and lemons. Their actions infuriated McCarthy, who was crabby about playing on a rainy day so dark and gloomy that the outfielders were hard to make out.

Going into the doubleheader, the Yankees were in third place with twenty-one games remaining. They had not been in first place, even for a single day, all season—but now the possibility stood before them if they could sweep. When they arrived at the ballpark, Detroit was first, 77–57, Cleveland was second, 76–57, a half game out, and the Yanks third, 75–57, one game out. A sweep of the twin bill could put them in first.

In game one, they beat Bob Feller 3–1 for rookie right-hander Ernie "Tiny" Bonham's fifth straight win. At 9–3 with a 1.90 ERA, the 215-pounder, who gripped a lead ball in the dugout to make the real ball feel lighter, was proving to be a big-game pitcher. The win put them in first place for a few hours, the only time they would be there all season.

For the second game, amid the falling rain and fruit and vegetables, Ruffing pitched against Al Smith.

"It was disgraceful," said McCarthy of the fans. "It should have been stopped." At one point McCarthy almost threw a lemon back into the stands, but thought better of it.

With one out in the third inning and the Yankees leading 2–0, Dahlgren, at first base, dropped a throw from Crosetti, allowing Ben Chapman to get to second. A double and single followed, and then Ruffing threw the wet ball into center field on what could have been a double play. The inning continued, and when it was over, the Indians had a 5–2 lead. They won 5–3 when the umpires stopped play due to darkness and increasing rain after six innings. Instead of first place, the Yanks were still in third.

That was their shot. They were 12–8 the rest of the way and finished third, two games behind Detroit. Except for DiMaggio's second straight batting title, a .352 showing, it was an "off year" for most of the regulars. When they lost on the final Friday of the season, they were eliminated. Arthur "Red" Patterson, in the *Herald-Tribune*, wrote, "The king is dead— long live the king." The streak of four consecutive world-championship seasons was done.

The season ended in Washington and the Yanks took the train home. The next day, McCarthy was cleaning out his office. A bunch of New York writers were there too.

One was John Drebinger of the *Times*. I was sitting with Drebby in the Yankee press box some thirty years later. We talked about Gehrig, and the conversation shifted to Dahlgren.

"McCarthy thought he had short arms," he said. "Not really a good first baseman, in his view."

I'd never heard about short arms before. But that started Drebinger talking.

"You know," he said, "McCarthy always felt that the error he made in Cleveland that opened up the floodgates cost him the pennant. He always believed that if Dahlgren catches that throw from Crosetti, the Yankees win the game, go into first, and stay there."

I wasn't familiar with the play; it really wasn't well known. But Drebby was on a roll.

"Furthermore," he said, "McCarthy said that if Dahlgren wasn't a marijuana user, maybe he catches the ball. The darkness, the rain, and his dulled reflexes all made him miss that throw."

This was pretty amazing stuff, and in the style of the day, "off the record" meant "off the record." No one wrote it, although John Kieran of the *Times* wrote, "Marse Joe McCarthy's motto in baseball is . . . 'Never throw out the dirty water until you have the clean water in.' So he must have known something when he let Babe Dahlgren go to the [Boston] Bees."

Yes, McCarthy let Dahlgren go, and one can be certain he told Barrow what he thought. Plenty of unprinted whispers followed, and Dahlgren's career was all but over.

Years later, his family tried to restore Babe's reputation by bringing the whole incident to light in a book called *Rumor in Town* by Dahlgren's grandson Matt. The very idea that a baseball player might have been using marijuana in 1940, when it seemed limited to jazz musicians and bohemian poets, seemed ludicrous. Certainly it was common in the seventies (a few years behind the trend). But in 1940?

The Yankees went on to win pennants in 1941, 1942, and 1943. If they had won in 1940, it could have meant eight pennants in a row, an unthinkable record. Could one dropped throw truly have prevented such a feat?

McCarthy thought so.

IF THE YANKEES were to right themselves in 1941, McCarthy was determined to try it with rookies. Not since 1926, when Lazzeri and Koenig found themselves at second and short, had such an adventure been undertaken by the team, but Marse Joe was now prepared to hand regular jobs to second baseman Gerry Priddy and shortstop Phil Rizzuto from the Kansas City Blues.

The plan was to move Gordon to first to replace Dahlgren; if needed, Johnny Sturm would also come up from the Blues. As it developed, Priddy was less than the doctor ordered and Gordon returned to second, while Sturm took hold of first.

Young Phil Rizzuto had to displace the popular veteran Crosetti, who, although only twenty-nine, had batted just .194 in 1940.

Such was the Yankee way of doing things that Rizzuto would not easily displace the veteran. Batting-practice swings were tough to come by. He waited for someone to say, "Let the kid hit." It was DiMaggio who finally spoke up.

The kid hit.

Rizzuto, the son of a streetcar motorman, came from the border of Brooklyn and Queens—Dill Place and Seventy-eighth Road—and played high school ball at Richmond Hills for Al Kunitz, who had been a Yankee batboy before Eddie Bennett. Kunitz had arranged for Rizzuto to have a tryout with Brooklyn, but Casey Stengel, the Dodgers' manager, told him, "Get a shoeshine box"—he was just too small.

He *was* small. But he had terrific baseball instincts to go with speed, arm strength, range, positioning, and a toughness that his impish, phobia-filled, almost naïve personality belied. He was five foot six and about 150 pounds, a throwback to the Kid Elberfeld days, and maybe that's what made Ty Cobb tab him as the rare player who could have starred in his day. He put his gum on the top of his cap when he batted for good luck. He was probably the best bunter the Yankees ever had, and a fine base stealer as well. He was a fan favorite almost at once, and continued to be so on through his fifty-seven years with the team, as a player and then as a popular broadcaster.

Kunitz got Rizzuto another tryout, this time at Yankee Stadium under the eyes of Paul Krichell. The Yankees liked tryout camps, trusted their scouts, and ran them well. If you made it through one of them, your future was bright.

So Rizzuto went off to the minors and won Minor League Player of the Year honors in 1940, hitting .347. Twenty-four of the twenty-nine players on the Kansas City roster that year saw major league service. It was a terrific collection of talent.

Rizzuto started on opening day in '41 in front of President Roosevelt in Washington. He never tired of talking about it. He was basking in the amazement of being a Yankee.

"Listen, Scooter," Gomez said to him one day, addressing him by his new nickname. "Your parents coming to the game today? I want you to come over to me on the mound like you're giving me advice. That will impress them; their son, giving advice to the great Gomez."

As was McCarthy's wont, he let Rizzuto play for a few weeks, then benched him for Crosetti. He wanted his new shortstop to sit next to him in the dugout and learn some finer points of the game.

"Don't look at the scoreboard—quick, what's the count?" he'd say to Phil. He wanted his head in the game at every minute.

On June 16, Crosetti was spiked in a game and Rizzuto returned to short. The position was now his.

Phil would be the butt of practical jokes: insects in his glove, shoes nailed to the floor, his fan mail torn up. He was the little boy afraid of lightning, but he was one tough competitor on the playing field. One day the Yankees would win five world championships in a row with him at shortstop.

Priddy didn't live up to expectations. His was disrespectful of Gordon, which didn't ingratiate him with his new teammates. He played only two years as a sub for the Yanks, and then elsewhere until 1953.

In 1973, he was convicted of extortion, threatening to put a bomb on a steamship unless he received $250,000. He spent nine months in prison. "That wasn't the Gerry I knew," said Rizzuto, sadly.

Sturm was the team's regular first baseman throughout '41 and in the World Series, but it would be his only major league season. He enlisted in the military after the season and badly injured his right hand; two fingers were amputated. He came back to play in the minors but never saw major league action again.

As for Rizzuto, he had a wonderful rookie season and the Yankees tied the major league record for double plays with him at short. DiMaggio took him under his wing. In fact, when the season ended, DiMaggio asked him to fill in for him at a communion breakfast in Newark, where Phil would meet his future wife, Cora. It was all a grand adventure come true for the hometown boy.

Meanwhile, DiMaggio had started the year slowly in defense of his two batting titles, and when he went 1-for-4 on May 15, nobody thought much about it. But when he passed his own personal best with a twenty-four-game hitting streak on June 8, people started to notice.

The club record of twenty-nine, held by Peckinpaugh (1919) and Combs (1931), was broken on June 17. Now radio newscasts were beginning to keep listeners informed. There were no game broadcasts in 1941.

Forty was the next milestone—George Sisler's modern record. And when he tied and then beat it in a doubleheader on June 29, all of America became captivated by Joe's streak. This was no longer for the sports pages.

In a nation with its eyes on the possibility of impending war, with fears of Nazi invasions dominating discussions, it was a delight.

"He's just a man and not a freak . . . Joltin' Joe DiMaggio," went a popular hit record quickly recorded by Les Brown's big band, with the vocal by Betty Bonney.

There was the story of Joe's bat being stolen, and then, mysteriously, recovered. It sold a lot of newspapers!

The pre-1900 mark of Wee Willie Keeler was next. That was forty-four, and Joe made it to forty-five on July 2. Now the record was all his. But how far could he go? Maybe to the professional record of sixty-one, which he set himself in San Francisco?

At League Park in Cleveland on July 16, Joe ran the streak to fifty-six with three hits. He had batted .408 during the 56 games with 91 hits, 56 runs, 55 RBI, and 15 homers. He'd struck out only five times. A few times it took him until his last at-bat, but then he'd come through and the crowd would sigh in relief, then cheer madly. There were no radio broadcasts of the game—the Yankees couldn't get a sponsor! But it was said that Heinz 57 varieties was ready to pay Joe a lot of money when the streak got to fifty-seven.

For game fifty-seven, DiMaggio shared a cab to Municipal Stadium with Gomez, and the cab driver said, "Make sure you get a hit your first time up. If you don't, you will be stopped." DiMaggio tried to ignore the suggestion.

Al Smith, the same man who beat Ruffing in the Dahlgren game ten months before, was on the mound for the Indians. DiMaggio's first time up, third baseman Kenny Keltner caught a tough grounder deep at the base and threw him out from the foul line. He walked his second time up, as Smith drew boos from the crowd. His third time up he hit another screamer to third, and again Keltner came through with a fine play to nail Joe.

In the eighth, now hitting off Jim Bagby Jr., he hit a bouncer to Lou Boudreau at short. Boudreau turned it into a double play, and the streak was over unless the Indians could tie the game and send it into extra innings. They did make it 4–3, but it wasn't enough and the streak ended at fifty-six.

It remains, more than seventy years later, maybe the toughest record of all to break, save for Cy Young's 511 victories. And when it was ruled that no hitting streak could be counted if it spread over two seasons, it meant that a run at fifty-six would have to begin before August 1, or forget it.

On June 3, 1941, Lou Gehrig died at his home at 5203 Delafield Avenue in Riverdale, age thirty-seven. Those who were monitoring his health knew the end was imminent. He had worked at his job at the parole board until just weeks before, but no one had written that the end was near.

The Yankees were in Detroit, where his playing streak had ended twenty-five months earlier. McCarthy and Dickey left the club to fly back to New York. At Briggs Stadium, the Yankee players stood before their dugout, caps over their hearts, as flags flew at half staff.

Five thousand lined the streets of Riverdale near Christ Episcopal Church. Stadium manager Charley McManus manned the door to make sure only the invited entered the service. Babe Ruth was there along with four physicians from the Mayo Clinic, Miller Huggins's brother Arthur, George Ruppert, Barrow, Weiss, the actress wives of DiMaggio and Gomez (neighbors on West End Avenue), batboy Timmy Sullivan, Bill Terry, and Eddie Collins. A floral arrangement was delivered from the "redcaps of Grand Central Terminal."

Gehrig would be cremated and his remains buried in a grave at Kensico Cemetery, where Ruppert had been laid to rest.

On July 4, a monument to Gehrig, matching Huggins's, was dedicated in center field, unveiled by Dickey and McCarthy. Connie Mack was among the speakers. McCarthy told people that the position of captain "has died with Lou. There will never be another one of the Yankees."

Seventy years after his death, neither a cause nor a cure for Lou Gehrig's disease, ALS, has been found.

Nervousness over war was evident through news reports about players' draft physicals and by the introduction of "The Star-Spangled Banner" to precede all games. It was Barrow's idea to do it daily, not just on holidays. The advent of the PA system allowed recorded music to be played, so a live band wasn't necessary. In 1941, it was performed on "I Am an American Day" by Lucy Monroe, who would become a fixture at the stadium over the next twenty-five years, dressed in mink and performing the anthem on opening day, holidays, and during the World Series.

On June 28, the Yanks beat Philadelphia 7–4 behind Atley Donald and began a fourteen-game winning streak that stretched to twenty-nine out of thirty-two. They wound up winning 101 and finishing seventeen games in first.

DiMaggio won the MVP Award despite Ted Williams hitting a titanic .406. The hitting streak and the .400 season came to grow in legend with the passage of time, as did the larger-than-life reputations of these two giant figures in American culture.

"The difference between the Yankees and the Red Sox," said Dom DiMaggio to author Leigh Montville, "was that the Yankees always were run as a business. They made sound business moves. The Red Sox, under Yawkey, were a hobby. He always kept friends around too long and made decisions according to who he drank with."

IN THE NATIONAL League, Brooklyn won its first pennant since 1920. The "Bums," despite so many losing seasons, had a great fan base, a charming little ballpark in Ebbets Field, a dashing manager in Durocher, and cunning owner Larry MacPhail. They also had a young shortstop named Pee Wee Reese to complement the Yanks' Rizzuto.

Much had been made over the years of the Yankees-Giants rivalry. Sharing such close quarters, they were natural rivals. But now came the first World Series between the Yankees and the Dodgers, a Subway Series with about fifteen miles between them. The fans were very different. Dodger fans were the little guys, the underdogs, the working stiffs from the borough of churches whose players lived in the neighborhood and seemed like regular guys. The Yankee fans were the Wall Street business crowd, better dressed, cockier, and not expecting to really meet any of the players on the street. Their ballpark was staid, proud, awe-inspiring. Ebbets Field was a place you snuck into after five innings, maybe wearing a T-shirt. You might sneak down into a box seat when no one was looking. At Yankee Stadium, you did so at your own peril.

After some talk about maximizing attendance by playing all the games at Yankee Stadium (loudly overruled by Dodger fans), the Series opened October 1 in the Bronx, and once again Ruffing rose to the occasion and won 3–2 with a six-hitter. Ruffing was thirty-seven now, but what a postseason player he was; this win made him an unbeaten 6–0 in World Series play.

Whit Wyatt beat Spud Chandler in game two, 3–2, ending the Yankees' ten-game World Series winning streak. Game three, in Ebbets Field, was a 2–1 complete game win for Marius Russo, won in the eighth on singles by

Rolfe, Henrich, DiMaggio, and Keller. (This was the first season in which DiMaggio-Keller-Henrich formed the regular outfield.)

Now game four. With two outs in the ninth, it was 4–3 Brooklyn, and they were one out from knotting the Series at 2–2.

Hugh Casey now faced Henrich. With a full count, he unleashed—a curve? A spitball? People have debated it since. Whatever it was, Henrich swung and missed, but made it to first on a passed ball by Mickey Owen.

"Five o'clock lightning." You didn't give the Yankees a fourth out, not these Yankees. DiMaggio singled, Keller doubled to score two, Dickey walked, and Gordon doubled to score Dickey. Suddenly it was 7–4 New York, and Murphy retired three straight to nail it down in the last of the ninth. The Yankees took a 3–1 Series lead.

"Hugh Casey didn't even know how to throw a spitball," said Durocher to his biographer, Ed Linn, in 1974. "Why should he? Casey had a natural sinker—that's why he was a relief pitcher . . . [He] made a great pitch and then everything went wrong. Mickey Owen reached for the ball instead of shifting his feet as he should have, and the ball went off the end of his glove and rolled behind him. It didn't roll that far, either. If there had been grass behind the plate, there is no question in my mind but that Henrich would have been thrown out at first base."

Bonham beat Wyatt 3–1 the next day and the Yankees had their ninth world championship. Gordon hit .500 in the Series and walked seven times.

Although the teams played another game, the Owens play came to represent the end of the Series—and with it the end of the prewar era of major league baseball.

Two months after the World Series, the Japanese bombed Pearl Harbor, and World War II began. Baseball had little choice but to support the war effort, try to stay vital, show pride when its stars went off to service, and hope that the game still existed as an important part of American culture whenever the war ended. Just holding its own would test its mettle. These were going to be rough years.

Chapter Eighteen

THE WAR DIVERTED EVERYONE'S attention for the next four years, and baseball was lucky to be able to continue. And so after a decade of the Great Depression, baseball was still unable to realize its full potential as an entertainment industry. Attendance and revenues would be flat for the better part of fifteen years, but still the Yankees found a way to succeed.

After dismissing Doc Painter as trainer after the '41 Series and replacing him with Eddie Froelich of the White Sox, the Yanks managed to stay mainly intact in 1942, while players on other teams were getting called up and sent off to war.*

The Yanks lost only Henrich and Sturm to military duty in 1942, and Henrich not until August 31. Tommy played a final game on August 30 during which PA announcer Jack Lenz proclaimed, "Ladies and gentlemen, Tommy Henrich has been ordered to report for active duty with the Coast Guard. This is his last appearance in a Yankee uniform until the war is over." A thunderous ovation followed, which Henrich called "one of the most touching salutes I've ever received."

That took him out of the pennant race, but the Yankees were eight games up when he left.

Red Rolfe, thirty-three, became a part-time player after developing chronic

---

* Painter, bitter after receiving no explanation for his firing after thirteen seasons, went to see McCarthy in Buffalo, but to no avail.

ulcerative colitis and retired after the season. At the time, he was probably the best third baseman in the franchise's history, a lifetime .289 hitter who played for six pennant winners in ten seasons. He would immediately go on to coach baseball and basketball at Yale, come back to coach for the Yankees in 1946, and then manage the Tigers for four seasons. Crosetti wound up playing a lot of third base next to Rizzuto.

Buddy Hassett, born in Manhattan, raised in the Bronx, and a semipro player in Brooklyn, had first been signed by the Yankees in 1936, then came back to play first base in Sturm's absence after six National League seasons. His teammates loved to hear his beautiful tenor voice; he could have been a professional singer. He hit a credible .284 in his final year in the big leagues, and then went into the service.

The pitching leadership of Ruffing and Gomez was surpassed in '42 by Bonham (21–5), Chandler (16–5), and Hank Borowy (15–4), with Atley Donald going 11–3. Gomez concluded his Yankee career with a 189–102 record. After the season he took a job at a GE plant in Lynn, Massachusetts.

Lefty, with his signature high leg kick, went out with an 11–2 win at Philadelphia on August 14 and never pitched again, save for one appearance for the Senators in '43. He would remain a fixture in baseball long after his retirement, first as a manager in the Yankee system (where he gave Eddie Ford the nickname "Whitey"), then as a representative of Rawlings sporting goods. He always thanked Johnny Murphy for saving so many of his wins, and said, "The secret to my success is clean living and a fast outfield!" "I'm the guy who made DiMaggio famous," he would tell audiences, adding, "I'd rather be lucky than good!"

Tiny Bonham was 79–50 in seven seasons and a two-time All-Star with the Yankees. He was traded to the Pirates in 1947 and gave Pittsburgh three solid seasons before being sidelined by an appendix attack in September of '49. During surgery he was found to have intestinal cancer and died a week later. He was only thirty-six.

DiMaggio, booed even at home after a wartime spring holdout, had an off year in '42, hitting .305/21/114.

A rookie, twenty-five-year-old Johnny Lindell, who was the Minor League Player of the Year in '41, made 23 appearances on the mound with a decent 3.76 ERA, but the following year moved to the outfield, a rare conversion that harkened back to Babe Ruth's switch. McCarthy simply felt that the USC product, a Bill Essick signing, lacked big-league stuff, but saw his potential as an everyday player. Joe's instincts were good: Lindell, a handsome six foot four and 217 pounds, was a solid outfielder for seven seasons with the Yanks and a fan favorite as well. He led the league in total bases in 1944 when he hit .300/18/103. (Lindell would finish his career in 1953 as a pitcher, going 6–17 for the Pirates and Phillies.)

The Yankees, as well as other teams, had to deal with the possibility of an air raid during a game. Air-raid wardens were always present. Bulletins were placed throughout the park to instruct fans to "sit tight, follow the green line or the red line," and to know where barrels of water, pails of sand, and fire extinguishers were. Fifteen thousand fans could be protected from bombs under the grandstand. No one would be permitted to leave in the event of a raid. SEE SCORECARD FOR ALERT INSTRUCTIONS, it said on the facing of the mezzanine. (It would seem to make the five-cent purchase worthwhile.)

The threat also led to one of the game's most curious rules: In the event of an air raid or a bomb attack, whichever team led after five innings would be declared the winner.

Fortunately, there was no need to redefine "Bronx Bombers" over the coming years.

Prior to a home game on April 29, across the street from the Bronx County Courthouse at the Grand Concourse, a road divider was named Lou Gehrig Plaza, with Eleanor Gehrig, Lou's parents, McCarthy, Dickey, and several teammates on hand to dedicate the plaque. Eleanor was dressed as an ambulance driver; she was in the process of working with the city to develop a fleet of Lou Gehrig ambulances with the number 4 painted on their sides. (The plaza was upgraded in 2009.)

Additionally, *Pride of the Yankees* was released during the season, starring Gary Cooper as Lou (a terrific casting decision), Teresa Wright as Eleanor, and Babe Ruth, Mark Koenig, Bill Dickey, and Bob Meusel as themselves. The movie, directed by Sam Wood and based on a Gehrig biography by Paul Gallico, was extremely well received and garnered eleven Oscar nominations. Many would watch the film over and over as the years passed, always moved by the presentation of Cooper/Gehrig's farewell speech and his slow walk toward the dugout for the last time. It was one of those cultural events in America that took baseball to the mainstream, and in the process made a household name of Gehrig and greatly increased interest in ALS.

For Teresa Wright, making only her third film in a twenty-eight-feature-film career, it was just another contract assignment, and she admitted to

not being much of a fan. But in her later years she became an avid supporter, and was lovingly introduced at games and at the Yogi Berra Museum
in the 2000s.

On August 21, Babe Ruth donned a Yankee uniform (with NY on the
jersey, for the first time), and took to the field for the first time since his
playing days. He was taking practice swings for a war bonds exhibition in
which he would bat against Walter Johnson. Of the current team, he knew
only the coach Earle Combs. He called him Kid.

Now forty-seven, Ruth suited up again on the twenty-third before 69,136
fans to bat against fifty-four-year-old Walter Johnson. On Johnson's fifth
pitch, Babe gave the fans what they wanted, a drive into the lower right-field
stands. On the seventeenth and final pitch from Johnson, he hit one into
the upper deck in right for the first time, and although the ball curved foul,
he circled the bases, waved his cap, and saluted the crowd. Ruth and Johnson walked off together to a terrific ovation. The game raised some $80,000
for the army-navy relief fund. That would be Babe's last trip around the
bases at the House That Ruth Built.

IN A SHOCKING vote at year's end, Joe Gordon, who had delivered a fine
.322/18/103 season, beat out Triple Crown winner Ted Williams (.356/36/137)
for MVP honors. A year after hitting .406 and losing to DiMaggio, this
time Williams lost to Gordon by twenty-one points. The vote was hotly debated for months and was the most controversial since the Baseball Writers'
Association began polling in '31. With Williams also leading the league in
runs, walks, and slugging percentage, it seemed clear that a lot of the voting writers simply did not like Teddy Ballgame. Gordon, as some pointed
out, only led in strikeouts, grounding into double plays, and errors.

Gordon described himself as "floored" by the award. "It's an honor I've
always had ambitions to win, like any other ball player, but I never thought
it would come this season," he said.

In his autobiography, Williams wrote, "The voting tends to go to the
team that wins, which is right. But I have to think the reason I didn't get
more consideration was because of the trouble I had with the draft."

He did spend much of 1942 trying to overturn his 1-A classification,
which won him few fans among the press or the public.

THE YANKEES WERE in first place from May on, and won by nine games. They now prepared to face the Cardinals for the first time since 1926. They had managed to avoid playing the Gashouse Gang, the great Cardinal teams of the '30s, but now faced a young team largely with players in their twenties, including Stan Musial, twenty-one. The Yankees, winners of eight straight World Series showdowns and 24–4 in Series games under McCarthy, were the heavy favorites.

The Series opened in St. Louis with Ruffing beating Mort Cooper, holding the Cards hitless until Terry Moore singled with two out in the eighth. But that was the high point for the Yanks. The Cardinals proceeded to win four in a row, with the finale a 4–2 victory, Johnny Beazley over Ruffing, who had been 7–1 in World Series play going into the game. Rizzuto, in his final game before going off to the navy, hit a first-inning home run, and the score was 2–2 in the ninth when Whitey Kurowski homered with a man on, just inside the left-field foul pole.

In the last of the ninth, the Yanks got two men on, but soon-to-be MVP Gordon was picked off second to end the rally.

To lose like that, in Yankee Stadium, on a pickoff, was a devastating blow.

EVERYTHING FELT DIFFERENT about 1943, starting with traveling secretary Mark Roth missing his first spring training in thirty-five years due to illness. Rex Weyant, Winnie's brother, assumed his duties and supervised the move to an abbreviated version of spring training at Asbury Park High School in New Jersey. Commissioner Landis had ordered limited travel, and thus the annual spring trek to St. Petersburg was on hold. (The Yankees trained in Atlantic City in 1944 and 1945.) The team headquartered at the Albion Hotel and played only one exhibition game on the high school grounds, against their Newark club. The fans who braved the chilly weather to see the Yankees work out didn't see DiMaggio, Rizzuto, Selkirk, Hassett, and Ruffing, who went into the service, but guys like Bud Metheny, Bill Zuber, Marv Breuer, Tommy Byrne, Tuck Stainback, and Oscar Grimes. A lot of glamour was missing, and there were a lot of holes for McCarthy to fill.

Ruffing, thirty-eight, a nineteen-year veteran who had lost four toes before embarking on his baseball career, was a surprise inductee, but he was chosen for non-combative duty and worked at an aircraft factory.

DiMaggio's entry into the army was particularly noted, especially since he could have sought an exemption as married with a son. There was a lot of confusion over his departure, and it seemed to catch Barrow by surprise. Pictures of Joe being sworn in ran in every newspaper in the country.

Crosetti, thirty-two, took over his old spot at short and Lindell took over in center. A rookie, Billy Johnson, was given third base. A pickup from the Phillies, Nick Etten was handed first. Dickey, at thirty-six, split the catching with Rollie Helmsley and batted .351. Metheny replaced Henrich in right. Patchwork? Sure. But every team had to deal with it. This team didn't hit much—Dickey was the only .300 hitter. But muscular Charlie Keller (who hated his nickname "King Kong") belted 31 homers. Etten drove in 107 runs. Gordon fell to .249, and Crosetti, suspended the first thirty days for shoving umpire Bill Summers in the '42 World Series, struggled and was often spelled by rookie infielder George "Snuffy" Stirnweiss, up from the champion Newark Bears.

Etten, twenty-four, out of Villanova, had played two seasons for the Athletics and two for the Phillies (then called the Blue Jays) before the Yankees sent them two journeymen and $10,000 to obtain his contract. "Christmas came early this year," he told his wife when informed of the trade. He would give the Yankees four seasons, leading the league in homers one year and RBI another, making him one of the team's better wartime players. He had an odd batting stance, almost completely facing the pitcher, which he said made it possible for him to follow the pitch with both eyes. He was certainly a good find for the Yankees during these fill-in years. He was classified 3-A in the draft (married with a child, like DiMaggio), which made him a "safe" acquisition.

Johnson, twenty-four, who was born in Montclair, New Jersey, on the same day Ted Williams was born in San Diego, had toiled in the Yankees' minor league system since he was seventeen, always hitting around .300 or better but never getting "the call." In '42 he hit .290 at Newark and was ready. He played every game for the '43 Yankees, hit .280 with 94 RBI (a new club record for third basemen), and fielded his position well. He finished fourth in MVP voting, a fine rookie accomplishment. But then he too would be off to the military for the next two years. He then returned to play the position regularly for five stellar years, four of them pennant winners.

Snuffy Stirnweiss, also twenty-four, was so named for his fondness for chewing tobacco. The son of a New York City policeman, he stood just five foot eight but played college football at North Carolina and was drafted as a halfback by the NFL's Chicago Cardinals. Born in Manhattan, raised in the East Bronx, and a graduate of Fordham Prep, he signed with the Yanks in

1940 and moved quickly through the farm system. Snuffy's draft status seemed secure; he had a wife and a mother to support, and his brother was in the service. He was never called.

The only real tune-up after training in Asbury Park was a three-way doubleheader at Yankee Stadium on April 14, with the Dodgers beating the Yanks in the opener and then the Giants in the second game before 35,301. The proceeds, some $75,000 including radio rights, went to the Civil Defense Volunteer Office.

Attendance fell to 645,006 for the season, the lowest it would ever be at Yankee Stadium, and naturally there was concern about the future of both the game and the country. Drawing nine thousand fans, on average, to a stadium that could hold seventy thousand was distressing. Any thoughts of selling the team were surely on hold now, its postwar value uncertain.

The Yanks were in first place all season and won their fourteenth pennant by thirteen and a half games, winning ninety-eight—seventeen with what are now called walk-off hits. With no Ruffing or Gomez to anchor the staff for the first time since 1929, Spud Chandler stepped up and delivered a 20–4 season with a club-record 1.64 ERA at age thirty-five, sparkling enough to earn himself the MVP Award, the only Yankee pitcher ever to accomplish the feat. He held opponents to a .215 batting average and was 10–2 both at home and on the road. He was only the fourth pitcher in AL history (with Johnson, Grove, and Gomez) to lead the league in both won-lost percentage and ERA.

At the All-Star Game that year, McCarthy, criticized in '42 for naming nine Yankees to the team (six starters), decided to select six Yankees but to sit them all. He still won 5–3, with not a Yankee in the box score.

The Yankees were delighted that the Cardinals repeated in the National League—a chance to avenge the 1942 embarrassment. With wartime travel restrictions in place, the first three games were in New York, with the next four scheduled for St. Louis. Chandler won the opener, but Barrow was taken to the hospital that day with a heart attack. Robust and vital, baseball people had to be reminded that "Cousin Egbert" was in fact seventy-five years old. But he would recover and return to work in eight weeks.

Bonham lost game two to Mort Cooper, an emotional game in that Mort and his brother Walker, his catcher, had lost their father to a heart attack that very morning. The Cooper brothers chose to play on in his memory, and the nation cheered their win.

Borowy won the third game, aided by a bases-loaded triple from Johnson, to send the teams to Missouri with the Yanks up 2–1.

From there, New York made quick work of it, Marius Russo winning game four and Chandler getting the clinching win in a 2–0 shutout. The old Yanks played key roles in this one, with Dickey, at thirty-six, hitting a two-run homer off Cooper in the sixth for all the scoring. For a final time, Art Fletcher would lead the clubhouse in singing "The Sidewalks of New York," "Beer Barrel Polka," and "Pistol Packing Mama" as relief pitcher Jim Turner and Etten hoisted Commissioner Landis onto their shoulders to sing along.

McCarthy was celebrating the team's tenth world championship—his seventh and last.

After the season, a contingent of big leaguers headed for the Pacific theater to play games for U.S. troops, and the Yankees on the team included Chandler, Johnson, Keller, Dickey, and Gordon. Along with Marius Russo, all of them would find themselves in the service in '44.

DESPITE ALL OF these roster losses, no one would dare speak of this in the face of the greater good of serving the country. Every team was affected, and no one questioned the commitment to the nation. It was just the way it was.

And so whatever 1944 would bring, baseball was happy to still be going. Whatever the attendance would be (789,995 in the Yankees' case), it was great relief and entertainment for the war workers, and that overrode anything else.

1944 would not produce a fourth straight pennant. In the final year of the Ruppert estate ownership, there was a resumption of radio broadcasting, with Don Dunphy and Bill Slater on WINS, but no champions to cheer for.

On January 28, Mark Roth died at sixty-two. He had been traveling secretary since 1915; first as a teen newspaperman and then in his current position, he had seen almost every game the team had played since its founding. He could have written the team's history, because he had a great knowledge of it, and Frank Graham's well-received 1943 book *The New York Yankees* leaned heavily on his memories.

His replacement, Rex Weyant, led a small contingent to Atlantic City to inspect the makeshift training facilities the team would encounter. Barrow wasn't yet ready to travel and McCarthy had dropped a log on his foot in

Buffalo and couldn't make the trip either. So the farm director, Weiss, went there along with Jackie Farrell, who ran the team's speakers' bureau; Charley McManus, the stadium manager; and Walter Owens, the head groundskeeper. Owens would supervise conversion of Bader Field from football to baseball, but the bad weather allowed the Yanks only six outdoor sessions all spring, including games against the Phillies and Dodgers. The indoor practices were held in an armory, and the team stayed at the Hotel Senator. The following year, the Red Sox would join them and share the facility.

Apart from his log accident, McCarthy missed the first three weeks of the season with a gallbladder attack. Fletcher managed the club.

This was an almost unrecognizable Yankee team. Stirnweiss took over at second, Etten manned first, but there was Mike Milosevich and Crosetti sharing short, Metheny, Lindell, and Hersh Martin in the outfield, Oscar Grimes at third, Mike Garbark and Helmsley catching, and even oldsters like Paul Waner, forty-one, Johnny Cooney, forty-three, and Jim Turner, forty, getting action. Dickey had gone off to the navy.

The pitching was a little more recognizable, as Borowy, Bonham, and Donald made 74 starts. Rookie Walt "Monk" Dubiel, up from Newark, was 13–13.

On June 26, 1944, the Polo Grounds hosted a most unusual exhibition game: Yankees vs. Giants vs. Dodgers. A different team took the field each inning. The Yanks and Dodgers shared the visiting dugout. In the end, with a truly bizarre scoring system, the Dodgers won 5 to 1 to 0.* The most emotional part of the afternoon was a wonderful ovation for Dickey, now a naval lieutenant, who managed to be at the ballpark.

And Dickey lived up to his billing—an officer, gentleman, and ballplayer. A newspaper conducted a popularity poll to select a favorite all-time player, with each vote costing $25 to buy a war bond. Lou Gehrig won with 320 last-minute votes: Dickey had wired a pledge of $8,000 and cast all his 320 votes for his old pal.

The '44 Yanks, a shadow of their former selves, still found themselves in first place for a week after Labor Day. On Friday, September 29, they were in Sportsman's Park, St. Louis, trailing the Browns and Tigers by three games with four games left on the schedule. A "crowd" of 6,172 turned out for the biggest games in Browns history as Bonham and Borowy went down in a

---

* The teams rotated against each other, with the total runs for each team's seven innings at bat producing a winner: Dodgers 5, Yankees 1, Giants 0.

doubleheader loss, 4–1 and 1–0, to eliminate the Yankees. The Browns won the only American League pennant in their history. (They moved to Baltimore in 1953.)

It was tough to lose to the Browns, and McCarthy saw no good side to it. To have won with his makeshift lineup would have been quite a feat, and certainly would have set aside his "push-button manager" knock. The Yanks finished third, six games out.

Chapter Nineteen

L ARRY MACPHAIL BEGAN THINKING about buying the Yankees in March of 1944. They had been, in his mind, "available for the right price" ever since Ruppert's death. He felt that ownership couldn't go on forever under the arrangement in Ruppert's will.

MacPhail was an unlikely man to own the Yankees. They were as conservative an organization as existed in sports, and the tone set by Barrow and McCarthy was all business: Give the fans a good team, and they will come. There would be no place for the flamboyance of a MacPhail, who was always thinking promotion.

MacPhail, now fifty-four, had run the Cincinnati Reds from 1933 to 1937, where he had originated night baseball, hired Red Barber to do broadcasts, and instituted air travel to road games. He moved to the Dodgers in 1938, brought Barber with him, led the team to the 1941 pennant, and then resigned in 1942 to reenlist, serving as a lieutenant colonel in the service of the undersecretary of war, Robert Patterson.

He was no stranger to the military, having served in World War I, and in a memorable act that typified his daring and his flamboyance, he hatched an ambitious plot to kidnap the kaiser shortly after the war's conclusion. He wanted to turn him over to Allied forces to put him on trial.

Kaiser Wilhelm II of Germany had taken refuge in a chateau in Holland. MacPhail, along with Lieutenant Colonel Luke Lea (a former U.S. senator), reached the castle under the pretense of needing to speak personally to the kaiser. When it became evident they were never going to see him, they decided to make a run for it. MacPhail swiped an ashtray on the way out as proof that they were there. (The ashtray is still in the family.)

During the years that James Farley had been trying to execute a purchase, $4 to $6 million was the price range bandied about in the press. (Red Sox owner Tom Yawkey was thought to be interested in buying the team as well, but his general manager, Eddie Collins, talked him out of it.)

MacPhail thought the bargain price of $2.5 million would do it, which he estimated to be the value of the real estate on which Yankee Stadium and the two Ruppert Stadiums—Newark and Kansas City—stood. Everything else—the major and minor league players, the office equipment, the playing equipment, the value of having a major league team in the biggest population center of the country—would be a bonus. He even wrote down on his checklist that while the Giants and Dodgers almost always had another team in town when they were home, the Yankee schedule had only about ten conflicting dates a season.

He was also banking on baseball becoming bigger than ever following the Great Depression and the war. June 6 was D-Day. Although Allied forces suffered terrible losses, the result was clear in the minds of Americans: The war was entering its final phase.

(Only one major leaguer was part of the Normandy invasion—or, more properly, a future major leaguer. Seaman First Class Lawrence Peter Berra was on the USS *Bayfield,* providing cover.)

Back on the home front, MacPhail took his lengthy summary of the team's value to Manufacturer's Trust, the estate trustee. Inheritance taxes were too great for the team—or even for the brewery—to cover. These laws would be changed over time, and when George Steinbrenner died in 2010, there were no such problems with inheritance taxes. But in the 1940s, these laws were backbreakers. It was reported that the estate owed more than $1 million.

Manufacturer's Trust was leery that MacPhail himself had the money. Baseball had made few people rich; it was still a very small industry. MacPhail, though, had a partner, John Hertz, who owned taxi fleets in Chicago, thoroughbred horses (his wife owned Triple Crown winner Count Fleet), and the Hertz Drive-Ur-Self Corporation, which would become Hertz Rental Cars. When Manufacturer's learned that Hertz was involved, the bank seemed ready to approve the sale.

But Hertz's racing interests were not going to pass muster with Commissioner Landis. MacPhail needed a different partner.

And so at the 21 Club on West Fifty-second Street in New York, he happened upon marine captain Dan Topping, who was on leave from Pacific duty. Topping, always well tanned and handsome, was just thirty-two. He was an heir to a tin fortune and was married to the champion ice skater Sonja Henie (already his third of six marriages, producing nine children).

Dan co-owned the NFL's Brooklyn Tigers, which had paid rent to MacPhail to play home games in Ebbets Field.

Topping quickly agreed to go into the purchase with MacPhail and suggested that Bing Crosby, the nation's number-one movie star, might also be interested. Crosby, however, also had racing interests (he owned Del Mar Racetrack) and was no more likely to gain approval than was Hertz. (Crosby did wind up with a piece of the Pittsburgh Pirates.)

It was Crosby, however, who suggested Del Webb, forty-five, as a third partner. The two of them had invested in three films together, including *Abie's Irish Rose*. Webb was a land developer who had moved to Phoenix in 1928 to recover from typhoid fever and started his construction company there. Webb casually got to know MacPhail when his construction company landed a big contract from the War Department to build a Japanese internment camp near Parker, Arizona. He also owned the Arizona Brewing Company.

Webb, a friend of Howard Hughes, would build the Flamingo hotel for Bugsy Siegel in Las Vegas—it would open in 1946—the Sahara in 1952, and the Mint casino in 1961, receiving "points," or part ownership, as part of his payment. He would also build the retirement community of Sun City, Arizona, in 1960. He took part ownership of the Flamingo when Bugsy was gunned down in June 1947, owing Webb a lot of money. His partners were Meyer Lansky and Gus Greenbaum, who lost his share of the place when he was found with his throat slit.

"I consulted with [J. Edgar] Hoover for a long time before we went into Vegas," Webb said, "because we were worried about the gangster element. Hoover encouraged us to go in."

The irony of baseball turning away people with racing interests while approving Webb despite his mob associations was not lost on critics.

The sale price was $2.8 million. The three Ruppert heirs received $2.5 million of it; $300,000 went to Barrow. George Ruppert retained a 3.12 percent interest in the team until he died in November 1948.

The announcement was made, appropriately, at the 21 Club on January 26, 1945. Topping was not present, having returned to duty in the Pacific, and was represented by his lawyer, J. Arthur Friedlund, who would become the secretary-treasurer of the team. MacPhail, in uniform, was there, as was the tall and judicious-looking Webb, with Barrow representing the Rupperts. Webb was charming, talking of his days as a pitcher in a California "outlaw league," while MacPhail, no stranger to anyone in the room, said, "Mr. Barrow and I are in full accord on the policy of the club and he will continue to direct affairs until such time as I can permanently take over my new duties."

Landis died in November 1944, his views on Webb unknown. The office was now vacant, pending a search for a new commissioner. Webb, however, proved to be a good citizen of the game, truly an absentee owner who was generally seen in New York only on opening day, Old-Timers' Day, and the World Series. He had no office among the Yankee complex and seemed perfectly content to let others run the team and its business interests and live his life in real estate development out West. The Yankee ownership, for him, was essentially good PR for his other business interests.

MacPhail was clearly going to run the show now, although Weiss was promoted to general manager. Few thought Barrow and McCarthy would get along with him. Barrow, now almost seventy-seven, was mentioned as a possible commissioner, but he recognized that his time to retire had come. He created no controversy in turning over the running of the team to MacPhail, and was named chairman of the board.

"McCarthy and MacPhail are as different as night and day," wrote Arthur Daley in the *Times*. "They may even be as insoluble as oil and water . . . But it's impossible to visualize the tempestuous redhead firing McCarthy as constantly as he fired Leo Durocher in the old days. With Marse Joe that first battle probably would be the last. And McCarthy never would stand for the slightest bit of front-office interference."

As for an office location, the 55 West Forty-second Street office would hardly do for a big idea man like MacPhail. He leased better space on the twenty-ninth floor of 745 Fifth Avenue (the Squibb Building), across the street from the Plaza Hotel, bringing Barrow's longtime secretary Elizabeth King (who would assume that job for George Weiss), an office manager (Emmet "Pop" Tuttle, who would retire in January 1946 after thirty years with the team), a bookkeeper, a ticket director, and a telephone operator. It was a good arrangement, allowing MacPhail and Topping to enjoy the finest Manhattan restaurants for lunches and cocktail hours. Barrow would never have been comfortable in that environment; he usually had lunch, packed by his wife, in the Harry M. Stevens office.

For a showman like MacPhail, a publicist was critical, and there had been no real publicity director to this point. After Mark Roth died, Jackie Farrell answered reporters' questions, but he was called to be the head of the speakers' bureau, booking players for appearances or making them himself, telling Babe Ruth stories. People expected John McDonald, who had worked for MacPhail in both Cincinnati and Brooklyn, to become the team's first official PR director, but instead MacPhail selected former sports-writer Red Patterson, who had been the National League's PR chief the year before. Patterson, who later served briefly as traveling secretary, was handed the additional role of public-address announcer.

There was also an expectation that Red Barber would come over, but he made a new deal with the Dodgers and stayed. (He moved to the Yanks in 1954.) Rex Weyant, Winnie's brother, stayed on as traveling secretary but would be succeeded in 1946 by MacPhail's son Bill, later the head of CBS and then CNN Sports. His other son, Lee, would operate the Kansas City Blues following his military discharge, and after 1947 became the farm director. Lee went on to become general manager of the Orioles and the Yankees, a top aide to Commissioner Spike Eckert, American League president, and head of the Players Relations Committee. He would eventually join his father in the Baseball Hall of Fame: the only father-son pairing in the Hall.

Faced with moving all the team's files to the new offices, MacPhail made a decision to toss almost all of it into the trash. This would not have only been the Barrow files, but all the records back to the Highlanders that had been maintained by the Yankees.

While there was hardly a "collector's market" in the mid-forties, the maintenance worker whose job it was to toss the trash spotted the endorsed checks and knew a good thing when he saw it. He sold off most of the haul to a book dealer and gave a lot of the canceled checks to friends. He also sold a lot of items to a former news editor for the *World-Telegram*, and eventually the material trickled into a larger marketplace. The early records and letters from Ban Johnson involving the formation of the team would vanish, but some material did survive, including letters involving the purchase of Ruth and the Carl Mays case.

Barrow moved from Larchmont to Rye, New York, and settled into retirement. He was seldom seen at baseball gatherings, although one Old-Timers' Day was staged in his honor by the Yankees. His personal life had not been free of tragedy. A son-in-law, Coca-Cola vice president Frederick Campbell, had committed suicide in 1933 by consuming carbon monoxide fumes in his New Rochelle garage. Frederick's widow, Audrey, the Barrows' only child, left with two small children, married for a fourth time in 1940, but this husband died in 1950 of a heart ailment. She then committed suicide herself in 1951, leaping to her death from an eleventh-floor window at 1161 York Avenue in Manhattan.

Barrow himself died on December 15, 1953, at the age of eighty-five, three months after his Hall of Fame election. He received a plaque to match Ruppert's on the outfield wall in 1954. He was buried in Kensico Cemetery in Valhalla, near Ruppert and Gehrig.

THE 1945 SEASON was another for playing 4-Fs, hoping for early discharges, and trying to stay competitive. Spring training was again held in Atlantic City and the team went "north"—126 miles—with an opening-day lineup of Stirnweiss at second, Hersh Martin in left, Russ Derry in right, Lindell in center, Etten at first, Joe Buzas at short, Don Savage at third, Mike Garbark catching, and Atley Donald pitching. These were hardly major leaguers, but they were determined to do the best they could. Derry actually hit four homers, two of them grand slams, in April and briefly got people excited about him.

On the roster with Bill Dresher, Herb Crompton, Mike Milosevich, Al Gettel, and Bill Zuber was Paul Schreiber, forty-two, the team's batting-practice pitcher since '37. He was on a big-league roster for the first time since 1923, a twenty-two-year gap between appearances. Zuber, from a German-speaking farming family in Iowa, could barely speak English, something McCarthy had to overcome. Tom Villante, a batboy on the team and later the head of broadcasting and marketing for Major League Baseball, recalls a day that "McCarthy was concerned that Zuber might lose his concentration after six innings, which had happened before."

> When Zuber headed for the mound in the seventh, he forgot to pick up his glove on the way. Players would leave their gloves on the field in those days, and there was Zuber on the mound, with his glove sitting on the grass between the foul line and the dugout.
>
> So Zuber pretends to tie his shoelaces, but broke one, so he had

to come in for a new pair. On the way back, he would pick up the glove and no one would notice.

But McCarthy never missed anything. He sat there shaking his head. This was wartime baseball.

World events in 1945 overwhelmed baseball, making some wonder why they were even bothering with it. The death of President Roosevelt in April postponed games and left the nation in mourning. But there had been jubilation with V-E Day as there soon would be with V-J Day, marking the end of combat and, for baseball fans, the eventual return of the players. It was not an overnight process, of course, and some teams—like Detroit, getting Hank Greenberg back early—fared better than others. Greenberg's homer on the last day would win them a pennant.

Instead of gaining players, the Yankees actually lost Lindell, who was inducted in June while fighting continued in the Pacific. And then came something from the front office that McCarthy had never heard once from Barrow.

"The players aren't hustling," said MacPhail.

Guys who couldn't hit or field was one thing. If hustling was the issue, that was aimed directly at the manager. McCarthy's health started to go bad. Gallbladder. Exhaustion. Drinking. He needed to get away. So he took a "leave of absence," went home to Tonawanda, New York, to rest, and put Fletcher in charge.

While he was gone, MacPhail sold his best pitcher, Borowy, to the Cubs for $100,000.

Borowy, from Fordham University, was 10–5, the ace of the staff, a very serious worker, and a real professional in the old Yankee way. He was twenty-nine and had compiled a 56–30 record for the Yanks, including 17 wins the year before. He'd won a big game for the Yanks in the '43 World Series. Now he was gone, just like that? This was a most un-Yankeelike roster move.

The sale remained controversial throughout the summer, particularly as Borowy continued to win with the Cubs. Elder statesman Clark Griffith, seventy-five, the Senators' owner, derided the waiver rule that allowed star players to escape to the other league where they couldn't hurt the Yankees. He demanded a change, although he acknowledged that he could have claimed the pitcher on waivers but hadn't bothered since "it was a foregone conclusion the name would be withdrawn." MacPhail called Griffith's criticism "silly."

There was clearly nothing wrong with Borowy, although McCarthy was supposedly grousing about his inability to complete games. He denied the team needed the money, claiming they had "$600,000 in the bank!"

The *World-Telegram*'s Dan Daniel, a good listener, had heard MacPhail say, "Borowy is through around here," after a bad home outing on July 15 in which he gave up an upper-deck homer to Zeb Eaton of Detroit, hardly a star player. The sale came twelve days later.

Being sold "came as a great surprise to me," said Borowy. "First thing I heard about it was after today's game when Larry MacPhail told me the news."

John Drebinger questioned whether McCarthy had approved it. "We doubt it," he wrote, "simply because this has never been the way that Joe McCarthy does things, and in the past fifteen seasons this observer has come to know Marse Joe and his way of doing things pretty well."

Wrote Daniel, "The sale of Borowy to the Cubs marked the end of an era. Col. MacPhail has been waiting for the opportunity to dash in and take hold of his outfit. He got it with Joe McCarthy's enforced vacation. From now on, MacPhail will make the big decisions, and from now on his opinion of players will dominate the Stadium situation."

McCarthy returned on August 9 after three weeks. Now he had to make do without his ace, and to top it all, had to watch as Borowy went 11–2 for the Cubs to make him a 21-game winner over two leagues. He even won two World Series games for Chicago, though they lost in the end.

McCarthy had offered to quit while he was home, but MacPhail, knowing the backlash it would have in his first season as owner, refused to accept the resignation.

He would carry on without Fletcher, sixty, who felt chest pains on September 12 and left the team, never to return. This had been his trusted coach since coming to the Yanks in 1927. Rolfe would leave Yale and return in '46 to replace him as third-base coach.

An exciting element of the strange season was the batting race. Averages were way down, but Tony Cuccinello of the White Sox went into the last day of the season with a .308 average, while Stirnweiss, nursing ulcers, was hanging in there at .306. The White Sox would be rained out on that last day and the game was not to be made up, since it had no effect on the pennant race.

Stirnweiss, at home against Boston, doubled his first time up. In the third he hit a grounder to third that was bobbled by Jack Tobin. Official scorer Bert Gumpert of the *Bronx Home News* called it an error, which Tobin later agreed with. But hometown scoring was as old as baseball, and other writers who liked Stirnweiss rushed to Gumpert to try to get him to reverse his call. He did; it became a hit.

Snuffy was retired his next two times up, and then on his last at-bat of the season singled to right. He was 3-for-5 and wound up at .3088, rounded off to .309, topping Cuccinello for the title. It was the only day of the entire season he was on top of the leaderboard, and it was the lowest average for a league leader since 1905. Stirnweiss, third in MVP voting, also led the league with 33 stolen bases, and his 22 triples were the most by an American Leaguer since Combs hit 23 in 1927.

The Yankees finished fourth, just six and a half games out of first in the final war year. Every Yankee fan felt that normal life meant a return to the World Series.

MACPHAIL'S BODY OF work in remaking Yankee Stadium was breathtaking. While Topping and Webb agreed to the expenses, it was all Larry's show.

He built a new home-team clubhouse, taking the Yankees from a street-level clubhouse on the third-base side to one on the lower-level, first-base side. It was carpeted and had a large trainer's space, a player lounge, a good-sized office for the manager, and plenty of storage space. It easily led to the first-base dugout, to which the Yankees moved in '46, at which time the bullpens also shifted, the Yankees now in right field.

MacPhail had new, permanent, curved-back box seats installed. The new seats were painted a lighter green than the ones that were scheduled to be upgraded later, marking the only time that there was "color coding," so to speak, in the stadium. Eventually, all would be the lighter green. He renumbered the sections so that lower numbers indicated choicer seating around the infield. (The original numbering system was restored when the new Yankee Stadium opened in 2009.) The loose Windsor chairs were painted a lighter green and scattered throughout the inner workings of the ballpark. As a general rule, collectors who purchased curved-back seats after the 1973 season were buying seats installed in 1946. The straight-back seats, located in the last rows behind the pillars, went back to 1923 (with some from 1928 and 1937).

There was a new press dining area near the Yankee clubhouse, where the food and drinks were always on the house.

A private restaurant called the Stadium Club was opened on two levels—the street level (the former Yankee clubhouse) serving a full menu for season box holders or VIPs, while a private room for parties or press conferences opened on the mezzanine level. That room was said to have the longest bar in New York. MacPhail had historic Yankee photographs blown up to serve as decor throughout these rooms and in fact throughout the stadium, so that Ruth, Gehrig, et al were never far from view.

He added a great deal of storage space and working space for the concessions business; built shops for the plumbers, electricians, painters, and carpenters; and had large storage rooms for old photos, trophies, pennants, even uniforms—except for the ones passed down to the minor leagues.

("We never gave a thought to taking home uniforms after the season," Yogi Berra said years later. "What would we need them for?" So they went down to the minors where they sewed on the Newark name, or whatever. Minor leaguers would wear DiMaggio's uniform.)

A smaller, electric scoreboard to the left of the existing one, paid for with advertising for Longines watches, was added because of the necessity of having a countdown clock for football games, including those played by Topping's New York Yankees football team, which played in the All-American Football Conference from 1946 to 1949.

MacPhail never got around to replacing the original scoreboard from 1923—that didn't happen until 1950, when the hand-operated classic was replaced by a $100,000 all-electronic board, paid for by Ballantine Beer.

MacPhail commissioned a new Yankee logo to complement the interlocking NY. This alternate logo, designed by Spencer Marketing graphic artist Lon Keller, would first appear as the script word *Yankees*, the "k" in the shape of a bat, topped by a red-white-and-blue Uncle Sam hat.

An early version may have been sketched on a napkin at the 21 Club by in-house portraitist Sam Friedman. It appeared on the 1946 spring training roster. Friedman's family said he drew it at the bar for Topping and Sonja Henie. If accurate, his version was embellished by Keller, circled by a baseball. It first appeared on the 1946 scorecard and throughout the stadium.

As expected, MacPhail soon put light towers on the roof of the stadium and put the team in the air for road trips, although after he departed, the Yankees returned to rail travel more than most clubs.

The addition of lights was especially welcomed by the New York *Daily News*, which called itself "New York's Picture Newspaper" and prided itself on spectacular action photos in its centerfold and on its back page. The *Daily*

News made a deal with the Yankees to pick up the electric costs for any day games in which the lights would be turned on, ensuring them better photos. The deal lasted almost twenty years. The *News* also used homing pigeons to pick up film at the stadium and fly it down to their Forty-second Street building.

With spring training never having been much of a moneymaker, MacPhail scheduled exhibition games in Panama and Texas to pick up a large guarantee and at least make training camp a break-even venture.

He also instituted Old-Timers' Day as an annual event, beginning in 1947. He called that one the "second annual," making Lou Gehrig Appreciation Day of 1939 the first. They have been held continuously ever since. Other teams have tried them, but all eventually ceased, while the Yankees' event has succeeded largely on the fans' enduring interest in the team's past. For many years there was a "theme," and the invited guests included both Yankees and opponents. Always on the field were Yankee owners and officials presenting gifts to the attendees. (When Gabe Paul went to the field in 1974, he encountered too many old-timers who had experienced nasty contract disputes with him on other clubs. It was decided that no team officials were necessary on the field.) Later on it evolved into an all-Yankee event. But over the years no less than Cobb, Mack, Griffith, Young, Speaker, Hornsby, Baker, Terry, Sisler, Frisch, Ott, Traynor, Robinson, Feller, and a long roll call of immortals made their way to the event, often en route to Cooperstown, where annual induction ceremonies followed a week later. Thus each year's new Hall of Fame class was also included.

Lucy Monroe remained a fixture performing the national anthem, and Yankee Stadium would be her ticket to fame, at least among Yankee fans. She sometimes played to mixed reviews. Wrote *Newsweek* in 1958: "The National Anthem is meant to rouse feelings of pride and re-dedication in American listeners, not to provoke laughter. It is our duty to report that the Lucy Monroe public address system version of *The Star-Spangled Banner* at the World Series in Yankee Stadium last week was a musical fright which brought embarrassment, smirks and giggles to attending thousands and listening millions across the country. It's time to send Lucy to the shower."

MacPhail never tinkered with the Yankee uniform, and brought Mel Allen back in '46 after his discharge to work both home and road games with Russ Hodges on WINS, replacing Bill Slater and Al Helfer, who did the '45 broadcasts.

Among people he brought over from his Brooklyn days was a top scout, Tom Greenwade, signing him to a contract on December 5, 1945, not long after he had scouted Jackie Robinson for the Dodgers. Greenwade would be the scout who discovered Mickey Mantle.

MacPhail's modernization helped the Yankees draw 2,265,512 in 1946, a new major league record and the first time the Yankees had topped a million since 1930. (On August 4, 74,529 paid to see Chandler beat Feller 2–0, a gate called the largest "accurately-counted crowd ever to see a baseball game.") Of course, the end of the war was the big reason, but MacPhail made sure that returning servicemen saw a greatly improved stadium over the one they remembered.

If there was one area where MacPhail showed no progress, though, it was in integrating the roster. As early as opening day 1945, his first game as owner, picketers marched around the stadium with signs saying IF WE CAN PAY, WHY CAN'T WE PLAY? and IF WE CAN STOP BULLETS, WHY NOT BALLS?

MacPhail, hardly alone in his thinking, met with the protestors, who said that negro fans constituted 25 percent of attendance, yet there were no negro employees in the Yankee organization. (Apart from service staff in the restaurants and maintenance, Pearl Davis, a secretary to Howard Berk, broke the color line in the front office in the sixties, and Doris Walden did it at the switchboard in the seventies.) MacPhail heard them out but made no hires. He later said that "agitators" who were just after their own self-interests were creating the clamor.

When NYU sociologist Dr. Dan Dodson, serving as executive director of the Mayor's Committee on Unity in New York City, tried to meet with the Yankees, MacPhail called him a "professional do-gooder" who didn't know anything about baseball.

A Major League Committee on Baseball Integration was formed in 1945, which included black sportswriter Sam Lacy, Branch Rickey of the Dodgers, MacPhail of the Yankees, and Joseph Rainey, a magistrate from Philadelphia. MacPhail never attended a meeting and the committee disbanded. Rickey, of course, was already thinking of signing a black player, and within months would meet with Jackie Robinson and begin the process of integrating first the International League in '46—and then in '47, the National League.

MacPhail, carrying forward accepted major league standards, earned no plaudits for his work in this area. His public position was that efforts to integrate the major leagues would undermine the Negro Leagues, perhaps putting them out of business. (That did, of course, happen.) He wanted no part of "political and social-minded drum beaters."

Besides, the Yankees had been collecting rent checks from the Negro Leagues, leasing the stadium since July 5, 1930, including a 1939 competition of five doubleheaders between Negro National League teams, with the ultimate winner to receive the Ruppert Cup. All the great stars of the Negro Leagues passed through Yankee Stadium, and Josh Gibson may have even hit a fair ball out of the stadium, a story undocumented but often told. The last recorded Negro League game was an East-West All-Star matchup at Yankee Stadium on August 20, 1961, with Satchel Paige pitching.

In other areas, MacPhail was quite enlightened. In '46, he prepared a confidential memo on the sacred Reserve Clause, which four years later came to light during congressional hearings before Brooklyn congressman Emanuel Celler. In the memo, he stated that the clause in baseball contracts binding players to their teams beyond the expiration of the contract itself "could not be enforced in the courts," and that salary disputes should be resolved through arbitration (which came to be twenty-seven years later). He also voiced support of expansion to six major leagues as opposed to the established two.

MOST OF THE $600,000 in changes to Yankee Stadium took place over the winter of 1945–46, and so dramatic were the changes—and so well received— that Arthur Daley of the *Times* suggested that MacPhail "ought to arrange inspection tours for [fans], a fifty-cent tour . . . in the Radio City style."

Forty years later, the Yankees did in fact initiate tours, run by team historian Tony Morante, who with his father had earlier been part of the Mantle security escort after games.

There was fan discontent over the rebranding of a number of reserved seats to box seats, and price increases to $2.50 for box seats, $1.75 for reserves, and $1.25 for general admission. The old prices—$2.40, $1.80, and $1.20—were "too slow for ticket sellers to make change from," explained MacPhail. He pointed out that the stadium had 39,520 low-priced seats, more than all but two other ballparks.

The team sold twenty-five hundred season box seats, and each purchaser got a brass nameplate affixed to their box railing, a practice that delighted the fans who would bribe ushers to sneak down to find themselves in, say, the Merrill Lynch box. Four hundred box holders signed up for membership in the new Stadium Club restaurant.

The MacPhail touch for promotion was evident when five hundred pairs of nylon stockings were given away at the first Ladies' Day of the season, and by hiring four barbershop quartets to serenade the fans.

The $250,000 lights on the stadium roof would leave only Fenway without lights in the American League. The six towers contained 1,245 reflectors, each with a 1,500-watt bulb. (Forbes Field in Pittsburgh had 864 reflectors and had been the park with the most.) The Yanks would play fourteen night games in that first illuminated season.

McCarthy found spring training unsettling, even with his stars back. MacPhail, looking to cover his spring costs, booked nine games in Panama against U.S. Army teams, while two simultaneous spring training camps operated in Florida to accommodate the large number of players, one in St. Petersburg and the other, run by coach Johnny Neun, in Bradenton.

The camp included a twenty-one-year-old med student from Tulane University named Bobby Brown, whose father was an old friend of Weiss's. Brown was a much-heralded shortstop at the time and received a $35,000 bonus to sign with the Yankees. He attended high school in Maplewood, New Jersey, and would go on to play a fine third base for the Yanks while also completing his studies to become a cardiologist. He would return to baseball years later as president of the Texas Rangers and then, in a final act, as president of the American League.

At Newark, he roomed with promising outfielder Larry Berra. One night, while studying his medical text, Berra asked him, "How'd your book come out?" It was an early Yogi-ism.

ON APRIL 30, Bob Feller no-hit the Yankees 1–0, the first time the Yanks had ever been no-hit at Yankee Stadium and the first time they had been no-hit anywhere since 1919. Frankie Hayes hit a ninth-inning homer off Floyd "Bill" Bevens to break a 0–0 tie.

The Yankees made their first regular-season flight on May 13. Harold Rosenthal of the *Herald Tribune* was aboard to report a takeoff from LaGuardia Field at 3:15 P.M. and a landing in St. Louis's Lambert–St. Louis Airport at 6:47 P.M. Four men, leery of flying—Ruffing, Crosetti, Bevens, and Bill Wight—were given permission to take the old-fashioned train.

The Yanks had chartered a DC-4 from Douglas Aircraft, calling it the

Yankee Mainliner. The rail age was winding down for teams; the camaraderie of the card games in the dining car, the friendships formed between writers and players, would be a thing of the past.

It wasn't embraced by everyone. In 1947 there was talk that MacPhail would make anyone who went by rail pay for his own ticket, but he backed off and said, "No one on our ball club ever has been told that he must fly."

Henrich took a leadership role here, befitting his seniority, his likability, and his intelligence. Tommy was an organizer, and whether it was barbershop quartet competitions back home in Massillon, Ohio, bridge tournaments on the trains, or a role in creating a player pension plan, he was never shy. At one point MacPhail wanted to expand the schedule to 168 games. Tommy opposed it and publicly challenged his boss's position. When it came to flying, he led a vote by the Yankee players with the majority opposing it. The vote was overruled. Eventually, most of the players flew, and those who wanted to use trains would get reimbursed.

Meanwhile, for others discovering the glamour of the early days of passenger travel, the flights added excitement to being a big leaguer. Mel Allen would alert fans to assemble at LaGuardia Field to welcome the team home, and sometimes, if the hour was right, the airport receptions were fantastic, with thousands greeting their heroes.

ON MAY 24, McCarthy's long run as Yankee manager ended.

McCarthy had gone home from Cleveland four days earlier, citing a flareup of his gallbladder trouble. He had a miserable cold and was generally run-down. He had been short-tempered with Rolfe, with his rookie pitcher Joe Page, with a Detroit cabbie, and even with Red Sox owner Tom Yawkey. He telegraphed MacPhail, "It is with extreme regret that I must request that you accept my resignation as manager of the Yankee Baseball Club, effective immediately. My doctor advises that my health would be seriously jeopardized if I continued. This is the sole reason for my decision which, as you know, is entirely voluntary on my part." He recommended Dickey as his successor.

MacPhail dispatched George Weiss to Tonawanda to visit with Marse Joe in person. It was an appropriate courtesy and the right gesture for this Yankee legend. But McCarthy had made up his mind.

"The retirement of McCarthy was not without advance warning and it occasioned no real surprise," wrote Red Smith in the *Herald Tribune.* "Yet it is going to be difficult to conceive of a Yankee team without him." As for Dickey, Smith wrote, "All but the first few months of Dickey's big league career was served under McCarthy, so it is to be expected the Yanks will go on being the same sort of ball team McCarthy had, which is the best and most skillful and most exquisitely polished team that can be built."

"The McCarthy stamp was indelibly imprinted on his team, his YAN-KEES," wrote Arthur Daley. "This grim-visaged man was in a class by himself . . . you can't improve on perfection. Joseph Vincent McCarthy was exactly that."

Dickey, with the team in Boston, became the Yanks' first player-manager since Bill Donovan had pitched one game in 1916 and the last they've had since. Dickey's last 15 appearances were all as a pinch hitter: He caught his last game on June 12.

The first Yankee home night game was played on May 28 following a rainout the night before. On a chilly evening before 49,917, in what would be Dickey's home debut as manager, Clarence "Cuddles" Marshall had the distinction of pitching for the Yanks, losing to Washington knuckleballer Dutch Leonard, 2–1. The first pitch was delivered by Charles E. Wilson, president of General Electric, whose engineers had designed the system.

The next day, McCarthy showed up at the stadium to say good-bye to everyone, to assure all that he and MacPhail had never exchanged a "rough" word, and that "I'm still a Yankee and I think the ball club will win with Dickey—no reason why it shouldn't."

THE TEAM, MEANWHILE, was underachieving. Stirnweiss fell to .251 and Etten to .232, leading people to label them "wartime" players who couldn't fare well against the returning first-rate pitching. What was more disheartening was seeing DiMaggio hit .290/25/95, Rizzuto .257, Gordon .210, and Henrich .251. Had they lost it?

Chandler was 20–8, while Bevens won 16. Bevens spent just three full seasons with the Yanks. The big right-hander from Oregon spent seven years in the minors before making it to New York, and then five more after his big-league career, pitching mostly in the Pacific Coast League.

The 1946 season would be Johnny Murphy's last with the Yanks; he was released after spring training of 1947. Johnny had given the team twelve sterling seasons out of the bullpen and helped bring glamour to the reliever's role. Murph had also served as the Yankees' and the American

League's player representative on matters involving the new pension program being instituted for ten-year major leaguers, based on proceeds from the All-Star Game and radio rights for the World Series.

ALTHOUGH AT DICKEY's hiring it had been reported that he was engaged "through 1947," this was apparently not the case. On September 2, according to MacPhail, Bill had "demanded a showdown on just where he stood for 1947. I told Bill the only thing I could tell him was what I told him when he was appointed, that a decision as to the management of the club in 1947 would be made as soon as possible after the close of the present season."

On September 9, MacPhail hired longtime manager Bucky Harris to serve in an advisory capacity, citing a need to do a better job in scouting their own minor league players for potential trades. MacPhail had visited with Harris in Buffalo in August, where Bucky was serving as general manager of the Bisons, seemingly done as a major league manager after twenty seasons, the last in 1943. "He is not considered for any kind of a job on the field," said MacPhail. "Bucky will be the contact between myself and the club, doing a job that I have found neither myself nor George Weiss has had time for this year."

MacPhail later reported that Durocher had sought out Dan Topping in early August to put his hat in the ring for the Yankee job.

On September 11, Dickey asked not to be considered for the managing job in '47, and two days later he quit and went home to Little Rock. He cited personal reasons, saying only that "I don't *think* Bucky will manage the Yanks. I don't know though—he might."

"I regret exceedingly leaving New York," he said as he checked out of his Detroit hotel. "I have played only with the Yankees and they will always be my team. I am very grateful to the fans in New York for the way they have treated me through the years. I am sorry my New York association ended just when it did. As Colonel MacPhail said in his statement it is 'unfortunate,' but the circumstances made no other action possible on my part."

With only fourteen games left on the schedule, coach Johnny Neun was named to finish the season (he went 8–6). The Yanks finished third, seventeen games out.

On September 20, the Yankees released Ruffing, the winningest pitcher in their history. He caught on with the White Sox in 1947, pitched nine games for them, and called it a career. Although Whitey Ford later passed him, his 231 victories remained a record for Yankee right-handers, a record likely to last a very long time. (Ruffing had passed Bob Shawkey in 1939, and thus by 2012 had held the mark for seventy-three years, with no challenger in sight.)

ACCORDING TO MACPHAIL, Harris was off scouting the Brooklyn playoff series with the Cardinals and recommended Durocher for the Yankee job.

Then, MacPhail said, he persuaded Harris to take the managing job on October 23, but held up the announcement as a favor to Leo, who was in negotiations with Brooklyn over a new contract. On October 26, he called Durocher to say he couldn't hold up on the announcement any longer and would have a press conference on Election Day.

On Election Day, November 5, in the club's Fifth Avenue office, Harris, fifty, was introduced as the new manager for 1947–48, with Charlie Dressen named as a coach. Both were present.

"When I hired Harris I had no idea of his managing the club," MacPhail said. "In choosing a manager, I felt a deep responsibility to my two partners, Del Webb and Dan Topping. I did not want to be hurried. I wanted to come up with the best available man. I think Harris is the best available man."

Wrote Arthur Daley, "Harris is an eminently sound choice, a chap wise in the ways of baseball. The baseball writers will applaud his selection because Bucky is a blunt, outspoken fellow who never equivocates. Nor will he take any nonsense from MacPhail, if that impulsive character ever should try to stick his finger in the pie."

"MacPhail offered me the Yankee job," said Durocher.

"Leo was never asked to become the new Yankee manager," said MacPhail. "But . . . he sent word to me that he would like to manage the club. I did not tell Leo he could have the job. I did not think he would be the logical man for it."

Crosetti was made a coach, replacing Rolfe. He'd hold that third-base coaching spot for the next twenty-one seasons.

JOE MCCARTHY TOOK it easy for all of 1947. By '48, he was ready to work again, and the Red Sox hired him to manage.

He managed Boston for two and half years, and then retired to his "Yankee Farm" in Tonawanda, where he lived until his death. He was elected to the

Hall of Fame in 1957. In planning the remodeled Yankee Stadium in the mid-seventies, it was decided to erect a plaque for Casey Stengel, who had died in '75. "Order one for McCarthy too," Gabe Paul told me. "Let him know about it and enjoy it while he's alive."

I called McCarthy and invited him to the unveiling, but he wasn't up to the trip. So I asked him to record a thank-you greeting for the fans, which went over nicely when we played it on the stadium's PA system on April 21, 1976. He died January 13, 1978, at ninety.

Chapter Twenty

Bucky Harris had managed four teams, having been the "Boy Manager" in Washington, leading them to the World Series in 1924 and 1925 while still playing second base. But his managing career had seemed to run out of gas after '43 in Philadelphia. He was still just fifty years old, but his career went back to 1916 and it seemed to some as if he had run out the course. Now he reemerged with the best job in baseball. And it was going to get better.

On October 11, 1946, the Yankees traded Gordon to Cleveland straight-up for right-hander Allie Reynolds. This was a blockbuster by any measure, a one-for-one deal involving two All-Star-caliber players. Both were thought to be twenty-eight, although it later turned out that Reynolds was really thirty. Gordon had played in exactly 1,000 games for the Yankees and recorded exactly 1,000 hits.

(The move shifted Stirnweiss back to second, where he set records by playing seventy-one straight errorless games and handling 382 consecutive errorless chances.)

Gordon and Reynolds were both coming off poor seasons. Both were vulnerable, and the deal freshened both of their careers. It was DiMaggio who told MacPhail to get Reynolds rather than Red Embree, who Cleveland owner Bill Veeck was dangling. "He's their best, outside of Feller," said Joe.

Reynolds was one-quarter Creek Indian, which of course led to his being called "the Big Chief." He was the son of a Nazarene evangelist minister and had a strict conservative upbringing, even forced to wear long-sleeved sweatshirts and sweatpants for his high school basketball games. Born in

Bethany, Oklahoma, he went to Oklahoma A&M (renamed Oklahoma State in 1957), where he played baseball for Hank Iba, the school's great basketball coach who went on to win two NCAA titles. To that point, Allie had not played anything more than fraternity-house baseball. Iba turned him into a pro prospect, and he signed with the Indians in 1939, reaching the majors in '42.

With the Yankees, he would emerge as the leader of a new starting rotation that would include Vic Raschi and, a year later, Eddie Lopat. Reynolds, whose best pitch was a rising fastball ("Today you'd call it a cutter," said Berra), would go 19–8 in his first Yankee season, but by completing only 17 of his 30 starts, he came to be paired in people's minds with the hard-drinking Joe Page, who handled the primary relief role on the team and who would emerge as a star in his fourth season.

"[Page] has 18 suits . . . and owns 11 pairs of shoes," wrote Milton Gross. "His shirts are made to order . . . His rayon undershorts are loud. He has five wristwatches. He is always immaculately groomed. He could pass for a man of distinction."

Page's entrances to games became rituals. He'd hurdle the low right-field bullpen fence and, jacket over shoulder, walk to the mound, glancing over his shoulder to get the game situation from the new auxiliary scoreboard, tossing the jacket to the waiting batboy and taking his warm-ups. There was no musical accompaniment, but the fans loved the show.

In Reynolds's eight Yankee seasons, he would start 209 games and relieve in 86, easily adapting to whatever the situation called for.

Raschi, from Springfield, Massachusetts, and nicknamed "the Springfield Rifle," played basketball at Springfield College, where Dr. James Naismith invented the game. After three years at the school he was signed by scout Gene McCann, who had been watching him play baseball since high school. (He would earn a B.S. degree from the College of William and Mary in off-seasons.) His move up the ladder was halted by Army Air Corps service, and in '46 he split the season between Binghamton, Newark, and the Yankees. He made the big-league club full-time in July of '47.

He arrived at the same time that the veteran Bobo Newsom joined the team. The colorful Newsom, thirty-nine, had debuted in 1929 and had changed teams thirteen times—with more to come before he retired at forty-five.

Not only did they both win as surprise starters in a doubleheader, but they found themselves in the middle of a nineteen-game winning streak, the longest in the American League in forty-one years. Raschi's win was number fourteen in the streak. He would go 7–2 for the season.

In January 1947, the Yankees also signed free agent George McQuinn to play first base after his release by the Athletics. McQuinn, thirty-seven, had originally come up through the Yankee organization but spent most of his career with the Browns, including during their their '44 championship. Despite a chronically bad back that even made sleeping difficult, he hit .304 in '47, bettered only by DiMaggio's .315, making it a brilliant acquisition by Weiss.

LARRY BERRA WAS interchangeably known as Larry and Yogi for the first few years of his career, but "Yogi" was so unique that it eventually won out. (He even wound up signing an anniversary card to his wife, Carmen, "Love, Yogi Berra.")

Some of the stories about Yogi were made up by his childhood neighbor Joe Garagiola, who also grew up on Elizabeth Avenue on "the Hill" in St. Louis and became a big leaguer.

But Yogi was an American original and, in fact, maybe the Great American Success Story. He was a genius in his field. Even in his eighties, he could see a different game from the rest of us, subtle points that would escape even baseball insiders.

He became one of the best-known figures to emerge from American sports, appearing in TV commercials beginning in the early fifties and still going in the 2010s. He knew the core American values of family and hard work, instilled by his Italian-immigrant parents. Paulina and Pietro Berra were married in Italy, but their five children were born in St. Louis. Larry left school in eighth grade to earn money for the family, a common occurrence during the Depression.

He loved to play ball as a kid and had a habit of sitting in a yoga position on the ground while his team was at bat. His friend Bobby Hofman (later a major league infielder, and the Yanks' director of scouting and player development in the eighties) called him "Yogi," and when the story emerged, that became his nickname. It was his ticket to national fame.

His malapropisms became treasured, even landing him in *Bartlett's Familiar Quotations*. Arguably the best known were "It ain't over till it's over," "It's déjà vu all over again," and "When you come to a fork in the road, take it." There was always logic to what he said, but you had to ponder it yourself.

A good and decent man, Yogi would be in a separate room at the Hall of Fame for baseball saints if such a thing were created. (He even seemed to perform miracles: snagging his second chance at a Ted Williams foul pop to save an Allie Reynolds no-hitter, coaching the 1969 Miracle Mets, delivering the Yanks a long-missing pennant when he returned as a coach, having George Steinbrenner apologize to him after a long falling-out, and seeing David Cone pitch a perfect game on Yogi Berra Day after he borrowed Joe Girardi's catcher's mitt for the first-pitch ceremony.)

When Ted Williams first saw him crouching behind the plate, he said, "What the hell is this, your shin guards are up to here, your mask is down to there, you're a ballplayer?" When he first reported to the Yankees' clubhouse, still in his naval uniform, Pete Sheehy said, "He didn't even look like a sailor!"

Yogi signed with the Yankees in 1943 when his hometown Cardinals, whom he loved, wouldn't give him the same deal they gave Garagiola. It was a matter of pride, something that Yogi never compromised. He had pride and he had integrity, and no one ever had better instincts for life decisions. It was always said that if Yogi canceled a plane reservation, you didn't want to take that flight.

Berra's stock seemed to rise with the Yankees when Mel Ott, managing the Giants, offered MacPhail $50,000 for him. MacPhail summoned Yogi to his office at 745 Fifth. He was expecting more than a five-foot-seven bow-legged figure. He told others that he looked like the "bottom of an unemployed acrobatic team."

Yogi hit .314 at Newark in 1946 and was called up to the parent club for the final weeks of the season, just as Dickey was turning the team over to Neun. Dickey may not have been there to bring him along—then—but he would be back in spring training to make a special student out of him, to "learn him" the finer points of catching, as Yogi was still moving between the outfield and the catching positions, finding his way.

In spring training, Berra impressed people with his play in left, enabling Henrich to move to first. But on May 6, with Aaron Robinson nursing a sore back, Yogi caught Reynolds and essentially began his eighteen-season Yankee career, during which he would make the All-Star team every year from 1948 to 1962. He would play more World Series games than any player in history, and would come to be seen as the team's "assistant manager," even while still a young player. There came a time when almost every other team in the league was using a catcher developed by the Yankees, unable to unseat Yogi. Gus Triandos, Sherm Lollar, Clint Courtney, Lou Berberet, Darrell Johnson, Hal Smith, and Gus Niarhos had all wound up playing elsewhere. It was a testament to the quality of Berra's play and the strength of the Yankee lineup.

One day at his museum, Yogi showed me how his glove manufacturer would remove the web in his catcher's mitt and replace it with heavy-gauge shoelaces so he could better view pop fouls. "Yogi, you had every advantage going for you, and you had to add to them?" I asked. But he was never one to miss a trick. He was believed to be the first to put his index finger outside the catcher's mitt for extra protection, and the first to pad the center of his mitt with a woman's falsie.

MEANWHILE, MACPHAIL WAS a tempest in a teapot, so unlike the staid Yankees of recent vintage.

New baseball commissioner Happy Chandler convened a hearing in late March of '47 to sort through assorted disputes between the Yankees and Dodgers. The press called it the "Battle of the Century."

Branch Rickey was angered that MacPhail had signed two of his coaches, Dressen and Red Corriden, who had been under contract to Brooklyn.

On March 10, the Dodgers left Havana after two games with the Yankees, with MacPhail claiming they had pledged to stay for a third.

MacPhail's flirtation with Durocher as manager (or was it the other way around?) seemed to be in violation of a contract.

Durocher was in trouble for palling around with gamblers, but MacPhail was seen in the company of Memphis Engelberg and Connie Immerman, both alleged gamblers, during one of the Havana games.

There was no love lost between Rickey and MacPhail, and these were two of baseball's glamour franchises. So Chandler hauled them all in.

Six days before the start of the regular season, the Yankees and the Dodgers were fined $2,000 each, Dressen was suspended for thirty days of the regular season, and Durocher was suspended for the full season, Jackie Robinson's historic rookie year.

Chandler found that the alleged gamblers in Havana were not guests of MacPhail.

Twice during the year, MacPhail had to report to Chandler's office in

Cincinnati to explain why he was breaking a pledge of silence not to discuss the charges and the discipline.

FRED LOGAN DIED on February 8 at sixty-seven, leaving Pete Sheehy in charge of the home clubhouse at Yankee Stadium for the next forty years. Logan was the last employee to go back to the origins of the team, the first season at Hilltop Park. He gave them forty-four seasons.

The Yankees began TV broadcasts in 1947, receiving $75,000 from WABD (Dumont Television) to cover all seventy-seven home games plus eleven selected games from Washington, Boston, and Philadelphia, with Bill Slater as the sole announcer. Mel Allen and Russ Hodges handled the radio on WINS, which still had a much bigger audience.

APRIL 27, A Sunday, was declared Babe Ruth Day by Commissioner Chandler. Fifty-eight thousand packed Yankee Stadium to see Babe in person, while fans in other ballparks heard the ceremonies via radio over their PA systems. It was a rare appearance for the Babe, who was showing the effects of a battle with throat cancer. Chandler's office said it was the first national commemorative day for a baseball figure since founding father Harry Wright had one in 1896.

Chandler was widely booed by Yankee fans, and even MacPhail instructed Mel Allen, the field announcer, to emphasize that "this is Babe Ruth Day, with other personalities on the program entitled to respect as well." Five thousand dollars of the day's proceeds was presented to Ruth, who turned it over to the Ford Foundation for a program sponsoring kids. Many in the press admired not only the way Chandler took the booing, but that his first words were "This is Albert B. Chandler."

Ruth required assistance to climb the dugout steps. He wore his now familiar camel hair coat, and removed his matching hat before speaking. He was coughing quite steadily, but managed to say,

> Thank you very much, ladies and gentlemen . . . you know how bad my voice sounds. Well, it feels just as bad. You know this baseball game of ours comes up from the youth. That means the boys. And after you're a boy, and grow up to know how to play ball, then

you come to the boys you see representing themselves today in your national pastime.

The only real game, I think, in the world is baseball. As a rule, some people think if you give them a football or baseball or something like that, naturally, they're athletes right away. But you can't do that in baseball. You've gotta start from way down the bottom, when you're six or seven years of age.

You can't wait until you're fifteen or sixteen. You've gotta let it grow up with you, and if you're successful and try hard enough, you're bound to come out on top, just like these boys have come to the top now. [He pointed to the current Yankees, kneeling on the field.]

There's been so many lovely things said about me, I'm glad I had the opportunity to thank everybody.

There weren't many dry eyes in the house. Ed Barrow, who had retired as a director in December, sat in a mezzanine box and wouldn't go down on the field. "I never did like to cry in public," he told Dan Daniel.

Babe was just fifty-two, but he seemed eighty. It was apparent that he was gravely ill, and indeed he had had throat surgery at Memorial Hospital in New York. "His health," wrote Shirley Povich in the *Washington Post*, "has been of national concern for weeks."

Every appearance from then on seemed it could be his last.

THE REGULAR SEASON started slowly but the Yanks took over first place on June 15 and never lost it, their nineteen-game winning streak essentially putting an end to any pennant race. They won by twelve games. Harris must have thought he'd died (three years in Buffalo) and then ascended to heaven (where he was handed the Yankees' managing job).

In May, MacPhail leveled a hundred-dollar fine on DiMaggio for missing a film shoot with Army Signal Corps newsreel photographers. Other players were fined lesser amounts for missing club-mandated dinners. It was another case of MacPhail upstaging the manager. DiMaggio, fined? Publicly embarrassed? Under McCarthy, who never went public with discipline and who always handled such matters without front-office interference, it would have been unimaginable.

"I needed batting practice badly and did not want to give up that time to anything else," said Joe.

"When Larry told me what he planned to do, I told him to forget it," said Harris. "Don't fine them. Let me talk to the boys."

But MacPhail fined them anyway. To some, it was an outrage. DiMaggio didn't bite back. But it was a most undignified act against this towering figure.

ON SEPTEMBER 28, the final game of the season, the Yankees held their "second annual" Old-Timers' Day.

This one featured Ruth (the only one who didn't suit up), Cobb (thrown out on a bunt at age sixty-one), Speaker, Young, Sisler, Simmons, Mack, Cochrane, Foxx, Lajoie, Grove, and a host of former Yankees going back to Peckinpaugh and Pipp. Dickey, now managing his hometown team in Little Rock, did not attend. The proceeds went to the Babe Ruth Foundation. Ruth thanked the crowd "in a husky voice that could scarcely be heard," said the *Times*.

BROOKLYN WON THE National League pennant, so Rickey and MacPhail would be in a Subway Series, the first to be televised. Gillette was the principal sponsor, and their brassy opening theme—"To LOOK sharp!. . . ."—became almost an anthem of big-time sports coverage for the next decade and a half.

In game one, the Yankees started their own rookie standout, Connecticut's Frank "Spec" Shea, "the Naugatuck Nugget," who burst onto the scene with a 14–5 record. The twenty-six-year-old right-hander was 15–5 in 1946 for Stengel's Oakland Oaks and made the jump to the majors with ease. His nickname had nothing to do with wearing glasses, which he didn't. His father had freckles and was nicknamed "Speckle," which was eventually shortened.

Shea, with four innings of relief from Page, won the opener 5–3. Reynolds won game two, and the Dodgers won game three at Ebbets Field, although Berra hit the first pinch-hit home run in Series history, in this, the forty-fourth World Series.

In game four, the unlikely Bill Bevens stood on the verge of baseball history. Despite a 7–13 regular season, and despite a sloppy outing that would see him walk 10 batters, the big thirty-year-old righty led 2–1 with two out in the ninth and a no-hitter on the line. Not everyone realized it was a no-hitter, given all the baserunners in the game.

But he was nevertheless on the verge of immortality as he worked from the stretch with pinch runners Al Gionfriddo and Eddie Miksis on base, facing pinch hitter Cookie Lavagetto. Gionfriddo's steal of second helped set up the inning, and some blamed the inexperienced Berra for allowing the steal. Dickey would help eliminate that problem in a hurry the following year.

Harris added to the controversy by having Bevens intentionally walk the next batter, defying the conventional wisdom to never put the winning run on base.

With a 1-and-1 count, "I pitched him high and away," said Bevens. "It looked like a lazy fly ball to right. I thought Tommy [Henrich] would catch it. But it stayed up in the air. I saw Tommy jump and the ball land about four feet over his glove."

On the radio, Red Barber screamed, "And here comes the tying run, and here comes the winning run . . . ," as the Dodgers won the game 3–2.

So much for the first no-hitter in World Series history.

Wrote Dick Young in the *Daily News*, "That's when God's Little Green Acre became a bedlam. The clock read 3:51, Brooklyn Standard Time—the most emotional minute in the lives of thousands of Faithful. There was Lavagetto being mobbed—and off to the side, there was Bevens, head bowed low, walking dejectedly through the swarming crowd, and completely ignored by it. Just a few seconds earlier, he was the one who everybody was planning to pat on the back. He was the one who would have been carried off the field—the only pitcher ever to toss a no-hitter in a series. Now he was just another loser."

"Look," reflected Bevens, years later. "Every kid has a dream, right? Mine was to meet Babe Ruth, be a Yankee, and pitch in a World Series. Well, I reached all three, so how can I complain? Of course, it would have been nice to know all those years ago that Lavagetto couldn't hit a low inside pitch. But what the hell."

The Series returned to Yankee Stadium, the Yanks up 3–2, but the Dodgers tied it, helped by a remarkable catch by Gionfriddo at the left-field bullpen, robbing DiMaggio of a three-run homer. Red Barber called, *"Back, back, back, back, back, back . . . he makes a one-handed catch against the bullpen! Oh, Doctor!"* to his amazed audience.

In a rare display of emotion on the field, the Yankee Clipper kicked at the dirt as the ball was caught, just as he was approaching second base. It was a body-language "shucks." Death Valley had done him in again. He managed only 148 Yankee Stadium home runs in his thirteen-season career, none in the World Series.

Shea, on just one day's rest after a complete-game win in game five, had nothing in game seven, but relief from Bevens (2⅔ innings) and Page (five shutout innings) gave New York a 5–2 win, and the Yankees had their eleventh world championship. Bevens, Gionfriddo, and Lavagetto would never play another major league game.

And then came the fireworks.

MacPhail, listening with writers to the final half inning in the press room, drinking and anticipating the upcoming celebration, suddenly told the press, "That's it. That does it. That's my retirement," as the game-ending double play was recorded. And with that, the writers suddenly couldn't leave for the clubhouse. MacPhail was now the story.

"I'm through. I've got what I wanted and I'm through. I can't take any more of this. My health won't stand it."

Writers who had been covering MacPhail for years couldn't be sure if he meant it, knowing he was capable of outlandish statements, sometimes fueled by liquor. But all they saw was beer, tears, and emotion.

He went into the clubhouse, and the writers followed. The players were into their celebration, hugging, posing for photos, singing, drinking beer.

MacPhail found Weiss. "Here! You!" he said, and then he turned to the writers, who didn't know for sure whether the world championship or MacPhail was the story. "I want you to say this in your story. I built the losing team out there, but he's the guy who built the winners."

Weiss smiled but was unsure what was going on as MacPhail worked the room, congratulating the players and telling them all that "I'm through."

Topping and Webb didn't know what to make of it. It was news to them. Red Patterson didn't have a clue. They'd lived through so much with MacPhail. One night, it was said, Topping and Tom Yawkey got drunk at 21 and traded DiMaggio for Ted Williams. The next morning, sober, they called it off. It was a roller-coaster ride, to be sure, and not always Macphail's doing.

Attention turned to the celebration. There was rookie Bobby Brown, the med student who had three pinch hits, celebrating with the handsome hero Joe Page. This was a first Series for many of them, and of course the first Yankee triumph for Harris.

Rickey went to the Dodgers' clubhouse to thank his men for their effort.

As he left, he bumped into MacPhail. They'd never been on easy terms. But MacPhail wrapped his arm around Rickey and began talking about what a great Series it had been.

What Rickey said could be heard clearly by those within a few feet. "I am taking your hand," he said, "only because people are watching us. Don't you ever speak to me again."

Now it was everybody downtown to the Biltmore Hotel for the official party, the celebration of the triumph. And there would be held the Battle of the Biltmore.

The stately Biltmore, a classic New York hotel near Grand Central, was often the site of baseball gatherings. League meetings, writers' dinners, welcome-home dinners, and now a World Series celebration. When MacPhail arrived, he downed a few more beers. People were annoyed with his behavior. He had upstaged the players, upstaged Harris, upstaged everything.

At the party was John McDonald, MacPhail's old aide in Cincinnati and Brooklyn. Now retired due to bad health, McDonald had written a story for the *Saturday Evening Post* about MacPhail, one that Larry took exception to. Spotting McDonald, to whom he had sent a telegram calling him a Judas, he berated him in person and then punched him in the eye. This wasn't a first for MacPhail by any means. He was arrested during the '45 World Series for assault and battery against the manager of the local telephone company near his estate in Maryland.

What was next? He spotted Weiss, there with his wife, Hazel. And he proceeded to give Weiss a stern lecture, may have socked him, and definitely fired him. On the spot. Weiss, the faithful Yankee since 1932, left the party in tears, no easy occurrence for the emotionless GM.

Then MacPhail got into an argument with Topping. Some felt blows were exchanged, but it was done in a room off to the side and no one was quite certain.

Not only was MacPhail resigning, now he was being pushed. Topping and Webb summoned their attorneys and gave MacPhail until 6:00 A.M. to accept a $2 million offer for his one-third share and get out of their lives.

Lee MacPhail, Larry's son, was twenty-nine and earning his stripes at the minor league level. A possible irritant in the Larry MacPhail–Weiss relationship could have been an attempt to bring Lee to New York as general manager, with Weiss reporting to him. Both Dan Daniel in the *World-Telegram* and Milton Gross in the *Post* reported that to be so. That would not have gone over well.

Said Lee in his book, *My Nine Innings*, "As soon as I walked into the ball-room I knew that something had happened. But people were reluctant to tell me the sorry details—that my father had argued with and then hit both Weiss and Topping. Everyone was still there and I was soon thrust in the middle of it. Dad had told Weiss he was fired and I remember telling George to ignore it, that he didn't mean it. However, the damage was already done . . . I wondered what would happen to me. I am sure that under the circumstances, Topping, Webb and Weiss would have welcomed my resignation. But I had a wife and two kids and needed the job and just waited to see if the ax would fall. George eventually talked to me and said I could stay but they would want me to return to Kansas City, rather than coming to New York."

LARRY MACPHAIL LIVED thirty-one more years and never ventured into the baseball universe again. For a while his name would come up if a team was for sale, but in time he faded off the radar. Seldom was he seen at baseball events. One night in the early seventies, Bob Fishel tapped me on the shoulder and pointed to Lee MacPhail's box. There as Lee's guest was his father, in his first return to the stadium since the Battle of the Biltmore. No longer the Roaring Redhead, he sat quietly. There was, I thought, sadness to the picture. He'd been battling cancer and alcoholism for many years, and had what is now known to be Alzheimer's disease. He had been raising cattle and breeding horses, but all of that was now gone; he lived in a VA nursing home.

He died in 1975 and was elected to the Hall of Fame in 1978. His grand-son Andy has carried on the MacPhail name in baseball as general manager of the Twins, Cubs, and Orioles.

Chapter Twenty-One

THE FUTURE OF BUCKY HARRIS was tenuous at best after MacPhail's departure. This was now George Weiss's team, and Harris had been MacPhail's selection. After the Battle of the Biltmore, Weiss, now fifty-two, was immediately "rehired" as vice president–general manager of the club, with Topping assuming the presidency. Topping never had much of an interest in the day-to-day affairs of the team, even if he reported to his office on a fairly regular basis. He pretty much turned over the company checkbook to Weiss, putting him in charge of the roster, the minors, club policy, and the office staff. In other words, he was now Barrow. The farm system would be run by Lee MacPhail, Gene Martin, Paul Krichell, and Eddie Leishman.

Despite a dour disposition, Weiss was a hardworking company man. Though players saw him as cheap with salaries ("You'll make up for it with your World Series share," he'd tell them), he was nonetheless a respected figure in the game who had a keen eye for picking good scouts and following their direction.

(Yogi Berra used to sign his contracts early, "Before all the money was gone," he said.)

Weiss did make mistakes, just not too many of them. In December of 1948, he picked up pitcher Fred Sanford from the Browns (with catcher Roy Partee) for three minor leaguers and $100,000, an enormous sum. Sanford was coming off a 21-loss season, and whatever Weiss had heard about his potential didn't play out. He never could crack the Yankees' starting rotation, and he was traded to Washington in midseason of 1951, having won only 12 games in two and a half years with New York.

Weiss was hardly a visionary. Player endorsement agent Frank Scott (who was Yankee road secretary in 1949) once presented Weiss with a plan for a Cap-Day promotion, in which all kids would receive a Yankee cap upon buying a ticket. It would serve as good advertising for the team long after they went home.

Weiss was said to have pounded a fist on his desk and said, "Do you think I want every kid in this town walking around in a Yankees cap?"

So much for the early days of marketing.

Yet Weiss was smart enough to acknowledge that MacPhail's efforts had taken the team to over two million in attendance in both 1946 and '47, even if fueled by baseball fans' postwar hunger. He toned down MacPhail's extensive spring training travel, but expanded things like Stadium Club dining membership. He added auxiliary scoreboards at field level outside the two bullpen gates, a touch that was restored in the 2009 stadium. He retained Old-Timers' Day. He expressed admiration for MacPhail's knack for using profits to improve Yankee Stadium. And he appreciated the Yankees' first-class way of presenting themselves. "We always wore fresh uniforms in second games of doubleheaders," said Berra. "Not every team did that. And if Weiss spotted a player in a torn uniform, he'd phone downstairs and make sure we changed between innings."

JUST AS SPRING training was arriving in February 1948, Weiss sprung a brilliant deal with the White Sox, sending Aaron Robinson, Bill Wight, and Fred Bradley to Chicago in exchange for the southpaw Eddie Lopat.

Edmund Lopatynski, 50–49 during four seasons in Chicago, was not a hard thrower, and it took a keen judge of talent to see past that and see that he knew how to win ballgames. Some called him a "junkball" pitcher, but that shortchanged his ability to mix up pitches and throw nasty breaking balls. "He didn't have much of a fastball," said Berra, "but he had good movement on it."

Lopat had an easygoing personality that seemed to match his tantalizing slow curves. He was born on the Lower East Side of Manhattan, grew up at Ninety-eighth and Madison, and went to DeWitt Clinton High, which had no baseball team. Stickball in the New York streets was his game. Now, at thirty, he was hardly a star, but he was about to become part of Reynolds-Raschi-Lopat, as good a three-man rotation as the team had ever enjoyed. And in '48, their first year together, the trio each started 31 games and had a 52–26 record. By the time they had their final year together in 1953, they had a 307–143 record, a .682 won-lost percentage, and five world championship rings. And no finer examples of professionalism ever wore the Yankee uniform. They were always ready to take the ball, always ready to reward the fans with a top effort.

ON MAY 24, the Yankees announced plans to celebrate the twenty-fifth anniversary of Yankee Stadium by making it their Old-Timers' Day theme, at which time they would also retire Babe Ruth's number 3. Only Gehrig's 4 and Carl Hubbell's number 11 on the Giants had been retired at this point, although many found it odd that players like Bud Metheny, Eddie Bockman, Hal Peck, Roy Weatherly, Allie Clark, Frank Colman, and Cliff Mapes had succeeded Selkirk in wearing number 3, rather than having it put out of circulation long before.

Mapes would happily yield the number and become the second Yankee to wear the "unlucky" 13, because, as Pete Sheehy told me years later, " 'Clifford Mapes' was thirteen letters long." (Mapes was also the last to wear number 7 before Mickey Mantle, having abandoned 13.)

Those close to Babe Ruth knew that he was in his final months. He looked just awful, his weight had fallen dramatically, and his public appearances were few. He cooperated as well as he could with radio personality Bob Considine on an autobiography that would become the first baseball book to ever make the *New York Times* bestseller list. (In keeping with his reputation, when Considine asked him to sign a copy for him personally at the book party, Ruth had to say, "What's your name again?")

On Saturday, June 12, after losing a doubleheader to the Indians, a party was held on the eve of Old-Timers' Day at the Ruppert Brewery, hosted by George Ruppert. The next day, as many members of the '23 team as could travel returned to New York. Still relatively young men in their fifties, they included Hoyt, Pipgras, Bush, Pipp, Meusel, Schang, Jones, Mays, and Witt. Ed Barrow was on the field with Arthur Huggins, Miller's brother. They squared off for two innings against latter-day "old-timers" including Zachary, Koenig, Selkirk, Collins, Sewell, Powell, Rolfe, Hadley, Hoag, Allen, Moore, Chandler, Borowy, Bonham, and the Indians' active player Joe Gordon. "Once a Yankee, always a Yankee," said Hoyt.

It was a miserable, drizzly day, but Ruth gave it his all. He dressed at his old metal locker at an "auxiliary" locker room apart from the new Yankee clubhouse. With the help of a male nurse and another aide, he managed to put on a Yankee uniform for one last time. The photographers had full access to him, and no one thought to protect him from the prying lenses.

Babe was to come from the third-base dugout. He took a Bob Feller bat for support, dropped his overcoat, and walked onto the field as he was introduced. More than forty-nine thousand chilled fans stood and cheered what would be his final appearance in Yankee Stadium.

The principal photographer that day was David Blumenthal, the Yankees' "official" photographer for special occasions. Nat Fein of the *Herald Tribune* was filling in for the paper's regular sports photographer and chose to position himself behind the third-base line so that he could shoot the Babe from the back. Ruth wore number 3 for only six of his seasons, and he never wore the NY that was on the front, but still, this was the Babe in full dress, the way fans wanted to see him. His dark hair appeared to be dyed.

Fein, using a Speed Graphic camera and working with available light and no flash, went to work. As twenty Yankee pennants hung over the facade, and with tears running down most everyone's cheeks, the Babe was saying good-bye. Fein shot one of the most famous sports photographs in history.

Babe made his way to the microphone and said in a barely audible voice, "I am proud I hit the first home run here. God knows who will hit the last one. It is great to see the men from twenty-five years ago back here today and it makes me feel proud to be with them."

(The Lord, if he is truly all-knowing, must have observed then that it would be Duke Sims hitting the last one in 1973, and that Jose Molina would do the honors in the remodeled stadium in 2008.)

Will Harridge went to the mike and said, "As president of the American League, I declare Yankee uniform number three retired. It never will be worn again in this stadium, or on the road."

Back in the clubhouse, Babe saw his pal Joe Dugan and said, "Joe, I'm gone."

ELEVEN DAYS AFTER Old-Timers' Day, Babe checked into Memorial Sloan-Kettering Hospital. His cancer had spread and the end was near. A film based on his life was produced in Hollywood with William Bendix as Ruth, a terrible casting choice and by all measures an artistic failure. The movie premiered at the Astor Theater on Broadway and Forty-eighth Street on July 26, with Ruth in attendance, having left the hospital for the evening. The movie's official release date was to be September 6, but given Babe's health, the premiere was rushed so that he could attend. But he was unable, or couldn't bear, to stay for the complete screening.

He died in the hospital at 8:01 P.M. on August 16, 1948. He was only fifty-three years old.

The Yankees made arrangements to have his body lie in state inside gate 4, behind home plate, surrounded by floral offerings. There his fans could view him one last time. For two days and two nights, between 75,000 and 100,000 people turned out and filed by respectfully. Nothing like this had ever taken place in a ballpark. Fathers brought small children so they could say that they saw him.

The funeral was held on August 19 at St. Patrick's Cathedral, and the burial was at Gate of Heaven cemetery in Hawthorne, Westchester County.

"No game will ever see his like, his equal again," wrote Grantland Rice. "He was one in many, many lifetimes. One all alone."

"Ruth possessed a magnetism that was positively infectious," wrote Hoyt. "When he entered a clubhouse or a room, or when he appeared on a field—it was as if he was a whole parade. There seemed to be flags waving, bands playing constantly."

A nation's flags would be at half staff in the summer of '48 for the greatest baseball hero ever. The Yankee players wore wide black armbands.

A Ruth monument would join Huggins's and Gehrig's in the outfield on April 19, 1949. In June of '49, the metal lockers of Ruth and Gehrig were presented to the Hall of Fame in a pregame ceremony at home plate. A year after his death, Babe Ruth Plaza was dedicated on a median along 161st Street between Ruppert Place and Gerard Avenue. The full team, in uniform, walked outside to the area for the dedication, which was marked by four diamond-shaped designations above bronze posts.

Ruth remained the supreme Yankee icon even as decades passed. Had he lived to be one hundred, he would have seen the arrivals of Jeter, Rivera, Williams, Pettitte, and Posada into the organization. Imagine the hand he would have received each year at Old-Timers' Day.

ON THE DAY Ruth died, the Yankees were in an unaccustomed fourth place. A seven-game winning streak immediately after and a nine-game winning streak surrounding Labor Day moved them to contention. They tied for first on September 24 with just seven games remaining, but they would win only three of those games. On Saturday, October 2, in the next-to-last game of the season, Jack Kramer of the Red Sox beat Tommy Byrne 5–1 at Fenway Park, and it was over. It was a 94-win season but a third-place finish, in contention until the final twenty-four hours.

This would prove to be a bigger miss than just losing a pennant race. Had they found a way to win in '48, they might have won seven straight world championships. And Bucky Harris might have managed all of them and been thought of as one of the greatest managers in history.

While DiMaggio had his best postwar season—.320/39/155—and while Berra, Henrich (who hit four grand slams), Lindell, and Brown also hit .300, the decline of Joe Page from his magical '47 season was thought by most to be the big reason for the drop-off. Page was 7–8 with a 4.26 ERA and had only 16 saves. And while he almost approached DiMaggio in popularity with the fans, his teammates began to turn from him, put off by his playing the role of DiMaggio's shadow, always seen running after Joe.

"Page was so dependent upon DiMag he wouldn't leave a hotel for a plane or train without the Jolter," wrote Milton Gross. "When bags were being unloaded from a plane, while the Yankees waited in their bus, Page would wait outside, not only for his bag but for Joe's as well, although DiMag was embarrassed by this attention."

Two DAYS AFTER the season, Harris was dropped as manager. Berra and other players heard that a rift had developed with Weiss, oddly, over Harris's refusal to provide his home telephone number for Weiss. Because September rumors of a rift between Harris and his boss had also led to speculation about either DiMaggio or Henrich succeeding him, the Yankees' statement on the matter concluded, "Several candidates, not including any player active with the Yankees in 1948, are being considered for the post."

Harris's career wasn't over yet; he'd manage the Senators (for the third time) from 1950–54 and the Tigers (for the second time) in 1955–56. He certainly had nothing to be ashamed about for his two-year Yankee stint: a .620 winning percentage and a world championship. But he was bitter, being dropped after a world championship and such a narrow miss in '48.

THERE BEING FEW opportunities for left-handed dentists, Charles Dillon Stengel, nicknamed "Casey" for his hometown of Kansas City—K.C.— dropped out of dental school and began his baseball career in 1910. He batted .284 in fourteen journeyman seasons as a semiregular outfielder with five of the eight National League teams.

As a manager, he had five minor league stops, including Worcester of the Eastern League in 1925. That was where he got to know Weiss, who operated New Haven. At thirty-four he led Brooklyn, and then went to Boston for a total of nine NL seasons, every one of them in the second division, and only one of them (77–75) over .500. At both stops he'd been paid to not manage in the final year of his contract. He was now fifty-eight years old but wrinkled and bowlegged and used antiquated and politically incorrect expressions; one could easily take him for seventy-eight. It was hard to imagine him drawing much respect from the old-line McCarthy guys like DiMaggio, Henrich, Keller, and Rizzuto. In fact, those players would find the adjustment difficult and would always cite McCarthy as the best they ever played for. Stengel briefly put DiMaggio at first base one day, embarrassing the legend who had no practice time there. It was an example of the disconnect between him and the old guard.

So what was this career National Leaguer, this failed manager and ordinary player, this fellow with a reputation as a bit of a clown (once letting a bird fly out from under his cap), going to be doing in a Yankee uniform?

Arthur Daley, writing in the *Times*, said, "The hiring of the tremendously popular Casey is a smart move because it takes some of the heat off the firing of the tremendously popular Harris. It's going to take a long time before the boys in the press box stop seething about the summary departure of Bucky."

Weiss was high on Stengel as he watched him take Oakland to the PCL pennant. He had Devine and Essick scout the Oaks for whatever they might learn of Stengel, and they came back with a favorable report. Topping was a bit wary, not aided at all by Casey calling him "Bob" at his 21 Club introductory press conference, but Webb, who usually didn't play much of a role in such decisions, signed on early as a Stengel supporter and years later told people, "My sole contribution to the Yankees was signing Casey Stengel as manager." He recounted observing Casey holding court in a hotel lobby, talking baseball with anyone who cared, and thinking, "If he cared that much about baseball he must be a terrific manager."

His support helped to bring Topping around.

Chapter Twenty-Two

BILL DICKEY RETURNED TO THE Yankees as a coach in 1949 and immediately set about making Berra a better catcher. Yogi had already impressed everyone with his bat, his ability to hit bad pitches and make contact. But his defensive game needed work, and Dickey proved to be a terrific instructor. Yogi would ultimately set records for consecutive errorless games (148) and chances (950), apart from most homers by a catcher (313, later broken by Johnny Bench).

Yogi and Casey understood each other and went to battle together. Casey trusted his pitch calling, as did the great pitching staff, and although Yogi was still only twenty-four, he was a team leader, a presence. He came to be considered Casey's "assistant manager."

As a rookie he had once failed to run hard on a ground ball. "Hey, we're all hustling here, how about you?" Keller said. It never happened again. The Yankees policed each other and protected their brand.

And this core of players, about to learn Casey's ways, would go on to win five consecutive world championships.

It hadn't happened before, and it hasn't happened since.

Twelve of the '49 Yankees would be on the roster for all five seasons: Rizzuto, Berra, Raschi, Reynolds, Lopat, Brown, Hank Bauer, Gene Woodling, Charlie Silvera, Johnny Mize, Joe Collins, and Jerry Coleman. (Also worth noting: Batboy Joe Carrieri was there from 1949–55, and later the author of a remembrance of his time.)

Mize joined the team on August 22, 1949. He was thirty-six, a lifetime .320 hitter with 315 home runs, sixth on the all-time list at that point behind only Ruth, Foxx, Ott, Gehrig, and Greenberg. (DiMaggio would pass him within a couple of weeks.) He still held sixth place by the time he retired.

Mize was related to Ruth by marriage into Claire's family, and Johnny's acquisition through the waiver route marked the first in a run of late-season Yankee pickups that would help fill a need and invariably seemed to produce strong results. Mize was the poster boy for the late-season pickup.

Outfielders Hank Bauer, who hit right-handed, and Gene Woodling, who hit left, were perfect players for Stengel. He played the two with finesse against righty or lefty pitching, mixing and matching as the game progressed, in what came to be called platoon baseball. He loved players who could play multiple positions. Today managers rely on computer-generated stats that show every batter versus every pitcher, where they tend to hit the ball and what count they can expect a fastball—but Stengel just intuitively knew it. He himself had been a platoon player in his career, and while he didn't love it and didn't expect his players to love it, it developed into a formula that worked.

His manipulation of the lineup seems so logical today, but at the time it was trend-setting, and this idea came to define his managing style. The handsome rookie Coleman, another Yankee from San Francisco, was a perfect Stengel player, able to play multiple positions.

The '49 Yanks would really test Casey's ability to mix and match and overcome, as the team listed seventy-one injuries, big and small, filling Gus Mauch's training room and Dr. Gaynor's medical ledger. Only fifteen times did DiMaggio, Henrich, and Berra appear in the lineup together. But Casey's work would net him Manager of the Year honors in his first year with the Yankees, which may have been his best managing job. There could be no assumption that anyone else could have managed this team of walking wounded.

As for his propensity to criticize his players through the press, the players hated that. But Stengel had "my writers," the core group he could trust and also use to belittle a player, which he thought was a beneficial tactic. Often the best place to get such insight was in the hotel bars that he frequented with his coaches but banned players from using.

"He was a hard man to play for," said Bobby Richardson, who came up in '55. "He would make you mad."

Billy Johnson hated playing for him.

Stengel's maneuverings were hardly "push-button," but rather often so obscure that only Stengel seemed to understand them. He'd pinch-hit for weak-hitting infielders in the first inning if he felt he could blow open the game early. He'd bat a good-hitting pitcher eighth, no matter how embarrassing for the ninth hitter.

He didn't even pronounce his players' names correctly, which could be considered insulting. Henrich was *Handricks*. He also resorted to ethnic terms for players, even DiMaggio, which spoke to a time in America in which he'd grown up that would eventually fall out of fashion. But it wasn't yet something that resulted in criticism; younger writers entering the scene would cringe but give him a free pass.

His mispronunciations of names were considered part of Stengelese, a rambling, illogical stream-of-consciousness language that Casey would use in talking to the press, the public, or, on one occasion, the U.S. Congress, if he wanted to duck a question. There were hints at his message if you listened carefully, but mostly he would take the listener down unexpected paths of dialogue, leading nowhere. It was all a show, of course, for his conversations with players showed none of that. He would talk to them directly and intelligently when he chose to.

"He was always clear to us," said Berra.

WOODLING CONCEDED THAT platooning may have made him a better player, although he was never one who lived and died by wearing a Yankee uniform. He was a blue-collar ballplayer from Akron, Ohio, who had come up with Cleveland after winning four minor league batting titles.

(Woodling later played for Stengel on the original Mets. He told me one day of sitting in the dugout during a typical pasting the Mets were receiving, when Stengel made eye contact with him, winked, and murmured, "Ain't like the old days, is it.")

Bauer, Woodling's counterpart in the outfield, was a tough four-year marine veteran of the Pacific who didn't like anyone "messing with my World Series money."

Bauer was scouted by both Lee MacPhail and his brother Bill. Bill was not really a scout, but they watched Bauer play for the Kansas City Blues and both felt he would be Keller's successor one day. The Kansas City stop was a good one for Hank—he hit .313 and .305 there in two seasons and married the club's office secretary.

IN 1948, THE New York Yankees of the All-American Football Conference, owned by Dan Topping, signed the black All-American Buddy Young. In February 1949, the baseball Yankees made a decision to enter the Negro League market and announced the signing of both infielder Artie Wilson of the Birmingham Black Barons (who was missing a finger on his throwing hand), and the dark-skinned Puerto Rican outfielder Luis Marquez of the Homestead Grays. The deals proved to be complicated; Cleveland also claimed to have signed them both, and when the deals were reviewed by Commissioner Chandler, Wilson was awarded to New York and Marquez was sent to Cleveland.

But Wilson didn't want to take the pay cut the Yankees were offering him to play for Newark, and he wanted a piece of the purchase price as well. So five days later he was sold to the Indians organization after all. In his place, the Yanks signed Frank Austin, a Panamanian shortstop, from the Philadelphia Stars. So who was the first black player in the Yankees organization? Both Austin and Marquez started the season with Newark in '49 and share the distinction, but both were out of the organization by May. Only Marquez would see brief major league action some years later.

IN 1949, JOE DIMAGGIO and Ted Williams became the first American League players to earn a $100,000 salary. (Hank Greenberg's Pittsburgh contract in 1947 was valued at $100,000.) But for the eighth time in eleven seasons (sometimes salary holdouts, sometimes injury), Joe would miss opening day. This time it was a heel injury, which would keep him out of the lineup until an eventful Tuesday, June 28.

Even without DiMag, and despite the mounting injuries, the Yanks were where they were expected to be: first place, four and a half games up. The Red Sox, now managed by Joe McCarthy, were in third, six out.

Feeling improved, Joe decided he was ready to play. He caught a mid-afternoon flight to Boston in time for the night game. Stengel, as surprised as anyone, put him in the lineup to hit cleanup, and DiMag responded with a homer in a 5–4 Yankee win.

On Wednesday, he homered twice as the Yanks won 9–7. And on Thursday he homered again as the Yanks swept the series. It was one of the most dramatic returns to the lineup anyone could remember. Even *Life* magazine would do a story on it. As if his legend already wasn't made, this capped it.

But the Red Sox weren't dead, and after they took two from the Yanks on

September 24–25, there were six games left on the schedule and the teams were tied for first. The Yanks fell one behind after losing to Philadelphia on the thirtieth, and now came the final two games of the regular season, Yankees vs. Boston at Yankee Stadium.

ON SATURDAY, OCTOBER 1, 69,551 paid to see Mel Parnell oppose Reynolds on Joe DiMaggio Day, scheduled after the storybook comeback in June at Fenway.

Player "days" were fairly common, some forgettable, some indelible. On some clubs, if a fan club or a hometown bought enough tickets, it was, "Sure, you can have a day." We had a Danny Cater Day when I was with the Yankees when people of Williamsport, Pennsylvania, his wife's hometown, bought a lot of tickets. Danny cried when he made his acceptance speech, but few others remember it.

Joe was already thought of in the same breath as Gehrig and Ruth, and since *their* days were historic, everyone wanted this one to be just as memorable, even if the circumstances were better. Unfortunately, Joe had to get out of a sickbed. He had pneumonia and a 102-degree fever, but he intended to play.

He accepted two cars, a boat, and lots more, and then said,

> Ladies and gentlemen, when I left San Francisco to come to the New York Yankees I did not know what was in store for me. Of course, all were strangers to me—nobody knew me. But Lefty O'Doul told me, "New York is the friendliest town in the world." My mother, who is here today to meet my friends, told me the same thing. She said, "People are the same everywhere." And I will say that this day proves that New York City is the friendliest town in the world.
>
> I have played under three managers and everyone has taught me something. I cannot begin to name the friends who took me along the road when I was a rookie—they certainly helped me.
>
> I'd like to say to Joe McCarthy [turning to Red Sox dugout], if it's not settled today, it will be tomorrow. If we couldn't do it, I'm glad that you did. On a day like this, I'm even friendly to our enemies— the Boston Red Sox. They're a grand team and a great bunch of guys—and that's not forgetting a fellow out there in center field

[his brother Dominic] who spends all the time robbing me of base hits.

Today, I'd like to thank a lot of people—Casey Stengel and my teammates. They're the gamest, fightingest bunch of guys that ever lived. And I'd like to thank my friends who arranged this day and all you fans here present. You certainly have been very good to me.

In closing, I'd like to thank the good Lord for making me a Yankee. This day certainly proves it's great to be a Yankee.

The "good Lord" sentence would be painted on the walls in Yankee Stadium more than forty years later as an inspiration to current players, none more than Derek Jeter.

As for the big game, Reynolds was knocked out in the third and Stengel turned to Joe Page, who was enjoying a terrific comeback year, one that would lead to him being named the best pitcher in the American League by the *Sporting News*. "How far can you go," asked Stengel as Page arrived on the mound. "A long way," he answered, and he proceeded to shut out the Sox for 6⅔ innings. Johnny Lindell homered in the bottom of the eighth, the Yanks won 5–4, and the teams were tied going into the final game. DiMag was 2-for-4 with a double.

On Sunday, October 2, it was Raschi (20–10) against Ellis Kinder (23-5) with the winners going to the World Series and the losers going home. This historic finish would have 68,055 witness.

Rizzuto's first-inning triple gave the Yanks a 1–0 lead, which held up through seven. Once mocked by Stengel at a Dodger tryout, the Scooter was on his way to being named Player of the Year by the New York chapter of the Baseball Writers' Association. In the top of the eighth, McCarthy removed Kinder for a pinch hitter and then brought in Parnell, Saturday's starter.

"We wanna hit . . . we wanna hit," shouted the fans, in the rhythmic chant of the day.

The first batter Parnell faced, Henrich, belted a home run. It was a great moment for Tommy, who had fractured his second and third lumbar vertebrae crashing into the outfield wall in late August and was now playing first base. By the time the inning was over, the Yanks had a 5–0 lead, helped by a three-run double by Coleman.

In the ninth, the Red Sox closed the gap when DiMaggio failed to run down a long drive by Bobby Doerr, and the score stood at 5–3. DiMag waved to

Stengel: He was hurting the team and he was taking himself out. Casey sent Woodling out to center as the crowd wildly cheered Joe's return to the dugout.

There was no closer that day despite Page's great season. With two out, Raschi bore down and got Birdie Tebbetts on a pop-up to Henrich. The Yankees were going to their sixteenth World Series.

Fans lingered on the field as the scoreboard operators kept up the out-of-town results, and after half an hour, they were able to see that the Dodgers had won the National League pennant with a victory in Philadelphia.

Hungry ticket scalpers were talking about getting fifty dollars a ticket, and a few movie theaters were showing the TV picture on large screens for $1.20.

DiMaggio had batted .346 in his 76 games, driving in 67 runs. And while Raschi, Reynolds, Lopat, and Tommy Byrne had gone 68–33, it was Page, 13–8 with 27 saves, who was the toast of the town. And now it was the Yankees and the Dodgers in the Series for the third time.

In game one, Henrich connected off Don Newcombe in the ninth for the first walk-off homer in World Series history, and the first time a homer had decided a 1–0 game since Stengel's homer against the Yanks in '23.

Preacher Roe won game two by the same 1–0 score, but the Yankees took the next three, the deciding game being a 6–4 victory for Lopat at Ebbets Field with a save for Reynolds. Bobby Brown hit .500 and drove in five runs for the Yanks to lead all hitters.

It was the Yankees' twelfth world championship, and their first under the ownership of Topping and Webb, with Weiss as GM and Stengel as manager. Their joy-filled presence in the clubhouse and at the victory party would become a familiar sight over the next decade. Those were the only times Topping, Webb, and Weiss would enter the clubhouse.

Charlie Keller, troubled by a bad back since '46 and demoted briefly to Newark in 1949, didn't even pinch-hit in the World Series. He was released in January 1950 and signed with the Tigers. He'd return as a Yankee coach in '52. Keller hit 184 homers in his Yankee career, which trailed only Ruth, Gehrig, DiMaggio, and Dickey on the team's all-time list at the time.

THE VENERABLE YANKEE scoreboard behind the bleachers, which dated back to 1923, was finally replaced by an electric board in 1950. It was "state of the art," seventy-three by thirty-four feet, but contained nothing that hadn't been on the hand-operated board other than light bulbs and a countdown clock for football. It would be in place for nine seasons.

In February, Major League Baseball passed a uniform height regulation for the pitcher's mound. Until that point, the mound "could not exceed 15 inches" and everyone had liberty to do what they wished with that. At Yankee Stadium it had been twelve inches, although in some earlier seasons it was nearly flat.

Another Stadium Club restaurant was added, where the visitors' clubhouse had been, and a new visitors' clubhouse was built behind the third-base dugout.

A small change that would have ramifications a year later was improvement to the outfield drainage system, beginning with a water well in the left-field bullpen.

A new press box was added as an overhang to the mezzanine, giving the writers and broadcasters privacy from the fans. After years behind home plate in the "coop" next to the players' wives' section, they had then sat in the first rows of the mezzanine until this enhancement.

Occupying the broadcast booth would be a crew from WABD, Channel 4, along with radio engineer Pappy Durkin from WINS, as Mel Allen and Curt Gowdy called the action. P. Ballantine & Sons was back for a fourth season as the team's beer sponsor and had prominent signage on the new scoreboard it paid for. And man, oh, man, could Mel Allen sell that Ballantine. He would pour it—perfectly—during live commercials, and the sponsor loved it. Home runs were "Ballantine blasts." "Baseball and Ballantine": What a combination that would be for twenty years.

Gowdy would leave for Boston after the season, and speculation focused on Henrich as a replacement, but it would be Art Gleason (joined in 1952 by Bill Crowley, later PR director for the Red Sox). The grammatically challenged ("slud" instead of "slid") Dizzy Dean was recruited to do pre- and postgame television shows.

Diz would be a fixture in American homes, calling the Game of the Week from 1953 to 1965 (first on ABC, then CBS), the majority of the games featuring the Yankees. This was largely unknown to New York–area fans, as the games were blacked out locally. But many across the nation would get lively exposure to the Yanks through the work of Dean, along with his partners Buddy Blattner and later Pee Wee Reese. It was the beginning of a true national fan base for the team.

Henrich made 1950 his final season, but it was injury-riddled and unsatisfying, and he would retire after eleven years in pinstripes, his home run total just one shy of Keller's for sixth on the Yankee list. Tommy coached for the Yanks in '51, and later for the Giants and Tigers. He would live to be ninety-six, the last of Lou Gehrig's teammates to die, when he passed away in 2009.

The 1950 season would also mark the end of the great association with the Newark Bears. Feeling only one triple-A team was needed, Weiss chose to keep Kansas City in the system. Newark became a Cub farm team and was shifted to Springfield, Massachusetts.

The dawn of the new decade saw major league attendance plunge 16 percent across the board, owing to a softening economy and perhaps enough time after the war for the baseball-is-back excitement to have subsided. And, yes, some spoke of the increased ownership of television sets and continued to warn about the dangers of the games being on free television. (Attendance would fall another 16 percent the following year.) The Yanks did top two million for the fifth straight year, a total they would never again approach in their remaining twenty-four seasons in the original stadium.

For the Yankees, 1950 marked the debuts of Whitey Ford, Jackie Jensen, and Billy Martin, and they would also swing a good trade with the Browns at the June trading deadline to bring pitchers Tom Ferrick and Joe Ostrowski to New York, giving up Stirnweiss in the process. Both pitchers would be big pennant-race pickups.

(Stirnweiss was out of baseball by 1952, and on September 15, 1958, he died tragically at age thirty-nine while a passenger on a New Jersey commuter train that plunged off the Newark Bay Bridge after leaving the Elizabethport station. He was working as a foreign freight agent, and was headed for a lunch appointment in New York.)

No 1950 deal was bigger than a waiver deal described as "inexplicable" by the press. Somehow, Pittsburgh first baseman Johnny Hopp went unclaimed by all National League teams and wound up with the Yankees on September 5. Hopp, a .335 hitter in '49, was hitting .340 at the time, second in the National League. A twelve-year veteran, he was, like Mize the year before, a perfect pennant-stretch pickup for New York.

How could this have happened? Lips were sealed. No explanation ever came forth. Like other surprising waiver deals, it would go the grave with Weiss, who never wrote a memoir.

"Baffling," wrote Arthur Daley. "The Giants could have used him and the Cards could have used him. But a 'gentlemen's agreement' presumably is more important than expediency and thus was Hopp waived out of the league."

Roland Hemond, who would join the Braves' front office the following summer, suggested that given Hopp's age (thirty-three), his salary ($20,000), his lack of power, and the fact that he was a good addition for a pennant contender but no one else, the waiver deal was not surprising. "Most teams had their first baseman, and wouldn't have really needed a Johnny Hopp," he said.

Hopp would play in 19 games down the stretch and hit .333 with eight RBI, including a pinch-hit, game-winning grand slam. The rest of his Yankee career was insignificant, but the 1950 waiver deal was an annoyance to those who resented the Yankees' seemingly endless ability to get whatever they needed.

Jensen and Martin both played for Oakland in 1949, and were both sold to the Yankees right after the season. Martin had played for Stengel there in '48; Jensen had not. Jackie was an All-American football and baseball star at Berkeley, a handsome blond athlete who had finished fourth in Heisman Trophy voting while also playing on the first College World Series–winning team in '47. Before Mickey Mantle was converted to the outfield, Jensen was thought of as a successor to DiMaggio in center. His Yankee career would last only three seasons; he would go to Washington and then Boston, where he'd win the American League's MVP Award in 1958. But his fear of flying made it impossible for him to fully enjoy his gifts, and his career never played out to its full potential.

Martin was "Casey's boy." Stengel would be the father figure that Billy never had, and since Stengel as a young man had enjoyed the same high times that Billy did, they got along famously. While Stengel would rein Martin in when necessary, he also seemed to enjoy watching his brash behavior. More than anyone, Martin would be the prime example of exceeding one's abilities simply by donning the Yankee uniform.

His teammates loved his fire and will to win, although not many could keep up with him on his nightly rounds. Those who did, including Mantle and Ford in the years to come, were seen by management as under his bad influence. Billy was just arriving on the scene in 1950, but he had no problem needling DiMaggio (unheard of among veteran Yankees) and making his presence felt. There was no ignoring Billy Martin in Yankee history, this 165-pound second baseman who would hit just .262 in seven seasons with the Yankees and .251 in four seasons away from them, but .333 in 28 World Series games.

Ford was just as street-smart as Martin, but more politically correct and more in the image of how a Yankee should conduct himself. He was enormously gifted, and would be the only twentieth-century pitcher under six feet to go to the Hall of Fame. That speaks to his confident mound intelligence, something that ultimately led Elston Howard to call him "the Chairman of the Board." Perfect.

Ed Ford was raised in Astoria, Queens, and went to the Manhattan School of Aviation. He was a first baseman in youth baseball, and attended a tryout session at Yankee Stadium under the eyes of scouts Paul Krichell and Johnny Sturm. It was Sturm who suggested he try pitching, being, in his eyes, too small to play first. Some months later, Krichell signed him for a $7,000 bonus.

Assigned to Binghamton in 1949, his manager was Lefty Gomez, who nicknamed him "Whitey." He'd also be known as "Slick" because Stengel called him "whiskey slick," a vague reference to his urban sophistication.

Ford was slick enough to call the Yankees from a Binghamton phone booth in 1949 to inform them that he was 16–5 with a 1.61 ERA and should be called up. It didn't happen, but he did get the call the following June after going 6–3 at Kansas City. And he then made one of the great debuts in Yankee history, winning his first nine decisions and assuming his place with Raschi, Reynolds, and Lopat in the starting rotation of the defending world champions.

His only loss would be in his final decision, a relief appearance against the Athletics on September 27. It was the second-to-last victory of Connie Mack's managing career.

The biggest of Whitey's nine victories came on September 16, an 8–1 triumph over Detroit that put the Yanks in first place to stay. They wound up winning by three games over the Tigers (managed by Rolfe) and four over Boston (managed by McCarthy until he retired for good on June 23). (Washington, managed by Harris, finished fifth.)

The Yankees' seventeenth pennant broke a tie with the Cubs for most pennants won, the Cubs having won six of theirs in the nineteenth century.

DiMaggio, .301/32/122, would enjoy his last big year, but it was Rizzuto, setting a record with fifty-eight consecutive errorless games and hitting .324, who would win the league's MVP Award. Mize, despite missing a month of the season, drove in 72 runs on 76 hits while belting 25 home runs. Berra, at .322, and Bauer, at .320, made the lineup formidable. A discouraging note among the pitching staff was the fall of Page to a 5.07 ERA, which would mark the end of his Yankee career after seven seasons.

The 1950 World Series featured the Whiz Kids, the surprising Philadelphia Phillies, but the Yankees were too good and too experienced for them. The Phils started Jim Konstanty, their ace reliever, in game one, but Raschi outpitched him 1–0, with Coleman's sacrifice fly in the fourth driving in Bobby Brown. In game two, DiMaggio homered in the top of the tenth to give the Yanks a 2–1 win as Reynolds bested Robin Roberts. Game three was a 3–2 Yankee win behind Lopat, with Woodling, Rizzuto, and Coleman singling in the last of the ninth for the winning run. Then Ford got the ball in game four and won the 5–2 clincher, with Stengel calling on Reynolds to get the final out, the fans booing Casey for removing Ford. The Phillies had made every game close, but the Yankees prevailed for their thirteenth world championship and second in a row under Casey.

Chapter Twenty-Three

IMAGINE YOU'RE A BASEBALL SCOUT with the lonely existence of driving long distances to see game after game, year after year, players in shoddy conditions in ragtag uniforms, all starting to look the same. Occasionally one stands out, you sign him to a contract, and then he becomes one of the 95 percent who never gets to the majors and is never heard from again.

You are earning less than $10,000 a year plus a few cents a mile for your gasoline, but you're in your element, you like the open road, and, hey, you're a baseball lifer.

And then one day you drive up to Baxter Springs, Kansas, and see, for the first time, Mickey Mantle. No other scouts are there. This is the moment a scout lives for.

It really can't happen anymore. Scouting is sophisticated; prospects are shuttled into eminent schools and programs; the value of young talent is simply too recognizable. There may never be another Mickey Mantle moment.

A minor league pitcher himself, Tom Greenwade had moved with MacPhail from the Dodgers in '46. In 1948, he stumbled on a sixteen-year-old Mantle playing for the Whiz Kids in Baxter Springs, twelve miles north of Mantle's home of Commerce, Oklahoma. Greenwade spoke to Mantle, and when Mickey said he was a junior at Commerce High, he decided to back off, knowing league rules prohibited him from negotiating with high school prospects—but he kept an eye on him.

"The first time I saw Mantle," Greenwade would say, "I knew how Paul Krichell felt when he first saw Lou Gehrig."

The Mantle story became familiar to baby boomers, the postwar children. Their dads loved DiMaggio, but Mick was their own.

He had a bad high school football injury that led to osteomyelitis. He was an erratic shortstop. Greenwade signed him in the backseat of his car in Baxter Springs the day he graduated high school for an $1,150 bonus. Mickey's alternative was to join his father and work in the zinc mines.

"[Greenwade] got me excused from the commencement exercises so I could play for the Whiz Kids that night," Mantle recalled.

> The game was in Coffeyville, Kansas. I had a good game—two singles and hit a pair of home runs, connecting from both sides. You'd figure I had it made, yet Greenwade comes over to Dad after the game and says very solemnly, "I'm afraid Mickey may never reach the Yankees. Right now, I'd have to rate him a lousy shortstop. Sloppy. Erratic arm. And he's small. Get him in front of some really strong pitching . . ." Then, without blinking an eye, he says, "However, I'm willing to take a risk." He stuck a contract in Dad's hand. "All right Mutt, I'm ready to give Mickey four hundred dollars for playing at Independence the rest of the summer." Dad winced. "He can make that much playing Sunday ball and working in the mines during the week." Greenwade started scribbling something on the back of an envelope. Finally he says, "Tell you what, we'll throw in an eleven-hundred dollar bonus."

He reported to Independence, Missouri, in the KOM League, where Harry Craft was his manager. He *was* a terrible shortstop, but he was on his way.

In 1951, the Yankees swapped spring training sites with the Giants, Del Webb being anxious to bring his team to his hometown. That put Mantle in Phoenix and Willie Mays in St. Petersburg for their first big-league camps. Mantle, still a teenager, was a heralded switch-hitter, but he was clearly not a big-league infielder. He was moved to the outfield where Stengel himself, a former outfielder, tutored him. By the end of camp, which included hitting a prodigious homer at an exhibition at USC that may have reached six hundred feet, he made the team and was already being called the successor to DiMaggio. He would play right while Joe spent his final season in center.

Mantle had it all. He got handsomer as his awkward teen years moved to maturity. The name, the appearance, seemed created by Hollywood. No switch-hitter ever hit with such power from both sides of the plate. No power hitter ever ran with such speed. His shy persona was a winner with fans.

He was timed running to first in an amazing 3.1 seconds. "We'd all stop to watch him in Arizona that first year," said Berra. "Everything about him."

Carmen Berra added, "We kept hearing about how handsome he was. Then one day that year we were in the lobby of the Concourse Plaza Hotel and he came out of the elevator. It was the first time I saw him up close. Oh my God!"

He would be the first superstar of the burgeoning television era of the game, and thus could be seen in homes across the country, a privilege Ruth, Gehrig, and DiMaggio had not enjoyed. And his fame would be national because he would play in twelve World Series in his first fourteen seasons, becoming as much a fall network TV star as Milton Berle. By 1952 he was already a third-place finisher in MVP voting.

His handsome face graced the cover of *Life* magazine and he'd appear on *The Ed Sullivan Show*. *Sports Illustrated* came along in 1954 and sold more copies with him on the cover than anyone else.

DiMaggio fans were somewhat disdainful. He struck out too much. Joe didn't do that. And Joe had more "class."

DiMaggio, seventeen years Mantle's senior, was not much of a mentor. He may have resented the attention, or, seeing all the strikeouts, resented the idea that this could be his successor. "I never volunteered any advice to Mickey or any other ballplayer," said Joe. "Sure, when he came up as a green kid I tried to help him in the outfield, but that's different from presuming to give unasked advice to a recognized star."

When I assisted Bowie Kuhn with his memoir in 1984, he paused in reflection while speaking of the game's accomplishments during his sixteen years as commissioner, and said, ". . . and we did it all without ever finding another Mickey Mantle." Such was the power of the Mantle story.*

MICKEY'S REPUTATION THROUGHOUT his playing career was one of a clean-living family man, a wholesome hero. Fans learned after his career that this wasn't quite the case. But by then, an entire generation had embraced him

---

* Of course, he still suspended Mantle (and Willie Mays) from their jobs as spring training instructors for taking post-career PR jobs with Atlantic City casinos.

as the true successor to the unbroken line of Yankee greatness. By the time he retired, with the most games played in Yankee history despite a long list of injuries, he was third on the all-time home run list, behind only Ruth and Mays.

Mantle's best friends on the Yankees would be Ford and Martin, guiding Mantle into big-city life and all the pluses and minuses associated with it. Ford would be drafted into the army and would not actually be a Mantle teammate until '53, so Billy had Mick to himself in those first two seasons and the bond between the two was set.

All didn't go smoothly in '51. He was given uniform number 6—pressure enough for a nineteen-year-old, to wear the "next number" after 3, 4, and 5—and when he hit a 452-foot homer in Chicago on May 1, it only raised expectations. But he struggled at bat and had to be returned to the minors to get his confidence back. After hitting .361 in 40 games for Kansas City, he returned to the Yanks, was given number 7 (Cliff Mapes, the previous 7, was sold to the Browns, and Bobby Brown, back from military duty, took his old number 6), and never again wore any other uniform but the Yankees'.

The struggles, and the return to the minors, allowed another Yankee rookie—versatile infielder Gil McDougald—to earn the Rookie of the Year Award in '51.

McDougald, another San Francisco native for the Yankees, was signed by Joe Devine for a $1,000 bonus and replaced Billy Johnson at third. Employing an odd batting stance that would gnaw at Stengel whenever he slumped, he wound up making the All-Star team at second, short, and third during his career.

ANOTHER NEW ARRIVAL in Yankee Stadium in 1951 was a public-address announcer, a forty-year-old speech teacher and former quarterback from St. John's University named Bob Sheppard. His debut coincided with Mantle's.

PA announcements had long been handled by the rotund Jack Lenz, a frequent object of teasing from players as he left his seat next to the dugout and paraded around with his megaphone: Yankee Stadium didn't have an electronic PA system until 1936. (George Levy, who had teamed with Lenz at the Polo Grounds, stayed behind to handle just the Giants when Yankee Stadium was opened.) Lenz was said to have handled more than two thousand consecutive games.

PR director Red Patterson handled the chore prior to Sheppard's hiring.

It wasn't much for him to slide the PA mike over to his seat in the press box, when all that was required was announcing the starting lineups and substitutions.

Sheppard's role was much the same for almost twenty years. But by 1967 the Yankees, recognizing the commanding dignity of his magnificent voice, had him announcing each at-bat. He had been doing between-inning commercials on matters such as upcoming home games or Yankee yearbooks for sale. (Never would the stadium make announcements about lost children, engines running, or lost bus drivers. They would sometimes, but not always, make announcements in the event of an emergency.) Fans had little idea what Sheppard even looked like until I happened to put his photo in the 1971 yearbook, recognizing the obvious—he was by now part of the Yankee Stadium experience.

His reputation grew. People enjoyed imitating his delivery. He was now instructed to announce every batter, every at-bat. Players considered it part of the big-league experience to have Sheppard say their names. And he was a perfectionist, always checking with visiting players to make sure that he got their names right.

Bob Sheppard would continue as "the Voice of God," as Reggie Jackson nicknamed him, until his late nineties. His introduction of Derek Jeter, however, continued via a recording that Jeter requested for the rest of his career. He was honored with a plaque in Monument Park in 2000, and always said that all that a PA announcer needed to be was "clear, concise, and correct."

THIRTY MONTHS AFTER being hired amidst snickers, Casey Stengel entered the season with a chance at a third straight world championship. He was suddenly a genius, and his system of platoon baseball was hailed as revolutionary.

The Yankees and the Indians were in a tight race for much of the '51 season, a season in which all home and road day games were televised on WPIX, owned by the *Daily News*, "New York's Picture Newspaper" (hence, PIX). The Yankees thus began a forty-eight-year run on Channel 11, the longest-running business arrangement the team has had with any company save two—Harry Stevens's concessions and Allied Maintenance, employers of the ground crew and maintenance workers.

With Whitey Ford lost to the army for two years after his spectacular 1950 debut, the Yanks essentially relied on Reynolds-Raschi-Lopat, who won a combined 59 games, with no one else winning more than nine. On July 12, Reynolds hurled a 1–0 no-hitter in Cleveland, beating Bob Feller. It was the first by a Yankee since 1938.

On August 29, the Yankees traded a kid pitcher, Lew Burdette, to the Boston Braves for the veteran Johnny Sain, the hero (with Warren Spahn) of the Braves' 1948 pennant.* Again it was a wise late-season veteran pickup, as Sain appeared in seven games, winning two and saving one. (A decade later, Johnny would be the Yankees' pitching coach for three pennant winners, 1961–63.)

Burdette, too, would be heard from again.

The Indians were a game ahead of the Yankees on the morning of Sunday, September 16, as 68,760 poured through the stadium turnstiles to see Reynolds and Feller in a rematch of the earlier no-hitter. Reynolds emerged the winner again, this time 5–1, creating a tie for first.

The teams met again the next day, first place on the line, Lopat against Bob Lemon.

In the ninth inning with the bases loaded and the score tied 1–1, Lemon threw a pitch near Rizzuto's head, but Scooter dropped down a perfect bunt and DiMaggio raced home with the winning run as Lemon fielded the ball too late to throw anywhere. It may be the most famous bunt in baseball history. Lemon fired the ball and his glove against the backstop in frustration.

Mantle, on deck, was just as delirious, jumping up and down. "I was going crazy because I didn't have to bat next," he said. "I think Casey would have me bunting too."

Rizzuto didn't have a helmet on that day, but during that season he became the first Yankee to wear one. Helmets were being constructed by a company started by Branch Rickey, and Phil had agreed to try one out.

The Yanks won nine of their last twelve and won the pennant by five games. The clincher was a classic in itself. On Friday, September 28, in the first game of a doubleheader, Reynolds faced Boston's ace, Mel Parnell. The Yanks had an 8–0 lead through eight, so the outcome was clear. What kept the fans on edge was Reynolds working on another no-hitter. No one had pitched two in a season since Johnny Vander Meer of the Reds in '38 (his were consecutive).

With two out in the ninth, Reynolds had to retire Ted Williams. Ted

---

* "Spahn and Sain and pray for rain" was the rhyme that made them famous.

swung on an 0-and-1 pitch and hit a pop-up behind home plate. That would be it—except Yogi became disoriented under the pop-up, began to lose his footing, dropped the ball, and fell down. The great Williams would be given a second chance. Yogi wanted to crawl into a hole.

The crowd of 39,038 sighed as one. They commiserated with the popular catcher; they didn't boo. He was Yogi, and he was beloved: He would win his first of three MVP awards in 1951. Reynolds helped him to his feet and patted his rump. It would be okay, he assured him.

Remarkably, Reynolds induced Williams into hitting another pop foul. It seemed like a miracle. This one was near the Yankee dugout, and Yogi caught it and clutched it tightly. It was both a second no-hitter for Reynolds and an eighteenth pennant for the Yanks. It was also a moment frozen in time for all who saw it in person or on TV.

The Dodgers and Giants tied for first in the National League, forcing a three-game playoff; they split the first two. That led to the decisive game at the Polo Grounds on October 3, and Berra was among a group of Yankees who went to the game to scout the teams in preparation for the World Series.

It was perhaps the most famous game in baseball history, as Bobby Thomson hit the "shot heard round the world" in the last of the ninth, turning a loss to a win, as the Giants won the pennant. As for Yogi, who would become famous for saying "It ain't over til it's over": He left early to beat the traffic.

The World Series featured a matchup of rival rookie stars as Mantle and Mays opposed each other for the first time. The Series, however, ended early for Mantle. In the fifth inning of game two, Mays flied to right center and Mick badly injured his knee, coming to a sudden stop and then falling as his foot hit a year-old sprinkler-system drain, with DiMaggio calling him off the play.

The torn ACL was severe and would change Mantle's career. He didn't have it repaired for two years, playing on it for two full seasons before finally undergoing surgery in '53. His rookie season was the only year he played at relatively full strength. He would always have a little bit of a limp; he would never be the Mantle he might have been. His blazing speed was diminished. It was the start of a host of injuries that would plague him. This one forced him to play with his leg wrapped tightly in Ace bandages for every game for the rest of his career.

In the fourth game, DiMaggio hit the final home run of his career in a 6–2 Yankee win that evened the Series at 2–2. McDougald's grand slam in game five helped the Yanks to a 3–2 edge, and in game six, reliever Bob Kuzava induced pinch hitter Sal Yvers to line out to Bauer in right with two runners on, Bauer catching it while sliding on the seat of his pants.

The Yankees won the game 4–3 for Casey's third consecutive world championship, and the Yankees' fourteenth.

DiMaggio waited until December 11 to make his plans public. Similar to what Ruth had done after his last Yankee season, he toured Japan and Korea with a traveling U.S. team. But when Red Patterson alerted the New York press to come to the team's Fifth Avenue office in the middle of the Christmas shopping season, they knew this was the day that Joe would retire.

"I've played my last game of ball," he said.

Joe never wanted to be embarrassed on the field, and hitting .263 with 12 homers on a painful heel was not a DiMaggio season to be proud of. His mother had died in June. The two scouts who had arranged for the Yankees to acquire him, Joe Devine and Bill Essick, had died twenty days apart in the fall. A magazine had published a scouting report on Joe that said he'd become very ordinary in some areas. He exited on his own terms, dignity intact. He probably wished he had quit a year earlier.

DiMaggio played only thirteen seasons, having lost three to the war. In ten of them, the Yanks played in the World Series. He hit .325 lifetime, but the rest of his lifetime stats reflected just thirteen years of play, not the long career he could have had. It didn't matter to people who loved the game and knew perfection when they saw it. He would be the standard of on-field excellence for a generation.

The "retirement" of a player was rare; most got released when it was time to go. Before the breakdown of baseball's Reserve Clause in 1976, a retirement created the oddity of a player still bound for life to a team. Had DiMaggio chosen, say, to come back at age forty-four seven years later as a pinch hitter for the San Francisco Giants, he would have found that the Yankees still controlled him. Over the years, the Yankees' list of "retired players" was small, but technically they held lifetime control over anyone who left that way—like Reynolds, Brown, Coleman, McDougald, Collins, Kubek, Richardson, and Mantle, plus a few lesser names.

DiMaggio would replace Dizzy Dean on Yankee pregame telecasts, looking awkward in the process, and in 1954 would marry Marilyn Monroe for 274 days, sealing his place in American history as not just a baseball star but as an iconic figure in American culture. Ernest Hemingway would write about him in *The Old Man and the Sea*. Gay Talese wrote a landmark piece about him for *Esquire* magazine. Paul Simon would use his five-syllable name in "Mrs. Robinson." He attended all but one Old-Timers' Day for the rest of his life, which lasted forty-eight more years. (After 1988, he ceased wearing a uniform at those gatherings; he took his last at-bat in 1975.) His Yankee association always trumped any other commitment; he loved the connection and still loved hearing the roar of the crowd. Though some believed he could be difficult, he understood his place in American lore, and when all was said and done, there was only one Joe DiMaggio.

Joe was elected to the Hall of Fame in 1955 (with Home Run Baker) in his third year of eligibility. First-round elections were rare in the days when the Hall was still young and still catching up with a half century of elections never held. Also, while there was no formal five-year waiting period (as enacted in 1954 but waived for Joe), electors seemed not to want to vote for newly retired players, something that helped bring about the five-year rule. DiMaggio, in fact, was only the fifth, and the last, player (besides Ruth, Hubbell, Hornsby, and Ott) elected in fewer than five years after retirement. (Gehrig was a special selection and the waiting period was waived for Roberto Clemente.)

ANOTHER DEPARTURE IN 1951 was that of Commissioner Happy Chandler. Chandler always felt that Del Webb was behind his ouster. He had begun an investigation of whether Webb held a financial interest in Bugsy Siegel's Flamingo casino in Las Vegas. The plain-talking Chandler wrote, "My abortive investigation of Webb's reported Las Vegas connections, of course, turned him flatly against me. In the end, he teamed up with [Lou] Perini, [Fred] Saigh, and other skunks to put me on the skids before I could get them."

"It took me about 48 hours to get enough votes to throw him out," said Webb. "It was the best thing that ever happened to baseball."

Chandler's successor was Ford Frick, the National League president who had covered the Yankees and who was among those who had been a ghostwriter for Babe Ruth.

IN THE YANKS' fiftieth season, 1952, Bell Telephone assigned a new phone number to Yankee Stadium—CYpress 3-4300—but calls for tickets were dropping. Despite the success, attendance fell by more than three hundred thousand in 1952, with more homes owning television sets and DiMaggio gone. (That number would still be in place when the Yankees moved into their new home in 2009.)

The Yankees would go after a fourth straight world championship that year, a quest to equal their all-time record. Most of the twelve players who were part of this run of championship clubs felt that the '52 team was the best of the five.

Martin had been drafted into the army in 1951, but after successfully applying for a hardship discharge (to care for his new wife and ailing stepfather), he had spent most of the season on the Yankee bench, and most of the evenings forming a friendship with Mantle. On April 30, 1952, Coleman was called off for military duty in Korea, and second base was Billy's. Two early-season brawls—one under the stands with Boston's Jimmy Piersall and one on the field after he broke Clint Courtney's glasses with a tag— quickly established Billy's reputation as a hot-tempered player. Although a product of Berkeley, California, Billy was like an Old West gunslinger, and his image evolved over the years into that of a Texan—and one you better not mess with. Mantle would say, "He was the only guy I ever met who could *hear* somebody give him the finger."

Billy had played in the Arizona-Texas League in 1947, and perhaps his self-image had been shaped there. He didn't reappear in Texas until he managed the Rangers in 1973, but by then he was all cowboy and would have been repelled by the liberal thinkers from Berkeley. He didn't even like tennis players, because to him tennis wasn't a manly sport. He even opened a Western-wear shop in New York.

Of course, Billy had his vulnerable side, too, something the fans seemed to realize. He was the skinny kid taking on the big fellows and doing his damnedest to succeed. These dueling personas—the sympathy-inducing Billy and the take-on-all-challengers Billy—would define his Yankee career for the next forty years, with time-outs for periodic exiles.

IN THEIR FIFTIETH season, the Yanks won a close pennant race with Cleveland, clinching when they won fourteen of fifteen in the final weeks of the season. The big game in that run came on Sunday, September 14, when 73,608 jammed Municipal Stadium to see Lopat beat 20-game winner Mike Garcia 7–1 with a 3⅔-inning save from Reynolds and a homer and a double from Mantle. The win put the Yanks two and a half games ahead instead of just half a game. The Indians would have no opportunity to narrow the lead head-to-head, and the Yanks kept rolling.

Berra, who set a catcher's record with 30 home runs, won his second MVP Award and was now in a remarkable streak of ten consecutive seasons in which he finished no worse than fourth in MVP voting.

THE '52 WORLD Series pitted the Yanks against Brooklyn for the fourth time, and this time the Flock (a nickname used by New York writers who recalled the Dodgers' days as the Robins) had become what author Roger Kahn would come to call the Boys of Summer.

With the Series knotted at 2–2, Stengel made a decision to start sidearmer Ewell Blackwell in game five. Blackwell, often called one of the toughest pitchers in the National League during his career with Cincinnati, had pitched in only five games for the Yankees since coming over from the Reds on August 28. Carl Erskine outpitched him, but the game went into extra innings, with the Dodgers winning 6–5 in the eleventh. Raschi, with a save from Reynolds, then won game six 3–2, and the tight series went down to a seventh game at Ebbets Field.

This game, preserved on a kinescope, is the oldest surviving full game known to exist on film.

Mantle, still just twenty years old, broke a 2–2 tie in the sixth with a home run and drove in another run in the seventh for a 4–2 Yankee lead.

In the last of the seventh, the Dodgers loaded the bases. As in '51, Stengel brought in Kuzava. This time, facing Jackie Robinson, Kuzava induced a high pop-up between the mound and first base. Collins, the first baseman, seemed to lose it in the October sun, and it appeared as though it might drop and score the tying runs. Suddenly, Martin raced in from second to catch the ball knee-high, saving the day for the Yankees. It was a quick-thinking, athletic play, a rare feat that showcased Martin's talents.

Kuzava got the last six outs for the second year in a row as the Yankees took their fourth straight world championship, equaling the feat of the 1936–39 teams. Mize, with homers in three consecutive games and a .400 average, was the hitting star for the Yankees, and Raschi and Reynolds each won two games.

WITH FIFTY YANKEE seasons having passed, Arthur Daley chose an all-time Yankee team for a lengthy *New York Times* magazine feature. He selected Gehrig, Lazzeri, Rizzuto, and Rolfe in the infield; Dickey catching; Ruth, DiMaggio, and Meusel in the outfield; and Gomez and Ruffing as the lefty and righty pitchers. The Yankees also asked all their regular sportswriters to vote, and the results were the same, adding Crosetti as a utility man, Murphy as a relief pitcher, and Pennock in a tie with Gomez as the left-handed starter.

WHITEY FORD WAS back in '53 from two lost years in the service, making 1953 the only full season in which Raschi-Reynolds-Lopat-Ford were together, although Reynolds was now spending more time in relief. Whitey, 18–6, led the staff in victories; Sain's 14–7 mark (19 starts, 21 relief appearances) was a pleasant surprise from the thirty-five-year-old; and Kuzava pitched the game of his life when he no-hit Chicago for eight innings before a 68,529-strong Ladies' Day crowd in August.

While not a regular, another player of note on the '53 Yankees was Willy Miranda of Cuba, purchased from the Browns in June. Miranda would be the first postwar Latino player on the team. (His brother Fausto was an important sports editor both in Cuba and the U.S.)

Also worthy of note in 1953 was the briefest of brief Yankee careers. Frank Verdi, who would later manage the team's triple-A clubs, made his debut on May 10, playing shortstop for one inning after Collins hit for Rizzuto. He handled no chances. But when Boston changed pitchers with Verdi due to hit, Casey summoned him back to the dugout and sent up Bill Renna. That would be Verdi's entire big-league career. Casey's platoon system could be cruel.

(Verdi fared better than some Yankees, lost to history, who were called up and never got into a game. This happened with regularity when catchers had weekend army reserve duty and an emergency triple-A player was called up—just in case.)*

Mickey Mantle 's reputation as one of the great sluggers of all time really took shape on April 17, 1953, when he hit a Chuck Stobbs pitch out of

---

* Perhaps the most notable of these "Phantom Yankees" was Pitcher Robin Roberts, who spent two weeks with the team in April 1962, without an appearance. He does not appear on the club's all-time roster.

Griffith Stadium in Washington, leading to the invention of the term "tape-measure home run."

The clout, accomplished right-handed with a borrowed Loren Babe model bat, left the ballpark after grazing the small scoreboard at the rear of the left-field bleachers. Everyone who saw the blast was in awe—no one thought they had ever seen its like.

Red Patterson knew a good story when he saw one. According to accounts of the time, Red left the press box, left the ballpark, and tracked down young Donald Dunaway on 434 Oakland Place, who was holding the ball. Dunaway showed Patterson where it landed, and gave him the ball in exchange for some cash.

Red would later tell me that he walked it off with his size-eleven shoes to determine the distance, each step being twelve inches. Reports said he'd used a tape measure. Red returned to the press box and reported that the ball traveled 565 feet. It became part of baseball legend.

In researching her 2010 biography of Mantle, Jane Leavy found the frail sixty-nine-year-old Dunaway. Dunaway told Leavy that he watched the home run from the bleachers, and then left the park to retrieve the ball. He returned to the park to give the ball to Mantle, and was escorted by an usher to the visitor's clubhouse. There he ran into Patterson, who never left Griffith Stadium.

The ball didn't get anywhere near the backyard of 434 Oakland that Patterson described, and was probably more like 505–515 feet. Still, Mantle's legend as the tape-measure home run king was made.

THE '53 YANKS coasted to their twentieth American League pennant by winning 99 games and finishing eight and a half games ahead of Cleveland. The season was effectively over on June 14 when the Yanks ran their winning streak to a club-record eighteen, completing a four-game sweep of the Indians and taking a ten-and-a-half-game lead. Lopat and Ford each won four during the winning streak, a streak that lost a little of its luster when the Yanks proceeded to drop nine straight to narrow the lead to five.

The Yankees won the World Series over Brooklyn in six games, Mantle hitting a grand slam in game five, then wrapping it up the next day behind Ford and Reynolds when Martin singled home Bauer in the last of the ninth for a 4–3 win over reliever Clem Labine. It was Martin's twelfth hit of the series and gave him a .500 average (with two homers and eight RBI), as Billy once again answered the call in October with a memorable performance.

This was the Yankees' fifth consecutive world championship, a feat unprecedented in baseball. More than a half century later and counting, no team has managed to win even four straight.

"You would think we would have had one of those ticker-tape parades after all those years," said Ford. "But we never had a single one. People just expected us to win, and we did, and then it was on to next year. We had our victory celebrations, we got our rings, but there was never a parade. It would have been fun! I would have liked to have been in at least one!"

IN NOVEMBER, THE Yankees made their way to the United States Supreme Court in the case of George Earl Toolson vs. New York Yankees et al. The case was a test of baseball's reserve system, and the structure of organized baseball was on trial. The Yankees were named because Toolson had been a Yankee pitcher at Newark in 1949 and believed he had major league abilities (he was 26-26 in triple-A), but because of the Reserve Clause he was being held back in the minors, unable to find a major league job on his own. When Newark dissolved, he was transferred to Binghamton and placed on the ineligible list when he refused to report. That was when he decided to sue.

By a 7–2 vote, the court ruled that any change in the system could not come from them but from Congress, although it was the court that had granted baseball its antitrust exemption in 1922.

IN DECEMBER, THE Yankees and Athletics completed an eleven-player deal, the Yanks giving up Vic Power, the American Association's batting champ at .349. "Power was the key player," said Weiss. "The Athletics mentioned his name and then wouldn't hear of anybody else. Apparently they are going to make a bid for Negro fans and figure Power will help them at the gate." The key additions to New York were pitcher Harry Byrd, who had been Rookie of the Year in '52 with 15 victories (but 11–20 in 1953), and Eddie Robinson, a slugging first baseman. The A's, who were desperate to stave off bankruptcy, happily took $25,000 in cash as part of the deal.

Power, a dark-skinned Puerto Rican with exceptional fielding skills at first base (he popularized one-hand catches), was a victim of scouting reports that included charged words like "showboat," "flashy," and "dates white women." Whether the latter was true or not, just "flashy" would probably have disqualified Power from ever making it to New York, regardless of the racial climate at the time. It just wasn't Yankee style, and so long as the team kept winning in the accepted manner created during the Barrow-McCarthy years, things weren't about to change.

In February '54, Vic Raschi was sold to St. Louis. The Springfield Rifle had gone 120–50 for the Yanks, despite pitching with bone chips in his pitching arm and a painful ligament injury in his right knee. But after going 13–6 in 1953, he refused to agree to a 20 percent pay cut and was sold, learning about it from reporters who came to his house in St. Petersburg. The great run of Raschi-Reynolds-Lopat was over.

Raschi did not pitch well for the Cardinals (he yielded Hank Aaron's first career homer), and he was done the following year. He retired to Conesus, New York, and operated a liquor store in nearby Geneseo. Vic died in 1988 at sixty-nine.

Chapter Twenty-Four

I N 1954, A BOOK WRITTEN BY Washington Senators fan Douglas Wallop was published called *The Year the Yankees Lost the Pennant*. It was well received and prophetic, for indeed, the Yankees won 103 games in 1954 but finished eight games behind Cleveland, ending their streak. Wallop's book was set in 1958 and involved a Senators fan selling his soul to the devil in order to reclaim his youth and, as a strapping Joe Hardy, lead his Senators to victory. The drama, of course, came when it was time for the devil to collect his debt.

The book was made into a Broadway musical in 1955 called *Damn Yankees*, and into a movie in 1958. Wallop, who died in 1985, was never embraced by the Yankee organization, who found nothing amusing about losing.

The 103 victories had only been bettered three times in team history, but it was Cleveland's year, as the Indians went 89–21 against everyone but the Yanks and White Sox, and won 111 in all. New PR man Bob Fishel even prepared a four-page handout for fans for the final weekend, featuring the five straight team photos and a "letter of apology" of sorts for failing to win a sixth straight.

One could hardly find fault with this team, but Stengel refused to take a salary increase in a new two-year contract that was paying him $80,000 annually. Even as late as September 5, the Yanks were just three and a half back. But on September 12, they lost a doubleheader at Cleveland before 86,563 fans. After that, they knew it was time to roll press with the "apology brochure."

The brochure was one of Fishel's first suggestions. He had a strong moral compass and a promotional sense from his days as Bill Veeck's publicist with the Browns, where he had helped sign the midget Eddie Gaedel to a one-day contract. Gaedel signed the pact in the backseat of Fishel's Packard.

An advertising executive by training in his native Cleveland, Fishel was a very well-liked and respected figure by the press, an old-world gentleman whose Christmas-card list topped nine hundred. After the Browns left for Baltimore, Bob was a good baseball man with no job. The timing was perfect for the Yanks to grab him.

"I think I was hired because we had a lot of Jewish writers covering the team, and Weiss thought it would be good to have a Jewish PR director," Fishel told me. What Weiss (who wasn't Jewish) didn't know was that Fishel was a non-practicing Jew, and that it was irrelevant—he had a wonderful relationship with all newspaper guys, whether they were named Dan Daniel (real name Markowitz), Ben Epstein, Hy Goldberg, and Milton Gross or Joe Trimble, Kenny Smith, and Til Ferdenzi. Dick Young was half Jewish and liked Fishel just fine.

Red Patterson's time with the Yankees came to a close on July 27 when he had a dispute with Weiss, allegedly over free tickets for an elevator operator at 745 Fifth Avenue. He quit and went to the Dodgers, first as assistant general manager and then as PR director. He stayed with the Dodgers on to Los Angeles, then became president of the Angels to round out his distinguished career. With the Yankees, he had created their first yearbook (called a Sketch Book) in 1950, "invented" the tape-measure home run, served as PA announcer, and produced the annual Old-Timers' Days. He initiated a monthly four-page newsletter called *Yank*, a nice summary of news, photos, and ticket information that would run for twenty years and eventually morph into *Yankees* magazine, a high-end monthly produced by a separate publications department in the front office.

Fishel would create the Yankees' first press guide in 1955. He was a lifelong bachelor who enjoyed Broadway and great restaurants. Mantle loved to tease him with practical jokes, especially if they shocked his sensibilities.

The mild-mannered Bob tore off his glasses and was ready to jump into a fight when the Yanks toured Japan after the '55 season, even though they staged it just to get his reaction. When the team visited Venezuela in spring training in 1972, Bob and White Sox traveling secretary Don Unferth were held hostage until a ransom of phony "taxes" was paid to the government. Lee MacPhail left him a blank check to assure his return. He was never far from adventure, but always a wise presence in the Yankee camp. And of course he brought me to the Yankees when he hired me in 1968. When he died twenty years later, a memorial service was held on the field at Yankee Stadium, with most of his Christmas-card list in attendance.

RED BARBER, DEFECTING from Brooklyn, joined the Yankee broadcast team in '54 (Jim Woods had come aboard the year before), leaving behind a young Vin Scully to carry on. Barber had been disappointed over not getting better support from Dodgers owner Walter O'Malley in seeking a higher World Series fee in '53. He would provide a reportorial style in contrast to Allen's more home-team enthusiasm for the next thirteen seasons.

THE 1954 SEASON saw the debut of Bill "Moose" Skowron at first base. An altar boy and marbles champion from Chicago, the gentle giant had been nicknamed "Moose" after Italian dictator Mussolini because he wore his head closely shaven. But he was also a "big Moose" character without the World War II reference; he had the look of a guy who spent a lot of time in locker rooms.

Skowron caught Stengel's eye in a pregame high school contest at Comiskey Park in 1950, and Stengel told him he'd make a Yankee out of him in three years. Moose walked away from a Purdue football scholarship and signed a $22,000 bonus contract with the Yanks. He hit .328 in three minor league seasons, then joined the Yanks in '54 to platoon at first with Collins. Fans started chanting *Moooooose* when he came to bat, which to strangers sounded like booing. It wasn't. Fans really took to him, especially when he hit .340 as a rookie and over .300 in his first four years.

Bob Grim was a twenty-four-year-old rookie right-hander in 1954 who replaced Raschi in the starting rotation and posted a 20–6 record to earn Rookie of the Year honors. He was the first Yankee rookie in forty-four years to win 20. Grim had gone 16–5 at Binghamton in 1951 but then went off for two years of military service, so no one saw this coming. Alas, although he would have some fine days out of the bullpen, he never truly reclaimed his magic, as arm trouble curtailed his career.

Oakland's Andy Carey, twenty-two, became a regular at third and responded with a .302 average, while Irv Noren got in enough outfield platooning to bat .319 in 125 games. Noren, twenty-nine, had come to the

Yanks in 1952 in a trade with Washington for Jensen and Spec Shea, and this was a breakout season for him. Cardinals star Enos Slaughter, a hero of the '46 World Series, was obtained on April 11 for three Yankee farmhands (including Bill Virdon) and would go on to two tours of duty in New York. He was one of the few players who ever shed tears when he learned he was traded to the Yankees. His Cardinals stay had been a very satisfying one.

Stengel did the best he could. He sent 262 pinch hitters to the plate and they responded with a .292 average. The other seven clubs' pinch hitters combined to hit .198. It was just the Indians' year.

ARNOLD MILTON JOHNSON, born in 1907, was a Chicago-based business-man, one of those gifted people who knew how to buy things with other people's money. At one point he owned as many as twenty companies, but he was never on anyone's wealthiest-Americans list. He just knew how to do deals, and he became an important figure in Yankee history.

J. Arthur Friedlund, secretary–general counsel of the Yankees, brought Johnson together with Topping and Webb, getting them all to purchase the Automatic Canteen Company, a vending company for candy and cigarettes. (Not surprisingly, Automatic Canteen grew into the concession business and would replace Harry M. Stevens as the Yankees' concessionaire in 1963, ending an association that went back to 1903.)

In December 1953, in what was called the "biggest real estate deal in baseball history," Topping and Webb sold Yankee Stadium and its land to the Arnold Johnson Corporation for $6.5 million.* Johnson then leased Yankee Stadium back to the Yankees for a total of $4.85 million spread over twenty-eight years. He sold the land on which Yankee Stadium stood for $2.5 million to the Knights of Columbus, finding it cheaper to lease the stadium than to pay taxes on it. The Knights, tax-exempt, paid no property taxes.

Johnson set up a matching twenty-eight-year lease arrangement with the Yankees totaling $11.5 million, netting him a profit of $6.65 million.

(Topping and Webb also dissolved the corporation that owned the Yankees

---

* The price included $650,000 for Blues Stadium, formerly Ruppert Stadium, in Kansas City, where the Athletics would now play.

in favor of a two-man partnership between them, a move designed to permit them to personally benefit from capital gains.)

In November 1954, Johnson purchased the Philadelphia Athletics from the Mack family and moved them to Kansas City. At the time Johnson's hope, with Webb's encouragement, was to move the team to Los Angeles. Webb always had his eyes on the L.A. market.

The Yankees aided Johnson's purchase by refusing to move the Blues out of Kansas City unless the city bought Blues Stadium. That ploy worked, giving him a home for the Athletics. The Yanks then waived any reimbursement for their territorial rights to the market, but got Johnson to reimburse the Western League $56,843 so that the Yankees could sell the Blues to Denver for $78,000 and make the team part of the American Association.

Not everyone was thrilled with Johnson's purchase. Walter Briggs of the Tigers was very vocal in calling it a conflict of interest, so long as Johnson owned Yankee Stadium. Clark Griffith agreed. Topping defended it, saying, "We hold a long-term lease with him and it is on a flat rental basis. A percentage arrangement might cast a different light on the lease." Commissioner Frick concurred.

Still, Johnson needed to win the votes of Briggs and Griffith, so he promised to sell off Yankee Stadium within ninety days. He didn't meet that deadline, but he did finally sell the ballpark to Texas businessman John W. Cox just before the 1955 season. Cox, who owned the General Packaging Company, was a Rice University graduate. In 1962 he donated Yankee Stadium to his alma mater, stating, "I hope that my gift will encourage others to support Rice."

And so rent checks from the Yankees became payable to Rice University. (In March of 1971, New York City exercised its right of eminent domain and paid Rice $2.5 million to take over the ballpark in anticipation of remodeling it.)

In the meantime, Johnson hired Lee MacPhail's brother Bill, the former Yankee traveling secretary, to be his PR director and hired Parke Carroll as general manager. Carroll too had worked for the Yankees for years, serving as business manager in both Newark and Kansas City. And to improve Blues Stadium to major league needs, he convinced the city council to hire the Del Webb Company to reconstruct it into Municipal Stadium. Between Johnson, Carroll, MacPhail, and Webb, there were plenty of incestuous relationships to go around.

Johnson would die of a cerebral hemorrhage in March 1960, with his estate eventually selling the Athletics franchise to Charles O. Finley. Johnson was only fifty-three, and he owned the team for only five seasons. Parke Carroll, fifty-six, died eleven months later.

In those five seasons, the Yankees and Athletics would make sixteen trades involving fifty-nine players, with the Yankees basically giving up players who were no good to them and obtaining players who were. Observers hated this cushy arrangement and called the Athletics little more than a Yankee farm club. Over the years the Yankees obtained Art Ditmar, Bobby Shantz, Clete Boyer, Ryne Duren, Harry Simpson, Duke Maas, Virgil Trucks, Murray Dickson, Hector Lopez, Ralph Terry, and finally Roger Maris, all of whom contributed to pennant winners. When he took over, Finley declared war on all that the Yankees stood for and stopped the pipeline, although his new general manager, Frank Lane, did let Bud Daley join the list and go to the Yankees in June 1961. But Finley meant business, and he fired Lane a few weeks later. The pipeline was cut.

ON NOVEMBER 17, 1954, the Yankees completed the biggest trade in baseball history, with seventeen players changing teams. But it wasn't with the Athletics—it was with the Orioles, following their first season in Baltimore. The key additions to the Yankees were Don Larsen, Bob Turley, and shortstop Billy Hunter, while the Orioles received Harry Byrd, Jim McDonald, Miranda, Hal Smith, Gus Triandos, and Woodling. The trade took two weeks to complete in full.

REYNOLDS RETIRED AFTER the '54 season. Like Raschi, he too had his salary fights with Weiss. He had to get Stengel to intervene to assure him that his salary wouldn't be cut when he took on bullpen responsibilities, knowing his victory total would fall. Allie had hurt his back in a bus crash and found the very act of conditioning to be a challenge. He said he pitched one year longer than he wanted to anyway.

He was 131–60 for the Yankees with 41 saves, and 7–2 in World Series play.

A bright fellow (he was the American League's player representative), Reynolds became successful in the oil-field business and later president of the American Association. But in 1984, his son and grandson were killed in a plane crash. He lost his wife of forty-eight years, Earlene, and then developed lymphoma and diabetes.

Allie received a plaque in Monument Park in 1989 and died in 1994.

Lopat would thus be the last of the great starting trio to retire. The 1955 season would be his final one for the Yanks, who traded him to Baltimore on July 30 to reacquire Jim McDonald. When he walked off the Yankee Stadium mound on July 27, an era ended. Steady Eddie was 113–59 for New York over eight seasons, and 4–1 in the World Series. He would be a baseball lifer, working as a pitching coach, a major and minor league manager, and a scout before passing away in 1992.

THE 1955 SEASON would mark the last time that the Yankees ended spring training with a week of games against southern minor league teams as they worked their way north. The practice went back to the Ruth-Gehrig days and was lucrative for the Yanks, who kept 60 percent of the receipts. Stengel had gone along with it, but preferred spending the final week in Florida.

Hastening the decision was a ruling by the Southern Association to end these games in their parks. And the reason was likely the Yankees' addition of Elston Howard.

In their fifty-third season, the Yankees were ready to integrate.

The Yanks were the thirteenth of the original sixteen teams to have an African-American player on their team, with the Phillies, Tigers, and Red Sox still to come. Aside from Howard and Power, and Austin, Marquez, and Wilson back in 1949, the Yanks had signed Bob Thurman and Mickey Taborn from the Kansas City Monarchs, but observers thought those men never had a chance.

(In 1953, Bill McCorry, a scout who passed on Willie Mays and who was by then traveling secretary, told John Drebinger, "I don't care what he did today or any other day. I got no use for him or any of them. I wouldn't want any of them on a club I was with. I wouldn't arrange a berth on the train for any of them.")

Once Vic Power had been traded, attention turned to Howard as the logical "first." He was, first of all, enormously talented. The Yankees also saw him as fitting in well, for he could play the outfield, first base, and catcher. He was also immediately popular with his teammates, no matter what their backgrounds or prejudices. Mickey Mantle, raised during the Dust Bowl in Oklahoma, told people, "I haven't had a roommate since Billy Martin, but if I did, it would be Elston Howard." Stengel, born just twenty-five years after the Civil War, didn't always say the right things ("I finally get a nigger and he can't run"), but clearly liked Howard.

A native of St. Louis, Howard had played for the Monarchs in the Negro American League and was signed by the Yankees in 1950. In taking him, Tom Greenwade passed on his teammate Ernie Banks.

Howard made it to the Yankees' spring training camp in '54. The sight of a dark-skinned ballplayer in a Yankee uniform was eye-catching, to be sure. Ellie made favorable impressions and hit .351, but was farmed out on April 1. The Yanks kept Ralph Houk and Charlie Silvera as backups to Berra.

Elston then hit .331 for unaffiliated Toronto in 1954, winning the International League's MVP Award and finishing second to Bill Virdon in batting.

No doubt there were people in the Yankee organization who feared that having negro players would keep away white patrons. Objections to the Yankee "policy" on maintaining an all-white team had gone on for years in the negro newspapers and among civil-rights activists. The argument might have carried more weight had the Yankees not been winning every year with what they had. Perhaps failing to win in '54 played a part in moving Elston up.

Lee MacPhail, then the Yankees' farm director, reflected on this years later. "I will agree that the Yankees may have perhaps dragged their feet a little bit," he told author Jules Tygiel. "I can't agree there was any racial bias there at all. The Yankees were very anxious that the first black player that they brought up would be somebody with the right type of character whom they felt was ideal. Elston was ideal."

Wrote Arthur Daley in the *Times*, "Howard doesn't carry a chip on his shoulder the way the aggressive Robinson does. Nor is he a hearty hail-fellow-well-met the way the popular Roy Campanella is. Elston is a nice, quiet lad of 25 whose reserved, gentlemanly demeanor has won him complete acceptance from every Yankee."

Like Yogi before him, Elston got special catching instruction from Bill Dickey and would eventually be ready to succeed Berra behind the plate. In the meantime, he gave the Yanks tremendous versatility.

ON MARCH 21, Fishel announced that Howard had made the team. Fishel's Yankee yearbook presented Howard as just another rookie in '55, although in '56, he would write, "Elston came up to the New Yorkers last spring amid publicity and furor. Despite the pressure, he just played ball and won his manager's and teammates' confidence."

The "publicity and furor" was most noticeable during spring training, when Howard was not allowed in the Soreno Hotel and instead resided in the home of Dr. Ralph Wimbish Sr., the president of the NAACP in Florida. But there would be trouble in the north as well. When the Howards wanted to build a home in Teaneck, New Jersey, there was community resistance, spray-painted epithets on their walls, and silent treatment from some neighbors. But there was also a warm greeting from many others, perhaps owing to Elston's fame as a Yankee or just people doing the right thing.

Wimbish published a notice in the *St. Petersburg Times* calling on the Yanks and the Cardinals (who shared St. Pete) to lead the fight to end discrimination in the Florida camps, notably the ban on negro players in the team hotels.

Six years later, Dan Topping, disturbed by the lack of progress St. Petersburg had shown in accommodating all the Yankee players equally, announced his intention to move the team's spring training to Fort Lauderdale. He didn't reference matters of race, but rather to having a city to themselves. Topping's action was at least in part a response to the rising voices of the civil-rights movement that were focusing on the absurdity of having men like Howard living in colored boarding houses where they had to answer a dinner bell to eat, rather than sharing a plush dining room in the team's headquarters hotel with their teammates.

Howard was not, of course, what Robinson was to the Dodgers—the face of the team, the man who brought thousands of negro fans to home games. Nor was he what Mays was to the Giants—the most exciting player on the field. Ellie was a high-quality role player at first, not one who garnered headlines, not one who brought out hoards of new fans. During his time with the Yankees, the population of the Bronx was shifting, the African-American population going from just under 100,000 to more than 350,000 between 1950 and 1970, while the white population dropped from 1.3 million to 1.1 million. But it wasn't reflected in ballpark attendance. Yankee Stadium remained a "white" place to be. The Major Deegan Expressway, begun in 1937, was finally opened in 1956, providing major highway access from New Jersey, Westchester, and Connecticut to the parking lots around Yankee Stadium, while those in walking distance generally stayed at home.

Howard was no shrinking violet when faced with prejudice, nor did the Yankees expect him to be. His wife, Arlene, could be particularly outspoken about injustice; the people knew not to mess with Arlene.

On April 14, 1955, Ellie entered the game at Fenway Park in the sixth inning after Noren had been ejected. He "came through with a run-scoring single on his first trip to the plate in the big league," noted the *Times*. "Howard thus became the first Negro to play for the Yankees in a league contest. He received a fine ovation."

It was not an easy season for him. Team hotels in Kansas City, Chicago, and Baltimore required him to find a separate "negro hotel" to stay in. But on a second trip to Kansas City, Stengel, in the city of his birth, told him to just go into the Muehlebach Hotel like everyone else and get a key. He roomed by himself—he wouldn't have a roommate until Harry "Suitcase" Simpson became the Yankees' second black player in 1957—but it was progress. And on the trip to Japan after the season, Howard and Skowron roomed together. Rizzuto and Berra became his very close friends. Bauer was very accepting. In fact, unlike the Dodgers when Robinson broke in, there were no incidents of any players demanding to be traded. It was, by that account, a very easy transition.

WHITEY FORD, now the undisputed leader of the staff, had an 18–7 season in '55 and hurled consecutive one-hitters. It marked the first time that fewer than 20 wins would lead the league in victories. Turley was 17–13, and his 210 strikeouts were the most by a Yankee since 1910, although he also walked 177. Tommy Byrne (who had once walked 179) made a terrific comeback with a 16–5 record for the league's top winning percentage.

Billy Martin returned from the army on August 31 to give the Yanks a boost down the stretch. On May 13, Mantle had the only three-home-run game of his career, and his first of a record ten games in which he switch-hit homers. Berra won his third MVP Award in five seasons.

As THE YANKS battled defending champion Cleveland, the Indians went 13–9 against New York, the first time in seven seasons that Stengel's Yanks lost a season series to anyone.

On Sunday, September 18, the final home date of the schedule, the Yanks beat Boston 3–2 before 54,501 on Phil Rizzuto Day. The day seemed to energize the team. They were on a run of ten wins in eleven games, and they managed to win their twenty-first pennant by three games.

Once again the World Series pitted the Yankees against the Dodgers, who'd never won a championship and had lost four to the Yanks. Might the "wait 'til next year" have finally ended?

It certainly didn't appear so after Ford and Byrne won the first two games, even with Mantle sidelined with a pulled leg muscle. Howard homered in his first World Series at-bat, but Robinson was the star of game one, stealing home on a play that Berra argued forever was a wrong call by the umpire.

No team had ever come back from an 0–2 deficit to win a seven-game Series. But moving to Ebbets Field without a travel day, the Dodgers won all three of their home games and led 3–2.

The Series returned to the Bronx, and Ford had the responsibility of saving the Yanks. He responded with a four-hitter, won 5–1, and set the stage for game seven, October 4, before 62,465 at Yankee Stadium.

A good number of Dodger fans were on hand. With season-ticket sales not anywhere near the heights of coming decades, World Series tickets could be had if one was willing to wait out long lines, perhaps overnight. And the New York newspapers loved the photos of the fans "camping out."

This would be Johnny Podres against Byrne. The Dodgers scored in the fourth and sixth and led 2–0. In the last of the sixth, Sandy Amoros went to left field to replace Jim Gilliam, who had moved to second base in place of Don Zimmer.

Martin, hitting .333 in the Series, led off with a walk, and McDougald beat out a bunt to put two men on. Berra then lined one down the left-field line that had extra-base hit written all over it. It would surely tie the score. But Amoros, who was shading toward center, raced across the outfield grass and made a catch for the ages. At once he whirled and fired to Pee Wee Reese, the cutoff man, who pegged it to Gil Hodges for a double play on McDougald. The ball was hit so hard, and the catch seemed so improbable, that almost any change would have resulted in a hit. Many viewers felt that if Amoros's glove had been on the other hand, he couldn't have reached the ball. It was a turning point.

Time was running out. Podres was pitching the game of his life. He set the Yanks down in the eighth and in the ninth got Skowron on a comebacker, Bob Cerv on a fly to left, and Howard on a grounder to Reese at short. "Next year" was here, as the Dodgers won their first and only world championship in Brooklyn.

After the Series, the Yankees headed on a twenty-five-game tour of Hawaii, Japan (including a game in Hiroshima), the Philippines, and Guam, winning twenty-four and tying one. Almost the entire roster and a good part of the front office went, with newlyweds Andy Carey, Johnny Kucks, and Eddie Robinson making honeymoons out of it, and Casey and Edna Stengel celebrating their thirty-fifth anniversary.

FOR BASEBALL FANS in 1956, four words said it all: Triple Crown, perfect game.

Mantle was still just twenty-four and had already been making his mark. In his first full season, 1952, he was third in MVP voting. He was the homer king in 1955 with 37. He was starting to show up on magazine covers regularly. Kids were taping his photo to their walls; Mickey Mantle T-shirts were available. He appeared on the *Perry Como Show*. Teresa Brewer recorded "I Love Mickey."

During spring training in '56, he hit a ball perhaps 590 feet into an area in right center at Al Lang Field surrounding the St. Petersburg Fountain of Youth. The regular season was no less impressive, with Mantle becoming the first switch-hitter to win a batting title (.353), and to this adding the homer (52) and RBI (130) titles for a Triple Crown and his first of three MVP awards.

On May 30, Mantle, batting left-handed, reached the facade above the upper right-field seats with a shot off Pedro Ramos that had a chance to be the first ball to ever clear Yankee Stadium. The ball struck the green frieze (as some called it) 107 feet above the ground.

He hit only five homers in September; up until then, it looked as if he might break Babe Ruth's immortal record of 60. He ended August with 47, whereas Ruth had ended August of 1927 with 43. People hadn't focused on anyone breaking Ruth's record since Hank Greenberg hit 58 in 1938. (Ralph Kiner had 54 in 1949 and Willie Mays had 51 in 1955, but neither was ahead of Ruth's pace throughout the summer as Mantle was.)

With eight games left in the season, Ted Williams was leading Mantle in the batting race, .356 to .352. Mick went 4-for-11 in the final week to Ted's 4-for-24, and wound up eight points over Williams.

An era came to a close on August 25—Old-Timers' Day—when a batboy found Rizzuto and told him that Stengel and Weiss wanted to see him. Phil hadn't been playing much, but when he arrived before his two bosses, he thought they were seeking his opinion on a roster move. They said they had a chance to pick up a big bat for September and wondered who on the roster he thought might be expendable.

Whether naïve to the process or in denial, he named everyone he could think of before realizing it was to be him all the time. He was shocked. He'd been there since 1941 and was being released on Old-Timers' Day, with many of his old teammates in the house. What further humiliated him was that he was being released to make room for the return of Enos Slaughter (from Kansas City)—a player older than he was!

It was Phil's good fortune that he bumped into Stirnweiss, who walked him out to his car and told him not to talk to writers and to just give himself a day to cool down. This proved to be perfect advice. Instead of knocking the Yankees, he stewed quietly at home. Not long after, the people from Ballantine Beer and WPIX approached him about moving to the broadcast booth the following year.

It was the start of a new forty-year career for the Scooter, who became one of the most popular sportscasters ever. At first intimidated by working with Mel Allen and Red Barber (Barber had little respect for ex-players becoming overnight broadcasters) and by those unhappy with his forcing Jim Woods out of the booth, Phil cautiously learned the craft. He was at first a very good, almost classic announcer, learning as he did from Allen and Barber. But when he became the senior broadcaster, he developed an endearing manner that turned generations into Yankee fans. He was a pro when it came to reading commercial copy, and his lack of ego made all of his many partners into stars in their own right; but he was Peck's Bad Boy when it came to slipping out early to beat the traffic, getting distracted by a gift of canoli, writing "WW" in his scorecard for "wasn't watching," calling enemy players "huckleberries," and proclaiming "Ho-leee cow!" for great moments. A great all-time Yankee and future Hall of Famer, he was at once your favorite uncle, teaching the game, decrying the lack of good bunters, and clearly rooting for the Yankees, who, after all, paid him without fail (except for World War II) from 1937 to 1996.

THE SUMMERLONG FOCUS on Mantle almost distracted from the pennant race and other accomplishments. Berra had a 30-homer season, Skowron and McDougald had .300 seasons, Ford was 19–6, and twenty-two-year-old

Johnny Kucks was 18–9. The Yanks were in first place all season and won by nine games. They were pleased that the Dodgers repeated in the National League; it was a chance to avenge the '55 Series.

Autumn in New York: a Subway Series. This may have been baseball at its peak; it certainly felt that way to New Yorkers. But baseball in the fifties still featured just sixteen teams, drawing now from the pool of black and white players. And with ten future Hall of Fame players on the benches (plus both managers), it was a classic in the making.

In New York, it was a rite of autumn. From 1949 to 1958, there was a World Series in town every year. And if you consider the Brooklyn fans who remained loyal after the Dodgers moved west in '58, the home-team streak extended to 1966: eighteen straight years.

The defending-champion Dodgers won the first two games at Ebbets Field, just as the Yanks had done the year before at Yankee Stadium.

Ford took the mound in game three and won a 5–3 decision, with Slaughter belting a three-run homer in the sixth. In the fourth game, it was the twenty-six-year-old sophomore right-hander Tom Sturdivant, a 16-game winner during the season, winning 6–2 to even the Series.

After the game, the devil-may-care Don Larsen went downtown with his sportswriter pal Arthur Richman of the *New York Mirror* to enjoy the city's nightlife. Don enjoyed a good time and Arthur was a friend to ballplayers throughout his life as a St. Louis Browns fan, a sportswriter, and then an executive for both the Mets and Yankees.

Despite future stories extolling a wild night of drinking, the two had dinner and a couple of drinks, and Larsen was back at the Concourse Plaza Hotel before midnight. He gave Arthur a dollar so that Arthur's mother could give it to her synagogue. He came to think of it later on as a good-luck move.

On Monday, October 8, 64,519 fans, including a sixteen-year-old Brooklyn kid named Joe Torre, made their way to Yankee Stadium for the game. In the Yankee clubhouse, just hours before game time, Casey Stengel gave the word to pitching coach Jim Turner: "Larsen." Crosetti dropped a baseball into Larsen's baseball shoe. That was how he knew he was pitching when he arrived at the park.

Was Larsen at his best that day? He was no champion of conditioning, no hero of early-to-bed training. He always gave a good effort. Lately, that effort included a no-windup delivery, encouraged by Turner as though he was pitching at all times with men on base. He had won four games in September with it.

Through the first three innings, Larsen and his opposite number Sal Maglie were both setting 'em down: no base runners for either team. The closest was a shot by Robinson off Carey's glove in the second, but it deflected to McDougald, who threw him out at first. In the last of the fourth, the first runner proved to be Mantle, who homered just inside the foul pole in right field for a 1–0 lead.

Minutes later, Mantle raced far toward left field to pull in a long drive by Gil Hodges, a play that would become a part of history.

On they played. Bauer drove in a run in the sixth for a 2–0 lead. Now the game went to the seventh and the fans were into every pitch. They knew what was going on, but baseball superstition forbade speaking the words "no-hitter." Even in the Yankee dugout, it wasn't uttered.

In the seventh, Gilliam grounded out, Reese flied deep to center, and Duke Snider flied to left. Six outs to go.

In the eighth, Robinson grounded back to Larsen, Hodges lined to third, and Amoros flied to deep center.

Larsen led off the last of the eighth to a thunderous ovation, but Maglie struck him out, along with Bauer and Collins, to send the game to the ninth.

Newsreel cameras were rolling. Carl Furillo flied to Bauer in right. One down. Campanella grounded to Martin at second. Two down. Up came pinch hitter Dale Mitchell to bat for Maglie. Mitchell, a longtime Cleveland Indian and a fine hitter, was concluding his career with this Series. He stood between Larsen and immortality.

A ball, outside. The fans groaned. A called strike one! The fans cheered. Strike two swinging! One and two. A foul ball. *Ohhhhhhhh!* Still one and two.

Then came the ninety-seventh pitch. It was, according to home-plate umpire Babe Pinelli, a called strike three! In the radio booth, Bob Wolff shouted, "A no hitter! A perfect game for Don Larsen!"

"I had to say no-hitter first," he explained later. "A lot of people were watching who weren't hardcore baseball fans. There hadn't been a perfect game in the major leagues in thirty-four years. Not everyone knew what it meant."

Berra, who called the game with equal perfection, couldn't contain himself. He ran out and leaped into Larsen's arms like a child. It was bedlam in the Bronx!

All the reporters crowded into the Yankee locker room to begin writing the game story of their lives. Dick Young of the *Daily News* whispered a lead to beat writer Joe Trimble, who typed, "The imperfect man pitched a perfect game yesterday." Shirley Povich, in the *Washington Post-Times and Herald*, wrote, "The million-to-one shot came in. Hell froze over."

Even Dodgers owner Walter O'Malley came into the clubhouse to get an autographed baseball.

And that night, Don went out and celebrated. It was okay.

Don Larsen was no immortal. He wasn't going to go to the Hall of Fame. He would have an 81–91 career record and never win more than the 10 he won the following season. But he had pitched a game that could never be bettered—the greatest game, by most measures, ever pitched. Roy Halladay pitched the second no-hitter in postseason history fifty-four years later, but it wasn't perfect and it wasn't a World Series. Larsen stood alone. For the rest of his life, on every milestone anniversary of the game, he was the centerpiece of Old-Timers' Day.

THE DODGERS CAME back the following day as Clem Labine beat Turley 1–0 in ten innings, Robinson hitting a walk-off single to score Gilliam. So it was game seven again, just as in '55, and this time, Johnny Kucks found the baseball waiting in his shoe when he got to the clubhouse. Kucks, just twenty-two, bucktoothed and raw, was born in Hoboken, New Jersey, which many historians consider the birthplace of baseball.* Winner of 18 games in just his second season, Kucks had pitched twice in relief in this Series and was a surprise starter, with Ford having had three days off.

Don Newcombe, so often brutalized by the Yanks (and particularly Berra), fell behind 4–0 after three and left the game. It was all Yankees from there. Skowron hit a grand-slam homer in the seventh to make it 9–0 and that's how it ended, with the Yankees back on top of the baseball world as champions, the Brooklyn Dodgers making their final World Series appearance, and Jackie Robinson striking out to end the game, and his career.

---

* Cooperstown gained the honor thanks to the tale of General Abner Doubleday inventing the game there in 1839. The tale was debunked by the time the Hall of Fame opened in 1939, but the setting was deemed just right to celebrate the game's origins.

Chapter Twenty-Five

SEVENTEEN GAMES INTO THE '57 season, Cleveland was the fourth stop of a five-city road trip for the Yanks, and they arrived at cavernous Municipal Stadium on Tuesday, May 7, for a night game with the Indians.

There were 18,386 on hand, which as usual made the huge ballpark feel almost empty. If anything, this was a good crowd for the Indians, since the Yankees were always a good draw, and the Tribe's ace, Herb Score, would be pitching.

Score, a handsome twenty-three-year-old southpaw born in Queens, burst onto the scene in '55 and came through with a 16–10 Rookie of the Year season followed by 20–9 in '56. In both years he led the league in strikeouts, with 245 and 263 respectively. He was the talk of baseball, the latest overnight phenom in the game's history of love affairs with flamethrowers. The Red Sox had reportedly offered $1 million for him after the '56 season, an offer the Indians rejected.

He would be making his fifth start of the year, his first against the Yanks, against whom he had been 3–1 in nine career starts with two shutouts.

He took the mound in the first inning, got Bauer on a ground ball, and then faced the shortstop, McDougald. The fans had barely settled into their seats when Gil hit a line drive right back at the mound. It got Score square in his right eye, and he dropped to the ground. A silence fell over the ballpark as the ball was retrieved by third baseman Al Smith, who threw to first for the out.

Score's nose was shattered and the hemorrhaging in his eye was frightening.

Gus Mauch, the Yankee trainer, rushed to the mound along with the Indians' medical team as the public-address announcer pleaded, "If there is a doctor in the stands, will he please report to the playing field." Within a minute, six physicians were headed for the field, clustered around the mound. Score never lost consciousness as he was taken off on a stretcher.

"He was the fastest pitcher I ever saw," said McDougald to author Dom Forker. "I just flicked my bat at the ball. The ball shot back at him. Herb didn't have time to get into his follow-through, because the ball hit him on the wrong eye. I saw the blood spurt. I didn't know whether to run to first or run to the mound. After the game I made a statement to the press, 'If anything happens to Herb, I don't want to play anymore.' The press blew it up. But that's the way I felt. It couldn't have happened to a nicer guy. He's such a beautiful person. C.I. Thomas, his doctor, called me in every town that I traveled to, to let me know Herb's condition. His mother called me the next day and said, 'Gil, you had no control over what happened. Don't ever think of quitting.' When people are that nice to you, you say, 'Hell!' But it took the starch out of me."

(Ironically, in August 1955 Bob Cerv hit McDougald with a line drive during batting practice. It ultimately cost McDougald his hearing, forcing him to resign from his postcareer job coaching baseball at Fordham. A cochlear implant in 1994 would restore his hearing.)

The game went on as if in a fog. The Indians won 2–1. Score would return the following season but was never again a star pitcher. He was 19–27 over the next six seasons before retiring to a long career as a Cleveland broadcaster.

The game was not televised, and no film or video existed of the play to be forever replayed. But for years, any drive up the middle that made contact with the pitcher would recall for many the night McDougald's liner hit Herb Score.

ABOUT A WEEK later, Thursday, May 16, after Turley beat the Athletics in New York, a group of Yankees and their wives went out to celebrate Billy Martin's twenty-ninth birthday. Joining Billy were former Yankees Irv Noren and Bob Cerv, now with Kansas City, plus Mantle, Berra, Ford, Bauer, Kucks, and their wives. They had dinner at Danny's Hideaway, then went to the

Waldorf-Astoria for another round and to see singer Johnny Ray's show at 10:30. As Cerv and Noren said good-night, the remaining group headed for the Copa, New York's premier nightclub, to see Sammy Davis Jr. perform the 2:00 A.M. show.

The nightclub was full, but the maître d' opened a special table at the front and seated the party of eleven. After all, this was New York royalty.

At a nearby table, members of a party of nineteen from a bowling league were celebrating, and probably resented this new table being unfolded in front of them. As Davis began to perform, taunts arose from the bowlers' table, seemingly racial, and in any case disruptive.

"One thing about Yogi," said Carmen. "He never stood for heckling; he always wanted respect shown for entertainers."

Bauer gave the bowlers a stern "shut up" in expletive terms.

The hostility found its way to the men's room, where one of the hecklers, Edwin Jones, was found unconscious on the floor. What would a Billy Martin party be without someone unconscious on the floor?

New York Post columnist Leonard Lyons led the players out of the club, and the next day, Bauer was charged with felonious assault. He maintained that he never hit anyone and that in fact Kucks and Berra were holding his arms. The charges were eventually dropped, but the Yankees fined each player $1,000, and Kucks, whose salary was much smaller, $500. The Copa brawl put the Yankees on the front pages of the city's tabloids.

Martin had a feeling the Yankees were running out of patience with him. They had his replacement ready in Bobby Richardson. Richardson and Tony Kubek had come up together from Denver as a second baseman–and–shortstop combo. Martin could see the writing on the wall and felt he was doomed after the Copa incident, even though no one accused him of hitting the fallen bowler.

"I'm gone, pard," he said to Mantle the next day.

MAY TURNED INTO a momentous June for the Yankees as they faltered, then regained their lead in the standings. On June 4, their chief scout Paul Krichell, who had been recruited from Boston by Ed Barrow in 1920, died at his home in the Bronx at seventy-four.

The same day, the Yankees obtained third baseman Clete Boyer from Kansas City to complete a deal that began in February when pitchers Art Ditmar and Bobby Shantz went to New York, with Tom Morgan and Noren going to the A's. Shantz, just five foot six, had been an Athletics mainstay since 1949 and the league's MVP in '52, when he went 24–7 for a 79–75 team. Boyer's brother Ken was an All-Star player on the Cardinals.

On June 13 in Chicago, Ditmar was facing the White Sox when he knocked down Larry Doby with a tight pitch. Words were exchanged, both benches emptied, and a lot of punches were thrown. Enos Slaughter, not even in the game, practically had his jersey ripped off his body in the fracas. With peace seemingly restored, Martin yelled something more at Doby and another fight broke out, this time settled by the Chicago police, who had to escort Martin off the grounds. Doby, Slaughter, and Martin were all fined $150, Ditmar $100. Topping said he would pay the Yankees' fines, but when league president Will Harridge threatened him with a $5,000 fine, he backed off.

"The pitch I threw to him was a foot over his head," said Ditmar. "Since it got past my catcher, I had to cover home. When I got there, Doby said to me, 'If you ever do that again, I'll put a knife in you.'"

Ditmar claimed umpire Larry Napp heard the exchange and told White Sox manager Al Lopez about it, but Lopez turned and walked away.

Martin played the next day in Kansas City, going 1-for-4 in a Yankee win. The fifteenth was the trade deadline. His name wasn't in the lineup that day; Richardson was playing second. Billy decided to sit in the bullpen, but in the seventh inning, Stengel walked over and said, "Billy, can I talk to you?"

"I followed the old man into the clubhouse," he said in his autobiography with Phil Pepe, "and Arnold Johnson, the owner of the Kansas City club came in a few moments later."

> Casey is talking to me and he's having trouble getting the words out.
> He couldn't even look me in the eye. But I knew what was coming.
>   "Billy," he said, "you're going to Kansas City . . . I couldn't . . .
> Mr. Johnson, let me tell you about this kid, he's one of the best . . ."
>   "You don't have to say nothing," I barked at Casey, cutting him
> off sharply. "I'll play for you, Mr. Johnson. I won't dog it on you."

(Lee MacPhail claimed he was the one who told Billy, as Stengel didn't have the heart.)

"I was crying," said Martin. "Mantle came over to me later and he was crying. Ford started crying. We got on the team bus to go back to the hotel and everybody on the bus was real quiet. They all knew. I saw Bobby Richardson sitting by himself, so I slipped into the seat next to him and said, 'You're going to be the second baseman now, son. Carry on the tradition.'"

Martin wore an Athletics uniform against the Yankees the next day. The biggest crowd of the season in Kansas City turned out. He went 2-for-5 and scored three runs.

Everyone felt terrible. It began eighteen years in the baseball wilderness for Martin, always carrying the Yankees in his heart, always feeling betrayed by Stengel, who he felt could have stopped the trade. He was, after all, "Casey's boy." They didn't speak for years. Ford and Mantle were like his brothers.

Billy would play for six teams before embarking on a managerial career that would eventually take him back to New York long after Weiss, Stengel, Topping, and Webb had departed. Much has been made of the times he was fired as Yankee manager, but his first "firing" was really on June 15, 1957, as a player, and he never got over it. He was never the same player again. More than anyone else, he basked in the Yankee uniform, and it inspired him to achievements far beyond his natural abilities.

WITH SHANTZ'S 2.45 ERA leading the league, earning him Comeback Player of the Year honors, Sturdivant going 16–6, Kubek winning Rookie of the Year, and Mantle winning his second straight MVP Award, the Yankees won their third straight pennant and the eighth for Casey.

A spectacular defensive moment during the season found Bauer, deep in right center, unable to glove a long drive—but in position to slap it barehanded to Mantle, who briefly bobbled it but held on for the putout. "That's a play we've been working on," said Bauer.

Mantle's .365 season, his career high, did not include a repeat of his Triple Crown, as his homers fell from 52 to 34 and his RBI from 130 to 94. This was enough for Weiss to send him a contract for 1958 with a $5,000 pay cut and, during negotiations, a threat to be traded. Eventually Mick got a raise to $75,000, but his distaste for Weiss was forever sealed.

Weiss was a distant figure who didn't like to know the players personally. "I never even met him," said Richardson. "His assistant Roy Hamey was assigned to deal with all but a few of us."

The Yankees took on the Milwaukee Braves in the '57 World Series, MVP Hank Aaron having led them to their first pennant since moving from Boston in 1953. The Yanks had never faced the Braves before, but when Ford beat Warren Spahn 3–1 in the opener at Yankee Stadium, it looked like business as usual for New York.

Game two featured Lew Burdette against Shantz. Few remembered that Burdette had actually once been Yankee property, traded to the then–Boston Braves for Johnny Sain. Although playing in the Yankee system for five seasons, he had only made two relief appearances for them in 1950 before moving on. On this day Burdette, who was often accused of throwing a spitball, stopped the Yanks 4–2 to even the series.

Game three was a homecoming for Kubek, a graduate of Bay View High in Milwaukee. Tony rose to the occasion with two homers and a single and drove in four as the Yanks won 12–3.

Spahn won game four, going the distance in a ten-inning, 7–5 Milwaukee win when Eddie Mathews hit a walk-off homer off Grim; then Burdette won his second in game five with a 1–0 win over Ford.

Back in New York, Turley came through with a 3–2 victory in game six to even the series and to set the stage for a deciding game seven. A crowd of 61,207 turned out as Burdette, working on two days' rest, took on Larsen, the World Series MVP of the year before.

It was the Braves' day. They scored four in the third and wound up winning 5–0 as Burdette won for the third time, a feat accomplished only twice before in World Series play.

THE CLOSE OF 1957 marked a lot of changes for New York baseball. Jerry Coleman, just thirty-three, retired to become assistant director of player development. He would work in the front office for five years, become a Yankee broadcaster for seven, and then move to San Diego, where he would become a legendary Padres announcer. "Being a Yankee was never a job," he reflected. "It was a religion."

Another who moved on after '57 was first baseman Joe Collins, thirty-four, who was sold to the Phillies but chose to quit. "If I can't be a Yankee, I don't want to play this game anymore," he said, even though he lived in Union, New Jersey, and a shift to the Phillies would not be of great geographic upheaval.

First-base coach Bill Dickey would retire in spring training of 1958, going home to Little Rock, Arkansas, to become a securities dealer for Stephens and Company. Denver manager Ralph Houk would replace him as first-base coach.

The biggest change of all was the departure of the Dodgers to Los Angeles and the Giants to San Francisco. This shocking development, removing two classic teams from the nation's biggest market, left New York alone to the Yankees.

No doubt some felt the Yankees would now scoop up National League fans and enjoy box-office success as never before. But the fans were hardly willing to cheer for their archrivals. And the Yankees, knowing better, made no extraordinary effort to win them over. They could find Yankee Stadium if they wished. No associations were formed with former Dodgers and Giants other than providing a television program for Roy Campanella, the great Dodger catcher who was paralyzed in an auto accident before he could ever move west. Campy, once he had sufficiently recovered, hosted a show between games on doubleheader days.

In 1958, with the New York territory all to themselves, the Yankees' attendance actually dropped seventy thousand from '57.

IN '58, RYNE Duren became the Yankees' first pure "closer" since Joe Page. Stengel had managed by using Reynolds as a starter-closer, with different pitchers filling the role each season. Now, in the hard-throwing, control-challenged right-hander who came over in the Billy Martin trade, Casey would have his man.

Duren wore what were always described as Coke-bottle eyeglasses. The Yankee Stadium ritual of scaling the low right-field bullpen fence, glancing at the auxiliary scoreboard to check the situation, tossing the warm-up jacket to the waiting batboy, kicking the dirt off his spikes against the rubber, and then firing his first warm-up pitch into the backstop (to frighten the waiting hitter) gave him high style points. The fact that the twenty-nine-year-old rookie would save 20 games, win another six, record a 2.02 ERA, and strike out 87 in 76 innings was a most welcome surprise. He had shown nothing along the way to make anyone think this was coming.

He was, unfortunately, also a bad drunk. At the same time that milkshake-drinking Richardson and Kubek were establishing themselves, Duren was trying to fit in as a guy who liked his liquor. But players who respected guys who could "hold their liquor" saw the distinction. He wasn't one of them.

His most notorious moment was aboard the Yankees' pennant-celebratory train in '58, in which he knocked a cigar out of coach Ralph Houk's hand. (The Yanks still took trains on occasion; they were one of the last to go all-airline, as neither Weiss nor traveling secretary Bill McCorry was a big fan of airline travel. This was an odd thing about Weiss, who'd nearly been killed in a train wreck in 1923.) Houk, Duren's manager in Denver who had bailed him out of overnight lockups on more than one occasion there, reacted by punching Duren and opening a cut over his eye. The moment was witnessed by several Yankee beat writers, who uncharacteristically reported it the next day.

But so long as he was going well—and to everyone's amazement, he was—such incidents could be swept under the rug. It was when he stopped going well that his baseball career wound down rapidly. After his career, Duren cleaned up, got active in AA, and by the 2000s actually looked more fit and healthy than most of his teammates.

Stengel juggled his pitching staff throughout the season, calling on a trio of forty-one-year-olds—Sal Maglie, Virgil Trucks, and Murray Dickson, plus twenty-nine-year-old Duke Maas—to augment the regular rotation. He still preferred to spot-start Ford, generally keeping him out of Fenway Park, which was tough on left-handers. Whitey would have preferred working on a regular rotation, as he won only 14 games in '58, half of them shutouts, posting a 2.01 ERA, the best of his career.

The year belonged to Bob Turley, who was 21–7 with six shutouts and a 2.97 ERA, all good enough to deliver the Cy Young Award to him at season's end. With his no-windup delivery and blazing fastball, the handsome twenty-seven-year-old right-hander became one of the most marketable players on the team. Mantle, with his 42 home runs, was still at the top of picture packs sold to fans, of course.

Nobody appreciated this more than Manny Koenigsberg, who opened Manny's Baseball Land on River Avenue in the late forties and who seemed to have a monopoly on Yankee souvenirs outside the ballpark until he retired in 1978. (The place later became Stan's, but by then it had a lot of competition up and down the block.)

Manny was a visionary, capturing a market long before licensing took hold of the souvenir industry. He specialized in Yankee caps, yearbooks of all teams (official and unofficial), and all sorts of fifties souvenir items like thermometers, decals, pens shaped like bats, buttons, badges, banks, snow globes, picture packs, bobbleheads, and Topps cards. No trip to Yankee Stadium was complete without first stopping at Manny's. (The "unofficial" yearbooks, first published in conjunction with the team, were issued by Jay Publishing, owned by John Jackson. The company ended with a 1965 American Airlines crash just north of Cincinnati that took fifty-eight lives, including Jackson and Jack Flynn, who sold Yankee commercial time for WPIX.)

The 1958 season also saw the introduction of the character Yogi Bear by animators Hanna-Barbera, a clear move by the company to capitalize on Yogi Berra's popularity without having to pay royalties. And while most people believed that Yogi had an ownership interest in Yoo-Hoo chocolate soft drink, he was simply paid an endorsement fee, and a small one at that. Still, his business deals were far more successful than Mantle's, who never seemed to catch a lucky break.

On July 9, the day after the All-Star Game in Baltimore, Stengel, Webb, Mantle, Ted Williams, and other baseball people went to Washington to testify before the Senate Subcommittee on Antitrust and Monopoly, which was investigating baseball's antitrust exemption. The hearings, led by Senator Estes Kefauver, were televised, and gave Casey the opportunity to put on a display of Stengelese the likes of which the Congressional Record had never seen. All it took was, "Mr. Stengel, you are the manager of the New York Yankees. Will you give us very briefly your background and views about this legislation?" To everyone's amusement and to no one's understanding, Casey went on for forty-five minutes and seven thousand words, much of it drowned out in laughter. When Mantle followed, he played his part well, simply stating, "My views are just about the same as Casey's."

THE YANKS LED wire to wire in '58 and had a seventeen-game lead by early August. A bump on the pennant trail was a no-hitter thrown against them in Baltimore on September 20 by knuckleballer Hoyt Wilhelm, normally a relief pitcher. This was the sixth no-hitter against the Yankees in their history, and there would not be a seventh for forty-five years.

(Amazingly, Wilhelm would come close again a year later. On May 22, 1959, only an eighth-inning single by Jerry Lumpe kept him from doing it in consecutive years.)

The 1958 World Series, again against the Braves, was considered the most satisfying for those of the Stengel era. Even though it was a practice to give World Series rings only to the players and not to front-office people, the occasion of Bob Fishel's sixty-fifth birthday in 1979 found him receiving (with Yankee approval) a '58 ring. He had tears in his eyes as he explained, "This was the best of all the championships; I couldn't have gotten a better gift than this."

Things started poorly for the Yanks, as Spahn and Burdette won the first
two games in County Stadium. Bauer saved the third game in Yankee Stadium, driving in all four runs in a 4–0 win behind Larsen and Duren, but
then left fielder Norm Siebern lost two fly balls in the sun and the Braves
won game four 3–0, Spahn besting Ford. It was 3–1 Braves.

Game five had Burdette poised to seal the world championship, but
Turley beat him with a 7–0 shutout, as Howard made a clutch catch on
his knees in left.

Game six had Ford and Spahn on the mound with just two days' rest.
Bauer's fourth home run of the Series, coming in the first inning, ran his
World Series hitting streak to a record seventeen (going back to 1956), but the
Yankees needed a tenth inning and a save from Turley to even the series 3–3.

The next day it was Larsen against Burdette, two former World Series
MVPs. The Yanks had a 2–1 lead in the third, but the Braves got two on and
Stengel went to his bullpen to summon Turley, pitching for the third time
in four days.

Bullet Bob set down the Braves with one run and two hits in 6⅔ innings,
nailing down a 6–2 win and the Yankees' eighteenth world championship—
Stengel's seventh and last. Skowron's three-run homer in the eighth sealed
the win, as well as Turley's position as the game's reigning pitching star.

"I think this World Series might be the greatest thrill I ever experienced
in baseball," wrote Lee MacPhail in his memoir. Lee left the Yankees as
player personnel director after the season to join the Orioles and succeed
Paul Richards as general manager, adding the club presidency title a year
later. "Feelings were aroused in Milwaukee, as someone in the Yankee party
had reportedly referred to Milwaukee as a 'bush town.' All over the city there
were figures of Yankees hanging in effigy."

IN 1959 THE Yankees unveiled a new $300,000 scoreboard, replacing their
existing one after nine seasons. That one was sold to the Phillies and reas-
sembled at Connie Mack Stadium, where it remained in use as a hand-me-
down until Veteran's Stadium opened in 1971. The new scoreboard, designed
by Lon Keller (creator of the top-hat logo) and underwritten by Ballantine,
included the first "message board" in the major leagues, eight lines long
and eight characters across, each letter having to be keyed in separately.
The nimble fingers of the team's chief electrician, George Schmelzer,
would punch out messages throughout the games, none of which could be

preprogrammed as a computer would allow today. The Yankees would get fifteen seasons of use out of this board, using the top line in its final season to show the up-to-the-minute batting average of the hitter.

By Yankee standards, 1959 was a disaster: third place. It was the lowest finish of the Stengel era, and when the Yanks lost to their Detroit nemesis Frank Lary on May 20 (Lary was 28–13 lifetime vs. New York), the *New York Post* headline said it all: YANKS HIT CELLAR.

They spent eleven days there, mired in eighth place. Finally, Turley shut out the Senators on May 31 to raise them from last. From there to the end of the season, they were a decent 61–52. But the first two months defined their year. The White Sox, managed by Al Lopez, wound up with the pennant.

There would be fleeting moments when it looked like all was well, but Ford had his first double-digit-loss season, Mantle hit just .285/31/75, and Turley fell to 8–11, 4.32, which was viewed as the big reason for the drop-off. On the bright side, Berra set a catching record with 148 consecutive error-less games, going back to '57, Richardson hit .301, Duren had a 1.88 ERA, Duke Maas went 14–8, and they pulled off a nice trade (with the A's, of course), getting Hector Lopez and Ralph Terry for Kucks, Sturdivant, and Lumpe. Lopez, a poor-fielding third baseman from Panama, moved to left and gave the Yankees some solid seasons and some memorable World Series games as well. The Yankees thought he was twenty-six when they got him; it turned out he was twenty-nine.

An emotional moment for the Yankees came on May 7 when they flew to Los Angeles to play a benefit game against the Dodgers, the Dodgers' net proceeds to go for Roy Campanella's costly rehabilitation. (The Yankees kept their share, but figured their presence had obviously produced a big crowd and allowed the Dodgers to make big money.) A baseball-record 93,103 fans packed the Los Angeles Coliseum, and between the fifth and sixth innings, everyone held a lit match or flicked a lighter as the stadium lights were doused. Reese wheeled Campy onto the field on an enormously dramatic day in baseball history for a much-beloved figure.

This was the Yankees' first trip to the West Coast since spring training of 1951. The game found most of the fans dressed casually: open shirts, bareheaded, sport clothes. It was still unthinkable that that would become East Coast style, but over the next five or six years, fans going to Yankee Stadium began to shed their business attire and bring a more casual appearance to a day at the ballpark. The days of men in suits and hats and white shirts was coming to a close as America relaxed its dress code.

A minor event during the season would prove to be a sports milestone. On Friday evening, July 17, Ralph Terry no-hit Chicago through eight innings in a 0–0 ballgame. This was the first year that WPIX was saving game highlights on something called videotape for use on the postgame *Red Barber Show*.

White Sox outfielder Jim McAnany led off the eighth and promptly broke up the no-hitter by dropping a single in front of Siebern in left center.

On the air, Mel Allen asked his director, Jack Murphy, if the base hit could be played back right then, as opposed to waiting for the postgame show. The WPIX tape engineers quickly rewound the moment, and on the air went the McAnany single, with Mel explaining that viewers weren't watching another single, but a replay of the hit that broke up the no-hitter.

And that was the birth of instant replay.

The fifties were the era when television coverage of baseball was expanding the game to new audiences. A center-field camera, introduced in 1957, became usable once its lens was long enough to see the pitcher-catcher action; then it became the primary pitch camera. Lenses kept bringing the view closer and closer to the player's faces, until 70:1 ratio lenses showed every skin pore. The station began broadcasting the games in color in 1965. Cable TV made rabbit-ears antennas and bad reception obsolete in the early eighties. By the late eighties every game of every team was televised, meaning no plays were ever missed, no highlights lost. By 2009, games became available on computers and handheld devices.

ONE AFTERNOON, JUST after Labor Day, Harry Craft was seeing the handwriting on the wall and his days as Athletics manager dwindling. He happened on Stengel during batting practice and mentioned, "If you have an opportunity, you ought to try to get my right fielder. Maris is much better than his numbers show; he's a terrific ballplayer." Craft, who had managed Mantle in the minors, would find that he was making a very good contribution to the Yankees' future with this scouting report. Of course Roger Maris, being an Athletic, may have simply found his turn in line to go to the Yankees anyway. Parke Carroll was ready to do business, and on December 11, the Yankees were able to swing the deal. They traded Bauer, Larsen, Siebern, and Marv Throneberry to the Athletics for Maris, Kent

Hadley, and Joe DeMaestri. Bauer, a great Yankee in his time, knew that younger players replaced older ones in well-run organizations, and the fact that he lived near Kansas City made the deal okay with him. As it was, he got to be a player-manager for the A's, starting him on a managerial career that took him to a World Series with Baltimore.

Ah, but the sweet-swinging Maris, he of keen defensive skills, a strong arm, good baserunning instincts, and more power in his bat than was realized at the time, was the key. He would prove to be just a terrific addition.

Weiss sent Mantle a contract for 1960 calling for a $17,000 pay cut. Mickey had to hold out for two weeks in spring training before settling for a $7,000 cut.

Chapter Twenty-Six

ROGER MARIS WAS A SENSATIONAL Yankee, but a poor match for New York. Raised in Fargo, North Dakota, a state that had produced only five major leaguers by the time he debuted, he seemed very comfortable playing for Kansas City and would, in fact, maintain his winter home there during his Yankee years. The glare of the spotlight would be gentle in 1960, his first Yankee season, as he raised his game to new levels.

At age twenty-five, Maris was a shining star. Seemingly out of nowhere, he led the league in RBI and slugged 39 home runs, just one behind Mantle for the league lead. He won a Gold Glove (he played left field throughout spring training, but Casey opened the season with him in right, and there he stayed), and then nosed out Mantle for the league's MVP Award, getting 225 votes to Mantle's 222, although Mantle had ten first-place votes to Roger's eight.

Mantle was important in helping Maris transition to the Yankees, as he too was still a middle-America kid at heart, a little awkward in the bright lights but now, as a ten-year veteran, a mature mentor to Roger. People were already calling them the M&M Boys and posing them in photos together. Seventy-nine home runs together was an impressive showing.

IT WAS ALSO during the 1960 season that Howard began to catch more often than Berra, with Yogi seeing more action in left field and Johnny Blanchard taking Howard's place as the backup catcher. Clete Boyer took over at third. A key addition to the Yankees turned out to be a Puerto Rican screwball pitcher and former National Leaguer named Luis Arroyo.

Arroyo, thirty-three, had been pitching for the Havana Sugar Kings. The takeover of private industry by Fidel Castro forced the Sugar Kings to hastily move to Jersey City, and Arroyo was purchased by New York on July 20. (Twenty-four of thirty players from that roster made it to the majors.) He made 29 appearances for the Yanks, went 5–1 with seven saves, and positioned himself to succeed Duren as the ace of the bullpen.

IN 1960 THE affable Bruce Henry, who had been business manager of the Richmond Virginians, a Yankee triple-A club, succeeded Bill McCorry as traveling secretary.

During the season, the Yankees also hosted the second of two All-Star Games, a bad idea, as it turned out, with only 38,362 paying customers buying into the two-game experiment.*

The '60 pennant race got a surprise entry with the emergence of the Baltimore Orioles, skippered by Paul Richards and with Lee MacPhail as general manager. A host of homegrown young players were turning the Orioles into a team that would be a model franchise for more than three decades, and they tested the Yankees' will in '60 by finishing just eight games out of first. It took a four-game sweep over Baltimore in mid-September to finally open up the race, the Orioles having arrived in New York just one game back. But wins by Ford over Steve Barber, Jim Coates over Chuck Estrada, and then a doubleheader sweep before 53,876 with Ditmar over Jack Fisher and Terry pitching a 2–0 shutout over Milt Pappas put the Yankees on a roll toward winning Stengel's tenth pennant. Coates's win, in relief, made him 12–3 for the season. The sweep opened up a fifteen-game winning streak to close the season. Even after the pennant was clinched and Stengel rested his regulars, the Yanks still won their last six. Among those who got to play then was Dale Long, who batted .366 in 26 games, another fine late-season pickup for the Yanks.

The Pirates won their first pennant since 1927 and would face the Yankees in the World Series. Stengel opted to start Ditmar in the first game at Forbes Field. Ditmar, 15–9, had been his big winner in '60. The Yanks managed to win 97 games without any pitcher winning 16.

---

* The second game was added in 1959 to increase contributions to the players' pension fund. The experiment ended after four years.

Ford, 12–9 and in everyone's mind still the leader of the staff, continued at the top of his game. He had had six days off before game one.

Ditmar lasted just a third of an inning as the Pirates won the opener 6–4. The second-guessing had begun.

Turley started game two and got things even as the Yanks triumphed 16–3, pounding out 19 hits.

Ford started game three in Yankee Stadium and pitched a four-hit shutout, winning 10–0. Richardson, who drove in only 26 runs in the regular season, hit a grand slam in the first off Clem Labine and drove in two more in the fourth on a bases-loaded single. The six RBI in a game—and, ultimately, 12 RBI for the Series—were both new records, and they were still standing more than half a century later.

The Pirates won the next two and led 3–2. Ford then pitched another shutout, this one 12–0. So the three Yankee wins were 16–3, 10–0, and 12–0, and yet it was going to take a seventh game to decide the champion. And for this, neither Ford nor Ditmar would be available, Ditmar having lost game five.

The seventh game would by many measures be one of the most memorable in baseball history. It had everything, so it seemed, except a strikeout. It was the only World Series game ever played without one. (When a kinescope of the game recorded and saved by Bing Crosby emerged from his archives in 2010, it was hailed as a major historical find.)

This decisive game, October 13 in Forbes Field, had Turley starting against Vern Law. But Turley was removed in the second. At various times it appeared that home runs by Hal Smith or Rocky Nelson of the Pirates, or Berra or Skowron of the Yanks, might be game changers. The Yanks had a 7–4 lead in the last of the eighth behind great relief pitching, fielding, and even hitting from Shantz. But a potential double-play grounder to short hit a pebble and smacked Kubek in the throat, sending him to the hospital. The Pirates would rally for five runs and a 9–7 lead, the big shot being a three-run homer by Hal Smith, who had been part of the seventeen-player trade to the Orioles in 1954.

For years, many felt Jim Coates's failure to cover first that inning on a grounder by Roberto Clemente was as costly as the freak "pebble play" on Kubek. But the ball was hit between where the second and first baseman would go for it, and Coates tried to field it before breaking to first. It was like a perfectly placed bunt, where all you could do was eat the ball.

"[The play] will always be remembered as a time of hesitation and indecision," wrote Coates in a 2009 memoir. "It has been the source of criticism, blame and second guessing over the years, of which a big part should be seen as undeserved once the details of the play have been properly reviewed."

"We had Coates wrong on that one," said Richardson after seeing the kinescope fifty years later. "He couldn't be blamed after all."

In the ninth, the Yanks rallied to tie the score when Mantle dove back into first to escape a double play. Nelson speared a hard shot by Berra; Mantle froze, not knowing if it was caught on a bounce or a liner. Instinctively, he dove to first, evading Nelson's tag. Then McDougald, pinch-running in his final moment on a baseball field, was able to score and tie it 9–9. Had Nelson tagged Mantle, the game would have ended and Smith's homer would have decided it.

Terry pitched the last of the ninth. On his second pitch, Bill Mazeroski homered over the left-field wall to give the Pirates the world championship. The most famous home run in Pittsburgh history and the first walk-off in a deciding World Series game had led to a shocking defeat of the Yanks, who had outscored the Bucs 55–27 in the Series. Many Yankee players, including Mantle, had tears in their eyes in the clubhouse.

Because the vote was taken before the game ended (the voting writers had to go downstairs for postgame coverage), Richardson was the MVP, the only losing player to be so honored as of 2011. (The award began in 1955.) The Pirates' star reliever, Roy Face, upon learning that Mazeroski had not won the MVP, threatened Yankee PR man Bob Fishel, convinced Fishel had cooked the vote.

"Great, great, great is the only word to describe the ballgame that today made the incredibly Cinderella-ish Pirates the 1960 champions of the baseball world," wrote Dick Young.

Had Nelson tagged Mantle, Mazeroski's legendary home run would never have happened.

FIVE DAYS AFTER the Series ended, Fishel and his new assistant Bill Guilfoile called reporters to a press conference at the Savoy Hilton Hotel, across Fifty-eighth Street from the Yankee offices where the General Motors Building and the Apple store now stand.

Casey was there, looking prosperous in a blue suit, and Topping took charge. He began to explain a profit-sharing payout waiting for Casey, and the fact that his last two-year contract had included an understanding that he could retire if he wished after one year. The writers were getting restless.

One finally yelled out, "Is he through, Dan? Has he resigned?"

The question went unanswered. It was Casey's turn to speak.

"Mr. Webb and Mr. Topping have started a program for the Yankees, a youth program," he said. "They needed a solution as to when to discharge a man on account of age. They have paid me off in full and told me my services are not desired any longer by this club. I told them if this was their idea not to worry about Mr. Stengel, he can take care of himself."

"Casey, were you fired?" shouted another reporter.

"No, I wasn't fired; I was paid up in full. Write anything you want. Quit, fired, whatever you please, I don't care."

This wasn't going as planned. Topping had been unable to make sweetness out of this send-off moment.

Joe Reichler of the Associated Press had already phoned his desk with the story.

"Casey, an AP bulletin says you've been fired . . ."

"What did the UP say?" asked Casey, referring to the old United Press (now UPI).

So the Yankees had fired Stengel after ten pennants and seven world championships in twelve years. What would have happened had he won the seventh game of the Series? No one ever learned the answer to that. "I'll never make the mistake of being seventy again," said Casey.

Indeed, the Yankees were now instituting a mandatory retirement age of sixty-five for employees. And sure enough, on November 2, George Weiss resigned as general manager, to be replaced by his assistant Roy Hamey. Weiss, however, would get a five-year consulting deal and had nothing bad to say.

"Gigantic organizations such as General Motors and United States Steel have retirement deadlines, but they have sense enough to use them with flexibility," wrote Arthur Daley. "However, a puny organization like the Yankees blindly adheres to the letter of its own law. It's a new law, too. It could have waited for implementation until Casey had decided to quit of his own will."

A night after his firing, the New York writers threw a party for Casey at the Waldorf-Astoria. He had filled their notebooks and made their jobs a pleasure for a dozen years.

Possible successors included Al Lopez, who had won the pennant both times the Yankees didn't finish first in the Stengel era; Birdie Tebbetts; and coaches Jim Turner (who had moved to the Reds), Eddie Lopat (who had succeeded him with the Yankees), Frank Crosetti (the ever-present third-base coach), and Ralph Houk (who had filled in for Casey for two weeks in 1960 when he was ill).

Internally, employees knew Houk was going to be their guy. Even Stengel knew he would one day be his successor. Beloved by the players, a champion manager in Denver (where he had managed Richardson, Kubek, Blanchard, Terry, and other top prospects), he was rumored to be headed to Boston to manage the Red Sox. Kansas City was also said to be interested in him, with a new owner, Charles O. Finley, having taken over the team. Topping and Webb didn't want to lose him. If anything, it hastened their decision to fire Stengel.

On October 20, once again at the Savoy-Hilton, Houk, forty-one, was announced as the team's new manager. The onetime bullpen catcher was now the boss.

Houk had won a Bronze Star, a Purple Heart, and a Silver Star at the Battle of the Bulge, and had risen to major in the army; hence, he was called the Major. Everyone agreed he was a good choice, but the fans were enormously sympathetic to Stengel. There would be no learning curve for the rookie manager: The expectation was to win at once.

IN AUGUST 1960, expansion was on the owners' minds. Dan Topping took a leadership role by demanding that the American League put a team in Los Angeles as a counterbalance to allowing the National League to reinstate one in New York. Webb, sensing an opportunity to build the new ballpark in L.A., concurred. The other AL owners closed ranks behind them, and the awarding of a franchise to Gene Autry—the Los Angeles Angels—was a victory for Topping. (When Anaheim Stadium was built in 1964–66, the contractor was the Del Webb Company, which had also retrofitted Los Angeles Coliseum for the Dodgers in 1958.)

The other AL franchise went to Washington, where a new team would replace the "old" Senators, who were granted permission to move to Minnesota. In the expansion draft, held December 14, 1960, the Yankees lost Eli Grba, Maas, Cerv, and Ken Hunt to the Angels, and Shantz, Long, and Bud Zipfel to the Senators. (Cerv would be traded back to the Yanks in May.)

McDougald, who had gone 9-for-21 as a pinch hitter in 1960 in addition to being an experienced role player, packed it in after the season. The Angels wanted him—Autry called him four times—but he knew he was through. "I got tired of traveling and putting on the uniform," he said. "When you get to that stage, you better get the hell out. I knew I was no longer a good ballplayer."*

1960 WAS NOT only the last year of the Stengel Yankees, but the last year of eight-team leagues and 154-game seasons, the new total being 162. It was also Ted Williams's final season, and Mantle became the uncontested superstar of the league.

Although the National League would not expand until 1962, New York's new National League team—the Metropolitans—would be spending 1961 getting prepared.

And what announcements they would have.

On March 12, 1961, they hired Weiss to be their general manager, and after much persuasion, Weiss named Stengel to be his manager on October 2, using the same suite at the Savoy Hilton Hotel to make the announcement. It was a stroke of genius. As good as Casey was with a talented roster, he was the perfect man to deflect attention away from a losing bunch of ballplayers while charming the media, wooing fans, and turning the Mets into instant hits in New York. The battle lines were drawn, with Weiss and Stengel prepared to snub their noses at the Yankees while winning over fans at the Mets' temporary, two-year home at the Polo Grounds.

They also took Gus Mauch, the Yankees' trainer (Joe Soares would succeed him), as well as a number of old Yankee front-office employees and even some retooled players like Gene Woodling and Marv Throneberry (a younger player from Houk's Denver champs, whose flubs and miscues would delight the press and help create the hapless but lovable Mets image). Casey could deflect bad play away from the players and help establish the Mets as "lovable losers," something no other expansion team in any sport has been able to duplicate.

Houk was a "player's manager." The mantra was "We'd run through a wall for Ralph Houk." Stengel had been well liked enough and certainly respected, but Houk was adored by his players. He never criticized a player

---

* A brief return to the Yankees came in 1974 when Home Box Office, still a small regional cable service, presented nineteen Yankee games, with Marty Glickman, Dick Stockton, and McDougald sharing the booth with the Yankee announcers.

in the media, he kept the bench players happy, and he didn't get involved with the pettiness of room checks and evenings out, something Stengel famously harped on.

Houk made two other key changes in '61. He told Mickey Mantle that while the Yankees hadn't named team captains since Lou Gehrig died, he was the de facto one—the guy who was to lead the team by example. "I'm not reviving the post of captain," he told Dan Daniel. "I want him to lead the club. He is 29, mellowed, certainly not complacent." He also put him in the cleanup slot in the batting order, protecting Maris in the third spot. Except for Ford and Berra, Mantle was now the senior player on the roster, already a Yankee immortal. (Berra was the only player to span the full Stengel era.)

Then he told Ford that he would be pitching every fourth day, and that he would not be held back and strategically placed in favorable ballparks. In short, he would treat him like the elite starter he was. And so after averaging fewer than 30 starts a year since his first full season, he would make 39 in 1961—and would respond with his first 20-win season. He went 25–4, leading the league in wins, winning percentage, and innings pitched while striking out a career-high 209 and winning the Cy Young Award.

If nothing else, changing the psychology of Mantle and the work habits of Ford elevated what had been a very good team into a legendary one.

Houk dropped Lopat as pitching coach and brought in Johnny Sain, who was developing a reputation as the best in the game. He added Wally Moses as hitting coach. (Sain lasted three seasons; when he wanted a $2,500 raise in '64 and was denied, he went elsewhere.)

The 1961 Yankees would perform so well that they immediately entered into the debate of "greatest Yankee team ever" with the '27 and '39 squads. They set a major league record with 240 home runs and coasted to the pennant. Their 109 victories were the second highest in franchise history, although this was the first year of an expanded schedule.

On September 1–3, before crowds totaling 171,503, the Yanks swept three from the Tigers as Arroyo won two and saved one. Arroyo was the best relief pitcher in the league, with a screwball as baffling as his arm was tireless. He appeared in a then-club-record 65 games, going 15–5 and saving 29 (AL relief records for both wins by a reliever and saves) with a 2.19 ERA. Forty of his appearances were for more than one inning, including a 6⅔-inning appearance of shutout ball on July 30. He was there so often to save Ford, it brought back memories of Gomez-Murphy, and Whitey loved it. On Whitey

Ford Day, held on September 9, Arroyo was driven in from the bullpen under a giant Life Savers package to everyone's amusement. Thirty-nine years later, at a second Whitey Ford Day, Arroyo was there again. Ford hadn't seen him in many years, and Whitey had tears in his eyes as they embraced. He loved Looie.

The sweep of the Tigers was the start of a thirteen-game winning streak for the Yanks, who wound up winning the pennant by eight games. They were an amazing 65–16 at home.

The regular lineup was essentially intact from 1960, although two new starters entered the rotation. Bill Stafford, just twenty-one, was 14–9, and Rollie Sheldon, twenty-four, was 11–5. Bud Daley, the "final" Kansas City acquisition, was obtained at the trading deadline in June for Ditmar and Deron Johnson, and won eight games.

Sheldon, from the University of Connecticut, was 15–1 at class-D Auburn in 1960 and made the jump to the majors after a fine spring training. He had lied about his age, telling scout Harry Hesse that he was twenty, but a phone tip to Bob Fishel by a sportswriter who had seen him play in Connecticut brought about a four-year adjustment.

Howard, Berra, and Blanchard, all catchers by trade, hit 60 homers between them, with Berra playing most of his games in the outfield. Howard hit .348, to lead the team. Skowron belted 28 homers. The infield—Skowron, Richardson, Kubek, and Boyer—was among the best defensively ever assembled.

But the real story of 1961 was the challenge to Babe Ruth's record of 60 home runs by Mantle and Maris. Few baseball events ever managed to capture all of America's interest as this did. The race to 60 was featured on the cover of *Life* magazine, reported on the network newscasts, discussed everywhere.

Mantle emerged as the wide favorite among fans and baseball insiders. Mick seemed "worthy," having challenged the record five years earlier, having worn the Yankee uniform for his entire career, having already won four home run titles, and having made his reputation as one of the great sluggers of all time.

Maris, twenty-six, seemed unworthy. He was in his fifth season, and only his second with the Yankees. He seemed to wear a scowl on his face, and his frank answers to questions he thought to be dumb rubbed writers the wrong way. Maris had hit only 97 home runs going into the season, few of them "tape-measure."

Among his chief critics were Mrs. Babe Ruth and old-timers like Rogers Hornsby and Frankie Frisch, who questioned whether he could even be on the same field with players of their era.

Mantle and Maris, who shared an apartment in Queens with Bob Cerv, tried to ignore the attention and just keep hitting. Roger didn't homer until the eleventh game of the season, but by July 4, the traditional halfway point of the baseball calendar, Maris had 31 and Mantle 28. (Maris lost one in a game rained out before five innings were completed.) Newspapers started to show graphs to track their progress, reminding people that Ruth had hit 17 in September. Pete Kalison, the Yankee statistician, worked overtime to find new twists in the chase. Bill Kane, just starting as Mel Allen's stat assistant in the broadcast booth, was frantically filling out three-by-five note cards each time one of the M&M Boys hit one.

On July 26, with Maris at 40 and Mantle at 38, Commissioner Ford Frick made a dramatic announcement. The onetime ghostwriter for Ruth said, "Babe Ruth's mark of 60 home runs, made in a schedule of 154 games in 1927, cannot be broken unless some batter hits 61 or more within his club's first 154 games." It came to be known as the "asterisk" decision (although the books showed both records, and Frick never used the word).

On they went, entering September with Maris at 51 and Mantle at 48. Mantle faded, limited by injuries, but still hit a career-high 54. Attention turned to Maris. He heard booing, even at home. The 154th game was in Baltimore on September 20 (actually, with an earlier tie, it was number 155). Roger needed two and he got one, grounding out weakly on his last chance off Wilhelm. He had 59 in the allotted time, and a sigh of relief went out from Ruth and Mantle fans.

That wasn't the way it should have been. Frick's decision, whether fair or not, had robbed baseball of the thrill of the final eight games and the grand chase. There was no real sense of marketing in baseball at the time; it was still an industry of "open the gates and they will come."

What should have been a thrilling finish felt anticlimactic. Maris hit his 60th against Jack Fisher of the Orioles on September 26, with just 19,401 on hand at Yankee Stadium. His teammates appreciated it—they coaxed him out of the dugout to wave his cap in appreciation of the applause, an unprecedented curtain call.

On the season's final day, only 23,154 turned out, many of them packed into the lower right-field stands, hoping to catch number 61 and receive $5,000 from a West Coast restaurateur. And Maris, with the pressure of the season having even caused some hair loss, delivered. He belted his 61st homer off Boston's Tracy Stallard in the fourth inning, as the Yankees won 1–0 for their 109th win. Again he made a curtain call. In right field, a Brooklyn teen named Sal Durante, there with his girlfriend, caught the ball. He was taken to the Yankee clubhouse where he tried to give the ball to Maris.

"Get what you can for it, kid," said Roger.

Sal collected the reward, married his girlfriend, and became a school-bus driver and the answer to a trivia question. (Baseball trivia has become a bit of a passtime all its own, with avid fans enjoying the challenge of the game's most obscure details.

Frick's decision was not only a bad marketing call, but history would prove that the expanded schedule did not play havoc with the record book. It was, of course, not anything that Frick could anticipate. Whereas Ruth's record of 60 had lasted thirty-four years, Maris's 61 lasted thirty-seven more, until broken by Mark McGwire and Sammy Sosa in 1998 and then again by Barry Bonds in 2001. Roger's widow, Pat, and her children were in St. Louis when McGwire hit his 62nd, a very emotional moment for baseball fans, who had come to respect Maris's accomplishment at last. (He still held the American League record.)

Not until 1991 did Commissioner Fay Vincent finally declare that the record belonged to Maris, no asterisk required. (Bonds, of course, has a ball in the Hall of Fame literally branded with an asterisk—his 756th career homer. McGwire's and Sosa's feats have been linked to performance en-hancing drugs as well.)

With his ruling defusing the thrill that the final games might have pro-vided, Frick contributed to what had to be considered a very unimpressive year at the gate for the Yankees. They were still the only team in town. The home run showdown had been an enormous story all summer. There was a good pennant race and a fantastic team. Where were the fans? The Yan-kees drew only 1,747,725, up just 120,000 from the previous year, an aver-age of about 1,600 more per date. It was not an impressive showing.

In later years, Bob Fishel would blame himself for the problems Maris faced with the press, feeling that he could have made things easier by creat-ing an "interview room" in a more controlled setting so that Maris wouldn't be cornered at his locker after games with the endless string of "Think you can do it?" questions. But no one had done this yet. It would later become standard practice in the NFL and then in the MLB at big events, and eventually carried out on the team level. Bob was hard on himself for not creating the idea to help shield Roger.

(Forty years after this great home run race, Billy Crystal produced, with Ross Greenburg, an Emmy-winning HBO film, *61**, with Thomas Jane as Mantle and Barry Pepper as Maris.)

Maris hit another homer in the World Series against the Cincinnati Reds, although the injured Mantle was limited to just six at-bats. The Yanks won the Series in five games, with Bud Daley winning the decisive game with 6⅔ innings in relief of Terry (16–3 in the regular season). Ford ran his World Series consecutive-scoreless-innings streak to 32, breaking the mark set by Babe Ruth back when Ruth pitched for Boston. It was the Yankees' nineteenth world championship. Houk won Manager of the Year honors, coming through under the pressure to succeed Stengel.

Maris again edged Mantle in MVP voting, this time by just four points, getting seven first-place votes to Mantle's six despite a .269 batting average to Mantle's .317. Roger also led the league in RBI with 141.

But even in losing the home run and the MVP Award, Mantle emerged, at long last, as the rightful heir to DiMaggio and a fan favorite. From 1961 through the remainder of his career, the boos turned to cheers. He would be the most popular player in the game, whether at home or on the road.

AFTER THE SEASON, a script was hastily written for a low-budget movie called *Safe at Home*, in which Mantle and Maris played themselves. The film was shot in the beautiful new Fort Lauderdale Stadium, known locally as Little Yankee Stadium, prior to the Yanks setting up their first spring camp there.

After training in St. Petersburg almost continuously since 1925, the Yanks decided to move east to Florida's Atlantic coast. Topping said, "Howard, Lopez and [rookie catcher Jesse] Gonder mean as much to our ball club as any other ball players and we would very much like to have the whole team under one roof." Other black players were coming along, including pitcher Al Downing, who debuted in '61 as the first African-American pitcher on the team.

Fishel made it clear that they were talking about the Soreno Hotel, whose assistant manager said, "We have always enjoyed having the New York Yankees with us. We hope to have them with us for many years to come on the same basis."

The "same basis" was the key. It meant separate housing for the team's negro players. But the clock had run out on that. The times they were a-changin'.

At spring training in 1961, Fishel said, "We hope eventually to break down the segregation which now exists in spring training. But it has been apparent that we would not be able to accomplish that this year, although we feel the Yankees have made more of an effort than any other club."

Fort Lauderdale was an up-and-coming city celebrated in teenage beach movies. The city fathers were anxious to lure a major league team there.

The Yankees comfortably moved into an integrated hotel on the beach called, appropriately, the Yankee Clipper. The Yankee presence in Fort Lauderdale for thirty-four springs put that city on the tourism map for vacationing New Yorkers.

The Yankees were changing, too. The staid, conservative style was going to be compromised by the addition of four rookies to the 1962 team.

With Kubek off on army duty for the first few months of the season, Tom Tresh and Phil Linz were to compete for the starting shortstop job.

Linz, a free spirit who wound up perfectly content to be a "supersub" utility player, was a likable guy who fit in well with New York nightlife, later opening his own nightclub, Mr. Laff's. Tresh, the more traditional of the two, came from a baseball family. His father Mike had caught for eleven seasons, mostly with the White Sox, and Tom had been a batboy when his father managed in the minors. A switch-hitter, Tom had that Yankee "look" and pop in his bat. His time at shortstop would be temporary—Kubek returned to the team on August 7—but he then shifted comfortably to left field and played it as though he'd always been there. He would wind up being Rookie of the Year.

Father-and-son combinations in the major leagues became quite common in the coming decades, but in the sixties it was still fairly rare, and Tresh was one of the first sons of a big leaguer to exceed his father's career achievements.

Jim Bouton, twenty-three, known as "Bulldog" for his gritty determination, was also a rookie in '62, having won 27 games in 1960–61 in the lower minors. Houk and Sain liked what they saw in spring training and decided to keep him. Born in Newark, he went to high school in Chicago Heights and college at Western Michigan. Bouton was unlike most players in that he was a true fan as a kid. Most players cared little about going to games, reading about them, or learning stats and history. Bouton grew up with the fan experience. Most of his teammates thought he had a left-hander's mind trapped in a right-hander's body, southpaws generally considered more zany in baseball. (Pete Sheehy would flick his left hand to excuse odd behavior.) He was also off to the left politically from his teammates, and an attempt to be elected player representative a few years later went about as well as George McGovern's presidential bid in '72.

Bouton's big break came in his 14th appearance of the season. On June 24, a Sunday, the Yankees played the longest game in their history, a twenty-two-inning affair in Detroit, won after seven hours on the only home run of reserve outfielder Jack Reed's career. That day, Bouton entered the game in the fifteenth inning and hurled seven shutout innings to get the win. Both his spot on the team and his "Bulldog" nickname were assured on that memorable evening.

The fourth rookie was a Brooklyn kid named Joe Pepitone who could hit "four sewers" in stickball and who was shot in his belly at Manual Training High School by a friend who was "kidding around." With incredible good luck, no vital organs were pierced, and after twelve days in the hospital, Joe was back. He got a $20,000 bonus from the Yankees and would be the first Italian-American Yankee of significance since the 1946 debuts of Raschi and Berra. Joe had terrific talent both at bat and in the field, but his work ethic was sometimes questionable: His own autobiography, years later, was called *Joe, You Could Have Made Us Proud*. He also hung out with people the Yankee front office thought of as "shady." On several occasions Joe showed up just minutes before game time, with Houk and the office in full panic mode, having called their police department contacts to search the city. But he always showed up.

Joe also embodied "style" on the Yankees, getting his uniform to fit as tight as the flannel material would allow. The trend toward form-fitting uniforms had begun with Willie Mays and Tito Fuentes of the Giants, who had a personal tailor perform alterations. It quickly spread around the country, and the once-baggy uniforms now looked much more fashionable on players. Even traditionalists like Mantle and Maris joined in. The whole process would change the "look" of the game over the next few years, foreshadowing the incorporation of tight double-knit uniforms, first adopted in 1972, with the Yankees following a year later.

Four rookies in one season, at least three of them a little off-center, would certainly be enough to give McCarthy, Dickey, and DiMaggio pause.

Joe could pause in person, as he was a spring training instructor now. In

'62, he was even accompanied by Marilyn Monroe, which certainly turned heads. (She died five months later.)

(Yogi Berra remembers going to dinner with Joe and Marilyn. When I asked him to tell me every detail, he said, "You know how they usually give you just five shrimp in a shrimp cocktail? That night they gave us eight!" He didn't remember anything else about the evening.)

IN 1962, THE Mets were born. They drew an "amazin'" 922,530 that season to the Yankees' 1,493,574. The total was certainly skewed by the return visits of the Dodgers and Giants, who accounted for 51 percent of the Mets' total draw in just fifteen games: The remaining fifty home dates averaged only 9,009. They were 40–120, the worst record of the century, but they clicked with the fans. Casey talked about how the "youth of America should play for the Mets," about how their new ballpark in Queens would have "escalators, so no more heart attacks going to your seats," and how little children would say "Metsie Metsie Metsie" as their first words. The press loved it.

Dick Young in the *Daily News* began to write about the "new breed" of baseball fans in town, a more ragtag bunch of people who were heading out to the Polo Grounds with enthusiasm unseen in the Bronx. Met fans began to bring banners to the games extolling Marvelous Marv Throneberry and Choo Choo Coleman.

By 1963, competition between the two resulted in a true cultural clash. The Mayor's Trophy game, which the Yankees had long played against the Dodgers and Giants, was revived. The proceeds went to benefit sandlot baseball in New York.* The "historic" first clash would be at Yankee Stadium, but when Met fans arrived with their banners (Casey called them "placards"), Yankee security people attempted to confiscate them. Yankee policy was no banners in the stands, obstructing others' views.

The press made a huge deal of the Yankees' confiscations. Eventually, it had the inevitable effect of softening Yankee policy, so that by the end of the decade the Yankees were staging "banner days" just as the Mets did. But the Mets were determined to make an impact, and make it they did.

---

* More than fifty-three thousand fans welcomed the world champion L.A. Dodgers to Yankee Stadium in June 1960 for the game's resumption, the Dodgers' first return to New York.

The Mayor's Trophy games eventually got a little stale. They were played from 1963 to 1979, then there was a two-year hiatus, and then they resumed in 1982–83 before shutting down. The real problem was that baseball economy pretty much ended doubleheaders, creating fewer mutually available off-days on which to play the game. The teams continued to contribute to sandlot baseball without playing the game. The trophy itself would get passed back and forth to whichever team won. The Yankees won the final one in 1983, so somewhere among Yankee possessions rests the actual trophy.

THE YANKS' FOLLOW-UP to the great '61 season was less spectacular. Although they took over first place to stay on July 8, they never had a lead of more than six games, and they seemed ripe for the taking all year. But when they had to win, they won.

Mantle won his third MVP Award in five years, to go with two razor-thin second-place finishes. He claimed that Bobby Richardson (who finished second) was more deserving, hitting .302 and becoming the first Yankee since Rizzuto in 1950 to register 200 hits.

Mick had a .321/30/89 season and at one point hit seven homers in 12 at-bats, but it was clearly well off his '61 showing, as was Maris's .256/33/100, with the fans and press beating him up verbally and in print most of the season.

Arroyo, troubled by a sore arm, had one win and seven saves, and the bullpen had only nine saves all season. While Ford went 17–8, it was Terry, 23–12, who would lead the league in wins.

The World Series was the first between the Yankees and a former New York team, as the San Francisco Giants beat the Dodgers in a three-game playoff series, just as in 1951, to win the National League pennant.

In game one, Ford allowed a run in the second inning, bringing his scoreless-inning record to a close at $33\frac{2}{3}$ innings, but he won the game 6–2. The Series was low-scoring, and the hoped-for Mantle-Mays matchup was a disappointment, Mantle hitting .120 and Mays .250, with neither of them homering. Bad weather forced three days of postponements, but it finally came down to a game seven in San Francisco, a game decided with no RBI.

The Yankees scored a run in the fifth when Kubek hit into a double play, scoring Skowron in what would be Moose's final game as a Yankee.

In the ninth, with Terry having pitched a two-hit shutout to this point,

Matty Alou beat out a bunt. Terry then fanned both Felipe Alou and Chuck Hiller.

That brought up Mays, who doubled to right, where Maris made a fine play and got the ball in to hold Matty at third.

Now the tying run was on third and the winning run on second. Up came Willie McCovey. Terry had been in this spot before: He had yielded Mazeroski's walk-off just two years earlier.

This time Terry would be carried off the field, as McCovey hit a hard liner to Richardson's left. Bobby snared the drive and saved the Series. Another foot and it might have been a two-run single and a Giants championship. Instead, San Francisco would not win a World Series for forty-eight years.

It was the Yankees' twentieth world championship—and while they couldn't have imagined it, their last for fifteen years.

Chapter Twenty-Seven

THE TRADE OF SKOWRON TO THE Dodgers after the 1962 season not only broke his heart, but it delivered a mixed message to Yankee fans. On the one hand, this was good baseball management: out with the old, in with the new, to perpetuate the success of the team. Joe Pepitone, a homegrown product with a quick bat and terrific fielding skills, was ready to take over—and was ten years younger! Heartless though it must have felt to the sensitive Moose, this was how successful teams flourished.

On the other hand, only a few people noticed that the rookie class of '62—Pepitone, Linz, Bouton, and Tresh—seemed to be the end of the supply chain. Al Downing and Mel Stottlemyre followed in the next few years, but where was the endless pool of players waiting to take over? The guys who kept the regulars on their toes, looking over their shoulders? Keen observers knew the Yankee system was faltering.

Quietly, Topping and Webb had begun talking to Lehman Brothers about underwriting a dramatic public sale of the team, in the fashion of the Green Bay Packers, who were "community owned." The talks were ongoing, but it seemed clear that there was an exit strategy brewing.

In exchange for Skowron, the Yankees got starting pitcher Stan Williams, a 14-game winner for the Dodgers in '62. But expectations weren't reached in 1963, Williams would go only 9–8 for the Yanks, and it was bringing up Downing (13–5) in early June that really saved the pitching. Arroyo, with a bad arm, had lost his effectiveness, and Hal Reniff, a hard-throwing righty, emerged as the bullpen savior.

But then there was Ford, who would go 24–7 for his second and last

20-win season, and Bouton, 21–7 with six shutouts, who kept knocking the cap off his head with each pitch.

Howard would win the league's MVP Award with a .287/28/85 season, leading the team in homers and winning a Gold Glove behind the plate, as Berra, now a first-base coach/pinch hitter, wound up his playing days with a .293 showing in 64 games. Howard was the first black player in the American League to win the MVP—the National League had already had eleven, indicative of the better jump it had on signing African-American stars.

Despite these success stories, who would have thought the Yanks could win when Mantle and Maris appeared in the lineup together only thirty times? Maris, bothered by a bad back, played only 90 games. On May 22, Mantle, now a $100,000 player, took hold of a Bill Fischer pitch and for the second time reached the upper right-field facade, calling it "the hardest ball I ever hit." But two weeks later, he fractured his left foot on the chain-link outfield fence in Baltimore, which would limit him to just 52 games in the outfield for the season.

On September 1, the Yanks were back in Baltimore, and Mantle, while activated, was on the training table for most of the game, having had a tough evening with Ford the night before. He was not expecting to play. But in the eighth, with the Yanks trailing 4–1, Houk sent him up to hit against Mike McCormick. Mantle delivered a line-drive homer into the left-field bleachers that helped send the Yanks to a 5–4 win. The "hangover homer" would become part of Mantle legend. "Those people have no idea how hard that really was," he told his laughing teammates on the bench as the Oriole fans applauded this dramatic return to their ballpark.

Mantle's elevation to the $100,000 level put him in a class with Greenberg, DiMaggio, Williams, Musial, and, as of that same year, Mays. It would be his annual salary for the rest of his career.

The Yanks would somehow win 104 games in 1963 and their third straight pennant under Houk, and would head to the World Series against the Dodgers, who still retained a few Brooklyn players, including their pitching ace, Sandy Koufax. And there would be the strange sight of Skowron playing first.

Houk's three pennants in his first three seasons were unprecedented in major league history. But his attempt at a third straight world championship came up short. The Dodger pitching was just too much.

In one of the most heralded matchups in World Series play, game one at Yankee Stadium would feature Koufax (25–5 in the regular season) against

Ford. But the day belonged to Koufax, who struck out a Series record 15, including the first five Yankees he faced. Richardson, who struck out only 22 times in 668 plate appearances during the regular season, fanned three times. Skowron drove in two, and the Dodgers were off and running.

Old nemesis Podres won game two, Don Drysdale pitched a three-hit shutout in game three, and Koufax came back to win game four, 2-1, again besting Ford, the Yanks' only run coming on a Mantle homer. In the last of the seventh, Pepitone missed Boyer's throw from third, claiming he lost it in the background of white shirts, and the error led to the winning run. It was an embarrassing sweep for the Yanks.

Unbeknownst to all but a few trusted insiders, '63 would be Houk's final year as manager. Roy Hamey was planning to retire after the season, and Topping wanted Houk to move up to the front office and succeed him. Ralph wasn't happy—he was a field guy—but he was a loyal employee, and if that was what they wanted, they'd get it.

Sixteen days after the World Series, the Yankees crossed the street to the Savoy Hilton and announced Hamey's retirement and Houk's ascension to the front office. Hamey would retire with three pennants in three years as GM.

The next day came Yogi Berra's elevation to the managing job. Another trek to the Savoy Hilton for a press conference. He too had been in on the plan since spring training. He was to receive a pay cut from his player salary, $45,000 to $35,000, and he took the occasion to announce his retirement as well. (His peak salary as a player had been $55,000.)

The announcement was greeted with some skepticism. A beloved figure and an immortal Yankee, he was not necessarily considered the "manager type," whatever that meant. Despite all the clever things he allegedly said, his communication skills were suspect. A typical conversation meant a lot of grunts and nods. Then there was the question of whether his former teammates could view him as the boss. All of that would have to be determined. What was unquestioned was his knowledge of baseball. He didn't miss a thing.

Topping and Houk may have seen the hiring of Yogi as a counterpunch to the Mets' popular success with Stengel. But Yogi was not the man widely quoted by the press who would sometimes stretch the truth to come up with a new Yogi-ism. He was not going to steal the cameras away from Casey.

Yogi got a one-year contract, which he claimed to be happy with. He wanted to prove to himself he could manage—and then get a big raise if he was successful.

He named Ford as his pitching coach in addition to continuing his regular turn on the mound. And while retaining Crosetti and Jim Hegan, he added Athletics scout Jimmy Gleeson as first-base coach. Gleeson had been his manager at the New London submarine base when Yogi was stationed there in the forties. Yogi called him two hours after his press conference ended. It was Berra displaying loyalty and friendship, two of his best traits.

And so Yogi's eighteen-year Yankee playing career drew to a close. Three MVP awards, more World Series games and hits than anyone, the home run record for catchers with 358, and a certain Hall of Fame plaque. Was he better than his mentor, Dickey? Dickey outhit Berra .313 to .285, but in many ways they were fairly equal. When it came time to retire Yogi's number 8, it was decided that Dickey, having worn it earlier, should get equal recognition. So the two 8s retired by the Yankees is unique in baseball. (In May 1965 Yogi would "unretire" and play four games for the Mets, a decision he later regretted.)

THE YANKEES OPENED the '64 season without Harry M. Stevens as the stadium concessionaire, a relationship that went back to 1903. Stevens was replaced by National Concessions Service, a division of Automatic Canteen Company, the company Art Friedland had brought Topping and Webb into some years before. It had grown into a full-service ballpark concessionaire, and the stadium menu was augmented by new items like shrimp rolls, pizza, fish sandwiches, and milkshakes. Automatic Canteen evolved into Centerplate, which handled Yankee Stadium until it closed in 2008, at which time the Yankees entered into a new company with the Dallas Cowboys called Legends Hospitality. A joint video with Cowboys owner Jerry Jones and George Steinbrenner, released October 20, 2008, would be the last business announcement Steinbrenner would be personally involved with. (In 1994, Aramark acquired the Harry M. Stevens name.)

THINGS DID NOT go smoothly for Yogi at first. Third in the standings in mid-August, the Yankees got a lifeline in Stottlemyre, called up from Richmond, a move reminiscent of Ford's debut fourteen years earlier.

Mel, a tall, poker-faced right-hander from Washington State whose best pitch was a sinker, started against Chicago on Wednesday afternoon, August 12, and won 7–3. He was aided by one of the longest home runs of Mantle's career. It was, in fact, the longest measured homer in Yankee Stadium, 502 feet, soaring over the twenty-two-foot screen in the batter's eye in dead center, a screen that would occasionally be removed to seat people in that bleacher section in the days before batter safety was taken more seriously.

Mel went 9–3 in 12 starts for the Yanks with a 2.06 ERA. Downing won just 13 but also struck out 217, the most on the team since Chesbro in 1904. Ford, doubling as pitching coach, was 17–6 with eight shutouts, and Bouton led the staff with 18 wins. The bullpen, though, needed shoring up. Pete Mikkelsen joined Reniff and Steve Hamilton, but the trio was no sure thing.

To many, a turning point in the season came in Chicago after a 5–0 loss to the White Sox, the team's fourth straight. Now they were in third place, four and a half out, and sinking.

On the bus to the airport, where the code of baseball called for contemplative silence following a loss, Phil Linz pulled out a new Hohner harmonica he'd been learning and began to play "Mary Had a Little Lamb." It was a silly moment, but it infuriated the old guard at the front of the bus—including Berra, whose nerves were frayed anyway.

"Shut that thing up," he yelled.

"What did he say?" asked Linz.

Mantle, not capturing the seriousness of the moment, responded to Linz: "He said play it louder." And Linz did.

That felt like defiance to the manager. Perhaps goaded by Crosetti, who called it "the worst thing I've seen in 33 years with the team," Yogi walked to the back of the bus and knocked it out of Linz's hands.

"I said put it away! You'd think we just *won* four games."

The writers, who traveled with the team in those days, witnessed the activity from their front seats. "Why are you getting on me?" said Linz. "I give 100 percent on the field. I try to win. I should be able to do what I want off the field."

Grumbling under his breath, Yogi returned to his seat and the team headed for Boston. Linz was fined $200, but would wind up on the back cover of the Yankee yearbook in '65, posing for an ad by Hohner. Did the show of managerial power snap this veteran team to attention? Did it turn things around?

That became the conventional wisdom. In fact, the Yankees lost their next two in Boston to run the losing streak to six. But then they began to play better. They won seven of their next nine. They won eleven straight in September. From the harmonica "incident" to the end of the season, they were 30–13.

On September 5 (too late to be eligible for World Series play), the Yankees traded Terry and Daley to the Indians for the veteran Pedro Ramos.

Ramos, master of the "Cuban palmball" (a spitter?), was a flamboyant character who wore a cowboy hat and boots, smoked Cuban cigars, and was forever challenging Mantle to a race, which the Yankees strictly forbade. A starting pitcher for most of his ten-year career, Ramos responded to his bullpen assignment with a win and eight saves in 13 appearances. He was an overnight hit with the fans and his teammates.

(He was also the last Cuban on the Yankees until Luis Tiant in 1979. Steinbrenner would try to take his team to Cuba in 1977 to open relations there and perhaps find a way to sign Cuban players, but Commissioner Bowie Kuhn stopped him, saying only an All-Star team could go. Steinbrenner made a later trip with Ford and took in a game with Fidel Castro, but couldn't open up the process in the Yankees' favor.)

THE YANKS WON their twenty-ninth pennant by just one game. It was their fifth in a row (under three managers), and a triumph for the rookie manager and the rookie general manager. But it was a close call.

Mantle had rebounded from his injury-riddled '63 with a .303/35/111 season, his last big year and his fourth 100-RBI campaign. Pepitone hit 28 homers and drove in 100. But the winds were shifting. Brooks Robinson of the Orioles won the MVP Award. The Yanks were starting to play "old."

The Cardinals, managed by Johnny Keane, won on the last day in the National League, when the Phillies collapsed. The Cardinals were a terrific team, though, and Berra was going to get to manage in his hometown against the team he grew up rooting for.

The Yanks didn't have Ramos, who sat in the stands in his cowboy gear. Ford, ailing, lost game one 9–5. Kubek, out with a sprained wrist, was replaced by Linz at short. Stottlemyre beat Bob Gibson in game two with Linz homering. The Series moved to New York.

In game three, the score was tied 1–1 going to the last of the ninth. Knuckleballer Barney Schultz came in to pitch, with Mantle leading off.

"I'm gonna hit one outta here," Mickey said to no one in particular. He was mostly talking to himself, although Bouton, who had tossed a six-hitter, heard it clearly.

And he did. He sent the first pitch into the upper right-field seats for a walk-off Yankee victory. He had 13 walk-off homers in his career, including this one: They were rare because he tended to get walked a lot in such situations. The drama of this, winning a World Series game, would become his "greatest moment" whenever asked (although Mick sometimes playfully recounted a few ribald non-baseball stories as his "greatest moment.")

The homer was his 16th in World Series play, breaking Ruth's record. Mantle would hit two more in that Series to finish with 18, a record unlikely to be broken. (It became common to lump "postseason home runs" together on television graphics once playoff baseball began in 1969.)

Another win by Bouton in game six tied it up and set up a game seven at Busch Stadium, the rookie Stottlemyre against the great Gibson. Linz got another homer off Gibby, as did Clete Boyer, but Gibson was able to tough it out and hold on to a 7–5 win and a Cardinals championship. For the second year in a row, the Yanks had lost the World Series, although this one was no blowout. The last time they had lost back-to-back World Series was 1921–22, their final years in the Polo Grounds.

IN THE SUMMER of '64, Lehman Brothers told Topping and Webb that this was not a good time to consider a public sale. "Baseball is in a down period," they were told, according to Dan Topping Jr., who was working as Houk's assistant. "If you can find a private buyer, you should do that."

Topping, being a man about town, knew William S. Paley, the chairman of the Columbia Broadcasting System, and began discussing a sale of the team with him. CBS was expanding beyond television and radio. They had purchased a toy company. They owned Columbia Records. They owned guitar-maker Fender. They invested in the Broadway show *My Fair Lady*.

In truth, CBS actually tried to buy the Yankees' tenants, the football Giants. They already had broadcast rights to the NFL. The Giants had been playing at Yankee Stadium since 1956, and with CBS televising their games, they had a close relationship. But the NFL did not permit corporate ownership, and Paley turned to the Yankees.

News broke on August 13 that Topping and Webb were selling 80 percent of the team to CBS for $11.2 million. The deal would become effective on November 2. CBS had an option to buy the remaining 20 percent for $2.8 million, making the total value of the team $14 million. Topping would remain president until such time as he sold off his shares. Webb would sell off his 10 percent by February of '65.

No one knew for certain what this corporate ownership would mean for the Yankees. The first thought was that games would be shown on WCBS-TV, not the long-standing WPIX. But they weren't going to preempt their prime-time lineup for baseball.

There were objections from other owners about the sale, some thinking that this would infuse so much money into the operation of the Yankees that the divide between them and the rest of the teams would become insurmountable. As an owner, CBS would have the ability to know how network negotiations were progressing with the Commissioner's Office, learning too much about rivals NBC and ABC in the process. There was general unease throughout the game.

Judge Roy Hofheinz, owner of the Houston Colt .45s (later the Astros), called it the "blackest day for baseball since the Black Sox scandal."

Topping and Webb agreed to a league meeting in Boston on September 9 to hear the arguments against the sale. But the five-hour meeting resulted in an 8–2 approval vote, and the deal was on.

ON OCTOBER 15, as soon as game seven was wrapping up in St. Louis, Bob Fishel placed a long-distance call to the Savoy Hilton. "Warm up the coffee, we have a press conference tomorrow."

Just twenty-four hours after losing a seven-game World Series, the Yankees were going to fire Berra as manager. He thought he was being called into the office to be given a raise, but Houk told him he was out.

At the same time, in St. Louis, the winning manager, Johnny Keane, was sticking it to his bosses and quitting his job. He'd been second-guessed all season, and when it appeared the Phillies were going to win the pennant, he figured he would be fired. Now he was being proactive.

Yogi didn't attend his press conference, even though he was being "moved" to a position as "special field consultant" at $25,000 a year for two years. Houk and Topping were present, and Houk said, "Losing the World Series had nothing to do with [this]. The decision was made before the World Series." He also said the decision was his and Topping's, and that CBS was consulted but played no part in it.

Berra, playing golf with friends in New Jersey, was stunned. In addition, it had to sting that the man who had been his third-string catcher a decade before, when Yogi was racking up MVPs and world championships, was firing him.

Yogi didn't express any of that to reporters. "I feel pretty good. I suppose I'll be doing some scouting. If another offer turns up, I'm free to take it. And hey, we won the pennant and it took seven games to beat us in the Series."

Years later, he told sportswriter Bill Madden, "The way I looked at it, the Yankees had given me a job they wouldn't even trust Babe Ruth with." He said he smoothed things over with Houk "through the years."

Houk told Madden, "Worst thing I ever had to do . . . Every time I'd see him at some public function, I felt awful."

Fans were in shock, and adding to it was the hiring of Keane the very next day. Everyone sensed this had all been in the works for weeks, with Yogi the only one not in on the plan. Keane was coming aboard at a moment of triumph, but to the fans he was an unknown, whereas Yogi had always been an enormously popular figure. And sure enough, within a month, the Mets offered Berra a coaching job and he took it. He'd be back in uniform, and back with Stengel for 1965, paying two tolls to drive to Shea Stadium instead of just one to Yankee Stadium.

IF THE FIRING of Stengel in 1960 had been a little sloppy, and the firing of Berra in 1964 a little cold, the firing of Mel Allen was just . . . empty.

On September 21, Mel was called up to Topping's twenty-ninth-floor office in the Squibb Building and told he wouldn't be offered a new contract for 1965. The news was devastating to Mel, a lifelong bachelor whose whole adulthood had been the Yankees. Still just fifty-one years old, he was the Voice of the Yankees, and those who understood marketing knew that the right announcer could be bigger than the players, bigger than the owners, perhaps the most talked-about man in town.

Maybe that was the problem.

Mel was never given a reason. Suddenly his friendships and allies on the team weren't there.

He wasn't the same announcer he had been in his heyday. He had begun to ramble on air; his stories became too long, too predictible. He was more short-tempered.

He was brutal to his young stat guy, Bill Kane, unforgiving of errors large and small.

A lot of people who used to enjoy his company would cross the street if they saw him coming.

There was even a problem with Ballantine, the team's principal sponsor. Business was bad. As the fees to advertise increased, sales were decreasing with the coming of national brands like Budweiser and Miller and their big ad budgets.

"They were being marketed as 'premium' beers," explained Tom Villante, the former batboy who became head of the Schaefer account at the BBDO ad agency. "They weren't really—the consumer was being asked to pay more for them to cover the cost of trucking them around the country. The consumer thought a higher price meant a premium flavor, and those brewers were happy to go along. Local beers like Ballantine, Rheingold, and Schaefer were feeling the pinch."

Ballantine, which had been sold since 1840, would hang in there with the Yankees until 1966, but then the brand faded from the marketplace. If Mel had still been there, it would have been very hard to attract a new beer sponsor, with Mel's voice so identified with Ballantine.

There were other bad marks on Mel's ledger. In 1961 he'd referred Mickey Mantle to his doctor for a "cure-all" injection, ultimately resulting in the infection that caused him to miss games in that fateful September home run chase.

In '63, he had lost his voice during the World Series telecast, and some thought that psychologically he was losing it—he couldn't bear to see the Yankees get swept, and had lost his instrument. There were also whispers of excess drinking and homosexuality, but they were nothing more than rumors.

There really was no single reason ever given to Mel or to the fans, and none ever materialized over the years. Mel had apparently just gotten annoying, and maybe too expensive, to the people who employed him.

The Yankees told NBC that Rizzuto should broadcast the '64 World Series, which broke Mel's heart, even though he knew by then he was done. That was a big deal, and began a series of news stories suggesting he might be gone. But the Yankees didn't formally announce his firing until December 17.

"There is no point in going into any details as to why we made the change," said Houk. "We just thought that a change would be beneficial."

Mel's replacement was Joe Garagiola, Yogi's childhood pal who worked the '64 Series with Rizzuto, who was a familiar face on the *Today* show and the author of the hit book *Baseball Is a Funny Game*. It was a wise choice because Garagiola was well liked and didn't suffer from comparisons to Mel. When Joe left after three seasons, Frank Messer came up from Baltimore and brought a fine, no-frills professional style with him, suffering not at all from Mel Allen comparisons thanks to the Garagiola span between them.

But for more than a decade, the most asked question among fans was always, "Why was Mel Allen fired?" And no one ever stood up with an answer.

Mel remained a somewhat saddened figure for the rest of his life. The Yankees meant the world to him. "I carry my heart on my sleeve," he'd tell people. He had a second act as the voice of *This Week in Baseball*. The Yankees even brought him back as a cable broadcaster in 1978, and he called Dave Righetti's no-hitter in 1983. When I was the WPIX producer, I had him do a few innings in 1990 so that he could be a "seven-decade announcer," and I had him record our opening so that each telecast began with his signature, "Hello there, everybody, this is Mel Allen . . ." But he died an unhappy figure in 1996 despite a plaque in monument park and lifetime ownership of the title "Voice of the Yankees," and as the first broadcaster (with Red Barber) to win the Ford Frick Award, presented in Cooperstown on induction day. But he had lost his great love at age fifty-one and it was never the same.

So in one eventful year, the Yankees changed ownership, fired Berra, and fired Allen. Ballantine was on the way out. Anyone who believed in curses had plenty to work with.

Chapter Twenty-Eight

IN JUNE 1965, A YOUNG FAN WROTE a letter to the editor of the *Sporting News*, saying, "Why is everyone giving up on the Yankees? They always come through in the end. They will be fine."

I know because I was that fan.

The letter writer was wrong. Johnny Keane had arrived at what would be a turning point in Yankee history. When he was handed the key to the manager's office, he couldn't have known that the dynasty was over. The team had collapsed, and would spend the next decade trying to rebuild itself for the first time since Babe Ruth arrived.

Even baseball experts didn't see it coming. It came to be said that Topping and Webb, knowing they were going to sell, had let the farm system run dry. But that was an oversimplification. Did they cut back on scouts? No. Did they reduce the number of farm clubs? No. Did they cut back on bonuses? No. In fact, they gave $100,000 to Ole Miss quarterback Jake Gibbs, signing him as an infielder and converting him to a catcher. And they offered a pitcher named Bob Garibaldi $125,000, only to see him sign with the Giants. The effort was still there.

But maybe they were a little gun-shy.

In 1948 they signed their first bonus player, pitcher Paul Hinrichs, for $40,000. He never pitched an inning for them. Two years later, $80,000 to pitcher Ed Cereghino. Never made it. In the fifties they signed Frank Leja and Tommy Carroll, men who would take up space on the roster, contribute little, and ultimately prove to be less than quality players. In 1960, $65,000 to Howie Kitt, who had been 18–0 at Columbia. Nothing. They had a pitcher named Bob Riesener who went 20–0 for Alexandria in 1957 but never made the majors. So they had been burned a little, and maybe they didn't reach out often enough for bonus players. Maybe they could have signed Frank Howard, Ron Fairly, Rick Reichardt, or Bob Bailey, who went to other organizations prior to the introduction of the amateur draft.

The collapse was due to a combination of factors. No one could point to an elite player the Yankees skipped because he wanted too much money. The hard fact was that Lehman Brothers was right: Baseball had hit a rough patch. It was no longer the sport of choice for elite high school players. Football was really taking hold of the nation, and basketball was building.

One could almost say that in the mid- to late sixties, baseball found only three "superstar" players: Reggie Jackson, Tom Seaver, and Johnny Bench. The greatest athletes were going elsewhere.

The Yankees' scouting director, Johnny Johnson, who would later be the president of the minor leagues, acknowledged this. "We don't have the quality of player we used to have," he said. "But neither does anyone else, because it just isn't there anymore."

Further hurting the Yankees was the installation of the game's first amateur draft in 1965. The draft, which excluded Latin America, was a system by which the last-place team would pick first from all eligible high school and college players. Thus, in the first such draft, the Athletics chose Rick Monday, who would have a fine career, and the Yankees, who chose nineteenth, selected pitcher Bill Burbach, who would have an undistinguished one.

So good players were getting away from the Yankees. But by dropping into the second division for five straight years—1965–69—the Yankees had better selections. They just didn't always work out. (An exception was Thurman Munson in 1968.)

By the sixties, superior scouting was no longer the answer; everyone knew who the best players were. Having top scouts was marginalized. There were no more Mickey Mantles to find when no one else was looking.

The draft was a very inexact science. No team was "brilliant" in this area on a consistent basis. Each team had high-round draft choices that never made it and low-round choices that fooled everyone. The finest baseball minds, relying on good scouting reports, were still gambling that an eighteen-year-old might evolve into a star. All too often, they didn't. The draft put the Yankees on equal footing with everyone else in this regard; they had no edge in signing players, even with the glamour of their name.

Another problem was the race issue, which finally caught up with the

Yankees. Once their white stars grew old, they were on equal footing with the other American League teams, who were equally slow to sign blacks.

While National League teams had been signing African-American players the caliber of Mays, Aaron, Banks, McCovey, Gibson, Frank Robinson, Billy Williams, Lou Brock, Ferguson Jenkins, and Willie Stargell and dark-skinned Latino stars like Clemente, Orlando Cepeda, Juan Marichal, Tony Perez, and more, the American League wasn't even close. The Yankees had let all those players get away.

Players of color on the American League's 1965 All-Star team included Howard, Mudcat Grant, Tony Oliva, Willie Horton, Felix Mantilla, Zoilo Versalles, and Earl Battey. Not a Hall of Famer in the lot. The NL squad had nine.

It also hurt the Yankees' image that the Mets, playing in their new Shea Stadium, were outdrawing them. New stadiums tended to produce strong attendance, Stengel had given the Mets a "fun" reputation, and they were building a strong fan base among affluent Long Island residents. Their open, well-lit parking felt more fan friendly than the dark streets of the Bronx did.

There could be no denying that the Yankee Stadium neighborhood was changing. The welcome-home dinners were moved to Manhattan in 1958. The Concourse Plaza had fallen into disrepair and was accommodating the homeless. By '68 it would be strictly a welfare hotel, (although Horace Clarke preferred to live there and walk to work). Joyce Kilmer Park, across the street, was becoming a drug haven. A lot of people were fleeing the neighborhood and moving to Co-Op City, a housing development on the grounds of a failed amusement park, Freedomland. As minorities moved into the apartments, the New York Times was running stories with subheads like TRANSITION FELT TO BE POSING THREAT TO STABILITY OF AREA, which would only make more people move out.

The media took a liking to the Mets, and suddenly, Yankee stories tended to use words like "collapsed," "crumbled," and "failure." The younger writers, dubbed "Chipmunks" and led by Stan Isaacs, Larry Merchant, and Leonard Shecter, weren't shy about delving into the team's woes. The old guard was much more protective of the Yankee brand. (Other Chipmunks included Phil Pepe, Vic Ziegel, George Vecsey, and Steve Jacobson.)

While the collapse was a blow to Yankee fans, for whom first place was almost a birthright, the end of the Yankee dynasty was joyous news to fans in the league's nine other cities. Suddenly, opportunity knocked.

In '65, the season of disbelief, injuries hit the team hard. Elston Howard hurt his elbow in spring training and was out until June. When he came back, he had a .233/9/45 season. Maris missed four weeks early and then 49 games during the summer. He was .239/8/27. Mantle played 122 games and suffered his worst season, .255/19/46. For Mick, it would prove to be the beginning of the end. The 1964 season, at age thirty-two, was his last as "Mickey Mantle." The remaining four years of his career were very ordinary.

Stottlemyre won 20 games, Ford went 16–13, and Ramos proved a capable and colorful reliever over the full season, but otherwise the pitching wasn't there, and the Yankees endured their first second-division finish since Babe Ruth's bellyache of 1925.

Bouton was just 4–15.

"In those days," he reflected, "before pitch counts and four days of rest, maybe I had just been overworked the previous two seasons. I wasn't a big guy, but I'd pitched 520 innings and 23 complete games in those years. After '65 I went to my own doctor and sure enough, I had a low-grade chronic strain of the brachialis, which connects the bicep to the bone."

"I felt badly for Johnny Keane," he added. "He was a religious man and we were a party team. That was okay with Houk and Yogi, but he wasn't a good fit for a team like us that could party and win. Except we were no longer winning."

Seen as an outsider who didn't understand the culture and chemistry of the team, Keane's relationship with the players was tense and distant. The players tended not to take him seriously. He issued fines they thought of as silly, like $250 to Mantle for drinking too much at an airport bar during a long flight delay. Keane was probably right in feeling that the "parties" needed wins, or else. But he lacked the respect that would have been needed to back it up. "Mickey was a superstar, but Keane didn't give him that much respect," said Ramos. "Instead of asking, 'You think you can play today?' Mickey had to find out if he was in the lineup." It was just a bad marriage.

Down 92,000 on the year, the front office sprang into action. It could have been more had not 71,245 turned out for the team's first Bat Day on June 20, with a second on August 14. When the fans responded to Bob Sheppard's request to hold the bats high for photographers, the sea of wood was a remarkable sight both for its visual content and its acquiescence into the land of promotion, so long avoided by the Yankees.

There was a quickly arranged Mickey Mantle Day, notable for the sight of

DiMaggio turning his back on Senator Robert F. Kennedy, said to be over matters involving Marilyn Monroe.

When Mantle came to bat that day in the first, Detroit pitcher Joe Sparma walked in from the mound to shake his hand. This was the esteem in which Mantle was now held throughout baseball. Everyone appreciated how he played in pain and played the game right. He never showed anyone up. He was, in fact, a great teammate and a great opponent.

In his eighteen-year career, Mick was hit by a pitch just 13 times. This is not to say that being hit shows a lack of respect or a vindictiveness, but such a startling statistic must have a little of "Mantle respect" built in as well.

At the end of the year, Tony Kubek, just twenty-nine, retired, and the Yankees pleaded with Richardson not to do the same lest they lose their middle infield in one swoop. They even offered Richardson a rare two-year contract to stay on, but he agreed to only one more year and then retired at thirty. Kubek retired because of injuries and Richardson because he hated the separation from his family. The Yanks got nothing in return for these two All-Star players.

Kubek had an unlikely post-playing career. A shy, even difficult interview as a player, he was hired by NBC for Game of the Week and World Series duty, pulled no punches, and became a respected broadcaster who would one day win the Frick Award. From 1990 to 1994 he even broadcast Yankee games, and wasn't shy about criticizing management.

Richardson continued his work with the Fellowship of Christian Athletes and the Baseball Chapel, spoke at Billy Graham crusades, scouted for the Yankees, coached college ball at South Carolina and two smaller schools, and ran an unsuccessful campaign for Congress.

The season began a procession of second-line players who barely resembled Yankees, and rookies with dim prospects. The team even had its first true knuckleballer in Bob Tiefenauer, which forced the team to buy an oversized catching mitt for Howard.

Two rookies did debut who would have a positive impact down the road, but in 1965 it was too early to see the promise in Roy White and Bobby Murcer. Another debut was by Horace Clarke, seen as the successor to Richardson at second.

AND JUST WHEN you thought is couldn't get worse . . .

The Yanks finished dead last in 1966 for the first time since 1912.

A team with Mantle, Maris, Ford, Pepitone, Richardson, Howard, Stottlemyre, and Boyer—last. In two years they had gone from first to tenth.

Bob Fishel pointed out that no last-place team had ever won 70 games before, but that thought barely resonated.

When they started out at 4–16, Keane was fired. He was sacked on a Friday night after a loss in Anaheim, and the timing helped bury the story in New York, where most people didn't catch up with it until Sunday's papers had a sad photo of Keane heading one way—for a taxi—while the players headed the other way, for the team bus. (Keane would die just eight months later; many wrote "of a broken heart," although it was a heart attack.) It was the first time the Yankees had fired a manager in midseason since Chase replaced Stallings in 1910.

Houk named himself as successor, with Dan Topping Jr. elevated to GM. Houk's move was well received when the Yanks won 13 of his first 17 games. But it was an artificial boost. This was a bad club, with Stottlemyre's 12–20 record tying rookie Fritz Peterson's 12–11 for most wins on the team. Ford, bothered by circulation problems, won just two. Jim Turner's return to the team as pitching coach after five years in Cincinnati was no tonic.

Mantle and Maris hit just 36 homers between them.

Clarke spent most of the year at shortstop and then took over at second in September as Richardson prepared for his retirement. His first two homers (he hit only 27 in his career) were both grand slams.

Clarke, a mild-mannered twenty-six-year-old, was just the fourth major leaguer from the Virgin Islands. Over the next decade, the press would view him as the symbol of all that had gone wrong. Criticized for bailing out on double plays, he nevertheless led the league in assists six times, putouts four times, fielding percentage once, and never in errors. A decent offensive player, he led in singles twice. In 1970 he broke up three no-hitters with ninth-inning singles in a course of four weeks. His 151 stolen bases in ten Yankee seasons spoke to some speed. The problem, of course, was that he was just a very ordinary player, and even his fielding honors could be attributed to limited range. It wasn't his fault that nobody better came along.

The fact that Houk stuck with him year after year came to be dispiriting to fans. Not once did he take a chance on a rookie just to "shake things up" out of spring training. Clarke was his guy, and the fans would groan.

Gloomy as the 1966 season was, the low point came on September 22 when only 413 fans were in the park for a weekday makeup game against the

White Sox. It was only three days after Michael Burke became the new team president.

Such a game would usually not have been on the broadcast schedule, but the season had run out of dates on which to make up the rainout, and so the WPIX cameras were there for the lackluster 4–1 loss in a continuous drizzle.

In the Channel 11 booth, Red Barber was thinking like an unbiased journalist and knew that the attendance was the story. It was hard to hide it. He spoke to director Jack Murphy between innings about paying more attention to the crowd. Murphy was hesitant. Barber became insistent. He talked about the small total on the air. He wanted Duilio Costabile, the cameraman at his side, to pan the stands.

Fishel asked Topping Jr. about inviting the 413 fans back for another game.

"We don't do things like that," he answered.

ON BURKE'S SEVENTH day with the team, he invited Barber to breakfast in the Edwardian Room of the Plaza Hotel. The team had played its final home game the day before, and Red was scheduled to do broadcasts in Washington before driving home to Florida.

Some small talk ensued. At last, Burke took a deep breath and said, "There's no use in our talking this way. I have to tell you we're not renewing your contract."

Red said he was stunned, although he'd seen Mel Allen shown the door two years earlier. But he had figured that CBS knew professionalism and would retain him. His partners, Rizzuto, Coleman, and Garagiola, were amateurs in his mind, ex-players. He never made it comfortable for them in the booth. And his patrician style also felt a bit condescending to younger fans, whom the Yankees were now desperate to reach.

Barber had not been beloved like Allen, but he was erudite and respected. This was a rough way for Burke to break in, although he told people the decision had been made before he got there. It came to be believed that Red's insistence on showing the 413 fans was the final straw.

"I inherited [the decision]," said Burke. "But I agreed with it. I believe that for every man there is a time to come and a time to go. In my opinion it was Red's time to go."

Barber did the games in Washington and bristled at Burke's concern that there was a danger in letting him go on the air. His professionalism was being needlessly questioned.

BURKE BECAME PRESIDENT on September 19. Topping sold his 10 percent interest to CBS and departed. Suffering from emphysema, he would die in May 1974. Del Webb died less than two months later.

Topping Jr. was replaced by Lee MacPhail, a move widely hailed. It would now be Burke-MacPhail-Houk charged with fixing everything.

The press immediately took to Burke's charm, style, good looks, progressive ideas, and colorful background. He gave them his home number to call whenever they needed him. They never cared for Topping's aloof style, which to many emboldened the staid Yankees corporate image.

Burke played halfback at Penn and won a Silver Star and a Navy Cross in World War II. Gary Cooper (who played Gehrig in *Pride of the Yankees*) played Burke in *Cloak and Dagger,* a film about his adventures in Italy with the Office of Strategic Services (the forerunner to the CIA).

After the war he became general manager of Ringling Bros. and Barnum & Bailey Circus, putting them in big arenas instead of tents. He joined CBS in 1962 as vice president in charge of diversification, and was involved with the purchase of the Yankees.

He found a way to dress fashionably for the times while still maintaining a CBS corporate look. He drove a Datsun 260Z and dated thin young actresses. He rode horseback in Central Park and got along well with Mayor John Lindsay.

Mostly, he had a manner that was thought to appeal to a younger generation of fans. That same appeal almost made Burke commissioner. In 1969, when looking for a new commissioner to replace William Eckert, the American League backed Burke; the National League Charles Feeney. The compromise candidate was National League lawyer Bowie Kuhn, who could get a consensus.

Paley thought Burke perfect to both revive the Yankees and compete with the Mets. In MacPhail, coming off a year as Executive of the Year for his work running the Commissioner's Office, he had a guy who could focus on the roster, while Burke attended to image and ballpark matters.

With Burke from CBS came Howard Berk, who had worked in the stadium's mail room in 1949 and was now returning as a vice president to give the team a more contemporary marketing focus.

One of their first moves was to bring in Lou Dorfsman, creator of the CBS "eye" logo, considered a genius in the design field. He was asked to help spruce up the stadium. Dorfsman walked into Burke's office, studied samples, and pointed to dark blue as the new color of the stadium seats. Over the winter of 1966–67, the entire stadium would be freshened up: blue paint covering the green seats, white paint covering up the outer brown concrete. Fiberglass bleachers replaced the wooden ones. Additional lighting was installed outside.

The neighborhood would follow suit as the "Yankee blue" was applied to the subway station and, in 1972, even the neighboring Macombs Dam Bridge. The ticket kiosks had blue roofs—although that was the choice of Dr. Frank Stanton, CBS's president. Dorfsman preferred a candy-stripe look.

The dark blue became the "team color," although the team's jackets, caps, and sweatshirts had been dark blue for years.

New graphics were selected for signage and a "telephonic Hall of Fame" was installed where fans could lift a telephone receiver and hear great moments in Yankee history. One such moment, hastily added, would be Mantle's five hundredth home run, belted in Yankee Stadium on May 14, 1967, which made him only the sixth player in history to reach that milestone.

Burke arranged for the stadium offices to move to Yankee Stadium, shutting down 745 Fifth Avenue and building offices for everyone along the 157th Street side of the park.

An enhanced sound system was installed at the stadium with a top CBS sound engineer, Paul Veneklassen, overseeing its quality. A deal was struck with Lowrey in 1965 to add live organ music, and the organist was Toby Wright for two years, with Eddie Layton coming along in 1967 to play a Hammond. Eddie played for the CBS soap operas in the afternoon and then hustled to Yankee Stadium for night games. Stadium "hostesses" patrolled the stands to look pretty and answer questions.

Burke hired a house photographer, Michael Grossbardt, to shoot every home game and to provide more artistic photography for team publications, some published by CBS-owned Holt, Rinehart & Winston. (Previously, the Yankees would use photographers like David Blumenthal, Luis Requena, Neil Leifer, or Bob Olen and then would ask newspapers or wire services for use of game action photography.) The New Studio was hired to design the annual yearbook, instead of just relying on the printer, Terminal Printing of Hoboken.

Columbia Records recorded a theme song, "Here Come the Yankees," written by Bob Bundin and Lou Stallman and recorded by a house band, Sid Bass and his Orchestra, with vocals by Mitch Miller's famous "Sing Along with Mitch" chorus.

They got opera star Robert Merrill to record the national anthem, and, beginning in 1969, he often performed it live, sometimes in his own Yankee uniform with 1½ on the back.

Promotion days proliferated. Aside from Bat Day, Ball Day, and Cap Day, there was Postcard Day, Keychain Day—anything one could imagine, and eventually they were offered to sponsors who added their logos to the products and picked up the cost. Senior Citizens' Day was added, around the same time that Ladies' Day disappeared after a few men sued over discrimination.

MacPhail, paying attention to his area, traded Clete Boyer to the Braves for outfielder Bill Robinson, and sent Maris to the Cardinals for third baseman Charlie Smith after the '66 season. Boyer's eight years with the Yanks saw him become the best-fielding third baseman in the team's history.

Smith was a journeyman who was just the best the Yanks could get for Maris at the time. Roger's skills had faded. He would claim the Yankees had not properly informed him of a hand injury that severely affected his play, and his parting was bitter.

Maris's injury prevented him from gripping the bat properly. He was in pain. Once Dr. Sidney Gaynor ruled out a broken bone, the front office thought it was taking Maris too long to get back into the lineup. They dropped hints that he might be "jaking it."

"For three months, everybody questioned if Roger was really hurt," recalled Al Downing to Maris biographers Tom Clavin and Danny Peary. "That is a long time to be ridiculed. He wanted to play but he just couldn't hit or throw. The sixties was the last decade before there was any kind of sports medicine. Today they'd do an MRI and it would've been taken care of."

Roger finally saw his own physician and an X-ray revealed a fracture of the hamate bone at the base of the hand. When Roger went to Houk with the evidence, Houk said, "Rog, I might as well level with you. You need an operation on that hand." As Clavin and Peary wrote, "The words 'I might as well level with you' etched themselves in Maris's brain. He would quote them often over the years to convey his sense of betrayal by Houk and a Yankee organization that had known the severity of his injury but kept it from the press, the fans, and him."

Maris played two final years for St. Louis, regained his love for baseball, and played in two more World Series before retiring to Florida, where appreciation for his career finally blossomed.

AFTER A WINTER spent fretting over the state of the team, the Yankees played their opening game in Washington in '67, with President Johnson throwing out the first ball. In the third inning, in his second at-bat, Bill Robinson homered to break a scoreless tie, and the Yanks went on to win 8–0 behind Stottlemyre.

Robinson was a personal favorite of Burke's. He wanted him to succeed badly. He was tall and rangy, he was black, and he seemed like a good statement for a team "moving in new directions" (wink).

But that was the high point of his season.

The team moved up to ninth place with two more victories than the year before, 72. Robinson never got going: He batted .196 with just six more homers and lost his outfield job to another promising but ultimately disappointing player, Steve Whitaker.

Ford, who had passed Ruffing as the winningest pitcher in Yankee history in 1965, ran out of gas in '67 and retired.

After breaking the record, Ford won only four more games. One of his last two wins was a shutout against the White Sox, the 45th of his career, and his ERA for his final season was 1.64, but he was getting by on cunning and wile, and at age thirty-eight he wanted to leave with dignity. His .690 career winning percentage was the highest in history for any 200-game winner.

ON 1967 OPENING DAY in New York, a Boston rookie named Bill Rohr had a no-hitter into the ninth when Ellie Howard broke it up with a base hit. Each time the Yankees went to Boston that season, Howard was booed.

On August 3, the Yankees traded him—to Boston! They didn't get much in return, but they cleared the roster of another aging player and Jake Gibbs, a converted infielder, became their catcher.

Few players have ever been traded so kindly. Praise and affection were heaped on Howard for his Yankee service. He was sent to a nearby team that was going to the World Series. He was essentially promised a job with the Yankees whenever his career ended. (He would indeed return as first-base coach two years later, the first black coach in the league.)

Just the same, Arlene Howard told the media her husband had been treated unjustly. "The Yankees are not the Yankees we knew and loved. It's a completely different organization," she said. "I could never get used to mediocrity, and that's what we have now." It was another low moment for a team that just couldn't seem to get it right anymore.

That left only Mickey Mantle from the Stengel years on the '68 team, and that was where I came in, hired by Bob Fishel to answer Mantle's fan mail. I had written a letter looking for a summer job and was assigned to an office not far from the clubhouse catching up with about forty cartons of unopened mail. Fishel knew every unanswered letter represented a possible future Mets fan.

There was a sign near my office that said, ABSOLUTELY NO WOMEN BEYOND THIS POINT. That meant the clubhouse was near; the taboo would be broken in 1978 when a court ordered the clubhouses open to all journalists.

That summer, I walked in the outfield to look for the drain on which Mantle tripped in '51. I was shocked to discover that the outfield wasn't flat, but contained many small hills and gullies, as you'd find on a golf course. I discovered storage areas in the basement where old trophies and photo blowups were stored. Employees and groundskeepers would bring bag lunches and sit in the stands. It was remarkable what a different feel the park had when it was empty.

Mantle treated me well. He saw right through my scheme of saving up "important mail" to review with him personally. There was no important mail. Everyone just wanted an autographed baseball.

It was sad to watch Mick in what would be his final season. No announcement was made, but there was a feeling. It was his fourth straight bad year. What was Mickey Mantle doing hitting .238? And who were these teammates? What was he doing batting behind Andy Kosco?

The '68 team had a shortstop named Gene "Stick" Michael, purchased from the Dodgers, and a third baseman named Bobby Cox from the Braves organization. No one would have thought that there were two future Hall of Famers on that year's team—Mantle and Cox—but Bobby went on to an illustrious managing career. Cox and Mantle even pulled off a triple play, started by pitcher Joe Verbanic, and it would be the last triple play the Yankees would execute for forty-two years.

Michael went on to one of the most multifaceted careers in history, as player, coach, scout, minor league manager, major league manager, general manager, and special advisor. His later influence would be huge. In the meantime, he'd emerge as the team's regular shortstop, pairing with Clarke in the middle of the infield for seven years.

Stan Bahnsen was 17–12 and won Rookie of the Year honors, Stottlemyre had a 21-win season, and Roy White became a regular and hit 17 homers.

Mantle hit 18. Much to his disappointment, his lifetime average dropped to .298. His 535th homer became somewhat "notorious" in that Detroit's Denny McLain, en route to a 31–win season, "grooved" a pitch for him to enable him to break a tie with Jimmie Foxx for third place.

Wrote Red Smith, "When a guy has bought 534 drinks in the same saloon, he's entitled to one on the house."

White, a switch-hitter who often choked up, came from Compton, California, where he played sandlot games with a stuffed sock and formed a double-play combination with Reggie Smith. It was hard to believe that he'd briefly been a gang member in L.A. (the Van Dykes), as soft-spoken and polite as he was. Signed by the Yankees in 1962, he was converted to the outfield, played for the Yanks in '65 and '66, and then was farmed out to Spokane in 1967, where he could have been forgotten. But he hit .343, returned to New York, and went on to enjoy a fifteen-year career, sticking around long enough for the team's return to the World Series. He would become one of the most respected players in town and would rank high on many Yankee lifetime offensive charts, including fifth in games played at the time he retired.

The '68 Yanks finished fifth in the last year of one-division, ten-team baseball, and in the Year of the Pitcher, they scored two runs or fewer in 73 of their 162 games.

FOR 1969, THE centennial of professional baseball, the American League added teams in Seattle and Kansas City (managed by Joe Gordon), the pitching mound was lowered, and Frank Crosetti left the coaching lines after thirty-seven years as a Yankee to join Seattle. Cro was the last link to the Ruth and Gehrig teams.

In Seattle, Crosetti would be joined by Jim Bouton, whose time in New York had also run out, and who would learn a knuckleball and have a second act with the expansion Pilots. (A brawl between the Yankees and the Pilots at the aptly named Sicks Stadium was a memorable moment of the Pilots' only season.)

The Yankees hoped to coax Mantle into another season, happy to pay him $100,000 just to suit up. He had played first base in his final two years, taking to the position quite nicely once his chronically painful legs made the outfield impossible for him. As his popularity remained high, his skills continued to diminish. "I just can't hit anymore," he told Dick Young, who prematurely headlined his retirement months earlier.

As spring training opened in Fort Lauderdale, Mantle made it official at a packed press conference. Despite all the injuries, he left with the most games and most at-bats of any Yankee, and ranked third all-time among everyone in home runs with 536, trailing only Ruth and Willie Mays. He was the greatest switch-hitter in history and the most popular player of his time.

A second Mickey Mantle Day was held on June 8, 1969, beautifully choreographed by Fishel. Important figures in Mickey's life were present, including George Weiss, Harry Craft, and Tom Greenwade. Mick's mother, Lovell, was there, but not Stengel, who was still boycotting the Yankees since his firing. Maris's name was booed when emcee Frank Messer mentioned it.

There was a sustained ovation of ten minutes for Mick, followed by a humble speech delivered without notes. "Today I think I know how Lou Gehrig felt," he said, recalling the "luckiest man" speech. After, he was driven around the running track in a golf cart by groundskeeper Danny Colletti. A crowd of 60,096 helped make the season attendance 1,067,996, a drop of 118,000 from his last year as a player.

The day was emotional for another reason as well. Mel Allen was invited to introduce Mantle from the dugout. He had been on the field for the Gehrig, Ruth, and DiMaggio days, and now this. (Mel, along with Berra, Weiss, Topping, and Webb, had all been back for Old-Timers' Day in 1967, a sweet year for reunion.)

BOUTON KEPT A notebook on his season in Seattle, and in collaboration with Leonard Shechter wrote *Ball Four*, a breakthrough book that spent seventeen weeks on the *Times* bestseller list, helped by a dressing-down from Commissioner Kuhn for telling tales out of school.

Bouton's book was considered scandalous for its violation of the so-called code of clubhouse silence, and it was the first time that fans learned that Mickey Mantle was not always the all-American boy. The book made Bouton persona non grata in the Yankee family and throughout all of baseball. But as controversial as the book was, it heralded a new wave of open sportswriting that forever changed how people saw the game. And while Bouton would remain on the outside looking in, many people, including the next generation of sportswriters, claimed to have fallen in love with baseball because of his revelations about the "inner game" going on, the struggle of journeymen to survive, the nightmares over imagined injuries, the appreciation for everything "big league." (Bouton, a clever entrepreneur, would later copyright the term "Big League" and would use it to market bubble gum and trading cards.)

Ball Four was an appropriate coda for the sixties, when the nation's core beliefs were in upheaval, along with the Yankees' place in the standings.

Chapter Twenty-Nine

To those whose mood changed with every Yankee victory and defeat, the years 1965 to 1975 were painful. There is a tendency to lump them together as the "lost years," a bad memory, an abomination.

But there were also millions of fans, born in the early sixties, who got their first exposure to Yankee baseball in this period, and it wasn't all bad. Unaccustomed to winning every year, these people enjoyed baseball for what it was really intended to be: the national pastime, a team to root for, a recreational diversion from daily life that was a big part of American culture. Each game was a new adventure. There were come-from-behind wins, heartbreaking losses, misplays and great plays. There was the hope behind a fresh rookie or the arrival of a familiar veteran who has a little more left to contribute.

There was still the classic uniform, the inspiring stadium, the great days at the ballgame, or the fun of listening to the playful Phil Rizzuto, the wise Bill White, and the smooth pro Frank Messer broadcast the games.

White, hired in 1971 on the recommendation of Howard Cosell to Burke, was a wonderful foil to Rizzuto, reining him in if he was going too far, chiding him for "thinking like an American Leaguer," or acknowledging a point well made.

White didn't care much for the attention on his being the first African-American to broadcast for a team (Jackie Robinson had done network commentary). But Burke convinced him that with the stadium so close to Harlem, he would be a role model for so many kids growing up there, knowing that when they grew up they could do what he was doing. So he accepted it.

And, of course, for fans in Minnesota, Boston, Detroit, Baltimore, and Oakland, there was the joy of celebrating a championship while the Yankees were down, a chance that had rarely come along before. The four-team 1967 pennant race, barely noticed in New York, provided among the most thrilling finishes to a season in the league's history.

THERE WAS ALSO a growing awareness in baseball that the "industry" could be better marketed. To those ends, Kuhn formed the Major League Baseball Promotion Corporation and, working with the Licensing Corporation of America, got into the licensing business in 1968. Burke was named president of the Promotion Corporation, while keeping his day job. At that point, the twenty teams saw team merchandise as not much of a business, but knew they were being "ripped off by a handful of nobodies," according to Joe Grant of LCA, who said Burke was "paramount to the success of the operation." And so the teams agreed to share equally under a managed program of granting licenses to legitimate businesses to produce quality merchandise.

Sharing equally seemed fine for the 1968 Yankees, but eventually their merchandise far outsold everyone else's. Still, they always participated on an equal basis.

In 1969, professional baseball celebrated its centennial and fans voted on their all-time local teams as well as overall all-time teams. For the Yankees, this was the first such measurement since 1950. It came out with an infield of Gehrig at first, Lazzeri at second, Rizzuto at short, and Rolfe at third; an outfield of Ruth, DiMaggio, and Mantle; Dickey catching; and Ruffing and Ford as the righty and lefty pitchers. On the all-time major league team, Gehrig, Ruth, and DiMaggio earned first-team honors, while DiMaggio, Dickey, and Stengel were among the "greatest living." Babe Ruth was named the greatest player ever, and DiMaggio the greatest living player, an honor he loved and requested whenever he was introduced.

The '69 Yankees hoped to spring two new heroes on the fans, both home-grown prospects who had been off on military duty and were now ready to take regular positions in the lineup. One, Jerry Kenney, didn't work out as hoped. The other, Bobby Murcer, would become the most popular Yankee of his time, and a hero to that generation born around the time Maris was breaking the home run record.

Murcer had been scouted and signed by Tom Greenwade, just as Mantle had. He came from Oklahoma, just like Mantle. He was an infielder who was moved to the outfield, just like Mantle. So the Yankees gave him Mantle's locker and Bobby Richardson's uniform number 1, and built him up to be the successor to Ruth-Gehrig-DiMaggio-Mantle.

Bobby wasn't going to be a Hall of Famer and wouldn't live up to that sort of buildup, but such pressure never bothered him. He was a quality player who lost two years to the service that could have been spent sharpening his tools. Still just twenty-three after rejoining the team (he'd been with them briefly in both '65 and '66, time enough to be a teammate to Mantle and Maris), he hit 49 homers in 1969–70. He became an immediate fan favorite to a fan base desperate to have someone to cheer. And the fans were good with him: They didn't boo him for not being Mantle, whereas Mantle was booed for not being DiMaggio.

1969 would see the departures of Tresh, Pepitone, and Downing, leaving only Stottlemyre and reliever Steve Hamilton from the pennant-winning era that ended in '64. Hamilton, the team's and the league's player rep and a very effective left-hander, developed a crowd-pleasing blooper pitch called the Folly Floater, which he threw perhaps a dozen times with generally good results. Tresh stayed in the lineup despite a four-year slump after beginning with such promise. Loose cartilage in his knee, suffered during a '67 exhibition game, turned the Gold Glover into an "old man" quickly. Pepitone returned to first base after Mantle's retirement, and, after he rebounded to 27 homers in '69 (from a combined 28 in '67–'68), the Yankees seized on a chance to get something of value for him. For all his troubles, he was lovable and popular and famous for being the first Yankee to require an outlet in his locker for a hair dryer. Unfortunately, MacPhail miscalculated and got ex-Yankee farmhand Curt Blefary from Houston, who added little to the team and complained about Houk. Tresh went to Detroit for outfielder Ron Woods, whose career would be brief, and Downing was part of a deal with Oakland that brought Danny Cater to play first base.

Cater, it was said, could calculate his batting average to the fourth decimal point while running to first, which said a great deal about both his speed and his focus.

But if you were a baseball fan in New York in 1969, there was really only one story, and it was happening ten miles away at Shea Stadium. The Mets, a thorn in the side of the Yankees since the moment they hired Stengel in

'61, won the National League East in the first season of division play, the National League pennant, and then the World Series. All three clinchers came at home, bringing delirium to their fans and amazement to just about everyone. Gil Hodges had led the Miracle Mets from ninth place in '68 to the top of the baseball universe in '69.

A telegram went to M. Donald Grant, the chairman of the Mets, after the pennant was clinched: CONGRATULATIONS ON BEING NUMBER ONE—AM ROOTING FOR YOU TO HANG IN THERE AND TAKE ALL THE MARBLES. AS A NEW YORKER I AM ECSTATIC, AS A BASEBALL PERSON I AM IMMENSELY PLEASED AND AS A YANKEE I CONSIDER SUICIDE THE EASY OPTION. MICHAEL BURKE, NEW YORK YANKEES, INC.

THE KEY NEW face of 1970 was catcher Thurman Munson, twenty-three, who took command of the position after just 99 minor league games. An All-American at Kent State near his native Canton, Ohio, Munson was signed by scout Gene Woodling.

Thurman would enjoy an unusual relationship with Yankee fans. Grumpy and contentious with the press, he was no media darling. But the fans saw beyond that. They loved his commanding presence on the field and his aggressive play. He would get cheered no matter what the papers wrote. He even got cheered once when he gave the fans the finger.

Munson overcame a 1-for-30 start and wound up hitting .302 and impressing everyone with his defense and pitch-calling. He was the first AL catcher to win the Rookie of the Year Award. Although Stottlemyre, White, and Murcer were established big leaguers, Munson was the first building block on the road back to the World Series. It was still six years away and would require much more, but the feeling of having an All-Star catcher in place, indeed a likely successor to the Dickey-Berra-Howard tradition, made the front office breathe easier. This was a number-one draft pick that was right on the money.

With Cater hitting .301, White .296, Murcer belting homers in four consecutive at-bats, a 20-win season from Fritz Peterson, and 29 saves from veteran Lindy McDaniel, the Yankees won 93 games in 1970, good for second place, although fifteen games behind the Orioles. It had been so long since the team had anything to celebrate that they uncharacteristically doused each other with champagne after clinching second, an event that surely would have invited a stern look from Joe McCarthy.

Stengel? Well, he was back in good graces and might have been okay with it. Casey had broken his decade-long exile from the Yankees by agreeing to attend the team's Old-Timers' Day—at which his uniform number 37 would be retired—and he put on the Yankee uniform and trotted out at age eighty to the roar of the crowd. (Since all guests received small gifts, I was personally thrilled to get a postcard from Casey when he returned to California, saying, "Mrs. Stengel and I had a marvelous time and thank you for my prize.")

THE YANKEES LURED Mickey Mantle back as a coach for the final month of the season. Mick had been broadcasting for NBC's Game of the Week, wasn't enjoying it, and thought it would be fun to suit up again and travel with the guys. His assignment was to coach first base in the three middle innings, relieving Howard of his duties each day for that interlude.

It bothered Mickey that the arrangement was a little embarrassing for Elston, and he realized that he didn't really have much of a role. The experiment lasted to the end of that season, but we decided to reshoot the team photo so that he was included.

Of course, there were his annual Old-Timers' Day appearances, which continued uninterrupted until Bowie Kuhn banned him from the game for representing an Atlantic City casino in 1983. Kuhn had done the same with Mays, seeking to distance baseball from gambling. The ban didn't extend to Old-Timers' Days, only to employment with the team, but Mick chose to make a statement by not returning for the ceremonies during the time of his ban. (Commissioner Peter Ueberroth lifted the ban in 1985, and Mick immediately became a broadcaster for the Yanks for four seasons and once again an Old-Timers' Day fixture.)

Meanwhile, a controversy of sorts arose over the order of introduction at Old-Timers' Days. Joe DiMaggio had been introduced last since his first one in 1952.

In the first years after Mantle retired, his popularity was so high and his fans so much more youthful, that the cheers for him were louder than those for DiMaggio. So Fishel (with me in agreement), decided to reverse the order so that DiMaggio's "greatest living" introduction was heard clearly.

Bad call. DiMaggio, always easy to offend, considered it a slight and threatened never to return again. Assured that he would be introduced last, he returned again and again.

Mantle couldn't have cared less. The gatherings were just fun for him, like the time I encouraged him to play center field one last time, or the time he forgot to bring his number 7 uniform with him (and we put a piece of tape over the 1 in Gene Michael's 17), or the time he emerged from the clubhouse with a dangling earring, poking fun at Barry Bonds's fashion statement and at his own wholesome image.

THERE WERE NO major additions to the team in 1971, but the Yankees sadly parted with Bill Robinson. He never found his groove with the Yankees, and for his four years in pinstripes batted only .206 with 16 homers. As the Yankees believed, he would go on to play another twelve years and would shine for Pittsburgh and Philadelphia and earn a World Series ring in 1979. It would forever be a mystery as to what went wrong with Bill Robinson in New York and why that promise wasn't fulfilled.

The '71 team was led by Murcer's .331 season—second to Tony Oliva's .337—but the gains of '70 were erased in an 82–80 year, fourth place, in which the bullpen managed only 12 saves. The only thing that put them over .500 was a forfeit victory in the season finale in Washington, when most of the 14,460 bitter fans stormed the field in anger over owner Bob Short's decision to move the Senators to Texas. The umpires declared a Yankee victory in a game they were losing 7–5.

DESPERATE TO PULL off a big trade and reverse the team's sliding fortunes, Lee MacPhail decided that Stan Bahnsen was his best player to offer as trade bait to bring some punch to the lineup for 1972. Teams always sought quality starters, and in four full injury-free seasons with the Yanks, Bahnsen had won 55 games with a 3.10 ERA.

MacPhail got a second baseman from the White Sox—Rich McKinney, who had batted .271 with eight homers in 114 games. He'd looked good against the Yanks. The plan was to move him to third base, where Kenney had failed to impress.

"It was the worst trade of my career," MacPhail wrote in his memoir, *My Nine Innings*. "I did not know McKinney well enough . . . We figured he could make the switch to third. That should not be an automatic assumption. But more important than that, for us, he simply did not have the aggressive bear-down temperament that we had thought he had."

And so in one bad moment, the Yankees were out a starting pitcher with eleven years left in his career, and still had a big hole at third base. The deal was so bad, MacPhail wrote a poem about his mistake and read it at the baseball writers' annual "pre-dinner dinner."

After committing four errors in one game at Fenway Park, McKinney was essentially written off. It did not help McKinney that he had injured his thumb participating in roughhouse hockey games, in which players used bats as hockey sticks, in the Yankee clubhouse. The Yankees dug into the Mexican League on a tip by Tomas Morales, a Mexican sportswriter, and found a likeable guy named Celerino Sanchez. He had a tenacious approach to the hot corner, taking the toughest shots off his chest and rifling them to first. He had a winning smile and was the anti-McKinney, winning him immediate fan acceptance. He bought the Yankees some time.

One trade that did work, and that took a lot of pressure off MacPhail's blunder, was Cater for Sparky Lyle. Ralph Houk had coveted Boston's lefty reliever, twenty-seven, a free spirit who had ice water in his veins in pressure situations. With only days remaining in spring training, I rushed to Winter Haven, the Boston training camp, to get Lyle photographed for the Yankee yearbook, which was going to press in twenty-four hours. We had only the number 28 uniform available among lower numbers, because Ron Hansen had recently been released. Sparky had been 28 with Boston. It was perfect.

With Lyle in place, the veteran Felipe Alou aboard to share first with the colorful Ron Blomberg, and (it was thought), an able third baseman in McKinney, the Yanks couldn't wait for the season to begin.

And then the players went on strike, the first strike in the history of baseball. No one knew what to make of it because it was a new experience for everyone. The most important thing to come out of it was the solidarity of the players. The '72 strike was brief, but it established the union as the real deal, with the players prepared to lose money and stick together. That formula would see them through all the work stoppages to come.

Compounding the confusion was the shocking death of Mets manager Gil Hodges, only forty-seven, who, in the absence of spring training games, was playing golf with his coaches. Such were the logistics of the strike disruptions that the Yankees' plane, due to fly north to New York, would bring Gil's body back home for his funeral, since the Mets were to open on the road. (After the funeral, Yogi Berra was named Mets manager.)

The lost games, seven or eight per team, were not made up. It meant that

Billy Martin's Tigers would win the AL East by half a game over Boston, since they didn't play an equal number of games.*

After having to cancel a four-game opening homestand against Baltimore, which included opening day and a Sunday Cap Day, the Yankees' home attendance for the year would be 966,328, ending a run of twenty-six straight seasons in which they had topped a million at a time when such a figure was worthy of an annual press release.

When play began in '72, the Yankees looked good. With Lyle wowing the crowds with heart-stopping saves, Murcer hitting 33 homers, and Stottlemyre, Peterson, and Steve Kline winning 49 games, there were positive signs. The role of the fourth starter came to be shared by the free-spirited Mike Kekich and Rob Gardner, who won 18 between them.

There was much drama to Lyle's appearances, and at one point I asked a musician friend if he might suggest a "theme" to accompany Lyle's dramatic entrances. The Datsun bullpen car would emerge from the bullpen, drive down the first-base running track, then Sparky would fling open the door and fire his warm-up jacket at the waiting batboy and stomp to the mound. My friend thought that since it foretold the culmination of the game—the save!—"Pomp and Circumstance," aka the graduation march, might work.

It caught on almost immediately. Toby Wright on the organ (Toby came back in 1971 when Eddie Layton had a full soap-opera schedule) would take my signal, and on his first chord the fans would respond with thunderous cheers. The music became synonymous with Lyle. Sparky asked me not to play it after that season, citing "too much added pressure," but he later came to say that the music had played a big part in creating the concept of the closer, and of course in having theme music for particular players. It was a prelude to "Enter Sandman" for Mariano Rivera in later years.

(The Datsun would be succeeded by Toyota; the idea of vehicles delivering relief pitchers lasted about ten years.)

Lyle's season produced a record 35 saves and nine victories, with a 1.92 ERA. Responding to his heart-stopping moments, like a nine-pitch, three-strikeout save against Detroit, the Yanks were only a half game out of first on Labor Day, and we were making postseason plans. Tickets, programs,

---

* Martin may have managed the Tigers, but he remained a New Yorker at heart. One Friday afternoon, stuck in horrendous Third Avenue traffic, he pulled his starting nine off the team bus and led them to the Lexington Avenue subway, just in time to arrive for the game. Few managers could claim to know where to find the 4 train to the Bronx.

press pins—lots of preparations had to be made, and most of us had not been there in '64, the last time the team went through this.

But soon after, the Yanks lost six of seven and retreated in the standings. Mike Burke coveted Billy Martin as manager and was prepared to dump Houk, maybe even "trade" him to the Tigers for Martin. But MacPhail wouldn't go for it.

When they lost their last five games of the season, they fell back into fourth again, this time 79–76 in the shortened season. Some were able to see progress, but for the fans it was just another disappointment, and patience with Houk was running thin.

THE FIRST SIGN that there might be structural problems with Yankee Stadium came on a Bat Day. Young fans would pound their bats on the concrete flooring to try and stimulate a rally. What they were stimulating, in fact, was the need for an upgrade of the aging ballpark. Mayor John V. Lindsay and Burke had first discussed it in general terms while sitting together at the 1970 Mayor's Trophy game.

The pounding of the bats was resulting in chunks of concrete falling. No one was hurt, but the maintenance crews were making the Yankees aware of the problem. Burke, Berk, Fishel, and MacPhail came to the conclusion that safety was going to be an ever-increasing issue with the current structure. Besides, people were expecting more amenities from their facilities—safer passageways, better lighting, escalators, and certainly unobstructed views. The concept of luxury suites was also emerging.

The stadium and its land was owned by Rice University and the Knights of Columbus, but as the City of New York had provided a new facility for the Mets, so too did the Yankees hope that the city might step up and do the same for them. No threats were made, but small notices would appear about offers from New Orleans, which was seeking a major league team for its new Superdome—or perhaps from New Jersey. I was part of a small contingent that inspected the Superdome during the Winter Meetings to determine its usage for baseball. (Bad sight lines).

Mayor Lindsay was no baseball fan, but he knew that he didn't want the Yankees leaving the Bronx on his watch, as the Dodgers and Giants had left under his predecessor, Robert Wagner. He especially didn't want them suggesting a departure while he was running for president, since he was going to seek the Democratic nomination in 1972. Lindsay and Burke were similar in manner and got along well from their first introduction. It did not take a lot of persuasion to get Lindsay on board with a plan to renovate Yankee Stadium, and in the process save the South Bronx.

The first cost estimate for the renovation was $24 million—the cost of building Shea Stadium a decade earlier. With inflation, and with this being less than a ground-up operation, $24 million was a figure people could "hang their hat on."

Fishel used to organize a winter "caravan" on which a band of Yankee front-office people, a broadcaster, Houk, and a new player to showcase would visit five outlying areas in five days to meet the media in towns like Albany, Cheshire and Stamford, Connecticut, White Plains, and Trenton. It began in 1961 and continued until the gasoline shortage of 1974. In January 1972, we made the trip with McKinney (who asked me where in New York he could buy good marijuana. Hello? I work here). At each of these stops, the show-stopping announcement was the plan to renovate Yankee Stadium.

The idea was for the city to acquire the land and the ballpark through condemnation proceedings, paying Rice and the Knights of Columbus a fair market price for the property and taking on ownership, just as they owned Shea. The renovation would include removal of all the pillars in the ballpark that caused obstructed views, a matter of removing the existing roof and creating a new configuration for the seating. The city would improve access roads and make the subway station safer. There would be new lighting, new parking garages, about a dozen luxury suites, and a great new scoreboard. The Yankees would sign a thirty-year lease, ending all talk of moving elsewhere.

The work would begin the day after the 1973 season ended and the stadium was to be ready in time for opening day of 1976. In the meantime, the Yankees and Mets would share Shea Stadium for two seasons.

Burke insisted that the new design not lose the facade that ringed the current ballpark. He wouldn't sign off on anything that didn't include it. The architects, Praeger-Kavanagh-Waterbury, placed a replica facade above the billboards at the rear of the bleachers. Burke had recognized the facade as almost a fourth logo for the team—apart from the interlocking NY, the pinstripes, and the top hat.

Part of the fallout of all of this was the end of the football Giants' days at Yankee Stadium. Unwilling to commit to a thirty-year lease, the Giants followed the call of the Meadowlands of New Jersey, where they would move into their own park in 1976. It would end a sixteen-and-a-half-year residency at Yankee Stadium, with the Giants playing two September games from their 1973 schedule in the Bronx before demolition began.

The Giants' departure also empowered opponents of the renovation, who could now argue that the park would be empty for half the year, reducing the number of jobs the stadium provided and affecting the economy of the neighborhood. The press on the caravan stops were learning of this even before the New York media, who were briefed when the caravan ended.

The 1972 Yankee yearbook had featured a two-page spread of an artist's rendering of the new stadium, although the final product would look somewhat different. The plans were in place, but two seasons, 1972 and 1973, in the historic old structure still remained.

Chapter Thirty

G ABE PAUL HAD BEEN WHEELING and dealing in the game for decades, going back to his days in the thirties as the Reds' traveling
secretary. He moved through the Cincinnati organization, briefly to
the presidency of the new Houston Colt .45s, and then to Cleveland as
president of the Indians. There may not have been a better politician in
baseball, and Gabe was a champion survivor no matter how many times
ownership above him changed. Mostly, he knew how to operate a team on a
tight budget, for that had been his fate in the game: He'd never worked for
owners with deep pockets when it came to baseball.

And that's why he perked up one day in the summer of 1972 while sitting with Al Rosen on a flight to New York. Rosen, the former Indian star,
knew all the movers and shakers in Cleveland, including an up-and-comer
named George Michael Steinbrenner III. Rosen had introduced Steinbrenner to Indians owner Vernon Stouffer, who'd made a handshake deal to
sell him the team. The deal would have made Steinbrenner Gabe's boss, so
Gabe was anxious to hear more about the fellow, even after the Cleveland
sale fell through when Stouffer had a change of heart.

"Is he for real?" Paul wanted to know. Assured that he was, or at least had
the ability to raise money among other Cleveland businessmen, Paul said,
"He asked me if I ever heard of a club for sale to let him know. And I know
of a club for sale."

Told it was the Yankees and that CBS was ready to sell, Rosen shared the
news with Steinbrenner. Paul and Steinbrenner began communicating

directly, and Paul met with Mike Burke on September 17, 1972, at the Plaza Hotel. At that meeting Burke confirmed that William Paley said he could buy the team himself if he could find investors. Burke agreed to meet Steinbrenner.

Steinbrenner had turned forty-two on July 4; Gabe was sixty-two and hadn't really considered a "next act" in the game. But Steinbrenner was a powerful force, a can-do sort of guy who had already owned a pro basketball franchise in the American Basketball League. He had been an assistant football coach at Northwestern and Purdue. He was now running American Ship Building, a company started by his father. Sports was his passion. He pronounced "athlete" with three syllables as though to add an extra beat of admiration. He was in the family business because "We're German, that's what we do."

Jacob Ruppert would have understood.

MEANWHILE, GABE PAUL went about running the Indians, whose best player was Graig Nettles. Nettles drove in 70 runs that year, tops on the club, and played an exceptional third base. Knowing the Yankees had barely gotten through the McKinney-Sanchez season at third, he let it be known that Nettles was available. All of Gabe's players were always available. And if he could shed some salary in the process, all the better.

At the Winter Meetings on November 27, in the middle of the Steinbrenner-Burke-Paul talks, Gabe traded Nettles to the Yankees for Charlie Spikes, Rusty Torres, John Ellis, and Jerry Kenney. All four had won the James P. Dawson Award as the top spring training rookie, an award presented annually since 1956 and named for the former *Times* reporter who had died during spring training in 1953. All had engraved Longines watches. There would be a good chance that between the four of them, they wouldn't be late for games.

Gabe would be the first to say that a deal wasn't a deal until the papers were signed, so despite later rumors about "knowing he'd be a Yankee too," the deal was legal and uncontested. But it was Gabe at his best, working the hallways and the back rooms.

Nettles, twenty-eight, had a sweet left-handed swing for Yankee Stadium and also a sarcasm and wit that reminded some of Roger Maris's "red-ass" reputation. And although Pete Sheehy hadn't taken Maris's uniform number

9 out of circulation, I saw a connection at once, and for the first and only time in my years with the Yankees, went into the clubhouse and said, "Pete, you gotta give Nettles number nine! He's Maris." It was a perfect fit.

On December 19, Steinbrenner stood before William S. Paley and told him that he had the partners and the financing and was prepared to make a deal. In ten days, it would be finalized.

The next meeting included Steinbrenner, Burke, and Paley. They agreed on $10 million as the sale price, which included several neighborhood parking garages and lots owned by the team. The city purchased the garages shortly after, making the sale of the club just $8.8 million. Steinbrenner's personal cost for his share was $168,000.

Paley wanted the announcement to cover his $13.2 million purchase—to make it seem that with the depreciation of player contracts, the network had essentially broken even.

But the truth was, at least since the Great Depression, and perhaps back to the beginning of Major League Baseball, this was believed to be the only time a team had ever been sold at a loss.

Although Gabe loved to leak stories to the press, particularly to Milton Richman of UPI, the talks about the Yankees being for sale became one of the best-kept secrets in New York sports history.

Just before Christmas, the Yankees held their employee Christmas party in the Stadium Club at Yankee Stadium, with farm director Johnny Johnson presiding over his annual slide show where funny captions pertaining to current employees were applied to stock photographs. Among those present, only Burke knew about the impending sale. MacPhail, to his disappointment, was not asked to come aboard as a partner. Even Howard Berk, Burke's closest confidant within the front office, hadn't been forewarned. The deal was signed on December 29.

Bob Fishel was informed on January 2, 1973. The next morning, I began my task of calling the media—we were still using rotary-dial phones and dealing with busy signals and no voice mail—to summon them at once to Yankee Stadium for an urgent announcement.

Lunch was prepared in the Stadium Club, a podium was moved in, and Mike Burke announced the purchase of the team, introducing his new partner George Steinbrenner, a shipbuilder from Cleveland, and promising to introduce all the other limited partners in another week.

"We plan absentee ownership as far as running the Yankees," said Steinbrenner in his first exchange with the New York media. It was what he had told Paley. "We're not going to pretend we're something we aren't. I'll stick to building ships."

The words would come back to haunt him as he'd grow more involved over the years. Some never let him forget it. Ignored was the fact that he knew and loved sports, and may have been answering politely because those currently running the team were right there in the room. It was not the way to tell them that their time had come to move on.

In fact, another statement that day caused greater internal consternation. Forgetting Paley's request to make the deal come out favorably to CBS shareholders, Steinbrenner said, "It's the best buy in sports today. I think it's a bargain!"

The statement felt like a great betrayal to Burke, whose loyalty to Paley was enormous. He was devastated. The styles and beliefs of Steinbrenner and Burke were probably never meant to coexist as a partnership, but on day one, mistrust had already emerged.

ON JANUARY 10, the limited partners were introduced at the 21 Club: powerful titans of business and industry, seated humbly, side-by-side on armless chairs, with Steinbrenner and Burke presiding. Another point of tension had shockingly emerged: Gabe Paul was a limited partner in the deal. (Rosen would become a limited partner a year later.)

Still more aggravating was Steinbrenner's decision to place Paul into a high front-office position. It nearly derailed the 21 Club event. Paul wanted to be announced that day as team president. Steinbrenner assured him that would be the case, with Burke as chief operating officer, responsible for such things as the new stadium project.

To Burke, this hadn't been agreed upon. Now, with Paul pointing his finger at him in the backseat of the car to 21, the two reached a hasty compromise. At the press conference, Burke would say, "Gabe is sixty-three and has a nice home in Florida where he and his wife, Mary, will retire in a few years. This is a nice swan song for him to end his baseball career."

Gabe sat there and accepted it, feeling Steinbrenner would ultimately make his feelings known. For the time being, it would just simmer.

As for the other partners, there were Gabe people and George people, many from Cleveland, some not. It was a hastily assembled group. One, James M. Nederlander, was the head of a theatrical family producing Broadway shows. He would bring Steinbrenner in as an investor for one of them—ironically, a revival of *No, No, Nanette*, the show linked to the Babe Ruth sale first produced by Harry Frazee.

It was Nederlander who told Steinbrenner, "New York likes big stars, never forget that." He and his brother Bob were important in integrating Steinbrenner into New York's proper "circles."

Over the years, a number of partners would rise to significant advisory roles, however temporary or long lasting they might be. Ed Greenwald would be involved in the signing of Catfish Hunter. Lester Crown's guidance would be frequently sought, and his family would own the second largest share of the team. Daniel McCarthy and Bob Nederlander would become caretaker general partners. Barry Halper, the acknowledged king of memorabilia collectors, would buy a piece of ownership with his neighbor Marv Goldklang and briefly run the front office. Later arrivals to the ownership team like Ike Franco, Jerry Speyer, Leonard Wilf, Mort Olshan, and Howard Rubenstein would also be involved in important decisions.

There were some partners whose lives would become unglued. John De-Lorean, Nelson Bunker Hunt, Marvin Warner, and the group's attorney Patrick Cunningham would all be brought up on criminal charges.

Ultimately, partners would come and go, although some would remain for many years. John Henry was a limited partner before winding up with part ownership of the Red Sox. The same for John McMullen of the Astros. The partners were generally happy with what proved to be handsome annual returns on their initial investments. A typical annual meeting, required under terms of the partnership, found them each handed profit and loss statements for a quick review, with the pages quickly collected so that no information left the room. There were never any leaks.

THE YANKEES' ANNUAL winter press caravan took off to showcase Nettles to the suburban media and answer questions about the new ownership and the plans for Yankee Stadium's fiftieth anniversary and final year. During one stop, the news broke that the American League had passed a new rule, permitting the use of a "designated hitter" to bat for one man in the lineup (the pitcher, obviously) each time he was due to hit.

This was breaking news, although not everyone at these outlying stops "got it."

One reporter asked Houk, "How often do you plan to use this?"

The DH was not passed in the National League even though the Players'

Association had to approve any changes to the rule book, the DH was a sure thing in the AL: The union would never eliminate the DH jobs. It was first listed as "experimental," and MacPhail explained that American League hitting had been so lackluster that a boost was really needed to add some scoring to the game. "I never expected it would be forever," he said. "I thought it would last a few years until some parity with the National League was reached."

The DH was used in spring training, and then officially on opening day, when the Yankees were in Boston with the day's earliest starting time. The Yankees, of course, batted first. Ron Blomberg, intended to be a platoon first baseman on the team, had suffered an injury that prevented him from playing the field, and he was the number-six hitter in the lineup against Luis Tiant.

Blomberg, who would bat .329 that year, got to bat in the first when the three batters ahead of him all reached base. And so Sherm Feller, the Fenway PA announcer, got to make history too, reciting, "The designated hitter . . . number twelve . . . Ron Blomberg." (Scoreboards had no way to show "DH," so at Yankee Stadium, for instance, it was just shown as "B," as in "batter," since the "B" was available to show 1B, 2B, and 3B.)

Blomberg was a high-energy guy, always talking, always eating. The nation's number-one draft choice in 1967 was extremely popular with New York's Jewish community, and he hit some prodigious drives in batting practice, even reaching the facade as Mantle had done. So long as he was facing right-handed fastball pitching, he was a monster hitter.

But on this at-bat, he walked, driving in a run. After the game I retrieved his bat and sent it to Cooperstown, where it would be the only bat on display representing a walk.

He would later write an autobiography called *Designated Hebrew* and talk with exaggerated humor about the day he ruined the game of baseball.

SPRING TRAINING OF 1973 would have a drama all to its own, and had Steinbrenner been approved by the other American League owners, he would no doubt have weighed in on the matter. But silenced by the waiting period, he simply listened in as the baseball world was jolted by news that Fritz Peterson and Mike Kekich, the team's left-handed starters who wore numbers 18 and 19 and had become very close friends, had in the off-season decided that they were in love with each other's spouses more than their own and would participate in a "wife swap," which would be, in fact, more of a "life swap"—involving homes, cars, kids, pets, and possessions. The wives went along, but by the time the story broke, things had already ended between Kekich and Marilyn Peterson. The two pitchers were barely speaking.

The news broke just as spring training was starting (Peterson was a holdout). At first, the Yankees decided to treat the matter as private, something between the players and not for public information. It would be unimaginable in a later age of tabloid television, Facebook, and Twitter that such a story could hold. But in 1973, it was considered possible.

It "held" for less than a day, and then the story was headline news across the country for a week.

Ballplayers can handle the news of most any behavior in a matter-of-fact style, but this one shocked even the pitchers' teammates, who naturally had to discuss it with their wives. Suddenly, the fun-loving Fritz and Mike were not the same guys who organized hockey games using baseball bats in the clubhouse. Kekich wanted to call the whole thing off, but it was too late for Fritz and Susan Kekich, who were genuinely in love and who celebrated thirty-eight years of marriage in 2011.

One thing was certain, now that the two were at war: One had to go. And that would be Kekich, who was traded to Cleveland on June 12, a sad turn of events in that it removed him from proximity to his children, who now lived with Peterson and his ex. Peterson was never the same quality starter again, and ten months later, after Kekich had moved on to Japan, he was traded to Cleveland too. Fritz left with the lowest ERA in Yankee Stadium history, 2.52.

ON APRIL 15, 1973, the Yankee players lined up along the first-base line at Yankee Stadium for its golden-anniversary celebration, with Mel Allen doing the introductions. A fiftieth-anniversary patch graced the sleeves of their new double-knit uniforms, highlighted by the frieze design. (The Yanks had joined the Expos and the Royals as the last teams to change from flannel to knit.) Bob Shawkey threw out the first pitch to Whitey Witt; Claire Ruth joined Betty Houk in placing wreaths at the monuments. All the fans received replicas of the inaugural 1923 program.

The players were all neatly trimmed. At the opener, a week before, the new co–general partner, George Steinbrenner, furiously wrote down the numbers of all players he thought wore their hair too long. The Yankees, to his thinking, had grown apart from the traditions that made them stand out—a fault of the careless leadership of the long-haired Burke. He had bristled at Burke's appearance in Fort Lauderdale for a yearbook photo, Burke arriving in a blue denim shirt, his long gray hair blowing in the wind, while Steinbrenner wore a sharp navy sport jacket and a close-cropped haircut. A team needed discipline before it would begin to win. It was going to begin with haircuts, and Steinbrenner had his list delivered to Houk with orders to restore a more dignified appearance. Under Steinbrenner's watch, Yankee players would be permitted mustaches but no beards (Wade Blasingame was the first to wear a mustache in late '72), would wear conservative and dignified clothing while traveling, and would comport themselves as he had been trained at Culver Military Academy. The free-spirited, long-haired style represented by the world champion Oakland A's would not be acceptable for the Yankees. As for winning, Steinbrenner told fans he would deliver a championship to them within four years.

Fan behavior at the games was an issue in the early seventies, as it was throughout big cities. In 1970, the Yanks instituted a "Good Kids" program to reward good behavior, run by Howard Berk. It helped a little, but it was a time when respect was not a given in society. The graffiti-laced subway system and the graffiti-laced outer walls of Yankee Stadium spoke to that.

As an example of diminishing good behavior, the Yankees had obtained a pitcher named Jim Hardin from the Orioles in '71. He drove up from Baltimore with all of his possessions in his car and parked it outside the players' entrance on 157th Street. He went downstairs to "check in" with Pete Sheehy, and then back to the street to retrieve his stuff. It was all gone. Someone had broken into his car in the ten minutes he was in the clubhouse and taken everything in broad daylight.*

Discipline became Steinbrenner's style with the stadium environment as well. George told Pat Kelly, his stadium manager, to buy lots of white paint and cover up the stadium graffiti every morning.

"We'll outlast them, and we'll win," he said. "We can buy a lot more paint than they can."

---

* Clancy the doorman (who had a line in the film *Bang the Drum Slowly* as himself), hadn't seen the caper.

It worked. The graffiti artists surrendered and found other places. It was one of the first victories New York would experience with this public nuisance.

THE HOME OPENER featured another conflict between Steinbrenner and Burke. When Bobby Murcer (whose number was on the haircut list) made the game's next-to-last out, Steinbrenner bristled. "There's your goddamn hundred-thousand-a-year ballplayer," he shouted.

Murcer signed a $100,000 contract in spring training, joining DiMaggio and Mantle as the only Yankees at that level.

ON APRIL 25, nineteen days into the season, Burke resigned as co–general partner. I distributed a simple release in the press box during a day game. Burke requested that he become a limited partner and make a settlement on his personal-services contract. That was done, and Burke got into his 260Z and drove off. His Yankee days were over.

He would go on to run Madison Square Garden, where he found the going equally rough with the Knicks and Rangers. Ultimately his reputation was that he had "humanized" the Yankees, made them a more fan-friendly team, but just couldn't produce winners

The media always liked him, but acknowledged his shortcomings. Howard Berk followed him to Madison Square Garden soon after, making him the first employee to leave the team after the new ownership arrived. Many would follow.

In 1982 Burke retired and moved to Ireland, where he died in 1987. I attended his memorial service at St. Patrick's Cathedral and found myself sitting next to author Kurt Vonnegut. Maybe that was all you needed to know about Michael Burke; he could attract Vonnegut but never did find a second baseman to replace Clarke.

As FOR THE Yankees of 1973, they were in first place from June 20 to August 2, and once again we got busy with playoff and World Series preparations. On July 20, in a twi-night doubleheader with the White Sox at Yankee Stadium, knuckleballer Wilbur Wood started and lost both games. (He was knocked out early in the first game; Fishel leaned over to me in the press box and predicted he'd start the nightcap.) The fiftieth-anniversary season was shaping up as a thrilling one.

Gabe Paul moved into Howard Berk's office, and although MacPhail was still the general manager, Paul clearly had become an influential force. At the trading deadline, the Yankees got Sam McDowell from the Giants and Pat Dobson from the Braves, two proven workhorse starting pitchers.

"If we don't win now, we only have ourselves to blame," said Murcer.

McDowell was the hardest-throwing Yankee starter since Bob Turley: A 10-strikeout game for him was routine. He had built his reputation under Paul with the Indians but now was in need of a comeback. Unfortunately, alcohol was consuming his life and seriously damaging his career. Dobson, a tenacious right-hander, had been one of four Oriole starters to win 20 in 1971.

But the two additions won only 14 games in the second half of the season, and the team went into an overall collapse, winning just 20 of 52 after their high-water mark. Not only did bad play doom them to fourth place in the AL East, but the fans had had it with the manager, and Houk heard boos and saw banners at every home game. Those three pennants in 1961–63 were now a distant memory.

Not only that, but the Mets, managed by Berra, were in a close race, and despite an 82–79 record—just two wins better than the Yankees—won the NL East, beat the Reds in the NLCS, and took the World Series to seven games before losing.

ON AUGUST 1 at Fenway Park, in the ninth inning of a 2–2 game, Munson barreled hard into Boston catcher Carlton Fisk. The collision quickly escalated to punching, emptying the benches into a big brawl. Both catchers were ejected.

Despite their geographic proximity, Boston and New York did not yet have the "rivalry" that would become the best one in sports. A true baseball rivalry requires that both teams be strong (unlike traditional college football rivalries), and, going back to the sale of Babe Ruth, the Red Sox seldom were. The exception, in the late forties, came and went.

But now, with Munson and Fisk emerging as stars, a rivalry was taking hold. Both had come up briefly in 1969. Munson had won Rookie of the

Year in 1970, Fisk in '72. Their teams were getting better. The Sox almost won the division in '72 as the Yanks challenged, and in '73, the Yankees were playing better baseball into the summer months. One could almost feel tensions rising. Munson and Fisk would genuinely come to dislike each other and embody the growing enmity, which is still in place forty years later. Many felt it first come together in that bang-bang play at the plate.

The Yankees played their final game in the original Yankee Stadium on September 30. Duke Sims, a backup catcher purchased six days before, hit the last home run in the park where Ruth had hit the first.

A crowd of 32,238 came out for the finale, and each fan received a record album, *Yankee Stadium: The Sounds of 50 Years*, narrated by Mel Allen.

Sadly, Houk had to go to the mound to relieve Peterson in the top of the eighth, and the fans really let him have it.

"It was like thousands of people booing my own dad for something he didn't do, right in front of me," wrote Peterson in his memoir.

The Yanks lost 8–5, finishing with an 80–82 record after all those weeks in first place. Mike Hegan, obtained in August, made the final out. With that, the fans set about taking Yankee Stadium home with them. Those who didn't storm the field for pieces of sod wiggled their seats loose from the concrete, breaking the legs in the process and going home with a mangled souvenir.

Seats were made available to season-ticket holders, and then what was left were sold by E.J. Korvette's department store for $5.75 plus five proofs of purchase from Winston cigarettes.

Much of the other treasures of the park were purchased by collector-author Bert Randolph Sugar, who gave Yankees controller (and later president) Gene McHale $1,500 in two checks for the right to first inspect what was available, and then to haul it off. At the time, there was no real "collectibles" market, and the Yankees were faced with paying to store the material or disposing of it for a quick payday. "I put two kids through college with the stuff and had plenty left over," said Sugar, who proved to be a visionary when it came to memorabilia.

WHILE THE FAN mayhem on the field continued, we gathered all the media into the press room for an unexpected announcement. I had been phoning the New York TV stations since the third inning to tell them to be at the stadium at the end of the game. Amazingly, they weren't planning on being there for the final out. In fact, UPI had asked me to send the final summary and box score to them and I had to call them and say, "Look, I can't cover the postgame story for you—you have to send someone!"

Into the press room, still in his number-35 uniform, came Ralph Houk. He stood by the bar and announced with sadness that after thirty-five years in the organization—including his distinguished war service—he was resigning. (His boat in Florida was called *Thanks Yanks*.)

The press did not expect this. Neither did the team employees, some of whom were weeping.

But no tears need have been shed for Houk. A pretty good politician in his own right, he had already made a deal to manage Detroit in 1974, having spoken with Tiger general manager Jim Campbell about it during the waning weeks of the season. Eleven days after the Yankee announcement, he was announced as the new Tiger manager. He would later manage the Red Sox, too, but took neither team to the postseason.

Houk's departure from the Yankees was certainly tied to his new working conditions. He didn't like the new owner questioning his moves. He'd had it pretty good for a long time. First Topping, then Burke, and certainly MacPhail, never second-guessed him. Suddenly he felt like an employee and didn't like the change in structure one bit. He complained to close friends about it, citing Steinbrenner as an outsider who "didn't know anything about baseball." He resented Steinbrenner bringing in the baseball clown Max Patkin to entertain fans between innings. He resented Steinbrenner criticizing his veteran bench players, particularly an aging Johnny Callison. When rumors cropped up that MacPhail might leave to succeed the retiring Joe Cronin as American League president, that was all he needed to hear.

Demolition of Yankee Stadium began the very next morning, October 1.

While the outer wall would stand, the interior would essentially be gutted and restyled to allow unobstructed views from every seat. There was a small ceremony that Monday morning, at which Claire Ruth received home plate and Eleanor Gehrig received first base. Mayor Lindsay made the presentations. Sam McDowell, of all people, represented the players. He was just there to clean out his locker.

The front-office staff would move to the Parks Administration Building in Flushing Meadow Park, across the street from Shea. I had spotted the building from the Grand Central Parkway and suggested it in a memo to Lee MacPhail. It had been the World's Fair headquarters building a decade before, and Gabe Paul would take Robert Moses's corner office. MacPhail, in his waning weeks before succeeding Cronin, would occupy a smaller office across the hall, and then his place would be taken by Tal Smith as executive vice president, reporting to Gabe, who was now officially the team president.

Tal would bring Pat Gillick with him from Houston as coordinator of player development and scouting, and he, like Smith, grew to be among the most respected men in the game. Their stays, however, were brief.

And now we had a manager to hire and a new ballpark to share with the Mets.

Chapter Thirty-One

O AKLAND BEAT THE METS IN THE '73 World Series, and Dick Williams emerged from it with the reputation as the game's best manager. But he couldn't take Charlie Finley's meddling, and so, like Johnny Keane nine years earlier, he quit right after the triumph.

Using a middleman named Nat Tarnopol, a record-company executive, Gabe Paul made overtures to Williams and began to sense that this could be Houk's successor. (Tarnopol employed Williams as a VP and was a Yankee season box holder.) It would be a blockbuster announcement, to be sure.

In the weeks following the Series, as speculation increased on Williams coming to New York, pressure was also growing on Bowie Kuhn to follow the progress of Steinbrenner's Watergate-related entanglements. Although all allegations had occurred prior to his coming into baseball, Kuhn was concerned about integrity issues involving an owner. On August 23, 1973, Steinbrenner pled guilty to authorizing $25,000 of illegal campaign contributions to the Nixon reelection campaign, filtering the money through American Ship Building employees as phony bonuses that allowed him to exceed the contribution limit. He also pleaded guilty to being an accessory after the fact by attempting to cover up the crime—obstruction of justice.

Steinbrenner, who was also a regular contributor to Democratic senator Ted Kennedy, was doing what he felt the shipbuilding business required, and had been instructed on procedure by Nixon operatives. It was a bad decision. He was hardly alone in the scheme; he was the seventeenth person indicted under similar charges, and AmShip was the fourteenth corporation so charged.

A week later he was sentenced: two fines totaling $15,000, and a $10,000 fine for the company. There was no jail time, but it was a felony conviction. (He was pardoned by President Reagan in 1989.)

It was the obstruction of justice portion of his crimes that bothered Kuhn, and the settlement put it front and center on the commissioner's desk.

Steinbrenner had voluntarily removed himself from daily activity with the team after his indictment, pending the outcome. But on November 27, Kuhn suspended him for two years, saying, "Attempting to influence employees to behave dishonestly is the kind of misconduct which, if ignored by baseball, would undermine the public's confidence in our game."

For a true absentee owner, suspending him from daily involvement with the team would have rung hollow. But clearly, in his eleventh month of ownership, Steinbrenner had demonstrated enough hands-on activity so that Kuhn felt the punishment would indeed be one with teeth, not just a meaningless pronouncement.

Steinbrenner was shocked. He quickly named Yankee counsel Patrick Cunningham, head of the Bronx Democratic Party, as the acting general partner. And while Steinbrenner was to have no contact with Gabe Paul or anyone else in the front office, it became clear that he had the means to weigh in on major decisions. Kuhn admitted to me some years later, "Of course I knew, and I couldn't object to his involvement in big money decisions. So long as he didn't flaunt it."

THE WINTER MEETINGS arrived, and the Yankees still had no manager. I had been instructed to prepare a few releases for people under consideration, among them Williams, Frank Robinson (still an active player), our coach Elston Howard, sixty-one-year-old Birdie Tebbetts, and sixty-five-year-old Al Lopez. But no announcement was made at the meetings. Howard would have loved the opportunity to make history as the first black manager and had many supporters.

On Monday, December 16, Gabe summoned me to his office and told me to arrange an elaborate, well-catered press conference to announce the signing of Williams. Even at a dollar a shrimp, he approved a shrimp bowl. Already settled in our modest offices in Queens, which really had no room for a lavish event, we chose Feathers in the Park restaurant in nearby Flushing Meadow, an exquisite setting.

On the eighteenth, we introduced Williams as the new Yankee manager for 1974, and then took him to Shea to photograph him in a Yankee jersey. It was the first time we'd been there since Fishel and I had met with Mets VP Jim Thompson to determine the logistics of a shared arrangement. (The Yankees would be using the New York Jets' cramped clubhouse down the right-field line.) Thompson, who had been fired as a Yankee executive years before, loved this moment.

Joe Cronin, leaving the AL presidency on December 31 to be succeeded by MacPhail, didn't like the deal and squashed it. Williams had walked away from his Oakland contract and was taking the Yankee job. Finley was screaming that he deserved compensation. He insisted on rookie prospects Scott McGregor and Otto Velez.

"They're our crown jewels!" screamed Gabe. "Never!"

MacPhail later said he didn't agree with Cronin's decision and would not have stopped the signing. Had that been known, the Yankees might have finessed the announcement until after the first of the year, and presumably been in the clear. But MacPhail did not want to be involved in anything quite so devious, and did not make his feelings known.

In the end, the Yankees gave up. It would have been nice to have Williams and it would have been nice to get their money back from Feathers in the Park, but it wasn't to be. Williams would go on to manage other teams, make the Hall of Fame, and then finally join the Yankees as a special advisor from 1995 to 2001.

Plan B was Bill Virdon, not Howard, a decision that dismayed Ellie, his former teammates, and the many who knew him and respected him greatly. This had been his shot.

Dismissed as Pirates manager late in '73 after winning the Eastern Division title in '72, and already signed to manage Denver, Virdon had a long-forgotten Yankee pedigree. He had been signed by Tom Greenwade in 1950 and then traded to St. Louis in '54 for Enos Slaughter. It qualified him to be a member of the newly formed Yankees Alumni Association, administered by Jim Ogle, the longtime beat reporter for the *Newark Star-Ledger*. (The Yankees stood alone in reaching out to alumni in such organized fashion.) Now his charter membership would include the manager job.

Modern fans remembered Virdon as a fine center fielder for the Pirates, who hit the "bad hop" grounder to Kubek in the '60 World Series that turned game seven around.

There would be no Feathers in the Park event for Virdon. That budget was spent. Instead, desks were shoved aside in the group sales office and the press invited back for sandwiches (no shrimp) with Virdon on January 3, the first anniversary of the CBS sale. Newly elected Hall of Famer Whitey Ford was named pitching coach. (Ford and Mantle had just been elected together.)

The Williams-Virdon episode was more than just the hiring of a new manager. It was a signal that many Yankee moves in the future would come with complications. There would be contested draft choices, aborted signings of players, trades restructured—all sorts of angst in getting deals done. Fans would come to recognize that Yankee deals would often be drawn out.

ALTHOUGH NEVER SEEN at games and never granting interviews, Steinbrenner was known to be unhappy with Virdon from the start.

He wasn't fiery enough, didn't excite the fans, and didn't seem to excite the players either. It bothered Steinbrenner that Ford would go to the mound and make pitching changes, and that Dick Howser, the third-base coach, would take the lineup cards out at the start of the game. Where was Virdon?

Bill had a laid-back style that didn't play well with the man they would soon be calling "the Boss."* Still, he had Gabe Paul's support—and he was winning!

The '74 Yanks were again in the pennant race, despite the failing of Murcer to solve Shea Stadium's dimensions. Murcer was horribly frustrated by the new ballpark, and did not hit a home run there until September 21, the 153rd game of the season—and then he hit another one the next day.

A key to the team's success had occurred the previous December, when the Yanks traded Lindy McDaniel to the Royals for Lou Piniella. It was Lee MacPhail's final Yankee trade. First signed in '62, Piniella had been in five organizations before joining Kansas City in 1969. Now he was thirty, and the Royals thought they could replace him with Jim Wohlford, something his new teammates never let him forget. Lou was quickly a team leader, easy to tease, easy to like, and a guy the fans took to at once. He hit .305 in his first year with the Yankees.

---

* This nickname was first used in print by Mike Lupica.

Then came a big trade three weeks into the season that brought Chris Chambliss and Dick Tidrow to the Yankees, as they bade farewell to "half our pitching staff," as Munson said. Munson was not happy about the deal, in which Peterson, Steve Kline, Tom Buskey, and Fred Beene went to the Indians, but Paul certainly knew what he was getting in Chambliss and Tidrow.

Chambliss, twenty-five, a soft-spoken son of a navy chaplain and a star at UCLA, replaced Mike Hegan at first base. Piniella, Munson, and Chambliss had been Rookies of the Year from 1969 to 1971 and were now all in the Yankee lineup. Tidrow, with a fierce mustache and the nickname "Dirt,"* could start or relieve, and would prove to be a key addition.

The team got a lift on July 8 when Sandy Alomar was purchased from the Angels, bringing the Horace Clarke Era to a close. For nearly ten years, Clarke had been a fixture in the lineup. If for no other reason than "need for a change," the arrival of Alomar was welcomed.†

On May 26, Virdon decided to put slick-fielding Elliott Maddox in center field, moving Murcer to right. Maddox, obtained from Texas during spring training, came from East Orange, New Jersey, and had studied prelaw at Michigan. He was studying for conversion to Judaism. Virdon was certainly one to appreciate the value of a top defensive player in center—he had been one himself.

This didn't sit well with Bobby, a Gold Glove winner two years earlier, but it was a move Virdon made without much procrastination. It just made sense to him, even though "center field, New York Yankees" had so much history behind it. That wasn't a big deal to Virdon. To him, Maddox was just a better option. And when Maddox took advantage of everyday play and hit .303, it was hard to argue with the move.

Pat Dobson and George "Doc" Medich, a med student as Bobby Brown had been twenty years earlier, each won 19 games, while newly acquired starter Rudy May had a 2.28 ERA and Lyle had a 1.66 figure in relief.

A big setback for the team was the breakdown of Mel Stottlemyre's arm in his 15th start of the season. It happened suddenly, as if his supply of

---

* His appearance conjured memories of a TV commercial for motor oil, showing "Mr. Dirt" gumming up engines.

† Over the years, some of the children of Yankee players who ran around the clubhouse were Roberto Alomar, Sandy Alomar Jr., Barry Bonds, Ken Griffey Jr., and Prince Fielder.

pitches—forty-five thousand over his career—had run out. He lifted his left hand to his right shoulder and rubbed. Trainer Gene Monahan came out with Virdon, and the three of them left the mound together. (Monahan helped usher in a more sophisticated era of athletic training after succeeding Joe Soares in 1973.)

Save for two relief innings in August, Stottlemyre never threw another pitch. Rotator-cuff surgery might have enabled him to continue, but Mel's injury came right before several important breakthroughs in sports medicine. MRIs, arthroscopic surgery, and rotator-cuff repair were all just in their infancy or not yet fully tested and approved.

Mel completed his Yankee career with 164 wins, 40 of them shutouts. He tried to return in 1975 but was released in spring training, a release he bitterly claimed came in the face of being told to take his own time recovering. (His partial salary would be due if he was not released by a certain date.)

The end of Stottlemyre's tenure marked the last connection the roster had with the Topping-Webb days and with the last pennant winner of the 1921–64 dynasty. Mel had five All-Star selections and three 20-win seasons. He returned as a pitching coach two decades later, recouped some money he felt was owed to him, and garnered four more rings. That helped complete the Yankee story for Mel.

THE 1974 TEAM, with so many new faces, played hard. They occupied first place from September 4 to 22. On a couple of occasions, Virdon was required to play tapes recorded by Steinbrenner to rally the team. They seemed to demonstrate the Boss's feeling that Virdon didn't have the means to fire them up himself.

With reserve catcher Bill Sudakis's boombox blaring Paul McCartney's "Band on the Run," the Yankees went town to town and kept winning. A particularly gratifying win came on September 10 when newly acquired Alex Johnson hit a twelfth-inning homer in Fenway Park to give the Yanks a 2–1 win, a game in which Chambliss had been struck in the arm by a dart thrown from the stands.

Johnson, a former batting champ and brother of Giant running back Ron, had no use for the media and was dressed and gone by the time the press arrived in the locker room. He didn't really talk to teammates, either. He just liked Bill Kane, the traveling secretary. No matter. The Band on the Run gang was still going.

Two games were left in the season, and the Yankees were one game behind Baltimore. They would have to win both games in Milwaukee and hope that the Orioles lost their last two.

The trip to Milwaukee did not go well. Some excessive drinking took place. In the lobby of the Pfister Hotel at the late-night check-in, some words between Munson's two backup catchers, Sudakis and Rick Dempsey, turned into a brawl, with lamps flying and chairs overturning. Murcer tried to play the role of peacemaker and broke a finger. He would be unavailable to play the next night.

The Yankees lost that game 3–2 in ten innings on a single up the middle by George Scott off Medich. In Detroit, Baltimore beat Houk's Tigers 7–6 with a run in the ninth. It eliminated the Yankees from the race with one game remaining. It was a disappointing end to an exciting season, displaced as they were from their home ballpark. Virdon was named Manager of the Year by the *Sporting News*, something that amused Murcer, Munson, and Nettles, as they had spent much of the summer ignoring his signs and giving their own.

On June 26 in Pompton Plains, New Jersey, in the Township of Pequannock, a baby named Derek Sanderson Jeter arrived, the first child for Charles and Dorothy Jeter. He would be heard from again.

Bob Fishel left at season's end to join MacPhail in the American League office as its chief publicist. He'd served for twenty years, and the writers gave him a Horace Clarke number-20 Yankee jersey as a parting gift. He loved it.

Steinbrenner, although suspended, called and asked if I felt capable of succeeding Fishel. I'd been elevated to PR director in '73 when Fishel became a vice president (just in time for Peterson-Kekich), but now I'd have the top job. I said I could do it because I had been lucky enough to observe Fishel for six years. He was the best PR man in the game. And so George Steinbrenner made me, at twenty-four, the youngest PR director baseball had ever had, and the third in franchise history.

The Shea Stadium experience for the Yankees was not a satisfying one. The Mets were accommodating, but it was clearly their home.

The clubhouse safe that had been in Hilltop Park, the Polo Grounds, and then Yankee Stadium never made it to Shea and disappeared forever. There went the last link to the Highlanders. It wasn't a part of Bert Sugar's haul, and it never appeared at auction. It had just vanished in the demolition, its historical value never realized.

Even Met fans were down on Shea, a utilitarian ballpark built for football and baseball and ideal for neither. Little was done to make Shea feel more "Yankee" during Yankee home games. A sign atop the scoreboard displayed the Yankees' logo instead of the Mets'. Some billboards were purchased in Queens to alert area fans that the Yankees would love to have them come to games, but there was little indication that such attempts at recruitment helped. Compounding the problem was the gasoline crisis of '74, which created lines at gas stations and forced people to cut back on travel. A lot of the Yankee fan base from New Jersey, Westchester, and Connecticut was going to sit out this sojourn to Queens.

The Yanks drew just 2,561,123 for their two seasons at Shea, while the Mets drew 3,452,775.

One of the great fiascos of the Shea years was Salute to the Army Day on June 10, 1975, which featured a twenty-one-gun salute from cannons placed in the outfield. Unfortunately, the firings blew a section out of the outfield wall while another section caught fire. The fire was quickly doused, which was a good thing because the Yankees and Mets would have been out of ballparks at that point, but the start of the game was held up for more than a half hour while boards were brought in and hammered into place.

Three days later, Elliott Maddox became a victim of the swampy outfield when he severely injured cartilage in his knee. Maddox, hitting .305, had to undergo surgery and was never the same player again. He wound up suing just about everyone—the doctors, the City of New York—but his real goal, to return to the form he showed in 1974–75, eluded him.

DURING THE 1974 World Series, a distraction arose that would change baseball forever.

An agent named Jerry Kapstein stepped forward to claim that his client, Jim "Catfish" Hunter, the best pitcher in the league, had not received an insurance-annuity payment in time from the Oakland owner, Charles O. Finley. The late payment, claimed Kapstein, was enough to void Hunter's contract and make him a free agent. People laughed.

But Kapstein was right. When the matter fell into the hands of arbitrator Peter Seitz, Hunter was declared a free agent. And while some thought the penalty too severe, the owners had signed on to the arbitration process when they okayed it for salary negotiations in '72.

In December '74, every team—including the A's—hustled to Hunter's farm in Hertford, North Carolina, and his nearby lawyer's office in Ahoskie, to show off their checkbooks.

"Gabe," I said to Gabe Paul during the early stages, "could this possibly reach a million dollars?"

"Damn right it could," he thundered. "This is war!"

Paul, who had worked his whole career with shoestring budgets (he had me mimeographing our daily press notes while every other team used Xerox copying, claiming it would "save hundreds a year!"), was suddenly rolling up his sleeves and playing with the big guys now that he had a well-financed ownership group behind him. And he was loving it.

If he could get Hunter, he would be adding a second superstar to the roster in a matter of weeks. On October 22, he had called me into his office as he phoned Murcer in Oklahoma City. He wanted a witness.

"Bobby? Gabe Paul. Listen, I have some news for you . . . I hope you'll think it's good news . . . We've traded you to San Francisco."

I could tell Murcer was speechless, but eventually the news settled in, and Gabe was telling him about all the fine restaurants in the city. At the very end, Bobby asked, "Who did you get for me?"

The answer was Bobby Bonds.

It was one of the biggest one-for-one trades in baseball history.

Murcer was in shock: Steinbrenner had told him he'd always be a Yankee.

But, as Tal Smith noted, anytime you can get one of the five best players in baseball, you find a way. And that was where people ranked Bonds at the time. His '74 totals had fallen to .256/21/71, but he had been the closest baseball had ever come to being a 40-40 man (40 homers, 40 steals), had been an All-Star Game MVP, and with Willie Mays had been the only player to twice reach the 30-30 club. He had been Mays's protégé, as Murcer had been to Mantle in New York.

For a new generation, Murcer was the franchise. He would be leaving behind a large base of young fans who adored him.

Bonds had more natural ability than Murcer, and Bob Fishel noted that some of the Yankees' PR during Murcer's career may have helped influence Horace Stoneham of the Giants into thinking the two were equal.

With Bonds in place, the pursuit for Hunter went on, and the Yankees had an ace up their sleeve. Their major league scout, with the unlikely name of Clyde Kluttz, was the very scout who signed the teenaged Hunter for Kansas City a decade before. Now, by good fortune, he was working for the Yankees. And Hunter loved him.

Kluttz, a major league catcher for nine years, was also a fellow North Carolinian. He was practically a father figure to Hunter, a straight shooter. The Yankees were fortunate indeed to have this going for them, and sure enough, on New Year's Eve, the media was called to the Parks Administration Building for a huge signing announcement.

Limited partner Ed Greenwald was busy drafting the contract as Hunter, his lawyers, and Kluttz flew to New York on a private plane registered to Steinbrenner. Even when they got to Gabe Paul's office, nothing was final. Talks continued while I mimeographed our press release and kept the media at bay. We were messing with everyone's New Year's Eve plans.

At last, Hunter took a nineteen-cent Bic pen and signed a five-year contract for about $3.35 million, a figure that included premiums on life-insurance policies for his children. There was, of course, no doubt that Steinbrenner had signed off on this, suspension or not, and Kuhn later admitted he would certainly not have denied him that right.

The signing rocked the sports world. Hunter was suddenly a household name in America. The most important thing about the signing was that it demonstrated what a free agent was now worth, seven years after Ken Harrelson, a top hitter, became a free agent and signed a $150,000 contract with Boston. It was enough to get everyone's attention, especially the Players Association. The free market had spoken, and it was suddenly clear that the existing salary structure in the game was artificially low.

Many would point to this signing as the day baseball lost its compass, and blamed Steinbrenner's spending for it. But most of the teams were bidding at or near this figure. If the San Diego Padres could offer $3 million, then the money was there.

While the Hunter signing preceded the formal ground rules of free agency that would follow, it did establish the multiyear contract as a normal course of business, the use of an agent as expected and accepted, and million-dollar deals to be affordable.

IF THE MANAGER OF THE YEAR just added Bonds and Hunter to his roster after finishing two games out, 1975 surely had high expectations. Which also meant little margin for error.

After getting off to a scary 0–3 start, Hunter was exactly as advertised: a brilliant pitcher on the field, a classy leader off it. He had competitiveness that harkened back to the old Yankees. There was a maturity to Hunter, the youngest of nine children, that belied his twenty-nine years of age, but at the same time a playfulness that made him a fun teammate.

In 1975 he went 23–14 (a fifth straight 20-win season), pitching 328 innings and 30 complete games, a figure never since equaled. In a sense it marked the end of an era when such numbers were recorded, certainly on the Yankees. And it would really be the only one of his five seasons in New York in which his stats inspired the awe that seemed to go with the contract. Still, he was a force throughout his years in New York, the guy who "showed us how to win," according to many. In his remaining four years he would only go 40–39. Some thought he left it all on the mound in year one, so anxious were the Yankees to recoup their money. But no one looking back on his legacy suggested that he was overpaid or over-hyped.

Bonds, meanwhile, was a remarkable athlete. He was a five-tool player, although he struck out a lot, and in '75 he broke Mantle's single-season Yankee record with 137 punch-outs. But he enjoyed being a Yankee. On one occasion, he represented the team at the State House in Boston, speaking out against a plan to introduce a baseball lottery in Massachusetts. He showed pride in the game when the Yankees were opening-day opponents in Cleveland, where Frank Robinson became the first black manager.

He didn't get off to a quick start at the plate, but in late May he started to show his greatness. On May 27 he began an eleven-game hitting streak, all on the road, during which he batted .408 with eight home runs, showing how he could carry a team. The Yankees won nine of those games. But then on June 7 in Chicago, he ran into the Comiskey Park wall running down a long drive and badly hurt his knee. He missed the next week, and his hot streak was interrupted.

He played the rest of the season hurt. That brief look at what might have been, all accomplished on the road, would remain forever as a quick image of a year that wasn't. The Bonds that the Yankees saw in 1975 was not Bonds at full strength.

For the season he hit .270/32/85 with 30 stolen bases, and despite the injuries he would be the first Yankee to record a 30-30 season. (Mantle's stolen base high had been 21.)

ALTHOUGH STILL UNDER suspension, Steinbrenner used his proxies to cast an important vote that summer—for the reelection of Bowie Kuhn as commissioner, a surprise to many.

"Let me tell you," he said to some New York writers when the vote was announced, "things are going to change now. The American League is going to get more respect from the Commissioner's Office after this. You watch."

Was this all part of some backstage deal with Kuhn to get his suspension lifted early? To many, Steinbrenner's explanation appeared pretty flimsy. But more realistically, other American League owners had come around the night before the vote was cast, and an anti-Kuhn vote by Steinbrenner would not have caused him to lose. It would have accomplished little more than pouting. Steinbrenner, who became skilled at last-minute vote shifts, more than likely sized up the situation and decided a "yea" vote would produce more for him in the long run than the momentary satisfaction of a meaningless "nay."

AS FOR THE '75 team, they had a 12–20 start but began to play better and reached .500 and second place on June 4. Briefly, in late June, they took over first. But then a seven-game losing streak set the vultures in motion over Virdon's days as a manager.

The worst thing that could have happened to Virdon was when Texas fired Billy Martin on July 20. Martin by now had earned a reputation as a quick-fix artist whose managerial skills generally produced better-than-expected results wherever he went. He'd already shown this in Minnesota, Detroit, and Texas.

He was eighteen years removed from his trade following the Copa incident. No one was left in the organization from 1957 save for some ticket-office employees. Those who were there cared little about his earlier exit, or even about his reputation for being high maintenance. Gabe Paul did not like a manager who might seek a voice in trades, but he was starting to feel the pressure from Steinbrenner to "do something!" All signs pointed to Martin, who craved a chance to return to the Yankees.

On a spring training boating trip that very year, he had told Bob Fishel, in front of his own owner, Brad Corbett, "I'd give anything to manage the Yankees."

Paul dispatched his longtime employee and now Yankee scout Birdie Tebbetts to find Martin, who was on a hunting trip in Colorado.

On Friday night, August 1, the night before Old-Timers' Day, the Yanks won their third straight to go to 53–51. But Virdon's fate was sealed. He was summoned across the street to Paul's office and told he was being replaced.

And so on Old-Timers' Day, Billy Martin returned to the Yankees after his exile, introduced to the cheering crowd of forty-four thousand in what was one of the happiest days of his life.

DiMaggio shook his head as I walked him to the clubhouse at Shea and told him the news, as though knowing what was to follow in coming years. He didn't look any happier when Martin was introduced after him, violating the "always last" agreement that had been struck years before.

IN AN EFFORT to breathe life back into the '75 Yanks, Billy arrived with a plan to evaluate what he had and make the best of what remained in the season. Martin was always a manager who quickly decided whether a player was his kind or not. He was especially loyal to veterans who had gone to "the wars" with him, to coaches who had long-term relationships with him (and weren't after his job), and to young players he thought could be molded.

For the injured Maddox, the hiring of Martin was not good news. He was a player Billy had not liked when he managed him in Detroit and Texas, and he had ordered him thrown at during spring training in '75, which led to a brawl.

Martin was only 30–26 in finishing out the '75 campaign, but he kept telling people, "Wait until I get a full season, with my own spring training."

ON SEPTEMBER 29, the day after the season ended, Casey Stengel died in Glendale, California, at eighty-five. Martin, whose relationship with "the old man" was strained after his trade, was emotional over the loss. He flew to California as the representative of the Yankees at Casey's funeral and slept in his bed that night. In 1976, he alone would wear a black armband on his uniform to honor Casey. The two men had reconciled without ever discussing the trade.

The Yankees' two seasons at Shea quietly came to a close, a piece of their history largely forgotten. One manager, Virdon, and one star, Bonds, would be on a short list of post-1923 Yankees who never appeared at Yankee Stadium as a member of the home team. When Shea Stadium came down after the 2008 season, retrospectives showed two concerts by the Beatles, but nary a mention of the 159 Yankee home games, nor the destruction of the outfield fence on Salute to the Army Day.

Chapter Thirty-Two

O N NOVEMBER 21, 1975, AN ARBITRATION hearing that would shake the foundation of Major League Baseball took place at New York's Barbizon Plaza Hotel. Peter Seitz, who had decided Catfish Hunter's fate, would decide whether Andy Messersmith and Dave McNally were free agents, too, having gone through the season without signing a contract. (Sparky Lyle had almost been "the one," having gone until the final days of the '74 season with an unsigned contract before finally agreeing.) The Players Association argued that that constituted their option year, and that the Reserve Clause should not bind them permanently to their team. Major League Baseball felt cautiously optimistic that Seitz would decide that court rulings, which included Curt Flood's Supreme Court defeat, would prevail.*

MEANWHILE, THE WINTER MEETINGS were held at the Diplomat Hotel in Hollywood, Florida. The week was passing with few announcements, and the media was hungry for news.

Finally, on Thursday, the Yankees broke the silence with not one, but two major trade announcements.

First was the announcement that Bonds, after just one season as a Yankee,

---

* Flood had refused a trade from St. Louis to Philadelphia and sued Major League Baseball, but ultimately lost in the Supreme Court by a 5–4 vote in 1970. The court seemed to be saying, "Congress needs to resolve this, not us," but MLB saw it as a vindication of the status quo and was hoping the arbitrator would agree.

was going to the California Angels for center fielder Mickey Rivers, who had led the league with 70 stolen bases, and 16-game winner Ed Figueroa, who had previously spent eight seasons in the minors.

Then came the trade of Doc Medich to Pittsburgh for starting pitchers Dock Ellis and Ken Brett and a rookie second baseman, Willie Randolph, who'd batted .339 in triple-A.

Because Randolph was fairly unknown, having played just 30 games for Pittsburgh, his name was overlooked by even some of the more astute media. "Medich for Ellis and Brett," was one report heard on New York television. Others said, "Medich for Ellis, Brett, and a minor league prospect." Gabe knew better.

"We know he can field," he said, "and anyone who comes up in the Pirates organization can hit."

Randolph, although born in South Carolina, had gone to Tilden High in Brooklyn. He brought New York street smarts with him. When he was assigned number 23 in spring training, he asked for 30, which he had worn for the Pirates.

"We're keeping that out of circulation in honor of Mel Stottlemyre," said Pete Sheehy. Randolph, all of twenty-one, looked at the legendary Yankee equipment manager and said, "I don't care about Mel Stottlemyre, I want thirty." He got it. When Stottlemyre and Randolph were both coaches on the Yankees in the nineties, it was Randolph who wore 30.

Ellis, thirty-one, had been a fixture with Pittsburgh since 1968. Sometimes controversial and always outspoken (he later claimed to have pitched a no-hitter while high on LSD), Dock would be a key contributor. Figueroa spoke little English and never quite got comfortable in New York, but Munson took a leadership role in making him feel part of the team. He would one day write a book called *Yankee Stranger*.

In one day, Paul added four key players to the roster. Both Bonds and Medich would go on to play for six more teams, never quite reaching their earlier promise.

The Yankees also traded Pat Dobson to Cleveland for outfielder Oscar Gamble, who brought a perfect Yankee Stadium swing with him. Gamble also brought the biggest afro hairdo in the game, and as soon as he arrived in spring training, Gabe Paul knew it had to go. He assigned me the task of getting it trimmed—immediately—on a Sunday afternoon.

"If he reports to camp looking like that, we won't let him work out," said Gabe. "He'll file a grievance with the union, and he'll win. That will be the end of the haircut policy and all discipline on this team. So it will be a PR problem, and that's why you better get it done."

Somehow, I found a barber and a very cooperative Oscar Gamble. With Ellie Howard along for moral support, we got it accomplished. Before-and-after photos ran all over the country.

During the Winter Meetings, Martin and Paul battled over a pitching-coach selection. Billy wanted his drinking buddy Art Fowler—Paul adamantly refused. So it went to the affable Bob Lemon, in the year he was elected to the Hall of Fame.

Additionally, the Yankees brought Yogi Berra back as first-base coach. Yogi had been fired as Mets manager the previous summer, and to have Yogi back "where he belonged," twelve years after he'd been fired as Yankee manager, was a feel-good announcement in New York. There were certainly some who thought the return of Yogi could mark the lifting of a "curse" placed on the Yankees after his dismissal. "Back to one toll," noted Yogi, who no longer had to cross two bridges to get to work from his New Jersey home. He began calling me daily for the latest gossip.

ON DECEMBER 23, Seitz declared Messersmith and McNally free agents. The monumental announcement changed the face of baseball. After more than a century of players belonging to teams "forever," with annual renewals, they were now, technically, all free.

Marvin Miller, fresh from his greatest union triumph, knew that a system was needed, something other than setting every player free every year. That would be a glut on the market and would not work in the players' best interests. Baseball faced an urgent need to come up with a mutually agreeable plan, and the owners decided to lock out the players from spring training until such a plan was found.

ON MARCH 1, Kuhn lifted Steinbrenner's suspension. He said that the Yankees' financial woes after two years at Shea (no parking or concessions money) would be "significantly alleviated by his reinstatement and attendant benefits to the team and Yankee fans."

"It's something I have to live with," Steinbrenner told author Nathan Salant in a 1978 interview. "I've regretted it time and again, but what's done is done. Hopefully, there are other ways I can make up for it."

Steinbrenner had been lobbying hard for this, and he saw it coming. With so many critical matters on his plate—including the new stadium—Kuhn had given him permission to conduct staff meetings at the Carlyle Hotel in January.

It was at these meetings that Steinbrenner looked at Martin and said, "Now this is your call, Billy, and I'm not saying this is necessarily a good idea or a bad idea, but sometimes it's good to appoint a team captain. It's not always the star, not always the obvious guy, but it's something you might want to consider."

As the PR director, I spoke up and said that it had been Joe McCarthy's wish to have the captain position retired with Lou Gehrig—that no one would have it again.

Steinbrenner listened, collected his thoughts, and said, "Well, if Joe McCarthy knew Thurman Munson, he'd know this was the right time, and this is the right guy."

So Munson, when informed, shrugged his shoulders, basically said, "Oh, okay," and became captain in 1976.

Kuhn ordered the spring camps opened for an abbreviated training period, and the Yankees quickly made a move to sign Messersmith. It failed, as Messersmith seemed to have a change of heart after an apparent agreement. Steinbrenner quickly issued a statement saying, "For the Yankees to pursue [Messersmith] at this time, in view of Andy's stated feelings about not wanting to play for the Yankees, would be totally inconsistent with what I am striving for—it would not be fair to the other men on the Yankee team—past and present."

He let him go, but he also sent a strong signal that he would be active in the free-agent market. He had bought into a system where no such market existed, but now that it was there, he was going to lead the way with it. Ultimately, he would be the last owner standing who predated free agency.

The Yankees' plunge into free-agent baseball would be one of the major developments of the game's history. Steinbrenner viewed the new ruling as a way to improve his roster annually as new stars became available, and as a better alternative to nurturing drafted amateur players. If he could get someone on the free-agent market, or trade minor league prospects for a player approaching free agency, or lock up a pending free agent by offering a big contract, he was game. He saw quickly that with a high-revenue-producing team, he could establish the market value on almost every player.

The Yankees' ability to land just about anyone they wanted was remarkable. No matter what players said, they usually went for the highest offer, and if the Yanks were determined to sign someone, they would spend the money. Messersmith turned down the Yankees to join the Braves in 1976, Greg Maddux turned down the Yankees to join the Braves in 1993, and then Cliff Lee did the same in joining the Phillies for 2011. If such events could be spread out once every eighteen years or so, the Yankees were operating on a very high success level.

The Yankees weren't alone as a big-market team, of course. The Mets could have been in the same position, and they were arguably richer when the system began, outdrawing the Yankees and more closely removed from World Series play. And the Los Angeles and Chicago teams had a lot of revenue sources to tap into. But the Boss seemed to take control of his position with zest.

Others, especially Kuhn, saw him as artificially sending salaries higher than they needed to be. If another team seemed to overpay for a player, it was seen as "the Yankee factor": If they didn't, the Yankees would. And every agent wanted his player to be coveted by the Yankees, driving up the value.

Kuhn was no fan. "I would certainly rank George ahead of Miller in terms of their respective contributions to player prosperity," he wrote in his memoir. "Finley set the stage with his guerrilla tactics. Miller opened the coffers with a lucky assist from Seitz. Steinbrenner then took charge by inaugurating the reign of fiscal insanity that ensued, impoverishing club operations—including his own—pushing up ticket prices and enriching the players beyond their imaginations."

Steinbrenner always ranked among both the most liked and most disliked people in baseball. Players and agents loved him for paying big salaries. Yankee fans loved him for providing teams with big stars (even if sometimes they were offended by his public criticisms of them). The media, with a few exceptions, loved him because he was always good copy, sold a lot of newspapers, and created excitement (even if they sometimes had to work their tails off running down his stories). Other teams begrudgingly accepted him because he filled their ballparks when the Yankees were in town. His own players loved him because he generally surrounded them with top players.

The Commissioner's Office did not like that the Yankees sometimes operated like a rogue nation, casting dissenting votes on matters that didn't favor them. But they had to acknowledge that the Yankees were creating big revenue for the industry through their aggressive enhancement of the Yankee brand with all of its international implications, and that the game was moving into an era of previously unimagined revenues.

Steinbrenner's own employees had it harder. He was a very demanding boss, and compliments weren't his strong suit. Job security was tenuous. Still, he created more jobs than any other team in baseball and brought a lot of good young people into the game. Many with Yankee pedigrees went on to high-level positions at other teams, at MLB, or in other sports. It was a line on the résumé that got favorable attention.

Some members of the press never warmed up to him. He found few allies at the powerful *New York Times*. Red Smith seldom had a good word for him. Murray Chass disliked his treatment of players, although as a strong union supporter, he recognized the benefits he was providing to the workforce.

The *Daily News*'s Dick Young and ABC's Howard Cosell hated each other but generally liked Steinbrenner, and he recognized their power and could be very charming with both of them. Bill Gallo's cartoons in the *Daily News* could skewer "Von Steingrabber's" ways, but ultimately showed admiration.

THE EBB AND FLOW of labor issues always turned eyes to the Yankees. In 1972, salary arbitration was introduced to baseball. It seemed of little consequence at first, but it was the genie emerging from the bottle. When salaries later soared, the clubs were still stuck with it, and even young players were able to garner the equivalent of free-agent-like salaries through the process. Even without having the case heard by an arbitrator, settlements were often extraordinary. Steinbrenner did not like to lose at arbitration, and would often turn on a player who had beaten him in the process.

In 1976, the free-agent draft was instituted, setting in place the system that Steinbrenner dominated. Not every signing worked out, but by and large this proved a very successful system for the Yankees.

Major League Baseball was found guilty of collusion after free-agent offerings decreased between 1985 and 1987, and the resulting penalties made the owners extremely cautious about ever repeating such an event. This produced a new explosion of salaries, a graph that seemed to rise continuously, always seemingly driven by the Yankees' desire to spend on stars.

The bitter baseball strike of 1994–95, resulted in the creation of a revenue-sharing plan, under which a team's local revenue (ticket sales, local broadcast money, signage, and concessions), minus its debt obligations and operating expenses for its ballpark, would be shared with the low-revenue teams. The Yankees were overwhelming contributors in this process.

In 1996, MLB created a central marketing department to greatly increase the industry's revenue, with the money divided evenly across the teams. As with the original licensing plan in the sixties, the Yankees suffered by getting a much smaller portion of revenue than sales of Yankee merchandise produced, but at the same time, the total sales were greatly increased through the performance of this very strong wing of MLB.

Over 1996–97, a luxury tax was added to the baseball landscape, based on payroll. In this case, teams exceeding a certain threshold had to pay a "tax" to MLB, who divided it among teams that stayed under the payroll threshold. The Yankees always had to pay this tax and had to budget for it when they determined their player payroll for the year. Occasionally, another team or two had to contribute, but generally speaking, the luxury-tax rule was directed at the Yankees. Through 2011, they had paid over $200 million in luxury taxes, with the Red Sox next at approximately $18 million.

Yet it seemed to do little to hold back spending.

IN THE SECOND game of 1976, in Milwaukee, rookie Dave Pagan gave up a ninth-inning homer to the Brewers' Don Money. Poor Pagan, who was a frail-looking kid from tiny Nipawin, Saskatchewan, where his home phone number was 8. Billy Martin came storming out of the dugout to argue that time had been called. (He won the argument.) Pagan, however, thought Martin was coming at him after yielding the homer, and started to run away from the mound.

THE "NEW" YANKEE STADIUM opened on Thursday afternoon, April 15, 1976, an unusually hot April day. Toby Wright, the Yankee organist from 1965–66 and 1971–77, entertained the fans as they settled into comfortable new "Yankee blue" plastic seating. There were community activists outside the park demonstrating against what had soared into more than a $100 million renovation. (The Yankees responded by sending Jimmy Esposito and his ground crew to renovate some surrounding baseball diamonds and basketball courts, posting signs saying WE CARE.)

There was a ticket-takers labor action that forced the gates to be closed until well beyond the stated opening hour, but Gabe Paul resolved it with the union.

Steinbrenner personally created the guest list for on-field introductions, all guests bearing Yankee Stadium heroics on their résumés. Included were football stars from Notre Dame, Army, the Giants, and the Colts, along with boxing legend Joe Louis and baseball heroes including DiMaggio, Mantle, Berra, Martin, and Howard. Mrs. Ruth and Mrs. Gehrig were there. (Claire Ruth would die six months later; Eleanor Gehrig in 1983.) Bobby Richardson read the invocation. Bob Shawkey, who started the 1923 home opener, threw out the first pitch as Whitey Witt, the first Yankee hitter in '23, stood in the batter's box. Surrounding Shawkey as he did the honors were Jim Farley, Toots Shor, Pete Sheehy, and Mel Allen. The clubhouse was named for Sheehy that day.

Minnesota jumped out to a 4–0 lead as Dan Ford hit the first home run in the renovated park, but the Yankees rallied and won 11–4, with Dick Tidrow pitching five shutout innings for the win and Lyle earning a save. A crowd of 52,613 was on hand in a Yankee Stadium with luxury suites and no obstructed views. The capacity was listed at 54,028, and there were no seats in the left-field bleachers, situated beyond the bullpens—the area was thought to be too distant for seating. That would change in October when Steinbrenner's friends, developers Zachary and Larry Fisher, personally paid to install bleacher seating there.

Also new to Yankee Stadium was the area called Monument Park, where the monuments for Ruth, Gehrig, and Huggins were placed, with a growing number of plaques moved to the wall behind them. They would no longer be on the playing field.

The field itself was lowered eight feet so that the lower-deck box seats had better sight lines.

Fan reaction to the new ballpark was very positive, although in the coming years, owing perhaps to nostalgia, it came to be thought of as "not as good" as the original stadium, a perspective that seemed to take for granted amenities of the new park such as unobstructed views, escalators, and a video-replay board that put focus on fan entertainment. Baseball would no longer just open the gates and expect the game to be the whole show. (Early on, under Steinbrenner's orders, controversial replays would be shown, sometimes making the umpires look bad. The American League office quickly stopped the practice of replaying anything close.)

THE SEASON GOT off to a strong start for the Yankees, making the move to Billy Martin look both prophetic and wise. From the very first week, it looked as though the Yankees were a team on a mission. By winning five of their first six games, they took over first and never lost it. After so many years in the wilderness, it suddenly seemed easy.

The Boston rivalry again took center stage when Piniella barreled into Fisk, resulting in another brawl. Boston's Bill Lee dislocated his shoulder in the dustup, having been thrown to the ground by Graig Nettles. The rivalry hit a low point the next morning when Lee spoke of Martin and Steinbrenner as Nazis with a brownshirt mentality.

As good as things were going, Steinbrenner and Paul still sought improvement. On June 15, the trading deadline, they bought Vida Blue from Oakland; Finley was also selling Joe Rudi and Rollie Fingers to the Red Sox.

Blue, a longtime teammate of Hunter's, was one of the most electrifying pitchers in the league, and his purchase—for $1.5 million—would give the Yanks a rotation of Hunter, Blue, Ellis, and Figueroa. (Rudy May had been the fourth starter, but Martin wouldn't speak to him after he questioned being removed from a game.) That would have been quite formidable. But Kuhn wasn't having it. Injecting himself into the transactions, he called out Finley for holding a liquidation sale.

Finley argued that he was shedding salary on soon-to-be free agents so that he could sign new players next off-season. Yet Kuhn didn't trust that Finley would do that, and he blocked the sales. Finley sued and lost. Blue remained with the A's for the rest of the season, and the Yankees played on. Kuhn had prevailed and made sure that future deals included players, and not just cash.

On the same day as the ill-fated Blue purchase, the Yankees and Orioles completed a rare intradivisional ten-player deal, their biggest since the seventeen-player swap of 1954. The Yankees sent Scott McGregor, Rick Dempsey, and Tippy Martinez to the Orioles—all three would become long-term, popular Orioles—along with Rudy May and Dave Pagan.

The Yankees obtained two reliable starting pitchers, Ken Holtzman and Doyle Alexander, along with the veteran catcher Elrod Hendricks, pitcher Grant Jackson, and a minor leaguer. Holtzman, the winningest Jewish pitcher in history (174 victories, to Koufax's 165), never got along with Martin, but he did win nine games over the balance of the season, while Alexander went 10–5 in 19 starts.

On July 25, Chambliss hit a walk-off homer to beat Boston, and the fans wouldn't leave until he took a curtain call from the dugout and waved his helmet. This was believed to be the first "curtain call" by a player since Maris's 61st home run fifteen years earlier.

The Yanks were driven all year by their new captain, as Munson enjoyed a .302/17/105 season and was a force in each game. It earned him the league's MVP Award and more than justified the idea of making him captain. He was the first Yankee since Howard in 1963 to win MVP; Mickey Rivers finished third.

Nettles, with 32 home runs, won the league's home run title, the first Yankee since Maris in 1961 to accomplish the feat. At the final home game of the season, Sal Durante, who had caught Maris's 61st homer fifteen years earlier, threw out the first pitch from the location of his seat in the old stadium. Nettles, the number 9 on his back, took the throw standing in right field.

Although the Yankees were still associated with power—hence the perpetual use of "Bronx Bombers"—they hadn't led the league in home runs since that 1961 season of 240, and would not lead outright again until 2007: forty-six seasons! (They tied in 2004.)

With the combination of the new stadium and a championship-bound team, with Rivers proving to be a great table setter and enormously popular with young fans, with rookie Randolph making the All-Star team, with all the trades working out well and Billy Martin looking like the outstanding in-game leader that he was, the Yankees drew 2,012,048 fans in 1976, making them the first team in the American League to top two million since they had done it twenty-six years earlier.

All of Major League Baseball enjoyed the sudden renewed interest in the game, and many claimed the surge was directly tied to the thrilling 1975 World Series between Boston and Cincinnati. And while that may certainly have been true to a degree, there was no doubt that the return of the Yankees to pennant-winning baseball along with the new Yankee Stadium was also a big contributor. Baseball as an industry was always strongest when the Yankees were winning, filling ballparks on the road and attracting big television ratings.

Another cultural phenomenon was occurring that helped spike attendance. The presence of women at games was increasing substantially.

"The women's movement gave them permission to work, to not need to have an escort, to listen on the radio themselves and not be thought of as tomboys," explained Suzyn Waldman, who would give up an acting career to pursue baseball broadcasting.

Waldman would eventually become a pioneer in the broadcast field. She was the first woman to hold a full-time broadcasting position in Major League Baseball when she joined John Sterling in the booth in 2005. Steinbrenner saw her coming. "Waldman," he said, "one of these days, I'm going to make a statement about women in sports . . . You're *it*, and I hope you can take it!"

IN JULY, ABOUT three months before his contract with the Yankees was to expire, Pat Gillick was approached by Peter Bavasi, president of the expansion Toronto Blue Jays, about becoming his general manager. He knew it was a violation of tampering rules.

Gillick had been doing good work building the scouting and minor league departments, and he was focusing special attention on Latin America, which was free from the amateur draft.

Steinbrenner found out about Bavasi's overtures to Gillick when Pat began recruiting scouts, and called the head of the beer company Labatt, also the lead owners of the Blue Jays. He yelled, "You should fire Bavasi at once. He just tampered with the best young baseball mind in the game; he's trying to hire my brightest baseball person!"

Recalled Bavasi, "My guy says, 'Who is this young baseball genius Bavasi is trying to hire?' George screamed, 'Gillick! Pat Gillick!' My man says, 'Never heard of him. But I will tell you this—if Bavasi is trying to hire the best and brightest young baseball guy at the Yankees, we will not fire him. We're going to give him a raise and a bonus.'"

"George actually loved telling this story," continued Bavasi. "He was great to me after I was fired in Toronto, promoted me for league president, hired me as a consultant, invited us to Thanksgiving dinner at his home, and when I went to run the Indians, he opened doors for me and introduced me to all the right people."

Gillick took Elliot Wahle, his next-in-command, to Toronto. On that one, Steinbrenner was less than magnanimous. He threw Wahle out without even allowing him to clean out his office.

THE YANKEES CLINCHED their first Eastern Division title with almost two weeks left, plenty of time for Martin to prepare the team for its first appearance in a League Championship Series. The winning margin was ten and a half games. The Western opponent, also in their first LCS visit, was Kansas City.

After splitting the first four games in the best-of-five series, the two teams played for the pennant at Yankee Stadium on October 14. Figueroa, who led the staff with a 19–10 record, overcame a shaky start and held a 6–3 lead when Grant Jackson relieved him in the eighth. Figueroa left to a loving fan chant of "Ed-die, Ed-die, Ed-die." But Jackson yielded a crushing three-run homer to George Brett to tie the game 6–6, which is where it stood in the last of the ninth.

Mark Littell was on the mound to face Chambliss, who had enjoyed a monster playoff series. Chambliss then proceeded to belt Littell's first pitch over the right-field wall for a pennant-clinching, walk-off home run. The historic shot, which gave him a .524 average for the LCS, induced thousands of fans to storm the field, making his run around the bases such an adventure that all hope to touch home plate would have to be abandoned as he bolted for the dugout in a mad dash after touching third. The rules, which doubtless stated he needed to circle the bases, were joyously overlooked, although Chambliss later went out and touched the plate with the mob still on the field. This was hardly a walk-off homer; it was more of a run-for-your-life one. The Yankees were going to their thirtieth World Series. And for no one was it more special than for Roy White, who had been there since the Horace Clarke Era began in 1965. The wait was over.

The Yankees headed to Cincinnati the morning after the LCS win, having partied and celebrated through the night. The Reds could not be taken lightly: They were the Big Red Machine, one of the great teams of the twentieth century. As the Yankee team bus headed for Riverfront Stadium, Dock Ellis kept everyone amused, reading passages from his newly published autobiography, which told of his adventures against Cincinnati. (He'd been ejected from a game two years earlier for hitting the first three batters: Pete Rose, Joe Morgan, and Dan Driessen.)

Martin named Doyle Alexander to pitch game one, bypassing the well-rested Holtzman and bristling when asked to explain it. Mystery clouded the selection, and the Reds won the game 5–1 behind Don Gullett. A controversy developed during the game when the Reds objected to the Yankees using scouts with walkie-talkies in the press box to position players. Commissioner Kuhn ordered the practice halted.

Steinbrenner had been doing this for much of the season; it was certainly regularly done in football. One day in Chicago, he had Gene Michael posted in the press box for the assignment. Bill Veeck, no fan of Steinbrenner's, ordered Michael removed. He assigned him to a seat adjacent to the press box for the rest of that series, but artfully hired a clown, in full clown garb, to sit next to Michael as he did his job.

Michael had retired as a player earlier that season, released by Boston after never appearing in a game for them. I mentioned to Steinbrenner that Michael would be a good addition to our operations, and he told me to have him come in to see him. That began a long and distinguished career for Michael in a variety of positions as he became one of the most respected figures in the game.

Furious over the loss and the embarrassment over the walkie-talkies, Steinbrenner confined everyone to their rooms at the team's far-off motel that night, saying that "parties are not for losers." This included Gabe Paul, who disregarded the punishment.

Catfish Hunter pitched well in game two but lost 4–3 on a single by Tony Perez with two out in the ninth. Game three, on a cold night in a boisterous Yankee Stadium, saw the Reds beat Ellis 6–2 for a 3–0 lead, and the fourth and final game was a 7–2 thrashing as Johnny Bench belted two long home runs, including a three-run shot in the ninth to seal the win and send the Yankee fans home, much quieted.

Munson, still in MVP form, batted .529 with nine singles in the four games and took exception to a response from Reds manager Sparky Anderson in the postgame press conference, when Anderson said, "Ain't nobody can compare to Johnny Bench." Munson took it personally and railed against Anderson, leaving the room with bitterness. It well reflected the deflated spirit of the Yankees after such a shining season. Martin himself had been ejected in the final game after rolling a baseball toward the home-plate umpire in frustration. Bruce Froemming, umpiring at first, said, "What are you doing?" Martin replied, "It's none of your business," to which Froemming responded, "It's my business now—you're outta here," and sent Martin packing. He was the only Yankee to ever be tossed from a World Series game.

Steinbrenner summoned everyone to work early the next morning, saying the entire organization should be ashamed of what had just occurred, and made no secret of his desire to improve the team in 1977 with the addition of a big hitter in the middle of the lineup. Chambliss had hit just 17 home runs in the cleanup slot in '76.

There was no doubt that the man Steinbrenner most coveted was the premier free agent of the first free-agent class, Reggie Jackson.

Chapter Thirty-Three

W ITH THE DAWNING OF free agency, it was hard to ignore a shift in the way baseball was being covered by the media.

Coverage of the Yankees by their own beat reporters had generally been respectful and even obedient. Occasionally, like in the 1957 Copa brawl or, later, the Peterson-Kekich affair, there was too much to ignore. But as a rule, the writers who traveled, ate, and drank at the team's expense were practically members of the family and kept secrets nicely.

Following an example set by *Newsday* in the fifties, the *Times* prohibited its reporters from serving as official scorers or voting on awards and the Hall of Fame, feeling it a conflict of interest.

While Dick Young remained the symbol of a hard-hitting reporter, his influence waned when he jumped from the *News* to the *Post*, and he seemed to grow more wrapped up in feuding with television (sometimes blocking their shots by stepping in front of their cameras). He came to champion the owners' side on disputes.

Things changed dramatically in the mid-seventies. While our daily press notes and occasional press releases once formed the day's news agenda, reporters were now stepping out on their own to discover what the news was.

No one was more prominent in this regard than Murray Chass of the *Times*. But given the growing national influence of the paper, its respect in journalism circles, and its being the paper of choice by affluent season box holders, Chass's reporting took team coverage to important new levels.

I started covering the Yankees late in 1970. I loved being a reporter, not just a baseball reporter. And it was my good fortune that at the time I was covering the Yankees, two stories were presented to me that had it all—the growing importance of labor and free-agency, and the oversized personalities of the Yankee personnel. It was a reporter's dream.

From time to time Mr. Steinbrenner would stop talking to me, but then he knew you couldn't just ignore the *Times*. I wouldn't let him bully me, I was always there, and I was always trying to get his reactions, even if he wasn't returning my calls that day. While he was busy playing the *News* against the *Post*, promising them both exclusives in exchange for planting some story, I was forced to call other teams and developed a great network of contacts, especially agents. Eventually, he came to respect me, I think, and we found a way to live together.

Moss Klein [of the *Newark Star Ledger*] was in step with me in terms of hard-hitting coverage. Sometimes we'd just wink at each other as though to say, "I got something." And by day's end, we may have both had it—or we were on two separate stories of importance.

Relations with the press became an important dynamic. Steinbrenner learned how to use it, how to steal column inches away from the Mets, how to reward certain writers and punish others.

Coverage of the Yankees would never be the same.

THE PURSUIT OF Reggie Jackson would be different from that of Hunter, because now George Steinbrenner led the Yankees' pursuit—not Gabe Paul, not Clyde Kluttz, but the owner himself. And Reggie gave every indication that he wanted to be courted. If it took a Rolls-Royce to sweeten the deal, that would be okay with George.

Everyone saw New York as the perfect city for Jackson, who helped Oakland win five straight division championships and who had an ego that fit "the city that never sleeps." The pursuit took three weeks. The Montreal Expos, owned by Seagram's Edgar Bronfman, actually made the best offer: almost $5 million for five years. San Diego, owned by Ray Kroc of McDonald's, offered $3.4 million.

Reggie had lunch at the 21 Club with Steinbrenner and felt the power and lure of New York all around him. Afterward, they walked the streets of New York: fans calling out to them, urging Reggie to sign with the Yankees. Steinbrenner didn't get him that day—he made a low offer—but he got him a few days later, for $2.96 million over five years plus a Rolls-Royce. The Yankees had their cleanup hitter.

At his press conference at the Americana Hotel, Reggie said he would wear number 42 in honor of Jackie Robinson, then decided on 20 before spring training, and then switched to 44 because the number looked so good on the backs of Hank Aaron and Willie McCovey.

Jackson was one of the great power hitters in baseball history, but he could be streaky. He would never hit 30 home runs in two consecutive seasons over his twenty-one-season career. He was by no means a sure bet, and the Yankees were betting a lot on him. So looming was his presence, though, that he wound up with a Yankee cap on his Hall of Fame plaque, a retired number, and a Monument Park plaque despite only four good seasons in New York.

To the captain and MVP, Munson, he was a great addition. Not only did Munson encourage Steinbrenner to "go get the big guy," but he believed that he had an understanding with Steinbrenner that he would be the highest-paid player on the team no matter which free agents were signed (with the exception of Hunter), and that his contract would be adjusted accordingly. That didn't happen, and it became a matter of conflict between the owner and his captain.

As if to add to it, Reggie did an interview with a *Sport* magazine writer during his first spring training, in which he questioned Munson's leadership and extolled his own, stating, "I'm the straw that stirs the drink; Munson can only stir it bad."

"Maybe he was misquoted," suggested teammate Fran Healy.

"For six [expletive] pages?" answered Munson.

Jackson was far too media-savvy to have fallen into a trap, although he always claimed that the journalist, Robert Ward, led him astray. Jackson felt the story had been sensationalized, but it seemed clear to all that he did in fact utter those words.

The magazine didn't come out until the season was under way, but with the publication of that article, the stage was set for a year of enormous disharmony.

With nearly twenty-three teammates siding with Munson (and Healy trying to side with both), Jackson was an outcast in the Yankee clubhouse during his first season. The drama that was beginning to unfold would be chronicled almost three decades later in the book *Ladies and Gentlemen, the Bronx Is Burning* by Jonathan Mahler, and in an ESPN miniseries, *The Bronx Is Burning*.

Jackson's problem extended to Martin as well. Billy didn't feel he needed Jackson. Didn't want him, didn't like him. But Steinbrenner went out and got him, and Billy was stuck. Martin and Jackson could read each other well—they knew the situation. Billy's least marketable skill was hiding his feelings. Reggie's was hiding his ego. One could almost feel this was a collision course.

On June 18, Jackson appeared to have loafed on a short fly ball to right in a nationally televised game at Fenway Park. Martin took him out of the game on the spot, sending Paul Blair out in the midst of the inning. This resulted in a nasty confrontation in the Yankee dugout as Jackson called Martin an "old man," and Martin prepared for a fight. The coaches—Howard, Dick Howser, and Berra—had to intervene to keep the two from a barroom brawl right on network TV. It was a scene replayed over and over across the country. Berra held Martin in a bear hug. Nobody could hold Reggie, although some tried. He left the dugout and, wisely, the ballpark.

For a month, newspapers speculated that Jackson was going to be the cause of Martin being fired—that George would back his big investment and that Martin had embarrassed the franchise on national TV by going after him in the dugout. Reggie had days when he wanted out. Billy refused to bat him fourth in the lineup, which was why he was signed in the first place. Munson went to Steinbrenner and asked him to "get off Billy's back or fire him, but don't leave him twisting in the wind."

There was a lot of secondary "good" to all of this. The team was winning, the turnstiles were clicking, and the Yanks were dominating the sports pages.

Jackson wasn't the only addition to the '77 Yanks. As each team was allowed to sign two free agents, the Yanks first considered Bobby Grich but then signed Don Gullett, the Reds' best starter. They traded a discontented Dock Ellis to the Athletics for Mike Torrez. Just before opening day, they traded LaMarr Hoyt (an eventual Cy Young winner) for Bucky Dent, a "heartthrob" shortstop who would replace Fred Stanley in the regular lineup and provide good defense, if not much pop. Stanley, an unsung hero of the '76 championship, got a touching standing ovation when he was announced as "now playing shortstop" in the ninth inning on opening day.

"Looking at the likes of Bucky Dent didn't hurt," said Suzyn Waldman, explaining the increasing female attendance at games.

Munson enjoyed his third straight .300 average/100 RBI season, something no one had done in the American League since Al Rosen in 1952–54, nor in the majors since Bill White in 1962–64. And Munson did it with only 47 homers over the three years, a tribute to his clutch-hitting abilities.

The Yanks also signed Houston star Jim Wynn, who electrified the crowd on opening day with a titanic shot into the center-field "black" portion of the bleachers. It would prove to be one of the longest home runs hit in the remodeled Yankee Stadium, but it would be Wynn's only Yankee homer, and the last of his career. (Detroit's Juan Encarnacion off Ramiro Mendoza on July 24, 2001, and one by Barry Bonds off Ted Lilly into the upper deck in right during an interleague game on June 8, 2002, both measured about five hundred feet).

Ron Guidry broke into the starting rotation with a 16–7 record, including five shutouts. Few had seen this sort of ability in the lanky left-hander known as Gator. Just a year before, barely noticed on the team, he had been sent back to Syracuse for more seasoning, and told his wife, "Let's pack, we're going home." They were driving to Louisiana when Bonnie Guidry turned to her husband and said, "Is this what you really want?"

"I guess I needed a push, and Bonnie gave it to me," he said. He turned around and went to Syracuse, then finished the season with New York. It was a good thing Bonnie spoke up.

The pitching star of the '77 team was not one of the starters but Sparky Lyle, who had a 13–5 record in 72 appearances with 26 saves and a 2.17 ERA. So dominant was his wicked slider that he would win the Cy Young Award, the first Yankee to do it since Ford and the first relief pitcher to win it in AL history.

The '77 Yanks won 100 games and the division title, but Billy Martin looked much more like a man who had taken each of the 62 defeats as a sock in the face. Hidden behind dark glasses, losing weight, drinking excessively, he had been through hell and back.

A season that was filled with so much drama came to a head in the final game of the League Championship Series. Again it was the Yankees and the Royals. This time, Martin benched the slumping Jackson in the decisive fifth game. But Martin sent him up to pinch-hit in the eighth, and he delivered a base hit, scoring Randolph. The Yankees went on to score three in the ninth, Roy White scoring the winning run, and they won their thirty-first pennant with a 5–3 win. Lyle won twice, allowing one run in 9⅓ innings, while Rivers hit .391.

Nine days later, during a memorable Yankees-Dodgers game during-six World Series night in New York, Reginald Martinez Jackson hit three home runs on three pitches against Burt Hooton, Elias Sosa, and Charlie Hough. The one off Hough sailed into the black, seatless portion of the center-field bleachers, nearly five hundred feet away. It marked four consecutive homers on four swings, going back to game five. And it was five home runs in the Series, the first time that had ever been accomplished. With that one huge night that even got Munson smiling in the dugout, Reggie earned the nickname that would appear on his Hall of Fame plaque: "Mr. October."* The Yankees won their twenty-first world championship and their first in fifteen years. As champagne was poured and the game was recounted, thoughts went back to what this team had been through. It would be the only world championship of Martin's managing career, and it was a painful one.

MAYOR ABE BEAME, taking a cue from the '69 Mets, decided on a ticker-tape parade for the Yankees after the World Series, a joyous celebration through lower Manhattan that would be a first for the Yankees after so many championship years. There had been subdued welcome-home parades preceding the 1961 and 1962 seasons, but they lacked the spontaneous enthusiasm that something a day later could provide. Whitey Ford didn't even remember those earlier parades. So the '77 Yankees had their moment, perhaps on behalf of the twenty previous world championship Yankee clubs who never had the thrill of going through the "Canyon of Heroes." Joe DiMaggio joined them for the parade.

But perhaps the sweetest coda to the season was the raising of the pennant on opening day of '78. After twelve years of self-imposed exile, Roger Maris accepted George Steinbrenner's invitation to join Mantle and raise the '77 championship flag. The flag raising, a tradition that was discontin-

---

* The nickname actually grew from a sarcastic remark made by Munson during the ALCS when Martin sat the slumping Jackson. "Billy probably just doesn't realize Reggie is Mr. October," he said.

ued when the Yanks won in 2009,* was always emotional, but never more than on the day Maris was welcomed back, a fully recognized Yankee hero. He received a prolonged and thunderous ovation on this unannounced moment. In the early and mid-seventies, I had phoned him each year to invite him to Old-Timers' Day. He'd say, "Why should I come back to be booed?" I told him I really didn't think that was going to be the case; a lot of feelings had changed. But now Steinbrenner had personally asked him back, and he accepted.

He became an Old-Timers' Day regular, and in 1984 had his uniform retired and a plaque dedicated. He died a year later, a cancer victim at fifty-one, two years younger than Babe Ruth was when he died. His funeral, in two-degree weather in Fargo, North Dakota, drew Mantle, Ford, Boyer, and Skowron among the pallbearers, and was followed by a memorial service at St. Patrick's Cathedral, with former president Richard Nixon in attendance.

RICH "GOOSE" GOSSAGE was the most attractive free agent available after the 1977 season, and despite having the best relief pitcher in the game in Lyle, the Yankees went after him. Although he would come at a high cost, this effectively showed that the Yankees planned on regularly pursuing the top free agents, particularly if they could go younger in their pursuit of continuing success. Again it was Steinbrenner in pursuit, Gabe Paul having sold his interest in the team and returned to run the Indians. Al Rosen, who became a limited partner in 1974, succeeded Paul as team president, returning to baseball for the first time in a daily capacity since he retired as a player in 1956.

Gossage, just twenty-six, was already a six-year veteran and was coming off his only National League season, a 26-save, 11-win showing for the Pirates with a 1.61 ERA. He had 151 strikeouts in 133 innings. Big, strong, hard-throwing, all arms and legs with a high-effort delivery, he was a sure thing as long as he didn't get hurt. This was the beauty of playing the free-agent market as opposed to developing minor league talent. Even the top draft choices and the best triple-A players always came with the element of "What if he can't make it in the big leagues?"

---

* Not out of any lack of respect for tradition: The flagpoles in the new stadium were no longer easily accessible for such a ceremony.

Lyle was thirty-three and not very happy about this at all. "He went from Cy Young to Sayonara," quipped Nettles. And Lyle's reaction proved correct: Gossage became the principal reliever and had 27 saves in his first Yankee season, while Lyle had only nine.

Gossage signed for $2.8 million over six years, and it came to be considered one of the best free-agent signings in baseball history. Lyle's summer of discontent would be told in a bestselling book called *The Bronx Zoo*, whose name came to characterize the whole late-seventies era of Yankee baseball, when the team achieved success despite mountains of controversy. The title was conceived by Larry Freundlich, an editor at Crown; the idea was hatched by Billy Martin's agent, Doug Newton, and Peter Golenbock was the coauthor. The book spent twenty-nine weeks on the *New York Times* bestseller list, the bestselling baseball book in history until George Will's *Men at Work* in 1990.

Gossage did not get off to a good start. In spring training, Martin went to the mound to tell him to "drill" Texas infielder Billy Sample, whom Martin disliked. He used a racial epithet to describe Sample, and Gossage, with no history against Sample, refused to carry out the mission. Martin immediately saw a weakness in his new reliever that set him on his bad side. When the regular season began, Gossage wasn't lights-out as advertised. In April he blew two leads and lost three times. He didn't get his first save until May 3.

A moment to remember came at the home opener of '78, when all fans received free Reggie bars, a product arranged by Jackson's agent Matt Merola after Reggie said, "If I ever play in New York, they'd name a candy bar after me." (Baby Ruth candy bars were "not named" after the Babe, so that the manufacturer could avoid paying royalties, similar to the case of Yogi Bear and Yogi Berra. Merola made sure that this time the player controlled the product's profits.)

When Reggie homered on his first at-bat, the fans showered the field with their free candy bars, making for a long game delay while the groundskeepers went into cleanup mode.

The team wasn't playing like defending champions at all. Although the Yanks were now drawing huge and enthusiastic crowds, their performance was quickly slipping. By July 19 they had fallen to fourth place, fourteen games out of first, and the Red Sox looked as if they were going to run away with the division.

Only two starters were holding their own. Ed Figueroa was on his way to becoming the first native Puerto Rican to win 20, and Ron Guidry was having a career year. Gator was almost untouchable, with a hop to his fastball that completely defied his 160-pound physique. Never was the magic of his season more apparent than in a 4–0 win over the Angels in Yankee Stadium on June 17 when he struck out 18, breaking Bob Shawkey's fifty-nine-year-old club record of 15 and setting a league record for left-handers. On that day, as the strikeout total rose, and as broadcaster Phil Rizzuto first called him "Louisiana Lightning," the fans began to stand after two strikes, lending their enthusiasm for a third. The practice, born that afternoon, continues to this day.

Guidry won his first 13 decisions, breaking Atley Donald's club record of 12; ironic in that Donald was the scout who signed him.

Troubles between Martin and Jackson continued. On July 17, Martin ordered Reggie to sacrifice, something Jackson hadn't done in six years. After one pitch, Martin removed the bunt sign, but Reggie decided to continue bunting. He popped out.

After the game Martin read a statement: "Reggie Jackson is suspended without pay effective this moment."

Billy was in a deep depression; Jackson was getting to him. In June, AL president Lee MacPhail had actually suggested to Steinbrenner and Bill Veeck that the Yankees and White Sox trade managers—Martin for Bob Lemon. It was Veeck who turned it down, but he fired Lemon anyway on June 29.

Jackson's suspension was lifted on July 23 as the Yankees won their fifth straight. The media circus at his locker—and the presence of a dozen roses someone had sent—fueled Martin's disgust with the whole situation. He didn't put him in the lineup. After the game, drinking in the press room, he read what Jackson had told reporters: "I never considered what I did an act of defiance. I didn't think people would get so upset at what I did. I was surprised the way they had taken it." Martin handed it back to the reporter in disgust.

At O'Hare Airport, Martin took Murray Chass and Henry Hecht aside and acted out an imaginary conversation with Jackson: "We're winning without you. We don't need you coming in and making all those comments." Then he said, "If he doesn't shut his mouth, he won't play, and I don't care what George says. He can replace me right now if he doesn't like it."

Billy insisted all he was saying was on the record. He continued: "I let him drive his Rolls-Royce to Miami, Vero Beach, Fort Myers. I let him fly

home to Oakland. He's a born liar. The two of them [Jackson and Stein-
brenner] deserve each other. One's a born liar; the other's convicted."

When the team's commercial flight landed in Kansas City, Chass and
Hecht called Steinbrenner and read Martin's comments. He had crossed
the line by referring to Steinbrenner's Watergate-related conviction. Hecht
said that his speech were slurred. But all the reporters insisted on asking
Martin if his words were "on the record," and when told that he was quoted,
he "grinned broadly," according to Chass.

(At this time the Yankees flew partly commercial, partly charter. The
commercial flights often meant long delays at the ballpark or at the airport.
Delays did not work well for Martin or, occasionally, for players with too
much idle time. Eventually, teams flew almost exclusively charter, and usually without writers aboard.)

Al Rosen was now preparing to fly to Kansas City to confront Martin directly. In the meantime, he reached out to his old Cleveland teammate Bob
Lemon to see if he would be ready to take over. Lem and Rosen had known
each other for almost forty years.

Mickey Morabito, who succeeded me as the team's PR director (I resigned in early '77 with Joe Garagiola Jr., the team's in-house attorney), was
sent to bring Martin to Rosen's room. Morabito discovered that Martin was
preparing to go to the media-filled lobby to announce his retirement, but he
managed to head him off and summoned Rosen to Martin's suite.

"Tell George I didn't say those things," Billy said to Rosen. Wearing dark
glasses, he proceeded to the level above the lobby and, breaking into tears,
read his resignation statement. "I don't want to hurt this team's chances for
the pennant with this undue publicity. The team has a shot at the pennant
and I hope they win it. I owe it to my health and my mental well-being to re-
sign. At this time I'm also sorry about those things that were written about
George Steinbrenner. He does not deserve them, nor did I say them. I've had
my differences with George but we've been able to resolve them. I would like
to thank the Yankee management, the press, the news media, my coaches,
my players and most of all . . . the fans." With that he broke down, and Phil
Rizzuto led him away.

Billy was gone. The organization he loved, the organization that hurt
him so much when they traded him in '57, the only team he wanted to manage, his dream job—gone. The defending world champion manager had
self-destructed.

Third-base coach Dick Howser managed for one game, and then Lemon took over what appeared to be a doomed season.

For days, Steinbrenner fretted over what had happened. On the one hand, he had little choice but to dismiss Martin for insubordination. On the other hand, the fans loved Martin and rallied around him most when he was down. He was a very sympathetic figure.

Finally, he decided on a dramatic plan, one that he didn't even share with Rosen. He decided to sneak Martin back to the stadium on Saturday—Old-Timers' Day—and introduce him as Lemon's successor, effective in 1980, when Lemon would become general manager. Lem, in his fifth day as manager, wasn't in on this either, and he and Rosen were shocked as they stood side by side in Indian uniforms during the ceremonies.

So three years after his Old-Timers' Day hiring, Billy was squirreled into the stadium and hidden until the moment when Bob Sheppard stunned everyone in the house by reading the announcement about the changes. Billy would be back, Lemon would be "kicked upstairs," and Rosen would be left wondering how he'd fallen out of the loop. The active players, sitting in the dugout, looked anything but thrilled. Billy took his bows and left.

For days afterward, the media wanted to interview Martin. Morabito finally went to Steinbrenner to plead for a luncheon—anything—to meet their needs in a controlled environment.

Steinbrenner reluctantly agreed. "But if anything goes wrong, it's on your head," he told Morabito.

Something went wrong. Martin needed little prodding to start attacking Jackson all over again. The reporters couldn't wait to call Steinbrenner, read Martin's quotes, and get his reaction.

Steinbrenner confronted Morabito. "If this Reggie stuff gets in the paper tomorrow, you're fired," he told him. Mickey, knowing it would make the papers, stopped at the mail room, picked up some cartons, and headed back to his office to begin packing.

That night, the New York newspapers went on strike. There would be no coverage of Billy's remarks except in the suburban papers, and Steinbrenner didn't care about them. A miracle had saved Morabito's job.

Not only that: Without the pressure of the daily newspapers chronicling every controversy, the Yankees began to win. It may have been coincidental, but it was hard to ignore. By September 7, as the Yankees arrived in Boston for a four-game series, the Red Sox lead had slipped to four games. Lemon had brought calm to a talented team, and was also manipulating the bench very well. Rivers, Randolph, and Dent were injured and out of the lineup; Munson was playing hurt.

A procedure by team physician Dr. Maurice Cowan somehow brought Catfish Hunter back to health, and he won six straight. The Red Sox, while not in free fall, felt the Yankees breathing down their backs.

In what came to be called the Boston Massacre, the Yankees won all four games of the series, 15–3, 13–2, 7–0, and 7–4. The shutout by Guidry in the Saturday game made him 21–2.

"This is," said NBC broadcaster Tony Kubek, "the first time I've seen a first-place team chasing a second-place team."

On September 13 the Yankees moved into first, but the Red Sox wouldn't die. With one game left in the season for each team and the Yankees up by a game, Boston won and the Yankees lost. There would need to be a one-game playoff to decide the division, the first time in their history the Yankees needed to play a tiebreaker.

Earlier in the month, Rosen lost a coin toss at the American League office, meaning if a tiebreaker was necessary, it would be played in Fenway Park. Steinbrenner couldn't believe Rosen could lose a coin toss. As Rosen recounted later to Bill Madden for his Steinbrenner biography, Steinbrenner shouted, "What did you call?" Told it was heads, he screamed, "Heads! You [expletive] idiot! Everyone knows it comes up tails seventy percent of the time!"

As the Yanks were losing the season finale, Steinbrenner summoned traveling secretary Bill Kane to his darkened office and asked him about the flight to Boston. "Where's the plane?" he asked. "Newark," responded Kane, "same as all season."

"Newark! No good. Move it to LaGuardia," said the Boss.

Angry words led to Kane's quitting—or being fired—at that very moment. After calling on Gerry Murphy, a former traveling secretary now in the ticket office, to take over, cooler heads eventually prevailed. The team went to Boston from Newark, under Kane's watch.

Monday, October 2, a day game in sunny Fenway Park, found Guidry, 24–3, on three days' rest, taking on ex-teammate Mike Torrez, who had gone to the Red Sox as a free agent after winning the final game of the '77 World Series. It would be a watershed moment in the Yankee–Red Sox rivalry. A full house in historic Fenway Park; the greatest rivalry in sports; a last-minute game with a pennant on the line. And it delivered.

Boston held a 2–0 lead through six. In the top of the seventh, with Chambliss and White on, Dent, hitting ninth in the lineup, fouled a pitch off his foot, cracking his bat. In pain, he borrowed a Roy White model bat from on-deck hitter Mickey Rivers. On the next pitch, as Bill White described it from the broadcast booth: "Deep to left! Yastrzemski . . . will not get it! It's a home run! A three-run homer by Bucky Dent! And the Yankees now lead by a score of three to two!"

Dent had hit 22 home runs in his career to that point, four that season. It's interesting to recall Rosen's coin toss at this moment: Had the game been in Yankee Stadium, the ball might not have gone out. It might have been an Al Gionfriddo moment. Now Fenway fell silent as the most unlikely man in the Yankee lineup rounded the bases.

The Red Sox would still rally, Jackson would homer, and Gossage would save the game, aided by a "blind catch" in the impossible sunlight by Piniella in right. Yastrzemski popped out to Nettles to end it, a 5–4 Yankee win.

The win made Guidry 25–3, the best winning percentage (.893) by a 20-game winner in history. His 1.74 ERA was the lowest by a lefty since Koufax's 1.73 in 1966, and the second lowest by an American League left-hander in history, Dutch Leonard having had a 0.96 ERA in 1914. For the season, in which the league batted only .193 against him, Guidry fanned 248, breaking Jack Chesbro's 1904 team record, and threw nine shutouts, a team mark and the most for an American League left-hander since Ruth had nine for the Red Sox in 1916. He was the unanimous winner of the Cy Young Award, won the *Sporting News* Man of the Year and the Associated Press Male Athlete of the Year—but not the MVP, won by Jim Rice with twenty first-place votes to Guidry's eight.

The Yankee franchise, blessed as it was over the decades with elite hitters, never did possess a Young, a Mathewson, a Johnson, an Alexander, a Grove, a Feller, a Spahn, or a Koufax. But for one season, Guidry outdid them all.

He never approached this performance again, but he would remain a beloved figure in Yankee history and would ultimately have his number-49 uniform retired and a plaque in Monument Park. Without the intervention of his wife just two years earlier, it never would have happened.

The Yankees beat Kansas City for the third year in a row in the LCS, doing it in four games with Guidry winning the decider. Munson found previously undiscovered power in game three and belted a homer off Doug Bird that landed by the Babe Ruth monument, about 475 feet away. It was the Yanks' thirty-second pennant.

For the second year in a row, the Yankees faced the Dodgers in the World Series. Randolph, injured, was replaced by Brian Doyle at second base, who batted .438. Dent hit .417 and was the Series MVP as the Yankees claimed their twenty-second world championship in six games, with Hunter winning in the finale at Dodger Stadium and two more Series home runs from Jackson. Nettles's brilliant fielding at third was a highlight, as was a baserunning maneuver by Jackson, deflecting a throw with his right hip while running to second. Gossage was on the mound for the final out in the play-off game at Fenway, the pennant clincher against the Royals, and the world championship against the Dodgers.

It was an especially sweet triumph for Lemon, fired in midseason by the White Sox and now able to enjoy a wonderful coda to his Hall of Fame pitching career as a world champion manager.

It wasn't a happy time for Sparky Lyle, however. Lyle did not appear in the World Series at all, and his time as a Yankee came to a close on November 10, when he went to Texas in a deal that brought Dave Righetti to the Yankees.

Chapter Thirty-Four

WHEN THE PHONE RANG AT Joe Garagiola's Phoenix home ten days after the '78 World Series, it marked the beginning of a horrible stretch for the Yankees that found the joy of a hard-earned championship transformed to ongoing grief.

"Joe, it's Lem," said the Yankee manager to the onetime Yankee broadcaster. "It's the worst, Joe . . . my son Jerry's been killed in a car accident near you. Can you go to the hospital and be there for me until Jane and I can get there?"

Jerry Lemon was twenty-six, their youngest of three sons. To Lem, it rendered meaningless the great triumph of just weeks before. But few in baseball were as well liked as Bob Lemon, and the friendship and support of the baseball community held him up.

Spring training would go on—Tommy John and Luis Tiant were exciting new free-agent additions to this world championship club—but this was not a team that was going to run on all cylinders.

Tommy John, four years removed from the career-saving elbow surgery that would come to bear his name, was at this point a fifteen-year veteran with 169 victories. Few thought that he had eleven years and 119 more victories left, but he would go 21–9 and 22–9 in his first two Yankee seasons. He would win more games for the Yanks—91—than for any other team he played for.

Tiant, the first Cuban Yankee since Pedro Ramos, was an almost mythical figure in Boston, one of the most popular and emotional players in Red Sox history. Defecting to the Yanks was huge. But El Tiante, who was at least thirty-eight at the time, would repeat his 13–8 '78 season by going 13–8 again. These were the bright spots.*

Catfish Hunter, in the final year of his five-year deal, would have the deaths of his father and Clyde Kluttz to deal with as he wound down the clock with a very unproductive 2–9 showing.

Was Lemon's heart no longer in his assignment? Now fifty-eight, he had come at Al Rosen's request to hurriedly take over for Martin the year before. Now, his son's death was a tough one to get through. Some felt the listless play of the Yankees under his watch was because he was distracted. He never really said, and no one asked.

The old gang was beginning to leave. Tidrow was traded to the Cubs in May, having done a fine job as a starter and reliever over five seasons. He'd later go on to a long career as a player personnel executive with the Giants.

Elite pinch hitter Cliff Johnson had a foolish tussle with Gossage in April, causing Goose to injure his thumb and miss three months. Johnson was traded to the Indians, almost certainly as a punishment.

Ron Davis, 14–2 with nine saves, filled in as a closer, but settled back into the role of a setup man; he was one of the first to be identified as such. Davis was a good find, and his Yankee career might have gone longer than three years had he not made an unwise speech during a winter appearance in New England following the 1981 season in which he criticized interference by Steinbrenner. When someone faxed the local newspaper carrying his remarks to the Boss, Davis was gone, hustled off to the Minnesota Twins. (His son Ike would later play for the Mets.)

Mickey Rivers went to Texas, which brought back Oscar Gamble for a second tour of duty and ended all too soon a wonderful Yankee stay for Mick the Quick, whose drive and desire seemed to have waned. Perhaps being the subject of trade rumors for much of the season was the cause.

On June 18, with the Yanks 34–31, Steinbrenner decided to relieve Lemon of his managerial duties and bring back Martin a year early. This was viewed as a necessary move, done with more kindness than most managerial firings. Lemon, in uniform, even stood with Martin at the press conference. The American League quickly moved to allow Lemon to manage the

---

* Also: the playing of Frank Sinatra's version of "New York, New York" after Yankee victories, which began in the late seventies; Liza Minnelli's version played after losses.

All-Star team a month later, despite his dismissal. No one could say enough about Lemon, who remained on the Yankee payroll for the rest of his life.

Martin was back for Billy II, despite an off-season fight in Reno with sportswriter Ray Hager. Billy's scrappy nature, often alcohol-induced, had a certain appeal to Steinbrenner, who liked his managers feisty. This time he was taking on a floundering team with many question marks and a roster in transition. Reggie Jackson asked to be traded, but agreed to stay on. Al Rosen himself quit a few weeks later.

On June 26, Bobby Murcer returned to the Yankees after four and a half years in exile with the Giants and Cubs. Bobby, thirty-three, was not the player he had been when he left, but his popularity was as strong as ever, and he'd give the Yankees six more seasons of limited role-playing, largely as a DH. His return was especially welcomed by his pal Thurman Munson.

Munson, thirty-two, was also not the player he had been. Never having spent a day on the disabled list, he was banged and bruised and carried the wounds of a ten-year veteran who played his heart out each day at the toughest position. Now, his knees shot, and bothered by other ailments, he was playing first, the outfield, DH, and talking openly about wishing to go to Cleveland to be close to his family and his business interests. He would have frank talks with Steinbrenner, into whose office he'd traipse after batting practice to talk business. "Get something for me before I leave as a free agent," he'd say. But Steinbrenner didn't want to lose his captain, and most felt that in his heart, Munson didn't really want to leave either.

Although he was a wounded warrior, the affection that showered down on him from the stands didn't fade. The fans had really connected with Munson over the years. He grumbled to the press, talked about leaving town, but they loved his game and they accepted him as the fourth great Yankee catcher, following in the tradition of Dickey, Berra, and Howard. He certainly seemed to be on a path for the Hall of Fame, if he could build his lifetime stats with five or six more productive seasons.

Thurman had begun flying propeller-driven planes during spring training of 1978. A small executive airport bordered Fort Lauderdale Stadium, making flying lessons convenient during spring training. Few among the media or the fans knew that Munson was flying home to Canton after games while other players were simply driving to their homes in Bergen or Westchester counties. Occasionally, he might mention it in an interview—he wasn't trying to hide it—but he did so few interviews, it was generally not known.

Munson would go home, spend time with his wife and three children, and then return to Teterboro Airport the next day and drive to the stadium. He loved the adventure of flying. When it came time to renegotiate a new deal with the Yankees in '79, he had the "no flying" clause removed from his contract. Steinbrenner reluctantly took it out, feeling it would stop Munson from dwelling on going to the Indians. Martin was very concerned that Munson was flying with team permission. "Does George know you're flying?" he demanded.

In late July, Munson and Piniella slept at Murcer's Chicago apartment during a series with the White Sox. Bobby and Kay Murcer then drove Thurman to small Palwaukee Airport north of Chicago after the August 1 series finale, in which Thurman played first base. Munson left after midnight and flew home to Canton, where, on just a few hours' sleep, he had breakfast with his kids, lunch with his father-in-law, and prepared to discuss a street naming in his honor with city officials.

Finishing lunch early, he went to Akron-Canton Airport to check on his newest plane—a Cessna Citation jet. He had moved up to an executive jet just three weeks before. He took it to the West Coast, with Reggie Jackson as a passenger. Martin and Nettles also went up with him. Many of his teammates, including Murcer, refused to go.

At the airport, Munson bumped into his business partner and fellow flying enthusiast Jerry Anderson, along with an instructor he knew, David Hall. He was anxious to show off the new jet to them, and as they walked around, Thurman said, "Let me show you how it performs," and offered to take them up. They agreed.

This was a Thursday off-day, and Munson didn't have to be back to Yankee Stadium until the following night. It was a carefree, blissful day for Munson, resting his sore body, being with his family, showing off his jet. He was in a good place.

Munson, with his two passengers, made three successful take-offs and touch-and-go landings, then took off for a fourth, turning right instead of left at the air traffic controller's direction. So things were different. And errors were being made. Both Anderson and Hall could sense it. Now they were coming in toward the runway, too low and too fast, and they sensed an imminent crash. Thurman knew it too, but despite his errors, he reacted quickly enough to save them from a crash. He brought it down hard into an adjacent field facing the runway, and fought to slow it down as it moved at high speed across the acreage.

"My God," thought Anderson. "We're all going to survive a plane crash."

"You guys okay?" Thurman managed to say.

But suddenly, the left wing hit a tree stump and jolted the aircraft to a halt. The force of the jolt tore Thurman's seat from its running track. His shoulder harness hadn't been fastened, and that caused his body to thrust forward, breaking his neck.

Hall and Anderson were determined to get him out. But Munson was paralyzed and unable to assist with his own rescue. The plane burst into flames, and Anderson and Hall had to make the horrible decision to flee for their lives and leave Thurman behind. Munson died in the wreckage. He, with Ed Delahanty and Ray Chapman, was the most prominent baseball player to ever die midseason. He was the captain of the defending world champions, a former MVP, a Yankee hero. He left a wife and three children.

It was late in the afternoon when the phone rang in George Steinbrenner's Yankee Stadium office. He absorbed the tragic news from the airport manager. He summoned his staff.

In his grief, his shock, and, yes, his anger, he took full control, barking directions and instructions. Almost in one breath, he said, "Call Cardinal Cooke—we'll have a memorial service before the game tomorrow . . . I'll write something for the message board—it will alternate with his photo . . . get black armbands for the players' uniforms . . . we're retiring his number . . . we'll put a plaque in Monument Park . . . we'll retire his locker . . . we'll take the team to the funeral . . . the wives . . . [Larry] Wahl, [Gerry] Murphy, you get the next plane to Canton and do whatever needs to be done there, go go go . . . Butterfield,* who are we bringing up from the minors to catch?"

Each player was called individually—Steinbrenner took the stars, and general manager Cedric Tallis the balance of the roster. Each call was its own separate shock. Billy Martin had to be called in from a lake on which he was fishing and told the news.

The next night, before the game with the Orioles, the Yankees stood at their positions with home plate empty, a steady drizzle falling, Yankee Stadium turned into a cathedral as Cardinal Cooke officiated in a memorial service. Then they played the game. They played Saturday and Sunday too, going through the motions, lost in grief.

---

* Steinbrenner was speaking to Jack Butterfield, the team's vice president of player development and scouting, who would himself perish in a Paramus, New Jersey, auto accident three months later. His son Brian would later manage in the Yankee organization and coach in the major leagues.

On Monday, August 6, the day of the funeral, the team went to the Canton Civic Center, where Murcer and Piniella read eulogies. Against plan, they boarded their buses and followed the funeral cortege to the cemetery. "We're going to be with him to the end," Steinbrenner decided, facing a forfeit if they didn't make it back for that night's game with the Orioles. But they made it.

On the flight home, Martin told Murcer to just go home; he'd been through so much on this very long day. But Bobby, only a part-time player at this point, said, "Skip, I somehow feel I've got to play tonight, if you'll let me." He put him in the lineup.

Playing listlessly behind Guidry, the Yankees trailed 4–0 in the seventh when Murcer hit a three-run homer, his first since returning to the team— his first in Yankee Stadium since 1973. Had the game ended right there, it would have been dramatic enough. But there was more.

In the last of the ninth, southpaw Tippy Martinez, the former Yank, was on in relief. Ordinarily, Murcer would have been pinch-hit for at this point, with a righty sent to bat. But Martin went against the book, feeling the emotion of the moment. Runners were on second and third.

Martinez felt the emotion too. He had loved Munson. He was thinking about him all day, even now as he threw two breaking pitches to Murcer and quickly went 0–2.

Suddenly, Tippy had a flashback. It was Munson coming to the mound, years before, with Ron LeFlore of Detroit at bat, a thirty-game hitting streak on the line, a Yankee win assured. "Give him a chance to extend the streak," extolled Munson. "Give him one he can hit."

Martinez knew he owed that to Murcer right there. Not a batting-practice pitch, but a major league fastball. Not over the middle but on the black. Something Murcer could hit.

Bobby swung and lined a shot down the left-field line, driving in Dent and Randolph with the tying and winning runs. Pandemonium! As Bobby left first base and fell into the arms of Yogi Berra, tears running down his cheeks, Martinez quietly exited and looked quickly at the heavens, saying to himself, "That one was for you, Thurman."

It may have been the only time in history that the fans left Yankee Stadium in tears after a Yankee win. It was the end of what was perhaps the most emotional five-day run in the team's long history. But now, their captain was gone.

———————

THURMAN'S TRAGIC DEATH alone did not end the Yankees' run of three straight pennants. It just wasn't their year. They were in fourth place, fourteen games out when Thurman died, and there they finished, despite going 55–40 and winning their last eight straight under Martin. Catfish Hunter was saluted with a day as his career wound down, but his speech, referencing the loss of his father, Clyde Kluttz, and Thurman within months of each other, took the cheer out of the day and cast another sad punctuation mark on the tragic season. Hunter himself would later meet his own tragic end, contracting Lou Gehrig's disease in 1999 and then dying from a fall before the full effects took hold. He was fifty-three.

THE FIRST MAJOR departure of the off-season was Billy himself, again. On October 23, he got into a fight with marshmallow salesman Joe Cooper in a hotel bar in Bloomington, Minnesota, and was fired five days later. "The marshmallow man I hit was saying bad things about New York and the Yankees," said Martin.

"We just can't keep having this kind of thing happen every two months," said Steinbrenner.

Sitting with Billy on a flight once, I asked him how many fights he thought he had been in that never made the newspapers, which had covered maybe fifteen of them. He thought for a long time before responding, and then said, "Probably about ten for every one you read about."

Martin was hired by Finley to manage Oakland, where over the next three years he would develop "Billyball," featuring aggressive baserunning and one last effort in the modern game to have pitchers work complete games.

The day Martin was sacked, Steinbrenner named Dick Howser manager and Gene Michael general manager, with Tallis becoming executive vice president.

Howser, forty-two, had coached third from 1969–78, and in '79 coached at his alma mater, Florida State. Well respected in the game, he had been offered the job in '77 during Martin's meltdown over Jackson, but turned it down. Now the time was right. Here, Steinbrenner opted for the bright former infielder who was 43–16 with the Seminoles.

Michael swung into action at once. On November 1, he completed two big trades, sending pitchers Jim Beattie and Rick Anderson, outfielder Juan Beniquez, and catcher Jerry Narron to Seattle for outfielder Ruppert Jones and pitcher Jim Lewis, and five hours later he sent Chris Chambliss to the

Blue Jays for catcher Rick Cerone, who would effectively replace Munson. Jones would effectively replace Rivers in center.

"We felt this coming," said Audra Chambliss, Chris's wife. "It was sad to leave, but we knew changes were in the wind. Thurman's death really changed everything."

Not every former Yankee led a happy life after baseball. Anderson was the International League's Pitcher of the Year in '79, going 13–3 with 21 saves and a 1.63 ERA for Columbus, which had become the Yanks' triple-A farm team that year. An eight-year veteran of the Yankee system, he pitched one game for the Yanks at the end of the season, and then five with Seattle in 1980. In 1989, he was found dead, living in a truck trailer in a boatyard in Wilmington, California, weighing over four hundred pounds. Obesity leading to heart failure was listed as the cause of death. He was holding a letter requesting an autographed baseball card when he was found.

The Yankees also signed Bob Watson to play first and brought back free agent Rudy May as Michael continued his whirlwind month.

Roy White, his contract up, went to Japan to continue his career. He spent fifteen distinguished seasons with the Yankees. The only Yankees who had appeared in more games than him were Mantle, Gehrig, Berra, and Ruth. Roy would later have three coaching stints with the Yankees, although once, when asked, he spoke favorably about playing conditions in Japan, helping pitcher Bill Gullickson decide to play there. Steinbrenner considered it an act of betrayal and never opened the doors widely for him.

A big midseason lead in 1980 was reduced to just a half game in late August, but the Yankees won when they had to, and behind John's 22 wins, Guidry's 17, May's league-leading 2.47 ERA, and 33 saves from Gossage, they never lost first place and wound up winning 103 games to capture the AL East. Jackson had a big year with 41 homers to tie for the league lead, while also hitting a career-high .300 and driving in 111. Randolph hit .294 and Watson .307.

But the LCS was a different story. This time, the Royals swept the Yankees in three straight, with George Brett hitting two homers. A key play was Randolph getting thrown out trying to score from first, a move that Steinbrenner considered a bad call by third-base coach Mike Ferraro. Howser defended Ferraro against a Steinbrenner tirade to the media, saying, "I coached third base for ten years, and I would have done the same thing." Randolph himself said he was going home no matter what.

"When Cincinnati swept us in the Series in '76, I vowed to myself that

that would never happen again," said Steinbrenner. "Now this. I was never so disappointed. It's embarrassing as hell to me. It was even more embarrassing than Cincinnati."

Howser had enjoyed the managing, but not the second-guessing from above. On more than one occasion he was seen hanging up on a Steinbrenner phone call, saying, "I'm busy," without getting into a discussion. Despite the most wins by the team in seventeen years, Steinbrenner was going to let him go.

A group of invited media were summoned to Steinbrenner's office for a spread of sandwiches. Howser sat in a chair well removed from the big round table that served as Steinbrenner's desk. Also present was Gene Michael, who would be announced as the new manager. Howser was being relieved of his duties, couched as a resignation in order for him to pursue a not-to-be-missed real estate deal in Florida.

"The door was open for Dick to return," said the Boss, "but he chose to accept this business opportunity."

"Were you fired, Dick?" asked a columnist, evoking memories of Casey Stengel.

"I'm not going to comment on that," he said.

He did say, as advice to his successors, "Have a strong stomach and get a good contract."

The Howser departure was viewed poorly by most after returning the team to a first-place finish the year after losing Munson. Critics of the incident were vindicated when Howser was hired by the Royals in '81 and won the Royals' only World Series in 1985, beating St. Louis.

Just a year later, he came down with brain cancer and died in 1987 at fifty-one.

Two weeks before Christmas of 1980, Elston Howard died of myocarditis, a heart ailment. He was also fifty-one. The beloved Yankee was mourned at Riverside Church, with Reggie Jackson and Whitey Ford as the principal eulogists. The first black Yankee and the first black coach in the American League, Ellie would have his number 32 retired and would receive a plaque in Monument Park. The 1981 team wore black armbands in his honor. Although the heart ailment had curtailed his coaching career, Steinbrenner had made sure he remained on the payroll until his death, and that Arlene, his widow, was always an invited guest on special occasions. A MAN OF GREAT GENTLENESS AND DIGNITY, read his plaque.

Also present for the Howard funeral was the newest Yankee, the most coveted free agent in baseball, Dave Winfield. He had signed a ten-year contract with the Yankees just two days before. Winfield, a remarkably gifted athlete who had pro offers in football, basketball, and baseball, spent eight seasons with the Padres before playing out his option, never having spent a day in the minors. In '73, as a San Diego rookie, he came to old Yankee Stadium prior to a Padres night game at Shea and I walked him around the old ballpark before it was torn down. He was clearly a man who appreciated Yankee tradition.

His contract signing would have long-term ramifications. The deal called for $1.4 million a year for ten years, plus a onetime donation of $3 million to the Dave Winfield Foundation. His would be the first $1 million salary on the Yankees. But Winfield's agent, Al Frohman, insisted on a cost-of-living increase on an annual basis because of the length of the contract. Because of the compounded increases, the real value of the deal would be enormous by the standards of the time, with the base salary eventually nearly double the $1.4 million understanding. In fact, what seemed like a $13.4 million deal might in fact be $25 million, as Murray Chass pointed out in his *Times* column the day after the press conference.

Chass's embarrassing column made Steinbrenner appear to have been had, and while portions of the deal were quietly renegotiated downward, and a buyout after eight years was inserted, Steinbrenner would never come to warm to his new left fielder through their long association. The marriage was off to a difficult start and would never be fully repaired.

"George Steinbrenner, it seemed, had no tolerance for all these details—the fine print, the escalators, the guarantees," wrote Winfield in a memoir. "He wanted me at any cost, and it resulted in an incredible courtship, with George at his most charming. Flowers, Broadway shows, dinner at the 21 Club, chauffeured limousines. Even telegrams in the middle of the night . . . 'We want you in New York.' Somewhere, maybe on the way to Elaine's restaurant from Lincoln Center, George said that he liked me a lot because I had class and he could take me places he could never take Reggie. Fantastic! Not only would I play for him, we'd pal around together."

It would never be.

THE YANKEES WON their thirty-third pennant in 1981, a work-stoppage season that resulted in them playing only 107 games. Winfield, batting .294, delivered, while Jackson, at .237, struggled. Jerry Mumphrey played center and hit .307. There was the now-accepted turmoil along the way, but there they were to face the Dodgers, the traditional rival, which somehow added a touch of legitimacy to an otherwise illegitimate season.

What made it illegitimate was the midseason strike that lasted from June 12 until August 10, wiping out about a third of the season. The issue was compensation for lost free agents, but the overriding passion for taking such a drastic step was, as always, the owners' desire to weaken the union and the union's desire to remain strong and not give back hard-won rights and benefits. The institution of a compensation system that did not automatically penalize a team signing a player was the compromise that ultimately brought the bitter strike to a close.

There remained the problem of how to proceed, and MLB decided to create a "split season," in which standings would start anew after the strike, and then the first-place winners of each half would play each other.

Despite a month-long injury to Cerone (who cursed in Steinbrenner's face after taking criticism from the Boss in a clubhouse meeting) and ever-increasing jabs at Michael from Steinbrenner, the team found itself in first place when the strike shut down the industry.

Once play resumed and the playoff rules were set, the second "half" of the season—fifty-three games, actually—mattered little to a first-half winner, other than an extra home game in the postseason.

The Yanks finished sixth out of seven in the meaningless second half, but Michael wasn't there to lead the team in October. After demanding that he be left alone or be fired, Steinbrenner dismissed him on September 6, and called on the retired Lemon to come back and lead the team. Lem went 11–14 and now had charge of the postseason bunch, despite Michael having won the half that got them there.

Gossage was exceptional in relief in the best-of-five Division Series against second-half winner Milwaukee, saving all three wins, while Rookie of the Year Dave Righetti won twice and Tommy John once.

The Yanks faced Billy Martin's Oakland A's in the ALCS and swept them in three straight, a big blow being a surprise homer from Willie Randolph (two homers all season), which proved to be the winning run in the deciding game. Winfield hit just .154 in the series. At the victory party afterward, the always sarcastic Nettles got under the skin of the always sensitive Jackson, resulting in a skirmish between the two. The traditions of the Bronx Zoo lived on and sold a lot of newspapers.

The World Series would be the only one in which Jackson and Winfield were teammates. The Yanks won the first two games in Yankee Stadium, despite not having Mr. October in the lineup—he missed the first three games with a calf injury. Game three pitted Righetti against Fernando Valenzuela, and Fernando went the distance for a 5–4 win. It was the first of three losses for Yankee reliever George Frazier in the Series.

After losing the next two, Steinbrenner arrived for game six with his thumb in a cast. Claiming to have taken on two drunk Dodger fans in the team's hotel elevator ("One of them slugged me with a beer bottle; I hit him back and knocked out a couple of teeth," he told his PR man David Szen), the thumb was broken.

What really happened in the Hyatt Wilshire Hotel was never known, other than confirmation of the broken thumb. The two protagonists never emerged. Had the Boss punched a wall in frustration over three straight losses?

It was back to Yankee Stadium now, but it was not a pretty story. Winfield had one single and one RBI to show for the first five games, and when he went hitless in game six, it made him 1-for-22, .045, an embarrassing showing. In 1985, Steinbrenner would refer to Winfield, sarcastically, as "Mr. May."

While the Yankees were going down for the fourth straight time, while Tommy John was screaming at Lemon in sight of everyone for pulling him in the fifth inning for Frazier (John had allowed only one run), Steinbrenner was in his office penning an apology to the fans.

> I want to sincerely apologize to the people of New York and to the fans of the New York Yankees everywhere for the performance of the Yankee team in the World Series. I also want to assure you that we will be at work immediately to prepare for 1982. I want also to extend my congratulations to Peter O'Malley and the Dodger organization—and to my friend, Tom Lasorda, who managed a superb season, playoffs and a brilliant World Series.
>
> Sincerely, George M. Steinbrenner.

Few were impressed by the obvious knock on Lemon's managing, or by the apology. It didn't go over well at all. Jackson said, "You play hard and you lose sometimes. I'm not apologizing to anyone. I've given my best since I've been here. Why not just be a pro and say the Dodgers beat us? Why make excuses? Be a man: Stand up and say, 'Hey, I did my best, but some-one else was better."

The first order of business after the Series would be deciding whether to keep Jackson, whose five-year contract was now up. Reggie didn't expect to be re-signed.

And nobody imagined how long it would take for the next pennant.

Chapter Thirty-Five

WITH THE CLOSE OF THE 1981 World Series, the Yankees entered a bleak period of their history, one that would keep them out of postseason baseball for fourteen years. Not since their very beginnings—their first eighteen seasons—had they hit such a dry spell.

In the eighties the Yankees would produce more regular-season victories than any other team in baseball, yet they couldn't find their way into the play-offs. Steinbrenner was fond of speaking of his "baseball men," the front-office band of qualified minds who seemed to be overwhelmed by the one vote that really counted, that of the Boss.

The baseball men as 1982 approached included Tallis, Bill Bergesch, Bill Livesey, and Rosen's successor as team president, Lou Saban, the well-regarded football coach who had employed Steinbrenner as an assistant at Northwestern in the fifties. Good baseball men would follow, moving in and out of the front office over the next decade, unable to please Steinbrenner or to bask in a pennant: Murray Cook, Woody Woodward, Bob Quinn, Harding Peterson, Syd Thrift, even Lou Piniella.

The Jackson decision loomed large, and if there was anything telegraphing what was to come, it was when the Yankees traded for Ken Griffey Sr. on November 4. Griffey, a lifetime .307 hitter with Cincinnati's Big Red Machine, was slated to be the team's DH, which seemed to squeeze Jackson out of the picture.

The Yankees ultimately made no effort to re-sign Reggie, and he went to the California Angels on January 22.

Steinbrenner came to call this the worst decision he ever made. With the passage of time, he yearned for the excitement Reggie could provide and for the way he could carry the team when he was hot. But the '81 season had been a bust. Steinbrenner even forced Reggie to take a day-long physical in August, questioning whether he was healthy. Reggie called it "harassment."

As much as Steinbrenner loved the way Jackson could "put fannies in the seats," Reggie was high maintainance, and it was time to go. The relationship mellowed over the years, and he became a special advisor to the team beginning in 1996.

Graig Nettles was named captain for 1982, but that was about the only thing that seemed to last from the start to the finish of this most dysfunctional season.

The Yankees added a number of players who could best be described as ill-fitting. Speedy Dave Collins, inspired by George's love of Billyball, was supposed to be a table setter in the Mickey Rivers tradition. Instead he stole just 13 bases and batted .253. Doyle Alexander returned for a second tour of duty and went 1–7, forcing Steinbrenner to say, "I'm afraid that some of my players will get hurt playing defense behind him."

John Mayberry, Butch Hobson, Lee Mazzilli, Roy Smalley, and Butch Wynegar, once good fits elsewhere, were not so on this team. The addition of Smalley made Bucky Dent expendable, and he went in the Mazzilli trade.

Dave LaRoche, who threw a blooper pitch he called "La Lob," put his stamp on the term "Columbus Shuttle," going back and forth to pitch for the Yankees and the Clippers four times.

Tommy John, 10–10, was shipped to the Angels in late August. He had taken the Yankees to salary arbitration, something that didn't play well with the team, which had been very supportive the year before when his son Travis fell from a window and clung to life. He would return four years later for the final years of his career.

In a deal barely noticed, a prospect named Willie McGee was sent to St. Louis for pitcher Bob Sykes. McGee would win the National League MVP Award in 1985 and hit .295 over eighteen seasons with 352 stolen bases. Sykes won three minor league games in '82 and then was out of baseball for good.

By the time the year ended, the Yankees also packaged Fred McGriff with Collins in a trade to Toronto for pitcher Dale Murray and a minor leaguer. McGriff would go on to hit 493 home runs—equal to Lou Gehrig's total— over nineteen seasons.

Gossage, now one of the senior members of the team in only his fifth season, took to calling Steinbrenner "the Fat Man" and claiming that he "treats us like animals" and has "made being here unbearable." He'd be gone after the '83 campaign.

Dave Winfield, enjoying a 37-homer season, sued Steinbrenner during the summer over late payments to his foundation, a matter later settled, but not without lingering bad feelings. By July, Steinbrenner was already missing Jackson and lamenting, "Winfield can't carry a team the way Jackson did."

During Jackson's emotional return to the stadium in an Angels uniform, fans could be heard chanting "Steinbrenner sucks!" after Jackson homered off Guidry in the seventh to seal a 3–1 win. It was a rare moment in Yankee history when a visiting player was so welcomed.

The chant was an early example of a changing ballpark culture in which the use of obscenities (now far more extravagant than "sucks") began to be heard, and not only by a few drunken fans. The power of thirty thousand people or more joining together was enabling, even if they would never speak like that outside the park. A freedom to be heard with more than "We want a hit!" was now part of the ballpark experience, and it seemed to have its origins in the mid-seventies. Curtailing beer sales after seven innings, or banning it altogether in the bleachers, which was to come, didn't make much of a difference. Society was allowing more obscenities into common usage, just as it had embraced a greater use of contractions and slang. Ballparks were sort of the testing grounds, since they came complete with built-in enemies.

At the same time, the less offensive "wave" was being hatched as a fan-participatory event (generally believed to have started for baseball in Oakland during the Yankees-A's playoff series of 1981). It involved sections rising in sequence, arms extended on high, creating a distracting but visually interesting effect.

While fans were getting more profane, the Yankees chose 1979 to introduce an ill-fated mascot to roam the stands. Hardly the success of Mr. Met, the San Diego Chicken, or the Phillie Phanatic, "Dandy" lasted three unspectacular years before sailing into mascot heaven. He wound up confined to the upper deck, where rumor had it that he was once beaten into submission by fans who were not necessarily drinking.

Chaos in the dugout made '82 painful for Yankee fans who longed for the days when the team's stability echoed its onfield professionalism and success. The '82 team employed three managers, three batting coaches, and five pitching coaches. One of the batting coaches was Joe Pepitone, who hadn't been in baseball since 1973. Lemon, assured during the off-season that he would manage the full year, was fired after starting the season 6–8 and replaced by his predecessor, Gene Michael, who had been scouting. When Lemon was rehired in December of '81, Michael was announced as the manager in waiting, with a deal to lead the team from '83 to '85. As with Martin's 1979 return, the schedule was advanced. Michael's first game was the game in which Jackson returned as an Angel, provoking the fan outburst.

Lemon could have been more aggravated by yet another abrupt dismissal, but it wasn't his style. "It's like Shakespeare," he said. "He writes the plays, and we act them out."

When the Yanks lost a doubleheader on August 3 and Bob Sheppard announced that fans were invited back for free to a future game, Stick knew he too was done. He was replaced by scout Clyde King, a onetime Brooklyn Dodger pitcher who had become a favored advisor to Steinbrenner. He would go 29–33 down the stretch as the team finished a humbling fifth, 79–83, sixteen games out of first. This would be the first time since 1946 that the Yankees had three managers in a season, and King wouldn't make it to '83—not with rumors that Steinbrenner was again coveting Martin, who was finishing his third year in Oakland. Baseball seismologists, knowing of the attraction between Steinbrenner and Martin, felt it was only a matter of time.

The year had one shining moment whose true significance was still to come. In the top of the ninth on September 8, Sheppard proclaimed, "Your attention please, ladies and gentlemen . . . playing left field and batting third, number forty-six, Don Mattingly. Number forty-six."

Mattingly, the nineteenth-round draft pick in 1979, made his major league debut, replacing Griffey in the lineup. On October 1, facing Boston's Steve Crawford, the twenty-one-year-old singled to right in the eleventh inning for his first of 2,153 hits. Trainer Gene Monahan, as was his self-appointed task, retrieved the ball, inscribed it, and presented it to Mattingly after the game. Something good was in the wind.

BILLY MARTIN'S THIRD shot at managing the Yankees began with a press conference on January 11, 1983, at which time he said, "I think George and I have a better understanding of each other than we did before."

Whatever. The Martin hirings and firings were now material for Johnny

Carson. Ticket brochures—box seats $675 for full season, $9 per game—arrived with Billy pointing to the number 1 on his back, beckoning you to follow him to the top.

THE YANKEES BROUGHT in free agents Don Baylor, Steve Kemp, and Bob Shirley for '83, and added Omar Moreno to replace Mumphrey in center. Baylor would be the team's DH for three years, and he hit .303 with 21 homers in his first season in pinstripes.

A memorable moment came on George Steinbrenner's birthday—July 4—when Righetti, battling New York heat and a tough Red Sox lineup, pitched the Yankees' first no-hitter since Don Larsen, first regular-season one since Allie Reynolds, and first by a Yankee southpaw since George Moridge. He struck out the tough Wade Boggs for the final out.

On June 20, preparing to recall the emerging Mattingly (who was hitting .340 at Columbus), the Yankees released Bobby Murcer and assigned him to the broadcast booth. Murcer's playing time had been limited to DH and pinch-hitting roles. He had barely made the roster in 1981, then smashed an emotional opening day pinch-hit grand slam. But he played only 50 games that year, and went to spring training in '82 as a nonroster player. Six days before opening day, he signed a three-year contract. It may have been an emotional signing by Steinbrenner, as Bobby again played just 65 games with seven homers. He hadn't played the field since 1980.

In '83, he had just four hits in 22 at-bats before his career closed down. Although inexperienced as a broadcaster, he was well accepted by the fans. Bobby continued as a broadcaster for the rest of his life (missing one season), and then fell victim to brain cancer, which claimed him at sixty-two in 2008. His popularity never waned among Yankee fans, and his wireless mike broadcasts from the field on Old-Timers' Days added a special dimension to those telecasts.

As bizarre moments go, few in baseball history ever approached what came to be known as the Pine Tar Game.

On July 24, Yankee nemesis George Brett belted a ninth-inning Gossage fastball for a two-run homer to give the Royals a 5–4 lead. Egged on by Nettles (who in 1974 had been fined for used a bat plugged with Super Balls), and by coach Don Zimmer, who seldom missed anything, Martin made his way to plate umpire Tim McClelland contending that Brett's bat was illegal: Its application of pine tar was too high on the bat's handle, well into the sweet hitting surface.

As Brett sat quietly in the Royals dugout, savoring his big homer, Mc-Clelland placed the bat beside home plate to take a measurement of how high the pine tar reached. Satisfied that Martin was correct, he waved his right arm to indicate "out," reversing the homer.

Brett made a frenzied leap from the dugout in attack mode. He was barely contained from hitting McClelland. It may have been the most re-played baseball moment since videotape arrived. The game would end with the homer excised, a 4–3 Yankee win. Brett, his manager Dick Howser, his coach Rocky Colavito, and teammate Gaylord Perry (who tried to make off with the evidence but was stopped by a stadium guard), were all ejected.

The Royals appealed to the league office, where Lee MacPhail presided. Feeling the call was in accordance with the rules but not in the "spirit of the rules," MacPhail reversed the decision and ruled that the game needed to be continued from the point of the home run, with the Royals leading 5–4. MacPhail acknowledged that it was unlikely that the presence of pine tar would do much to assist in hitting a home run.

Steinbrenner's reaction: "If the Yankees lose the pennant by one game, I wouldn't want to be Lee MacPhail living in New York. Maybe he should go house hunting in Kansas City."

Bowie Kuhn acknowledged that he came very close to suspending Stein-brenner over the remark, knowing that passionate Yankee fans might well interpret this as a call to physically go after MacPhail. In one of his last acts as commissioner, he fined Steinbrenner $300,000.

The matter went to court, twice. A few fans sued, claiming a separate admission to the remaining outs was not legal. The remaining four outs—an oddity in baseball history by any standard—were played before 1,245 people on August 18. Martin treated it like a joke, playing Guidry in center and the left-handed Mattingly at second, as the Royals recorded their only out, and then the Yankees went down 1-2-3 in the ninth to lose the game.

In the press box, Yankee PR man Ken Nigro handed out cans of pine tar and T-shirts reading, I WAS THERE FOR THE PINE TAR GAME, which did not go over well with Steinbrenner. Nigro was also planning to testify about Stein-brenner's involvement in recruiting fans to sue the league in State Supreme Court over the admission plans in an effort to derail MacPhail's agenda.

Nigro's days were numbered. Not only that, but Steinbrenner didn't attend a "roast" for all the former PR men after the season because of Nigro's presence. We would have liked to have had him there.

In early August, with the Yankees in Toronto, Winfield found himself under arrest after striking and killing a seagull at Exhibition Stadium while throwing warm-ups between innings. The charge was eventually dismissed.

On the day of the Pine Tar conclusion, Yankee shortstop Andre Robertson was involved in an auto accident on the West Side Highway near the George Washington Bridge, which left his female passenger paralyzed and altered his up-and-coming career. By the following season, he ceded the position to Bobby Meacham.

Despite all of these distractions, plus the ongoing bickering between Martin and Steinbrenner, the Yankees stayed in contention in 1983 until they dropped three out of four to Baltimore in early September and wound up second, seven games back. They drew almost 2.3 million fans.

Martin's future hung in the balance. There was no one moment this time, no punch-out, no ill-tempered remarks. It was just another year of Billy turmoil, picking a fight with a female reporter, battling over his buddy Art Fowler's dismissal as pitching coach, suspended for kicking dirt on an umpire, rebuked for smashing a clubhouse urinal at Cleveland Stadium.

THE YANKEES TRADED their big first baseman Steve Balboni to open the position for Mattingly in '84, but who would write Mattingly's name on the lineup card remained a question. On December 16, George pulled the trigger. Billy was out, again. And Yogi Berra, who last managed the Yankees in 1964, was the new manager.

Yogi knew, of course, what he was getting into. He'd been a coach for eight years and had seen it all. But as he said, "It was offered, it was home, and I thought I could win," which were all good reasons to take the job. To sweeten it, the Yankees even traded to get infielder Dale Berra, Yogi's youngest son, from the Pirates. It would be the first case of a player being managed by his father since Connie Mack managed Earle Mack from 1910 to 1914.

While Dale Berra was not a top-flight player, Yogi was blessed with the blossoming of Mattingly, who was. Yankee fans quickly fell in love with "Donnie Baseball"—the low draft pick who had defied the odds and stayed in the organization, unlike so many of his minor league teammates.

At five foot eleven and 185 pounds, one didn't expect big power numbers from Mattingly, and yet his swing was perfectly tailored to Yankee Stadium. Of course, if it was that easy, a lot of 185-pound left-hand hitters would have solved it along the way.

Mattingly's work routine included monotonous hitting off a tee into a net before the game. He carried himself with a soft-spoken dignity that belied his youth—he only turned twenty-three that April. He managed to play his game relatively free of controversy throughout the tumultuous eighties and nineties, save for an occasional dispute over the length of his hair. He was a player's player, and many who would reach the majors in the 2000s, like Mark Teixeira, would confess to having had a Don Mattingly poster on their wall growing up. (A popular one was him dressed like a mobster, with the legend "Hit Man.")

Lou Piniella retired as a player on June 17 and became the team's hitting coach. "I learned to be a power hitter from Lou," Mattingly told the *Daily News*'s Bill Madden. "My body was starting to mature from weight lifting and Lou taught me about weight shifting and how to incorporate it into my swing. I started pulling the ball. At the same time, Yogi just let me play. He'd told me that spring I was gonna be his swing man, going back and forth from the outfield to first base, but he started me at first and wound up leaving me there."

He went on to win six Gold Gloves at first base, exhibiting a range and a sureness that led to a great old New York baseball debate: Who was better, the Mets' Keith Hernandez or the Yanks' Don Mattingly?

What developed over the next six All-Star seasons would evoke the names of the greatest Yankees in history and put Mattingly right beside them.

In '84, the Yankees said good-bye to their captain, Graig Nettles, the greatest third baseman in the team's history to that point. He would be the last Yankee to have played in the original Yankee Stadium, and his 250 homers were sixth on the club's all-time list. He was also the league's all-time home run hitter among third basemen with 319.

But he would be forty that summer and the Yankees had planned to platoon him with Toby Harrah if they kept him. He wasn't happy about that, and the Yankees weren't happy with a book he wrote, *Balls*, published during the off-season, which criticized Steinbrenner's meddling. He went to his hometown, San Diego, on March 30 in a trade that brought starting pitcher Dennis Rasmussen to the Yanks. There, Nettles joined Gossage, who had gone to the Padres as a free agent after six seasons with the Yanks, and together they would help San Diego to its first World Series appearance. Goose had little good to say about Steinbrenner as he departed, but mellowed over the years and came to view him with affection. He'd return for one more tour of duty in 1989.

Righetti, in a much-debated decision, replaced Gossage in the bullpen and proved to be a worthy successor, saving 31 games. "Rags" found himself a teammate of Mike "Pags" Pagliarulo, who came up from Columbus on July 7 to play third base after Harrah failed to hit.

In 1984 the Yanks also added free agent Phil Niekro, who signed a two-year contract after spending his entire career with the Braves. He used his knuckleball to win 32 games for the Yanks over two seasons, with the final win being the 300th of his career. He became the first player to win his 300th while wearing a Yankee uniform.* By then the Yanks had added his brother Joe, also a knuckleballer, to the staff.

At the same time, they lost pitcher Tim Belcher as compensation in the free-agent draft. Belcher was selected by Oakland, even though the Yankees drafted him after the list of protected players was due. Belcher would win 146 games in the majors, and hurled eight shutouts in 1989.

The Yanks got off horribly and were twenty games out of first at the All-Star break. Steinbrenner took out his frustrations by firing the bullpen coach, Jerry McNertney, for "failing to impose discipline" in the bullpen, and by hauling Yogi and his coaching staff into his office to berate them for the team's performance. Exasperated, Yogi could take the lecture no more and flung a pack of cigarettes across Steinbrenner's desk and into his chest. He essentially dared the Boss to fire him, and shouted, "This is your [expletive] team, you put this [expletive] team together, you make all the [expletive] moves around here, you get all the [expletive] players no one else wants!"

Yogi wasn't fired. In the second half of the season, they had the best record in the majors, 51–29, but it was too little, too late, as they finished third, seventeen games out, with just 1.8 million in home attendance, their first time under two million (except for the '81 strike season) since they moved into the renovated Yankee Stadium.

During this period, a whole new segment of fans began to follow base-

---

* Roger Clemens became the second in 2003.

ball through fantasy leagues, where individual player performance mattered and team performance didn't. Because enrollment in the leagues involved a generally modest fee, it was a form of gambling that greatly increased interest in baseball. Gambling's relationship with baseball quietly went back to the nineteenth century, the low point being the Black Sox scandal. For years, NO BETTING signs loomed large in ballparks, and when state-run lotteries became legal, the sports leagues fought to keep their games off-limits.

No team was more wagered on than the Yankees, according to Danny Sheridan, *USA Today*'s sports gambling expert. "The Yankees are THE brand name in all sports," he said. "With that notoriety, comes a loyal following of bettors—probably up to a million nationally for a big series. Bookmakers know baseball bettors will wager on them at any price, especially at home, and they raise their odds on them accordingly."

DON MATTINGLY EDGED Winfield for the batting title on the final day of the season, a thrilling race between teammates won by Mattingly's .343 to Winfield's .340, when Don went 4-for-5 on the final day. After Mattingly's fourth hit, Winfield grounded out, forcing Don at second. A pinch runner went in for Dave allowing the two of them to come off the field together. They came off to a terrific ovation, arm in arm.

But there were overtones to the batting race in '84. Disappointed though he was about losing (he had never won a batting title), Winfield was hurt by the boos he heard when he came to bat, compared to the cheers for Mattingly. "Stuff like that hurts, believe me," he wrote. "It stays with you." While it was easy to see the fans rooting for the smaller guy, the guy who came out of nowhere to challenge the $21 million man, to pretend there weren't racial overtones would be to ignore that race still mattered and that most fans at the game were white.

Mattingly was the first Yankee batting champion since Mantle's Triple-Crown season of 1956—twenty-eight years—and the first left-handed Yankee since Gehrig in 1937 to hit .340 or better. His 207 hits were the first of three straight 200-hit seasons, which hadn't been done since Gehrig, from 1930–32.

Chapter Thirty-Six

Rᴵᴄᴋᴇʏ Hᴇɴᴅᴇʀsᴏɴ ᴡᴀs ᴀ Christmas Day baby who threw left, batted right, and was acclaimed as the greatest leadoff hitter in the history of baseball. He hit more leadoff home runs, stole more bases,
scored more runs, and walked more times than anyone who ever played the
game.

When the Yankees traded for him on December 5, 1984, giving up five
promising players and cash, he had already topped 100 stolen bases three
times by age twenty-five. He was arguably the best player in baseball, and
certainly the most exciting. He took his place atop a Yankee lineup that also
included Mattingly, Winfield, Griffey, Baylor, and Randolph. This was a good
team.

But all of these blessings wouldn't get Yogi into May. Despite promising
to trust him, Steinbrenner fired the Yankee icon when the team started
6–10, even though Mattingly, Winfield, and Henderson were all hurting.

GM Clyde King sought out Yogi in the cramped visiting manager's office
at Comiskey Park. He closed the door and delivered the news. Yogi had
been fired twice before, but at 6–10 in April? With his three best hitters
hurt?

The players reacted with a fury. Baylor threw over a garbage can. Curses
were hurled at the absent owner.

As for Yogi, he was a baseball lifer, and he knew how the game worked.
What really got him was the way in which it was done. This, to him, called
for a dismissal by the owner, not by King.

Yogi went on the first bus to the airport with the team, sitting up front as managers do. It took two buses to travel this party. This was the same route taken when Phil Linz played his harmonica twenty-one years before. Because Yogi would not be getting on the plane with the team and going on to Texas, the bus driver was instructed by Bill Kane to stop first at the passenger terminal before proceeding to the tarmac, where the players would get right off and onto the waiting charter.

At the passenger terminal, Yogi rose, collected his bags, and began to depart. Suddenly, hands began clapping—an ovation in the bus for the departing skipper, a beloved figure in baseball history. And, yes, the ovation, heard in the second bus, prompted the ovation to continue there. Dale Berra was crying in the back of the first bus. That was his dad.

The two buses circled around to go the tarmac. Players could see the lonely, unmistakable figure of Yogi Berra, alone on the sidewalk, entering the terminal to go home.

This one really hurt Berra, and this proud man decided that as much as he bled Yankee blue, he would never again return to Yankee Stadium so long as George Steinbrenner owned the team. He was first a man of principle, and this defied his principles.

He occasionally cheated and snuck back to the stadium to see Pete Sheehy, maybe to collect something for a charity auction, or just feel the presence of Yankee Stadium. But he never went back when Steinbrenner was there.

His New Jersey neighbor John McMullen, once a limited partner in the Yankees ("There is nothing as limited as being a limited partner of George Steinbrenner," he said), now owned the Houston Astros. He reached out and offered Yogi a coaching job with the Astros, and Yogi took it. The Astros won their first division title in his first season. He stayed until 1989, when he finally retired from full-time baseball work.

In 1998, the Yogi Berra Museum and Learning Center opened at Montclair State University, and it provided Yogi with a destination to talk baseball, meet fans, and feel honored and appreciated. It was just a short drive from the fork in the road that led to Yogi's home. As with many things in Yogi's life, the museum's success exceeded expectations.

And it was there, in 1999, fourteen years after his firing, that George Steinbrenner came to see him and to apologize. Broadcaster Suzyn Waldman brokered the deal. Yogi's family was encouraging him to accept the apology so that his grandchildren could see him get cheered at Yankee Stadium.

Steinbrenner arrived a little later than announced ("You're late," was the first thing Yogi said), but clearly everyone was ready to bury the hatchet.

The two, along with Carmen Berra, retreated into Dave Kaplan's museum director's office. Steinbrenner began by saying, "I made a big mistake," and Yogi interrupted him to say, "Oh, I've made mistakes too." By acknowledging that an apology was due and accepted, but by responding as he did, Yogi's wisdom had won the day. He put the Boss at ease in a most unusual situation for a man of his power. From then on, Yogi would be a fixture at special events, in spring training, and whenever he felt like taking in a game.

"I never saw Mr. Steinbrenner happier than on the drive back to the stadium after that meeting," said his media-relations director Rick Cerrone.

YOGI'S SUCCESSOR WAS Billy Martin, back for his fourth turn as manager. "George and I have the greatest relationship I've ever had with him," he said. The media, and most fans, let out a collective sigh, although to some he remained one of the top in-game managers in baseball.

One thing that Billy had this time was Henderson, who had thrived under him in Oakland. And Rickey delivered, scoring 146 runs, belting 24 homers, and stealing 80 bases, breaking Fritz Maisel's seventy-one-year-old club record. He was only thrown out 10 times. His run-scoring prowess was amazing. If he was on third, he would take a lead, almost willing home plate into his pocket. Henderson on third always felt like a sure run, and he'd often get there on a walk and a couple of steals. His runs-scored total was the most in the league since Ted Williams in 1950, and the most by a Yankee since DiMaggio in '37. He became the first player in AL history with 20 homers and 50 steals.

Martin also had Bobby Meacham and Dale Berra, who made the blooper reels for '85 when both were tagged out at home by Carlton Fisk on a single play. It made them look bad, but it turned out that Lou Gehrig and Dixie Walker, Yankee teammates in 1933, had done the same thing. It would have made the play less painful and more comical had it been known at the time.

A SAD NOTE in the summer of '85 was the death of Pete Sheehy at seventy-five. Pete suffered a heart attack, and his passing broke a link that went to the very origins of the team, as Pete had come aboard in 1927 to assist Pop Logan in the clubhouse, and Logan had gone back to the first season, 1903. Pete was Yankee history, and his funeral, at a small church in New Jersey, drew DiMaggio, Martin, Berra, Michael, Bobby Brown, McDougald, Roy White, Guidry, Mattingly, Righetti, Baylor, and a large contingent of front-office people and former employees. Steinbrenner sat quietly in the back row.

"I've known the man for thirty-five years and today was the first time I've met his wife," said Martin, one of the eulogists.

Knowing of Big Pete's secrecy with matters involving players, I waited a few seasons to gain his trust before I attempted to draw him out in conversation. One day in the early seventies, I finally said, "Pete, tell me about the Babe."

He was silent for a few moments, and then said, "He never flushed the toilet."

The Yankees wore black armbands on their sleeves for the remainder of the season after Pete died.

With his passing, his longtime assistant Nick Priore took charge of the Yankee clubhouse, with Rob Cucuzza succeeding him in 1998. Cucuzza's father, Lou Sr., had worked the visiting clubhouse since 1977, with Lou Jr. running it after starting as a batboy in 1979.

IN 1985, DON MATTINGLY won the league's MVP Award, the first Yankee to do so since Munson. He drove in 145 runs, the most by a Yankee since DiMaggio's 155 in 1948. He reached his peak in home runs with 35.

The Yanks played great ball throughout the summer, going 38–18 in July and August and scrambling into a good pennant race, with an eleven-game winning streak carrying them into September. Ron Guidry was rebounding from 10–11 to a 22-win season, while Righetti was on his way to 29 saves. By September 12, they had moved to within one and a half games of division-leading Toronto. But suddenly they lost eight straight, including three to the Jays, and by September 22 were six and a half out with only fourteen games left. And as the losing streak unfolded, Martin seemed to melt down with it.

The streak followed a dressing-down by Steinbrenner. "This is a test of Yankee heart and Yankee pride!" he said in the clubhouse, shortly after a confrontation with player-rep Winfield over distribution of material urging the players to support a drug-testing plan proposed by Commissioner Peter Ueberroth.

During the streak, the Yanks blew a 5–3 lead to the Indians when reliever Brian Fisher allowed six runs in the ninth. Martin blamed the game on third-string catcher Juan Espino's pitch calling.

In another loss, Martin ordered lefty-hitting Pagliarulo to bat right-handed. Pags struck out looking. Even he wondered what was going on.

Then there was the time Martin scratched Ed Whitson from his start, referring to him as "Whatchamacallit" to the press and claiming he had a sore arm. Whitson knew nothing about this.

Whitson had signed as a free agent with the Yanks after a 14–8 record with San Diego in '84. A seven-year veteran, the six-foot-three right-hander met all the Yankees' scouting requirements to move into the rotation. But he started out 1–6 with a 6.23 ERA after 11 starts, and the patience of Yankee fans was never their strong suit. Although he would go 9–2 from that point with two shutouts, he'd lost Martin's confidence. He would come to be the first name recited when people began to talk about the "New York factor," the supposed difficulty of transitioning to New York after pitching in other cities. It became a new gauge of mental toughness for pitchers—something that had previously been unidentified during the years of Giants-Dodgers-Yankees. Suddenly, even if the players were Hall of Fame–bound like Randy Johnson, or just successful elsewhere like Kenny Rogers, Terry Mulholland, Jack McDowell, or Javy Vazquez, the question "Can he pitch in New York?" became part of the dialogue.

By the following year, it was decided that Whitson would only pitch in road games. It had gotten that bad.

In loss number eight, in Baltimore, Martin forgot that rubbing his nose was actually a sign for a pitchout. He did it twice. Rich Bordi, pitching instead of Whitson, threw two pitchouts and wound up walking Lee Lacy before Cal Ripken delivered a game-winning single.

That night in the lounge of the Cross Keys Inn, where the Yankees were staying, Martin got into a verbal fight with two honeymooning young couples, apparently telling one that "your wife has a potbelly." Martin denied this, claiming he had said she had a "fat ass." Some shoving ensued, but when Billy suggested taking the fight outside, his opponent failed to show.

Sometime after midnight on Saturday night, back in the Cross Keys lounge, Whitson was engaged in an argument with another patron. Martin and Dale Berra went to his aid, at which point Whitson turned on Martin and they tumbled to the floor and had to be separated by other players. Martin questioned Whitson's claim that he had "sucker-punched" him, and suggested that Whitson couldn't "hold his liquor."

Whitson continued to scream at Martin, and Martin went back toward him. Players were holding Whitson back, but he managed to kick Martin in the groin. Said Billy, "Okay, now I'm gonna kill you, now you did it."

Round three continued outside, with Whitson, now unrestrained, rushing at Martin. The two crashed to the pavement, punching away. "You've tried to bury me here; you're trying to ruin me," shouted Whitson.

Whitson was sent home the following morning; Martin went off to the hospital with a broken right arm. Whitson, thirty, was a well-conditioned professional athlete. He should have had the sense to walk away. Billy, fifty-seven, was as thin as ever at 165 pounds, and too old for this stuff. Yet Billy could look in the mirror and see the same guy who had fought Clint Courtney almost forty years before. There was no gray hair, no potbelly. A challenge was a challenge. And his drinking never abated.

Whitson would pitch just once more that season, in a Yankee win at Toronto, which put them two out with two games to play. But they lost 5–1 the next day, officially knocking them out of the playoffs. Phil Niekro won his 300th on the season's meaningless final day. The Yanks wound up with 97 wins, and finished two out.

On October 27, the morning of the seventh game of the World Series between Kansas City and St. Louis, Billy was fired a fourth time. This one was announced by conference call from the Bronx to reporters in Kansas City. His replacement would be hitting instructor Lou Piniella, who had never managed before. Steinbrenner did not take part in the call; Clyde King made the announcement.

PINIELLA HAD LONG been a favorite of Steinbrenner's. A Tampa neighbor with a winning personality and a drive to win, he would ultimately go on to win more than 1,800 games as a manager, the fourteenth-best total in history.

Once, as a player, Lou, among others, had missed a photo shoot that Steinbrenner had arranged. Threatening retaliation, Steinbrenner went down the list of offenders one by one, citing, "no more free tickets," "no more favors," as the names appeared. Finally, getting to Piniella, he said, "Oh don't worry. I'm gonna *really* [expletive] him! I'm gonna make him the manager!"

The time had come. Being a favorite son had its disadvantages. He got a three-year contract.

But despite his expressions of confidence in Piniella, Steinbrenner kept

Martin as a close advisor in '86. The team came out of spring training with its pitching staff in ruins—new "ace" Britt Burns had a damaged hip and would never pitch for the team; Phil Niekro was released. Guidry had a horrible 9–12 season and the team never did settle on a shortstop or a catcher. Steinbrenner continued to complain about Winfield, both his performance and his foundation. Rasmussen, who Martin said was "soft," would be the team's only double-digit winner, going 18–6, while Righetti saved 46 games, a major league record.

Newcomer Mike Easler hit .302, and Henderson bettered his '85 performance by stealing 87 bases and hitting 28 homers, although his batting average dropped more than fifty points to .263. Pagliarulo added 28 home runs of his own.

But it was again Mattingly who was the team's best player, leading the majors with 238 hits, breaking Earle Combs's team record of 231 set in 1927. His 388 total bases were the most by a Yankee since DiMaggio in '37. His 53 doubles broke Gehrig's team record of 52, also set in '27. He lost the batting title to Wade Boggs .357 to .352, when Boggs sat out the last weekend with a sore hamstring and Mattingly went 8-for-29 in pursuit.

The MVP Award went to Roger Clemens of the Red Sox, who got nineteen first-place votes to Mattingly's five, a rare example of a pitcher winning the award over a position player. (Jim Rice had won the award over Guidry in 1978.)

The Yankees were just three and a half behind Boston on August 13, but proceeded to lose thirteen of their next twenty-one to blow their chance at a title, and in the end finished second with a 90–72 mark, a decent showing for a rookie manager. Unfortunately, the disappointment at losing out to the Red Sox was magnified by the Mets winning the pennant and then a memorable World Series against Boston. What had looked like a possible subway series in August (T-shirts were sold!) had faded.

The Yankees went to spring training in '87 with Piniella as manager and Harvey Greene as PR director—the first time since 1974–75 that the same twosome (in that case, Virdon and me) had returned. But it was hardly a sign of new stability on the team. The season featured a ten-game winning streak in April, and first place from May 12 to August 6 (save for a couple of days), but crashed with the comings and goings of forty-eight different players, and with Henderson spending fifty-five days on the disabled list amid accusations that the injuries weren't real.

The Henderson drama was central; the team could hardly lose their table-setting superstar for a third of the season and pretend they could cover it.

There was no question that Henderson missed Billy Martin, and Piniella was not always sure that his left fielder was giving it his all. When Rickey went on the disabled list for a second time over what he called "bad hammys" (hamstring muscles), Piniella suggested to several sources that he was "jaking it."

Steinbrenner finally intervened in the Henderson matter, issuing a long, rambling statement on the state of the team that exonerated Henderson, while undermining Piniella by revealing that he wanted Rickey traded.

The statement also criticized Piniella for not being available for a pre-arranged phone call. "I don't know of too many guys—even sportswriters—who, if their boss told them to be available for a call at a certain time, wouldn't be there!" the statement said. Many felt the statement essentially brought a close to the season, if not to Lou's tenure.

There was another record-breaking season from Mattingly (six grand slams, the only six of his career, and eight consecutive games with at least one homer). Obtaining Steve Trout from the Cubs ("I just won you the pennant," said Steinbrenner to Piniella at the time) resulted in not a single win, as Trout took his place beside Whitson as failures. Only Rick Rhoden (16–10) and the returning Tommy John (13–6) cracked double figures in victories. Pagliarulo led the team with 32 homers, and the Yanks finished a disappointing fourth.

The disappointments in 1987 were many. The "special relationship" between Steinbrenner and Piniella was tarnished. And Mattingly, despite the home run records and a .327 average, began to show signs of a back problem that would ultimately reduce him from one of the best players in baseball to just a good player.

"It's something that was there from the time I was a kid, and it's always gonna be there," Mattingly told Bill Madden. "When it first flared up in '87, it was a spasm. The funny thing was, right after that I went on that home run streak."

Mattingly missed eighteen games early in the year because of the back. He hit 30 homers in '87, but never hit more than 23 again. He would have two decent years in '88 and '89, but less than stellar by the standard he had set for himself. Starting in 1990, he put up fairly ordinary stats—just 58 homers in his final six seasons, and no more 100-RBI campaigns. His fielding remained superlative, and he would always be Donnie Baseball, but he would never again be the Mattingly of 1984–87.

Piniella was fired after the season and moved up to general manager to replace poor Woody Woodward (who'd failed at his main assignment: to trade Winfield).

Piniella's successor, sure to please Henderson, was Martin again. Billy V was anointed on October 19, an off day during the World Series, and also "Black Monday," the day the stock market plunged 508 points. After this, the Commissioner's Office ruled that there could be no major team announcements to interfere with the World Series.

The Yankees drew 2.4 million fans in '87 despite all the angst, the third-highest total in team history. The Mets, however, coming off their '86 championship, became the first New York team in history to top three million.* This was an unacceptable development for the Yanks, but the Mets would continue to outdraw them until 1994.

Even if the Mets were leading at the gate, in TV and radio ratings, and in revenues, a gasp went up throughout the industry when the Yankees signed a twelve-year cable-television deal in 1988 that drove a huge wedge between them and all the other teams. There was a buyout clause in the Yankees' SportsChannel deal that would enable them to open the television rights to the marketplace, and they exercised it. (They made a $50 million radio-rights deal in 1987 with WABC, the year the majority of telecasts moved to cable.)

The Yankees were in the fortunate position of being courted by three wealthy entities: Cablevision's SportsChannel (owned by HBO founder Charles Dolan), Madison Square Garden Network (owned by Paramount Entertainment, run by Bob Gutkowski), and their longtime over-the-air broadcaster, Tribune Company's WPIX (which, under its president Lev Pope, had once nearly bought the team, only to have Tribune nix the deal—Tribune later bought the Cubs).

MSG Network, desperate to have summer programming, won, bidding $493.5 million. This had a seismic effect on the Yankees' future: an influx of revenue that dwarfed everyone else's and assured their ability to sign top stars. It happened at a time when the Mets "owned the town" but were

---

* The Dodgers, by then a Los Angeles team, were the first to cross the threshold in 1978.

locked into a long-term deal with SportsChannel. It had been considered lucrative when they signed it, but by the time the Mets' deal expired, MSG Network had the Yankees, and three entities to bid up the cost weren't there.

The Yankees weren't the first New York team to embrace cable: MSG Network first provided home games of the Knicks and Rangers in the seventies, a novelty for the New York area that helped create the cable market. Yankee home games, of course, had long been televised. But the arrival of SportsChannel put every Yankee game on TV. In the eighties, the increasing number of games migrating from "free TV"—WPIX was down to forty games from as many as 140 in the late fifties—and the slow rate at which New York's outer boroughs (including the Bronx) were being wired for cable made this a polarizing issue. For the first time, a new medium (cable) was creating a situation in which fewer people could watch or listen to Yankee games.

The Yankees added free agent Jack Clark in 1988 after a stellar career in the National League, Clark responded by hitting just .242—with a team-leading 27 homers—and he was traded to San Diego right after the season. Another 1988 transaction was dealing outfielder Jay Buhner to Seattle for DH Ken Phelps. Buhner would go on to become a terrific player and nearly a cult figure in Mariners history; Phelps was a bust and the trade became grist for a joke on *Seinfeld*, which never missed an opportunity to parody Steinbrenner.

As for Billy V, a dangerous trip to Lace, a Dallas strip club, would pretty much be his last hurrah as a Yankee.

Billy had been thrown out of a 7–6 loss at Texas on a Friday night, May 6, and then went out with his pal Mantle (who lived in Dallas) and a couple of coaches. All but Martin left "early." He went to the men's room, exchanged words with someone, and the next thing he knew, he was being beaten up against the stucco wall outside the club, his ear dangling off his head.

Bad luck was with Billy as he made his way back to the team hotel, where he intended to quietly call Gene Monahan to get medical assistance. But despite the late hour, a fire alarm had sent everyone out of their rooms. Billy arrived to a packed lobby, bloodied and beaten, to be seen by all.

Piniella, wondering what he had been thinking, resigned as general manager three weeks later, turning the job over to his assistant Bob Quinn, whose grandfather had led a group that bought the Red Sox from Harry Frazee in 1923 and sold them to Tom Yawkey in 1933.

The next day, Martin, who had been fined for kicking dirt on umpire Tim Welke earlier in the season, repeated the action against umpire Dale Ford, but one-upped it by scooping up dirt and throwing it at his chest. Not only was Martin suspended for three games, but the umpires threatened further action to rein him in. And whatever action that might prove to be, one thing was certain: No close calls were going to go the Yankees' way with Billy as manager.

The Yanks got off to a fast 20–9 start, much of it attributable to Winfield's record-tying 29 RBI in April. (Only since 1982 had the schedule begun in the early days of the month.) Billy had embarrassed the franchise again. Steinbrenner waited until they lost seven of eight the following month, and fired him on June 23. "How many times can a man have his heart broken?" said Billy. Counting his trade in 1957, this would be six.

"He wasn't the same Billy Martin this time," said Steinbrenner, who quickly named Piniella, still under his three-year contract, as successor.

Without much pitching to work with (John Candelaria led the team with a 13–7 record), Piniella somehow kept the Yanks in contention. An inspiring eighteenth-inning home run by the productive Claudell Washington (.308) against the Tigers on September 11 put the Yanks in second place, just three and a half behind the Red Sox, and that's where they found themselves when they got to Fenway for a four-game series starting September 15.

(Washington hit just 26 homers for the Yankees over four seasons, but one of them, in April '88, was the ten thousandth in franchise history. While a lot of people contributed to that total, the team's all-time top twenty had themselves hit almost half of them: 4,888, with Ruth, Mantle, Gehrig, DiMaggio, and Berra hitting 2,407.)

Hopes for a repeat of the 1978 Boston Massacre were high, especially after a 5–3 win in the opener behind Rick Rhoden. But then the Yanks lost three straight, dropping them to fourth with time running out. When they lost four of their last five, dropping Piniella's record to 45–48, the team was done, and so again was Lou.

Chapter Thirty-Seven

THE 1989 SEASON WAS MARKED BY departures, beginning with Piniella's. His replacement was Dallas Green, fifty-four, a pitcher turned manager who led Philadelphia to the 1980 world championship, their first ever. From 1982 to 1987 he was general manager of the Cubs. At six foot five and 260 pounds, he was the biggest manager in Yankee history, and he arrived with no experience in the American League in a pro career that stretched back thirty-four years. He brought in five coaches, mostly with National League backgrounds.

Willie Randolph, co-captain with Guidry, was not re-signed after '88 and signed with the Dodgers as a free agent. He played another four seasons before retiring, hitting .327 for the Brewers in 1991. Randolph was thirty-four and the Yankees replaced him with free agent Steve Sax, twenty-nine, the Dodgers' second baseman for the previous eight seasons. While Sax hit .315 for the Yanks with 205 hits, he never enjoyed the same popularity that he had in Los Angeles. The fans missed Randolph, a five-time All-Star, who was an understated presence in the lineup—.275 in thirteen seasons— seldom struck out, and always played great defense.

I was in the Fort Lauderdale parking lot one day in spring training when I spotted Dave Winfield walk to his car and drive off while practice was still going on. It turned out his Yankee career was about over. He had back surgery on March 24 and missed the full '89 season. Few players could miss a full season at age thirty-seven and return in peak form. Winfield, a marvelous athlete, was able to do it, but his Yankee days were effectively done. He returned in 1990, but after an 0-for-23 slump in April, the Yankees traded him to the Angels on May 11 for Mike Witt, who would be an oft-injured starting pitcher for them.

In Winfield's eight-plus seasons, he batted .290 with 205 homers and 818 RBI, earning five Gold Gloves and selection to the All-Star team in each full season. He would go on to a twenty-two-season career and shed his "Mr. May" reputation by driving in the winning run in the 1992 World Series for Toronto. When he went into the Hall of Fame, he chose to have a San Diego cap on his plaque, a decisive blow to his relationship with the Yankees, who had already assigned his uniform number 31 to Hensley Meulens the year they traded him. He would be an occasional Old-Timers' Day guest, but it was never a very happy post-baseball relationship for the two parties.

Winfield and Steinbrenner sued each other in January of 1989 for the third time over payments not made to the Winfield Foundation. Lurking in the background was the presence of one Howie Spira, for whom the term "gambler" came to be used. It was actually a compliment: It implied he had a profession. In reality, Spira was a ne'er-do-well who thought he could make a killing offering incriminating information on Winfield to Steinbrenner, audaciously asking for payment in return. Steinbrenner was intrigued; he might be able to discredit Winfield as consorting with lowlifes like Spira, possibly even being involved with "gamblers." He began taking his calls. Aside from that, the Winfield Foundation lawsuits were settled in September. Sadly, this story still had legs.

VETERAN FRONT-OFFICE OPERATIVE Syd Thrift was hired as general manager during spring training of '89. Having gone through a stint as Charlie Finley's GM, he figured he could surely work for George Steinbrenner. Bob Quinn, promoted and demoted during this stretch, became the number-two man to Thrift, but then replaced him on August 29 when Thrift departed for "personal reasons."

Part of the personal reasons was the growing influence of an alternative front office emerging in Tampa. With George Bradley there as the vice president of player development and scouting (essentially the farm director), the Tampa office began a period in which it sometimes overrode decisions made by the New York "baseball people." This arrangement often caused inner turmoil in the management of the team, the Tampa people vs. the New York people, a problem that continued for many years until Brian

Cashman finally brought it to a halt in 2005 when his insistence on full authority became a condition of his re-signing as GM.

Quinn didn't last long in this latest stint as GM; he quit. Harding "Pete" Peterson became the team's newest general manager in October, but he too was handicapped by the Tampa operatives who sat down the hall from Steinbrenner.

Ron Guidry departed in 1989. He continued to struggle with shoulder problems, and was only 2–3 in 1988. In '89, he only pitched for Columbus, going 1–5 in seven starts, then announced his retirement in July. One of the great pitchers in Yankee history, he was fourth in wins and second in strikeouts, with a 170–91 career record. Ron Guidry Day was held in 2003, at which his uniform number 49 was retired.

Rickey Henderson departed in 1989. The gifted and popular left fielder stole 93 bases in 1988, but was not playing well in '89. In 65 games he was hitting only .247 with 25 steals, and at times looked lackadaisical in the field. Fans were starting to turn on him; management certainly was. Dallas Green questioned his work ethic when he didn't voluntarily report early for spring training as was requested. "Rickey Henderson is not going to run the Yankees in 1989," said Green. "Dallas Green is. We sent letters to everybody about when to report. Maybe Rickey can't read."

It was the final year of Henderson's five-year contract, and it appeared certain he'd leave at year's end for free agency, especially if Green was still managing. Instead he agreed to a trade back to Oakland on June 21, the Yankees getting pitchers Eric Plunk, Greg Cadaret, and outfielder Luis Polonia (who would hit .313 for them, but would be convicted of having sex with a minor two months after he joined the team; he served sixty days in prison after the season). Henderson would play another fifteen seasons in the majors and would be a first-ballot Hall of Famer, but his Yankee stint was just a brief stop in a twenty-five-year career.

Still, in the brief stop, he became the Yankees' all-time stolen base leader with 326, a mark that stood until Derek Jeter broke it in 2011.

Tommy John also left in 1989, released on May 30 with a 2–7 record. His appearances in 1989 gave him twenty-six major league seasons, including fourteen after his game-changing Tommy John surgery in 1975. Ninety-one of his 288 career victories came as a Yankee.

Cablevision's SportsChannel ended its relationship with the team after televising Yankee baseball since 1979, at various times employing Mantle, Martin, Allen, Hawk Harrelson, and Murcer as announcers. (MSG hired Tony Kubek, the former shortstop but frequent critic of Steinbrenner's; he lasted five seasons.)

Charles Dolan and Cablevision weren't out of the picture forever. Cablevision bought MSG Network in 1994, and some four years later made an agreement with Steinbrenner to purchase 70 percent of the team, a deal that would keep Steinbrenner running the Yankees, and also the Knicks and Rangers, while Cablevision essentially got free rights to the broadcasts through its ownership. But the deal was never consummated; Steinbrenner came to realize it was not in his best interests to lose the broadcast revenue and to be essentially working for Dolan.

BILL WHITE DEPARTED the Yankee broadcast booth in 1989, named to succeed Bart Giamatti as National League president. A Yankee broadcaster since 1971, his work with Rizzuto was loved by Yankee fans. Frank Messer had left the TV booth after 1984 (he did one year on radio only), and many felt the Rizzuto-Messer-White team of '71 to '84 was a perfect baseball broadcast experience. White was replaced by Met legend Tom Seaver, with George Grande being the third man in the booth, while MSG's new broadcast team would bring newspaperman Michael Kay into the studio for a wrap-up show, beginning his long career as a Yankee announcer. In 1992 he became a full-time broadcaster. Also new to the radio booth was John Sterling, a onetime sports talk host on WMCA in New York, and then an Atlanta Braves and Atlanta Hawks announcer. Sterling too would enjoy a long run on Yankee radio broadcasts, and his "*Thuuuuuuu* Yankees win!*" call after team victories became a signature part of the Yankee experience.

Another '89 departure was Dallas Green himself. He had been unable to make the team play better than it should have. Mattingly's back had robbed him of his power; Jesse Barfield, a star in Toronto, wasn't hitting much in New York, and only one pitcher—Andy Hawkins—was en route to a 10-victory season. (He would go 15–15.) Players like Alvaro Espinoza, the shortstop, and Mel Hall, an outfielder, appeared to be stopgaps. A team-record fifty players paraded in and out of action during the season. As the team kept losing, Steinbrenner decided he wanted to change Green's coaches. This had become a familiar tactic to force the manager out. Green wouldn't have it.

"Let's face it, there is absolutely no hope that their organization will be a winning organization as long as Steinbrenner runs the show," said Green to Bill Conlin of the *Philadelphia Daily News.* "It's sad. He has no organization there now. He has absolutely no pride. The ballplayers there now have no feeling of being a Yankee."

The statement would ordinarily have been enough to get Green fired, but it took a few more days. With the club nine games under .500 on August 18, Green was out.

Steinbrenner wanted Piniella back, but Lou turned him down and stayed in the broadcast booth, where he'd been consigned at the start of the season. So he turned to his Columbus manager, Bucky Dent, thirty-seven, the hero of 1978. It was the seventeenth managerial change in seventeen years for the Yanks. Dent went 18–22 for the remainder of the season, as the Yanks again finished fifth in the East, thirteen games under .500. The mood in the stadium had grown dark; attendance fell almost five hundred thousand from the previous year. Fans were turning on the owner.

People close to Steinbrenner felt that he was considering dropping Dent and bringing back Billy Martin for a sixth term. Piniella, meanwhile, was hired as the new Cincinnati manager when Bob Quinn emerged as their GM. He managed the Reds to the 1990 world championship, with Paul O'Neill his star right fielder. He won the Series on the night Steinbrenner was guest host of *Saturday Night Live.*

Piniella went on to manage Seattle, Tampa Bay, and the Chicago Cubs—a twenty-three-year managing career that included a 116-victory season with the Mariners.

BILLY MARTIN WAS killed in an auto accident on Christmas Day of 1989 on an icy road near his home in Binghamton, New York.

Billy's personal life was a mess. His fourth marriage, to Jill, quickly followed his third, to Heather, someone he'd begun seeing when she was sixteen. But he never returned home to her after the 1985 season.

His finances were in bad shape. His drinking was heavy and occurring before the nation took greater interest in alcoholism as a disease.

He died just two weeks after his feisty mother died in California, a devastating blow to the emotional Martin. At the time, he had been told that his parents had never married; this was later shown to be incorrect, but he didn't learn of the correction while he was alive.

He was also arguing with Jill, and instead of spending the holiday with her, he set off drinking with his pal Bill Reedy. Reedy's truck slid out of control as Billy shouted, "Hang on! Look out!" but he couldn't survive the accident. He was sixty-one.

Whether Reedy or Martin was actually driving became a matter of debate, settled in court by a jury that found Reedy guilty of drunk driving. There were Martin hair fragments in the passenger window, but his injuries suggested the steering wheel had gone into him. Like many things about Billy, there was mystery surrounding it.

Not only did Martin have a majestic funeral at St. Patrick's Cathedral in the presence of Richard Nixon, Steinbrenner, Mantle, Ford, Rizzuto, and others, but he was buried within a few feet of Babe Ruth at Gate of Heaven in Hawthorne, New York.

There was never a more prideful Yankee. Or a more complicated one.

IN 1990 THE Yankees dropped to last place with 95 losses. They had been last in 1966, 1912, and 1908, and that was it.

On July 30, Commissioner Fay Vincent imposed a second suspension on Steinbrenner. Having conducted an investigation into payments made to Howie Spira to dig up dirt on Winfield, Vincent concluded that a suspension was called for. Spira went to jail for twenty-two months on an extortion conviction. To everyone's surprise, Steinbrenner rejected the suspension and chose instead to remove himself from baseball, offering to be placed on baseball's permanent ineligible list. It was the preferred course of action for him if he wished to remain active with the United States Olympic Committee, an assignment he genuinely enjoyed. Bob Nederlander, a limited partner, was named general partner. Steinbrenner would be permitted to participate in matters "extraordinary and material" to the team.

Word reached the fans at Yankee Stadium during a game in progress. Fans did not yet have cell phones, texts, and e-mails at the ready in those days, but news quickly spread and a chant of "No more George" began to be heard. It was a bizarre moment, and of course it reflected the fans' frustration at how low the team had sunk. He was, in the minds of the fans, the fall guy for the sorry product they were watching that season. Yes, Steinbrenner had overseen some success, but the frustration had been growing a long time. The fact that the team passed two million in attendance was thought of as a small miracle.*

Daniel McCarthy, an original limited partner in the team, succeeded Bob Nederlander as the Yankees' "acting general partner" a year later, but Vincent rejected him when he and another partner, Harold Bowman, sued Vincent over the value of their Yankee stock being compromised by Steinbrenner's expulsion. The suit was dismissed, but McCarthy's time at the top was brief, and he was succeeded by Steinbrenner's son-in-law, Joe Molloy.

BUCKY DENT WAS a marked man from the time he arrived, and his tenure would be brief. He was fired on June 6, with the team 18–31. Sadly, the fir-ing came when the Yankees were in Boston, the scene of his greatest mo-ment. His replacement was Columbus manager Stump Merrill, then in his eleventh year as a minor league manager for the Yanks. The first game he managed was the first time he had been inside a major league stadium in his twenty-five years in the game, beginning as a catcher.

He inherited a falling club. Mattingly's big years were over—he had a .256 season with just five homers, and missed 60 games with a bad back. Only reliever Lee Guetterman managed to win 10 games. Tim Leary lost 19. Dave Righetti saved 36 of the team's 67 wins and Barfield hit 25 hom-ers, while Sax and Roberto Kelly teamed up for 85 stolen bases. A surprise DH find was Kevin Maas, who hit 21 homers in 254 at-bats.

So awful was the season that when Andy Hawkins no-hit the White Sox on July 1, he managed to lose the game 4–0. In the last of the eighth of a scoreless tie, two out, third baseman Mike Blowers made an error, and Hawkins walked the next two. Robin Ventura flied to left, but rookie Jim Leyritz misplayed it for an error, allowing all three runners to score. Then Ivan Calderon flied to right, where Barfield lost it in the sun for another er-ror and another run.

"What's going on here?" said a shocked Phil Rizzuto in the TV booth. It could have applied to the full season. As a home team with the lead, the

---

* The Yankees went twenty-two years—1981 to 2003—without leading the American League in attendance.

White Sox didn't have to bat in the ninth, which meant Hawkins's no-hitter was only eight innings, and not included in the record books. Talk about a bad year.

Merrill was 49–64 and there were few hopeful signs, except perhaps for the promotion to third-base coach of thirty-two-year-old Buck Showalter, who was thought to have a good baseball mind. Buck had previously been the team's eye in the sky, positioning players from the press level.

GENE MICHAEL RETURNED to the general manager's office in August 1990, but George Bradley, of the Tampa brigade, was brought to New York with similar duties. The two butted heads over a number of off-season roster moves, emphasizing how dysfunctional the operation had become. Dave Righetti left via free agency to finish his career with the Giants, with Al Rosen, now San Francisco's general manager, offering him four years to the Yankees' two.

In his place, Michael signed Steve Farr, who saved 78 games over the next three seasons. Michael also signed Scott Sanderson, who would be the team's leading winner (16–10), and took a chance on the oft-suspended Steve Howe, who'd battled drug and alcohol problems since a Rookie of the Year showing with the Dodgers. It was the move of a team desperate for pitching—at one point during the '91 season, the rotation included Wade Taylor, Jeff Johnson, and Scott Kamieniecki, all considered triple-A pitchers at that point.

Meanwhile, Bradley signed the fading Steve Sax to a four-year deal, something Michael opposed, causing further tension in the front office. Sax rebounded to go from .260 to .304. New faces also included catcher Matt Nokes (24 homers) and third baseman Pat Kelly.

In June, at the annual amateur draft, the Yankees gambled on a nineteen-year-old left-hander named Brien Taylor, who was advised by agent Scott Boras and represented by his mother, Bettie, a tough negotiator. The team's last-place finish in 1990 had earned them the top pick in the nation, and it was Taylor.

Bettie upped the pressure by saying, "Once Brien goes to college, the Yankees will have no chance at him. They have the opportunity now. If they want him, now is the time to get him."

As negotiations continued and she wasn't getting her price, she said,

"I'm beginning to wonder, is it because we're back here, we're poor and we're black?"

(Among those passed over by the Yanks was Manny Ramirez from neighboring Washington Heights, drafted by the Indians with the thirteenth overall pick.)

Taylor got a record $1.55 million signing bonus and spent two seasons in the minors, winning 19 games and showing good developmental progress for his age. The Yankees were delighted with his 13–7 season for Albany-Colonie in '93. But in December 1993 he got into a barroom fistfight defending his brother, and dislocated his left shoulder in the process. He was never the same, and never pitched an inning in the majors, becoming a UPS package handler instead of a Yankee Stadium star.

THE YANKS RETURNED to fifth place in '91 and stayed with Stump Merrill for the full season, the first time in four years they'd played a year under one manager. Merrill was fired at year's end, as was George Bradley. Stump continued to serve the organization in a variety of capacities for many years, including managing, but never again on the big-league level.

There was a breakthrough moment that arrived quietly. On July 7, in a home loss against Baltimore, the Yankees started Bernabe Williams in center field. Gene Michael thought Williams represented the kind of hitter the Yankees needed in the lineup—someone selective at the plate who could get on base a lot.

"Bernie," just twenty-two, batted eighth and had a single and a sacrifice fly in four plate appearances, driving in two. While Roberto Kelly was the team's regular center fielder (20 homers, .267), Williams played in 85 games, hit his first three homers, and stole 10 bases. The soft-spoken, switch-hitting product of Escuela Libre de Musica High School in Puerto Rico, who could play classical guitar, would be the first of the mid-nineties stars to arrive to begin the process of digging the team out of the hole it was in.

Chapter Thirty-Eight

WILLIAM "BUCK" SHOWALTER became the Yankees' manager on October 29, 1991. At thirty-five, he was the youngest in baseball and the youngest Yankee manager since Roger Peckinpaugh in 1914. He'd been a teammate of Mattingly's at double-A Nashville, where he led the league in hits, part of a seven-year playing career as a first baseman and outfielder. He began managing the Oneonta Yankees in 1985, and in five seasons in the organization, had four first-place finishes.

Showalter had a keen mind for detail and loved to get involved in all phases of the game. He was prepared, disciplined, and efficient, traits greatly admired by Steinbrenner, even in absentia. He received a one-year contract, but just three months into his first season, with the team barely at .500, he was given two more. He wound up finishing the 1992 season tied for fourth, ten games under .500, twenty games out of first. It was a five-game improvement over 1991. Gene Michael saw talent in Showalter, saw that the team was a work in progress, digging out from years of shipping off prospects for players who weren't a good fit, and he chose to retain Buck to continue the team's development.

Danny Tartabull was the big preseason acquisition, signing a $25.5 million, five-year contract, and as a right fielder and DH, he delivered 25 homers and 85 RBI, nine of them in one game. Catcher Mike Stanley was acquired from Texas to back up Matt Nokes, while Pat Kelly took over at second from the departed Sax, with Charlie Hayes becoming the regular third baseman.

The Yanks' number-one starter was to have been Pascual Perez, but he failed a drug test and was suspended for the full season. Instead his brother Melido became the de facto "ace," winning 13 to Sanderson's 12. Steve Howe, who started the season strong, also failed a drug test and suffered his seventh suspension, leaving Farr as the short man.

The Howe suspension caused another major split between the Yankees and the Commissioner's Office, when Showalter, Michael, and COO Jack Lawn testified on Howe's behalf at an arbitration hearing. Vincent threatened all three with their own suspensions for taking Howe's side, stating, "You have effectively resigned from baseball by agreeing to appear at the hearing." He later apologized for the appearance of intimidating future witnesses.

Vincent was shown the door three months later, after a series of actions that found other teams exasperated with his leadership. But on July 24, before he left office, he announced that Steinbrenner's suspension would be lifted and that he could return in 1993. (In November, Howe's suspension was overturned by an arbitrator.)

Vincent's departure found Milwaukee owner Bud Selig stepping in as acting commissioner, which would lead to a long run as permanent commissioner.

ON MARCH 1, 1993, Steinbrenner returned, riding a white horse and dressed in Napoleonic clothing for a *Sports Illustrated* cover. The photo op was considered "good sport," but fans feared that the return might also mean a return to the disorder of the eighties. Disorder, however, was more prevalent in Tampa, where American Ship was struggling to survive. The company filed for bankruptcy that November.

The baseball fears proved unfounded. Michael had steadied the operation. Showalter proved to be a good leader, and the team was about to break its streak of four straight sub-.500 seasons and begin one of the most successful eras in the team's history.

Prior to the season, the Yankees signed free agent Wade Boggs. While Boggs's biggest years and six batting championships were behind him in Boston, he arrived with a .335 lifetime average and was still a quality player. Both Boggs and the Yankees got a thrill from the scandalized reaction of Red Sox fans, and he lifted his average 43 points from 1992's .259 low point, back over .300, started the All-Star Game, and led the league in fielding.

Jimmy Key, thirty-two, was a free agent from Toronto who went 18–6 and took over leadership of the starting rotation. Key, winner of two games in the '92 World Series, was a second choice after the Yankees were spurned by Greg Maddux, who chose to go to Atlanta for less money. David Wells said of Key, "He's one pocket protector away from full-blown nerd status, but don't let any of that fool you. He's a tough competitor."

Jim Abbott, one of the great success stories in major league history, pitched a no-hitter on September 4. In a classy gesture, he summoned his catcher, Nokes, out of the dugout after the game to share equally in the cheers from the crowd.

Abbott had been born without a right hand, yet had overcome the handicap, pitching lefty and maneuvering his glove back onto his throwing hand afterward so he could field his position. He did it so effortlessly that one almost forgot the odds he'd overcome to attain big-league status. A star at the University of Michigan, he broke in with the Angels, and by the time he was traded to the Yankees, people had accepted his fortitude and expected big things. On that count, his Yankee career was middling, 20–22 over two seasons before he left as a free agent. Sadly, he was pretty much done at twenty-eight, going 2–18 back with the Angels.

A fourth new face on the club would be Paul O'Neill. A native of Columbus, Ohio, whose sister Molly wrote a food column for the *New York Times*, O'Neill had played for his "hometown" Cincinnati Reds since 1985. But by 1992 his numbers had slipped to .246/14/66, unproductive for a right fielder.

At the same time, the Yankees were feeling that Bernie Williams, or perhaps the unrelated Gerald Williams, might be as good as Roberto Kelly in center. Kelly, right-handed, would never attain big power numbers in Yankee Stadium, but O'Neill, left-handed, might. Michael made the Kelly-O'Neill deal on November 3, 1992, and it would prove to be one of the best trades in Yankee history. O'Neill returned to top form—even surpassing his best Cincinnati seasons—and would be a key part of the coming success of the team. His popularity with the fans, who enjoyed his Piniella-like intensity, was instant. In his first Yankee season, O'Neill hit .311 with 20 homers, and he would lock down the right-field position for the next nine seasons.

Bernie Williams would claim center field in '93, similarly taking hold of that spot for the long term.

"Mr. Steinbrenner was impatient about Bernie," said Michael. "Frankly, none of us saw the power that he had. But occasionally he'd crush one in batting practice, and we knew the raw tools were there. The fact that he could switch-hit broke the hold we had with right-handed hitters like Kelly.

That was big. We needed more patience from the Tampa people, George included. I think over the years I taught him patience while he taught me business. It was coming together. Bernie was the first step. And he became a good center fielder who could really run down a ball."

He would, in fact, become the most prolific postseason home run hitter in baseball history until Manny Ramirez passed him. And as far as crushing them in batting practice, whereas no one ever hit a fair ball out of Yankee Stadium in a game, on July 23, 2001, Bernie may have hit one onto River Avenue through the opening between the bleacher billboards and the grandstand during batting practice. It quickly became urban legend, but no one came forward who could absolutely attest to it.

"I didn't see it," said Williams, "but I noticed that it never came back, so that should have been some indication it was out . . . It was as hard as I ever hit one."

Mike Stanley, meanwhile, unseated Nokes as the team's number-one catcher, and his .305 showing with 26 homers made him only the tenth catcher in major league history to scale .300/25. Fans took to him quickly.

The Yankees also brought Willie Randolph "home" in '93, making him an assistant general manager after the All-Star break, and then moving him to third-base coach in '94 and bench coach in '04, a position he would hold until he was named manager of the Mets in 2005.

The '93 Yanks spent some time tied for first place, but yielded in September to Toronto. Still, they had put enough of a stake in the ground to claim that they were once again contenders. While some would claim that the foundation for the upcoming years of success was planted during the Steinbrenner absence, supporters of the Boss's reign could point to '93, the year he returned, as being the start of it all. Both sides had good arguments. And the team's attendance of 2,416,965 was almost seven hundred thousand more than in '92, and the fourth highest in Yankee history.

READY TO GO in 1994 with little turnover to the roster, the Yankees were enjoying a 70–43 season, first place, and a six-and-a-half-game lead when the season was suddenly halted by a devastating player's strike on August 12. The issue was the owners' desire to institute a salary cap for player salaries, something Steinbrenner supported, even when the end result meant his paying a special tax for exceeding the limit, designed to assist the lower-earning teams.

Key was 17–4; Steve Howe had a 1.80 ERA. O'Neill was hitting .359 (and

.400 as late as June 17), enough to win him a batting championship if the season did not resume. And it did not. The average would be the highest recorded by a Yankee since Mantle's 1957 season and remained so through 2011, fifty-four years after Mantle's .365.

As had been the history of bitter labor stoppages between union and management, this one was equally nasty with no end in sight. Finally Bud Selig had to accept the obvious and announce that for the first time in ninety years, there would be no World Series in 1994.

And so the Yankees had no championship to show for their aborted season, during which they'd been easily the best team in the AL and may have won the first in what would soon become a string of championships. With no pressure to achieve an agreement once the Series was canceled, the talks lingered on through the winter and into the following spring, when the teams decided to use replacement players—"scabs" was the union's term—to play spring training games.

One of the replacement players was Shane Spencer, a 1990 draft pick by the Yanks who would burst onto the scene in 1998 and earn three World Series rings. Another, Dave Pavlas, came up to the Yankees in July of '95 and was shunned by his teammates. A third, Cory Lidle, was in the Milwaukee organization at the time. He would pitch for ten organizations, but the Yankees would be his last. He was killed in a private-plane crash into a Manhattan apartment building right after the 2006 season.

Two quiet, classy players performed a small gesture of generosity at the close of the '94 season. Since there was no final game, the batboys would not receive their year-end tips from the players. Mattingly and Abbott went to the trouble of calling Kathy Bennett in the Yankees' accounting office to get the home addresses of the kids, and mailed them their tips.

1995 WOULD BE the last time the Yankees would gather in Fort Lauderdale for spring training. The once-beach-blanket-bingo town had lost some of its youth-oriented luster over the years, but Steinbrenner was frustrated by the city's inability to provide him with a full minor league complex adjacent to the major league camp. With Florida's east coast losing a number of teams, easy travel to road games had dissipated, and venerable Fort Lauderdale Stadium would lose its Yankees after thirty-four springs. (The Orioles moved in to replace them.)

The team moved to Steinbrenner's hometown of Tampa the following year with the opening of Legends Field (it became Steinbrenner Field in 2008), but the last roundup off Commercial Boulevard near Route 95 featured some promising rookies, including catcher Jorge Posada, nonroster shortstop Derek Jeter, and pitchers Andy Pettitte and Mariano Rivera. Pettitte would make it north with the team out of camp and win nine of twelve in the second half of the year; Rivera and Jeter would come up a month later, with Jeter making thirteen starts while Tony Fernandez nursed a rib-cage injury. Posada joined the team in September, as Jeter returned from Columbus, mostly to sit and observe. Jeter, the team's number-one draft choice in '92, was the Minor League Player of the Year in '95. After Pettitte retired in 2010, and Posada in 2011, Jeter and Rivera would be the last of the Fort Lauderdale–trained players on the team.

Rivera, not considered a top prospect early on, came from Panama and threw about eighty-nine or ninety miles per hour. One day in spring training of 1992, Michael drove him to the Dodger camp in Vero Beach to see Dr. Frank Jobe, who had pioneered Tommy John surgery. Jobe examined Rivera and decided he wasn't a candidate, but he did go in and clean out some bone fragments in his right elbow. Mariano pitched only ten games that year, had mixed success in '93, and a 5.81 ERA at Columbus in '94. In '95, he was twice sent to the minors between ten Yankee starts. On his second time down, Michael was reading reports and saw that the radar gun had him in the mid-nineties.

"Must be a mistake," thought Michael. But he asked around, and in a conversation with Tiger scout Jerry Walker, got a confirmation of the number.

"Yeah, that's what we thought," he told Walker matter-of-factly.

When Rivera was recalled, he was indeed throwing that hard. Whatever happened remained a baseball mystery.

"I told Buck I'd like him to start Mariano in Chicago on July 4," said Michael. "It was a day game, and it's a tough park for hitters by day. He came through with an eight-inning performance, just two hits and eleven strikeouts. We knew we had something."

"Maybe he just relaxed and was able to let it all out," Michael said. He was a new player. His career turned around.

SPRING TRAINING WITH "real" players lasted only twelve games, and the regular season was trimmed to 144 in what would be the first season of Commissioner Selig's new division alignments, with three division winners and a wild-card team making the playoffs in each league. The Yankees obtained Jack McDowell in the off-season to bolster the pitching staff, and then added defending Cy Young winner David Cone in July when Key needed rotator-cuff surgery. Cone had been a very popular New York Met in the late eighties, and then pitched for Toronto, Kansas City, and Toronto again from 1992 to 1995. (McDowell too was a Cy Young winner with the White Sox, for whom he twice won 20.)

Cone cost the Yanks Marty Janzen and two other minor leaguers. The Blue Jays insisted on Janzen, who had gone 10–3 at Tampa and showed a lot of promise. Going against others who wanted to keep him, and even against his own plan of holding on to prospects longer, Michael said, "We're the Yankees. We need Cone, and we should make this deal."

Janzen won six games for the Blue Jays and spent the rest of his career in the minors.

THEN THERE WAS the question of Don Mattingly's future. He was in the final year of his contract, and while still enormously popular, his offensive production had become too diminished for a power position. He went 192 at-bats between his first and second homers of '95 and was batting .203 with runners in scoring position. Many felt the Yankees might have to make the tough decision to not re-sign him at year's end.

It was a gloomy season for all of baseball, with embittered fans staying home after the strike. Everything was affected: baseball-card sales collapsed, television ratings plummeted, booing of the players increased. Slumping Danny Tartabull, making $5.3 million, was a special target as his game seemed rapidly in decline. Eventually he wouldn't even come out for batting practice, fearful of being singled out by the fans. On July 28, he went to Oakland for Ruben Sierra, who drove in 44 runs in 56 games.

A rare nationally celebrated event for fans came when Cal Ripken broke Lou Gehrig's consecutive-game streak, ending a Yankee hold on that mark that went back seventy-three years, including Everett Scott's mark preceding Gehrig's. When the record fell, Gehrig's teammate Joe DiMaggio was on hand in Baltimore to honor Ripken in the ceremonies.

MICKEY MANTLE, DEBILITATED from years of drinking, rehabilitated at the Betty Ford Clinic and received a liver transplant in Dallas on June 8. He did a soul-searching, "Don't be like me" press conference from the hospital when the baseball world descended on Dallas for the All-Star Game, suggesting that he could indeed be a role model—a negative one. He established an organ-donor drive. Baby boomers wept. This was the Mick, and he had touched that whole generation.

He couldn't make it to Old-Timers' Day on July 22 and sent a touching video message to the fans, wearing a uniform that no longer fit him well, saying that "I'll see you next year . . . maybe . . . hope."

In late July, cancer spread to his lungs and he went back to the hospital on the twenty-eighth. One by one, his teammates—Bauer, Blanchard, Skowron, Ford—came to the hospital to say good-bye. Richardson provided religious comfort.

He died on Sunday morning, August 13, and his funeral was carried live from Dallas by ESPN, with Bob Costas poignantly saying, "He was our guy."

"I just hope God has a place for him where he can run again," said Costas, making everyone remember the young teenage sensation who burst into America's consciousness forty-four years before. It seemed like every baby boomer in America wanted to play center field and wear number 7 in Little League. The Yankees wore a 7 on their sleeves for the balance of the season.

Phil Rizzuto did not make it to the funeral. WPIX had told him he was needed for the broadcast that night, and Phil, no fan of travel, was happy to have an excuse. But when he saw the funeral on TV, he had great regrets. He felt so badly, he resigned as a broadcaster, ending a thirty-nine-year run. "I've overstayed my welcome," he said. (He did reconsider and came back to do some games in 1996 to make it an even forty years as a broadcaster.)

As the Yankees battled for a playoff spot in the first year in which a wild-card team would make the postseason, attention fell on Mattingly. He would end the season with 1,785 games played—but would he ever have one in the postseason? There was a lot of sentiment for the Yankees because of him.

The Yanks won twenty-six of their last thirty-three games to clinch the first American League wild-card slot on the season's final day in Toronto. Pat Kelly's homer in the third-to-last game, a 4–3 win in the Skydome, kept them alive. In the last game, Sterling Hitchcock got the win; Mattingly homered, and the Yanks beat the Jays 6–1 for the clincher.

Cone had delivered, winning nine of eleven down the stretch. Pettitte was a 12-game winner. Bernie Williams hit .307 and John Wetteland saved 31 games after being picked up in a spring training trade with Montreal.

THE YANKEES FACED Piniella's Mariners in the Division Series after the Mariners won a one-game tiebreaker with the Angels. Seattle had played refuse-to-lose baseball all year, led to their first postseason by emerging stars such as Ken Griffey Jr., Edgar Martinez, Randy Johnson, Tino Martinez, and an eighteen-year-old phenom named Alex Rodriguez who rode the bench watching Luis Sojo play short.

The Yanks won the first two games at Yankee Stadium, the second decided on a fifteenth-inning home run by Jim Leyritz at 1:22 A.M. In that game, Mattingly hit his first postseason home run. He hit .417 for the ALDS and went out in a big way: His career would conclude with a .307 lifetime average, but sadly, the bad back had taken away the torque that had once made his swing so lethal. His final home run was a tremendously sentimental moment for a generation of Mattingly fans, who sensed he would not play again.

Things didn't go well in Seattle. Johnson beat McDowell in game three, the Mariners evened the series 2–2 in game four, and it all came down to a dramatic game five on October 8.

In the last of the eighth, with the Yanks up 4–2, Griffey hit his fifth homer of the series to make it 4–3. Three walks and a single let the Mariners tie the game. Into extra innings they went, and now Johnson and McDowell were pitching in relief. This was as tense a postseason game as could be remembered.

In the top of the eleventh, the Yanks' all-purpose Randy Velarde singled home a run to give them a 5–4 lead. Then, in the last of the eleventh, McDowell allowed singles to Joey Cora and Griffey. Edgar Martinez, who hit .571 in the series, doubled to left, scoring Cora, with Griffey following him in, sliding home with the dramatic winning run.

The victory was enormous for the Mariners. Many credited it with getting voters to approve financing for the new Safeco Field project to replace the Kingdome. It was a game that may have saved a franchise.

For the Yankees, it was a tough loss after winning the first two. McDowell was one of a number of players who were crying in the clubhouse after the game.

Another was Showalter, weeping at his desk. Steinbrenner walked in with Dr. Stuart Hershon, the former Harvard football player who had been the team physician since 1988.

"George was angry, but when he saw Buck crying, he became paternal," said Hershon. "He walked to him, patted him on the back, and said, 'It's okay, it's okay.'"

But Buck knew it wasn't okay. He had a very discontented owner who cared little about the team making the postseason for the first time in fourteen years.

"He knows the bottom line," said the Boss, who had refused to endorse a contract extension for Showalter during the season.

Hershon was at Steinbrenner's table for eight that night at the hotel restaurant. After the first two guests ordered, Steinbrenner threw down the menu and said to the waiter, "I can't eat; I'm too upset."

The first two rescinded their orders. Eight people sat quietly drinking water for dinner.

Chapter Thirty-Nine

THE SEARCH FOR A NEW MANAGER was somewhat half-hearted; many felt that the best man for the job was Showalter, and that a dismissal of the thirty-eight-year-old, who was still growing into the job, was uncalled for.

Michael, back to battling with Steinbrenner, agreed to step back as GM and become director of major league scouting, with the GM position going to the former Yankee first baseman Bob Watson, who had served a similar role with Houston.

Both Michael and his twenty-eight-year-old assistant, Brian Cashman, were supporters of retaining Showalter. Rather than fire Buck, Steinbrenner first told him that he could not name his own coaches. He sent him a two-year contract for $1.05 million on the condition that at least hitting coach Rick Down was to be let go. When Showalter rejected it, Steinbrenner considered it a resignation, not a negotiation, and moved on.

Michael, preparing for his departure, recommended Brooklyn-born Joe Torre, fifty-five, who had managed the Mets, the Braves, and the Cardinals after a fine playing career. The Cardinals had fired him in mid-June and many felt his managerial career might have been over after fifteen years.

Joe Molloy recommended Michael, but Stick promptly turned down the idea of a third term. "We never get along when I'm manager," he said.

Michael's idea of Torre was supported by Arthur Richman, a senior advisor. Richman had been the Mets' traveling secretary when Torre began his managing career. He was a true baseball character and onetime *New York*

Mirror reporter who left the Mets in a dispute and came to the Yankees in 1989. He was a guy who knew everyone in the game and had pictures on the wall of his office (my old office) to prove it. He maintained a list of his suggested pallbearers in his wallet, and George Brett even named a son after him. Arthur and his brother Milton, the UPI sports editor who died in 1986, were considered formidable power brokers in the game, and Arthur remained a Yankee advisor until his death in 2009.

So with Richman's influential endorsement, but with Michael's suggestion carrying the most weight, the Yankees gave Torre a two-year deal for the same $1.05 million offered Showalter. It was announced on November 2.

The press was rough. A *Daily News* headline, CLUELESS JOE, created by deskman Anthony Rieber, gave Steinbrenner pause. It came to be thought that the headline reflected on his abilities, but it was intended to be a warning about what he was getting himself in for. Steinbrenner even doubled back and considered rehiring Showalter, probably making Torre club president instead.

But Buck had moved on. He had a handshake deal with the new Arizona Diamondbacks to be their first manager, even if they were two years away from their first game. In a public statement, Steinbrenner said, "I am very upset by his leaving. I wish Buck and his fine little family nothing but the best."

Showalter went on to manage in Arizona, Texas, and Baltimore, never losing his reputation as a bit of a control freak, but always held in high regard by Yankee fans for being the manager as the team returned to playoff form.

BEFORE THE YANKEES opened their Tampa spring training site, they swung a big trade with Seattle, bringing Tino Martinez and reliever Jeff Nelson to the Yankees for third-base prospect Russ Davis and Sterling Hitchcock.

"The Mariners wanted either Hitchcock or Pettitte," recalled Michael, "and we were dealing with Woody Woodward, their GM, who knew our system from having worked here in the eighties . . . I liked Pettitte's determination and concentration just a little more. I managed to keep him, and we got them to agree to Hitchcock."

Martinez was just the sort of player the Yankees needed. He would bring a big RBI bat to first base after Mattingly's struggles. As successor to Mattingly, he had big shoes to fill, but he had talent, a winning personality, even what sounded like a New York accent, and the "right stuff" to just do his job, put up the numbers, and let his on-field play take care of any Mattingly comparisons.

He symbolized what Michael wanted in hitters: patience, the ability to run the count deep, a guy who got on base a lot. In his first year, he hit .292/25/117 and won over the fans.

The Yankees' on-base percentage in 1991 was .316. By 1996 it was .360. Boggs had been the first player to demonstrate the patience that Michael liked. Now it was starting to pay off up and down the lineup. It would be the hallmark of Yankee teams to come. It wore down starting pitchers and got the Yankees into the middle-relief men on a daily basis, often rendering the closers useless.

Meanwhile, Wetteland remained a very effective closer for the Yanks, saving 43 games in 1996. But his setup man, Mariano Rivera, was to many the team's MVP. Rivera preceded Wetteland 26 times in those 43 saves, pitching more than an inning in 20 of them. His stuff was dazzling; his fastball had pop, and his cutter was as tough on lefties as it was on righties. There was no need to go lefty-righty once he came in, keeping the rest of the bullpen—Nelson, Bob Wickman, and Australian Graeme Lloyd—effective earlier in the game. The formula worked well; the Yankee starters had only six complete games.

The Yanks re-signed David Cone as a free agent, and he was 4–1, 2.01 before going down with a frightening, career-threatening aneurysm. When he came back with his first start in September, he no-hit Oakland for seven innings before Torre took him out over pitch-count concerns. Pettitte was 21–8, while Kenny Rogers, the recovered Jimmy Key, and Doc Gooden won 35 between them. Ramiro Mendoza was an effective spot starter. Gooden, considered finished by some, hurled a no-hitter against Seattle on May 14, something he had never achieved with the Mets.

Additionally, second baseman Mariano ("We play today, we win today") Duncan led the team with a .340 average (he and Rivera were the only two "Marianos" in baseball history), and veterans Tim Raines, Cecil Fielder, and Darryl Strawberry were big contributors, Fielder having been obtained for Sierra on July 31.

Third baseman Charlie Hayes, who platooned with Boggs, returned in an August 30 trade with Pittsburgh, just in time to be postseason eligible.

"He might have been the best third baseman in the league when we had

Ed Barrow converted Babe Ruth to an outfielder while managing him in Boston, then came to the Yankees as general manager and presided over their dynasty until after World War II. "You'd tremble at those eyebrows," said Phil Rizzuto. (Rogers Photo Archives)

Larry MacPhail, in three seasons as one-third owner of the Yankees, modernized Yankee Stadium, put the team on television, sent them to road games by airplane, and, in a last act, punched out general manager George Weiss at the 1947 World Series party. He sold his interest in the team the next day and never returned to baseball. (Baseball Hall of Fame)

Bill Dickey (r) was (along with McCarthy and DiMaggio) symbolic of the Yankees' no-nonsense, businesslike approach to their profession. Here the great Yankees catcher is greeted by (l to r) co-owners Del Webb and Dan Topping, and general manager George Weiss, after agreeing to return to the team as a coach in 1949. (Rogers Photo Archives)

Infielders Billy Martin (front l) and Phil Rizzuto (r) celebrate the Yankees' 1953 world championship, their fifth straight. Martin hit .500 in the Series and drove in the winning run in the deciding game. In the background, fittingly, are Yogi Berra's backup catchers, Ralph Houk (l) and Charlie Silvera. (Baseball Hall of Fame)

The Yankees never had a trio of starting pitchers as successful and for as long as (l to r) Vic Raschi, Allie Reynolds, and Eddie Lopat. All were there for the five straight world championships, from 1949 to 1953, with Reynolds proving as adept at occasional relief as all were as starters. (Baseball Hall of Fame)

Ralph Houk (l), after winning three straight pennants from 1961 to 1963, became general manager and promptly signed Yogi Berra (r) as manager for 1964. Club owner Dan Topping presided over the signing. A year later, Houk fired Berra, and later returned to manage the club during a decidedly unsuccessful period in team history. (Rogers Photo Archives)

Billy Martin had five stints as Yankees manager and was fired five times—six, if you count his being traded as a player. Always combative, he knew how to work the fans into his corner, and there was always a strategy in his arguments with umpires. He'd bully the young ones and sweet-talk the older ones, part of his admired managerial skills. (Rogers Photo Archives)

Whitey Ford, Mickey Mantle, and Billy Martin (l to r) were teammates who played hard and lived fast. The Yankees of the early '50s were winning all the time while America was discovering baseball on television. Each October, it seemed, there were the Yankees on the NBC fall schedule, playing in the World Series. (Ozzie Sweet photo; courtesy of Randall Swearingen)

Bob Shawkey (l), who started the first game at Yankee Stadium in 1923, and came back for ceremonial-pitch honors in 1976, with Mickey Mantle. Shawkey, who also managed the Yankees in 1930, felt it was unjust that he was fired after one season, and thought, "I might have won all those pennants McCarthy won." (Michael Grossbardt)

The great Yankee infield of the 1960s featured (l to r) Clete Boyer at third, Tony Kubek at short, Bobby Richardson at second, and Joe Pepitone at first. Pepitone succeeded Moose Skowron at the position after 1962, as the Yankees constantly sought to replace older players with up-and-coming young stars. They were thrown for a loop when both Kubek and Richardson retired in the mid-sixties, with the Yankees getting nothing for them in return. (Baseball Hall of Fame)

The arrival of Roger Maris (r) in 1960 helped to turn Mickey Mantle (l) into the most popular player in the game for the rest of his career. And together, they captured the attention of America with their 1961 dual assault on Babe Ruth's single-season home run record. Maris did it, but baseball hadn't yet learned how to best market its current stars, and Maris's time in New York was not a happy one. (Ozzie Sweet photo; courtesy of Randall Swearingen)

After beating the Giants 1–0 in the seventh game of the 1962 World Series, Ralph Terry is carried off the field at San Francisco's Candlestick Park. Bobby Richardson caught the final out with the winning runs in scoring position, snaring a line drive by Willie McCovey. It would be fifteen years before the Yankees would win another world championship. (Rogers Photo Archives)

Fans take to the field after the final game in the original Yankee Stadium, September 30, 1973. In 1976, the refurbished stadium opened, two million fans turned out, and the Yankees returned to the World Series. But at the end of 1973, there was little to cheer, and fans were able to purchase souvenir seats for $5.75 from E. J. Korvette's department store. (Rogers Photo Archives)

Four generations of excellence at catcher helped the Yankees to many of their championships. Old-Timers' Day of 1976 was the first time this foursome could be photographed together: (l to r) Bill Dickey, Yogi Berra, Elston Howard, and Thurman Munson. Howard, the first African-American to play for the Yankees, was also the first to coach in the American League. Munson, named team captain that year, would die in a plane crash three years later. (Michael Grossbardt)

The signing of Jim "Catfish" Hunter on New Year's Eve 1974 changed baseball and jump-started the modern era of big salaries. It helped inspire the players to battle harder for free-agency rights, and created common usage of agents, the issuance of multiyear contracts, and million-dollar deals. Hunter won 25 games in 1975 and hurled 30 complete games. (Rogers Photo Archives)

Ron Guidry had a magical season in 1978, going 25–3 and winning the final, "Bucky Dent" playoff game in Fenway Park. Here he is on a float at the Yankees' ticker-tape parade up Broadway, which was made into a ritual by New York Mayor Abe Beame the year before. The great Yankee teams of the past had never had such a parade. (Michael Grossbardt)

Chris Chambliss (10), whose home run won the 1976 pennant for the Yankees, greets Reggie Jackson (44) after Jackson's third homer of the deciding game of the 1977 World Series. Jackson would lead the Yankees to the world championship in his first season with the team. He came to New York as a free agent to replace Chambliss as cleanup hitter, a move Billy Martin resisted for most of the season. (Michael Grossbardt)

Dashing Michael Burke, a CBS vice president, was put in charge of the Yankees by the broadcast corporation after its purchase of the team. But the Yankees were about to hit hard times, and as much as Burke charmed the press and humanized the team's previously cold image, it was a down time in Yankee history, known today as the Horace Clarke Era. (Rogers Photo Archives)

Southpaw starters and close friends Fritz Peterson (l) and Mike Kekich (r) were the stuff of tabloid dreams in 1973 when they traded lives—wives, children, and homes—believing each other's life would provide greater happiness. It worked for Fritz, but not for Mike, and both of their Yankee careers faded quickly. (Michael Grossbardt)

Gene Michael was a Yankee shortstop, scout, coach, manager, and general manager and, in the latter role, received many accolades for his work at restoring glory to a franchise that went from 1981 to 1996 without a World Series appearance. (New York Yankees)

Dave Winfield was one of the most gifted athletes to ever play baseball, and while his time with the Yankees was turbulent and resulted in only one World Series appearance, he was forever a threat at the plate, in the outfield, and on the bases. (Rogers Photo Archives)

Don Mattingly was the most popular player on the team during the "down time" of 1982–95, finally getting into a playoff series in his last season. By then, a bad back had robbed him of his power stroke, but his defense at first base remained dazzling, and to a generation of fans, he would always be "Donny Baseball." (Rogers Photo Archives)

Derek Jeter hugs Mariano Rivera following Jeter's 3,000th hit, July 9, 2011. The hit, a home run, was part of a 5-for-5 game that marked yet another highlight day in the Captain's storied career. Two months later, Rivera was the hug recipient when he broke the all-time saves record. (New York Yankees)

Joe Torre had never been to a World Series during a long career as player and manager. But the Brooklyn native changed all that with four world championships in his first five seasons as Yankees manager (1996–2000), dealing with a tough boss, an intense and expanding media, and a multinational roster of millionaire players on long-term contracts. (New York Yankees)

Bernie Williams took over center field in 1991, the first of a wave of homegrown talent that would turn the franchise around. A batting champion and, for a time, holder of the record for postseason home runs, he was a quiet but commanding presence in the lineup. (New York Yankees)

In-game entertainment developed into an art form in modern baseball, even when as simple as the Yankee ground crew performing to "Y.M.C.A." while sweeping the infield. The sign in the bullpen for Yankees.com was yet another aspect of baseball's using new media to reach its fan base. (New York Yankees)

The Yankees were proud of their homegrown talent, and the Core Four won five World Series together, one more than Babe Ruth: (l to r) Andy Pettitte, Derek Jeter, Mariano Rivera, and Jorge Posada. Jeter, Rivera, and Posada played seventeen seasons together for the Yankees—no three players had ever been teammates longer, anywhere. (New York Yankees)

The Yankees' twenty-seventh world championship came in the first year of the new Yankee Stadium (2009) and was the first for many players on the roster, including Alex Rodriguez and Mark Teixeira (embracing in front, center), and Series MVP Hideki Matsui (second from r). (New York Yankees)

George Steinbrenner (center) owned the Yankees longer than anyone and was the last owner in the game who purchased his team before free-agency rules kicked in. His teams won eleven pennants and six world championships, and he redefined the role of ownership in pro sports. Here he is at a banquet with two of the fifteen different men who managed for him: Yogi Berra (l) and Dick Howser (r). (Rogers Photo Archives)

The family of George Steinbrenner, now owners of the team, stand before his plaque in Monument Park at Yankee Stadium following its dedication. Daughters Jennifer Steinbrenner-Swindal and Jessica Steinbrenner are on the left, sons Hank Steinbrenner and Hal Steinbrenner are on the right, and George's widow, Joan Z. Steinbrenner, is in the center. (Associated Press)

him earlier, before losing him to Colorado in the expansion draft," said Michael.

Strawberry and Gooden were Steinbrenner reclamation projects. He had Arthur Richman charged with looking after them. They were two of the most talented players of the eighties when they came up to the Mets, but alcohol and drugs killed their Cooperstown-bound careers. They still had something to prove, and something to give to the Yankees.

Another addition to the team was bench coach Don Zimmer, whom Torre did not personally know very well. Zim was a baseball lifer who started as a Brooklyn shortstop and then carved out a long managing and coaching career in the game, including two coaching stints with the Yanks in the eighties. He proved to be a great strength to Torre, quick to observe things on the field and to make suggestions without seeking publicity or credit. Chubby, bald, Popeye-like in appearance, "the Gerbil" was a favorite of the TV cameras. The team's rookie shortstop, Derek Jeter, took a particular liking to Zimmer, rubbing his bald head for good luck.

Mel Stottlemyre and Chris Chambliss returned as pitching and batting coaches to provide a "Yankee pedigree" in the dugout.

JETER WAS NOT a sure thing to be the team's shortstop in '96. Clyde King, for one, thought he wasn't ready. Gene Michael thought he was. So did coach Willie Randolph, who knew something about playing the infield at a young age. The Yanks toyed with making a deal with Seattle to get Felix Fermin, and considered dealing Bob Wickman or Mariano Rivera for him. Tony Fernandez broke his elbow in spring training, jeopardizing second base at the same time.

Everyone seemed to think Jeter's time was coming, but not necessarily in '96. But Michael prevailed, and he got the job. He homered off Dennis Martinez on opening day in Cleveland and made an over-the-shoulder catch. He was hitting .340 after fifteen games. He was ready.

Born in New Jersey but raised in Kalamazoo, Michigan, Jeter was a Yankee fan from summer vacations back in Jersey, where he'd watch the games on WPIX. The product of nurturing parents in an interracial marriage, he had an easy personality, good looks, and star quality. He was observed in Kalamazoo by scout Dick Groch and then scouting director Bill Livesy, who held their breaths at the 1992 amateur draft as four teams passed and the

Yankees got him. "He wanted to be a Yankee," said Groch. "That's the thing he wanted."

From the beginning, he mastered the art of avoiding controversy in remarks to the media. He seemed to have perfect instincts for the game. His trademark movements—raising his right arm for a brief "time!" before each pitch (that began in his second season), his quarterback-like rifle throws to first while airborne in short left field, his line drives to the opposite field, and his unselfish approach all contributed to what was going to be a Hall of Fame career.

As he matured, his place among the all-time great Yankees was evident. He was named captain in 2003. He emerged as the team's spokesman at ceremonial events. His number-2 jersey would be worn by thousands of fans, many of them female (he was still a bachelor as 2012 arrived) and many of them youngsters. His image was perfect for the game, especially as steroid allegations stirred around other stars. And he, along with Torre, Williams, Martinez, Rivera, Pettitte, and Cone, began to confound traditional Yankee haters. These were hard guys to root against. It was a most unusual development for the franchise, and frustrating for those who had spent a lifetime finding the Yankees arrogant.

Jeter's highlight reel would be filled with memorable Yankee moments, and if there was a commercial to be made featuring a baseball player, there was a pretty good chance that Jeter was in it. Jeter T-shirts and jerseys were the best selling in the game.

While not considered powerful enough to hit in the middle of the lineup, he nevertheless hit more than 200 career homers to make the all-time top ten among Yankees, and hit 20 postseason home runs (through 2011), which was third all-time among all players.

TORRE BECAME THE figure to watch as the Yankees went into the postseason. He was a steady yet emotional man who connected well with New Yorkers, and fans were rooting for him to get to his first-ever World Series. He had been a calming presence all season, putting himself between his players and the front office, keeping them out of public criticism, changing the culture of the organization.

After Williams homered three times as the Yanks beat Texas in the Division Series, the Yanks faced Baltimore in the ALCS. In game one, trailing 4–3 in the eighth, Jeter hit a fly ball toward the first row in right field. Oriole right fielder Tony Tarasco set up to catch it on the warning track and later said he felt he could make the play, but a twelve-year-old New Jersey boy, Jeffrey Maier, reached out and deflected it into the stands. Umpire Rich Garcia called it a home run and the game was tied. It gave the Yankees life, and in the last of the eleventh, Williams hit a walk-off homer to give the Yanks the win. (On seeing the replay, Garcia admitted to blowing the call.)

Baltimore won game two behind David Wells, but then the Yankees took three straight, with Pettitte taking the clincher 6–4. The Yanks were off to their first World Series since 1981.

THE BRAVES AT first looked just too good for New York, with John Smoltz and Greg Maddux both winning in New York to go up 2–0 as the Series headed for Atlanta. The Yanks won the third game 5–2 behind Cone, but in game four, they trailed 6–3 going to the eighth and it appeared they would fall behind 3–1 in games.

But in the eighth, Bobby Cox brought in Mark Wohlers. Hayes and Strawberry both singled, and Jim Leyritz belted a three-run homer to left, another huge hit for the clutch Leyritz and a moment that gave definition to the impending era of Yankee baseball. If the bottom line was to win the Series, this was a bottom-line moment.

The Yankees won in the tenth inning and then won game five 1–0, Pettitte beating Smoltz, with Cecil Fielder driving in the only run. Now it was back to New York, and during the off day, Torre's bother Frank, a former Milwaukee Brave, had a successful heart transplant. It heightened the emotion, not only for Torre but for the fans as well.

Game six featured a clutch triple by the hustling catcher Joe Girardi in the third inning as the Yanks scored three runs off Maddux. "When I got on third base, I almost started crying," said Girardi later of his big hit. Girardi had emerged as both the team's regular catcher and a mentor to young Jorge Posada.

Rivera shut down the Braves in the seventh and eighth, and then Wetteland did it in the ninth for his fourth save of the Series. Charlie Hayes, the August 30 pickup, caught the final out, and the Yankees won their twenty-third world championship and heralded in a new "feel-good" era that would last into the next century.

Torre was teary-eyed in finally winning it all. The team took a victory lap around the field, with Wade Boggs jumping on a police horse. Bob Watson celebrated being the first African-American general manager to win a World Series. The city rejoiced as Mayor Rudolph Giuliani, a die-hard, Brooklyn-born Yankee fan, hosted a City Hall reception following the team's World Series ticker-tape parade.

To some, Torre would come to be considered the best manager in the franchise's history, surpassing the work of Huggins, McCarthy, and Stengel. Unlike them, he had to beat thirteen, not seven opponents to win the pennant, and he had to get through three rounds of playoffs to win the world championship.

He had to reckon with multinational, multiracial players with huge guaranteed contracts. He had to deal with the second-guessing that went with the emergence of sports talk radio, to be followed by bloggers and the twenty-four-hour news cycle provided by cable television and the Internet. His postgame comments were shown live on TV. And he had that very demanding boss. Neither Huggins, McCarthy, nor Stengel ever experienced any of that.

The Yankee organization established itself as polished and efficient during this era. Marketing and promotional innovations were admired, even the ground crew's dance performance of "YMCA" as they raked the field before the sixth inning (as suggested by Joe Molloy in 1996, after doing it with Tampa's ground crew in spring training).

The field was better maintained and achieved a beautiful look under head groundskeeper Danny Cunningham, who succeeded Frankie Albohn in 1994. The removal of the on-deck and fungo hitting circles, the creative alternate mowing patterns, and the painting of the classic NY logo behind home plate, maintained by Dick Kunath and his family, made the field look spectacular. Part of the reason, as well, was the decreasing use of chewing tobacco by players, which used to badly soil the field.

The Yankees were proactive in banning smoking in the stands and tobacco advertising on billboards starting in 1995, years before such things were mandated by law. Then, in an effort to deal with unruly fans, beer sales were cut off after seven innings, and stopped entirely in the bleachers (but restored in the new stadium in 2009).

Bob Sheppard's PA announcements still had their lordly dignity, but now the scoreboard helped make the game fun for younger fans: an animated subway race, various quizzes and games, and the playing of "Cotton Eye Joe" as a sing-along. Eddie Layton had a great sense of ballpark music, augmented by favorites direct from the pop charts.

Attendance went back over two million in 1996, and by 1999 cracked the three million mark. Just six years later, it hit an unthinkable four million. Ticket prices rose along with payroll, but not horribly, and well below Broadway prices. Box seats rose from $7.50 in 1980 to $12 in 1990 to $35 in 2000. The fans were being rewarded with great teams, and Yankee merchandise was worn all over. It was a very uplifting era in Yankee history, and it all began in 1996 when Torre, Zimmer, and Stottlemyre entered the dugout, when Jeter took over at short, when Rivera moved to the bullpen, when Tampa became the spring training home, and when "YMCA" began playing at the end of the fifth inning.

Universally, the game was undergoing changes. ESPN's *Baseball Tonight* was a staple for the ardent fan, while the proliferation of online stats and Web sites put information on overload. When blogs and Tweets came along, some players kept "in touch" with their fans with what felt like personal communications. Baseball cards became more high-tech, annual record books faded into online versions, and people could follow games on handheld devices while on the go.

Women continued to attend in growing numbers. "While the success of the team played a big part in this ascent, a combination of other factors was also at play," said women's sports historian Ernestine Miller.

> Women liked the game for their own enjoyment, but it was also relevant to them in their job, social, and family lives. A big change in traditional attitudes towards what women should and should not like was taking place.
>
> The Yankee brand was expanding and part of the marketing effort was directed at women with the manufacturing of apparel in women's sizes. Wearing T-shirts, caps, sweatshirts, and jackets with the Yankee logo not only showed support for the team, it was the ultimate fashion statement.
>
> And of course in a society that was becoming increasingly obsessed with athletes, players like Jeter and later Alex Rodriguez attracted legions of adoring women who wanted to know details about their lives that had nothing to do with baseball.

Having won the World Series in '96, and operating with a big payroll and a win-at-all-costs owner, the Yankees began to find themselves favored to win almost every year. And with the ability to acquire players in midseason to fill holes, especially free-agents-to-be with demands too high for their teams, their options became fertile with win-now players. The temptation to fix a problem area with an available veteran always made them part of the pennant picks.

The most interesting new face on the '97 Yankees was their first Japanese player, pitcher Hideki Irabu (his father was American), a right-hander who had put up big strikeout totals in the Japanese Pacific League. As far back as the seventies, the Yankees had tried to create ties with Japan, forming a working relationship with the Nippon Ham Fighters, who installed one of their employees in the Yankee offices to learn the U.S. business style for baseball. Unfortunately, the bond never led to any player signings.

San Diego purchased the rights to Irabu. The signing led to the creation of a "posting system" to better govern the movement of players from Japan to the U.S. Ichiro Suzuki, who went to Seattle in 2001, was the first big star and the first position player affected by this.

Irabu, meanwhile, only wanted to pitch for the Yankees and would not sign with San Diego. Recognizing the futility of trying to persuade him, the Padres finally sent him to the Yankees with infielder Homer Bush for pitcher Rafael Medina, Ruben Rivera, and $3 million. The Yankees gave Irabu a $12.8 million contract for four years.

Dispensing with Ruben Rivera, a cousin of Mariano, was noteworthy in that the highly regarded outfielder, rated the Yankees' top prospect by *Baseball America* from 1995 to 1997, was falling short of his promise. Rivera would bounce around without success before coming back to the Yanks in spring training of 2002, only to be caught stealing Jeter's glove and bat from his locker to sell to a sports-memorabilia dealer. The lapse in judgment resulted in his immediate release.

Irabu was less than expected. He did not get along with the huge Japanese media contingent that was assigned to cover him. It wasn't long before fans started suggesting the name meant "I rob you" in Japanese. Although he would twice be the American League Pitcher of the Month during his three seasons in New York, and although he had a 29–20 record with the Yanks, he was a disappointment. He was 5–4 in 1997 but had a 7.09 ERA. After four starts he went back to the minors, returning weeks later without improvement.

In spring training of 1999, he failed to cover first base before Steinbrenner's watchful eye and was labeled a "fat pus-y toad" by the Boss. He was pretty much finished in New York after that. He refused to travel to Anaheim to open the season, reporting instead for the season's third game in Oakland. In 2011, long retired at forty-two, he hung himself in his Southern California home.

Also new to the starting rotation was big David Wells, a free agent from the Orioles. He won 16 and was tireless on the mound. A big Yankee fan who once wore a game-used Babe Ruth cap on the mound (he had purchased it from a dealer, but was told to remove it after an inning), "Boomer" would be a challenge for Torre, as his renegade lifestyle didn't always conform to Joe's designs. Four weeks after he signed, he broke his hand during an "altercation" following his mother's funeral in San Diego. His mother, "Attitude Annie," was a Hell's Angel biker chick. The Yankees were his fifth team and he wound up pitching for nine altogether, but there was a lot to be said for his workhorse abilities and great control.

Martinez had the team's big bat in '97, belting 44 homers and driving in 141 runs. He even won the Home Run Derby at the All-Star break, beating Mark McGwire and Ken Griffey Jr. in the process. He was only the seventh different Yankee to reach 40 homers in a season.

With Wetteland off to Texas through free agency, the team turned over the closer's job to Rivera, confident that his spectacular work as a setup man in '96 would translate.

Still, there is something in the mind and heart of a closer that makes the assignment different, and Rivera had to prove himself. He gave up runs in three of his first seven appearances and had a 4.00 ERA. But he settled in and found his groove, becoming the Mariano Rivera that fans and opponents would come to revere over the next decade and a half: lights out. He finished that season with 43 saves and a 1.88 ERA, 68 strikeouts and 20 walks in 71⅔ innings. The stats seldom varied, year after year. He was the best closer to ever come along and he did it without the dramatic flamboyance associated with the position.

Each game's routine was efficient and businesslike. The stretches and the warm-ups in the bullpen. Entering home games to "Enter Sandman" by Metallica. But the rest of his "show" was all in his work, breaking bats, inducing weak pop-ups, fielding his position with precision, and calmly walking off after the final out. Hitters knew what to expect, with his fastball setting up his rising cutter, leaving them, lefty or righty, flailing away or making weak contact. He turned games into eight-inning affairs for Yankee opponents. Few players would be as respected by opponents as the deeply religious Rivera, who would also be the last active player to wear number 42.

The number was retired in honor of Jackie Robinson in 1997, except for players who were still wearing it.

"Enter Sandman" was selected by a group of Yankee employees who tested a variety of options after Stadium Operations Director Kirk Randazzo was impressed by Trevor Hoffman's entrances to "Hell's Bells" in San Diego at the '98 World Series. Randazzo "auditioned" six possible selections and the group agreed on "Enter Sandman" after Mike Luzzi brought it in. It was first used in 1999, but Mariano played no part in the selection.

The '97 Yankees were the wild-card team in the AL. They won 96, four more than in 1996, but were locked in second place all season. They finished two games behind Baltimore with a late-season run of five straight wins and thirteen out of sixteen.

The Yanks took on Cleveland in the ALDS, and led 2–1 after three games. Then in game four at Jacobs Field, the Yanks leading 2–1 in the eighth, Torre brought in Rivera for a five-out save situation. But Sandy Alomar Jr. hit a game-tying homer with the series just four outs from going the Yankees' way. In the ninth, with the score still tied, Ramiro Mendoza allowed another run, and victory would have to wait another day.

It didn't work out. In the deciding fifth game, Jaret Wright outdueled Andy Pettitte, the Indians won 4–3, and the Yankees went home, the Alomar homer still vivid in their minds. That would be remembered as the key moment of the series, and one of the few black marks on the career ledger of Rivera.

Chapter Forty

BRIAN CASHMAN BECAME THE YANKEE general manager on February 3, 1998, following the resignation of Bob Watson. Cashman, just thirty, would be the second-youngest GM in the game's history, topped only by Tal Smith's son, Randy, in San Diego. The appointment continued Steinbrenner's desire to "let the young elephants into the tent," and in this case also recognized that a change in the position was developing. No longer would the GMs in baseball be men recycled from team to team, operating largely on the gut instinct of veteran scouts. Now they would have to adapt to the emergence of sabermetrics (with Bill James as the guru) and the collection of computer-based data in evaluating talent.

Much of this was outlined in the book *Moneyball* by Michael Lewis, which put its focus on Billy Beane's business style in Oakland. Cashman, for five years an assistant to Gene Michael and then to Watson, would see his methods "assigned" to the younger GMs in the game, and his relationships were growing as these men built seniority. In Beane, Cashman was able to find someone to take Kenny Rogers off his hands.

Cashman, who grew up in Rockville Centre, New York, and Lexington, Kentucky, played baseball at Catholic University and joined the Yankees in 1986 as an intern in the minor league and scouting department. His father was in the horse-breeding business and knew Steinbrenner through that world.

Three days into his new job, Cashman swung a deal with another young GM, Terry Ryan, and got All-Star Chuck Knoblauch from the Twins to play second base. "Knoblauch was the best leadoff hitter in the game," said

Cashman, and he had to trade their 1996 number-one draft pick, pitcher Eric Milton, to get him. While Knoblauch's average dipped to .265, he hit 17 homers, a lot for a second baseman, and he also led the team with 31 steals. The following year he would develop an inexplicable mental block throwing to first, forcing an eventual move to the outfield.

The Rogers trade brought third baseman Scott Brosius to New York, coming off a horrific .203 season after hitting .304 in 1996. No one was quite certain about Brosius, who was originally thought to be a utility player taking Randy Velarde's role. But Brosius rebounded with a .300/19/98 season in New York and signed a new three-year contract before it was over. He would be an All-Star and win a Gold Glove, three World Series rings, and a World Series MVP Award.

His success made Mike Lowell expendable. Lowell, the team's Minor League Player of the Year in 1997, would spend the year at Columbus, hitting .304, and then was traded to the Marlins. He went on to a stellar career with Florida and Boston.

THE 1998 SEASON marked the seventy-fifth anniversary of Yankee Stadium, with April 18 to be the actual date of the commemoration. A special logo was designed for the occasion, and many of the gift days on the schedule revolved around the theme.

But on April 13, the date of the fourth home game of the season, a five-hundred pound chunk of concrete and steel—an expansion joint—fell fifty feet onto the loge level, pulverizing seat 7, Box A in Section 22 along the left-field line. Had anyone been sitting there, the result would have been tragic. But the accident occurred at about 3:00 P.M., two hours before the gates opened, and a disaster was averted. While city building inspectors rushed to the scene, the Yankees moved two games, playing one of them against the Angels at Shea Stadium and then shifting their weekend "anniversary" series to Detroit. Not only was the anniversary game not played at home, but the focus on the glorious history of the stadium was removed from the team's plans. Now the focus would be on Steinbrenner's growing push to have a new ballpark built.

It wasn't easy for the team's marketing people, led by Debbie Tymon. Trying to sell tickets to historic Yankee Stadium while dealing with reports of a failing ballpark made for a daunting assignment.

This was not a new campaign, but as concerns about security, lighting, and the neighborhood mounted, it became more determined. Five years earlier, Governor Mario Cuomo had embraced the concept of a new Yankee Stadium to be built over the Long Island Railroad Yard on Manhattan's west side, over Thirtieth to Thirty-third streets, a site later pushed by Mayor Michael Bloomberg for a Jets football stadium. The Yankees didn't discourage the talk.

But for all the complaining, they couldn't keep the fans out: The team on the field was extraordinary. The '98 Yanks were something special, and 2,919,046 fans poured through the turnstiles despite all the publicity about the aging facility.

"There was a quality to that season that seemed to defy a century of how baseball games play out," said Rick Cerrone, the team's media relations director from 1996 to 2006. "If we were down, say 5–3 after six, somehow you knew that was a game you'd win. You knew the opponent wasn't going to score any more off our bullpen, and you knew we'd surely get six runs."

With an eight-game winning streak, the Yankees moved into first place on April 30 and remained there for the rest of the season, finishing 114–48, twenty-two games ahead of Boston and 62–19 at home. It was the most wins in team history, with the 1927 club having gone 110–44 for a slightly higher percentage. The league record was 111 by the '54 Indians, done in 154 games. By August 1, the Yanks had lost only 27 times. As the year unfolded, the '98 Yanks became part of the discussion as to which was the greatest team in franchise history: 1927, 1939, 1961, or this one.

The Yanks hit 207 homers, but despite a year of record-shattering outputs from others, no Yankee hit more than 28 (Tino Martinez). The power was spread out among ten Yankees reaching double figures. Strawberry hit 24 in just 295 at bats. O'Neill (116) and Martinez (123) were the only ones to top 100 RBI, but Williams had 97 and batted .339 to win the league's batting title. Jeter hit .324 with 19 homers. Shane Spencer, a late-season recall, hit 10 homers in just 67 at-bats, three of them grand slams.

Mark McGwire's and Sammy Sosa's breaking of Maris's single-season record, a moment that came to be seen as tainted following baseball's steroid scandal, ended a seventy-eight-year hold on the homer record by a Yankee, going back to Ruth's 1920 season. Despite the many huge homer seasons during this era, Maris continues to hold the American League record with his 61.

Another milestone came on September 20, the final home game of the season for the Orioles, when Cal Ripken voluntarily ended his playing streak at 2,632. It seemed appropriate that the Yankees were the opposing team that day, and they stood at the top of their dugout steps and applauded Ripken as soon as it was realized that he was not in the lineup.

Rivera missed much of April with a strained groin muscle, but still saved 36 games. David Cone had his first 20-win season in a decade; Pettitte won 16, and even Irabu went 13–9. But the mainstay of the staff was David Wells, who led the league in winning percentage with an 18–4 record, including five shutouts, and who on Sunday, May 17, pitched a perfect game against Minnesota in Yankee Stadium. It was the Yankees' first perfect game since Larsen's World Series gem forty-two years before; interestingly, Wells actually attended the same high school in San Diego as did Larsen. And again it was an "imperfect" man achieving the feat.

Then there was Orlando Hernandez, also known as El Duque. Because of the mystery surrounding his background and perhaps his age (thirty-two?), he was somewhat of a Satchel Paige in a Yankee uniform, even throwing oddly as he lifted his left knee toward his chin before delivering an array of dazzling pitches. He was the half brother of Livan Hernandez of the Marlins.

According to reports, El Duque, kicked off the Cuban national team because they feared he would defect, had been spirited out of the island nation on a raft, or a ship, and was picked up by the U.S. Coast Guard on Anguilla Cay. Guided by a savvy scout, he took residence in Costa Rica, enabling him to avoid the draft and make himself a free agent.

The Yankees arranged for a visa and signed him to a four-year, $6.6 million contract. They sent him to Columbus, but he had to make an emergency start on June 3 against Tampa Bay. He went seven innings, allowing a run and five hits. He wasn't going back to the minors. He instead went 12–4 with a 3.13 ERA, becoming an overnight sensation and a fan favorite throughout his sometimes mystifying Yankee career, which covered six seasons, producing a 61–40 record. He was one of the best postseason clutch pitchers they had, with a 9–3 record.

El Duque's grit was immediately visible that fall. After sweeping Texas in three straight to win the Division Series, the Yankees faced Cleveland in the ALCS. The Indians had knocked them out the year before, and this time went up two games to one, with game four in Cleveland. The Yanks needed the win, and Hernandez delivered, hurling seven shutout innings in a 4–0 victory.

Following his win, the Yanks won their thirty-fourth pennant behind Wells, then Cone, with Rivera saving the final three games.

The Yanks took on San Diego in the World Series. In game one at Yankee Stadium, with the Yanks losing 5–2 in the seventh, Knoblauch (who had argued with an umpire during the ALCS against Cleveland while the ball sat on the ground and a run scored) hit a three-run homer and Martinez belted a grand slam. They would go on to sweep the Padres for their twenty-fourth world championship, with Brosius, who hit .471, earning Series MVP honors. By going 11–2 in the postseason, the Yankees were 125–50 overall for 1998, a spectacular showing.

COMING OFF A remarkable rookie season as general manager, Cashman had concerns about '99. He was worried about a letdown, worried about a fat-cat syndrome, and wanted to head that off with an even better team. With Bernie Williams becoming a free agent, he had a big task ahead of him.

One course of action was to pursue free agent Albert Belle, the gifted but troublesome hitting machine who had experienced great seasons with Cleveland. Belle carried a bad reputation and could certainly be a counterweight to such a feel-good team as the Yankees had become, but the onetime Eagle Scout was certainly worth considering. Williams was being offered $90 million for seven years by the Red Sox. It seemed like the Yanks would lose Bernie and sign Belle.

But Belle had a change of heart after agreeing to a Yankee contract. He recognized that he would have trouble with the New York media, and as Cashman reminded him, "That's part of the job here, it goes with the territory." He reconsidered and signed with Baltimore.

Meanwhile, the thought of losing Williams weighed heavily on Steinbrenner, and in his heart Bernie did not want to leave either. All he wanted was to be paid his free-agent value.

The Yanks offered $87.5 million for seven years, and he took it. He would remain a Yankee for the rest of his career.

Then came an opportunity for the Yankees to get Roger Clemens from Toronto. Clemens had been a longtime Yankee foe, an intimidating pitcher who never hesitated to throw hard and inside, one who never backed down from a challenge. Owner of five Cy Young awards, five 20-win seasons, five strikeout titles, and 233 victories, he had never been with a World Series winner. Cashman felt that was incentive enough to make him an even better pitcher in '99.

The price was high: David Wells. But it would take Wells, along with pitcher Graeme Lloyd and infielder Homer Bush, to make this happen, and Cashman pulled the trigger.

Sports talk radio, especially WFAN, was never as lively as it was the day of the trade. Brokenhearted fans, many of whom despised Clemens going back to his Red Sox days, were in high gear. But this was one of the game's elite performers, and this was what the Yankees did. It was a bold move no matter how one looked at it. And the fans were going to have to adjust to the sight of Clemens in pinstripes. The deal was made as spring training was opening.

Clemens would earn more than $45 million over the next five seasons with the Yankees, winning 77 games, including his 300th. And he proved to be a great teammate.

"Roger Clemens was a John Wayne type, an all-time hard worker," said Cashman. "He was just a great guy to have on the team. He intermixed so well with the clubhouse guys, with the lowest players on the roster . . . He'd always be doing things like buying a suit for a rookie, picking up checks . . . And if a teammate was underperforming, he'd get on him, especially if he felt he was cutting corners. He always did more than he had to do; he was one of the best people that we ever had here."

YOGI BERRA, NEWLY reconciled with Steinbrenner, came back on opening day in '99. Joe DiMaggio had died on March 8, and Yogi was now considered the "greatest living Yankee." He didn't refuse the designation, but he would say, "I don't know, you got Rizzuto, you got Ford . . ."

He was then honored with Yogi Berra Day on July 18. As part of the ceremonies, Don Larsen threw the ceremonial first pitch to Yogi, who borrowed Joe Girardi's mitt for the moment.

Then, with Larsen and Yogi looking on and Girardi calling the pitches, David Cone went out and hurled a perfect game, just as Larsen had done forty-three years before—and just as another David—Wells—had done on another warm Sunday a year before. Two Sunday perfect games in two years by two Davids. This one was against the Montreal Expos, and had Cone falling to his knees in disbelief at the end.

(Making the game even more unusual was the presence of broadcaster

Bob Wolff, a press-box spectator. Bob had called the '56 game on the radio.)

It was the peak moment of an outstanding career for Cone, but what followed was a decline with few high moments. He had only six more Yankee victories in him over the next season and a half.

As for Yogi, he would remain a fixture with the team, throwing out first pitches in postseason games, stealing the show on Old-Timers' Day, and visiting spring training every year, where Ron Guidry served as his driver and meal companion, wearing a "Driving Mr. Yogi" cap.

DiMaggio had died of lung cancer at eighty-four. His attorney, Morris Engelberg, had taken control of everything in Joe's life—and death—and kept the Yankees at arm's length. Joe himself developed paranoia about all things baseball, even in regard to his former teammates. They knew better than to even ask him for an autograph. "They're all making money off my back," he told Engelberg.

A small family funeral was held in San Francisco with no Yankee presence. Steinbrenner went to see him in his Hollywood, Florida, hospital six days before he died. The Yankees held a memorial service for Joe some weeks later, with Paul Simon singing "Mrs. Robinson," and its line "Where have you gone, Joe DiMaggio?" while standing with his guitar in center field.

Joe never really understood what the line meant. "I'm still here," he would tell people. When they finally met one day, Simon explained, "It's only about the syllables, Joe. I needed five syllables there." (After the song came out, Simon threw out the 1969 opening-day first pitch. He and Art Garfunkel were Columbia recording artists, and CBS owned the record label.)

DiMaggio's final appearance at Yankee Stadium was on the last weekend of the '98 season, on a hastily arranged Joe DiMaggio Day, at which he received eight World Series rings to replace those stolen from a hotel room. His speech was, alas, lost to the ages when the microphone failed to work. It infuriated him, his mood not helped by the illness now engulfing him, complicated by a fever. Older fans remembered that he had been ill at the first DiMaggio Day, at the end of the '49 season.

As in 1979, sadness was abundant in '99, and not only with DiMaggio's passing. Catfish Hunter died of ALS. The fathers of Brosius, Luis Sojo, and

O'Neill all died that year. Of Hunter, Steinbrenner said, "Catfish was the foundation on which our tradition here was built."

True to Cashman's fears, the '99 season wasn't living up to '98. With 98 wins, it was a drop-off of sixteen, which would have been disastrous if the standard hadn't been so high. In this case, it was good enough to win the division by four games.

The season began with a diagnosis of prostate cancer for Joe Torre, necessitating that Zimmer fill in as manager until his return. Zimmer was there for the last three weeks of spring training and was 21–15 as a fill-in during the regular season, until Joe returned on May 15, cancer-free.

Darryl Strawberry, a productive part of the '98 Yanks, was diagnosed with colon cancer on October 1, 1998, leading to a winter of chemotherapy after it spread to a lymph node. Then, on April 3, he was found in possession of cocaine while soliciting sex from an undercover policewoman. Major League Baseball suspended him for 140 days, and he was sentenced to twenty-one months' probation by the court in Tampa. He returned in time to qualify for the postseason, and homered twice in it, but his turbulent career was effectively over.

The '99 Yanks set a club record with 3,292,736 paid admissions, their first time over the three-million threshold. Williams came through with a .342 season, while Jeter hit .349 with 219 hits (the most ever by a shortstop) and 102 RBI, reaching base safely in his first fifty-three games of the season. Chili Davis, at thirty-nine, became a big contributor with 19 homers, while El Duque led the staff with 17 wins and Rivera had a 1.83 ERA to go with 45 saves. Clemens, 14–10, disappointed in his first year.

The Division Series was another three-game sweep of Texas, with Williams driving in six runs and batting .364 and Clemens winning the deciding game 3–0 with a save from Mariano.

Then it was Boston in the LCS, opening in Yankee Stadium, where a tenth-inning walk-off homer by Bernie Williams got things started. The homer followed a pregame "pep talk" in which Yogi told a worried-looking Bernie, "Don't worry . . . these guys have been trying to beat us for eighty years."

Then they took game two behind Cone, who came through when many questioned the choice of the fading veteran for such a big game.

After Pedro Martinez beat Clemens in game three in Fenway, Pettitte won game four and El Duque, the MVP of the series, won the pennant clincher for a trip to their thirty-sixth World Series.

The Series opponents were again the Braves, but this time it was an easy four-game sweep for the Yanks, giving them an 11–1 record for the postseason and twelve World Series wins in a row. Maddux, Kevin Millwood, Tom Glavine, and Smoltz all succumbed to the Yankees, with Rivera winning the MVP Award. The third game was the tightest, with Chad Curtis, known for his belly-flop throws from left, winning it with a walk-off homer.

With their twenty-fifth world championship, the Yankees were called the "team of the century." The twenty-five titles were captured in seventy-nine seasons, and the final title of the twentieth century was a fitting cap to a remarkable run.

TWO MONTHS AFTER the Series, Steinbrenner offered the vacant team presidency to Randy Levine, who took command on January 1, 2000, becoming the first to hold the title since Gene McHale in 1986. Levine, a powerhouse attorney, had worked in the Giuliani administration and led MLB's Player Relations Committee in reaching a settlement with the players after the 1994–95 strike.

During his time with the Yankees, he would greatly enhance the team's international brand, forging relationships with the Chinese Baseball Association, with the parent company of the Tokyo Giants, and with the Chinese Taipei Baseball Association. Ultimately, he would also forge a business partnership with the Dallas Cowboys—Legends Hospitality—that would handle concessions in the new stadiums of the two teams.

Chapter Forty-One

FOR THOSE WHO FELT THE twentieth century ended not in 1999 but in 2000, the Yankees gave them one more win with a twenty-sixth world championship. They would be the first team since the 1972–74 Oakland A's to win three straight.

Cashman made a terrific trade in 2000 that had much to do with the success. On June 29 he got David Justice from Cleveland for left fielder Ricky Ledee and pitchers Jake Westbrook and Zach Day.

Justice, once married to actress Halle Berry, had been with seven division winners in eight years between Atlanta and Cleveland (not counting the strike season). With the Yankees in 2000 he added another, playing 78 games and batting .305/20/60. Then he drove in 12 runs in the postseason.

The 2000 season was also when Jorge Posada took over as the team's regular catcher, taking his place in the catching lineage of Dickey, Berra, Howard, and Munson. The Puerto Rican–born switch-hitter, of Cuban-Dominican parents, had an uncle, Leo, who played for Kansas City in the sixties, while his father, Jorge Sr., played in Cuba. Jorge Jr. was frequently Robin to Jeter's Batman as the two became close friends, going back to 1992 at Greensboro. Posada was an All-Star five times in the 2000s. His 30 home runs in 2003 tied Berra for the most by a Yankee catcher, and he was third in MVP voting that year.

The 2000 Yanks won only 87 games, but it was enough to win the division by two and a half over Boston, despite winning just three of their last eighteen regular-season games. They went into the postseason with a seven-game losing streak. Torre could do little but shrug his shoulders and continue to write out a lineup card made up largely of All-Stars.

This was the postseason of unforgiving travel: six coast-to-coast trips to get to the World Series. (For the writers who traveled separately and accumulated some twenty thousand frequent-flier miles, it was a mixed blessing.)

The fifth and deciding game of the ALDS against Oakland saw the Yanks score six times in the first inning and apparently lock it up. But Oakland battled back, knocked out Pettitte in the fourth, and tightened the game to 7–5. From that point on, Yankee relievers Mike Stanton, Jeff Nelson, El Duque, and Mariano shut the door, and the Yankees took a deep breath and moved on.

Middle relievers Stanton, Nelson, and Mendoza were often the unsung heroes of this period. Workhorses who pitched often and never closed games, they were the bridge to Rivera and rightfully earned their rings. Stanton, a left-hander, spent seven years with the Yanks and was 31–14 with a 3.77 ERA, and fourth all time in pitching appearances. Nelson had a dazzling breaking ball and gave the Yanks six seasons, in which he had 334 strikeouts in 311 innings. Mendoza, always there for an emergency start and either short or long relief, gave the Yanks seven seasons of dependable work, highlighted by a 10–2 record in 1998.

Taking on Seattle in the ALCS, the Yankees got past a first-game loss and went up 3–1 behind strong pitching from El Duque, Pettitte, and Clemens as the Mariners scored only three runs in the games. Clemens's win in game four was a masterpiece: a complete-game, 5–0 victory in which he struck out 15, allowed only one hit, and walked two. Seattle's only hit was a line drive off Martinez's glove in the seventh by Al Martin. The complete game was a rarity for Clemens, who, despite being thought of as "old school," completed only four of his 193 Yankee starts covering the regular and postseason.

The Mariners won the fifth game, but the Yankees won their thirty-seventh pennant in New York on October 17 with a 9–7 win behind Hernandez and Rivera. Justice hit a big three-run homer into the upper deck in the seventh, which was enough to hold off an eighth-inning homer by Alex Rodriguez, playing his final game as a Mariner before going the free-agent route to Texas.

The 2000 World Series would be the first Subway Series since 1956, when the Yankees beat Brooklyn. The Mets, a wild-card team, won the National League pennant, and although the teams were regularly facing each other now in interleague play, which had begun in 1997, a Yankee-Met World Series was a treat for the city. (But not so for the nation; TV ratings were a record low.)

The Yanks won the opener 4–3 in twelve innings on a hit by reserve infielder Jose Vizcaino, and took game two 6–5 behind Clemens, who startled onlookers in the first inning by retrieving a shattered bat from Mike Piazza and hurling the jagged piece toward him as he ran to first on what was a foul ball. Earlier in the year, Piazza hit a grand slam off Clemens, then received a fastball to the helmet the next time they squared off. The bat-throwing incident, which cost Clemens a $50,000 fine, was bizarre and troubling,* but it didn't cost Roger his composure, as he allowed only two hits and no walks over eight innings in picking up the win. It was the Yankees' fourteenth World Series victory in a row, a major league record.

The Mets broke that streak with a 4–2 win in game three despite a 12-strikeout performance from El Duque, the most ever by a Yankee in a World Series game. Going into the game, Hernandez had an 8–0 record and a 1.90 ERA in postseason play. Later, Rivera would break Whitey Ford's "postseason" record for consecutive scoreless innings, running his total to 34⅓. (Ford's, of course, were all in World Series starts.)

Steinbrenner, disgusted by the run-down visitors' clubhouse at Shea, hired a moving company after the third game and took all of the Yankees' comfy leather clubhouse furniture from Yankee Stadium to Shea in time for game four. That's where he chose to sit and watch the game on television—when a pipe burst during the game and began to flood the clubhouse. At the game's conclusion—a 3–2 Yankee win fueled by a Jeter homer on the first pitch of the game—the players found Steinbrenner, deep in the rushing water, helping to bail the place out.

A critical moment in that game was Torre summoning David Cone from the bullpen with two outs in the fifth to face Piazza. Denny Neagle held a 3–2 lead, and the move cost him the victory, but Torre didn't want Neagle facing the Mets' best hitter. Zimmer put the notion in Torre's head earlier by asking, "Who do you want to pitch to Piazza?" When Torre said, "Who would you use?" Zim responded, "Coney."

Cone, the former ace of the Met staff, had gone 4–14 with a 6.91 ERA in

---

* Clemens later said he confused the piece of the bat with the ball, an odd claim that still doesn't explain why he threw it at Piazza.

2000 and for all purposes seemed done. He even suffered a dislocated shoulder in September. But he had one more moment in him to cap his Yankee career, and he got Piazza to pop up to second to end the inning as Nelson, Stanton, and Rivera stopped the Mets the rest of the way. It was just one batter—his last as a Yankee—but it was a huge out and a great exit for a great competitor.

The Yanks wrapped up the Series 4–2 the next day despite a tough performance by the Mets' Al Leiter, as they pushed two across in the ninth to break a 2–2 tie and then handed the ball to Rivera for his eighteenth straight postseason save. Jeter hit .409 in the Series with two homers and won the MVP, having earlier in the year won the All-Star Game MVP. It was the Yanks' twenty-sixth world championship.

It would be their last for nine years.

IN 2001, THE Yanks signed free agent Mike Mussina, the ace of the Oriole staff, to a six-year, $88.5 million contract. A durable right-hander and frequent Gold Glove winner, "Moose" would become only the ninth player in history to win 100 games with two different franchises, including 17 in his first year as a Yankee.

The Yanks were forced to move Knoblauch to left field, his throwing problems at second having gotten the better of him. (He went home after six innings during a 1999 game after three throwing errors.) Although Knoblauch adjusted well to his new position, he didn't hit with the kind of production the Yankees needed from an outfielder, and his career was quickly winding down. His second-base replacement, however, was Alfonso Soriano, a Dominican who had played ball for Hiroshima, Japan. His signing as a free agent had been contested by the Japanese Central League but approved by Commissioner Selig. Soriano stole 43 bases and hit 18 homers, but struck out a lot and hardly ever walked.

Tino Martinez led the Yanks with 34 homers and 113 RBI, Jeter hit .311, and Rivera saved 50 games, but Clemens was the year's big story, going 20–3 at age thirty-eight with 213 strikeouts in 220 innings to win his sixth Cy Young Award. Now earning over $10 million a year, it was his sixth and last 20-win season.

The Yankees swept a pair of three-game series from Boston in September and won the division by thirteen and a half games. The highlight of those victories came on September 2, when Mussina retired the first twenty-six Red Sox he faced at Fenway Park, outdueling David Cone, who had signed with Boston. Pinch hitter Carl Everett had a 1–2 count on him when he singled to left center to break up the perfect game. Mussina retired the next batter for a 1–0 one-hitter—one strike from perfection.

TUESDAY, SEPTEMBER 11, was a beautiful day in New York: sunshine, warm temperatures, and a night game against the White Sox scheduled.

That morning, America was attacked by terrorists using four hijacked commercial jets as suicide attack missiles, two of which were deliberately crashed into the World Trade Center in lower Manhattan. Among the many consequences of the attack was the stoppage of all sports in America.

Dave Szen, the team's traveling secretary, walked alone to the upper deck to peer through an opening to view the towers on fire. They were a little less than ten miles away. And from that vantage point, he saw them fall.

Two thousand six hundred and six people died in the towers, and about eleven hundred of the bodies were never found. Three of the victims, all of whom worked for Cantor Fitzgerald, had Yankee connections: John Swaine was the son of the Yankees' vice president of ticket operations, Frank Swaine, while Timothy and John Grazioso were sons of ticket seller Hank Grazioso.

The grandson of the late Marty Glickman, who had done pregame radio shows for the Yankees in the late fifties, also died in the attack.

Team president Randy Levine had been at a midtown meeting and was scheduled to fly to Milwaukee to represent the Yankees at an owners' meeting. With planes grounded, that was obviously canceled. He called Steinbrenner, who was at his Manhattan residence, the Regency Hotel on Park Avenue, and met him there.

From 10:00 A.M. to midnight, they sat together at the Regency, watching television and occasionally calling Mayor Giuliani to see if there was anything they could do. Finally the mayor had an idea. He didn't want the team to send anyone to Ground Zero, which was still in a state of confusion, but he suggested they send some players to St. Vincent's Hospital, where rescue workers were being treated, to the Lexington Avenue Armory, where families were identifying the dead, and to the Javits Center, where rescue workers were being housed.

On September 15, the first day the players who remained in town worked out at the stadium, PR man Cerrone organized O'Neill, Jeter, Posada, Rivera, Williams, Knoblauch, Cashman, Torre, and coaches Zimmer, Mazzilli, and Randolph to visit the three sites.

Williams encountered a grieving family at the armory, where many photos were hung showing the missing. Just weeks before, the armory had been the site of a big HBO party for the Billy Crystal film *61**, for which many Yankees were present. Introduced to a wife, looking desperately for her husband, he said, "I don't know what to say; all I know is, I think you need a hug." And that hug, widely reported, was part of the healing process that was to engulf New York as no event before had ever done.

Baseball shut down for six difficult days. The mayor spoke to Steinbrenner and Levine and asked them about doing a Prayer for America service at Yankee Stadium, which was set for September 23, when the team was on the road. It was a multi-denominational service filled with patriotism and sorrow as the city and the nation sought to find ways to recover. Home plate and the pitcher's mound were adorned with flowers; Oprah Winfrey, Placido Domingo, Marc Anthony, and Bette Midler were among those who led the event.

George Steinbrenner donated $1 million to the Twin Towers Foundation, and the Yankees sent their infield tarp to be used as a covering near Ground Zero.

On September 18, the Yankees resumed play in Chicago. The flight was uneventful, and Yankee charter flights had long been ahead of the field in terms of attention to security. At the game, a fan held a banner that said, I LOVE NEW YORK AND EVEN THE YANKEES. The Yankees wore FDNY and NYPD caps instead of their NY caps, and fans shouted, "USA! USA!" Indeed, the nation's sympathy for New York's fallen even extended to rooting for the Yankees, a development that would become the theme of an HBO Sports documentary on the days after 9/11.

September 25 was the first home game for the Yankees after the tragedy. A long line of city rescue teams stood near the home clubhouse waiting to go onto the field, and the players came by and hugged them and thanked them for what they were doing. Along the baselines before the game, Clemens walked the line and wished everyone well. A huge American flag was unfurled in the outfield.

The Yankees clinched the Eastern Division title that night but shook hands and raised a toast, instead of spraying each other with champagne, as had become sports tradition. "A lot of people were crying," said Rivera. "It was secondary," said Jeter. "It was great for the fans . . . it gave them something to cheer for, even if it was just a couple of hours each day."

There were mixed feelings about baseball at this time. Often it was said how insignificant the game seemed in the face of such tragedy. And yet it had such an uplifting impact on New Yorkers who so needed to be able to smile again. On balance, it was a great thing that baseball was there as an escape, and greater still that the Yankees were again going to the postseason and giving their fans another reason to continue cheering.

While the urge to show patriotism and hang American flags on cars lasted for about a year, the wave of patriotic feelings took hold at Yankee Stadium for years afterward. Kate Smith's version of "God Bless America," the rousing World War II anthem, was played daily in the seventh inning, with fans unfurling their own flags as it was played.

On September 11, 2002, a plaque commemorating 9/11 was dedicated in Monument Park. For many years an eagle named Challenger would dramatically swoop down from the bleachers to the mound and onto its handler's arm before postseason games. Similarly, Irish tenor Ronan Tynan would move the crowd with a live version of "God Bless America" on such occasions. (Alas, one errant flight by the eagle, and one overheard joke uttered by Tynan, thought to be in bad taste, and they were no more.)

Security was ramped up at all public landmarks and government buildings, and Yankee Stadium was certainly considered a target. Metal detectors were installed at every entrance, and no one was permitted to bring any bags or parcels, laptops, or (eventually) iPads into the ballpark. People had to remove their caps upon entering to show there was nothing hidden in them. Cell phones had to be turned on and shown to the security people. It was just a new way of life in America.

The regular season didn't end until October 7. In the ALDS against Oakland, the Yanks began their quest for a fourth straight world championship.

No TEAM HAD EVER lost its first two at home and come back to win a five-game series, but that was the tall order in front of the Yanks after two defeats at Yankee Stadium. Mussina and Rivera won a 1–0 game three on a Posada homer, a game best remembered for an unfathomable defensive gem by Jeter in the seventh. With Jeremy Giambi dashing home with the tying run, Jeter, dashing off to the right of home plate in foul territory, took an off-line throw from Shane Spencer and in one motion flipped it to Posada, who tagged Giambi on the back of his leg to preserve the lead. In a 1–0 win, facing elimination, the enormity of the play made it one for the ages.

"The kid has got great instincts, and he holds it together," said Torre after the game. Why was Jeter in just the right spot, so out of position from where a shortstop would normally be? He claimed it was a play they practiced, but even years later no one could cite a similar play in which Jeter just happened to be standing in foul territory on the first-base side for a possible cutoff.

El Duque went to 9–1 in postseason play, getting the win in game four to even the series. In the deciding game, back at Yankee Stadium, the Yanks won 5–3 with a big homer from Justice in the sixth as relievers Stanton, Mendoza, and Rivera pitched 4⅔ shutout innings to send the Yanks to the ALCS.

The Yanks' opponents were the Mariners, winners of a record 116 games in 2001 even with Randy Johnson, A-Rod, and Griffey having left. In this series, however, the Yankees dominated, winning four of five games for their thirty-eighth American League pennant. The big hit of the series was a game-four walk-off homer by Soriano that gave New York a 3–1 series lead. They won 12–3 the next day behind Pettitte, who earned MVP honors for the series with two wins, while Williams homered in three straight games. And thus the Yankees stood four victories away from a fourth straight world championship, which would set up 2002 as the year they could go after their record of five, from 1949 to 1953.

The Diamondbacks, their World Series opponents, reached the Series in only their fourth season of play. Former Yankee counsel Joe Garagiola Jr. was their general manager; Bob Brenly, their rookie manager, had replaced Showalter just that year.

This would be a Series with great sentimental support for the Yankees in the wake of 9/11, especially after coming home for game three, trailing 2–0.

Security was unusually tight for this game as President George W. Bush was to throw out the first ball. He had been to New York to visit Ground Zero, but this ceremonial moment, standing alone on the pitcher's mound before a packed Yankee Stadium, would prove to be one of the dramatic moments of his presidency.

Bush wanted to throw a few warm-up pitches before he went to the mound. The bulletproof vest he wore might make the pitch awkward, but he prided himself on being good at this task. (He'd been the lead owner of the Texas Rangers before entering politics.)

As he practiced under the stands, Jeter walked by and said, "Hey, Mr. President, are you going to throw from the mound or from in front of it?"

As Bush recounted in his memoir, "I asked what he thought. 'Throw from the mound,' Derek said. 'Or else they'll boo you.' . . . On his way out, he looked over his shoulder and said, 'But don't bounce it. They'll boo you.'

"I climbed the mound, gave a wave and a thumbs-up, and peered in at the catcher, Todd Greene . . . My adrenaline was surging . . . The ball felt like a shot put. I wound up and let it fly."

He unleashed a strike. "I was the definition of a relieved pitcher," he wrote. As he walked to shake Greene's hand and to meet Torre and Brenly by the Yankee dugout, the crowd began to shout, "USA, USA, USA . . ."

It was an indelible, post–9/11 moment for the national pastime and for the president.

The Yankees won that game behind Clemens, snapping an eighteen-inning scoreless streak.

In game four, the Yankees trailed 3–1 in the last of the ninth when O'Neill battled for a tough base hit, and then Tino Martinez electrified the crowd with a two-out, two-run homer off Byung-Hyun Kim to tie the score.

In the last of the tenth, the score still tied and the clock striking midnight, Jeter stepped in against Kim. Midnight meant this would be the first World Series game ever played in November. With two out and two strikes, Jeter fouled off three pitches—and then hit one down the right-field line for a game-winning homer. There was pandemonium in the stands: The swing tied the Series. One fan held up a sign that said, MR. NOVEMBER, and it remains a mystery why he had such a sign with him for a game that began October 31.

Yogi Berra once allegedly said, "It's déjà vu all over again," and that was the case in game five. Kim was again on the mound, sitting on a 2–0 lead with two outs in the ninth. This time it was Brosius who provided the miracle moment, with a two-run homer to tie the game, leaving Kim devastated as the fans tried to process what they were witnessing.

In the twelfth, Soriano provided the game winner with an RBI single to score Knoblauch, giving the Yanks a 3–2 win and a 3–2 lead in the Series, having won all three games in New York, the last two in miraculous fashion.

If scriptwriters in Hollywood—or even documentarians at HBO—could have their way the Series would have ended there, and New York would have had the post–9/11 moment of joy everyone seemed to crave.

But it was back to Arizona. And in game six, the D-backs crushed the

Yanks 15–2, setting the stage for a deciding game seven. And in this one, improbably, they beat Rivera, ending his streak of twenty-three consecutive postseason saves, when Luis Gonzalez dropped a single over the drawn-in infield in the last of the ninth for a 3–2 win and the world championship. Not since 1960, when the Yankees had outplayed Pittsburgh but lost, had Yankee fans felt so empty at the end. The dramatic homers in the middle games would live forever, but so too would a world championship trophy for Arizona.

THE *TIMES'* BUSTER Olney then wrote a prophetic book called *The Last Night of the Yankee Dynasty,* for this was indeed the end of something: for O'Neill (who'd been moved to tears by chants of his name in game five) and for Brosius, each of whom retired; for Martinez, who went to St. Louis via free agency; for Knoblauch, who as a free agent went to the Royals, where his odd career came to a close; and for popular Luis Sojo, who likewise had played his last game as a Yankee.

THE YANKEES' BREAKTHROUGH deal with MSG Network expired in 2000 but was extended for 2001. Years earlier, Tom Villante, the director of marketing and broadcasting for MLB, had warned Steinbrenner about long-term broadcast deals, telling him, "The landscape is changing—teams will one day be able to produce their own games." He was right.

In preparation for the end of the Cablevision contract, the Yankees and the NBA's New Jersey Nets formed YankeesNets in 1999. The primary purpose by now had evolved to forming a regional sports network of their own.

In spring training 2002, the Yankees Entertainment and Sports Network launched. The YES Network gave the Yankees control of their own broadcast fate after fifty-three years of selling their TV rights to others. The Yankees-Nets owned two thirds; Goldman Sachs and Providence Equity the other third. (YankeesNets dissolved in 2004 after the Nets were sold to Bruce Ratner, but the Nets were still broadcast by YES.) Leo Hindrey was the network's first CEO. The production value was first-rate, and the concept worked.

(A glitch in 2002 and early 2003 was a disagreement between the Yankees and Cablevision over terms to carry the games, and they were blacked out over a wide sheath of area homes during that span.)

Yankee Global Enterprises, the successor company to YankeesNets, separately owned the ballclub. Yankee Holdings, owned by the Steinbrenner family and the original limited partners (or those who acquired their shares), controlled Yankee Global and the Yankees' portion of Legends Hospitality. YES paid the Yankees a rights fee that exceeded that paid by MSG. The original Nets people, who sold to Ratner, retained their shares in the network. The network came to be valued at almost twice what the team was worth, according to a report in *Sports Business Journal*. "The total value of all YGE companies is about $5 billion, but YGE's share is roughly $2.75 billion," they wrote.

This was a long way from the days when Steinbrenner first bought the team, finding itself unable to even sell radio rights. The YES Network became the most lucrative regional sports network in the country, with a reported $435.2 million in revenues in 2010.

Chapter Forty-Two

THE YANKEES AGAIN WON THE AL East in their one hundredth season, but 2002 would not result in a fifth straight World Series appearance, as they lost to the Angels in the ALDS, going down in four games as Wells, Pettitte, and Mussina pitched poorly in the postseason.

Yes, David Wells was back, landing in the same rotation as Clemens. On January 17, Boomer spurned a handshake agreement with the Diamondbacks and returned to pinstripes, winning 19 games at age thirty-nine. He still caused Torre to shake his head, but the fans always loved the sight of the rumpled, 275-pound Boomer, battling away.

The Yanks third baseman in 2002 was Robin Ventura, who had played the previous three seasons for the Mets after nine years with the White Sox. It was unusual for the Yankees and Mets to trade first-line players with each other, but the Yanks sent David Justice to the Mets for him in a one-for-one deal. Ventura hit 27 homers and drove in 93 runs; the Mets sent Justice to Oakland.

Soriano continued to dazzle, leading the league with 128 runs, collecting 209 hits, stealing 41 bases, and hitting 39 home runs, the most ever for an American League second baseman. Rivera went on the disabled list three times in 2002, limiting him to just 28 saves, the fewest in his first fifteen seasons as a closer.

JASON GIAMBI, THE American League MVP of 2000, spent seven years at Oakland and then signed a seven-year, $120 million contract with the

Yankees beginning in '02. Arriving at age thirty-one, he hit 41 homers in each of his first two seasons, splitting time between first base and DH. The free spirit from Long Beach State was thought of as a motorcycle-riding, tattooed beach guy, but he adapted to the Yankees' conservative style and won over the fans with a dramatic walk-off fourteenth-inning grand-slam homer in a driving rainstorm on May 17 for a 13–12 win over Minnesota.

At six foot three and 240 pounds of muscle, Giambi was a left-handed presence in the lineup that put fear into opposing pitchers. As powerful as he was, he was always disciplined at the plate, twice leading the league in walks while a Yankee, and once in on-base percentage.

By 2002, after several years of whispers, the subjects of steroids and human growth hormones began to be spoken of more openly, particularly after published remarks by Ken Caminiti and Jose Canseco acknowledging their own use. People began to look at over-muscled sluggers with growing suspicion, especially during Barry Bonds's astonishing 73-homer year in 2001. Canseco, a teammate of Giambi's at Oakland (and briefly a Yankee himself in 2000), had been the subject of "steroid" shouts from Yankee Stadium fans as far back as 1991, when he proudly answered them by flexing his big bicep.

It was becoming increasingly clear that steroids were playing a big part in the game, and that MLB, the Players Association, and the media were ignoring the havoc it was causing to the record books, and to the health of the players, with their increasingly cartoonish physiques. The entire nation seemed asleep at the switch on this growing controversy. Among players, the subject was hushed. Even those who played "clean" wouldn't rat out a teammate. Talented minor leaguers were losing out on promotions that went to steroid users. It was a sorry time.

Giambi would experience some mysterious downtimes in his Yankee career. In 2004, he fell to .208 with 12 home runs and looked hopeless at the plate following the July discovery that he had a benign tumor. Prior to the start of the 2005 season, he delivered an apology to his teammates and fans at a Yankee Stadium press conference, apparently for using steroids, although he never explicitly said so. Then he came back to win Comeback Player of the Year in 2005, belting 32 homers.

In May of 2007, he apologized again, this time admitting to steroid use. He acknowledged his admission in grand-jury testimony in an investigation of the Bay Area Laboratory Co-Operative (BALCO), which had been accused of providing steroids and human growth hormones for athletes.

Fans disapproved of steroid use, but when it came to their hometown players, they were usually supportive—as long as they played well. Giambi never suffered from fan ire. By the time his seven-year contract expired, he had no world championship rings to show for his New York stay (nor did Mussina), but he did have 209 home runs, ninth all-time in Yankee history, and that bought him a lot of goodwill.

The Mitchell Report, issued in December 2007, named the players that former senator George Mitchell's committee had concluded were steroid or HGH users in baseball, and helped spur greater cooperation between MLB and the Players Association toward advanced drug testing.

Players with Yankee connections named in the report included Giambi, Gary Sheffield, Randy Velarde, Kevin Brown, Clemens, Jason Grimsley, Jerry Hairston Jr., Glenallen Hill, Justice, Knoblauch, Hal Morris, Denny Neagle, Pettitte, Stanton, Ron Villone, Rondell White, Canseco, and Darren Holmes. Also implicated for the use of steroids or human growth hormones but not mentioned in the Mitchell Report were Ivan Rodriguez, Matt Lawton, Sergio Mitre, Leyritz, and Todd Greene. Lawton, Grimsley, and Mitre were the only ones suspended by MLB; Mitre's punishment came in his first fifty days with the Yankees in 2009 for an infraction while with the Marlins. Lawton was suspended for ten games at the start of the 2006 season, by which time he had moved on as a free agent from the Yankees to Seattle.

Alex Rodriguez's name would emerge later.

Clemens issued an unconditional denial and later found himself locked in a legal battle over whether he lied to a congressional investigating committee about it. Pettitte admitted to using a growth hormone in 2002 to help recover from injury and received widespread forgiveness due to the manner in which he handled it. Knoblauch, Justice, Morris (a Yankee before the steroid era), Stanton, and Hairston denied the charges. Others refused to be interviewed.

It was a difficult time for baseball, particularly for the onslaught of suspect home run records. Every era of baseball had been different, due to segregation, air travel, night games, dead ball, lively ball, war, the DH, spitballs, or the lowered mound. But the steroid era would prove to be harder to get past, coming as it did with such ostentatious home run numbers. Yet as power stats declined and the problem seemed in retreat, the issue faded and fans seemed ready to move on. Hall of Fame elections remain a future obstacle, but otherwise the game did not seem to suffer in attendance, television ratings, or advertiser support. Baseball took a black eye, for sure, one of the worst in its history. But the basic game on the field continued to hold the fans.

THE SUCCESS OF Ichiro Suzuki with the Seattle Mariners, who entered the major leagues in 2001, had shown major league clubs that position players from Japan were ready to compete in the majors and achieve All-Star-level success. Ichiro had been MVP and Rookie of the Year in 2001, banging out 242 hits. Following the 2002 season, the Yankees signed Hideki Matsui, the premier power hitter in Japanese baseball.

Matsui, nicknamed "Godzilla," played ten seasons for the Yomiuri Giants, "the Yankees of Japan," and in 2002 was the Central League's MVP, hitting .334 with 50 home runs. At six foot two, he towered over his Japanese teammates. He was a black belt in judo, and in a country where honor ranks high as a standard of measurement, he was a national hero. While his English did not rise to high proficiency in the U.S., his dignity was measured in how he carried himself, right from the day he signed a three-year, $21 million contact in January 2003. (He would re-sign as a free agent in 2006 for another four years at $65 million.) The fans took to him at once, particularly after his grand-slam homer on opening day in Yankee Stadium won the game for the Yanks.

Matsui probably should have been Rookie of the Year in 2003, playing in every game and driving in 106 runs, but publicity about not truly being a rookie after ten pro seasons in Japan turned some voters away from him and he finished second. The matter had not come up during Ichiro's rookie season, nor during pitcher Hideo Nomo's ROY season with the Dodgers.

Matsui's respect for the game, and indeed for the Yankee organization, could be seen in an interview he did with a Japanese newspaper some years later. While extolling the honor of playing for the Yankees, he expressed shock that some of his teammates could be seen spitting their gum on the Yankee Stadium field. It was, to him, a dishonor to the historic ballpark.

The foreign media crush surrounding Matsui's arrival never abated. His every move was reported in the Japanese press. When he surprised his teammates by getting married during spring training of 2008, he good-naturedly sketched a stick-figure drawing of his bride, preserving her anonymity with great humor. In Japan, his father administered a museum bearing his name. And whereas Hideki Irabu had been rude and ill-tempered to the press, Matsui treated those same reporters with friendliness and respect. He also reached out to the New York media, taking them to dinner each spring training with his interpreter in tow, picking up the check for the large party and providing them with gifts.

"He was a joy," recalled media-relations director Rick Cerrone. "He was the anti-Irabu as far as the Japanese media was concerned. We had some sixty Japanese media to accommodate in spring training, and a large contingent following his every move. It was sometimes a larger group than New York media. And he was always great with them all."

Generally the team's left fielder, he filled in capably in center when needed, and ran his consecutive-game streak, covering Japan and the U.S., to 1,768 before fracturing his left wrist diving for a fly ball in 2006. The 518 consecutive games he played in the U.S. to start his career was a major league record, and it was the longest playing streak by a Yankee since Lou Gehrig's.

The Yankees also signed a four-year deal with Cuban exile José Contreras in 2003, one that didn't work out as well. Although he was 7–2, 3.30 as a starter, he made four visits to the disabled list and didn't provide the excitement that El Duque brought. After two seasons, Contreras moved on and achieved greater success with the White Sox.

In their centennial season of 2003, the starting staff, while old, was strong. Clemens and Wells, both forty, were 17–9 and 15–7 respectively. Mussina, thirty-four, was 17–8, and Pettitte, thirty-one, was 21–8. The Yanks won 101 games to capture their sixth straight division title. On June 13, Clemens won his 300th game before a rain-soaked crowd at Yankee Stadium, beating the Cardinals in an interleague game. The game featured the oddity of his also recording his 4,000th strikeout in the process. The Cardinals' Tino Martinez was about to bat for the first time as a Yankee Stadium visitor, but the applause for Clemens's accomplishment overshadowed the Martinez at-bat. Not to be deterred, the fans made sure that Tino got his standing ovation in his next at-bat—a "makeup" ovation.

The Yankee players gave Clemens a Hummer as a gift for his 300th win.

Another oddity during the season was a no-hitter thrown by six Houston pitchers on June 11 against the Yankees, as Roy Oswalt, Peter Munro, Kirk Saarloos, Brad Lidge, Octavio Dotel, and Billy Wagner hurled the first no-hitter against the Yankees since Wilhelm in 1958. The no-hitter "by committee" was necessitated by a strained groin muscle suffered by Oswalt in the second inning.

On June 3, with the team in Cincinnati, the Yankees named Jeter captain, a position vacant since Mattingly's retirement. It felt like a natural transition from untitled team leader. This followed a mild controversy from the previous December in which Steinbrenner had questioned Jeter's lifestyle, wondering whether the gossip columnists had it right about his being seen "on the town" so frequently. "When I read in the paper that he's out until 3 A.M. in New York City going to a birthday party, I won't lie. That doesn't sit well with me," said the Boss to Wayne Coffey of the *Daily News*.

Not only did they patch up the misunderstanding, but they got a clever television commercial out of it for Visa credit cards, which concluded with both of them being in a conga line at a nightclub.

(The Boss's oldest son, Hank, reprised this theme in 2011 when he said, "I think maybe they celebrated too much last year. Some of the players, too busy building mansions and doing other things, and not concentrating on winning." The reference was clearly to Jeter, who had just concluded the construction of a thirty-thousand-square-foot mansion on Davis Island in Tampa, known locally as "St. Jetersburg.")

AT THE JULY 31 trading deadline for the 2003 season, the Yankees decided to trade two players and cash to Cincinnati for third baseman Aaron Boone, a third-generation major leaguer whose father Bob and grandfather Ray had preceded him. (His brother Bret was also in the majors.) Ventura was traded to the Dodgers on the same day, and Boone would handle the position for the remainder of the season.

After winning a sixth straight division title, the Yanks lost the first game of the Division Series to Minnesota, but came back behind Pettitte, Clemens, and Wells to win the next three, Matsui's two-run homer in the Clemens game providing the margin of victory.

Then came another Yankee–Red Sox showdown in the ALCS, one that would prove among the most memorable. The series, which would ultimately go to seven games, was marked by a bitter fight in the third game in which Pedro Martinez shoved Yankee coach Don Zimmer to the ground. While it was hard to emerge with any sympathy for Martinez with a seventy-two-year-old man lying on the ground, Zimmer admitted later that "it all happened so fast, I didn't have time to realize what a fool I'd made of myself."

Martinez had given up a two-run double to Matsui and then hit the Yanks' Karim Garcia with a pitch that many people thought was intentional. Then he began pointing at his head and yelling at Posada, as though to suggest that Jorge was next to go down.

When Clemens threw high and tight to Manny Ramirez in the last of the fourth, both benches emptied. This is when Zimmer charged onto the field in search of Martinez. All Pedro could do was to shove him aside in self-defense.

It was thought best to get Zimmer to a hospital for precautionary X-rays, so there was Zimmer, being hauled out of Fenway Park on a stretcher, the latest drama in the Yankee–Red Sox wars.

Martinez tried to apologize the next day, but Zimmer said, "What does he have to apologize for? I was the guy who charged him and threw the punch!"

In game seven, the Yanks scored three times in the eighth to create a 5–5 tie, allowing a massive sigh of relief from the full house in Yankee Stadium. Many felt that Red Sox manager Grady Little had gone too deep into the game with Martinez, and the game-tying hit was a two-run double by Posada that finally drove Pedro out. (Little was fired by the Red Sox after the season.)

During that inning, Boone, who had been benched, ran for Ruben Sierra, then took over at third for Enrique Wilson.

Rivera set down the Sox in the ninth, tenth, and eleventh, a rare three-inning stint. Now the Yankees came up to face Tim Wakefield in the last of the eleventh, with Boone to lead off with his first at-bat of the night. It was 12:16 A.M. Bret Boone was a Fox broadcaster, watching his brother come to the plate. Aaron had gone 2-for-16 in the series and had six homers in 54 games during the season.

Boone swung at Wakefield's first pitch—and it was into the left-field seats for a pennant-winning home run, reversing a game in which Boston had been just five outs from going to the World Series.

"It was the greatest moment I've been here for," said Brian Cashman more than seven years later.

Boone's unlikely heroism sealed his place in Yankee history, reviving memories of Chris Chambliss and Bucky Dent. It brought the Yankees their thirty-ninth American League pennant, and sent them into the World Series against the surprising Florida Marlins.

As with most things Yankee-Boston, anything that followed felt anticlimactic. Beating the Red Sox felt like winning the World Series. But that wasn't how the rules worked. And Florida, like Arizona two years before, would leave the Yanks with a pennant, but not a world championship. Up three games to two and playing at a hushed Yankee Stadium, hosting its one hundredth World Series game, Josh Beckett topped Pettitte 2–0 with a complete-game triumph, bringing the Marlins a second world championship in just eleven years in the league. The Marlins hit only .232 in the six games and were outscored by the Yankees, but there would be no seventh game for the Yankees to recover.

That would be Joe Torre's last trip to the World Series as a Yankee. Zimmer, his relationship with Steinbrenner deteriorating since his interim managing stint in 1999, resigned. A lot of people thought his pairing with Torre in the Yankee dugout was an important ingredient to the Yankee success in the nineties and beyond. He didn't miss a thing.

It was also thought to be Clemens's farewell to the game, and he did nothing to discourage talk of his retirement. He accepted standing ovations in his last starts throughout the majors, and even got one from the Marlin players after departing game four, trailing 3–1, in what was believed to be his last time on the mound. Even the fans in Boston, known to despise him, had begrudgingly stood and cheered him in his "final" Fenway Park start during the LCS.

IN DECEMBER 2003, George Steinbrenner collapsed while attending the funeral of his friend Otto Graham, the great Cleveland Brown quarterback. While he recovered quickly, to many it was a milestone, signifying the start of a gradual health decline. His outbursts about performances would be less frequent. His availability to the media became more limited. An outside spokesman, Howard Rubenstein, was often the one who issued responses when requests were made. Newspapers took to assigning reporters just to follow Steinbrenner out of the stadium after games, hoping to catch a newsworthy remark. But he could no longer be counted on to be at home games or, in fact, at owners' meetings. His son-in-law, Steve Swindal, assumed a higher profile and was designated by Steinbrenner as his ultimate successor. (Unfortunately, a split from Jennifer Steinbrenner derailed those plans.)

Late in 2004, Steinbrenner was a guest on YES Network's *Centerstage* program, with Michael Kay interviewing him. It didn't go well. The old bombast was gone, and the questions were generally repeated as answers. He never did another such interview again. For a man who had learned to use the press to advance his agenda, to criticize a player or a manager, to chide another owner—it was a big void in the New York papers.

After 2007, Hank, forty-nine and the eldest son, stepped into the lead role, but a year later, acknowledging that Hal "has the head for this," the family moved Hal into a leadership position. Both Hank and Hal had gone to Culver Military Academy, as their father and sisters Jennifer and Jessica had. Hank, forty-nine, then went to Central Methodist College, and worked in the Yankees' front office in the eighties, but was generally occupied with management of the family's Ocala-based horse farm. Hal, thirty-eight, graduated from Williams College (like his dad) and got an MBA from the University of Florida. He served as chairman and CEO of Steinbrenner Hotel Properties.

Publicly, both children continued to defer to their father.

Chapter Forty-Three

THE OFF-SEASON OF 2003–04 WAS both controversial and momentous.

Andy Pettitte, coming off his 21-victory season and his game-six loss to Beckett, signed a three-year free-agent contract with Houston on December 16. An opportunity to pitch near his hometown of Deer Park, Texas, proved too enticing to refuse.

As soon as he signed, speculation began that Clemens would "unretire" and join him, which he did. The two had a close friendship, a shared workout routine, and a chance to get Houston to its first World Series: The Astros began play in 1962 and had never won a pennant. They finally won in 2005 with Clemens and Pettitte winning 30 games between them.

The Yanks replaced them with Javier Vazquez, whose 4.91 ERA would be a disappointment; Jon Lieber, only slightly better; and the heralded Kevin Brown, who was 10–6 in 22 starts, limited by a bad back. Tom Gordon came aboard as the eighth-inning setup man, a position in which he excelled over two seasons.

Brown had won 197 games over seventeen seasons with five teams. The Yanks got him in a trade with the Dodgers on December 13 and assumed his contract of nearly $16 million a year. He was not, however, a pitcher who was able to adjust to diminishing skills, and his Yankee stay was not a happy one.

The Yanks thought they would have David Wells back, having reached a verbal agreement. The next thing they knew, he signed with San Diego, spurning the Yankees as he had spurned the Diamondbacks two years before in similar circumstances.

"I'm not complaining," said Cashman. "This can happen when you're negotiating with David."

The Yanks also added Gary Sheffield, signing him as a free agent six days after the Brown trade. This was a deal primarily done out of the Tampa office, where Doc Gooden, Sheffield's uncle, had Steinbrenner's ear. In New York, Cashman had been pursuing Vladimir Guerrero.

The Braves, for whom Sheffield had produced two strong seasons, wanted him back. He decided to meet with them at Malio's, a favorite Tampa restaurant of Steinbrenner's; he wanted the Boss to see him dining with the Braves. His plan worked. Steinbrenner saw him with the Braves, and met with him right afterward. After a couple of tough negotiating sessions (which Sheffield did without an agent), he made a deal.

"The truth was that I wanted to play in New York and nowhere else," wrote Sheffield later. "I had to get New York out of my system."

In 2004, he finished second in MVP voting—to Guerrero—with a .290/36/121 season.

In February 2004, Aaron Boone, the toast of New York, was playing a pickup game of basketball and tore a ligament in his knee. It was a violation of his contract. He'd be out all year.

A lot of other players would invent ways to explain how they had gotten hurt. Not Boone. He called Cashman and told him the truth, knowing he would likely be released.

"He was man enough to admit what happened," said Cashman. "But I had to do my job."

Boone left with the distinction of being the first Yankee since Joe DiMaggio to be married to a *Playboy* Playmate of the Month. But now the Yankees needed someone to play third.

On February 16, they swung one of the most dramatic trades in the history of the franchise. They traded Soriano, their talented second baseman, to the Texas Rangers for Alex Rodriguez.

A-Rod was already one of the great players in baseball history. He led the league in home runs in each of his three seasons in Texas. With Jeter and Boston's Nomar Garciaparra, he was considered one of a trio of superstar shortstops that the American League had been blessed with in one era. With the Yankees he would have to move to third base, a move he willingly embraced, ceding short to Jeter.

His salary was another issue. Tom Hicks, the Rangers' owner, had given him a ten-year deal beginning in 2001 for a colossal $252 million—way more than anyone else was offering. As such, the deal was baffling to observers and seemed well out of line with what was necessary to sign him. Of course, A-Rod had jumped at it.

He later revealed that he used steroids in Texas, attributing it to the pressure the contract brought. He seemed well on the way to breaking Bonds's career home run record, an event baseball would celebrate to cleanse Bonds out of the record book. The future steroid revelation would complicate that, but to break the record as a Yankee, restoring the career record to Babe Ruth's team, seemed like a terrific idea.

He had always worn Babe's number 3, but as that was retired on the Yankees, he would wear 13.

The move was not as great a salary upheaval to the Yankees' payroll as it might have been. Not only were the Yankees shedding Soriano's contract, over $5 million in 2004, but the Rangers agreed to pay $67 million of the $179 million remaining on A-Rod's pact, which left the Yankees giving him about $16 million a year. Miguel Cairo would play second base and earn just $900,000. So they were only "adding" a net $12 million in payroll. This they could do.

BORN IN WASHINGTON HEIGHTS but raised in Miami, Rodriguez soon became the greatest third baseman in Yankee history. His right-handed power dwarfed even that of DiMaggio, who always seemed thwarted by the left-field dimensions of old Yankee Stadium. A 2005 home run by Alex, deep into the old visitors' bullpen, where the ambulance now parked, was thought to have traveled 487 feet. In the remodeled stadium, this was topped by only five players: Kirk Gibson (500 feet to the top of the right-field bleachers in 1985), Barry Bonds (500 feet into upper deck in right in 2002) Jay Buhner (492 in 1991), Juan Encarnacion (490 in 2001), and Fred McGriff (490 in 1987).

Rodriguez would bring eccentric moments to the field—yelling "Ha!" or "I got it!" to try to get an infielder to drop a pop-up, trying to slap a ball out of Bronson Arroyo's glove while racing him to first base in a Yankee-Boston playoff game, and annoying Oakland pitcher Dallas Braden, over whose mound he ran after making an out.

He dated starlets, including Madonna, Kate Hudson, and Cameron Diaz, and was a gossip-column regular. He did endorsement deals for private jets, but lacked the easy rapport that Jeter always enjoyed with the public.

No one doubted he was a unique talent, but even his friendship with Jeter had soured a bit while he was at Texas, after he told a magazine that Derek wasn't the guy in the Yankee lineup that people feared. It wasn't what friends did. Sometimes the on-field camaraderie between them seemed false.

The 2004 season was going to be a test of Torre's leadership. Good chemistry couldn't be counted on. It helped that old hero Don Mattingly returned as a coach after eight years away from the game, but the team was still a bit more like the old Yankees for Yankee haters.

Yankee haters, of course, were most in abundance in New England, and the rivalry between the Yanks and the Red Sox would call for both teams to step back and ban vulgar T-shirts and banners that fans brought into both parks. Scuffles in the stands were not uncommon; security was always tightened. Rhythmic, obscene chants were impossible to stop and became a part of the soundtrack for games between the two clubs. The team owners, who certainly enjoyed the sellouts created by the rivalry, didn't always stand back. In December 2002, Boston CEO Larry Lucchino referred to the Yankees as "the Evil Empire" after they signed José Contreras, a term that had been used by President Reagan in 1983 in reference to the Soviet Union.

Steinbrenner responded to Lucchino's charge by saying, "That's how a sick person thinks. I've learned this about Lucchino: He's baseball's foremost chameleon of all time. He changes colors depending on where he's standing. He's been at Baltimore and he deserted them there, and then went out to San Diego, and look at what trouble they're in out there. When he was in San Diego, he was a big man for the small markets. Now he's in Boston and he's for the big markets. He's not the kind of guy you want to have in your foxhole. He's running the team behind John Henry's back. I warned John it would happen, told him, 'Just be careful.' He talks out of both sides of his mouth. He has trouble talking out of the front of it."

THE YANKEES RESPONDED to "Red Sox Nation" by creating "Yankees Universe" in 2006, selling merchandise that benefited pediatric cancer research at Memorial Sloan-Kettering Hospital. (The Yankees Foundation, a charitable arm formed by Steinbrenner in 1973, benefits projects in the

Yankee Stadium neighborhood. A Yankee fantasy camp in Tampa is among the revenue streams that feeds the foundation.)

There had been many classic Yankee–Red Sox games over the years, including a 2–0 Yankee loss in a Martinez-Clemens complete-game matchup in 2000 decided by a ninth-inning homer by Trot Nixon.

But perhaps the ultimate matchup came on July 1, 2004, in Yankee Stadium, a tense, back-and-forth contest that went into extra innings. In the twelfth, Nixon lifted one down the left-field line. Jeter, never quitting, dove toward the ball and made the catch as his momentum carried him into the stands. He emerged with a bloodied face and suffered a bruised right cheek and right shoulder. He was taken to Columbia Presbyterian Hospital (on the site of old Hilltop Park) for X-rays and received seven stitches.

"I went to the hospital with him," said Dr. Stuart Hershon. "What you saw on TV—the stoic, matter-of-fact approach, the calm, this-is-how-you-play-the-game attitude—that's the way he was in the privacy of the trip. There was never a mention of, 'Maybe I shouldn't have put myself at risk like that.' He only knew one way to play baseball."

The Yankees won the game, and Jeter was back in the lineup the next night.

The Yankees opened the 2004 season with two games against Tampa Bay in Tokyo, seen on television in New York at 5:00 A.M. Matsui was the impetus for the games, and he rewarded his faithful Japanese fans (who regularly woke up early in the morning to watch the Yankees on live TV) with a two-run homer in the second game, giving Brown a victory in his Yankee debut.

The Yankees moved into first place to stay on June 1 as Rivera recorded 12 saves in an eighteen-game period. (He had 53 for the season, his career high.) They won 101 for the second straight year, making three straight 100-win seasons for the first time in their history, along with seven straight division titles. They set a new Yankee Stadium attendance record of 3,775,292.

Again it was Minnesota in the ALDS, and again, after losing the opener of the series, the Yankees came back to win three straight, the clincher coming in eleven innings when A-Rod, hitting .421, doubled and scored to provide the winning run.

Now it was again the Red Sox in the ALCS, the two highest-payroll teams in baseball going at each other. (The Yankees, the only team to pay a luxury tax on payroll in the system's first year, 2003, owed $25 million in 2004, with the Red Sox owing $3 million and the Angels $927,000. No other teams owed anything.)

Red Sox Nation looked on in anguish as the Yanks won the first three games 10–7, 3–1, and an embarrassing 19–8.

In game four, the potential clincher at Fenway, the Yanks led 4–3 going to the last of the ninth with Rivera on the mound. Kevin Millar led off with a walk, and Dave Roberts, pinch-running, stole second. Bill Mueller singled him home with the tying run, and the teams played on.

In the twelfth, "Big Papi" David Ortiz homered off Paul Quantrill and the Sox would see another day. (Quantrill pitched a Yankee-record 86 games in the regular season.) In game five, Ortiz, who would have 11 RBI in the series, homered in the eighth, and a sacrifice fly off Rivera tied the game at 4–4. Boston won it in the fourteenth when Ortiz singled home Johnny Damon off reliever Esteban Loaiza, working his fourth inning. Three games to two.

In game six, Boston held on to a 4–2 win as Curt Schilling went seven innings despite a torn tendon sheath, resulting in his bleeding through his white sanitary sock.

In game seven, the Red Sox were seeking to become the first team in post-season history to overcome a 3–0 deficit. And they did it, knocking Kevin Brown out of the box in the second inning, pounding him for five earned runs in 1⅓ innings, and winning 10–3 before a stunned, silent, and early-departing Yankee Stadium crowd. The big blow was a grand slam by Damon. It was certainly one of the most painful losses—both the game and the series—the Yanks had ever endured.

The Red Sox would go on to win the World Series in four straight and to end the Curse of the Bambino after having gone without a world championship since 1918.

WHILE WATCHING GAME ONE of the World Series on TV, opera great Robert Merrill, eighty-seven, a regular national anthem performer for the Yankees since 1969, died.

On the day after Christmas, Stadium organist Eddie Layton died at seventy-nine. He had been a beloved fixture at Yankee Stadium since returning in 1978 (his original run was 1967–70). His successors would be Paul Cartier and Ed Alstrom.

Willie Randolph, a Yankee coach since 1994 and bench coach after Zimmer left, got his long-awaited shot at managing when the Mets hired him on November 3. His successor was Joe Girardi, who had been a YES Network broadcaster in '04 following his retirement as an active player. (A year later, Girardi became Manager of the Year with the Florida Marlins.)

Tony Womack was to have been the Yankees' second baseman in 2005, but it wasn't working out, and in May Torre handed the job to rookie Robinson Cano.

Cano, born in San Pedro de Macoris, Dominican Republic, and named for Jackie Robinson (he eventually wore number 24 as a tribute to Robinson's retired number 42), would become one of the few players whose major league performance far exceeded his minor league one. So rapidly did his skills rise above expectations, that by his sixth season it was possible for observers to believe that on most days, the Yankees were fielding the best third baseman (A-Rod), best shortstop (Jeter), and best second baseman (Cano) in team history. Of course, careers take twists and turns, and injuries can happen, but his offense was already exceeding the two Yankee second basemen in the Hall of Fame—Lazzeri and Gordon—and he had a smooth flat-footed defensive style and strong throwing arm.

The son of Jose Cano, who pitched six games for the '89 Astros, he got a modest $150,000 bonus and hit .261 in three minor league seasons. He always made a postgame phone call to his father to analyze his performance, even after he became a star.* He was often in trade talks as a "throw-in" but he stayed in the system, and he was there when Womack failed. He began with a 2-for-23 showing but Torre built his confidence and told him the hits would fall. He wound up with a .297 average, and finished second in Rookie of the Year voting.

One of the trades he survived was the one that brought Hall of Fame–bound Randy Johnson to New York in 2005. Johnson, forty-one, a nine-time strikeout champion and five-time Cy Young winner, became, at six foot ten, the tallest Yankee in history.† He had 246 career victories, a perfect game, and a World Series ring from the 2001 Arizona triumph over the Yankees. He earned $32 million in his two years.

While Johnson won 34 games over his two Yankee seasons, there was a

---

* Jose was Robinson's selected pitcher in the 2011 Home Run Derby at the All-Star festivities. Robinson won it.

† Andrew Brackman, at six foot eleven, beat that record in 2011 and became the fifteen hundredth Yankee in the process.

sense that his skills were beginning to diminish. He wasn't "lights out," as he had been so often in his career, and his 5.00 ERA in 2006 confirmed what people were sensing. He got on poorly with the media, entering into a confrontation on a Manhattan street with a TV crew even before he pitched his first game. It was less than a good fit, and he was traded back to Arizona after two years, winning his 300th game with the Giants in 2009 before retiring at age forty-five.

He was joined on the Yankee staff in 2005 by Chien-Ming Wang, the fourth Taiwanese player in major league history and the Yanks' first. Wang (pronounced *Wong*, but playfully called "Wanger" by Jeter and others) had been the organization's Minor League Pitcher of the Year in 2004. He signed in 2000 and worked his way up through the system, beginning with the Staten Island Yankees, the Yankees NY-Penn League team that began play the year before at a new ballpark near the Staten Island Ferry dock. (The team moved from Oneonta, nineteen miles from Cooperstown, where for thirty-two seasons the Yanks had maintained a working relationship with the community-owned franchise.)

The Yankees brought Wang up from Columbus in late April and put him in the starting rotation. He responded with an 8–5 record in 18 games. Communication was difficult, but he managed press conferences in English without a translator.

Wang turned out to be a real find. He won 19 games in both 2006 and 2007 and became the most reliable pitcher in the rotation. When the new Yankee Stadium opened in 2009, he was among the players prominently displayed on exterior billboards heralding the star-packed roster. But in a 2008 interleague game at Houston, he partially tore a tendon in his right foot while scoring the only run of his Yankee career. He wound up on crutches and missed the rest of the season.

The baserunning snafu wasn't really the problem. Wang had some shoulder issues and ultimately, they did him in. He pitched the first exhibition game in the new stadium the following year, and then 12 regular season games afterward, but his 9.64 ERA said it all. His mechanics were off, and he was not the pitcher he had been. Sadly, he was cut loose after the 2009 season, with fans left to wonder what might have been, and reminded of how fragile a career can be.

Another "find" in 2005 was Aaron Small, thirty-three. The Yankees were his tenth organization. He had mostly pitched in the minors for seventeen long seasons. The Yanks called him up in July, and he became an inspiration to all players who just "hung in" over repeated shuffles through the minors and various organizations. Small went 10–0 with a 3.20 ERA before losing a game in the ALDS. He was a one-year wonder; the magic was gone in 2006, but to be ten games over .500 for a playoff-bound team was no small contribution.

Yet another free agent signing for 2005 was Carl Pavano; one this did not play out well. Pavano pitched against the Yankees in the 2003 World Series, and then went 18–8 for the Marlins in 2004. He signed a four-year contract for just under $40 million, and started the '05 season well. But then injuries followed injuries, rehab didn't go well, and when Pavano broke his ribs in a car accident and waited too long to tell the team, the relationship really soured. He refused a minor league assignment to give the Yankees a needed roster spot. Newspapers cleverly called him "American Idle."

His teammates began to speak about him in less than supportive terms. Mussina said, "Was everything just coincidence? Over and over again? I don't know." Torre used the word "sizable" to describe the work Pavano needed to do to get back in the good graces of his teammates. It was most unusual to find players not closing ranks around one of their own.

In the end, the Yankees let his four-year contract expire and just called it a bad signing. He managed to get another contract from Cleveland and got back his winning form there and in Minnesota. When he was a free agent after 2010, and the Yankees needed a starting pitcher—he was not considered.

His lifetime record with the Yankees in just 26 starts was 9–8, 5.00. He pitched just 145 innings over the length of the contract, at a cost of over $250,000 per inning. Throw in medical expenses and meal money, and Pavano was one of the least rewarding investments the team ever made.

A FAMILIAR FACE returned to New York in 2005 for one last season. With Giambi now seen as primarily a DH, the Yanks brought back Tino Martinez. Tino showed his old power early, hitting eight homers over eight games in May, but in the end hit only nine more and then retired. Al Leiter also came "home" to the organization at which he had begun his career, returning on July 17, sixteen years after being traded to Toronto for Jesse Barfield.

The 2005 Yanks got an instant MVP season from A-Rod, .321/48/130, in which he became the first Yankee in twenty-five years (since Reggie Jackson) to lead the league in home runs. He was the first right-handed-hitting

Yankee to win a home run title since DiMaggio in 1948, and it gave him 429 career home runs in the year he turned thirty.

The Yanks went 95–67, the same record as the Red Sox, but because they won the season series from Boston 10–9, they clinched the division on the next-to-last day of the season with an 8–4 win over the Sox. For eight years in a row now, they had finished first and Boston second.

On Sunday, September 25, the final home game of the regular season, a crowd of 55,136 poured through the gates to put the Yankees over four million for the first time in their history. It was an incredible accomplishment—almost a season of sellouts. When I had been the PR director, we would put out an annual press release hailing "the [blank] consecutive year in which the Yankees had drawn a million." Two million became standard when the remodeled stadium opened in 1976. Three million became the threshold in 1999. And now this. In each of the final four years of the remodeled Yankee Stadium, four million was surpassed.

The Yanks faced the newly renamed Los Angeles Angels of Anaheim in the Division Series. The Angels were always a tough opponent for the Yanks, and in this series they divided the first four games, with the Yanks' Shawn Chacon staving off elimination with a game-four victory. But in game five, Mussina allowed five runs in $2\frac{2}{3}$ innings, and Torre brought in Randy Johnson in relief. On two days' rest, Johnson pitched $4\frac{1}{3}$ shutout innings, but the Angels held on to win the game 5–3 and send the Yankees home. They hadn't missed two World Series in a row since the 1981–95 drought.

AFTER LOSING THE 2001 World Series, Steinbrenner had told Brian Cashman, "Okay, we've been doing it your way, now it's my turn," and he had created dual—some said dueling—front offices. The concept failed to produce another world championship.

"I kept telling George that he needed a general manager he would listen to," said Cashman. "If roster moves weren't working out, it was my problem, I was taking the blame, and in many cases, I hadn't signed those guys in the first place. Too many people were involved. In the military, you have a clear chain of command, and you consolidate authority. We needed that as an organization. And I told him I would leave—I had other offers. It wasn't a power play, it was just becoming more and more difficult.

"George was surprised by my position, especially when Randy Levine and [general partner] Steve Swindal told him I meant it."

Steinbrenner acquiesced. He didn't want to lose Cashman, and he agreed to tender him full authority for player decisions. He gave him autonomy and a three-year, $3 million contract.

"I stayed out of respect for him. I didn't want to go, I didn't want to disappoint him, but I couldn't exist in the current structure," he said.

Chapter Forty-Four

WITH SHEFFIELD AND MATSUI both sidelined for long stretches by injuries in 2006, the Yankees were lucky to come up with four unexpected replacements: Johnny Damon, who left the Red Sox to sign a four-year, $52 million contract; rookie Melky Cabrera, who brought young enthusiasm to the roster; Bobby Abreu, a fine offensive player obtained in July from the Phillies; and Bernie Williams, who signed a one-year, $1.5 million "last-round" contract and wound up playing 131 games.

When the season ended, Williams was disappointed not to be offered anything more than a spring training invite. So his career ended without him formally retiring, still hopeful of another shot.

Williams had five 100-RBI seasons and eight 100-run seasons. He was sixth on the Yankees' all-time home run list, fifth in games played, and no Yankee hit more postseason home runs.

Jeter enjoyed a big 2006 and finished a close second to Minnesota's Justin Morneau in MVP voting, his second runner-up finish. Jeter never played for awards, but this felt like a missing piece of hardware to a remarkable collection. Cano hit a robust .342.

Sheffield returned late in the season from his wrist injury, and Torre decided to try him at first base, feeling the outfield was now well manned with Damon, Matsui, and Abreu, with Giambi as DH (37 regular-season homers), and with Cabrera as a spare. But the team's ninth straight ALDS didn't go well for the Yanks; Sheffield was 1-for-12, A-Rod 1-for-14 (to increasing fan booing), Cano 2-for-15, and Damon 4-for-17. The Tigers knocked off the Yanks in four games with only Wang winning his start, and the Yankees went home early for a third straight year. Ex-Yank Kenny Rogers hurled seven shutout innings for the Tigers in game three.

Steinbrenner waited until three days after the season before offering Torre another contract, albeit at $7 million a year, the most ever earned by a manager. But patience was never his strong suit: It had been six years now without a world championship.

When pitcher Cory Lidle's private plane hit a Manhattan apartment building four days after the Yanks were eliminated, killing the pitcher and recalling the death of Thurman Munson, some reflected on how a win over Detroit would have kept the Yanks going: Lidle would not have been in the air that day.

TALK CONTINUED ON a new Yankee Stadium. In 1996 HOK, the renowned stadium architectural firm, proposed four sites for a new home: the rail yard on Manhattan's west side, Pelham Bay Park, Van Cortlandt Park, and the existing site (or across the street). By now Rudolph Giuliani had been elected mayor, and there never was a bigger Yankee fan in City Hall.

But despite having everything seemingly in place—a supportive mayor, a strong economy, a popular team, and a 1998 plan unveiled for a new Met stadium—it never happened during the Giuliani administration. In his final week in office, not long after 9/11, he brought forth a half-taxpayer, half-ballclub plan for both the Yankees and the Mets to have new ballparks, but that too was not what ultimately happened. One missing element was a supportive press. They didn't like the idea of public money going to the projects. And still, New Jersey beckoned. The *New Yorker* had a cover showing Yankee Stadium being lifted by helicopters and transferred to Jersey. But public opinion polls in New Jersey convinced Governor Christine Whitman to back down.

On April 5, 2006, the city council of New York approved plans calling for the Yankees to privately finance a new ballpark. The stadium was built through a combination of the state, the city, and the Yankees. The city formed a local development corporation that in effect provided the land to build it. The Yankees paid for construction through PILOT payments (payments in lieu of taxes), and the funding came via city-issued bonds, the Yankees making payments to the bond holders while contributing millions toward new parks and Bronx community-group programs. The city owned both the land and the building; the Yankees signed a forty-year lease.

On August 16, 2006, the fifty-eighth anniversary of Babe Ruth's passing, ground was broken just across East 161st Street from the existing ballpark for a new and larger Yankee Stadium, with no naming rights sold. It would eventually cost about $1.45 billion, with an additional $300 to $400 million for infrastructure improvements to be borne by city and state taxpayers.

Just like other teams with new ballparks, the Yankees could deduct their stadium-construction payments from their local revenue (broadcast, tickets, and concessions), from which their sharing obligations with the lower-revenue teams was determined.

A long-sought train station for Westchester and Connecticut commuters would be built, and beginning that very day, construction cranes arrived to begin a task scheduled for completion by opening day 2009.

THE STRUCTURE WOULD rise on top of city-owned land at Macombs Dam and John Mullaly parks, which dated back to 1899, with the current stadium to be torn down and replaced by three smaller diamonds, known together as Heritage Field. (Mullaly, who died in 1914, was known as the "father of Bronx parks.") In 2010, a new Macombs Dam Park opened atop the new Ruppert Plaza Garage, on the south side of 161st Street, across from the old gate 4.

"We're just happy that we're able to do this for the Yankees and happy to do it for you people," said Steinbrenner at the groundbreaking. "Enjoy the new stadium. I hope it's wonderful."

It was a ninety-minute ceremony on a very hot day. Yogi Berra and actor Billy Crystal sat behind him. Mayor Michael Bloomberg, Governor George Pataki, Bronx officials, Commissioner Selig, Steve Swindal, COO Lonn Trost, and team president Randy Levine all spoke. A photo op of hard-hatted dignitaries overturning the first dirt was followed by real excavation as soon as the invited crowd departed. HOK, who had designed the luxury suites in the 1976 stadium, was the architect, and Turner Construction did the building. For the next two seasons, a trip to Yankee Stadium would mean a sighting of the work in progress next door.

THE 2007 SEASON introduced a pair of homegrown pitchers who really stirred attention. Phil Hughes, just twenty, made his Yankee debut on April 26, and although he missed 85 games with a strained hamstring, the

Yankees won all five of his September starts as he positioned himself for a spot in the rotation. He was a first-round pick in the 2004 June draft right out of Foothill High School in Santa Ana, California.

Beefy Joba Chamberlain, a Native American raised in Lincoln, Nebraska, by a single father, was the feel-good story of the year. A product of the University of Nebraska, he was drafted as a starting pitcher in the compensation round of the 2006 draft. But after he went 9–2 in 15 starts for Tampa, Trenton, and Scranton/Wilkes-Barre, the Yankees called him up on August 7 and put him in the bullpen.

He didn't allow a run in his first 15⅓ innings, the longest Yankee streak for a newcomer since Slow Joe Doyle of the Highlanders in 1906. He finished with a 0.38 ERA in 19 appearances (just one earned run), with 34 strikeouts in 24 innings. With each big out he dramatically pumped his fist, his motion carrying him toward the first-base line. His wheelchair-bound father, who had been raised on the Winnebago Indian Reservation near Lincoln, became a fixture at home games, pumping his first in unison. By his fifth appearance, his entry onto the field had the fans howling. It was one of the great debuts in Yankee history, almost a gift from the baseball gods, especially since relief pitching was all new to him. By year's end, having Joba pitch the eighth and Rivera the ninth had shortened Yankee games to seven innings; if the opponent didn't have the lead by then, it was over.

For a mentor, Chamberlain and Hughes found themselves an unlikely teammate in forty-four-year-old Roger Clemens, who had pitched three years with Houston and seemingly retired again. But rumors began to swell that he was considering yet another comeback with the Yankees, and on May 6, during the seventh-inning stretch at Yankee Stadium, he stood up in a luxury suite with a microphone and said, "Thank y'all. Well, they came and got me out of Texas, and, I can tell you it's a privilege to be back. I'll be talking to y'all soon."

The odd moment was accompanied by his signing a deal worth $28 million for the season, but prorated to $18.7 million to cover his time with the team. He debuted on June 9 and went 6–6 in 17 starts. He was a great presence in the clubhouse, and was reunited again with Andy Pettitte (15–9), who also returned to the Yankees after three years in Houston.

The Yankees were not as lucky with another new arrival, Kei Igawa. A star pitcher in Japan, he was thought worthy of a five-year, $20 million contract after the Yankees paid the Hanshin Tigers $26 million for his rights. This was considered a runner-up prize, so to speak, as the Red Sox signed

Daisuke Matsuzaka to a six-year, $51 million contract after paying the Seibu Lions more than $51 million for his rights. Matsuzaka was the better signing, but neither pitcher adapted well to the American game. Igawa was a disaster. Even in 2008, when the Yanks were bringing up everyone with a pulse to fill openings in middle relief, Igawa was relegated to Scranton/Wilkes-Barre, which had replaced Columbus as the Yanks' triple-A farm team in '07.

Offensively, the season belonged to A-Rod, whose 143 runs scored were the most in baseball in twenty-two years, and who led the league with 54 homers and 156 RBI as he won his second MVP as a Yankee. He hit his 500th career home run on August 4.

ON AUGUST 13, 2007, Phil Rizzuto died in a New Jersey nursing home at the age of eighty-nine. In his final months, Yogi Berra would visit weekly to play bingo with him. Bill White sat with him and held his hand. He loved his canolis until the end. Because his career with the Yankees as a player and a broadcaster lasted from 1941 to 1996, fans born in the 1980s could feel connected to the Yankees of the forties through Rizzuto and would be able to maintain that connection until their old age in the 2070s and beyond. He had a powerful bond with fans, and the fact that he broadcast the '96 season, and spoke of Jeter, Williams, Posada, Pettitte, and Rivera in his final times on the air, also connected those players to his original teammates.

His 1994 induction speech at the Hall of Fame, at long last, was one of the most charming and memorable ever delivered.

THE 2007 SEASON was the first since 1997 without the American League East title, but the Yankees did manage to take the wild-card spot and make the playoffs for the twelfth time in Joe Torre's twelve years at the helm. It didn't come easily. They were 21–29 by the end of May and needed a big finish in September to pull it off. There was talk of Torre's job being in jeopardy early in the year, but he prevailed and the Yanks took on Cleveland in the Division Series.

All eyes were on A-Rod as the series unfolded. He had gone 3-for-19 in the previous two ALDS, and despite his big numbers the Yanks had not won a World Series since he arrived. Pressure was heavy on him, but he went 4-for-15 and heard boos with each out at Yankee Stadium.

The Indians' CC Sabathia beat Chien-Ming Wang 12–3 in the opener, and then the Yanks lost game two 2–1 in eleven innings, a game remembered as "the bug game." In a fluke of nature, swarms of midges attacked humid Jacobs Field in the seventh inning, a situation that would have sent any picnicker running for cover. But the players stayed on the field, interrupted only by Gene Monahan and Steve Donahue doing their best to help with bug spray. It probably made things worse. Everyone was flailing away wildly at the attack.

(In 1939, the Yanks similarly lost a doubleheader to the Red Sox in a futile attempt at fighting off Japanese beetles.)

Chamberlain, on the mound when the bugs arrived, soldiered on, trying to pretend that he wasn't covered with pests. But his sweat seemed to attract more. In the last of the eighth he gave up the tying run, setting up a chance for the Indians to win, and they did.

"It was my biggest mistake in twelve years as manager," said Torre. "I should have taken my team off the field."

The series moved to Yankee Stadium. On the morning of game three, *Bergen Record* columnist Ian O'Connor took a chance and called the Regency Hotel on Park Avenue and asked for George Steinbrenner. This was the Boss's New York home, as he never had a permanent residence in the city.

After a brief screening process, Steinbrenner was on the phone. He hadn't done an interview in ages. This would be his last one.

"Hi, Ian." O'Connor was startled, but he gathered himself and started asking his first of about ten questions, before he heard, "Okay, Ian, you got enough?" and that was the end.

He had enough. Steinbrenner said that he'd likely fire Torre if the Yankees lost the series. "His job is on the line," he said, giving O'Connor his headline and a story that was picked up everywhere. "I think we're paying him a lot of money . . . so I don't think we'd take him back if we don't win this series."

Steinbrenner did not blame Torre for not pulling the team off the field in Cleveland; he blamed Bruce Froemming, who was retiring as an umpire after thirty-seven years of service. "He won't umpire our games anymore. It was terrible," he said. "It messed up the whole team. Jeter, all of them."

Asked whether he had ceded control to his sons Hank and Hal and son-in-law Felix Lopez, who had married his daughter Jessica, he said, "I have full control. I'm doing all right. I'm fine."

While all of this was going on, Alex Rodriguez's agent, Scott Boras, was sending signals that his client, the richest man in the game, would likely opt out of his contract and become a free agent, presumably forcing the Yankees into the bidding at an increased rate. The publicity did not help in getting fans to back off booing A-Rod.

"I think we'll re-sign him," Steinbrenner told O'Connor. "I think he realizes New York is the place to be, the place to play."

Game three saw Clemens, in what really would be his final appearance, give up three runs quickly and Hughes enter in the third. Hughes, Chamberlain, and Rivera allowed one run over the last six innings, while the Yanks came back to win 8–4 to stay alive. But in game four, the Indians scored early on Wang, forcing Mussina into second-inning relief. It was to no avail; the Indians won 6–4. The Yankee Stadium crowd sat quietly as their team was eliminated for the seventh year in a row. Boston would win the World Series again.

In the coming days, attention turned to the rehiring of Joe Torre and the great dilemma of what to do about A-Rod. Hank Steinbrenner said the Yankees wouldn't negotiate any further with him. (The Yankees would be losing the $21.3 million that Texas was paying him under his original agreement.)

There weren't a lot of teams left who could pay the kind of money he was looking for, and A-Rod knew it. He would later say that opting out was "a mistake that was handled extremely poorly.

"I made mistakes. I've got to look in the mirror. If I had to do it again, I would've called Hank from day one and negotiated myself," he added. He did, indeed, drop Boras as his representative and handled the renewal with the two sons on his own, with assistance from a managing director at Goldman Sachs.

He didn't do badly at all. On December 13, Rodriguez signed a new ten-year contact for $275 million, which included bonus clauses if he passed Mays, Ruth, Aaron, and Bonds on the career home run list. The new contract to run through 2017, fluctuated year by year, peaking at $32 million in 2009 and 2010.

THE JOE TORRE saga played out quite differently.

Having not won a World Series since 2000, Joe was losing leverage each year. There were supporters in the front office losing patience with him. Although he had the twelve straight playoff seasons under his belt, he also perennially had the league's highest payroll, so success was expected. There was some resentment over his increasingly high profile—all the commercials, the magazine covers, the television interviews. The organization prided itself on success being a team effort, meaning the full front office.

In fact, although his popularity remained high, Torre was beginning to disconnect from Cashman, who, having gained full control of player decisions since his 2005 contract, was more and more impressed by the use of computer stats and the insight that they could provide. Cashman was seeing how lineups with the best chance of winning could be produced by computer output. Torre was still going by the gut instincts of a baseball man of nearly a half century.

"People used to think it was okay to smoke, or okay to drink during pregnancy," said Cashman. "We learn as we go forward."

Cashman felt the Red Sox were regularly playing better than they had a right to, and he saw in that the use of SABR stat guru Bill James, a Red Sox advisor. He brought in Mike Fishman as his director of quantitative analysis. His assistant general manager, Jean Afterman, was also a strong advocate of the far-reaching information computer stats could reveal. Sometimes Cashman would go to Torre to show him the value of the computer. "Look at this, Joe" he'd say. "We have a better chance against this pitcher with [Wilson] Betemit in the lineup instead of [Andy] Phillips." But he wouldn't get very far. Cashman was losing faith. He felt his manager needed to be on the same page he was.

Torre saw a growing divide. "We had a falling-out in spring training," he told Tom Verducci in his memoir. "I basically challenged him. Then I apologized a few days later, because I really like Cash . . . I would have really liked to have him trust me."

Still, it was Cashman who remained his biggest supporter when a group met at Steinbrenner's home in Tampa to discuss Torre's future. Cashman saw the public-relations fallout of dropping the enormously popular local hero. Steinbrenner, his sons, his son-in-law, and Randy Levine were ready to move on. But they decided to offer him a $5 million contract—a pay cut—that would still keep him the highest-paid manager, and would include incentives to get him to $8 million if he won the World Series.

Torre was hurt by the offer and asked Cashman if he could talk to the Steinbrenners in person. On October 18 he flew to Florida with Cash, and walked into Steinbrenner's fourth-floor office at Legends Field. He said he didn't think he deserved a pay cut.

Hal Steinbrenner said, "I'm sorry you feel this way, but we'd all still like you to stay with the Yankees and work with the network."

That was the end. By not taking the new offer, and then by holding his own press conference the next day to call the offer an insult, he was making his exit. He felt there was no negotiation intended. The Joe Torre era was over.

Not since Casey Stengel's 1960 firing had the public felt such a shock. Joe would soon take a job managing the Dodgers, moving to Los Angeles and returning the Dodgers to the postseason. His book with Verducci in 2009 burned a lot of bridges, took serious shots at the Yankees, and called A-Rod "A-Fraud," which was a tough thing to do to Rodriguez. Torre's excuse that "he's called that in the clubhouse all the time" didn't go over well.

The competition to succeed Torre came down to Torre's bench coach, Mattingly, and Joe Girardi, who had already been a National League Manager of the Year with Florida before getting fired there. Cashman knew Mattingly would be the popular choice, but in terms of embracing computer projections and being in sync with him, Girardi fared much better. Girardi got the job.

Mattingly went with Torre as a coach, and succeeded Joe as Dodger manager in 2011. Neither Torre nor Mattingly would be around to mark the final year of old Yankee Stadium or the opening of the new one.

Less than a month after the playoffs, Steinbrenner officially handed the top organizational duties to Hank and Hal as general partners, with George still listed as principal owner.

Chapter Forty-Five

2 008 WAS A YEAR-LONG CELEBRATION of the last season of Yankee Stadium, making little distinction between the 1923–73 version and the 1976–2008 renovated version. Older fans seemed to display greater affection for the original park, forgetting the times they had partially obstructed views, or had to reach the upper deck without escalators. At each game, the sight of fans posing for photos with the field behind them was an event that invited a shared experience with fellow fans.

The Yankees used a "countdown clock" all season, with special guests invited to pull on a placebo lever to knock another game off. Each guest had some connection to the park's history, and it was a popular daily event. Steinbrenner did the first one. The Topping and Sheehy families were represented. Longtime employees such as Tony Morante and Debbie Nicolosi took a turn. Celebrities such as Bob Costas, Ben Stiller and his father Jerry, Billy Crystal, and Lance Armstrong had a pull. The Bleacher Creatures were recognized. So was Buck Showalter. Former players included Billy Werber (from 1930), age one hundred, Coleman, Richardson, Murcer, White, Gamble, Dent, Jackson, and Boggs. Perfect-game pitchers Larsen, Wells, and Cone shared a moment. When there were no games remaining, the clock said FOREVER.

The historic season missed the voice of Bob Sheppard, who at ninety-eight was just too ill to work any longer, although he didn't officially retire. (His last game was September 7, 2007.) Jim Hall, a Sheppard sound-alike, was at the microphone all season.

Major League Baseball honored the legacy of Yankee Stadium by awarding it the 2008 All-Star Game, an honor often reserved to showcase new ballparks. The festive event would be best remembered for the Monday-night Home Run Derby, in which Texas slugger Josh Hamilton hit some of the longest drives ever witnessed in the park.

The game was attended by George Steinbrenner, who was given a ride to home plate on a golf cart, where a number of his old players embraced him warmly as the fans cheered. It would be his final appearance in old Yankee Stadium. (During spring training, Legends Field in Tampa was renamed George M. Steinbrenner Field.)

In midseason, I had an opportunity to bring Tom Stevens, Babe Ruth's grandson, and his son Brent to meet Lonn Trost, the Yankee official princi-pally charged with the new stadium's planning. It was a meeting intended to maintain a relationship between the Yankees and the Ruth family; the de-struction of the House That Ruth Built was not intended to be a metaphor.

The new stadium would amply honor Babe, with the exterior along 161st Street to be called Babe Ruth Plaza and dotted with appropriate signage and banners. The new facility was being called the House That George Built by the media, but it would well honor the team's legacy and would even in-clude a Yankees Museum, the focal point of which was a long display of baseballs signed by everyone the team could find who had played even one game for them. At either end would be statues of Don Larsen pitching and Yogi Berra catching, recalling the 1956 perfect game.

The 2008 Yankees did not go to the postseason, despite a 20–9 year from Mike Mussina in his final year before retiring. (He was the first pitcher since Sandy Koufax in 1966 to win 20 and then quit.) Instead, even with a $209 million payroll, they never managed to emerge from third place after mid-June. It was the first time they missed the postseason since 1993, save for the '94 strike year.

The failure to make the postseason actually presented a good situation. The final game at Yankee Stadium would be the last home game of the regular season. Had they gone into the postseason, there would have been no way of predicting when that last game would be, and it would have been impossible to schedule lavish ceremonies around it.

The Yankees paid the city $11.5 million to be able to sell off memorabilia from the stadium—the seats, the signage, and more. Collectors were sali-vating over the treasures that would come from vintage Yankee Stadium. A pair of seats was available for $1,500 through Steiner Sports, which had a collectibles partnership with the team. Season-ticket holders could own their own seats for an extra $500. Brian Cashman's desk chair cost $5,000. Sections of the outfield frieze were offered at $50,000. A twenty-by-twenty-foot chunk of outfield sod? $10,000. A display case with dirt? $50. Jeter got the sign in the tunnel to the Yankee dugout that quoted DiMaggio's "I want to thank the Good Lord for making me a Yankee," a sign he always touched as he headed for the field. The flagpole was retained by the Yankees and rests quietly under the new bleachers. Rivera wanted the bullpen bench. The foul poles were cut into two-inch sections and sold for $80 per section. Home plate was carried to the new ballpark. Thurman Munson's locker was moved to the new Yankees Museum. A group campaigned to save the massive concrete gate 6 as a landmark, but was unsuccessful.

And so the last game would be on a warm Sunday night, September 21, televised nationally by ESPN. Andy Pettitte got the honor of pitching against the Orioles, and got his 2,000th strikeout in the first inning. Bob Sheppard read the starting lineups, having recorded them earlier in the day at his home. The 1922 American League pennant, which was hung on opening day of 1923, was spread out in the unoccupied area of the bleachers.

I had lunch at Mickey Mantle's Restaurant in Manhattan with Julia Ruth Stevens and her family—she was to throw out the ceremonial first pitch a few hours later. The Babe's daughter was ninety-two, but sprightly and excited for her honor. My own father had died eight weeks earlier at ninety-two, and Bobby Murcer had lost his battle with cancer on July 12, failing to achieve his goal of seeing the new stadium open. So Julia's bright spirits on such a sentimental day certainly were appreciated. She would deliver her big pitch to Posada in about four hours.

I met up with my son, Brian, who came in from Boston, and we took our seats in the mezzanine over right field, section 33, to share the finale together. (I wished my daughter Deb was with us, but she was living in San Diego.) Bunting hung from the mezzanine and upper deck as though it was the World Series. Bobby Abreu was the Yankees' right fielder, and I pointed out to Brian that at my very first game, in 1956, I sat in right field with my father, and Hank Bauer was playing right.

"And if you scramble the letters in Abreu," I noted, "you get Bauer." "It's the Yankees," I explained. "Everything connects."

I also pointed out that this would be the last chance for someone to hit a fair ball out of Yankee Stadium.

The crowd that day put attendance for the season at 4,298,543, an all-time team record and the eighth straight year of growth. The gates opened seven hours early and the Yankees let the fans walk on the field and take photos. It was one of the highest-priced tickets ever offered by the reseller StubHub.

The pregame ceremonies began with a parade of Yankee employees in vintage flannel uniforms, representing the first 1923 lineup and popular Yankees of the past. Tony Morante, the team's historian and tour guide, got to wear 22 for his favorite, Allie Reynolds.

Former Yanks—real ones—were introduced by John Sterling and Michael Kay, and they ran to their respective positions to great cheers, especially Bernie Williams, back for the first time since his 2006 departure.

Winfield and Roy White were introduced and ran to left. Nettles, Boggs, and Brosius took third. To cheers of "REG-GIE, REG-GIE, REG-GIE," Jackson went to right with O'Neill, and "PAUL O-NEILL!" was chanted. They were joined by Roger Maris's son Randy. Skowron ("Moose!"), Chambliss, and Martinez took first.

Joining Gene Michael at shortstop was eighty-eight-year-old Cora Rizzuto, Phil's widow, who stood through the whole ceremony. She was escorted by Mariano Rivera. Great cheers rang out for Yogi at catcher, who was joined by Girardi; Cheryl Howard, Elston's daughter; and by Michael Munson, Thurman's son.

On the mound were Ford, Larsen, Guidry, Wells, Cone, Gossage, and Catfish Hunter's widow, Helen. Ford and Larsen scooped up dirt. Billy Martin Jr. joined Randolph and Richardson at second. Randolph, recently discharged as the Mets' manager, slid into second base. All the widows and children wore properly numbered jerseys.

Center field, that most hallowed ground, was the most emotional spot to fill. Besides the appearance of Williams, David Mantle, looking so much like his dad and running with his elbows high as Mickey did, went out, as did Kay Murcer, wearing a number-1 jersey, with her two children, Todd and Tori. It was their first time back and they shared emotional hugs with Bernie and Danny as the fans cheered and dabbed at their eyes.

The DiamondVision screen showed fast photos of some seven hundred Yankees by position, whether they were present or not. Omitted was Roger Clemens, who had recently suffered a huge fall from grace over allegations of steroid use.

Everything was the "last time in the old park." The last starting lineup was Damon, CF; Jeter, SS; Abreu, RF; Rodriguez, 3B; Giambi, 1B; Xavier Nady, LF; Cano, 2B; Matsui, DH; and Jose Molina, C. As the innings passed, the flashes from digital and cell-phone cameras constantly illuminated the old park.

Molina, who had been the team's regular catcher for most of the year with Posada hurt, hit the last home run in the fourth to put the Yankees ahead 5–3. It would be 7–3 by the ninth when the Yanks took the field for the last time. Metallica's "Enter Sandman" played as Mariano Rivera came in to finish the game. Everyone stood for the full inning.

The fans loved this perfect finish. To see the great Rivera in his familiar routine, staring at the baseball, readying himself, his concentration on his craft never broken, was one of the joys of being a Yankee fan in this era. His body facing north, knees bent, pulling the ball into his waist before the delivery: It was an image fans wanted to preserve forever. It couldn't go on forever, of course, and fans were now savoring each appearance, knowing one day this would end.

On the field in the ninth were Melky Cabrera in left, Brett Gardner in center, and Abreu in right. Cody Ransom had gone to first to replace Giambi, who had delivered the last hit in Yankee Stadium, which would in turn be the last hit of his Yankee career. His contract up, he would depart as a free agent and sign with Colorado.

Jay Payton grounded out weakly to short for the first out on a 1-and-2 pitch. Luke Scott grounded out to second on an 0-and-2 pitch. Two down. Everyone readied their cameras.

At this point Girardi took out Jeter, a dramatic flourish used on rare occasions when the manager clearly acknowledges the moment. He was allowing the captain to hear "DE-REK JE-TER" one more time as he jogged to the dugout. He emerged briefly for one more curtain call. Wilson Betemit went out to play short.

With flashbulbs popping, Rivera went 2-and-1 on Brian Roberts, and then delivered the final pitch in the history of old Yankee Stadium. It was 11:41 P.M. Roberts grounded to Ransom at first for an unassisted putout. The Yanks won 7–3, the victory going to Pettitte. And that was it.

But not quite. Few fans left. The Yankee players emerged onto the field and a microphone appeared. Jeter, honored before the game for breaking Lou Gehrig's record for hits in Yankee Stadium, addressed the crowd without notes.

> For all of us out here, it's a huge honor to put this uniform on and come out every day to play. And every member of this organiza-

tion, past and present, has been calling this place home for eighty-five years. It's a lot of tradition, a lot of history, and a lot of memories. Now the great thing about memories is you're able to pass it along from generation to generation. And although things are gonna change next year, we're gonna move across the street, there are a few things with the New York Yankees that never change. That's pride, tradition, and most of all, we have the greatest fans in the world. And we're relying on you to take the memories from this stadium, add them to the new memories to come at the new Yankee Stadium, and continue to pass them on from generation to generation. So on behalf of the entire organization, we just want to take this moment to salute you, the greatest fans in the world.

He doffed his cap to salute the fans and his teammates followed.

Jeter always seemed to get it right. The familiar sight of his postgame interviews, the little cough into his fist, the squeezing of the nose, the small smile, had become so familiar over the years. But it had taken his parents to tell him to enjoy it all a little more. "Make sure you enjoy this," they told him. "You don't want to look back and wish you'd done something different."

With that, led by Jeter, the team took a lap around the field, waving their caps, sharing the emotion. Security was tight, including police officers on horseback. Joba Chamberlain went back to the mound to slap the pitching rubber and wave to his dad. All the while, Frank Sinatra's "New York, New York" played over and over until the last fans had filed out, well past midnight.

The final message on DiamondVision: TO BE CONTINUED.

Chapter Forty-Six

S ELENA ROBERTS OF *SPORTS ILLUSTRATED* arrived at the University of Miami weight room on February 5, 2009, to seek out Alex Rodriguez. A-Rod was working out in the final weeks before spring training.

Roberts confronted him. She had learned he tested positive for steroids in 2003.

He directed her to the Players Association and chose not to speak about it any further.

Two days later, SI.com posted her story. A-Rod had not been named on any previous lists, and baseball was poised to promote him heavily as the ultimate successor to Barry Bonds for the lifetime home run record. This was a blow not only to A-Rod but to the Yankees and MLB.

Moving quickly to control the damage, A-Rod did an interview with Peter Gammons on ESPN on February 9. He said, "When I arrived in Texas in 2001, I felt an enormous amount of pressure. I felt like I had all the weight of the world on top of me, and I needed to perform, and perform at a high level every day. Back then, it was a different culture. It was very loose. I was young. I was stupid. I was naïve. I wanted to prove to everyone that, you know, I was worth being one of the greatest players of all time. And I did take a banned substance. You know, for that I'm very sorry and deeply regretful."

He reported to Tampa on February 17, and the Yankees set up a press conference in the tent outside the third-base side of Steinbrenner Field. Cashman, Girardi, and his teammates attended.

He didn't change his story about using the steroids only with Texas, leaving some wondering why he didn't feel the same pressure coming to New York. He mentioned a cousin who had administered the substance. "It was pretty evident we didn't know what we were doing," he said, but to another question he replied, "I knew we weren't taking Tic Tacs."

Cashman sighed. "We've got nine years of Alex remaining . . . And because of that, this is an asset that is going through a crisis. So we'll do everything we can to protect that asset and support that asset and try to salvage that asset.

"This story is going to be with Alex for a long time. It's going to be with him forever."

As it happened, it had its time on the nation's front pages and faded. Baseball's fan base was pretty much exhausted with steroid revelations at this point, although Hall of Fame voters will ultimately have the last word. As long as he produced on the field, the hometown fans cheered him. A-Rod, the Yankees, and MLB would have to move on. There was not much of an alternative.

IN PREPARATION FOR the new stadium, and after missing the playoffs, the Yankees made four key additions to the 2009 team.

Two were pitchers who went by their initials: CC Sabathia and A.J. Burnett. They were introduced at a joint press conference on December 19, the last one in the old stadium. During this month, the offices were being moved, and the media showed employees carrying trophies across the street. These would be two more, and they crossed 161st Street for photos in the new park.

Sabathia, twenty-eight, was a bear of a man, over three hundred pounds on a six-foot-seven frame, and he liked to wear his uniform baggy. He was the heaviest Yankee since 295-pound Walter "Jumbo" Brown in 1936, although David Wells may have weighed in on that debate. In eight seasons with Cleveland and half a year with Milwaukee, he had won a Cy Young Award and established a reputation for being able to pitch deep into games. (When he pitched a complete game in May 2011, it was the first for the Yankees in two years, a record streak of 341 CG-less games.) He signed a seven-year, $161 million contract with the choice to opt out after 2011.

Burnett, thirty-two, a beneficiary of Tommy John surgery, had been in the majors since 1999 with only one season better than three games over .500. He'd gone 18–10 with Toronto in 2008—his option year. He signed for five years and $82.5 million.

Next came Mark Teixeira, signing for eight years and $180 million. His press conference, with the now traditional donning of a pinstripe jersey, came on January 6. It was the first event in the new stadium. "Tex" proved to be a brilliant defensive first baseman with a great Yankee Stadium swing. He met the challenge in his first year with a .292/39/122 season, leading the league in RBI and total bases, tying in homers, and finishing second in MVP voting. It didn't take fans long to embrace the Georgia Tech product, who had broken in with Texas in 2003 and continued to improve as his career matured.

The fourth acquisition was outfielder Nick Swisher. His signing wasn't the big news the others had been; no press conference followed. He was coming off a .219 season with the White Sox and was thought to be a fourth outfielder. Only when Xaxier Nady had a season-ending injury did he find himself a starter.

The gregarious Swisher was the son of a major leaguer: His father, Steve, was a catcher for nine seasons starting in '74. So Nick grew up around the game, and then became a star at Ohio State. Michael Lewis's bestselling book *Moneyball*, which looked into how Billy Beane went about building the Oakland A's on a small budget, paid special attention to Swisher. Lewis related how much Beane coveted Swisher, how much he hoped he would last in the 2002 draft until Oakland could pick him. "Swisher has an attitude," said Beane. "Swisher is fearless. Swisher isn't going to let anything get between him and the big leagues. Swisher has presence." He wound up getting his man in the first round, the sixteenth pick, as compensation for the loss of Johnny Damon to the Red Sox.

Over his time with Oakland, Swish did not become the big star that Beane had hoped, but a good player who reached highs of 35 homers and 95 RBI in 2006. When he tailed off in '07, he was traded to Chicago. And there, Swisher slumped and became available again.

"We saw the .219, but we were able to tell that he was better than that," said Cashman. "Our stat-analysis department was a manifestation of how we were now going about doing our business. We realized that there was a lot more going on in this game than met the eye.

"The difference in Swisher's .219 in 2008 compared to his years in Oakland was largely bad luck. He had the third-lowest batting average in the majors on balls put in play, a statistic that varies greatly with luck. He had many fewer hits than he should have had. He still had great patience at the plate—4.5 pitches per at-bat. There was no decline in home runs, despite hitting only four in his first 185 at bats. Nineteen of his 24 homers came in home run friendly parks, as Yankee Stadium figured to be. I thought he was a great low-buy opportunity and a huge bounce-back candidate."

Cashman's homework paid off. He got him in a trade for Wilson Betemit and two minor league pitchers. All he believed proved correct, as Swisher found a new life in the Yankee outfield and turned into a clutch performer. He hit 29 home runs in each of his first two Yankee seasons, got his average up to .288, and restored his OPS—on-base plus slugging—from .743 in Chicago to .870 in New York. By his second year with the Yankees, he was on his first All-Star team, and although the switch-hitter's strikeouts were high, he would use up a lot of pitches getting them, helping to wear out pitchers.

OLD YANKEE STADIUM could fit into new Yankee Stadium. The difference wasn't in the seating capacity, which was actually smaller, but in the footprint of the park, which allowed for wider pedestrian paths and for a magnificent Great Hall—thirty-one thousand square feet along the first-base side, in which long banners hung honoring past Yankee greats.

The concourses behind the seating were festive, with a wide variety of concession booths and a clear view of the field. In the old park, the bleacher fans were cut off from the rest of the stadium; here they could walk the full 360. Weather-resistant cushioned box seats were a new amenity.

The outfield fences—318 to left, 408 to center, 314 to right, with the power alleys at 399 and 385—replicated the 1976–2008 stadium, although the fifty-two feet from the catcher to the backstop was a reduction from the original eighty-four.

Construction proceeded right up to the last minute. One unplanned interruption was the revelation that a worker—a Red Sox fan!—had buried a David Ortiz jersey in the concrete to cast bad luck on the team. The section was drilled apart and the jersey removed. No chances were taken.

The monuments were relocated to dead center field (as opposed to left center), where they were hidden by the fence lest they reflect in the batter's eye. Thus the best view of them came from the upper deck, not the lower seats.

The video board was breathtaking, both for its size—59' × 101'—and for the quality of its high-definition images. A 24' × 36' board was placed in the

Great Hall. A crew of twenty-five, led by Mike Bonner, elaborately planned in-game entertainment.

The player clubhouses were huge, along with all the requisite trappings of the modern game: indoor batting cages, video screening areas, state-of-the-art training facilities, and even secure, indoor parking to get the players in and out without concern over crowd control. That was one daily ritual that ended—fans greeting the players as they walked from the player lot to the player entrance at the old park.

The stadium was decorated with historic Yankee photographs from the archives of the *Daily News*, and the luxury suites, now wrapping end to end around the park, were branded with uniform numbers, with every player who ever wore the corresponding number listed on a plaque outside the suite. (Suite 4 had only one name, Lou Gehrig; fifty-two players had worn number 22, and still counting.) Those who feared the memory of the old Yankees would fade were relieved to see the homage to the old days. Even replica medallions, bearing eagles, went into holes in the concrete over the entrance gates, replicating the look of the 1923 park.

Auxiliary scoreboards showing the line score went back up at field level in right- and left-center fields, a reminder of the post-1947 stadium.

Nothing, however, made it more "Yankee Stadium" than the frieze that topped the upper deck. On the most important thing, the public was in agreement: It still felt like Yankee Stadium. The ability to connect the two parks was crucial, and it succeeded. It would still be the park visiting players wanted to play in, still be part of the reason free agents wanted to be Yankees, and it seemed to rightfully carry the history of the franchise with it. After all, it was still at East 161st Street and River Avenue. It was just across the street. And for the 2009 season, the two parks were up side by side, as demolition of the outer concrete at the old place did not begin until late in the year.

The first section of sod from DeLeo Sod Farms in Pilesgrove, New Jersey, was installed on October 15, 2008, giving the playing surface plenty of time to knit together. The front office moved in on January 23, retaining the phone number that it'd had since 1952.

Over the years, the demographics had changed for the ticket-buying public, with a more affluent crowd now, and often businesses prepared to pay well over Broadway-show prices for three hours of live baseball featuring a star-laden team.

Ticket prices were set between $500 and $2,500 for 4,397 premium seats. People in those seats would also receive access to restaurants under the stands, which gave the appearance of unsold seats, since many were "down below" during the games, indulging their appetites for shrimp and prime rib.

But then something unexpected happened: a stock market crash late in the 2008 season.

So bowing to the new reality, the team announced in late April that they were lowering prices, with the $2,500 seats halved, and the $1,000 seats along the base lines dropping to $650.

In the last year of the old stadium, the top ticket price had been $400, which covered the first eleven rows of the seats closest to home plate. There were sixteen different price points, all the way down to a $14 bleacher seats.

In the new park, bleacher seats were still $14 (and $5 for some partially obstructed views). Field-level box seats were $325, but then lowered to $235. There were $100 and $75 tickets as you moved toward the outfield, reaching down to $23 for the upper grandstand.

THE FIRST GAME in the new stadium, Friday, April 3, was an exhibition game against the Cubs, managed by Lou Piniella. In the spirit of 1923, bleacher seats sold for twenty-five cents and grandstand seats for $1.10.

The official opener would not come until April 16, a Thursday-afternoon game against the Indians, with Sabathia pitching against Cliff Lee.

There was no Bob Sheppard to announce this time, as he had now officially retired at ninety-eight. The job went to Paul Olden, a former Yankee radio broadcaster who had once famously asked Tom Lasorda what he thought of Dave Kingman's three-home-run performance against him, a hilarious audio tape that lives on in blooper compilations.

It was sunny and 56 degrees for the opening game. I arrived early and sought the exact spot outside the park where a photo would replicate the best-known opening-day photo of 1923, the one with cars driving by the first-base side. Satisfied that I had the shot, I joined one of my PR successors, Jeff Idelson, in a right-field, foul-territory section in time to catch the opening ceremonies. Jeff was now the president of the Baseball Hall of Fame and interested in what artifacts might be donated to the Hall from the game.

George Steinbrenner was in attendance and appeared on the giant video screen with a wave to the fans. He had lived to see the magnificent new ballpark open, although travel back and forth to Tampa had become very difficult. As he left after the game, he responded to a shout-out from Anthony McCarron of the *Daily News* by saying simply, "It's beautiful."

A statue of Steinbrenner was placed in the Yankee office lobby near gate 2, and a replica of it appeared outside Steinbrenner Field in Tampa prior to 2011 spring training. That one cited eleven pennants and seven world championships during his time of ownership. He might have vetoed mention of the eleven pennants, since it reflected four lost World Series.

The field ceremonies featured the West Point Marching Band performing John Philip Sousa songs, such as "Stars and Stripes Forever," to recall the '23 opener. John Fogerty performed "Centerfield" from center field on a baseball-bat-shaped guitar (later claimed by Idelson), and then Bernie Williams did a soulful acoustic guitar version of "Take Me Out to the Ballgame" to great cheers of "Ber-NIE, Ber-NIE, Ber-NIE." A huge flag was unfurled, and a military flyover accompanied the national anthem, which was performed by Kelly Clarkson, an *American Idol* winner. This was especially ironic when the Indians were introduced, for there was the "American Idle" himself, Carl Pavano, to a chorus of boos. No one thought to take their picture together.

The ceremonial first pitch was delivered by the beloved eighty-three-year-old Yogi Berra, who loved the honor but stood closer to home plate each year for the pitch.

The Yankees starting lineup was Jeter, SS; Damon, LF; Teixeira, 1B; Swisher, RF; Posada, C; Cano, 2B; Matsui, DH; Ransom, 3B; Gardner, CF.

Ransom was at third because Alex Rodriguez was out following surgery to repair a labral tear on his right hip. The news had broken as spring training opened, and it was believed that he would need a second surgery later on. His recovery was such, however, that the second surgery was deemed unnecessary. Whether it took a little of his game away was an open debate.

Ransom made two errors and hit into two double plays, hardly capitalizing on his opportunity before the pumped-up crowd.

At 1:06, it was "play ball," as Sabathia delivered a fastball to Grady Sizemore. Sizemore grounded out to Teixeira at first, unassisted, the same play that ended the previous season, with Ransom at first.

In the last of the first, as Bob Sheppard's recorded voice introduced Jeter as the leadoff hitter, a Babe Ruth bat was placed on home plate. Jeter picked it up and gave the fans a laugh as he handed his own bat to the batboy, but then he got down to business and flied out to center.

Damon had the first hit in the new stadium, a single. Posada hit the first home run, a shot to center field in the fifth. But it wasn't the Yankees' day. Sabathia, having thrown 122 pitches, left with two outs in the sixth, and then the Indians erupted for nine runs in the seventh, mostly off Damaso Marte. The outburst included a grand slam by Sizemore, which was thrown back onto the field, as had now become a Yankee Stadium custom.

The paid attendance of 48,271 was announced as a sellout, and it meant that 1) the days of fifty-thousand-plus were pretty much over—the stadium didn't hold that many—and 2) the days of drawing four million were over. The new stadium would produce more revenue, but the total crowd size would not approach the records that had been set across the street. Indeed, the season attendance for the first year of the new stadium would be 3,719,358, a drop of almost six hundred thousand despite a year of mostly sellouts. (They did manage to sell fifty thousand tickets during the post-season when fewer comp tickets were available.)

A-Rod returned to the Yankee lineup on May 8 and hit a home run his first time up. He missed twenty-eight games and the team was 13–15 without him. His return was a big reason for the team going 90–44 the rest of the year, and seldom has a player had a more dramatic day than A-Rod had on the last game of the season, when he hit two homers and drove in seven runs in one inning to give him 30 homers and 100 RBI for the season—the twelfth year in a row he reached both standards.

The season had its share of milestones: On June 28, Rivera recorded the 500th save of his career at the Mets' new park, Citi Field.

On September 11, Jeter passed Gehrig for the most hits recorded by a Yankee, 2,722, a record held by Gehrig for seventy-two years. His Yankee teammates leaped out of the dugout to embrace him, and even the Orioles' players applauded from their dugout. The charter franchises in the major leagues all had their hit leaders, and they had names like Cobb, Aaron, Lajoie, Banks, Musial, Mays, Rose, Yastrzemski, and Clemente.

2009 was a great year in Jeter's career. He batted .334, won a Gold Glove, and finished third in MVP balloting and hitting.

The Yanks set a major league record with eighteen consecutive errorless games, and they also hit 244 home runs in 2009, 136 of them at home. For most of the season, home runs were flying into right field in abundance, making many wonder what could possibly have brought about this oddity. The W.B. Mason office-supply company loved it; their outfield billboard was seen repeatedly in replay after replay.* Seven Yankees bettered 20 homers, and Jeter hit 18.

Engineers sought answers. There were open drafts to exits in this park that weren't in the old park. Could that have been it? There were 26 home runs hit in the first six games at the new park. Through June 18, an average of 3.5 home runs per game went out from both teams. But then, as mysterious as the power surge had been, it began to slow later in the season, and wasn't there by 2010.

"Guys obviously adjust," was Joba Chamberlain's take on the reduction. "You don't necessarily pitch away from your game. But you pitch a little different."

Chamberlain himself was adjusting. From his sensational debut in 2007, he had been a starter and reliever in 2008 and was now strictly a starter in 2009. Phil Hughes became the reliable setup man. The sensation was gone, even as the Yanks carefully followed the "Joba Rules" to limit his pitch count. He made 31 starts but was only 9–6 with a 4.75 ERA. The following year he would be back to the bullpen, but without his setup role. Careful as the Yankees had been, perhaps some undetected injury had snuck into his big frame and changed everything. He was still throwing in the mid-nineties, but the "magic" had faded. Then in June 2011, despite pain-free success on the mound, he was found to have a torn ligament in his right elbow, and Tommy John surgery ended his season.

Part of the home run oddity of 2009 was the propensity for the Yankees to deliver walk-off victories. They did it fifteen times, plus twice in the postseason, and part of the celebration was a "pie in the face" from A.J. Burnett (actually shaving cream in a towel). It was great fun, and the Yanks romped to a 103–59 record, eight games ahead of Boston, winning their first division crown in three years.

The Yankees knocked the Twins out in three straight in the ALDS, with Teixeira's walk-off homer in the eleventh winning game two, and Pettitte beating Pavano (now a Twin) in the clincher. But A-Rod was the story. Long maligned for not delivering in the postseason, he was in a zone at the plate

---

* Advertising signage in Yankee Stadium seemed to grow each year as new spots became available. Rotating signage behind home plate began in 1994, irritating purists, but it eventually became an accepted part of the modern stadium landscape.

that few had ever seen. Against the Twins, he batted .455 with two homers and six RBI.

Then he hit .429 in the ALCS against the Angels, with three more homers and six more RBI in the six-game series, the Yanks taking it behind two wins from Sabathia to go to the World Series for the fortieth time. By winning the pennant in a new Yankee Stadium, the team matched the feats of the 1923 and 1976 Yankees.

Joe Girardi had worn uniform number 27 all season, his mission being to win the Yanks' twenty-seventh world championship. With Steinbrenner watching for his final time from his box, it was Sabathia vs. Cliff Lee at Yankee Stadium, the same matchup as opening day, as Lee had since moved to the Phillies.

Lee hurled a six-hit complete game and Chase Utley hit two of what would be five World Series homers, tying Jackson's record from 1977. But Burnett won game two on homers by Teixeira and Matsui, with fans aware that Matsui might be playing his final week for the Yankees with free agency looming and the team likely to go for a younger replacement.

Matsui hit a pinch-hit homer in game three, a Yankee victory, and Damon, another likely free-agent departee, had three hits to lead the Yanks to victory in game four.

After Lee won again in game five, the Yankees won their twenty-seventh world championship in game six as Pettitte beat old nemesis Pedro Martinez, 7–3. Matsui hit .615 in the Series and was named MVP, and A-Rod drove in six more runs to add to his fabulous postseason performance.

It was time for another ticker-tape parade and a City Hall reception, as the team won its first World Series in nine years. Girardi changed to uniform number 28 for 2010. Much was made of the Core Four: Jeter, Rivera, Pettitte, and Posada, the guys who all been together since 1994 at Columbus and had now won a fifth ring together, one more Yankee ring than Babe Ruth.*

---

* The Core Four, along with the rest of the roster, participated in a community outreach program called HOPE Week, begun by Media Relations Director Jason Zillo in 2009—an annual weeklong program in which the team recognized individuals, families or organizations; visited them, brought them to the Stadium, and called attention to their special needs.

Chapter Forty-Seven

THERE WAS MEASURED SADNESS TO the winter departures of several key members of the world championship team.

Melky Cabrera was traded to Atlanta for reliever Boone Logan and the return of starter Javier Vazquez, who would disappoint again in his second time around.

But two emotional departures were Matsui and Damon. Neither wanted to go, and in both cases, the Yankees liked them and the fans loved them. But baseball is a business; they were getting older and making a lot of money. It was time to give Brett Gardner a regular job in left, and the Yanks obtained Curtis Granderson from Detroit to play center.

Matsui and Damon would be greeted as returning heroes with their first trips back to New York in 2010, but the Matsui return had a special resonance. He had signed with the Angels, and they were in town for opening day—the day the world championship rings were distributed. And so Hideki Matsui was called from the Angel dugout to receive his ring, as his Yankee teammates of the year before gathered to welcome the Series MVP "home." The fans had so connected to this Japanese star—his quiet leadership, his presence. He waved his red Angels cap, he gave everyone an embarrassed and modest smile, and then he bowed and returned to the Angel dugout. It was a very sentimental moment.

The day also featured the return of Yankee head athletic trainer Gene Monahan, a fixture since 1973 in the Yankee dugout and the senior trainer in baseball. Monahan had battled cancer and missed his first spring training since his minor league days in the sixties. He had sent a number of assistants over the years on to the top jobs on other teams. His assistant and ultimate successor, Steve Donahue, had been at his side since 1986. Monahan had, through his professionalism, elevated the profession to being much more than providing liniment rubdowns and ethyl chloride for bruises. Everyone in the game respected him, and the fans cheered his proud stance and military salute along the first-base line on this day. Monahan returned in midseason, then retired after the 2011 season.

While Teixeira, Jeter, Posada, Granderson, and A-Rod all underachieved at the plate in 2010, Cano became one of the elite players in the league and third in MVP voting. Burnett, Vazquez, and Chamberlain never found their hoped-for levels of excellence, while Hughes became a dependable starter and Kerry Wood a terrific one-year setup man. Rivera was still at the top of his game as he turned forty, with no sign of slowing up. Sabathia went 21–7, while Pettitte was 11–3 and seemingly headed for even better things before an injury sidelined him for much of the second half.

In the winter, he announced his retirement at a stadium press conference. He had 240 victories, and had his 37 wins for Houston come with the Yankees, he would have passed Ford as the team's all-time leader.

He was 19–10 in postseason play, the most wins in the postseason for anyone.

A-Rod hit his 600th home run on August 4, joining Bonds, Aaron, Ruth, Mays, Ken Griffey Jr., and Sosa as the only players to reach that level. At thirty-five, he was the youngest to do it, and only Ruth had done it in fewer games. Rodriguez missed twenty-five games due to injury, but managed to reach 30 home runs for the thirteenth year in a row (along with 125 RBI) when he hit four against Boston on September 24–26, the final home games of the year. In doing so he became the first player ever with fourteen 100-RBI seasons.

ON JULY 11, Bob Sheppard died at his home in Long Island, three months shy of his one hundredth birthday. Throughout his fifty-seven-year career, he had fought to keep his age a secret, but never denied playing football for St. John's University from 1929 to 1931. His voice announcing Jeter's every at-bat played on, and he had a plaque in Monument Park.

Just two days later, at his home in Tampa, George M. Steinbrenner III suffered an early-morning heart attack and was rushed by ambulance to St. Joseph's Hospital, two miles from Steinbrenner Field. He died at the hospital at 6:30 A.M. at the age of eighty, surrounded by his family. The Yanks had just celebrated his birthday on July 4 at Yankee Stadium without him present.

Steinbrenner had a form of Alzheimer's disease, but when I visited him in Tampa in November 2010, he knew who I was, and we talked about his early years with the team. It was the heart attack that claimed him.

His death came while baseball was gathering in Anaheim for the All-Star Game, and it was there that Girardi and Jeter held a press conference to express their warm feelings for the man who would forever be the Boss.

Steinbrenner would have been pleased by some of the circumstances on the day of his passing. He went out a winner. His team was the defending world champion and was in first place the day he died. Upstaging the All-Star Game would have made him smile, although not as much as if the Mets had been the host team.

Because there was no federal estate tax in effect in 2010, Steinbrenner's estate—some $1.1 billion—remained in the family.

The fans reacted with respect for his legacy, and many supported his consideration for the Hall of Fame. He did not get elected on his first attempt in 2011, but the talk was alive. He had won seven world championships, eleven pennants, seen the building of a new Yankee Stadium, and took the team—and the industry with it—to remarkable levels of business success. He was the senior owner in the game and owned the team longer than Ruppert had. He redefined the way owners involved themselves in club matters.

The family would continue to operate the team, with Hal the managing general partner, and Hank, Jennifer, and Jessica general partners. The four children, the executors, could not sell the team without a majority vote of unnamed trustees.

At the first home game after the All-Star break, on July 17, Rivera and Jeter led a memorial service of sorts, Mariano placing two roses at home plate in memory of both Sheppard and Steinbrenner, and Jeter addressing the crowd to say, "We gather here tonight to honor two men who were both shining stars of the Yankee universe." Led by Swisher, who hit a homer in the eighth and then a game-winning, two-run single in the ninth, the Yanks won the game. "On a day like this when we celebrate his life, we got to take him out with a 'W,'" said Swisher afterward.

On September 20, a 760-pound plaque mounted on a base was dedicated in Monument Park, directly behind the monuments to Ruth, Huggins, Gehrig, DiMaggio, and Mantle. The entire team walked out to the area where the Steinbrenner family participated in the unveiling, including the return of Steve Swindal. Also back for the unveiling were two visitors from the Dodgers: Joe Torre, in his final weeks as manager, and his appointed successor, Don Mattingly. Lonn Trost had invited them. Torre and Cashman hugged when they saw each other. The ice was broken.

"We've taken the steps to start to repair whatever got broke," said Cashman. When Torre's return for Old-Timers' Day in 2011 produced a tremendous ovation, it appeared as though whatever went wrong had been righted.

The team wore a patch on the sleeve for Sheppard, another over the heart for Steinbrenner, and then when Ralph Houk died on July 21, they added a black armband. In October, Bill Shannon, an official scorer at Yankee Stadium for thirty-two years, also died, in a house fire in New Jersey.

The team did not stay in first place after Steinbrenner died, finishing second by a game to the surprising Tampa Bay Rays but earning the wild-card spot for the postseason. They faced the Twins again in the ALDS and again swept them in three games, as Sabathia, Pettitte, and Hughes all won their starts, with Mo saving two of them. But in the LCS against Texas, the pitching wasn't there. The staff allowed 25 runs in 31⅔ innings and the hitters batted only .201 as the Rangers went on to their first World Series appearance. The only high point was a four-home-run output from Cano, who had eight hits and batted .348.

Girardi would have to wear number 28 in 2011 as they tried again.

THE YEAR 2011 began with the Yankees failing to sign free agent pitcher Cliff Lee—a rare occasion when the franchise lost out on a player it coveted—and with a difficult signing of Jeter to a new contract, a negotiation that took some awkward turns. His ten-year, $189 contract had concluded, and no one, including Derek, saw him going to any team other than the Yankees. But he had come off a disappointing season, was getting old to play shortstop, and the negotiations turned more public than either side might have liked. In the end he signed a three-year contract with a fourth-year option, with the total value of $51 to $65 million, depending on the option.

In a rare display, Jeter said he was unhappy with the negotiations going as public as they had, acknowledging that he was never entertaining any thoughts of finishing his career anywhere but with the Yankees. Jeter, Rivera, and Posada would make 2011 their seventeenth season as major league teammates, something no trio had ever done before.

The Yanks also signed free agent Rafael Soriano as a setup man, going against Cashman's desire to avoid losing a draft choice in the process, but as he acknowledged, he didn't own the team and sometimes had to face being overruled.

Soriano wound up as the team's seventh-inning pitcher when Chamberlain required surgery and David Robertson burst to prominence with a remarkable season. His 100 strikeouts in just 66⅔ innings was the best strikeout-inning ratio in league history for anyone with 100 Ks. He had a 1.08 ERA, recording 14 bases-loaded strikeouts. The pitching staff was full of surprises in 2011, as Hughes fought a "dead arm" and ceded his spot in the rotation to veterans Bartolo Colon and Freddy Garcia, both of whom had seen better days. They won 20 games between them, while rookie Ivan Nova, a twenty-four-year-old Dominican right-hander, went 16–4, including 8–0 after a month in the minors during a roster squeeze. Sabathia won 19.

The season produced a first-place finish and the team's fiftieth visit to postseason baseball, where they were upended in the ALDS when their bats slept in key situations against Detroit.

But it was a year of emotional statistical milestones, some of epic proportion.

There was, for instance, the day Cano, new catcher Russell Martin, and Granderson each hit grand-slam homers. Three in one game was unprecedented in major league history. Cano remained a sensational player both at bat and in the field, while Granderson led the league in runs (136) and RBI (119) while finishing second in homers (41).

Alex Rodriguez moved to within one grand slam of Gehrig's record 23, but injuries limited him to 99 games and just 16 homers, his worst major league season to date. Brett Gardner tied for the league lead with 49 stolen bases.

Posada, in a frustrating final year of his contract, caught only one game and, serving as a DH, tumbled to .235 with just six hits off left-handers. But he had one last hurrah in him when he pinch-hit for hot-hitting rookie Jesus Montero on September 21 and delivered an emotional single to right for the RBI that clinched the division title for New York.

"I just had a feeling about it; he knows how to play in the big moment," said Girardi.

His Yankee career ended with him sitting eighth on the team's all-time home run list with 275.

Jeter looked lost at the plate for the first half of the year, struggling to even hit fly balls. But after a brief stint on the DL, he returned on July 4 and hit .331 in the final three months, raising his average to .297 for the season. On July 9, he became the first Yankee to reach 3,000 hits, homering for the milestone hit (his first Yankee Stadium homer in a year). He went 5-for-5 that sunny Saturday afternoon, driving in the winning run for yet another highlight-reel day. The 3,000th hit was caught by Christian Lopez, a cell-phone salesman in the left-field bleachers, who returned the ball to Jeter without seeking any cash reward. Lopez's father, wearing a DiMaggio jersey, assisted with the catch.

During the year, Jeter also passed Mantle for most games played as a Yankee.

Two days before Posada's division-winning hit, Mariano Rivera passed Trevor Hoffman for the most saves in history, recording his 602nd in the year in which he also became the first player to ever hurl 1,000 games for a single team.

The fans were hungry to see Rivera make history in their presence, and so when Swisher grounded into a double play to end the eighth (maintaining the save situation), the fans actually cheered. It was a funny moment, and even the players laughed at the reaction.

Rivera did what he'd been doing for fifteen years and closed the game with ease. His teammates rushed the field to embrace him, and Posada pushed him to the mound, where he stood alone, acknowledging the cheers of the loving fans. Finally he spread his arms wide, a gesture that recalled Roger Maris's when he was pushed out of the dugout fifty summers earlier, one that seemed to say, "Okay? I'm feeling very embarrassed about this, may I go now?"

DAN CUNNINGHAM LIKED the moment before the game when he grabbed a hose and helped water down the infield, turning the light-brown dirt dark. It was a reflective time, very peaceful, before the Yankees took the field. There were moments when he'd be watering the infield and he'd think about Ruth, Gehrig, DiMaggio, Mantle . . .

It was hard to look up at that magnificent stadium, or the historic moments playing on the video board, and not be awed by what the park and the team represented—to the city, the fans, the sport, and to the nation's culture. It was daunting.

Danny wasn't familiar with Phil Schenck, who laid out Hilltop Park in

Washington Heights in 1903. The players came and went, but always there was the soil under their feet, the bases ninety feet apart, the pitching rubber sixty feet, six inches from home plate, and someone in charge of it all. At this time in history, it was Danny. And somewhere in the U.S., or in Latin America, or in the Far East, youngsters were running the bases, learning the game, falling in love with baseball.

Some would play on this very field one day. Or maybe, as the next century approached, at a new Yankee Stadium—built on the site of the original one, right across the street.

As Mel Allen would have put it, "How about that!"

Appendix: Yankees Year-by-Year Results

Year	Position	W-L	Pct	GA/GB	Manager	Home Park	Attendance	Postseason	Honors
1903	4	72-62	.537	−17	Griffith	Hilltop	211,808		
1904	2	92-59	.609	−1.5	Griffith	Hilltop	438,919		
1905	6	71-78	.477	−21.5	Griffith	Hilltop	309,100		
1906	2	90-61	.596	−3	Griffith	Hilltop	434,700		
1907	5	70-78	.473	−21	Griffith	Hilltop	350,020		
1908	8	51-103	.331	−39.5	Griffith/Elberfeld	Hilltop	305,500		
1909	5	74-77	.490	−23.5	Stallings	Hilltop	501,000		
1910	2	88-63	.583	−14.5	Stallings/Chase	Hilltop	355,857		
1911	6	76-76	.500	−25.5	Chase	Hilltop	302,444		
1912	8	50-102	.329	−55	Wolverton	Hilltop	242,194		
1913	7	57-94	.377	−38	Chance	Polo Grounds	357,551		
1914	6	70-84	.455	−30	Chance/Peckinpaugh	Polo Grounds	359,477		
1915	5	69-83	.454	−32.5	Donovan	Polo Grounds	256,035		
1916	4	80-74	.519	−11	Donovan	Polo Grounds	469,211		
1917	6	71-82	.464	−28.5	Donovan	Polo Grounds	330,294		
1918	4	60-63	.488	−13.5	Huggins	Polo Grounds	282,047		
1919	3	80-59	.576	−7.5	Huggins	Polo Grounds	619,164		
1920	3	95-59	.617	−3	Huggins	Polo Grounds	1,289,422		
1921	1	98-55	.641	+4.5	Huggins	Polo Grounds	1,230,696	WS-Giants L	
1922	1	94-60	.610	+1	Huggins	Polo Grounds	1,026,134	WS-Giants L	

1923	1	98-54	.645	+16	Huggins	Yankee Stadium	1,007,066	WS-Giants W	MVP-Ruth
1924	2	89-63	.586	−2	Huggins	Yankee Stadium	1,053,533		
1925	7	69-85	.448	−28.5	Huggins	Yankee Stadium	697,267		
1926	1	91-63	.591	+3	Huggins	Yankee Stadium	1,027,095	WS-Cardinals L	
1927	1	110-44	.714	+19	Huggins	Yankee Stadium	1,164,015	WS-Pirates W	MVP-Gehrig
1928	1	101-53	.656	+2.5	Huggins	Yankee Stadium	1,072,132	WS-Cardinals W	
1929	2	88-66	.571	−18	Huggins/Fletcher	Yankee Stadium	960,148		
1930	3	86-68	.558	−16	Shawkey	Yankee Stadium	1,169,230		
1931	2	94-59	.614	−13.5	McCarthy	Yankee Stadium	912,437		
1932	1	107-47	.695	+13	McCarthy	Yankee Stadium	962,320	WS-Cubs W	
1933	2	91-59	.607	−7	McCarthy	Yankee Stadium	728,014		
1934	2	94-60	.610	−7	McCarthy	Yankee Stadium	854,682		
1935	2	89-60	.597	−3	McCarthy	Yankee Stadium	657,508		
1936	1	102-51	.667	+19.5	McCarthy	Yankee Stadium	976,913	WS-Giants W	MVP-Gehrig
1937	1	102-52	.662	+13	McCarthy	Yankee Stadium	998,148	WS-Giants W	
1938	1	99-53	.651	+9.5	McCarthy	Yankee Stadium	970,916	WS-Cubs W	
1939	1	106-45	.702	+17	McCarthy	Yankee Stadium	859,785	WS-Reds W	MVP-DiMaggio
1940	3	88-66	.571	−2	McCarthy	Yankee Stadium	988,975		
1941	1	101-53	.656	+17	McCarthy	Yankee Stadium	964,722	WS-Dodgers W	MVP-DiMaggio
1942	1	103-51	.669	+9	McCarthy	Yankee Stadium	988,251	WS-Cardinals L	MVP-Gordon
1943	1	98-56	.636	+13.5	McCarthy	Yankee Stadium	645,006	WS-Cardinals W	
1944	3	83-71	.539	−6	McCarthy	Yankee Stadium	789,995		MVP-Chandler
1945	4	81-71	.533	−6.5	McCarthy	Yankee Stadium	881,846		
1946	3	87-67	.565	−17	McCarthy/Dickey/Neun	Yankee Stadium	2,265,512		

Year									
1947	1	97-57	.630	+12	Harris	Yankee Stadium	2,178,937	WS-Dodgers W	MVP-DiMaggio
1948	3	94-60	.610	-2.5	Harris	Yankee Stadium	2,373,901		
1949	1	97-57	.630	+1	Stengel	Yankee Stadium	2,281,676	WS-Dodgers W	
1950	1	98-56	.636	+3	Stengel	Yankee Stadium	2,081,380	WS-Phillies W	MVP-Rizzuto
1951	1	98-56	.636	+5	Stengel	Yankee Stadium	1,950,107	WS-Giants W	MVP-Berra ROY-McDougald
1952	1	95-59	.617	+2	Stengel	Yankee Stadium	1,629,665	WS-Dodgers W	
1953	1	99-52	.656	+8.5	Stengel	Yankee Stadium	1,537,811	WS-Dodgers W	
1954	2	103-51	.669	-8	Stengel	Yankee Stadium	1,475,171		MVP-Berra ROY-Grim
1955	1	96-58	.623	+3	Stengel	Yankee Stadium	1,490,138	WS-Dodgers L	MVP-Berra
1956	1	97-57	.630	+9	Stengel	Yankee Stadium	1,491,138	WS-Dodgers W	MVP-Mantle
1957	1	98-56	.636	+8	Stengel	Yankee Stadium	1,497,134	WS-Braves L	MVP-Mantle ROY-Kubek
1958	1	92-62	.597	+10	Stengel	Yankee Stadium	1,428,438	WS-Braves W	CY-Turley
1959	3	79-75	.513	-15	Stengel	Yankee Stadium	1,552,030		
1960	1	97-57	.630	+8	Stengel	Yankee Stadium	1,627,349	WS-Pirates L	MVP-Maris
1961	1	109-53	.673	+8	Houk	Yankee Stadium	1,747,725	WS-Reds W	MVP-Maris CY-Ford
1962	1	96-66	.593	+5	Houk	Yankee Stadium	1,493,574	WS-Giants W	MVP-Mantle ROY-Tresh
1963	1	104-57	.646	+10.5	Houk	Yankee Stadium	1,308,920	WS-Dodgers L	MVP-Howard
1964	1	99-63	.611	+1	Berra	Yankee Stadium	1,305,638	WS-Cardinals L	
1965	6	77-85	.475	-25	Keane	Yankee Stadium	1,213,552		
1966	10	70-89	.440	-26.5	Keane/ Houk	Yankee Stadium	1,124,648		
1967	9	72-90	.444	-20	Houk	Yankee Stadium	1,259,514		
1968	5	83-79	.512	-20	Houk	Yankee Stadium	1,185,666		ROY-Bahnsen
1969	5	80-81	.497	-28.5	Houk	Yankee Stadium	1,067,996		

Year	Place	W-L	Pct	GB	Manager	Stadium	Attendance	Postseason	Awards
1970	2	93-69	.574	-15	Houk	Yankee Stadium	1,136,879		ROY-Munson
1971	4	82-80	.506	-21	Houk	Yankee Stadium	1,070,771		
1972	4	79-76	.510	-6.5	Houk	Yankee Stadium	966,328		
1973	4	80-82	.494	-17	Houk	Yankee Stadium	1,262,103		
1974	2	89-73	.549	-2	Virdon	Shea Stadium	1,273,075		
1975	3	83-77	.519	-12	Virdon/Martin	Shea Stadium	1,288,048		
1976	1	97-62	.610	+10.5	Martin	Yankee Stadium II	2,012,434	ALCS-Royals W / WS-Reds L	MVP-Munson
1977	1	100-62	.617	+2.5	Martin	Yankee Stadium II	2,103,092	ALCS-Royals W / WS Dodgers W	CY-Lyle
1978	1	100-63	.613	+1	Martin/Lemon	Yankee Stadium II	2,335,871	ALCS-Royals W / WS-Dodgers W	CY-Guidry
1979	4	89-71	.556	-13.5	Lemon/Martin	Yankee Stadium II	2,537,765		
1980	1	103-59	.636	+3	Howser	Yankee Stadium II	2,627,417	ALCS-Royals L	
1981	1	34-22	.607	+2	Michael	Yankee Stadium II	1,614,353		ROY-Righetti
	6	25-26	.490	-5	Michael/Lemon	Yankee Stadium II		EDS-Brewers W / ALCS-Athletics W / WS-Dodgers L	
1982	5	79-83	.488	-16	Lemon/Michael/King	Yankee Stadium II	2,041,219		
1983	3	91-71	.562	-7	Martin	Yankee Stadium II	2,257,976		

1984	3	87-75	.537	-17	Berra	Yankee Stadium II	1,821,815	
1985	2	97-64	.602	-2	Berra/ Martin	Yankee Stadium II	2,214,587	MVP-Mattingly
1986	2	90-72	.556	-5.5	Piniella	Yankee Stadium II	2,268,030	
1987	4	89-73	.549	-9	Piniella	Yankee Stadium II	2,427,672	
1988	5	85-76	.528	-3.5	Martin/ Piniella	Yankee Stadium II	2,633,701	
1989	5	74-87	.460	-14.5	Green/ Dent	Yankee Stadium II	2,170,485	
1990	7	67-95	.414	-21	Dent/ Merrill	Yankee Stadium II	2,006,436	
1991	5	71-91	.438	-21	Merrill	Yankee Stadium II	1,863,733	
1992	4	76-86	.469	-20	Showalter	Yankee Stadium II	1,748,773	
1993	2	88-74	.543	-7	Showalter	Yankee Stadium II	2,416,965	
1994	1	70-43	.619	+6.5	Showalter	Yankee Stadium II	1,675,556	
1995	2	79-65	.549	-7	Showalter	Yankee Stadium II	1,705,263	ALDS-Mariners L	
1996	1	92-70	.568	+4	Torre	Yankee Stadium II	2,250,877	ALDS-Rangers W	ROY-Jeter
								ALCS-Orioles W	
								WS-Braves W	
1997	2	96-66	.593	-2	Torre	Yankee Stadium II	2,580,445	ALDS-Indians L	
1998	1	114-48	.704	+22	Torre	Yankee Stadium II	2,919,046	ALDS-Rangers W	

Year									
1998								ALCS-Indians W	
								WS-Padres W	
1999	I	98-64	.605	+4	Torre	Yankee Stadium II	3,292,736	ALDS-Rangers W	
								ALCS-Red Sox W	
								WS-Braves W	
2000	I	87-74	.540	+2.5	Torre	Yankee Stadium II	3,227,657	ALDS-Athletics W	
								ALCS-Mariners W	
								WS-Mets W	
2001	I	95-65	.594	+13.5	Torre	Yankee Stadium II	3,264,777	ALDS-Athletics W	CY-Clemens
								ALCS-Mariners W	
								WS-Diamond-backs L	
2002	I	103-58	.640	+10.5	Torre	Yankee Stadium II	3,461,644	ALDS-Angels L	
2003	I	101-61	.623	+6	Torre	Yankee Stadium II	3,465,585	ALDS-Twins W	
								ALCS-Red Sox W	
								WS-Marlins L	
2004	I	101-61	.623	+3	Torre	Yankee Stadium II	3,775,292	ALDS-Twins W	
								ALCS-Red Sox L	
2005	I	95-67	.586	o	Torre	Yankee Stadium II	4,090,692	ALDS-Angels L	MVP-Rodriguez
2006	I	97-65	.599	+10	Torre	Yankee Stadium II	4,243,780	ALDS-Tigers L	
2007	2	94-68	.580	−2	Torre	Yankee Stadium II	4,271,083	ALDS-Indians L	MVP-Rodriguez

2008	3	89-73	.549	−8	Girardi	Yankee Stadium II	4,298,543		
2009	1	103-59	.636	+8	Girardi	Yankee Stadium III	3,719,358	ALDS- Twins W	
								ALCS- Angels W	
								WS- Phillies W	
2010	2	95-67	.586	−1	Girardi	Yankee Stadium III	3,765,807	ALDS- Twins W	
								ALCS- Rangers L	
2011	1	97-65	.599	+6	Girardi	Yankee Stadium III	3,653,680	ALDS- Tigers L	

Bibliography

Books and Periodicals

Alexander, Charles. *Ty Cobb*. New York: Oxford, 1984.

Allen, Lee. *The American League Story*. New York: Hill & Wang, 1962.

——. *The Hot Stove League*. New York: A.S. Barnes and Co., 1955.

——. *100 Years of Baseball*. New York: Bartholomew House, 1950.

——. *The World Series*. New York: G.P. Putnam's Sons, 1969.

Allen, Lee, and Tom Meany. *Kings of the Diamond*. New York: G.P. Putnam's Sons, 1965.

Allen, Maury. *Roger Maris: A Man for All Seasons*. New York: Donald J. Fine, 1986.

Allen, Maury, with Susan Walker. *Dixie Walker of the Dodgers*. Tuscaloosa, AL: University of Alabama Press, 2010.

Allen, Mel, and Ed Fitzgerald. *You Can't Beat the Hours*. New York: Harper & Row, 1964.

Anderson, Dave, Murray Chass, Robert Lipsyte, Buster Olney, and George Vecsey. *The New York Yankees Illustrated History*. New York: St. Martin's Press, 2002.

Angell, Roger. *A Pitcher's Story: Innings with David Cone*. New York: Warner Books, 2001.

Antonucci, Thomas J., and Eric Caren. *Big League Baseball in the Big Apple: The New York Yankees*. Verplank, NY: Historical Briefs, 1995.

Appel Marty. *Baseball's Best: The Hall of Fame Gallery*. New York: McGraw-Hill, 1977.

——. *Joe DiMaggio*. New York: Chelsea House, 1990.

——. *Munson: The Life and Death of a Yankee Captain*. New York: Doubleday, 2009.

——. *Now Pitching for the Yankees: Spinning the News for Mickey, Billy and George*. Kingston, NY: Total Sports, 2001.

——. *162–0*. Chicago: Triumph, 2010.

Asbury, Herbert. *The Gangs of New York*. New York: Alfred A. Knopf, 1927.

Axelson, G.W. Commy. *The Life Story of Charles A. Comiskey*. Chicago: The Reilly & Lee Co., 1919.

Barra, Allen. *Yogi Berra: Eternal Yankee*. New York: W.W. Norton, 2009.

Barrow, Edward G., and James M. Kahn. *My Fifty Years in Baseball*. New York: Coward-McCann, 1951.

Barzilai, Peter, Stephen Borelli, and Gabe Lacques. *Yankee Stadium*. McLean, VA: USA Today Sports Weekly, 2008.

Bashe, Philip. *Dog Days: The New York Yankees' Fall from Grace and Return to Glory, 1964–1976*. New York: Random House, 1994.

Berk, Howard. *When My Boss Calls, Get the Name*. New York: iUniverse, 2008.

Berra, Yogi, and Dave Kaplan. *Ten Rings: My Championship Seasons*. New York: William Morrow, 2003.

Berra, Yogi, and Ed Fitzgerald. *Yogi: The Autobiography of a Professional Baseball Player*. Garden City, NY: Doubleday, 1961.

Berra, Yogi, and Tom Horton. *Yogi: It Ain't Over*. New York: McGraw Hill, 1989.

Bjarkman, Peter C. *Encyclopedia of Major League Baseball Team Histories: American League*. Westport, CT: Meckler, 1991.

Blomberg, Ron, with Dan Schlossberg. *Designated Hebrew*. Chicago: Triumph Books, 2006.

Bogen, Gil. *Tinker, Evers, and Chance: A Triple Biography*. Jefferson, NC: McFarland, 2004.

Borelli, Stephen. *How About That! The Life of Mel Allen*. Champaign IL: Sports Publishing, 2005.

Boston, Talmage. *1939: Baseball's Pivotal Year*. Fort Worth, TX: The Summit Group, 1994.

Bouton, Jim. *Ball Four*. Ed. Leonard Shecter. New York: World Publishing, 1970.

Brown, Warren. *The Chicago White Sox*. New York: G.P. Putnam's Sons, 1952.

Browning, Reed. *Cy Young: A Baseball Life*. Amherst, MA: University of Massachusetts Press, 2000.

Burke, Michael. *Outrageous Good Fortune*. New York: Little Brown & Co., 1984.

Burns, Robert. *50 Golden Years of Sports*. St. Louis: Rawlings, 1948.

Bush, George W. *Decision Points*. New York: Crown, 2010.

Cairns, Bob. *Pen Men*. New York: St. Martin's, 1992.

Cannon, Jimmy. *Nobody Asked Me, But . . . The World of Jimmy Cannon*. New York: Holt, Rinehart and Winston, 1978.

Carmichael, John P. *My Greatest Day in Baseball*. New York: A.S. Barnes & Co., 1945.

Carrieri, Joe, as told to Zander Hollander. *Yankee Batboy*. New York: Prentice-Hall, 1955.

Castro, Tony. *Mickey Mantle: America's Prodigal Son*. Dulles, VA: Potomac Books, 2002.

Cataneo, David. *Peanuts and Crackerjack*. Nashville: Rutledge Hill Press, 1991.

Chadwick Dean. *Those Damn Yankees: The Secret Life of America's Greatest Franchise*. New York: Verso, 1999.

Chandler, Happy, with Vance Trimble. *Heroes, Plain Folks, and Skunks*. Chicago: Bonus Books, 1989.

Chapman, Con. *The Year of the Gerbil*. Danbury, CT: Rutledge Books, 1998.

Chase, W. Parker. *New York the Wonder City*. New York: Wonder City Publishing, 1932.

Cherry, Thomas L. *Good Ol' Country Boy*. Ahosie, NC: Pierce Printing Co., 2000.

Clavin, Tom, and Danny Peary. *Roger Maris. Baseball's Reluctant Hero*. New York: Touchstone, 2010.

Coates, Jim, with Douglas Williams. *Always A Yankee*. West Conshohocken, PA: Infinity Publishing, 2009.

Cobb, Ty, with Al Stump. *My Life in Baseball—The True Record*. Garden City, NY: Doubleday, 1961.

Coberly, Rich. *The No-Hit Hall of Fame*. Newport Beach, CA: Triple Play Publications, 1985.

Columbia Presbyterian Medical Center. *Hilltop Park Commemorative Media Kit*. New York: 1993.

Cook, William. *Waite Hoyt*. Jefferson, NC: McFarland, 2004.

Cramer, Richard Ben. *DiMaggio: The Hero's Life*. New York: Simon & Schuster, 2000.

Creamer, Robert. *Babe: The Legend Comes to Life*. New York: Simon and Schuster, 1974.

———. *Baseball in '41*. New York: Penguin, 1991.

———. *Stengel: His Life and Times*. New York: Simon and Schuster, 1984.

Dahlgren, Matt. *Rumor in Town*. California (no city): Woodlyn Lane, 2007.

Daley, Arthur. *Kings of the Home Run*. New York: G.P. Putnam's Sons, 1962.

———. *Times at Bat*. New York: Random House, 1950.

Daniel, Dan. *Babe Ruth: The Idol of the American Boy*. Racine, WI: Whitman, 1930.

Danzig, Allison, and Joe Reichler. *The History of Baseball*. Englewood Cliffs, NJ: Prentice-Hall, 1959.

DeVito, Carlo. *Scooter: The Biography of Phil Rizzuto*. Chicago: Triumph, 2010.

———. *Yogi: The Life & Times of an American Original*. Chicago: Triumph, 2008.

Dickson, Paul. *The Dickson Baseball Dictionary*. New York: Facts on File, 1989.

DiMaggio, Joe. *Lucky to Be a Yankee*. Revised edition. New York: Grosset & Dunlap, 1957.

Durant, John. *The Yankees: A Pictorial History of Baseball's Greatest Club*. New York: Hastings House, 1950.

Duren, Ryne. *The Comeback*. Dayton, OH: Lorenz Press, 1978.

Duren, Ryne, with Tom Sabellico. *I Can See Clearly Now*. Chula Vista, CA: Aventine Press, 2003.

Durocher, Leo, and Ed Linn. *Nice Guys Finish Last*. New York: Simon and Schuster, 1975.

Durso, Joseph. *Casey: The Life and Legend of Charles Dillon Stengel*. Englewood Cliffs, NJ: Prentice-Hall, 1967.

Eig, Jonathan. *Luckiest Man*. New York: Simon and Schuster, 2005.

Epting, Chris. *The Early Polo Grounds*. Charleston, SC: Arcadia Publishing, 2009.

Eskenazi, Gerald. *The Lip: A Biography of Leo Durocher*. New York: William Morrow, 1993.

Fainaru, Steve, and Ray Sánchez. *The Duke of Havana*. New York: Villard, 2001.

Falkner, David. *The Last Yankee: The Turbulent Life of Billy Martin*. New York: Simon & Schuster, 1992.

Famous Slugger Yearbook. Louisville, KY: Hillerich & Bradsby Co., various years.

Figueroa, Ed, and Dorothy Harshman. *Yankee Stranger*. Smithtown, NY: Exposition Press, 1982.

Fischer, David. *A Yankee Stadium Scrapbook*. Philadelphia: Running Press, 2008.

Fleitz, David. *Ghosts in the Gallery at Cooperstown*. Jefferson, NC: McFarland, 2004.

Fleming, G.H. *Murderers' Row: The 1927 New York Yankees*. New York: William Morrow and Co., 1985.

Ford, Whitey, Mickey Mantle, and Joe Durso. *Whitey and Mickey: An Autobiography of the Yankee Years*. New York: Viking Press, 1977.

Ford, Whitey, with Phil Pepe. *Slick: My Life in and Around Baseball*. New York: William Morrow, 1987.

Forker, Dom. *The Men of Autumn: An Oral History of the 1949–53 World Champion New York Yankees*. Dallas: Taylor Publishing, 1989.

———. *Sweet Seasons: Recollections of the 1955–64 New York Yankees*. Dallas: Taylor Publishing, 1990.

Frommer, Harvey. *A Yankee Century*. New York: Berkley, 2002.

———. *The New York Yankee Encyclopedia*. New York: Mountain Lion, 1997.

Gallagher, Mark. *Day by Day in New York Yankees History*. New York: Leisure Press, 1983.

———. *Explosion! Mickey Mantle's Legendary Home Runs*. New York: Arbor House, 1987.

Gallagher, Mark, and Walter LeConte. *The Yankee Encyclopedia*. 4th edition. Champaign, IL: Sports Publishing Inc., 2000.

Gallico, Paul. *Lou Gehrig: Pride of the "Yankees."* New York: Grosset & Dunlap, 1942.

Gallo, Bill, with Phil Cornell. *Drawing a Crowd: Bill Gallo's Greatest Sports Moments*. Middle Village, NY: Jonathan David Publishers, 2000.

Gay, Timothy. *Tris Speaker: The Rough-and-Tumble Life of a Baseball Legend.* Lincoln, NE: University of Nebraska Press, 2005.

Gentile, Derek. *The Complete New York Yankees: The Total Encyclopedia of the Team.* New York: Black Dog & Leventhal, 2001

Gershman, Michael. *Diamond—The Evolution of the Ballpark.* New York: Houghton Mifflin Co., 1993.

Gilbert, Bill. *They Also Served.* New York: Crown, 1992.

Gipe, George. *The Great American Sports Book.* Garden City, NY: Doubleday, 1978.

Godin, Roger. *The 1922 St. Louis Browns.* Jefferson, NC: McFarland, 1991.

Golenbock, Peter. *Dynasty: New York Yankees 1949–1964.* Englewood Cliffs, NJ: Prentice-Hall, 1975.

Graham, Frank. *Lou Gehrig: A Quiet Hero.* New York: G.P. Putnam's Sons, 1942.

———. *The New York Giants.* New York: G.P. Putnam's Sons, 1952.

———. *The New York Yankees: An Informal History.* New York: G.P. Putnam's Sons, 1943.

Graham, Frank Jr. *Casey Stengel: His Half-Century in Baseball.* New York: John P. Day Co., 1958.

Greenberg, Hank. *Hank Greenberg: The Story of My Life.* Ed. Ira Berkow. New York: Times Books, 1989.

Gross, Milton. *Yankee Doodles.* Boston: Kent Publishing, 1948.

Guernsey's Auctioneers. *Yankee Stadium Auction Catalog: The Baker Collection.* New York: Guernsey's, 2008.

Guidry, Ron, and Peter Golenbock. *Guidry.* Englewood Cliffs, NJ: Prentice Hall, 1980.

Halberstam, David. *October 1964.* New York: Villard Books, 1994.

———. *Summer of '49.* New York: Morrow, 1989.

Halberstam, David J. *Sports on New York Radio.* Lincolnwood, IL: Masters Press, 1999.

Haley, Alex. *Baseball in a Segregated Town.* New York: Sport Magazine, 1961.

Handrinos, Peter. *The Truth and Ruth (And More): Behind the New York Yankees' Most Popular Myths, Legends, and Lore.* Unpublished manuscript, no date.

Henrich, Tommy, and Bill Gilbert. *Five O'Clock Lightning.* New York: Birch Lane, 1992.

Hermalyn, Gary, and Anthony C. Greene. *Yankee Stadium 1923–2008.* Charleston, SC: Arcadia Publishing, 2009.

Holtzman, Jerome. *No Cheering in the Press Box.* Revised edition. New York: Henry Holt and Company, 1995.

Honig, Donald. *The New York Yankees.* Revised edition. New York: Crown, 1987.

Houk, Ralph, and Charles Dexter. *Ballplayers Are Human Too.* New York: G.P. Putnam's Sons, 1962.

Houk, Ralph, and Robert W. Creamer. *Season of Glory: The Amazing Saga of the 1961 New York Yankees*. New York: G.P. Putnam's Sons, 1988.

Howard, Arlene, with Ralph Wimbish. *Elston and Me: The Story of the First Black Yankee*. Columbia, MO: University of Missouri Press, 2001.

Huhn, Rick. *The Sizzler: George Sisler, Baseball's Forgotten Great*. Columbia, MO: University of Missouri Press, 2004.

Hunter, Jim "Catfish," and Armen Keteyian. *Catfish: My Life in Baseball*. New York: Berkley, 1989.

Ijuin, Shizuka. *Hideki Matsui: Sportsmanship, Modesty: and the Art of the Home Run*. New York: Ballantine, 2007.

Istorico, Ray. *Greatness in Waiting: An Illustrated History of the Early New York Yankees, 1903–1919*. Jefferson, NC: McFarland & Company, 2008.

Jackson, John. *New York Yankees Unofficial Yearbook*. New York: Jay Publishing, 1956–1965 (annual).

Jackson, Kenneth T. *The Encyclopedia of New York City*. New Haven, CT: Yale University Press, 1995.

Jackson, Reggie, and Mike Lupica. *Reggie*. New York: Ballantine, 1985.

Jacobson, Steve. *The Best Team Money Could Buy*. New York: Atheneum, 1978.

James, Bill. *The New Bill James Historical Baseball Abstract*. Revised edition. New York: Free Press, 2001.

Johnson, Harold (Speed). *Who's Who in Major League Baseball*. Chicago: Buxton Publishing, 1933.

Jones, David. *Deadball Stars of the American League*. Dulles, VA: Potomac Books, 2006.

Jonnes, Jill. *We're Still Here: The Rise, Fall, and Resurrection of the South Bronx*. New York: Atlantic Monthly Press, 1986.

Kahn, Roger. *October Men*. New York: Harcourt, 2003.

Katz, Wallace B. *The New York Rapid Transit Decision of 1900: Economy, Society, Politics*. Washington, DC: Department of the Interior, National Park Service,

Kavanagh, Jack. *Ol' Pete: The Grover Cleveland Alexander Story*. South Bend, IN: Diamond Communications, 1996.

Kavanagh, Jack, and Norman Macht. *Uncle Robbie*. Cleveland: Society for American Baseball Research, 1999.

Kennedy, Kostya. *56: Joe DiMaggio and the Last Magic Number in Sports*. New York: Sports Illustrated, 2011.

Kennedy, MacLean. *The Great Teams of Baseball*. St. Louis: Sporting News, 1929.

Kerrane, Kevin. *Dollar Sign on the Muscle*. New York: Beaufort, 1984.

Kohout, Martin. *Hal Chase: The Defiant Life and Turbulent Times of Baseball's Biggest Crook*. Jefferson, NC: McFarland & Company, 2001.

Koppett, Leonard. *The Rise and Fall of the Press Box*. Toronto: Sport Classic Books, 2003.

Krueger, Joseph. *Baseball's Greatest Drama*. Milwaukee: Classic Publishing Co., 1943.

Kubek, Tony, and Terry Pluto. *Sixty-One: The Team, The Record, the Men*. New York: Macmillan, 1987.

Kuhn, Bowie, with Marty Appel, editorial assistant. *Hardball: The Education of a Baseball Commissioner*. New York: Times Books, 1987.

Lanigan, Ernest. *The Baseball Cyclopedia*. New York: The Baseball Magazine co., 1922.

Larsen, Don, and Mark Shaw. *The Perfect Yankee*. Champaign, IL: Sports Publishing, 1996.

Leavy, Jane. *The Last Boy*. New York: Harper, 2010.

LeConte, Walter. *The Ultimate New York Yankees Record Book*. New York: Leisure Press, 1984.

Lee, Bill, and Dick Lally. *The Wrong Stuff*. New York: Viking, 1984.

Levitt, Daniel. *Ed Barrow: The Bulldog Who Built the Yankees' First Dynasty*. Lincoln, NE: University of Nebraska Press, 2008.

Lewis, Franklin. *The Cleveland Indians*. New York: G.P. Putnam's Sons, 1949.

Lewis, Michael. *Moneyball*. New York: Norton, 2003.

Leyritz, Jim, Douglas B. Lyons, and Jeffrey Lyons. *Catching Heat*. New York: HCI, 2011.

Lieb, Fred. *The Baseball Story*. New York: G. P. Putnam's Sons, 1950.

———. *The Boston Red Sox*. New York: G.P. Putnam's Sons, 1947.

———. *Connie Mack—Grand Old Man of Baseball*. New York: G.P. Putnam's Sons, 1945.

———. *The Detroit Tigers*. New York: G.P. Putnam's Sons, 1946.

———. *The St. Louis Cardinals*. New York: G.P. Putman's Sons, 1947.

Lieb, Fred, with Bob Burnes, J.G. Taylor Spink, and Les Biederman. *Comedians and Pranksters of Baseball*. St. Louis: Charles C. Spink & Son, 1958.

Light, Jonathan Fraser. *The Cultural Encyclopedia of Baseball*. Jefferson, NC: McFarland & Company, 1997.

Linn, Ed. *Inside the Yankees: The Championship Year*. New York: Ballantine, 1978.

Lowenfish, Lee. *Branch Rickey: Baseball's Ferocious Gentleman*. Lincoln, NE: University of Nebraska Press, 2007.

Luisi, Vincent. *New York Yankees: The First 25 Years*. Charleston, SC: Arcadia Publishing, 2002.

Lyle, Sparky, and Peter Golenbock. *The Bronx Zoo*. New York: Crown, 1979.

Mack, Connie. *My 66 Years in the Big Leagues*. Philadelphia: John C. Winston Co., 1950.

MacPhail, Lee, with Marty Appel. *My Nine Innings*. Westport, CT: Meckler, 1989.

Madden, Bill. *Pride of October*. New York: Warner Books, 2003.

———. *Steinbrenner—The Last Lion of Baseball*. New York: Harper, 2010.

Madden, Bill, and Moss Klein. *Damned Yankees*. New York: Warner Books, 1990.

Mahler, Jonathan. *Ladies and Gentlemen, the Bronx is Burning*. New York: Farrar, Straus and Giroux, 2005.

Mann, Jack. *The Decline and Fall of the New York Yankees*. New York: Simon and Schuster, 1967.

Mantle, Merlyn, Mickey Mantle Jr., David Mantle, and Dan Mantle, with Mickey Herskowitz. *A Hero All His Life: A Memoir by the Mantle Family*. New York: HarperCollins, 1996.

Mantle, Mickey, with Herb Gluck. *The Mick*. New York: Doubleday, 1985.

Mantle, Mickey, with Mickey Herskowitz. *All My Octobers: My Memories of Twelve World Series When the Yankees Ruled Baseball*. New York: HarperCollins, 1994.

Mantle, Mickey, and Robert W. Creamer. *The Quality of Courage: Heroes In and Out of Baseball*. Garden City, NY: Doubleday, 1964.

Maris, Roger, and Jim Ogle. *Roger Maris at Bat*. New York: Meredith Press, 1962.

Martin, Billy, with Phil Pepe. *Billyball*. New York: Doubleday, 1987.

Mayer, Ronald. *The 1923 New York Yankees*. Jefferson, NC: McFarland & Company, 2010.

McCarigle, Bob. *Baseball's Great Tragedy*. Jericho, NY: Exposition Press, 1972.

McCough, Matthew. *Bat Boy: My True Life Adventures Coming of Age with the New York Yankees*. New York: Doubleday, 2005.

McGraw, John J. *My Thirty Years in Baseball*. New York: Boni & Liveright, 1923.

Mead, William B., and Harold Rosenthal. *The 10 Worst Years of Baseball*. New York: Van Nostrand Reinhold, 1978.

Meany, Tom. *Babe Ruth*. New York: A.S. Barnes and Company, 1951.

———. *Baseball's Greatest Teams*. New York: A.S. Barnes and Company, 1949.

———. *The Magnificent Yankees*. Revised edition. New York: A.S. Barnes and Company, 1957.

———. *The Yankee Story*. New York: E.P. Dutton & Co., 1960.

Mercurio, John. *Chronology of New York Yankee Records*. New York: Perennial, 1989.

Mize, Johnny, and Murray Kaufman. *How to Hit*. New York: Henry Holt and Company, 1953.

Montville, Leigh. *The Big Bam*. New York: Doubleday, 2006.

———. *Ted Williams*. New York: Doubleday, 2004.

Moore, Joseph Thomas. *Pride Against Prejudice*. Westwood, CT: Praeger, 1988.

Moreland, George. *Balldom*. New York: Balldom Publishing, 1914.

Mosedale, John. *The Greatest of All: The 1927 New York Yankees*. New York: Dial Press, 1974.

Munson, Thurman, and Martin Appel. *Thurman Munson: An Autobiography*. Revised edition. New York: Coward, McCann and Geoghegan, 1979.

Murcer, Bobby, and Glen Waggoner. *Yankee for Life*. New York: HarperCollins, 2008.

Murdock, Eugene. *Ban Johnson: Czar of Baseball*. Westport, CT: Greenwood Press, 1982.

Nash, Bruce, and Allan Zullo. *The Baseball Hall of Shame 3*. New York: Pocket Books, 1987.

———. *The Baseball Hall of Shame 4*. New York: Pocket Books, 1990.

———. *The Baseball Hall of Shame's Warped Record Book*. New York: Collier, 1991.

Neft, David, and Richard Cohen, *The World Series*. New York: St. Martin's, 1990.

Neft, David, Richard Cohen, and Michael Neft. *The Sports Encyclopedia: Baseball*. 23rd edition. New York: St. Martin's Griffin, 2003.

Nettles, Graig, and Peter Golenbock. *Balls*. New York: Pocket Books, 1985.

New York Yankees. *Play Ball with the Yankees*. Bronx, NY: New York Yankees, 1952.

———. Scorecards. New York: New York Yankees, 1903–1922.

———. Scorecards. Bronx, NY: New York Yankees, 1923–1973, 1976–2011.

———. Scorecards. Flushing, NY: New York Yankees, 1974–1975.

———. Sketch Books and Yearbooks. Bronx, NY: New York Yankees, 1950–2011.

———. *Yankees* magazine. Bronx, NY: New York Yankees, various dates.

New York Yankees Media Relations Department. *Media Guides*. Bronx, NY: New York Yankees, 1955–1973, 1976–2011 (annual).

———. *Media Guides*. Flushing, NY: New York Yankees, 1974, 1975 (annual).

O'Connell, T.S. *Legendary Yankee Stadium*. Iola, WI: Krause Publications, 2009.

O'Connor, Ian. *The Captain*. New York: Houghton Mifflin Harcourt, 2011.

Okkonen, Marc. *Baseball Uniforms of the 20th Century. The Official Major League Baseball Guide*. New York: Sterling, 1991.

———. "Hilltop Park: Home of the Highlanders." *Yankees* magazine, June 22, 1989.

Olney, Buster. *The Last Night of the Yankee Dynasty*. New York: Ecco, 2004.

O'Neal, Bill. *The American Association, 1902–1991*. Austin: Eakin Press, 1991.

———. *The International League, 1884–1991*. Austin: Eakin Press, 1992.

———. *The Pacific Coast League, 1903–1988*. Austin: Eakin Press, 1990.

Paper, Lew. *Perfect*. New York: New American Library, 2009.

Patten, William, and J. Walker McSpadden. *The Book of Baseball*. New York: P.F. Collier & Son, 1911.

Peary, Danny, ed. *Cult Baseball Players: The Greats, the Flakes, the Weird and the Wonderful*. New York: Fireside, 1990.

Pepe, Phil. *Talkin' Baseball: An Oral History of Baseball in the 1970s*. New York: Ballantine Books, 1998.

———. *The Yankees: The Authorized History of the New York Yankees*. Dallas: Taylor, 1995.

Pepitone, Joe, with Berry Stainback. *Joe, You Coulda Made Us Proud*. Chicago: Playboy Press, 1975.

Peterson, Fritz. *Mickey Mantle Is Going to Heaven*. Denver: Outskirts Press, 2009.

Peterson, John E. *The Kansas City Athletics: A Baseball History, 1954–1967*. Jefferson, NC: McFarland, 2003.

Pietrusza, David. *Judge and Jury*. South Bend, IN: Diamond, 1998.

———. *Major Leagues*. Jefferson, NC: McFarland & Company, 1991.

Piniella, Lou, and Maury Allen. *Sweet Lou*. New York: Bantam, 1987.

Pitoniak, Scott. *Memories of Yankee Stadium*. Chicago: Triumph, 2008.

Poekel, Charlie. *Babe & the Kid: The Legendary Story of Babe Ruth and Johnny Sylvester*. Charleston, SC: The History Press, 2007.

Povich, Shirley. *The Washington Senators*. New York: G.P. Putnam's Sons, 1954.

Prudenti, Frank. *Memories of a Yankee Batboy, 1956–1961*. Bronx, NY: Pru Publications, 2003.

Reach Official Baseball Guide. 1902–1940 (annual).

Reisler, Jim. *Before They Were the Bombers: The New York Yankees' Early Years, 1903–1915*. Jefferson, NC: McFarland & Company, 2002.

Rice, Grantland. "New York Yankees" in Ed Fitzgerald, ed., *The Book of Major League Baseball Clubs: The American League*. New York: A.S. Barnes & Co., 1952.

———. *The Tumult and the Shouting: My Life in Sport*. New York: A.S. Barnes & Company, 1954.

Richardson, Bobby. *The Bobby Richardson Story*. Westwood, NJ: Fleming H. Revell, 1965.

Ritter, Lawrence. *East Side West Side*. Kingston, NY: Total Sports, 1998.

———. *The Glory of Their Times*. New York: Macmillan, 1966.

Rivers, Mickey, and Michael DeMarco. *Ain't No Sense Worryin': The Wisdom of "Mick the Quick" Rivers*. Toronto: Sport Publishing, 2003.

Rizzuto, Phil, and Al Silverman. *The "Miracle" New York Yankees*. New York: Coward-McCann, 1962.

Roberts, Selena. *A-Rod: The Many Lives of Alex Rodriguez*. New York: Harper, 2009.

Robinson, Ray. *Iron Horse*. New York: Norton, 1990.

Robinson, Ray, ed. *Baseball Stars of 1961*. New York: Pyramid Books, 1961.

———. *Baseball Stars of 1962*. New York: Pyramid Books, 1962.

Robinson, Ray, and Christopher Jennison. *Pennants and Pinstripes*. New York: Viking Studio, 2002.

———. *Yankee Stadium: 75 Years of Drama, Glamor and Glory*. New York: Penguin Studio, 1998.

Rosen, Charley. *Bullpen Diaries*. New York: Harper, 2011.

Rosenfeld, Harvey. *Roger Maris*: A Title to Fame*. Fargo, ND: Prairie House, 1991.

Rosenthal, Harold. *Baseball Is Their Business*. New York: Random House, 1952.

———. Interview with Tom Greenwade. Typed submission version from his files, 1960, courtesy Bill Madden.

Ruth, Babe, and Bob Considine. *The Babe Ruth Story*. New York: E.P. Dutton & Co., 1948.

Ruth, Mrs. Babe [Claire] with Bill Slocum. *The Babe and I*. Englewood Cliffs, NJ: Prentice-Hall, 1959.

Salant, Nathan. *This Date in New York Yankees History*. Revised edition. New York: Stein & Day, 1983.

Schaap, Dick. *Steinbrenner!*. New York: G.P. Putnam's Sons, 1982.

Schnakenberg, Robert. *The Underground Baseball Encyclopedia*. Chicago: Triumph, 2010.

Schechter, Gabriel. *This Bad Day in Yankees History*. Cooperstown, NY: Charles April Publications, 2008.

Schoor, Gene. *Mickey Mantle of the Yankees*. New York: G.P. Putnam's Sons, 1958.

———. *The Thrilling Story of Joe DiMaggio*. New York: Frederick Fell, 1950.

Schwarz, Alan. *The Numbers Game*. New York: St. Martin' Press, 2004.

Selter, Ronald. *Ballparks of the Deadball Era*. Jefferson, NC: McFarland & Company, 2008.

Seymour, Harold, and Dorothy Seymour. *Baseball: The Golden Age*. New York: Oxford, 1971.

Shalin, Mike. *Donnie Baseball*. Chicago: Triumph, 2011.

Shapiro, Michael. *Bottom of the Ninth*. New York: Times Books, 2009.

Shapiro, Milton. *The Phil Rizzuto Story*. New York: Julian Messner, 1959.

Shatzkin, Mike, ed. *The Ballplayers*. New York: William Morrow & Co, 1990.

Shecter, Leonard. *Roger Maris: Homerun Hero*. New York: Bartholomew House, 1961.

Sheffield, Gary, and David Ritz. *Inside Power*. New York: Crown, 2007.

Shoemaker, Robert. *The Best in Baseball*. New York: Thomas Y. Crowell Co, 1949.

Silverman, Al. *Joe DiMaggio: The Golden Year, 1941*. Englewood Cliffs, NJ: Prentice-Hall, 1969.

Siwoff, Seymour, ed. *The Book of Baseball Records*. New York: Elias Sports Bureau, 2011.

Slaughter, Enos, with Kevin Reid. *Country Hardball*. Greensboro, NC: Tudor Books, 1991.

Smith, Curt. *Voices of the Game*. South Bend, IN: Diamond Communications, 1987.

Smith, Ken. *Baseball's Hall of Fame*. New York: Grosset & Dunlap, 1952.

Smith, Red. *Red Smith on Baseball: The Game's Greatest Writer on the Game's Greatest Years*. Chicago: Ivan R. Dee, 2000.

Smith, Robert. *Baseball*. New York: Simon and Schuster, 1947.

Smith, Ron. *Sporting News Presents a Century of Greatness: Yankees*. St. Louis: The Sporting News, 2002.

Society for American Baseball Research (SABR). *Baseball Research Journal*. Various.

———. *The National Pastime*. Various.

———. *The SABR Baseball List & Record Book*. New York: Scribner, 2007.

Solomon, Burt. *Where They Ain't*. New York: The Free Press, 1999.

Sowell, Mike. *July 2, 1903: The Mysterious Death of Hall-of-Famer Big Ed Delahanty*. New York: Macmillan, 1992.

———. *The Pitch That Killed*. New York: Macmillan, 1989.

Spalding Official Baseball Guide. New York: American Sports Publishing, 1903–1940 (annual).

Sparks, Barry. *Frank "Home Run" Baker*. Jefferson, NC: McFarland, 2006

Spatz, Lyle. *New York Yankee Openers*. Jefferson, NC: McFarland & Company, 1997.

———. *Yankees Coming, Yankees Going*. Jefferson, NC: McFarland & Company, 2000.

Spatz, Lyle, and Steve Steinberg. *1921: The Yankees, the Giants, and the Battle for Baseball Supremacy in New York*. Lincoln, NE: University of Nebraska Press, 2010.

Spink, J.G. *Taylor: Daguerreotypes*. St. Louis: Charles C. Spink & Son, 1961.

Sporting News Editors. *Baseball: A Doubleheader Collection of Facts, Feats & Firsts*. New York: Galahad Books, 1992.

Sporting News Guide. St. Louis: Charles C. Spink & Son, various years.

Sporting News Record Book. St. Louis: Charles C. Spink & Son, various years.

Sporting News Register. St. Louis: Charles C. Spink & Son, various years.

Stang, Mark, and Linda Harkness. *Baseball by the Numbers*. Lanham, MD: Scarecrow Press, 1997.

Stottlemyre, Mel, and John Harper. *Pride and Pinstripes*. New York: HarperCollins, 2007.

Stout, Glenn, ed. *Top of the Heap: A Yankees Collection*. Boston: Houghton Mifflin, 2003.

Stout, Glenn, and Richard A. Johnson. *Yankees Century*. Boston: Houghton Mifflin, 2002.

Sugar, Bert Randolph. *The Baseball Maniac's Almanac, 2nd Edition*. New York: Skyhorse, 2010.

Sullivan, Dean. *Early Innings: A Documentary History of Baseball*. Lincoln, NE: University of Nebraska Press, 1995.

Sullivan, George, and John Powers. *The Yankees: An Illustrated History*. Philadelphia: Temple University Press, 1997.

Sullivan, Neil J. *The Diamond in the Bronx: Yankee Stadium and the Politics of New York*. New York: Oxford, 2001.

Swanson, Harry. *Ruthless Baseball*. Burlington, IN: AuthorHouse, 2004.

Swearingen, Randall. *A Great Teammate: The Legend of Mickey Mantle*. Champaign, IL: Sports Publishing, 2007.

Tan, Cecilia. *The 50 Greatest Yankee Games*. Hoboken, NJ: John Wiley & Sons, 2005.

Tebbetts, Birdie, and James Morrison. *Birdie*. Chicago: Triumph Books, 2002.

Tofel, Richard. *A Legend in the Making*. Chicago: Ivan R. Dee, 2002.

Torre, Joe, and Tom Verducci. *Chasing the Dream: My Lifelong Journey to the World Series*. New York: Bantam, 1997.

————. *The Yankee Years*. New York: Doubleday, 2009.

Trachtenberg, Leo. *The Wonder Team. The True Story of the Incomparable 1927 New York Yankees*. Bowling Green, OH: Bowling Green State University Popular Press, 1995.

Trimble, Joe. *Yogi Berra*. New York: A.S. Barnes and Company, 1952.

Tullius, John. *I'd Rather Be a Yankee*. New York: Macmillan, 1986.

Turkin, Hy, S.C. Thompson, and Pete Palmer. *Official Encyclopedia of Baseball, 10th Revised Edition*. Cranbury, NJ: A.S. Barnes, 1979.

Tygiel, Jules. *Baseball's Great Experiment*. New York: Oxford, 1983.

Vaccaro, Mike. *Emperors and Idiots*. New York: Doubleday, 2005.

Vancil, Mark, and Mark Mandrake. *One Hundred Years: New York Yankees: The Official Retrospective*. New York: Ballantine, 2002.

Veeck, Bill. *The Hustler's Handbook*. New York: G.P. Putnam's Sons, 1965.

Vincent, Fay. *The Last Commissioner: A Baseball Valentine*. New York: Simon & Schuster, 2002.

Votano, Paul. *Tony Lazzeri*. Jefferson, NC: McFarland, 2005.

Waller, Spencer Weber, Neil B. Cohen, and Paul Finkelman. *Baseball and the American Legal Mind*. New York: Garland Publishing, 1995.

Ward, Ettie. *Courting the Yankees: Legal Essays on the Bronx Bombers*. Durham, NC: Carolina Academic Press, 2003.

Warfield, Don. *The Roaring Redhead: Larry MacPhail*. South Bend, IN: Diamond, 1987.

Weinberger, Miro, and Dan Riley. *The Yankees Reader*. Boston: Houghton Mifflin Company, 1991.

Wells, David, with Chris Kreski. *Perfect I'm Not*. New York: William Morrow, 2003.

White, Bill, and Gordon Dillow. *Uppity*. New York: Grand Central, 2011.

White, G. Edward. *Creating the National Pastime: Baseball Transforms Itself, 1903–1953*. Princeton, NJ: Princeton University Press, 1996.

White, Roy, and Darrell Berger. *Then Roy Said to Mickey*. Chicago, Triumph: 2009.

Williams, Ted, and John Underwood. *My Turn at Bat*. New York: Simon and Schuster, 1969.

Wind, Herbert Warren. *The Gilded Age of Sport*. New York: Simon and Schuster, 1961.

Winfield, Dave, with Tom Parker. *Winfield: A Player's Life*. New York: W.W. Norton, 1988.

Wray, John, and J. Roy Stockton. *Ban Johnson's Story of His Life*. St. Louis *Post-Dispatch* multipart newspaper series, 1929.

Yablonsky, Lewis. *George Raft*. New York: McGraw-Hill, 1974.

Zimmer, Don, with Bill Madden. *The Zen of Zim*. New York: St. Martin's, 2004.

———. *Zim: A Baseball Life*. Kingston, NY: Total Sports, 2001.

VIDEOTAPES

Various from Major League Baseball, YES Network, SportsChannel, WPIX, MSG Network, HBO Sports, ESPN, New York Yankees.

WEB SITES

(Some sites may no longer be operative.)

Abebooks.com, alabev.com, Alibris.com, allaboutbeer.com, baberuthcentral.com, ballparksofbaseball.com, Baseball-almanac.com, baseball-fever.com, baseballhall .org, baseballindex.org, baseballlibrary.com, baseball-links.com, baseballprospec tus.com, baseball-reference.com, Bioproj.SABR.org, books.google.com, captnsblog .wordpress.com, centerplate.com, earlyerabaseballphotos.com, historyoftheyan kees.com, homebrew.com, Jacobruppert.com, kansascitybaseballhistoricalsociety .com, members.cox.net/bngoldenl/baseballfirstsl.htm, mickeymantle.com, MLB .com, Newsday.com, No-smoking.org, Nycsubway.org, NYDailynews.com, Nyfood museum.org, NYPost.com, NYTimes.com, Retrosheet.com, Rice.edu, Savetheyan keegate2.com, SI.com, Sportsbusinessjournal.com, Sportsencyclopedia.com, The baseballpage.com, Thedeadballera.com, Themick.com, Thesmokinggun.com, Theswearingens.com, Ultimateyankees.com, Washington-heights.us, Wikipedia .com, Wirednewyork.com, Yankees.com, Yankeenumbers.com

ARCHIVAL NEWSPAPERS AND MAGAZINES

The American, Baseball, Baseball Digest, Beckett Baseball, Diamond, Evening Journal, The Herald, Herald-Tribune, The Journal, Journal-American, The National, Newsday, New York Daily News, New York Evening Telegram, New York Evening Telegraph, New York Mirror, New York Post, New York Times, The New Yorker, Plain Talk, Sport,

Sporting Life, Sports Business Journal, Sports Collectors Digest, Sporting News, Sports Illustrated, The Sun, The Telegram, The Telegraph, The Tribune, USA Today Baseball Weekly, USA Today Sports Weekly, The World, World Journal Tribune, World Telegram and the Sun, Yank, Yankees Magazine

AUTHOR'S AUDIO TAPES

Interviews with Fred Lieb, Roger Peckinpaugh, Thurman Munson, and Bowie Kuhn.

Index

(Incidental or passive references are not included.)

Aaron, Hank, 321
Abbott, Jim, 484, 486
Abreu, Bobby, 543, 554
Adkins, Doc, 24
air-raid drills, 228
air travel, 249–50, 323–24
alcohol problems
  Alexander, 148
  Bennett, 185
  Caldwell, 81–82
  Duren, 323–24
  Gooden, 495
  Howe, 480
  Mantle, 348, 488–89
  Martin, 429, 441, 466–67, 477
  McDowell, 393
  Meusel, 101
  MacPhail, 264
  Ruth, 144
  Strawberry, 495
  Whitson, 466–67
Alexander, Doyle, 419, 420, 453
Alexander, Grover Cleveland "Pete,"
  148–49, 162
Allen, Johnny, 176, 191
Allen, Mel, 204, 246, 355–57, 371, 390
All-Star Games, 181, 214, 232, 331
Alomar, Sandy, 401
ALS (amyotrophic lateral sclerosis), 208–12,
  445, 509

Altrock, Nick, 61–62
amateur draft, 359, 480, 495–96
American Architect magazine, 126
American League
  "designated hitter" rule, 388–89
  expansion, 335–36, 370
  founding of, 2, 3, 4
  and integration, 359–60
  monument for MVPs, 136–37
  and National League, 8–9
  pennant races, 33, 36–39, 68, 90–93,
    106, 108, 217–19, 446–47
amyotrophic lateral sclerosis (ALS), 208–12,
  445, 509
Anderson, Jerry, 442–43
Anderson, John, 34
Anderson, Rick, 445
Anderson, Sparky, 423
Angels, Los Angeles, 335
apology brochure, 301–2
Appel, Marty, ix, 369, 403, 412–13, 434
Aragon, Angel, 67
Arroyo, Luis, 330–31, 337–38
Athletics, Kansas City, 305, 328–29
Athletics, Oakland, 399, 404–5, 445, 513
Athletics, Philadelphia, 42, 55, 80, 161,
  172–73, 299–300, 305–6
Austin, Frank, 277
Austin, Jimmy, 50
Autry, Gene, 335

Babe Ruth All-Stars, 118
Babe Ruth Day, 260–61
Babe Ruth Plaza, 271
Bahnsen, Stan, 370, 378
Baker, Frank "Home Run," 80–81, 84,
    100–101, 111–12, 122–23
Balboni, Steve, 458
Ballantine beer, 281, 356
Ball Four (Bouton), 371–72
ballparks, 29
Ballparks of the Deadball Era (Selter), 22–23
Balls (Nettles), 459
Baltimore, Maryland, 4
Barber, Red, 204–5, 236, 303, 364–65
Barfield, Jesse, 476–77
Barrett, Charlie, 66
Barrow, Edward Grant "Ed"
    biographical info, 109, 232, 240–41
    as business manager, 107
    death and funeral, 297
    and Elberfeld, 32
    and Huggins, 109–10
    and Mays, 91
    and McCarthy, 168
    as part-owner of Yankees, 203
    and Ruppert's death, 202
    and Ruth, 95, 96
    and sale of Yankees to MacPhail, 238–39
    and scouting department, 144–45
baseball
    fantasy leagues, 461
    mascots, 454
    millennium changes, 498, 499
    women and, 93, 420–21, 429, 463, 499
    Baseball magazine, 18–19, 60, 64, 65,
        81–82, 101, 126, 156
Base Ball Players' Fraternity, 61
baseballs
    with cork vs. rubber center, 52
    juiced up, 96, 106–7, 113
    with Ruth's signature, 95, 119, 164
Baseball Writers' Association, 229.
    See also MVP awards
base stealing, 43
Bat Day, 361
batting helmets, 103–4

Bauer, Hank, 274, 275, 276, 326, 328–29
Bavasi, Peter, 421
Baylor, Don, 456
Beame, Abe, 430
Beane, Billy, 560
Bears, Newark, 174–75, 282
Beattie, Jim, 445
Beene, Fred, 401
"Beer Barrel Polka, The," 153, 215, 233
Belcher, Tim, 460
Belle, Albert, 507
Bell, Edward Everett, 55–56
Belmont, August, Jr., 7
Bench, Johnny, 359
Bengough, Benny, 151
Beniquez, Juan, 445
Bennett, Eddie, 112, 185
Bennett, Kathy, 486
Bentley, Jack, 138
Berger, Joe, 78
Berk, Howard, 365, 392
Berra, Dale, 458, 463, 464
Berra, Larry "Yogi"
    biographical info, ix–x, 249, 257–59, 274,
        344, 564
    coaching for Astros, 463
    fired from Yankees, 354–55, 462–63
    as first base coach, 413
    as "greatest living Yankee," 508, 509
    and Linz, 351
    as manager, 349–50, 458
    on Mantle, 288
    MVP awards, 292, 296, 310
    stats, 258, 327, 348, 350
    and Steinbrenner, 460, 463–64
    and Stengel, 274
Betemit, Wilson, 556, 561
Bevens, Floyd "Bill," 249, 251, 262–63
Beville, Monte, 24
Black Sox scandal, 90, 95, 109, 116, 461
Blackwell, Ewell, 296
Blefary, Curt, 375
Blomberg, Ron, 389
Blues Stadium, 304–5
Blue, Vida, 419
Bodie, Ping, 88

Boggs, Wade, 483, 494, 497
Bonds, Barry, 106, 203, 378, 401n, 524, 524, 558
Bonds, Bobby, 405, 407–8, 411
Bonham, Ernie "Tiny," 227
Bonner, Mike, 562
Boone, Aaron, 528, 529, 533
Boras, Scott, 480, 549
Borowy, Hank, 242–43
Borton, Babe, 66
Boudreau, Lou, 176
Bouton, Jim "Bulldog," 342–43, 361, 370, 371–72
boxing at Yankee Stadium, 126
box seats, 100, 115, 244, 248–49, 456, 499, 561, 563
Boyer, Clete, 306, 319, 367
Bradley, George, 474, 481
Braves, Atlanta, 497–98, 499–500, 510–11
Braves, Boston, 68, 80, 182
Braves, Milwaukee, 321–22, 325–26
Brett, George, 456–57, 493
Brett, Ken, 412
Briggs, Walter, 305
Broaca, Johnny, 194–95
broadcasting
    cable-television deal, 470–71, 475–76
    CBS as Yankees owners, 353–54, 365
    early TV broadcasts, 260, 281–82
    firing Allen, 355–57
    firing Barber, 364
    first female broadcaster, 421
    Ford Frick Award, 357, 362
    Home Box Office, 336n
    and instant replays, 328
    integration of, 373–74
    and MacPhail, 204–5
    Mantle's media splash, 288
    Rizzuto in, 313
    staff changes, 476
    teams producing own games, 521–22
    Yankees channel, 290
    See also media; radio
Bronx Zoo, The (Lyle), 432
Brosius, Scott, 504, 507
Brown, Bobby, 249, 274

Brown, Kevin, 532
Browns, St. Louis, 121–22, 234–35
Brush, John T., 5, 59, 63
"bug game," 548
Buhner, Jay, 471
Burdette, Lew, 291, 322, 326
Burke, James "Jimmy," 50, 172
Burke, Michael, 364–65, 374, 376, 381–82, 385–87, 391, 392
Burnett, A.J., 559–60
Burns, Britt, 468
Bush, Bullet Joe, 119, 122, 133, 144
Bush, Donie, 166
Bush, George W., 519
Bush, Homer, 500, 508
Buskey, Tom, 401
Butterfield, Jack, 443n
Byrd, Harry, 299–300

Cabrera, Melky, 543, 568
Cadaret, Greg, 475
Cairo, Miguel, 534
Caldwell, Ray "Slim," 52, 68, 78, 81–83, 90
Called Shot home run, Ruth's, 177–79
Cameraman, The (movie), 160
Caminiti, Ken, 524
Campanella, Roy "Campy," 323, 327
Candelaria, John, 472
Cano, Robinson, 538
Canseco, Jose, 524
Cardinals, St. Louis
    for sale, 86–87
    World Series, 146, 147–49, 161–62, 230, 232–33, 352–53, 422–24
Carey, Andy, 303
Carroll, Parke, 305, 306
Carroll, Tommy, 358
Casey, Hugh, 225
Cashman, Brian
    on A-Rod's steroid use, 559
    on Boone, 533
    as general manager, 474–75, 503
    roster development, 503–4, 512, 532–33, 541–42, 561
    and stat analysis with computers, 550, 560–61

Cashman, Brian (*continued*)
  and Steinbrenner, 541–42
  and Torre, 550–51, 570–71
  on Yankees pennant win over Red Sox,
    529
Cater, Danny, 375, 379
CBS as owners, 353–54, 365, 384–87
Cereghino, Ed, 358
Cerrone, Rick, 446, 449, 464, 505, 527
Chadwick, Henry, 4, 30
Chamberlain, Joba, 546, 566
Chambliss, Chris, 401, 422, 445–46, 495
Chance, Frank, 64–65, 67–69, 130
Chandler, Albert B. "Happy," 259–60, 294
Chandler, Spud, 197, 232
Chapman, Ben, 173, 180–81
Chapman, Ray, 102–3, 104–6
Chase, Hal, 43–44, 46, 47, 50, 53–56, 60,
  66
Chase, Nellie, 46
Chass, Murray, 425–26, 448
Chesbro, Jack, 25, 32, 35, 37–39, 49
Clark, Byron, 203
Clarke, Horace, 128, 362, 363, 401
Clark, Jack, 471
Clarkson, Kelly, 564
Clarkson, Walter, 34
Clemens, Roger
  biographical info, 513, 514, 515, 527
  leaving Yankees, 530
  MVP Award, 468
  playing for Astros, 532
  signing with Yankees, 507–8, 546
  and steroids, 525
Cleveland fans, 217, 218
Coates, Jim, 332–33
Cobb, Ty, 60–61, 105, 140
Cochrane, Mickey, 195
Coleman, Jerry, 274, 275, 322
Colletti, Danny, 371
Collins, Joe, 274, 296, 322, 453
Collins, Pat, 145, 151–52
Collins, Rip, 119
Collins, Dave, 453
Columbia Presbyterian Hospital, New York
  City, 62

Combs, Earle, 140, 142, 144, 145, 152,
  164–65, 185, 190
Comiskey, Charles, 89, 92
Cone, David, 488, 494, 514–15
Conlon, Charles, 35
Conroy, William "Wid," 24, 25, 124
Contreras, Jose, 527
Corbett–Sullivan championship fight, 2
Corhan, Roy, 104
Corum, Bill, 159
Courtney, Ernie, 24
Coveleski, Stan, 159
Cox, Bobby, 369
Cox, John W., 305
Craft, Harry, 328
Crane, Sam, 27
Cree, Birdie, 50–51
Cronin, Joe, 399
Crosby, Bing, 238
Crosetti, Frank, 175–76, 221, 370
Crown, Lester, 388
Cuccinello, Tony, 243–44
Cucuzza, Rob, 465
Cummings, Candy, 3–4
Cunningham, Danny, 498, 573
Cunningham, Patrick, 388, 398
Cuomo, Mario, 505
Curse of the Bambino, The (Shaughnessy),
  97
curveball, 3–4
Cy Young Awards
  Clemens, 507, 515
  Cone, 488
  Ford, 337
  Guidry, 437
  Johnson, 538
  Lyle, 429
  McDowell, 488
  Turley, 324
  Sabathia, 559

Dahlgren, Babe, 206, 207, 218–19
Daily News, 245–46, 493
Daley, Arthur, 239, 253, 273, 283, 297, 308,
  334, 352
Daley, Bud, 306

Damn Yankees (Broadway musical), 301
Damon, Johnny, 543
Daniel, Dan, 123, 243, 337
Davis, Pearl, 247
Davis, Ron, 440
Davis, Russ, 493
Davis, Tom, 50
Day, Zach, 512
deadball era, 22
Dean, Dizzy, 281–82
Deering, John, 24
Delahanty, Ed, 27
DeLorean, John, 388
DeMaestri, Joe, 329
Dempsey, Rick, 403, 419
Dent, Bucky, 428–29, 437, 438, 453, 477, 479
"designated hitter" (DH) rule, 388–89
Devery, Big Bill, 9–13, 68, 70, 74, 75
Devine, Joe, 187–88
Dewey, George, 13
DH ("designated hitter") rule, 388–89
Dickey, William Malcolm "Bill"
    and Berra, ix, 350
    biographical info, 251, 252, 322
    as coach, 274, 322
    debut, 161
    and Gehrig, 234
    ovation from fans, 234
    and Reynolds broken jaw, 176–77
    stats, 191, 192, 231
Dickson, Murray, 306
DiMaggio, Joseph Paul "Joe"
    in army for WWII, 230–31
    batting titles, 218, 221–22
    biographical info, 74, 189–92, 293–94, 509
    emotions on field, 263–64
    injuries, 277
    and MacPhail, 261
    and media, 188–89
    and Monroe, 189, 293–94, 343–44
    and "Mrs. Robinson" song, 509
    MVP awards, 212, 224, 285
    at Old-Timers' Day, 377
    recruiting, 187–88

and Rizzuto, 221
    salary disputes, 196, 329
    speech for Joe DiMaggio Day, 278–79
    stats, 187, 190, 193, 212, 227, 251, 280, 285, 293
Ditmar, Art, 306, 319, 320
Dobson, Pat, 393, 401, 412
Doby, Larry, 320
Dodgers, Brooklyn
    playoff vs. Giants, 292
    World Series vs. Yankees, 224–25, 262–64, 265–66, 280, 296, 298–99, 311–12, 314–16
Dodgers, Los Angeles, 323, 348–49, 430, 438, 450–51
Donahue, Steve, 569
Donald, Atley, 212
Donovan, William "Wild Bill," 75–76, 78, 82, 83, 85
Dougherty, Patsy, 34
Downing, Al, 341, 347, 375
Doyle, Slow Joe, 45, 546
Drebinger, John, 98–99, 131, 218–19, 243
Dressen, Charlie, 253
Dreyfuss, Barney, 5n
drug testing, 465, 483
Dugan, Joe "Jumping Joe," 120–21, 145, 156–57, 162
Dunaway, Donald, 298
Duncan, Mariano, 494
Durante, Sal, 340, 420
Duren, Ryne, 306, 323–24
Durocher, Leo, 56, 160–61, 252, 253, 259
Durst, Cedric, 166

Easler, Mike, 468
East Potomac Park monument, 136–37
Ebbets Field, 224
Ehret, George, 71
Elberfeld, Norm "the Tabasco Kid," 31–32, 38, 44, 45, 47, 48–49
Ellis, Dock, 412, 428
Ellis, John, 385
Elysian Field, Hoboken, New Jersey, 3
"emery ball," 52–53
Enright, Richard, 74

Essick, "Vinegar Bill," 101, 188
Etten, Nick, 231
Evers, Johnny, 64
Excelsior team, Brooklyn, New York, 3
exhibition games
  benefit for Campanella, 327
  for Civil Defense Volunteer Office, 232
  first game in new Yankee Stadium,
    563–64
  Giants–Yankees series, 55, 69
  Mayor's Trophy Game, 344–45
  for NYC's unemployed, 173
  in Panama and Texas, 246
  Ruth batting against Johnson, 229
  sandlot baseball benefit, 344–45
  San Francisco earthquake relief, 42
  silent fans for, 41
  survivors of *Titanic*, 42
  West Point, 154
  for WWI soldiers, 84
  Yankees vs. Giants vs. Dodgers, 234
  Yankees with their Kansas City farm
    team, 207–8

fans
  and A-Rod, 548, 549
  and banners, 344
  and Chandler, 260
  and Chase, 55–56
  and DiMaggio, 189
  dress becoming casual, 327–28
  exiting on Yankee Stadium field, 20, 192,
    280
  Gehrig's speech to, 210–11
  heckling and throwing food, 177, 217–18,
    454
  in lost years, 363–64
  and minor league games, 175
  and Senators move to Texas, 378
  and steroid use, 525
  storming the field for Yankees-Senators
    brawl, 180
  team-based differences, 224
  "wave," 454
  and Winfield–Mattingly batting title
    race, 461

fantasy leagues, 461
Farley, James, 216–17
farm system, 173–75, 196, 207–8
Farrell, Charlie "Duke," 9–13, 24, 42, 59,
  68, 70, 74–76
Farrell, Frank, 9–13, 20
Farrell, Jackie, 99, 234, 240
Farr, Steve, 480
Federal League, 67
Fein, Nat, 270
Feller, Bob, 249
Ferraro, Mike, 446
Ferrick, Tom, 282
Fewster, Chick, 104, 120
Fielder, Cecil, 494
Figueroa, Ed, 412, 422, 432
Finley, Charles O., 306, 397
Fishel, Bob, 301–3, 308–9, 325, 340–41, 382,
  386, 403
Fisher, Ray, 52, 78
Fishman, Mike, 550
Fisk, Carlton, 393–94, 419
Fitzgerald, John "Honey Fitz," 120
Fletcher, Art, 151, 165, 215, 243
Flood, Curt, 411
Fogerty, John, 564
food service, 20–21, 153, 350
football
  Giants team, 75, 353, 382–83
  popularity of, 359
  at Yankee Stadium, 126, 245
  Yankees team, 245, 277
Ford, Ed "Whitey"
  biographical info, 284, 368
  and Houk, 337
  and Mantle, 289
  as pitching coach, 350, 400
  on ticker-tape parades, 299
  Whitey Ford Day, 337–38
Ford Frick Award, 357, 362
Ford, Russell, 52–53, 104
Fort Lauderdale, Florida, 309, 342, 486
Franco, Ike, 388
Frazee, Harry, 90, 91, 95–97, 110, 119, 120
free agency for players, 404–6, 411, 413,
  414–16, 425–26, 449

free-agent draft, 416, 460
Freeman, Buck, 23
Frick, Ford, 294, 339–40, 357, 362
Friedlund, J. Arthur, 239, 304
frieze at Yankee Stadium, 126, 312, 390,
    554, 562
Froelich, Eddie, 226
Froemming, Bruce, 423
Fuchs, Emil, 182
Fultz, Dave, 24, 25, 44

Gallico, Paul, 136, 152
Gamble, Oscar, 412–13, 440
gambling and gamblers
    of baseball players, 43–44, 81
    and Chase, 43, 53–54, 66
    and fantasy leagues, 461
    and Gedeon, 81
    and MacPhail, 259
    and Magee, 81
    Mantle representing a casino, 377
    in National League, 3
    in New York City, 9–11
Ganzel, John "Popup John," 24, 25–26
Garagiola, Joe, 356–57, 439
Garagiola, Joe Jr., 519
Garcia, Karim, 528–29
Gardner, Brett, 568
Gardner, Rob, 380
Garvin, Ned "the Navasota Tarantula,"
    34–35
Gehrig, Henry Louis "Lou"
    biographical info, 135–36, 223
    as captain, 185, 207
    and Daily News "polio germ" comment,
        217
    deterioration and ALS diagnosis, 206–12
    on Huggins, 165
    MVP awards, 152, 191
    playing, 135, 142–43, 145, 162, 173
    signing with Yankees, 110
    stats, 144, 152, 155, 176, 179, 193, 212
George Earl Toolson vs. New York
    Yankees et al, 299
Giambi, Jason, 523–25
Giants football team, 75, 353, 382–83

Giants, New York
    about, 5, 32, 42, 55
    Giants–Yankees exhibition series, 55, 69
    and Highlanders, 59
    playoff vs. Dodgers, 292
    Polo Grounds as home field, 42, 55
    World Series vs. Yankees, 115–17, 122,
        137–39, 192, 195–96, 292–93
    Yankees vs. Giants vs. Dodgers exhibi-
        tion game, 234
Giants, San Francisco, 323, 345–46
Gibbs, Jake, 368
Gillette sponsorship, 262
Gillick, Pat, 396, 421
Gilmore, Jimmy, 67
Girardi, Joe, 497, 538, 551, 567
Giuliani, Rudolph, 498, 516, 517, 544
Gleason, Art, 281
Gleeson, Jimmy, 350
Goldklang, Marv, 388
Gomez, Vernon "Lefty," 166, 169–70, 171,
    176, 220, 227
Gooden, Doc, 494, 495
Gordon, Joe "Flash," 196, 229, 255
Gordon, Joseph W., 11, 46
Gordon, Tom, 532
Goslin, Goose, 141
Gossage, Rich "Goose," 431–32, 440, 449,
    453–54, 460
Gowdy, Curt, 281
Gowdy, Hank, 84
Grabowski, Johnny, 151–52
graffiti, 391–92
Graham, Frank, xiii–xiv, 101, 135, 136
Graham, Otto, 530
Grand Concourse, Bronx, 128
Granderson, Curtis, 568
Grant, Eddie, 165
Grant, M. Donald, 376
Grba, Eli, 335
Great Depression, 166, 167, 173
Greater New York Baseball Association, 14
Greenberg, Hank, 167, 242
Green, Dallas, 473, 475, 476–77
Greene, Harvey, 468
Greenwade, Tom, 286–87, 375

Greenwald, Ed, 388
Griffey, Ken Sr., 452
Griffith, Clark "Old Fox"
    biographical info, 15–16, 32, 44, 45–47
    criticism of, 30
    manager of Cincinnati, 47–48
    manager of Washington, 48, 61–62
    as owner of Washington, 15, 48
    playing for Americans, 24
    Senators win pennant, 141
    and uniform design, 26
    on waiver rule, 242
    and Yankees wins, 215
Grim, Bob, 303
Grimm, Charlie, 178
Groch, Dick, 495–96
Gross, Milton, 256
Grossbardt, Michael, 366
Guetterman, Lee, 479
Guidry, Ron "Gator," 429, 432–33, 437, 475
Gullett, Don, 428
Gumpert, Bert, 244

Hadley, Irving "Bump," 191, 195
Hadley, Kent, 329
Halas, George, 93
Hall, David, 442–43
Hall of Fame, Cooperstown, 186, 213–14,
    271, 316
Halper, Barry, 388
Hamey, Roy, 334, 349
Hamilton, Steve, 351, 375
Harding, Warren G., 119, 134
Hardin, Jim, 391
Harper, Harry, 110
Harrelson, Ken "Hawk," 406
Harris, Bucky, 252, 253, 255, 267, 272
Hartzell, Roy, 55, 57–58
Harvard Stadium, 2
Hassett, Buddy, 227
Hawkins, Andy, 456
Hayes, Charlie, 482, 494–95
Hegan, Mike, 394
helmets, 103–4, 291
Hemond, Roland, 283
Hempstead, Harry, 63

Henderson, Rickey, 462, 464, 469, 475
Hendricks, Elrod, 419
Henrich, Tommy, 193–94, 226, 250, 279,
    282
Henry, Bruce, 331
"Here Come the Yankees" (theme song),
    366–67
Heritage Field, 545
Hernandez, Orlando "El Duque," 506, 510
Hershberger, Willard, 214
Hershon, Stuart, 535
Hertz, John, 236
Hicks, Tom, 534
hidden ball trick, 175
High, Bunny, 78
Highlanders
    cheating, 51
    failing season in 1912, 60–61
    first games against Washington, 26–27
    Giants–Yankees exhibition series, 55, 69
    last game, 61–62
    name of, 18
    organizing, 7–8, 13–14
    pennant race, 1904, 35, 36–39
    safe for players' valuables, 21–22, 129
    and Sunday baseball, 41–42
    uniforms, 26, 28, 32–33
Hilltop Park (American League Grounds)
    amenities, 20, 21
    construction, 19–20, 22, 27
    dimensions, 22–23
    excavation, 16, 19–20
    first and last games in, 27–29, 61–62
    food service, 20–21
    location, 17
    and Sunday baseball, 42
    transportation to, 16–17
    World Series at Polo Grounds and, 55
Hinrichs, Paul, 358
Hitchcock, Sterling, 493
Hoag, Myril, 190
Hobson, Butch, 453
Hodges, Gil, 379
Hodges, Russ, 246
Hofheinz, Roy, 353–54
Hogg, Bill, 45

Holtzman, Ken, 419–20
Hoover, J. Edgar, 238
HOPE Week, 567n
Hopp, Johnny, 282–83
Hornsby, Rogers, 148
Houk, Ralph
  and Berra, 354–55
  biographical info, 393, 394, 571
  as first-base coach, 322
  as general manager, 349
  as manager, 335, 336–37, 363
  resigning from Yankees, 395
Howard, Elston "Ellie"
  biographical info, 307–10, 330, 447–48
  injuries, 361
  and manager position, 398, 399
  MVP Award, 348
  traded to Red Sox, 368–69
Howell, Harry, 24
Howe, Steve, 480, 483
Howser, Dick, 400, 435, 445, 447
Hoyt, LaMarr, 428
Hoyt, Waite, 110–11, 117, 133, 152, 164, 167, 271
Hubbell, Carl, 170, 192
Huggins, Miller
  biographical info, 115, 164
  and Huston, 90
  as manager, 86–87, 123
  monument for, 165
  on throwing games, 122
  Yankees win World Series, 138–39
Hughes, Phil, 545–46, 566
Hughes, Tom, 53
Hunt, Nelson Bunker, 388
Hunter, Jim "Catfish," 404–6, 407, 440, 445, 509–10
Huston, Tillinghast L'Hommedieu "Cap"
  biographical info, 72–73, 84, 124, 200
  and Huggins, 90, 107
  and Mays, 91–92
  and Ruppert, 74, 76, 79–80, 86, 87
  selling his share of Yankees, 123–24, 134–35

Idelson, Jeff, 563
Igawa, Kei, 546–47

Indians, Cleveland
  Chapman's death, 102–3, 104–6
  pennant races, 291–92, 301
  Score injury, 317–18
  and Speaker, 80
  vs. Yankees, for the pennant, 113–14
instant replay, birth of, 328
integration
  of broadcasting, 373–74
  committee on, 247–48
  as means to increase fan base, 299
  and MVP awards, 348
  National vs. American Leagues, 359–60
  views on, 197–98, 247–48
  of Yankees, 277, 308–10
International League, 98, 174–75, 247, 446
Irabu, Hideki, 500–501
Irwin, Arthur, 24, 25, 76

Jackson, Grant, 419
Jackson, Reginald M. "Reggie," 359, 426–28, 430, 450–53, 454
Janzen, Marty, 488
Japan, 302, 310, 312, 446
Jenkinson, Bill, 113, 132
Jensen, Jackie, 282, 283, 304
Jerome Cafeteria, New York City, 191
Jeter, Derek
  biographical info, 402, 487, 495–96, 543, 572–73
  as captain, 527–28
  dive into stands, 535
  "flip" play, 518
  most hits recorded record, 565
  MVP award, 515
  negotiations, 571
  and Rodriguez, 535
  Sheppard recording for introduction, 290
  speech at last game in old Yankee Stadium, 556–57
  3,000th hit, 573
Joe DiMaggio Day, 509
Johnson, Alex, 402–3
Johnson, Arnold Milton, 304–6, 320–21
Johnson, Billy, 231

Johnson, Byron Bancroft "Ban"
  and American League formation, 2, 3
  and Americans first year, 30
  ballpark site selection, 6–7
  and Comiskey, 89
  and Farrell, 10–11
  and Highlanders/Yankees, 5
  and Mays trade from Red Sox to Yankees,
    91–92, 108
  and new ownership for Yankees, 70–74
  and players for Ruppert, 73, 80
  and Stallings, 54
  and Yankee Stadium opening, 130–31
Johnson, Cliff, 440
Johnson, Hank, 159
Johnson, Johnny, 359
Johnson, Randy, 538–39
Johnson, Roy, 193–94
Johnson, Walter, 49, 104, 229
John, Tommy, 439, 450, 453, 475
"Joltin' Joe DiMaggio" (song), 222
Jones, Ruppert, 445
Jones, Sad Sam, 119, 133, 136, 138
Jorgens, Arndt, 177
Judge, Joe, 151
Justice, David, 512, 523

Kandle, Matt, 179
Kane, Bill, 436
Kansas City farm team, 207–8, 220, 282,
    305
Kapstein, Jerry, 404
Kay, Michael, 476, 530, 555
Keane, Johnny, 358, 361, 363
Keeler, Willie "Wee Willie," 23–24, 32, 35,
    47, 49, 124
Kekich, Mike, 380, 389–90
Keller, Charlie "King Kong," 212–13, 231,
    280
Keller, Lon, 245
Kelly, Little Ray, 99–100, 179
Kelly, Pat, 480, 482
Kelly, Roberto, 484
Kemp, Steve, 456
Kennedy, James C., 5–6
Kenney, Jerry, 374, 385

Key, Jimmy, 483–84
Kieran, John, 154, 158–59, 209–10
King, Clyde, 455, 495
Kitt, Howie, 358
Klein, Moss, 426
Kleinow, Red, 34, 38–39
Kline, Steve, 401
Kluttz, Clyde, 406
Knight, John, 53
Knoblauch, Chuck, 503–4, 515
Koenig, Mark, 101, 143, 145, 152, 167, 177
Koenigsberg, Manny, 324–25
Koufax, Sandy, 126, 348–49
Krichell, Paul, 50, 110, 135, 319
Kubek, Tony, 321, 342, 362
Kucks, Johnny, 316
Kuhn, Bowie, 352, 377, 408, 415, 419, 457
Kunitz, Al, 220
Kuzava, Bob, 293, 296, 297

Ladies' Day, 197, 249
Landis, Kenesaw Mountain, 108–9, 118, 138,
    193, 197–98, 236–37, 239
Lane, Frank, 306
Lannin, Joe, 79
LaRoche, Dave, 453
Larsen, Don, 314–16, 322, 326, 328–29
Lary, Lyn, 167, 173
Lasker, Albert D., 108
Last Night of the Yankee Dynasty, The
    (Olney), 521
Layton, Eddie, 366, 498, 537
Lazzeri, Tony, 145–46, 148, 155, 162, 191,
    195–96
League Award, 136
Leavy, Jane, 298
Ledee, Ricky, 512
Lee, Bill, 419
Lee, Cliff, 571
LeFlore, Ron, 444
Leiter, Al, 540
Leja, Frank, 358
Lemon, Bob, 291, 413, 433, 439, 440–41, 455
Lemon, Jerry, 439
Lenz, Jack, 289
Leonard, Dutch, 90, 251

Levine, Randy, 511
Lewis, Duffy, 90
Lewis, Jim, 445
Lewis, Michael, 503, 560
Lidle, Cory, 486, 544
Lieber, Jon, 532
Lieb, Fred, 43, 93, 119–20, 132, 155
Lindbergh, Charles, 154
Lindell, Johnny, 227–28
Lindsay, John V., 365, 381–82, 395
Linn, Ed, 225
Linz, Phil, 342, 351
Lloyd, Graeme, 494, 508
Logan, Boone, 568
Logan, Fred "Pop," 20, 149, 260
Lombardi, Ernie, 214–15
Long, Herman, 24, 26
Lopat, Eddie, 256, 268–69, 274, 307, 337
Lopez, Christian, 573
Lopez, Hector, 306
Lou Gehrig Appreciation Day, 208–11, 246
Lou Gehrig Plaza, 228
Lowell, Mike, 504
Lucchino, Larry, 535
Lueker, Claude, 60–61
luxury tax based on payroll, 417, 536–37
Lyle, Sparky, 379, 380–81, 429, 431–32, 438
Lyons, Leonard, 319

Maas, Duke, 306, 335
Maas, Kevin, 479
Mack, Connie, 78–79, 80–81, 120
MacPhail, Bill, 240, 305
MacPhail, Larry
    and Berra, 258
    and broadcasting, 204–5
    changes to Yankees and stadium, 239–41
    and DiMaggio, 261
    gambling charges, 259–60
    and integration, 247
    and McCarthy, 239, 242, 243, 249
    and media, 264
    purchasing Yankees, 236–39
    on Reserve Clause, 248
    retirement and death, 264–66
    and Rickey, 259, 264–65

MacPhail, Lee
    on 1958 World Series, 326
    as farm director, 308
    and father's attitude, 265–66
    focusing on roster, 365, 367, 378, 400
    and Pine Tar Game, 457
    and PR, 240
Madden, Bill, 355, 436, 459, 469
Maddox, Elliott, 401, 404, 409
Magee, Lee, 81
Maisel, Fritz, 65–66, 67
Major League Baseball
    All-Star Games, 181, 214, 232, 331
    amateur draft, 359, 480, 495–96
    Committee on Baseball Integration,
        247–48
    free agency for players, 404–6, 411, 413,
        414–16, 425–26, 449
    free-agent draft, 416, 460
    luxury tax based on payroll, 417, 536–37
    marketing baseball, 417
    and media access to players, 340–41
    new division alignments, 487–88
    pitcher's mound height rule, 281
    Player Relations Committee, 511
    and split season (1981), 449–51
    and steroids, 524, 525, 558–59
    steroids and/or human growth hor-
        mones, 524–26, 534, 558–59
    See also American League; National
        League
Major League Baseball Promotion Corp.,
    374
Manhattan Field, 6
Mantle, Mickey
    and Appel, 369
    biographical info, 173, 287–89, 292, 348,
        371, 377–78, 488–89
    as de facto team captain, 337
    discovery of, 286–87
    as first-base coach, 377
    as heir to DiMaggio, 341
    home runs, 298, 310, 352–53
    on Howard, 307
    and Maris, 330
    and Martin, 289, 295

Mantle, Mickey (*continued*)
  Mickey Mantle Day, 361–62, 371
  MVP awards, 312, 321, 345
  practical jokes, 302–3
  race to 60, 338, 339
  respect for, 362
  stats, 312, 321, 327, 352, 361
  and Weiss, 321, 329
Mariners, Seattle, 490, 519
Maris, Roger
  biographical info, 306, 348, 361, 430–31
  Craft's recommendation of, 328–29
  and Mantle, 330
  and media, 340–41
  MVP awards, 330, 341
  race to 60, 338–41
  traded to Cardinals, 367–68
Marquez, Luis, 277
Marsans, Armando, 67
Marshall, Clarence "Cuddles," 251
Martin, Billy
  biographical info, 282, 295, 296, 299,
    321, 477–78
  birthday celebration at the Copa, 318–19
  fired from Yankees, 434–35, 445, 467,
    472
  and Gossage, 432
  and Jackson, 428, 429–30, 433–34, 435
  and Mantle, 289, 295
  and Pine Tar Game, 456–57
  and Steinbrenner, 435–36
  and Stengel, 283–84
  trade to Kansas City, 320–21
  troubles, 319, 320, 423, 429, 471–72
  and Whitson, 466–67
  as Yankees advisor, 468
  as Yankees manager, 408–9, 413, 417,
    423, 440–41, 455–56, 458, 464,
    465–67, 470
Martinez, Pedro, 528–29
Martinez, Tino, 493–94, 501, 515, 527, 540
Martinez, Tippy, 419, 444
Martin, Jack, 104
Martin, Mike, 24, 48
mascots, 454
Mathewson, Christy, 55

Matsui, Hideki "Godzilla," 526–27, 536,
    567, 568
Matsuzaka, Daisuke, 547
Mattingly, Don
  biographical info, 455, 458–59, 461, 468,
    469–70, 486
  as coach, 535
  as coach for Dodgers, 551
  contract expiration, 488
  MVP Award, 465
  and Winfield, 461
Mauch, Gus, 318, 336
Mayberry, John, 453
Mayor's Trophy game, 344–45
May, Rudy, 401, 419, 446
Mays, Carl, 90–93, 102–3, 104–6, 108, 116,
    118, 140
Mazeroski, Bill, 333
Mazzilli, Lee, 453
McAnany, Jim, 328
McCarthy, Daniel, 388, 479
McCarthy, Joe
  biographical info, 168–69, 176, 242,
    250–51, 254
  and Dahlgren, 218–19
  and Gehrig, 206–7
  and Johnson, 193–94
  and MacPhail, 239, 242, 243, 249
  as Red Sox manager, 253–54
  and Zuber, 241–42
McClelland, Tim, 456–57
McCue, Martin, 42
McDaniel, Lindy, 400
McDonald, Jim, 307
McDonald, John, 265
McDougald, Gil, 289, 317, 318, 333, 335–36
McDowell, Jack, 488
McDowell, Sam, 393
McFarland, Herm, 24, 26
McGee, Willie, 453
McGraw, Bob, 91, 176
McGraw, John, 4, 15, 35–36, 55, 59, 100, 185
McGregor, Scott, 419
McGriff, Fred, 453
McGuire, Deacon, 34
McGwire, Mark, 505

McKinney, Rich, 378
McLain, Denny, 370
McLoughlin, Father Thomas, 42
McManus, Charlie, 76, 77, 102, 129
McMullen, John, 463
McNally, Mike, 110, 411, 413
McNamee, Graham, 153
McNertney, Jerry, 460
McQuinn, George, 257
Meacham, Bobby, 464
Meany, Tom, 111
media
    on 1927 Yankees, 151
    and baseball, 30–31
    and DiMaggio, 188–89
    and Fishel, 302
    and free agency, 425–26
    and Griffith, 30
    and Highlanders, 30–31
    on Hilltop field condition, 28–29
    and MacPhail, 264
    and Maris, 340–41
    and Matsui, 526–27
    on Meusel, 101
    name for NYC team, 18–19
    and Steinbrenner, 416, 530, 548–49
    and Stengel, 275, 334
    on Torre as Yankees manager, 493
    and transition to a new style of coverage,
        425–26
    and winter "caravan," 382
    World Series coverage, 115–17, 122
    Yankees annual press caravan, 388
    on Yankees purchase of Ruth, 97
    and Yankees vs. Mets, 360
    See also broadcasting; radio
Medich, George "Doc," 401, 412
Medina, Rafael, 500
memorabilia, 394
memorial plaques and monuments
    Allen, 357
    AL monument for winning players,
        136–37
    Barrow, 241
    commemorating 9/11, 518
    Gehrig, 223, 228

    Howard, 447–48
    Huggins, 165
    Maris, 431
    McCarthy, 254
    Monument Park creation, 418
    Munson, 443
    in new Yankee Stadium, 561
    Reynolds, 307
    Ruppert, 202
    Ruth, 100, 271
    Sheppard, 569
    Steinbrenner, 570
    Stengel, 254
Mendoza, Ramiro, 494, 513
Mercer, Sid, 117
Merola, Matt, 432
Merrill, Robert, 367, 537
Merrill, Stump, 479, 480, 481
Messer, Frank, 357, 371, 373, 476
Messersmith, Andy, 411, 413
Mets (Metropolitans), New York
    Berra as coach, 355
    founding of, 336–40, 344
    outdrawing Yankees, 360
    popularity of, 470
    winning seasons, 375–76, 393, 468
Meusel, Bob, 101, 118, 119, 120, 138, 145, 161,
        166
Michael, Gene "Stick"
    as director of scouting, 492
    as general manager, 445–46, 447, 480,
        492–93
    and Jeter, 495
    as manager, 455, 483
    and O'Neill, 484
    and Rivera, 487
    as shortstop, 369
    and Showalter, 482, 492
    on Williams, 484–85
Mickey Mantle Day, 361–62, 371
Mikkelsen, Pete, 351
Milano, "Bald Vinny," 56
Miller, Don, 151
Miller, Elmer, 78, 120
Miller, Ernestine, 499
Miller, Marvin, 413

Miranda, Willy, 297
Mitchell, Jackie, 172
Mitchell Report, 525
Mize, Johnny, 274–75, 285
Mogridge, George, 84
Molloy, Joe, 479, 492
Monahan, Gene, 455, 568–69
Moneyball (Lewis), 503, 560
Monroe, Lucy, 223, 246, 297
Monroe, Marilyn, 189, 293–94, 344
Montville, Leigh, 98
Monument Park, 418, 561. *See also* memorial plaques and monuments
Moore, Wilcy, 152, 154, 156, 179
Morabito, Mickey, 434, 435
Morante, Tony, 248, 552, 555
Moreno, Omar, 456
Morgan, Tom, 319–20
Morneau, Justin, 543
Moses, Wally, 337
MSG Network, 470–71, 475–76
Mumphrey, Jerry, 449, 456
Municipal Stadium, Cleveland, 217
Munson, Thurman
    biographical info, 376, 401, 423, 429, 437, 441–44
    and Fisk, 393–94
    and Jackson, 427–28
    MVP awards, 420
    plane crash and aftermath, 441–44
    as team captain, 414
Murcer, Bobby, 362, 374–75, 392, 400, 401, 405, 441, 444, 456
Murderer's Row, 153–54
Murphy, Johnny, 184, 227, 251–52
Murray, Dale, 453
music for entry of closer/relief pitcher, 380, 501, 502, 556
Mussina, Mike, 515–16, 527, 540
Myer, Buddy, 180–81
My Nine Innings (MacPhail), 266, 378

Nahon, Abe, 21, 50
Napp, Larry, 320
Narron, Jerry, 445
National Commission, 89, 92, 108

National League, 3, 4, 8–9, 359–60
Navin, Frank, 92
Neagle, Denny, 514
Nederlander, Bob, 388, 478
Nederlander, James M., 387–88
Negro Leagues, 248
Nelson, Jeff, 493, 513
Nettles, Graig, 385–86, 420, 453, 459–60
Neun, Johnny, 252
Newcombe, Don, 316
New Jersey and Yankee Stadium, 544
Newsom, Bobo, 256–57
Newsweek, 246
New York Americans, 18, 26. *See also* Highlanders; Yankees
New York City
    demographics, 3
    Grand Concourse, 128
    subway system, 16–17, 19, 37, 44, 58, 111 130–31
    Tammany Hall, 9, 13, 19, 71, 74
    and Yankee Stadium, 305, 381–83
New Yorker, 544
New York Post, 327
New York Times, 55, 125, 217, 297
Niekro, Joe, 460
Niekro, Phil, 460
night games, 186, 245–46, 249
Nigro, Ken, 457–58
9/11 terrorist attacks, 516–17
Nippon Ham Fighters, 500
no-hitters
    Abbott, 484
    Caldwell, 83
    Cone, 508
    Ellis, 412
    in Fenway Park, 84
    Gooden, 494
    Hawkins, 456
    Houston pitchers, 527
    Hughes, disallowed, 53
    Johnson, 538
    Jones, 136
    Larsen, 315–16
    Mogridge, 84
    Pearson, 197

Reynolds, 258, 291–92
Righetti, 456
Wells, 506
Wilhelm, 325
Young, 37, 49
Nokes, Matt, 480
Noren, Irv, 303–4, 319–20
Nova, Ivan, 572

Oaks, Oakland, 174, 262
O'Connor, Ian, 548–49
O'Connor, Jack, 7, 24
O'Doul, Lefty, 93, 120, 189
Olden, Paul, 563
Old Timers' Day
    25th anniversary of Yankee Stadium, 269
    about, 209, 246
    and DiMaggio, 294
    and Fisher, 52
    and Gomez, 171
    and Griffith, 48
    and Maris, 431
    Martin's return to Yankees, 409
    Rizzuto released on, 312–13
    Ruth featured, 262
    and Stengel, 377
O'Leary, Charley, 151
Olney, Buster, 521
Olshan, Mort, 448
O'Neill, Paul, 484
Orioles, Baltimore (American League), 5,
    13–14, 306, 331, 419, 505–6
Orioles, Baltimore (International League),
    98
Orioles, Baltimore (National League), 4,
Orth, Al, 34
Osborn Engineering, 124, 126
Ostrowski, Joe, 282
"Over There" (Cohan), 84
Owen, Mickey, 225
Owens, Walter, 234

Pacific Coast League, 89, 187–88
Pagan, Dave, 417, 419
Page, Joe, 256, 272, 279, 285
Pagliarulo, Mike "Pags," 460

Painter, Earle "Doc," 172, 226
Paley, William S., 353, 385, 386–87
Paschal, Ben, 144
Patterson, Red, 289–90, 298, 302
Paul, Gabe
    biographical info, 384–87, 431
    and Hunter, 405–6
    as team president, 396
    trades by, 401, 412
    and Williams, 397, 398–99
Pavano, Carl, 540, 564
Pavlas, Dave, 486
Pearson, Monte, 191, 197
Peckinpaugh, Roger, 44, 65, 69, 119
Pennock, Herb, 133–34, 141, 146, 178
pension program, 252
Pepitone, Joe, 343, 347, 375, 454–55
Perez, Melido, 483
Perez, Pascual, 482–83
perfect games. See no-hitters
Peterson, Fritz, 389–90, 394, 401
Peterson, Harding "Pete," 475
Pettitte, Andy, 487, 493, 519, 525, 532, 569
Pfeffer, Jeff, 104
Phelps, Ken, 471
Phil Rizzuto Day, 310–11
Piazza, Mike, 514
Piercy, Bill, 118, 119
Pilots, Seattle, 370, 371
pinch hitters, 304
Pine Tar Game, 456–57
Piniella, Lou, 400, 419, 459, 467–69, 471,
    472, 477
Pipgras, George, 155
Pipp, Wally, 78, 142–43
Pirates, Pittsburgh, 156–57, 331–33
Pittsburgh defectors, 7–9, 24
Plank, Eddie, 88
Plantania, Joe, 160
platoon baseball, 275, 276, 290, 303–4
player days, 278
player-development operation, 187–88, 220.
    See also farm system; scouts
players' strikes, 379, 449, 485–86, 488
Plunk, Eric, 475
Pollock, Ed, 156–57

Polo Grounds
    dimensions, 64
    fire, 58–59
    Highlanders' safe at, 21–22, 129
    Mets home at, 336
    Ruth on, 132
    ticket prices and Ruth, 100
    World Series at Hilltop and, 55
    as Yankees home field, 63–64, 77, 83
    Yankees playing at, 59
Polonia, Luis, 475
Posada, Jorge, ix, 487, 512, 572
Povich, Shirley, 316
Powell, Jake, 181, 191, 192, 197–98
Powers, Jimmy, 217
Power, Vic, 299, 307
Pratt, Del, 88, 110
Prayer for America service, 517
press caravan, annual, 382, 388
Priddy, Gerry, 219, 221
Pride of the Yankees (movie), 228
Priore, Nick, 465
Prohibition, 72
promotion days, 367. See also specific events
Pulliam, Harry, 8

Quinn, Bob, 471, 474, 475
Quinn, Jack, 50, 51, 89, 112, 119

radio
    broadcasting to Yankees fans, 204–5, 233
    increasing popularity, 147
    live broadcast of World Series, 122
    opening game, 1927, 153
    Ruppert on, 185–86
    Yankees announcers, 233, 246, 260
    See also broadcasting
Raft, George, 56
rainchecks, 28
Ramos, Pedro, 352
Randolph, Willie, 412, 473, 485, 495, 537–38
Rangers, Texas, 378
Raschi, Vic "the Springfield Rifle," 256–57, 274, 300
Rasmussen, Dennis, 459, 468

Rawhide, Gehrig in, 193
Reach Guide, 52, 92, 97, 113, 120, 135, 162, 179
Red Sox
    McCarthy as manager, 253
    pennant races, 33, 36–39, 277–78, 279–80
    and Ruth, 95–97, 98
    World Series, 90, 537
    and Yankees, 393–94, 419, 435–37, 528–29, 535, 536–37, 541
Reedy, Bill, 478
Reese, Jimmie, 167
Reese, Pee Wee, 224
Reggie bars, 432
Rehg, Walter, 78
relief pitchers, 154–55
Reniff, Hal, 350, 351
Reserve Clause, 248, 299, 411
Reuther, Dutch, 155
Reynolds, Allie "the Big Chief," 255–56, 258, 274, 291–92, 306–7
Reynolds, Carl, 176–77
Rice, Grantland, 87, 122, 271
Richardson, Bobby, 321, 333, 345, 349, 362
Richman, Arthur, 314, 492–93
Rickey, Branch, 45–46, 173–75, 247, 259, 264–65
Riesener, Bob, 359
Righetti, Dave "Rags," 449, 456, 460
Ripken, Cal, 488, 505–6
Rivera, Mariano, 487, 494, 501–2, 511, 523, 573
Rivera, Ruben, 500
Rivers, Mickey "Mick the Quick," 412, 440
Rizzuto, Phil "Scooter"
    on Barrow, 109
    biographical info, 274, 291, 313, 547
    on DiMaggio, 189
    discovery of, 219, 220–21
    on Farley, 216
    MVP award, 285
    Phil Rizzuto Day, 310–11
    as Player of the Year, 279
    released by Yankees, 312–13
    retirement from broadcasting, 489

Robertson, Andre, 458
Robertson, David, 572
Roberts, Selena, 558
Robins, Brooklyn, 86–87
Robinson, Bill, 367, 378
Robinson, Brooks, 352
Robinson, Eddie, 300
Robinson, Jackie, 133, 247, 316, 373, 427,
    502, 538
Robinson, Ray, 210
Robinson, Wilbert, 86, 87, 108, 135, 185
Rodriguez, Alex "A-Rod"
    biographical info, 534–35, 540–41, 547,
        564, 569, 572
    and fans, 548, 549
    and Jeter, 535
    MVP awards, 540, 547
    negotiations, 549
    and steroids, 534, 558–59
    traded to Yankees, 533–34
Rogers, Kenny, 503, 504, 544
Rohr, Bill, 368
Rolfe, Red, 184, 226–27
Ron Guidry Day, 475
Roosevelt, Franklin D., 220, 242
Roosevelt, Quentin, 47
Roosevelt, Theodore, 42, 47
Root, Charlie, 177–78
Rosen, Al, 384, 431, 434, 436, 441
Roth, Mark, 38, 45, 76, 77, 230, 233
Rotkin, Hyman, 191
Royal Rooters, 37
Rubenstein, Howard, 388, 530
Rue, Joe, 217
Ruel, Muddy, 110
Ruffing, Charley "Red," 166, 169, 170–71,
    224, 230, 252–53
Rumor in Town (Dahlgren), 219
Ruppert, George, 203, 269
Ruppert, Jacob, Jr.
    biographical info, 5, 70–72, 73, 200,
        201–2
    on Donovan's death, 85–86
    and farm system, 174
    and Huston, 87, 123–24, 134–35
    and Johnson, 73, 80, 108–9

and Mays, 91–92
on Pratt, 88
and Ruth, 183, 200–201
Ruppert, K. Jacob, 73–74, 204
Ruppert Stadiums, 174, 175, 237
Russell, Allen, 91
Russo, Marius, 212
Ruth, George Herman "Babe"
    abscess in left arm, 116–17
    and Babe Ruth All-Stars, 118, 119–20
    on Babe Ruth Day, 260–61
    biographical info, 94–95, 98, 135, 144,
        145, 182–83, 201
    Called Shot, 177–79
    death and funeral, 270–71
    and Hall of Fame, 100, 213–14
    home runs, 95–96, 102, 106, 131, 147,
        155–56, 157
    and Huggins, 94, 165
    and Johnny Sylvester, 147
    and mascot Little Ray, 99–100, 179
    MVP award, 136
    at Old Timers Day, 269–70
    and player-manager position, 166, 181, 183
    and Ruppert, 183, 200–201
    sale to Yankees from Red Sox, 95–97
    stats, 106, 112–13, 136, 141, 146, 152, 176,
        182
    on team quality, 153
    war bonds exhibition, 229
Ryan, Rosy, 138

Sabathia, CC, 559
Safe at Home (film), 341
Sain, Johnny, 291, 337
Saints, St. Paul, 143
Salute to the Army Day, 404
Sanchez, Celerino, 379
Sanderson, Scott, 480
Sanford, Fred, 267
San Francisco earthquake relief benefit
    game, 42
Sax, Steve, 473, 480, 482
Schaefer, Germany, 61–62
Schang, Wally, 110, 118, 145
Schenck, Phil, 1, 22, 128–29, 573

Schilling, Curt, 537
Schmelzer, George, 326
Schreiber, Paul, 241
Schrimpf, Charlie, 56–57
Schultz, Barney, 352–53
Schwert, Pius "Pi," 67–68
scoreboard at Yankee Stadium, 129, 245, 281, 326–27, 498, 561–62
Score, Herb, 317–18
Scott, Everett "the Deacon," 119, 142
scouts
    and DiMaggio, 187–88
    and Jeter, 495–96
    and Keller, 212–13
    and loss of quality players, 359
    and Mantle, 247, 286–87
    marginalization of, 359
    and Negroes, 307
Seals, San Francisco, 187
Seaver, Tom, 359
Seitz, Peter, 405, 411, 413
Selig, Bud, 483, 486, 487–88
Selkirk, George, 184–85, 213
Selter, Ronald, 22–23
Senate Subcommittee on Antitrust and Monopoly, 325
Senators, Washington
    American League pennant win, 141
    Americans first games against, 26–27
    forfeit, last game, 378
    Griffith as manager, 48, 61–62
    Griffith as owner, 15, 48
Senior Citizens' Day, 367
September 11, 2001, terrorist attacks, 516–17
Sewell, Joe, 172
Shannon, Bill, 571
Shantz, Bobby, 306, 319–20, 321, 335
Shaughnessy, Dan, 97
Shawkey, Bob, 78–79, 81, 131, 133, 166, 167–68, 253, 390, 418
Shea, Frank "Spec," 262, 304
Shea Stadium, 360, 403–4, 409–10
Sheehy, Michael "Big Pete", 149–50, 258, 260, 412. 464–65, 412
Sheffield, Gary, 533, 543
Sheldon, Rollie, 338

Sheppard, Bob, 289, 290, 455, 498, 569
Sheridan, Danny, 461
Shirley, Bob, 456
Shocker, Urban, 143–44, 146, 158–60
Shore, Ernie, 90
Showalter, William "Buck," 480, 482, 491, 492, 493
Siebern, Norm, 328–29
Sierra, Ruben, 488, 494
Silleck, Henry Garrison, Jr., 203, 216
Silleck-Holleran, Helen Ruppert, 202, 204
Silleck-McGuire, Ruth Rita, 202, 204
Silvera, Charlie, 274
Simpson, Harry, 306
Sims, Duke, 394
Sisler, George, 121, 122
61* (film), 341, 517
Skowron, Bill "Moose," 303, 347
Slaughter, Enos, 304, 313, 320
Small, Aaron, 539–40
Smalley, Roy, 453
Smith, Al, 42, 75, 222
Smith, Charlie, 367
Smith, Elmer, 120
Smith, Hal, 332
Smith, Red, 250–51, 370
Smith, Tal, 396, 405
Soriano, Alfonso, 515, 523, 533
Soriano, Rafael, 571–72
Sosa, Sammy, 505
Sousa, John Philip, 131, 564
Spalding Guide, 173
Spanish-American War, 13, 18
Sparma, Joe, 362
Sparrow, Harry, 76, 77, 101–2, 107, 130
Speaker, Tris, 79–80, 120
Spencer, Shane, 486
Speyer, Jerry, 388
Spikes, Charlie, 385
Spink, Taylor, 86
Spira, Howie, 478
spitball pitchers
    Caldwell, 52, 83
    Chesbro, 24, 25, 35, 38
    Grimes, 184
    Howell, 25

Orth, 34
Quinn, 51, 89, 112
Shocker, 143
split season (1981), 449–51
Sporting Life, 43, 64
Sporting News, 1, 65, 97
Sports Business Journal, 522
Stafford, Bill, 338
Stallings, George, 49, 50, 51, 53–54, 68
Stanley, Fred, 428
Stanley, Mike, 482, 485
Stanton, Mike, 513
stat analysis with computers, 550, 560–61
Steffens, Lincoln, 12
Steinbrenner, George Michael, III "Boss"
    apology for Yankees play, 450–51
    on attire and haircuts, 390–91
    and Bavasi, 421
    and Berra, 460, 463–64
    biographical info, 167, 415, 478–79, 530,
        569–70
    and Burke, 387
    buying the Yankees, 384–87
    and Cashman, 541–42
    and Davis, 440
    employees' difficulties, 416, 423–24, 436,
        452, 460, 467, 484–85
    and Green, 477
    and Howser, 446–47
    and Jeter, 528
    on losing, 446–47
    and Lucchino, 535
    and Martin, 434
    and media, 425–26, 530–31, 548–49
    and MSG Network, 476
    and Munson, 427, 443
    and new Yankee Stadium, 563–64
    and Nigro, 457–58
    on Pine Tar Game ruling, 457
    and Piniella, 467–68
    and Showalter, 491, 492
    and Silver Shield charity, 33
    Sports Illustrated cover, 483
    and Torre, 544, 548–49
    Watergate involvement, 397–98, 413–14
    and Winfield, 448, 450, 474

Steinbrenner, Hal, 531, 551
Steinbrenner, Hank, 528, 531
Stengel, Charles Dillon "Casey"
    and Berra, 274
    biographical info, 272–73, 409
    fired from the Yankees, 333–34
    and Howard, 307–8
    "lost shoe" home run, 137
    as manager of Mets, 336–37, 344
    and Martin, 283–84
    and media, 334
    at Old-Timers' Day, 377
    as player-manager, 275–76
    testimony to U.S. Senate, 325
Sterling, John, 421, 476, 555
steroids and/or human growth hormones,
    524–26, 534, 558–59
Stevens, Harry Mosley, 20–21, 131, 185, 350
Stevens, Julia Ruth, 554
Stirnweiss, George "Snuffy," 231–32,
    243–44, 251, 255, 282, 313
Stoneham, Charles, 100
Stottlemyre, Mel, 347, 350–51, 401–2, 412, 495
Stouffer, Vernon, 384
St. Petersburg, Florida, 141–42, 172, 309,
    341–42
Strawberry, Darryl, 494–95, 510
Sturm, Johnny, 219, 221, 226
Sudakis, Bill, 402, 403
Sugar, Bert Randolph, 394
Sullivan–Corbett championship fight, 2
Sullivan, John M., 12
Sullivan, Tom, 9
Sunday baseball, 40–43, 93
Superbas, Brooklyn, 41–42, 59
Supreme Court, New York State, 92, 457
Supreme Court, United States, 299, 411
Suzuki, Ichiro, 500, 526
Sweeney, Ed, 66
Swisher, Nick, 560–61
Sykes, Bob, 453
Sylvester, Johnny, 147

Tallis, Cedric, 443, 445
Tampa office vs. New York office, 474–75,
    480, 533

Tampa, spring training in, 486–87
Tannehill, Jesse, 24, 25, 32
Tarasco, Tony 496–97
Tartabull, Danny, 482, 488
Taylor, Brien, 480–81
Tebbetts, Birdie, 180, 334, 398, 409
Teixeira, Mark, 560
Terry, Ralph, 306, 328, 352
Thompson, Jim, 399
Thormahlen, Hank, 110
Thrift, Syd, 474
Throneberry, Marv, 328–29, 336
Tiant, Luis, 439–40
ticker-tape parades, 13, 154, 299, 430, 498, 567
Tidrow, Dick "Dirt," 401, 440
Tiefnauer, Bob, 362
Tigers, Detroit, brawl with Yankees, 140–41
TipTops, Brooklyn, 67
Titanic survivors benefit game, 42
Topping, Dan
    biographical info, 238, 267
    buying the Yankees, 238–39, 244
    and expansion of AL, 335–36
    financial dealings, 304–5
    on integration, 341
    and MacPhail, 264, 265–66
    selling the Yankees, 347, 353–54, 365
    and Stengel, 273, 333–34
Topping, Dan, Jr., 363
Torre, Joe
    biographical info, 510
    on "bug game," 548
    and Cashman, 570–71
    decision to hire as manager, 492–93
    leaving Yankees, 549–50
    as manager, 496, 498
    as manager for Dodgers, 551
    and Steinbrenner, 544, 548–49
    and Zimmer, 495, 530
Torres, Rusty, 385
Torrez, Mike, 428
Tresh, Tom, 342, 375
Trout, Steve, 469
Trucks, Virgil, 306
tryout camps, 220

Turley, Bob, 324
Turner, Jim, 363
Tuthill, Harry, 51
TV. *See* broadcasting
Twins, Minnesota, 335
Tymon, Debbie, 504

Ueberroth, Peter, 377, 465
Unglaub, Bob, 34
uniforms with numbers, 162–63

Vance, Dazzy, 79
Vander Meer, Johnny, 215
Vaughn, Jim "Hippo," 52, 53
Vazquez, Javier, 532, 568
Venezuela, 302
Ventura, Robin, 523, 528
Verdi, Frank, 297
Verducci, Tom, 550, 551
Vick, Sammy, 110
Vidmer, Richards, 153, 183
Vila, Joe, 1, 65, 116, 122, 123, 185
Villante, Tom, 241, 356, 521
Vincent, Fay, 340, 478, 483
Virdon, Bill, 399–400, 408–9

Wagner, Robert F., 92
Wahle, Elliot, 421
waiver deals, 133, 242, 282–83
Walden, Doris, 247
Waldman, Suzyn, 421, 429, 463
Walker, Dixie, 180
Wallace's Ridgewood Grounds, Queens, 41
Wallop, Douglas, 301
Walters, Al "Roxy," 81
Wang, Chien-Ming, 539
Wanninger, Pee-Wee, 142, 143, 145
Ward, Aaron, 101
Warhop, Jack, 50, 51
Warner, Marvin, 388
Watson, Bob, 446, 497–98
Webb, Del, 238, 265, 273, 294, 304–5, 347, 353–54
Weiss, George
    biographical info, 174
    and DiMaggio, 188

as manager, 267–68
and Mantle, 321, 329
as Mets general manager, 336
and players, 321
on Power, 299
retirement of, 334
and Steinbrenner, 265
in train accident, 85
and trains, 324
Wells, David "Boomer," 501, 506, 508, 523, 532–33
Welzer, Irv, 175, 211
Westbrook, Jake, 512
Western League, 2, 3
Wetteland, John, 490, 494, 501
Weyant, Helen Winthorpe "Winnie," 202–3, 204
Weyant, Rex, 203, 230, 233, 240
Whitaker, Steve, 368
White, Bill, 373, 476, 547
Whitehill, Earl, 180–81
White, Roy, 362, 370, 446
White Sox, 89, 320–21, 327
Whitson, Ed, 466–67
wife swap, 389–90
Wilf, Leonard, 388
Wilhelm, Hoyt, 325
Williams, Bernabe "Bernie," xi–xii, 25, 481, 484–85, 507, 543, 564
Williams, Dick, 397, 398–99
Williams, Jimmy, 24
Williams, Joe, 182
Williams, Ken, 121–22
Williams, Stan, 347
Williams, Ted, 224, 229, 258, 291–92, 312
Wilson, Artie, 277
Wiltse, Snake, 24
Wimbish, Ralph, Sr., 309
Winfield, Dave, 448, 454, 458, 461, 473–74
Witt, Mike, 474
Witt, Whitey, 119, 121, 131, 390, 418
Wolfe, Barney, 24
Wolverton, Harry, 60, 63
Womack, Tony, 538
women and baseball, 93, 420–21, 429, 463, 499

Woodling, Gene, 274, 275, 276, 336
Woods, Ron, 375
Wood, Wilbur, 392–93
World Series
    1910, Cubs. vs. Athletics, 55
    1914, Braves vs. Athletics, 80
    1918, Red Sox vs. Cubs, 90
    1921, Giants vs. Yankees, 115–17
    1922, Giants vs. Yankees, 122
    1923, Yankees vs. Giants, 137–39
    1926, Cardinals vs. Yankees, 146, 147–49
    1927, Yankees vs. Pirates, 156–57
    1928, Yankees vs. Cardinals, 161–62
    1932, Yankees vs. Cubs, 177–79
    1936, Yankees vs. Giants, 192
    1937, Yankees vs. Giants, 195–96
    1938, Yankees vs. Cubs, 198–99
    1939, Yankees vs. Reds, 214–15
    1941, Yankees vs. Dodgers, 224–25
    1942, Cardinals vs. Yankees, 230
    1943, Yankees vs. Cardinals, 232–33
    1947, Yankees vs. Dodgers, 262–64
    1949, Yankees vs. Dodgers, 265–66, 280
    1950, Yankees vs. Phillies, 285
    1951, Yankees vs. Giants, 292–93
    1952, Yankees vs. Dodgers, 296
    1953, Yankees vs. Dodgers, 298–99
    1955, Dodgers vs. Yankees, 311–12
    1956, Yankees vs. Dodgers, 314–16
    1957, Braves vs. Yankees, 321–22
    1958, Yankees vs. Braves, 325–26
    1960, Pirates vs. Yankees, 331–33
    1961, Yankees vs. Reds, 341
    1962, Yankees vs. Giants, 345–46
    1963, Yankees vs. Dodgers, 348–49
    1964, Cardinals vs. Yankees, 352–53
    1973, Oakland vs. Mets, 397
    1976, Reds vs. Yankees, 422–24
    1977, Yankees vs. Dodgers, 430
    1978, Yankees vs. Dodgers, 438
    1981, Dodgers vs. Yankees, 450–51
    1996, Yankees vs. Braves, 497–98, 499–500
    1998, Yankees vs. Padres, 507
    1999, Yankees vs. Braves, 510–11
    2000, Yankees vs. Mets, 513–15

World Series (*continued*)
  2001, Diamondbacks vs. Yankees, 519–21
  2003, Marlins vs. Yankees, 529–30
  2004, Red Sox vs. Rockies, 537
  2009, Yankees vs. Phillies, 567
World War I, 84, 88–89
World War II, 223, 225, 228, 236, 241
Wright, Teresa, 228–29
Wright, Toby, 366, 380, 417
Wynegar, Butch, 453
Wynn, Jim, 429

Yank (newsletter), 302
Yankee Global Enterprises, 522
Yankee Mainliner (DC-4), 249–50
Yankees football team, 245, 277
Yankees magazine, 302
YankeesNets, 521
Yankee Stadium
  25th anniversary, 269–70
  50th anniversary, 390
  75th anniversary, 504
  air-raid drills, 228
  All-Star Game at, 214, 331, 553
  celebrating last year of, 552–57
  christening by Ruth, 119
  construction and design, 124–27, 128–29, 130, 132
  deterioration, 360, 504
  dimensions, 127, 128, 561, 574
  food service, 153, 350
  frieze, 126, 312, 390, 554, 562
  graffiti, 391–92
  and integration, 309
  leasing to Negro teams, 248
  location, 127–28

  magic of, xii
  Monument Park, 418, 561 (*See also* memorial plaques and monuments)
  music for entry of closer/relief pitcher, 380, 501, 502, 556
  new stadium, 561–63
  new stadium opening, 539
  new stadium plans, 504–5, 544–45
  opening day, 130–32, 417–19
  pennant ceremonies, 120, 130–31, 430–31
  Prayer for America service, 517
  renovations, 111, 160, 192, 244–46, 248–49, 281, 366–67, 381–83, 394, 395
  sale and Yankees lease, 304–6
  scoreboard, 129, 245, 281, 326–27, 498, 561–62
  site selection, 5–7, 16
  structural problems, 381
  thunderstorm leads to two deaths, 163–64
  World Series decor, 137
  See also Hilltop Park
Yankee Years, The (Torre and Verducci), 551
Year the Yankees Lost the Pennant, The (Wallop), 301
YES Network, 521–22
Yogi Bear (cartoon character), 325
Yogi Berra Day, 508
Young, Cy, 37, 49
Young, Dick, 315–16, 333, 344, 425

Zachary, Tom, 156
Zeider, Rollie, 66
Zillo, Jason, 567*n*
Zimmer, Don, 495, 528–29
Zuber, Bill, 241–42